DOUGLAS HURD

——

Memoirs

LITTLE, BROWN

A *Little, Brown* Book

First published in Great Britain in 2003 by Little, Brown

Copyright © 2003 Douglas Hurd

The moral right of the author has been asserted.

A CIP catalogue record for this book is available
from the British Library.

ISBN 0 316 86147 2

The publisher acknowledges the Society of Authors as the
Literary Representative of the Estate of A.E. Housman.

Typeset in Sabon by M Rules
Printed and bound in Great Britain by
Clays Ltd, St Ives plc

Little, Brown
An imprint of
Time Warner Books UK
Brettenham House
Lancaster Place
London WC2E 7EN

www.TimeWarnerBooks.co.uk

Contents

Prologue

This book comes into the world late. The three prime ministers with whom I worked wrote their memoirs some time ago. The shelves are stacked with other published accounts of the events in which I took part. In a way this comes as a relief, for it means I can make my book more personal. This will not be the history of an age nor an account of British politics in the last quarter of the twentieth century. It is the story of my life up to July 1995, when I resigned as Foreign Secretary – one decision which I took in the right way at the right time.

The political parts of the story take their place among the rest. They do not swamp the book, any more than in my memory they swamp my upbringing, my family or my friends. Some of the matters with which I dealt will always be controversial. For as long as academics write, there will be no unanimity about the Suez campaign, the General Election of 1974, the Anglo-Irish Agreement of 1985, the Treaty of Maastricht in 1991 or Bosnia in the early nineties. Professors of hindsight will continue hard at work disputing one another's portraits of Ted Heath, Margaret Thatcher, John Major and dozens of others whom I knew well. I have read many, perhaps most, of the works which have so far resulted. If I were to set about analysing and commenting on these controversies, this book would be hopelessly distorted. Instead, I have preferred to set out as plainly as I can how things looked at the time and why we acted as we did.

I do not regard with total awe or admiration any of those with whom I worked. But nor am I a hater. Irritation and anxiety often, indignation occasionally, but hatred never dominated my feelings about individuals. I regard this as a fact rather than a virtue; I am not interested in manufacturing hates in order to give extra flavour to this dish. I hope there will be enough entertainment and interest in its natural ingredients without the need to add such artificial sauces.

I began keeping a diary at the age of eight. My Letts Schoolboy's diary of 1938 is a formidable document bound in cloth with black loop pencil and world maps, priced one shilling and sixpence. A long section on careers beckons its owner into the 'Indian Police' (medical and riding tests age 19–21; salary from R450 a month) or 'Banking' (salaries begin at about £80 and rise, for clerks, to £400 a year). There are tables of Latin, Greek and French verbs, an essay on bicycles, a list of ocean liners, many lists of sports records, and a page for personal memoranda. This showed that our telephone number was Pewsey 50, that I stood at four feet, six inches and weighed five stones, two pounds. Though invited, I did not record my size in collars or hats.

It is more or less true that every evening since 1938 I have written in bed an account of the day just ending. (Only more or less because I dropped the habit between 1939 and 1944, and have lost the diary covering most of 1956.) This claim perhaps creates an impression of a library crowded with stately volumes. On the contrary, all my diaries fit into two shelves of a bookcase in my study at Westwell. For most of these years the diary consisted of cheap, tiny booklets, usually with four or five lines for each day. In recent years I have moved to a stiff, but still economical, WH Smith diary with a page for each day. On dull days the page was not filled; very occasionally it overflowed. Writing my diary has become a habit, like brushing my teeth, the one ritual closely following the other. But unlike teeth-brushing it has had no clear purpose; it just happens. The diary is certainly not written for publication. This is not because it is full of improper scandal, but rather because most of it is scanty or even incomprehensible. Once or twice I tried the experiment of writing a day's entry the next morning, but I could not regularly find the time or the zest for this. A day later any vivid emotion has evaporated, any striking phrase been forgotten. So, however tired or full of wine I am, I make an entry the same evening, even though the pen sometimes drools in exhaustion down the page.

These diaries have been a huge help in two ways. First, they have pinned me down to accurate dates and sequences. Left to itself, my memory strays from the tracks, putting events in the wrong order, misplacing individuals, reorganising emotions. The diary enables me to put this right. Second, the diary from time to time perks up and provides some vivid detail not to be found in newspapers, parliamentary reports or official papers.

The drawback of a diary is that, unless edited later with hindsight, it provides an immediate but not a considered reaction to what happened. It does not reveal what the diarist really thought about a person or an event, just what he or she felt at the end of a particular day. A diary may contain only the residue of feeling, the reaction which was *not* expressed during the equally valid comings and goings of the day. This does not matter if the diary is simply gossip with no deeper pretence. The damage comes when a solemn historian following later takes a diary as revealing something serious or complete about a crisis or an individual. To treat the diaries of Alan Clark or Woodrow Wyatt as serious contributions to history would be deeply foolish. They are sometimes fun to read because they were written for fun. My diaries, bitty and unpolished, would not even be fun to read. They are a raw material, no more.

While completing this book I have read the Alanbrooke diaries, which show how this process works. Repeatedly, Alanbrooke records, for his wife's eyes only, damning late-night criticisms of Winston Churchill, his intolerable working methods, his wasting of time, his lack of strategic grasp. These are the extracts which most interested fun-loving commentators. But when he reread later what he had written, Alanbrooke often withdrew or qualified his verdict on Churchill. His considered view was not the same as that expressed in a diary entry at the end of a vexed day.

This relationship between the diary and the real world was often in my mind when writing this book. When I worked for them, I might go to bed exasperated beyond immediate endurance by the way Ted Heath or Margaret Thatcher had handled something about which I felt strongly. But I endured. Diary extracts of my frustrated scribbles would give a false account of how I really felt about these two prime ministers or the crisis of the day.

Several years ago a young Aberdonian academic wrote to me out of the blue, announcing that he intended to write my biography. In 1998 Mainstream published Mark Stuart's book with the title *The Public Servant*. The process of opening at least part of one's life to a total stranger is a curious one. In our case it worked well, and though his book is not a work of flattery, I enjoyed Mark's company. He did not read my diaries, but when he came to Westwell, we sat opposite each other across a desk and he asked me about particular events. I looked them up and answered. Sometimes I read him a sentence or two from the diary. His book – not least its criticisms – has helped me to a sober perspective. For example, he put into proportion in my mind the tangle of unrelated subjects which I dealt with in the Home Office.

I am grateful to all those concerned in the Foreign and Commonwealth Office, in particular Dr Christopher Baxter, in the Home Office, the Cabinet Office and the Northern Ireland Office for the painstaking way in which they have unearthed government papers; to the House of Lords Library for unfailing helpfulness; and to the late Mrs Rosemary Wolff for permission to quote one of her husband's letters. I must thank Anthony and Anne Mildmay White for letting me use their

Lutyens dining room at Mothecombe to write a crucial part of the book in the Indian summer of 2002.

I have written in longhand every word which follows and have sent chapters of my draft to individuals who lived through a stage of my life with me. I am particularly grateful for their lively interest and suggestions, to my brother Stephen, my first wife Tatiana, my eldest son Nicholas and his wife Kim, Lord Lloyd of Berwick, Jacky Shaw-Stewart, Sir Alan Donald, Lord Renton of Mount Harry, Chris Patten, Michael Maclay, Maurice Fraser, Anthony Howard, Mrs Mary Moore, Lord Waldegrave of North Hill, Lady Chalker, John Sawers, Lord Garel-Jones and Mats Berdal of the Institute of Strategic Studies. I owe much to Mr Anthony Seldon for the trouble he took in reading the manuscript: he manages to combine running a successful public school with much stimulating analysis of recent political history.

My editor, Alan Samson, and the prince of agents Michael Sissons have sustained me with wise advice and generous refreshment along the way. My manuscript, scribbled by different pens in a decaying hand, sometimes in trains or planes, has been valiantly transcribed on to the computer by my wife Judy, Julia Broad, Pauline Glock and Sue Townsend. Their patient and intelligent help has been indispensable.

Judy chose the illustrations. She has corrected my prose, pruned my adjectives and pointed out occasional contradictions in my views. She has in all ways encouraged and kept me going throughout this enter-prise, as she has through our married life. I dedicate the book to her.

And also to others. Michael Sissons advised me early not to include in the book too many spearcarriers, meaning individuals who were part of my life for just a few months or years. The advice was shrewd but impossible to follow. Anything I achieved and everything I enjoyed have been the result of those who were with me in each episode. So the book is dedicated with gratitude and affection to Judy and all those who helped me, whether they carried spears, shields or simply a red box.

PART I

GROWING UP

1

A COUNTRY CHILDHOOD

RAINSCOMBE FARM

We thought at the time that we lived an ordinary life in an extraordinary place. Going back there, I can see now that this semicircle of downland is not extraordinary, just pleasant, as many landscapes in England are pleasant. But to me it remains special. I have taken all my children there to climb the Giant's Grave and listen as patiently as they can to their father talking about the first seventeen years of his life.

The road from Marlborough south across Wiltshire towards Salisbury Plain falls steeply down an escarpment through beech woods to the village of Oare. On the left the bowl of downs called Rainscombe is formed by a promontory jutting into the Vale, on top of which a ditch and stockade were dug before the Romans came. This gives the promontory something like a human shape. Hence its name: the Giant's Grave. At the base of this bowl of downland lies a stylish Georgian house, Rainscombe Park. At the point where the drive from the house meets the main road a clutter of buildings embraces the farmhouse, which looks straight across the fields at the steep slope of the Giant's Grave. To that small, square, whitewashed farmhouse my father Anthony Hurd came, aged twenty-five, in 1926, having taken from the owner of Rainscombe Park the lease of the 450 acres which formed its estate. From there he courted Stephanie Corner, elder daughter of a distinguished surgeon, whom he had met because her parents and his aunt lived in the same road in Beaconsfield.

3 April 1928

My dear Stephanie,

I am so glad you enjoyed Sunday. You always seem to enjoy yourself
when you come down, so you'd better consider the possibility of
coming here for good! It is Leap Year you know. Sometime soon we
must fix up a dinner and dance in town, when Bobby comes back
from Italy.

I have returned to the sheep fold tonight, and I am afraid for several
nights more because Halliday's throat has developed into quinsy.

Bobby was my father's brother, and Halliday the peremptory Scots
farm foreman. I don't know who proposed to whom, but that autumn
he married Stephanie. My mother had early moments of uncertainty
as revealed to her uncle, who unexpectedly married at the same time.

My dearest of Uncles

Give the love of your devoted niece to your wife and tell her that I do
hope we shall have a chance of meeting each other some day soon.

What an old dog you are darling to hide your secret away like that
when mine was laid bare to the vulgar scrutiny of the world in general.
You make me a little envious when I think of all the smiles you must
have smiled up your sleeve and all the pleasures (unknown to your
curious friends and relations) you must have enjoyed in quiet moments.
I am all against publicity now – having learnt the value of intimacy.

Will you write to me and tell me a little about the lady. I know she
is charming already for I saw the family last week and you know how
skilfully they diagnose characters. I am so very glad there is someone
to look after you now – to prevent your winter cough and deliver you
from the Club Chef and his slow poisons – not to mention the Bishops
and lounge bores.

I am on the whole very happy. It would be foolish to say floating
blissfully on the tide of married life – for I feel I am still rather
uncertainly feeling and groping my way along – sometimes up on a
wave of complete happiness – then down in an awful trough of the
blues – does the sea calm down eventually? Looked at cold bloodedly
and apart – it is a profoundly interesting chapter of psychology isn't it –
I wish I had you here to talk tonight – Anthony is in town, it being his
office day and I am alone and you could tell me such a lot.

Good night and my love to you both dear

Stephanie Hurd

A letter to her father, also from these first weeks of marriage, gives a
glimpse of my mother, then twenty-four, entering a new world as a

farmer's wife and as the daughter-in-law of the local MP, whom she still called 'Mr Hurd'. Perhaps this letter sets the scene as well as any description.

My dearest Pop

Many happy returns of Monday from your married daughter. I am sending you a few mushrooms and lawyer's wigs – fruits of the land in due season – they are about the last we shall have and are getting rather musty I am afraid – but *tant pis* – they carry my very best wishes and love to you and I hope they will eat well.

We have had a wonderful week here with Mr Hurd with us. I got back quite safely Tuesday – the kitten soon escaped from her basket but she sat quite still on my lap for the rest of the way and was most good. I don't believe she has had a moment's home sickness since she arrived, being quite the most passive and ornamental creature in the place – Anthony is tolerating her.

Wednesday we went to 2 meetings with Mr Hurd and in both cases were cheered on our introduction. I felt rather shy and unusual, but A made a nice little thank-you speech and I tried to be as pleasant as possible to all the hard workers in the great cause – the first was a schoolroom with a small village attendance not very bright or enthusiastic but the second much more ambitious had a concert as well. Mr Hurd speaks extraordinarily well and is most popular. I admire his manner towards everyone tremendously. 2 speeches a night and workhouses and committees all day very hard work I think.

Last night however was our crowning glory – we drove there and joined Mr Hurd at a village concert 70 miles away – sat that out – supped gorgeously with the chairman who is the local Master of the Otter Hounds then A and I went on to the Imps dance at Devizes with Mr Jolliffe Mr Hurd's agent. There we had a tremendous reception (about 12.30) – about 300 young things in the Corn Exchange – who cheered us. A had to make a speech from the platform and I had to be introduced to all the lights – it almost turned a girl's head – one envious young ex-mayor's daughter asked Anthony if it was not rather fun to be a tin-god – he was so annoyed.

A fearful night – rain – and wind and we did not get home till 2.30 – to-day it all seems a dream. I'm a Devizes Imp however and have got to go to meetings there.

Mr Hurd says the Gen. Election is not likely to take place before September next – so we have still some time to go.

We are very happy – tomorrow some Marlborough Boys are coming out to lunch and tea and Tuesday I go to play bridge with Lady Biggs! How clever of you and Mum to win so much last Tuesday.

The eggs were greatly appreciated – our pullets at last are beginning
to lay – . . . and I am very busy planting bulbs.
My love to you, Pop dear –
Yours Ever
Stephanie*

At Rainscombe Farm three sons were born in quick succession: myself
in 1930, Julian in 1932 and Stephen in 1933. Born at 4.30 in the
afternoon on 8 March, weighing seven pounds, eight ounces, I began by
losing too much weight, so that a 3 a.m. feed was reluctantly added to
my routine. There were expenses: after one grandparental visit my
mother noted in her diary 'no mention of a pram, so we shall definitely
have to get one ourselves'. She also recorded a good many tears (hers
rather than mine), though it was a good sign that outside on the down
where the ewes were lambing it was an excellent spring for triplets. By
her own birthday in June my mother was 'very, very happy and pleased
with life'. Thereafter her diary shows a steady shift in that way of life.
As we children took up more of her time she rode less often, went to
fewer tennis parties and played less bridge with Lady Biggs.

To Rainscombe Farm came a steady flow of visitors. Most frequent
were my grandfather Percy Hurd and his wife Hannah. Sir Percy (he was
knighted in 1932) served as the local Conservative Member of
Parliament for the Devizes constituency from 1924 until he retired in
1945. He had no house of his own in Wiltshire and used ours as his
base. The son of a solicitor, he became a journalist, developed a
particular interest in Canada, and before the Great War edited the
weekly newspaper *Outlook for Canadians in Britain*, thus coming into
close sympathy with Max Aitken (later Lord Beaverbrook) and with the
cause of tariff reform. He married Hannah Cox, the daughter of a
distinguished Congregationalist minister in Dundee. My grandfather
prospered in London and bought an enchanting Georgian house on one
of the lanes which led up to Highgate Village from the Archway Road.
As children we often visited Hillside. I recall a fierce rocking horse; a cook
called Bella who gave us bagfuls of buns and breadcrumbs for our
expeditions to London Zoo; racing along the paths which traversed the
shrubs and trees of the steeply sloping garden; a streetlight hard for us
Wiltshire boys to live with as it shone outside our window; and glowing
coals settling with a quiet, friendly noise in the bedroom grate after
lights had been turned out. In April 1938 I noted in my diary (first

---

*Lady Biggs lived down the drive in the big house: Rainscombe Park. The Imps
were the forerunners of the Young Conservatives.

volume) that from Hillside we visited the Tower, the Natural History Museum, the Zoo, Kenwood, St Paul's, the Houses of Commons and Lords, and Westminster Abbey. On top of this torrent of improving tourism I recorded mysteriously, 'can now count to 499'. One would think that the next step would have been relatively straightforward.

There was one room at Hillside, the largest in the house, which we never visited. The drawing room was on the first floor – elegant, scrupulously tidy, with a grand piano in the corner. I suppose it was quite usual in the 1930s that children should not frequent the drawing room of their grandparents. But what struck us as strange even then was that our grandparents hardly used the room themselves. Although no one ever described it as such, the drawing room was a shrine, consecrated with photographs and medals. On 15 September 1916 my grandparents' eldest son, Captain Douglas Hurd of the Middlesex Regiment, was shot in the head by a sniper while leading an attack on a German position in the second phase of the Battle of the Somme. All the other company commanders of his battalion were killed on the same day. As was the Prime Minister's son, Raymond Asquith. A young officer named Harold Macmillan was badly wounded. It was a bad day on the Somme; but then on the Somme there were no good days. The colonel wrote a gentle, dignified letter to my grandparents. So, in pencil from the trenches or a military hospital, did several of the men whom my uncle had commanded. The King and Queen sent a telegram. Douglas's tutor from Corpus Christi, Oxford, wrote that he was 'in every way a splendid man, one of the strongest characters I have ever known'. These and many other letters and press cuttings were pasted into an album by my grandparents. At the front of the tattered volume the original message gives the news from the War Office in Hounslow. At the edge of the telegram form is written in pencil: 'Read first by mother, sitting by the garden door of the Dining Room at Hillside 18/9/16. What shall I do? What shall I do?'

In July 1997, when making a television series for the BBC called *In Search of Peace*, I found the cemetery where Douglas is buried, at Bronfay Farm on a secondary road which winds north above Bar sur Somme. The cemetery is small: about a hundred British officers and men are buried there, each marked with equal and meticulous dignity by the white stones of the Commonwealth War Graves Commission. Red roses soften the austerity of the plots. Most of these men were killed in the same week. On the day of our visit larks sang in a ripening wheat field on two sides; on another stood a grove of oaks. Across the road the farmer emerged from his buildings, his stomach straining against white shorts. His father had bought the farm in the twenties, but he had informed himself about the Great War. That barn, he said, pointing to a building opposite the farmhouse, was the field hospital. The colonel and others in mercy had told my grandparents that Douglas died on 15 September, the day the sniper shot him in the head, but the list at the Public Record Office in Kew and the gravestone above the Somme valley record that he died of wounds two days later, on the 17th. It was hard on a beautiful summer day eighty-one years later to imagine in what distress and pain my namesake spent his last two days in that barn.

Douglas was twenty-one when he was killed. His brother Jack reached that age eighteen months later, serving in the Hertfordshire Regiment on the front near Amiens. The Germans overwhelmed that sector in Ludendorff's final offensive of March 1918, and a few days after his birthday Jack was killed. The Germans swept over his position and the body was never identified with certainty. His ambition had been to grow roses in East Anglia.

My father Anthony was then nearly seventeen, at school at Marlborough. The war ended a few months before he too became eligible for slaughter.

My grandparents did not talk in our hearing about Douglas and Jack. Among the millions of dead there was nothing extraordinary about their sacrifice, but it changed their lives. My grandfather decided at once to put aside his career as a journalist and stand for Parliament. He was elected for Frome in Somerset in 1918, re-elected in 1922 and defeated in 1923, in the first election won by Labour. Frome was then in part a coal-mining constituency. The album of his press cuttings records in great detail the noisy, good-humoured hustings at which he was heckled by miners and gave back as good as he got. In those days candidates, by holding such meetings, which were reported verbatim in the local press, provided voters with a lively, locally based political education of which there is no counterpart today. After his defeat in Frome Percy Hurd was in 1924 elected for Devizes, half a county away to the north.

So far as I can make out, it was the loss of his two sons rather than any deep political thinking which pushed my grandfather into Parliament. He wanted a change of life, and to do something, probably nothing especially specific, for his country. He held the Devizes seat until he retired in 1945.

In the Commons his voting record was loyal to the Conservative Party of Stanley Baldwin and Neville Chamberlain. He was active on behalf of his constituents; he took a continuing interest in agriculture and in the affairs of the colonies and dominions. He saw politics essentially in terms of personalities, and entertained village meetings with a string of anecdotes about the colourful figures of the day: for example, Lady Astor (whom he disliked), Jimmy Maxton (leader of the Independent Labour Clydesiders) and David Lloyd George. In 1940 he introduced me to the seventy-seven-year-old Lloyd George in the Central Lobby of the House of Commons; I remember only his small stature and the fineness of his abundant white hair.

Because of his fund of stories, we called him 'Funny Grandpa'. In the 1935 General Election he arranged for his three small, solemn grandsons, dressed in bright blue coats, to sit in the front row of the Liberal candidate's meeting in Oare Village Hall, in the hope that we would put her off her stride. A little later it was my duty to present a bouquet to the Prime Minister's wife Mrs Baldwin in Devizes Town Hall. I was urged down an aisle which seemed a mile long, between loudly clapping Conservatives, towards a distant platform on which with relief I recognised my grandmother. Beside her stood a lady dressed in something brown and shiny who clasped me to her bosom. Despite this experience, I never thought of being anything other than a Conservative.

Although we saw her often, we did not know Percy's wife Hannah well because she was seriously deaf. When they were both old, my grandfather sometimes shouted at her when he was irritated. Yet once, soon after her death, he broke down when proposing her health at table. I was young and ignorant enough to be puzzled by this apparent contradiction. Before deafness set in, my grandmother had been the lively moving force of the family. I have the courtship letters which she and Percy exchanged in 1892 and 1893. In this last Victorian decade the daughter of the Dundee Congregationalist minister certainly takes and holds the initiative over the rising young London journalist. Bicycle trips played a large part in their wooing.

If my mother's parents came less often than the Hurds to Rainscombe Farm, it was not that our link with them was weaker. Her father was going blind and preferred his own house, where he knew each step of the staircase and each turn of the garden path. Edred Corner had practised as a surgeon at St Thomas's Hospital in London and lived then at the centre of his medical world in a big house at the corner of Harley and Queen Anne streets. We have a photograph of him in his Medical Corps uniform of the Great War: tall, heavy and bespectacled. There is a contrasting photograph of my grandmother from a little earlier: a beautiful hostess in a low-cut Edwardian evening dress. As his sight failed, Edred could no longer practise. The Corners, with their three children, left Harley Street and set up a nursing home at Woodlands Park in Buckinghamshire. The venture fared quite well but did not last long. By the time I was born my Corner grandparents were installed in Stratton End, a big, comfortable, mock-Tudor house at the edge of the new town of Beaconsfield. In those days Stratton Road petered out into bumpy gravel before Stratton End was reached. The garden sloped steeply down through a beech wood to open country, stretching towards Penn, all long since built over. We went often to Stratton End but Edred was as separated from us by his growing blindness as Hannah was because of her deafness. Surprisingly, he managed for several years to continue his passion for stamp-collecting, peering at his trophies through a strong magnifying glass in his study beside the staircase. My two brothers and I all collected stamps. I was particularly keen, constantly rearranging my British Empire collection, including the Jubilee (1935) and Coronation (1937) sets from each colony, carefully recording each stamp's value according to the highly optimistic figures in the Stanley Gibbons catalogue. I could not understand my grandfather's preoccupation with the watermarks on small, dull stamps of long-gone American presidents. Later he spent most of his time in a high chair in the drawing room, listening to the big, dark brown wireless set. Heavy romantic music of Brahms, Tchaikovsky and Rachmaninov floated out through the open garden door. But he did not confine himself to the house. By this time bent and unsteady, he managed to walk fifty yards to the wood shed using a rope installed alongside the path. There he would saw logs for hours on end, returning to the house with the same painful slowness for lunch or tea.

My grandmother Henrietta came from a large family of Hendersons, born and brought up in Blairgowrie, Perthshire. Her Scottish energy and kindness, prolonged to the age of ninety, provided a fixed point in our lives, taken for granted at the time, but (as I look back) remarkable and splendid. She throve on adversity. Before the Great War, married to a successful surgeon, she was running a fashionable Harley Street home with plenty of servants. By the time the next war came she was looking after a big house and garden in Beaconsfield with an ailing husband and no staff. She must have had someone to cut the grass, but certainly she cooked, cleaned, shopped, canvassed at elections in the Conservative interest (she won a national prize for her prowess) and drove her small car to district council meetings in Amersham.

The Second World War gave impetus to one of my grandmother's strongest instincts: a personal war on waste. Every human artefact was used carefully and then reused. Her letters might be written on the back of laundry bills and would certainly be posted in elderly envelopes secured with economy labels. When she and her two sisters spent Christmas with us at Rainscombe, after the presents had been opened the three old ladies would kneel and carefully fold the bright wrapping paper, tut-tut over careless rents made by impatient children, and rewind ribbon round rheumatic fingers to be placed in a drawer against next year. There was no meanness in this, for all three ladies were by nature generous. It stemmed from a belief, I suppose Presbyterian in origin, that all objects which God provided for us deserved the respect of constant and careful use.

This certainly included time itself; no hour was wasted. Whenever as a family we needed a refuge of some kind, because one of us was in quarantine for a childhood illness, or because our parents were briefly away together, it was my grandmother who received and looked after us at Stratton End. There we rode our bikes furiously until our knees were scarred with many falls, dammed the trickle of a stream which ran down from pond to pond through the beech trees, and in the evening played card games: hearts or rummy or love courted or even vingt et un. I see my grandmother coming in on a mild winter afternoon, green cardigan over long tweed dress, shapeless brown hat on her head, a basket of twigs gathered for kindling on her arm, calling us to light the drawing-room fire and lay the table for tea.

Oare Hill takes its name from the village sprawling at its foot, just out of the semicircle of downs which embraced us at Rainscombe Farm. Oare has some good houses but is not a beautiful village; the main road sweeps through it into the Vale of Pewsey. Oare House lies back from the road, connected by an avenue of limes, under which daffodils announce to the village the arrival of spring as authorised by the squire. The plain Georgian house built by a wine merchant in 1740 had been transformed in the 1920s by the fashionable architect Clough Williams-Ellis, best known for the creation of Portmeirion in Wales. Oare House became elegant, with added wings and high ironwork gates and railings. It was the home of my godfather Geoffrey Fry, created a baronet after long years of discreet service in the Treasury and as Private Secretary to the Prime Minister, Stanley Baldwin. Geoffrey Fry solved the problem of a young godson by treating me at all times as a grown-up. Book tokens or serious works of history or politics would arrive at conventional intervals. If, at the age of twelve or thirteen, I called at Oare House he would receive me with sherry: 'Let me know if you find it a little too dry.' He and his wife Alathea were resolute invalids. I recollect her hardly at all, and him as a frail, kindly figure, if outdoors wearing a thick cloak, if indoors sitting at one of the big windows covered by a generous rug, looking out over his meadows and woodland towards the downs. His conversation was fascinating and at a different level from my grandfather's. Sir Percy was the jovial anecdotal backbencher; the Commons was the centre of his working world. Sir Geoffrey was the laidback senior official talking naturally of SB (Baldwin) and Maynard Keynes, of Washington, Whitehall and Downing Street.

His main friend in Oare was the subtle historian of the Victorian age G.M. Young, who shared a modest thatched house of medieval origins further up the village with a lady historian, Mona Wilson. Occasionally we caught a whiff of gossip about the irregular manner in which G.M. and Mona shared the Old Oxyard; but to us children they were both so old, so learned, and in appearance so plain that no question of impropriety could possibly arise. Out of this friendship between Geoffrey and G.M. sprang the latter's biography of Baldwin, the least successful book he wrote. My godfather would later lament this ill-fated enterprise to me. G.M., who had shown himself so charitable and understanding of the great Victorian age, could not cope with the many layers of Baldwin's character and missed the essential point about the politics of rearmament in the 1930s.

For us, access to Oare House meant above all the swimming pool, which lay beyond the big lawn, protected by a tall yew hedge. We could reach the pool without disturbing the Frys. We parked our bicycles, having slipped in off the road past the tool shed, where each implement hung highly polished in its own place, down a path with a herbaceous border on either side. Lining the gravel stood a long regiment of lavender, murmuring with bees. The pool itself was large, elegant and edged with grey stone, the yew carefully trimmed. There was a diving board and white wooden garden seats were provided at either end for spectators. We changed behind the hedge, leaving our clothes in tidy heaps. There was one great difference from any swimming pool today: no chemicals were used and the water through the swimming season was never changed. As a result it turned dark green and achieved the consistency of steadily thickening soup. Little frogs and newts were our companions in the water but no one fretted. I think that occasionally one of us suffered from earache for a couple of days, but nothing worse, and the pool was simply considered a place of healthy refreshment. When during the war an army of boys came from Marlborough College to help us bring in the harvest they too jumped and splashed enthusiastically in the pool.

For us the most important house in the village was Bennetts, an old-fashioned thatched cottage at its upper end. This was the home of my grandmother's two spinster sisters, Anne and Isabel Henderson. They had moved there soon after my mother and father's wedding in 1928. Known to us as Aunt A and Aunt I, they became a channel for the overflow of boyish energy. When our games required an audience or more than three players, the aunts volunteered. They had to drink the cider which we brewed in buckets in the farmyard at Rainscombe; they bought expensive imaginary transatlantic passages on the *Normandie* or the *Queen Mary* when we used the advertisements in *The Times* to set ourselves up as travel agents. But the centre of the relationship was tea. We bicycled or walked to tea with the aunts several times a month, and a pattern established itself. Aunt A, older and plumper than her sister, spent her life indoors. When at an early age I found at home *The Forsyte Saga*, bound in red leather, I identified Aunt A as a village version of old Anne Forsyte. Aunt A specialised, like a true Scot, in baking. We could be sure of a massive cake, preceded by home-made scones and biscuits. In the aunts' small dining room hung a copy of Turner's *The Fighting Temeraire*. Glancing at the picture hundreds of times over many years, I always assumed it depicted the noble ship sailing into battle. It came as a great shock a few years ago to realise that the *Temeraire* was being towed to the break-up yard.

Aunt I had served as a nurse in France during the Great War. Her mind must still have been full of fearful sights and sounds. She spoke nothing of this as she lived her modest life in a Wiltshire village. Her domain was the garden, and while tea was being prepared we earned it under her direction. In summer the borders needed watering – not direct to the soil from the can but down a short section of pipe inverted vertically beside each plant in the border so that the water went straight to the roots. When it rained there were bricks to be pulverised in the garden shed with a special heavy hammer so that the red dust could later be scattered on the flower beds to lighten the heavy soil. We fought battles with brass water syringes capable of drenching any target at short range. Above all there were bonfires at all seasons, but particularly in the autumn. I have kept sadly few practical skills from those days, but this is one. Making a bonfire is a specialised and controversial art, and my own mastery of it is sometimes challenged by my family. But they are wrong; I am very good at composing a bonfire, placing the paper (firelighters are an abomination) at the right level and the correct position for the wind of the day and then feeding the flames – not overindulging them at first but gradually building that core of red at the heart which guarantees success.

At a Bennetts tea, Victorian card games culminated in the mild malice of 'old maid' and then it was time to walk home, a mile out of the village up the hill to Rainscombe. I associate this walk with dark winter evenings. Find the coats and galoshes, tie scarves round necks, put on woollen gloves, shine the torches on the garden path, and then out on the road, just the three of us small boys, for traffic was scarce and no other danger conceivable. As we entered the bowl of downs, leaving the last cottage of Oare behind us, a fox might bark from the Giant's Grave and the vixen reply from the opposing hillside under the frosty stars. We would be quite glad that we were wrapped up warm and only fifteen minutes from our own home lights and welcoming beds. On one evening my brother Stephen remembers plodding behind Julian and myself up the wintry road listening awestruck as we talked of the grown-up world of prep-school life which he had not yet entered.

Oare was big enough to support a school, the White Hart pub, a forge with pungent smells, a bakery famous for special jam sponge, a post office and a Victorian church. The aunts were Presbyterian but there was nothing to offend them in our services, and they both lie in Oare churchyard. My parents preferred the grey medieval church at Huish, a hamlet at the foot of the next fold of downs towards Devizes and there we were christened. On most though not all Sundays we went to one or other of the two churches (which shared a vicar). The phrases of the Book of Common Prayer worked their way into mind and heart. In advance of Christmas, Easter and Harvest Festival we would be involved in decorating the church. Midnight Mass on Christmas Eve was not yet fashionable, so stockings had to be unpacked and a family breakfast eaten in good time for Matins in Oare at eleven o'clock. 'And there were in the same country shepherds abiding in the field keeping watch over their flocks by night . . .' I find it hard to forgive those who have robbed our children and grandchildren of the magic of such sentences, which returned dependably at the right time in the right place year after year. But my keenest recollection is of Harvest Festival evening at Huish. The open door let in the evening sun, forming a link between the sheaves of corn round the pulpit and the harvested fields from which they had been brought. My favourite psalm was the sixty-fifth, though in recent years I have never heard the chant which I loved. 'The folds shall be full of sheep: the valleys also shall stand so thick with corn, that they shall laugh and sing.'

The village celebrated the Silver Jubilee of King George V in 1935 with a giant bonfire on the Giant's Grave. At this point the ridge of the down is narrow. The turf falls steeply away on either side of the fence which runs along that ridge. Anyone turning away that night from the brightness of the blaze into the darkness was temporarily blinded and at risk of a twisted ankle. Or worse, for Mrs Hall, the vicar's wife, tore her knickers in rather public circumstances as she clambered over the fence. Such happenings stay firmly fixed in the memory of a small boy. Two years later the Coronation of King George VI was also celebrated with a bonfire, but on the wider, less precarious plateau on the opposite down above Huish.

Our life as children in the thirties centred on the farm, so that the stages of that life were the changing seasons. In my mother's diary these are usually expressed in terms of weather and flowers. There was no inhibition then about picking wild flowers or indeed taking trowels to dig and transplant them to our own home or garden. First, snowdrops everywhere at the climax of each winter. Then primroses in one particular wood quite a long trek up the downs and across two fields beyond the ridge. My brother Stephen later bought and still owns that wood called Withy Copse. In Roman times the humbler Britons used it as a rubbish dump. In our time the rabbits were excellent archaeologists; with their help we collected each year many shards of pottery, terracotta, grey and charcoal-coloured, which we transferred into a museum of our own. They took their places on the shelves of a filing cabinet alongside bones found on the downs, and flints which might or might not have been shaped by human hand. Flints lay everywhere close to the surface on those upland fields, and we were always looking for round stones bigger than golf balls which, we were told, those fairly ancient Britons had used as money boxes. A fine hoard of coins would really impress the museum at Devizes, which was rather snooty about the humble pottery which we and the rabbits unearthed. Later in the year bluebells massed in the West Woods towards Marlborough. Then cowslips, plentiful on the steepest slopes of the Giant's Grave, where no plough came. In September blackberries, which required preparation and at least two wicker picnic baskets, for they were traditionally at their best two miles away at the back of Martinsell looking towards Savernake Forest. I have been a keen blackberry picker ever since. Of course, they have to be gathered before Michaelmas Day, when the devil spits on them and spoils their flavour. Finally, mushrooms in October. Botany was a hobby of the Corner family, indeed a lifework for my uncle, John, later a professor at Cambridge and fellow of the Royal Society. My mother's knowledge of which mushrooms are safe to eat has sadly vanished from the family. Spring, summer and autumn, her diary records how she took the children out on these quests, and the trophies with which we returned.

The sterner, more practical aspect of the seasons became increasingly important as we three boys grew. The 450 acres of the farm were partly steep down on which sheep grazed and hardy dark brown Sussex cattle were reared for beef. The thin land on top grew wheat, barley or oats, and in wartime flax. In the days before compound fertilisers in plastic bags most of our land needed home-grown richness. Wessex Saddleback sows were tethered to wooden arks which ranged across the fields. Sheds on cast-iron wheels housed the Rhode Island Red hens, whose eggs were collected in wicker baskets and carried down the hill by pony and trap. Farming required a specialised permanent workforce (Sidney for the chickens, his brother Jim on the tractor, Halliday for the sheep), increased in certain months by a rush of unskilled labour working against the clock to complete a particular task. As boys, my brothers and I were part of that amateur army. Potato planting in the spring involved long hours in the field near the house, filling a bucket with seed potatoes from strategically placed sacks, and dropping them at regular intervals in the allocated furrow. I cannot remember whether we were paid nine pence an hour and planted potatoes at intervals of fifteen inches, or the other way round. The hazard of the job would be a sack in which some of the seed potatoes had rotted, covering the others with a slimy mush into which we had to plunge our hands to fill our buckets.

The main effort came at harvest. The work that is now completed in one process by combine harvesters was then separated by several months. The binder cut the corn and left bound sheaves to be put together in stooks of six or eight sheaves, which stood drying until carried to build ricks at the edge of the field or in the farmyard. The stooks had to hear the church bells on three Sundays before they were ready (though not, of course, in wartime, when the church bells were reserved for the German invasion which never came, until they were rung for the victory of El Alamein). Stooking was a backbreaking job which needed to be done quickly. We boys (and during the war the team of bigger boys from Marlborough College who camped in the park) were usually allotted the edges of the field. The sheaves here tended to be lighter, but contained more thistles from the hedgerows. The mechanical binder was not infallible and often if its twine had run out we had to secure unbound sheaves with stems of corn twisted together. After a few days, particularly if the stooks had been unskilfully built without allowing for a through draught, the wind might knock them down, in which case the unskilled labour had to re-erect them, with curses. Barley was more difficult than wheat or oats because of the awns, the scratchy spikes which protect the barley ears and lacerate the arms and legs of short-trousered workers. A hot bath after a day's harvesting was a painful affair.

In late autumn or winter the threshing machine arrived, and the ricks were dismantled one by one. Our job then was to stand in a circle with short sticks and kill the rats which tried to escape from the bottom of each rick. The men on top tossing sheaves rhythmically into the machine on their pitchforks steadily lowered the level of the rick and brought nemesis closer to its tenants. These and lesser jobs, such as cutting kale and scything nettles, were undertaken and enjoyed as a natural part of our lives, halfway between work and recreation.

The arrival of three Hurd boys in just over three years changed the architecture of Rainscombe Farm. A schoolroom with extra bedrooms above was added to the main farmhouse, a small swimming pool was dug in the garden (five strokes long, three strokes wide), and a thatched shed built beyond it and called the garden house. There we were noisy, untidy and undisturbed as we organised intricate battles of lead soldiers which could continue day after day without being tidied up. Indoors there were stamp collections to be arranged and rearranged, and the new board games to be tried – Monopoly, Totopoly and later four war games of the period, one for each armed service, L'Attaque, Dover Patrol and Aviation, plus Tritactics on land, sea and air. I have played (and won) this last subtle and dramatic board game with all my sons in turn.

By unwritten principle we spent out of doors any daylight hours when the weather was passable. At an early age we began to use an airgun, graduating upwards to a 4.10 and a twelve-bore shotgun. Neither my father nor his successive landlords reared pheasants, but much time was spent stalking the hedgerows with my father in search of rabbits. In early years we had a pony called Nigger, a name which then gave no surprise or offence to anyone. On this pony I posed in a woollen yellow bathing costume for a good portrait of all three of us painted in 1937 by Keith Henderson, a family friend. In the background are the Giant's Grave and two stone griffins. My grandfather obtained these (legitimately, I'm sure) from the façade of the Palace of Westminster when this was being refaced. The griffins followed us from garden to garden, weathering decade by decade, and now stand guard outside the library at Westwell. The pony did not otherwise play a big part in our lives, and when he died was not replaced.

One of my mother's main interests during my childhood was Hilltop, a cottage perched right on the summit of Huish Down, about a mile's steep climb from Rainscombe Farm. Hilltop was the lone survivor of a bleak little hamlet, the rest of which had crumbled away. Snowdrops were habitually planted on a cottage path from the back door to guide anyone searching for the outside earth closet on a dark January evening. In our early years an eccentric architect lived at Hilltop in mystery. We never ventured close in those days because of a huge and frightening stuffed bear which he displayed in the upstairs window. The architect and his bear departed, my mother bought the cottage in 1938 for £150, and gradually, she brought it up to minimum standards, which remained austere. The wind constantly battered Hilltop; snow drifted to block the track which led to it; water had to be pumped by hand. An Easter which we spent there working on the garden was remembered as unbelievably cold. On clear days you could see the spire of Salisbury Cathedral from the down just beyond Hilltop. The solemn rumbling from the guns on Salisbury Plain was particularly impressive at that height.

My parents occasionally joined the Hurd grandparents on holiday on the Riviera or (once) Madeira. Our own holidays were solid south-coast English seaside. I did not go abroad till I was seventeen. Weymouth, Swanage, Seaview and Totland Bay on the Isle of Wight – the albums are full of paddling and castle-building photographs. (My youngest brother Stephen established a reputation by sitting firmly with his back to the sea.) Sunburn was a threat: I remember a railway journey where I could not lean my tortured back against the hot cloth of the seat. From the lawn of the small Hotel Seaview we could salute the stately Atlantic liners on their voyages to or from Southampton, having plotted the moment exactly from the newspapers. A favourite board game then was Blue Riband of the Atlantic: you placed your bets with white pebbles from the seashore on squares marked *Queen Mary*, *Bremen* and *Normandie* until the croupier called *rien ne va plus* and spun the wheel on which models of the great ships were mounted. One holiday, planned for 1939, was cancelled because of the outbreak of war, but strangely we all went with our grandparents for an orthodox bucket-and-spade holiday to Treyarnon Bay in Cornwall in August 1940, when the Battle of Britain was at its height.

At first my parents employed a married couple down at Rainscombe Farm; she cooked, he looked after the garden, including plenty of vegetables. Later the two jobs became separated. In her classic of the period, *The Provincial Lady*, E.M. Delafield showed how the lady of the house lost control of events: when entertaining, she was condemned to sit helpless with her guests wondering what was going on in the kitchen, when and in what form lunch would appear. The same flavour surrounds my mother's account of the visit of the Bishop of Salisbury to Rainscombe Farm in 1933: 'Long delay before lunch was announced, but B. an easy guest. With much worldly assurance and a great appreciation of good food when it did arrive – in fact the last 2 chocolates made his nose bleed.'

Until we three boys went to boarding school we had a nanny. These were not starched qualified professionals, but friendly girls recruited from nearby villages, beginning with Nanny Grace, recruited from Aldbourne, who became a long-lasting friend. The nannies shared with my mother the different chores connected with us. They tended to leave fairly quickly for marriage and babies of their own. The last in line, Rozelle, played 'Red Sails in the Sunset' on her guitar. Then briefly there was an experiment with a governess, Miss Edith, who tried in vain to teach us German and the piano. She had no gifts of inspiration or persuasion, and I suspect my parents took her on because she was a refugee from Slovakia. If this element of mercy existed, it was not communicated to us, and we were fairly merciless, with one exception. At this time, it must have been early 1939, Hitler was trying to create a satellite state in Slovakia, separated from the Czechs. This involved first an overprint on the normal Czechoslovak stamps, and then entirely new stamps for Slovakia itself. These were scarce among English schoolboys. We warmly encouraged Miss Edith's family correspondence with Bratislava.

Money matters were never discussed in our presence, and I have no recollection of financial ups and downs. The way of life I have described was comfortable rather than luxurious. Three boys born close together were privately educated. The farmhouse and garden were steadily improved, presumably by agreement with the landlord. Our wants as boys were not excessive, but we lacked for nothing that we desired. That way of life could not have been sustained in the 1930s off the income (after rent had been paid) of a farm of 450 acres of not particularly good land. My father had another, modest, source of income, which took him to London one or two days a week. He was already agricultural correspondent of *The Times*, with an article published each Monday, and during the thirties at various times worked for the *Field* and for *Farmer's Weekly*, before settling down to write for many years a column in *Country Life* under the pen name Cincinnatus. This agricultural journalism gave him much pleasure, widened his horizons, and built his reputation, but would not have been generously paid. He had no particular capital of his own at this stage of his life; nor did my mother. Twice during his twenty-one years as tenant of Rainscombe Farm the estate with the big house, as well as our own farmhouse, came on the market. Once at least, so I was later told, my father tried to find the capital to buy it. The figure must have been just beyond what he and my grandfather were able or willing to find, and he remained a tenant. No accounts survive, and my mother's diaries, like our family conversation, were dumb on the subject. But it seems inescapable that my grandfather, Percy Hurd, himself comfortably off rather than wealthy, gave his elder surviving son continuous support for several years to provide for our upbringing.

The war made little impression on Rainscombe. The Hurd family was much less exposed in 1939 than between 1914 and 1918. My father was thirty-eight when war broke out. His weakness from a polio attack in his twenties would have exempted him from soldiering even if he had not been a producer of essential foods. The Minister of Agriculture appointed him one of his advisers in administering new powers to encourage (and if need be compel) the greatest possible output farm by farm. The emphasis today is entirely different. Nowadays when I read about farm set aside or am invited to admire the environmental splendour of some field of nettles and thistles, my private reaction remains what my father's would have been: incredulity verging on scorn. He preferred a walking stick with a hoe on the end for 'spudding' thistles or other weeds disfiguring his pasture. He set us to scythe and scythe again nettles in the corners of fields or round the ricks or barns. Waste, weeds and untidiness were then prime enemies of the good farmer.

My mother was put in charge of the land girls brought on to the Wiltshire farms. We received evacuees for a time at one end of the farmhouse. We built an air-raid shelter in the garden, though the chalk roof subsided as the war proceeded, and we never used it in earnest. My father joined the Home Guard. A trench was dug and occasionally manned where the main road to Marlborough reached the top of Oare Hill. From here, come the invasion, the Home Guard would toss Molotov cocktails into the turrets of German tanks as they changed gear after a long climb. One morning we were told that the Germans had landed, and I sat up in bed fingering a heavy, silver-coloured toy revolver, loaded with explosive caps loud enough to frighten nannies if not the Wehrmacht. We were taken to see the wreck of a Dornier bomber displayed in Salisbury market place. The two closest tragedies occurred while I was away at boarding school. During the Battle of Britain a Spitfire blew up over a field of our wheat at the top of Oare Hill; for a long time we picked up fragments of twisted metal among the natural downland flints. Later a Wellington bomber returning at night from Germany had damaged instruments or a disabled pilot; he failed to notice the coming change in altitude and crashed into the side of the down behind Rainscombe House, killing all on board. For years after the burned turf faithfully reproduced the bomber's shape.

But on the whole life continued much as before. There were lesser changes. No summer holidays after Treyarnon Bay, no signposts, blackout strictly observed, dimmed headlights, petrol rationing, sweet rationing and points, National Savings stamps, no more tennis parties for my parents. The only real difference was that the family was focused more intensely on the farm itself. The tractor precariously ploughed pasture on steep slopes which had not given corn since the Napoleonic Wars. The Marlborough boys came in greater numbers to bring in the harvest, joined later by rather jolly Italian prisoners of war. The farm grew flax for the first time, for parachutes, we hoped. We were set to make butter, which on unfavourable days could mean boring hours turning the handle until the welcome golden specks appeared in the cream and the butter was on its way. We boys bred rabbits unsentimentally to supplement the meat ration. We passionately followed the progress of the war, particularly by moving flags on big wall maps. In the early days we stood up on Sunday evenings before the news when the BBC played the national anthems of all the allies, waiting in particular for the splendour of the 'Marseillaise'. Hitler's victories in 1940 increased the number of allies as neutral after neutral was invaded; the national anthems were abandoned. We never doubted that Britain would win the war. Hitler was a villainous buffoon; Mussolini just a buffoon. It would take a bit of time, but the outcome was sure. It was not until I got to Eton in 1942 that the heavier side of war began to form part of my education.

Before the outbreak of war my grandfather had told the Devizes Conservative Association that it was time for him to retire from Parliament. The local Conservatives began to consider their next choice and adopted the general principle that the new candidate, unlike my grandfather, should possess a butler and a park. My father had hoped to succeed his father in the seat, but was ruled out by this move back to the nineteenth century. He was quickly adopted for the neighbouring and safer constituency of Newbury, where the Conservatives preferred him to an obvious local candidate who had both butler and park. The Devizes Conservatives eventually chose the Roman Catholic author Christopher Hollis, *sans* butler, *sans* park, and so the tangled evolution of the Party continued. The consequence for us was that after the General Election of 1945 my father, the new MP for Newbury, began to look for a house in that constituency. He had, I think, outgrown his role at Rainscombe Farm and would probably have looked for a change anyway.

We left Rainscombe in 1947. I cannot from now on speak collectively for my brothers, but this was a sad revolution for me. Seventeen is a sentimental age, and I roamed the familiar ring of downs in desolate farewell. Fifty years later I took my son Philip up the Giant's Grave and photographed Rainscombe Farm from the top. By chance I chose the same vantage point as my mother had done when photographing it in 1947. The farmhouse, Rainscombe Park, the layout of the fields, hedgerows and woods spread beneath us were identical in the two pictures. The only difference was that in 1947 the stooks of corn stood neatly in the September fields, waiting for the sun and wind to dry them and for the army of human harvesters to cart them to the ricks.

It seems long ago. I have lingered on the Rainscombe theme, because the seventeen years I spent there shaped much of my view of life, and of this country. Certainly there was much missing. I knew the inside of most of the houses and cottages of Oare, where there was poverty, of a simple, straightforward kind which did not protest or shock. But I knew little of cities, or of mass unemployment or later of the grim financial state of Britain. With the possible exception of Geoffrey Fry, I knew no one who was grand or rich. The list of our friends and acquaintances was as small as the range of our travel. I knew something about the King and Queen, about the history of England, as embodied largely in earlier kings and queens, about the Conservative Party, and its genuine supporters from all walks of life, about the Church of England and its combination of boredom and beauty. These in different ways were already part of the background of my life, and all seemed harmonious and acceptable. My parents were thoughtful and loving. There was nothing to rebel against, plenty to attract loyalty. More positively, the

sum of these experiences, set physically against the changing seasons of
the year and the landscape of Wiltshire, suggested a settled and stable
future, not just for me but for the whole community of which I had been
part. In short, we were happy.

TWYFORD

To the visitor, the town of Marlborough has changed little in the last
half-century. Waitrose now prospers where once we went to the cinema
(1938: 'Elephant Boy good but scary. Victoria the Great v.g.'). The
Ailesbury Arms is no longer a hotel. The town still holds in autumn the
Little Mop and Big Mop fairs from which we returned home flushed
with excitement, clutching balloons and goldfish in precarious bowls.
Essentially Marlborough remains a warm, unpretentious market town
in red brick, notable for the generous width of its High Street and for the
college buildings clustered unobtrusively across the Bath Road beyond
St Peter's Church.

In Marlborough our education began. At the age of five I started to
attend Cray Court, a kindergarten on one of the roads running along the
northern slope above the High Street. It was run effectively on
traditional lines by Miss Kinder. Her reputation for sternness was
justified, though I do not remember her as unfair or unreasonable. Her
comments in my reports sometimes verged on the waspish, though she
remarked favourably on my hard work and general knowledge. 'Why is
he so nervous? Particularly when his mother is away.' I was just six at
the time. At the end of the following term: 'Douglas finds a good deal
of the work easy, which is lucky because he does not persevere when he
meets a difficulty. He asks for guidance on silly little points connected
with his work and so must be urged to be more self-reliant.' A year later
she relented: 'A very good term. Douglas does not fuss now, and looks
after Julian very well on Fridays.' But in my very first term at Miss
Kinder's a specific note was sounded which later became significant.
Handwork consisted of 'Raffia and Woollen Ball', and the verdict was
'Douglas should be made to use his hands – nothing finicky, or he will
be discouraged.' For better or worse (probably at that age for worse), I
was already more interested in affairs of state than in raffia work or
indeed woollen ball. This letter must have been written early in 1936
when my mother was away in London: 'Dear Mummie, I had a very
good time in the snow we have been having. I went to the town hall
today to see King Edward the VIII made King.' At the age of eight and
a half I was sent away to boarding school. I do not suppose there was
any particular discussion before the decision. It was taken for granted,

including by myself. The choice of school was, however, adventurous. Twyford School, two miles east of Winchester, is one of several which claim to be the oldest preparatory school in England. Certainly there was a Roman Catholic school there soon after the Restoration, hovering uneasily on the boundary of the anti-papist laws. It was attended by Alexander Pope, but faded away in the middle of the eighteenth century. In the nineteenth century Twyford was re-established under the ownership of the Wickham family, who provided, with interruptions, successive generations of Church of England clergymen as its headmasters. The main hazard to prep schools as they grew in the nineteenth century was not poor teaching or even bullying, but bad drains. In 1896 and 1897 two epidemics of diphtheria forced the numbers at Twyford down to twenty-eight. Three boys died, many parents withdrew their sons and the remnant were moved away from Twyford while massive new sanitation was installed. The Wickhams persevered; Twyford revived.

By 1937 there was a new crisis. The headmaster, H.G. McDonell, was humourless, inhibited and intensely conservative. He was particularly suspicious of electricity. Although he reluctantly installed it in his study, he insisted on having a paraffin lamp burning as well in case the electric light should go out. There was no question of installing electricity throughout the school; his sister Daisy explained that this would not be wise 'because it was so dangerous when it went round the corners'. Black beetles abounded and there was no bathroom in the private house. Neither the sanitation nor the curriculum had altered since the beginning of the century. Twyford continued to win top scholarships to Winchester, but in the thirties this was no longer quite enough. The school needed fifty pupils to be viable, and in 1937 had just thirty-seven. By then it was owned by Bob Wickham, a newly ordained schoolmaster of thirty-two teaching at Marlborough, with a young wife and no money. Bravely he took over the running of his family's school from the faltering headmaster and began, on the eve of a world war, the task of putting it to rights. I do not know how my father met Bob Wickham, but he must have been greatly impressed. Within a year I was at Twyford, and my two brothers followed. It proved an excellent choice.

October 1 1938

Dear Mother
Thank you very much for all your letters. I am sorry that I couldn't write before, as I could not find time. I am getting on very well and am not homesick. I sleep in the Long room Dormitory with five other people and I sit at meals second from the bottom at the left hand

table . . . At the present moment it is 2.15 (rest time) . . . This morning
we did Latin, English, French and Maths.

October 2 1938

Dear Julian and Stephen,
. . . Today we have all got our navy blue suits on and school ties. How
are all the pets getting on? . . . One of the great things to do here is to
collect stores of beech nuts . . . I have been fitted out with my school
cap and hat as well as my football boots.

October 3 1938

Dear Rozelle
This morning I pulled one of my front teeth out. It has been worrying
for 2 days . . . As you said I have found many friends, Watt,
Horseford, Sanger, Nightingale and E. Studd; but I like Studd best.
The chief form of punishment is to go into Coventry. This means that
you must not [talk] for some of tea. You can go in Cov. for 5 minutes,
10, 15 etc. You were quite right; tea consists of toast with fish or
something like that. Today I collected some 140 beech nuts.

This was the first batch of many unremarkable letters. I counted the
days which had to pass before the next holidays, because holidays were
clearly preferable to school. But neither on paper nor in my memory is
there any hint of misery. I was an accepting boy – or perhaps we were
an accepting generation.

Twyford looked like dozens of other English prep schools. A small
but dignified early eighteenth-century house formed the core in which
the Wickhams lived. Round it were assembled a chapel, hall, war
memorial library, classrooms, dormitories and an indoor swimming
pool. More vivid in my mind are the terraced playing fields, presided
over by the aforesaid beeches. The most formidable of the teachers was
Leslie Davies, known to us as Trotsky, presumably because of his
authoritarian instincts. His moustache was supposed to be stiff with
remnants of breakfast marmalade. His main weapon of instruction was
a silver propelling pencil, with which he whacked the heads of those
whose irregular verbs were out of joint. For Mr Davies taught French,
and somehow taught it just right. Later, at Eton, I was taught by Oliver
van Oss, who went on to be headmaster of Charterhouse and
introduced us to Lamartine, Victor Hugo and the civilisation of France.
But none of that would have been nourishing if Mr Davies had not
previously forced into my mind the structure of French grammar, the
beginnings of a vocabulary, and the essential distinction between
pronouncing '-ont' and '-ant'. Major Bull was the senior master, a

survivor from the McDonell days and guardian of the ancient (that is, Victorian) traditions of Twyford. But we could see that the real authority belonged to Bob Wickham. To us, a headmaster of thirty-three was by no means young, and the dog collar gave him extra gravity. He taught us Latin and Divinity and swam with us on summer mornings. He did not strive for a modern sort of familiarity and we had no notion that he was struggling to save the school. For our age and time he was a first-class headmaster.

Twyford in South Hampshire somehow seemed closer to the seat of war than Rainscombe in North Wiltshire, but even so it is remarkable how the rhythms of school life were sustained. We followed the progress of the war with great care. In one corridor there was a shelf to which was delivered each morning a copy of the *Daily Telegraph* destined for the masters' common room. Somehow we established or stole the privilege of glancing at this paper on our way to breakfast. One morning in June 1940 the headlines accurately reported that the French Prime Minister Reynaud had resigned; he was to be replaced by Marshal Pétain, who would seek an armistice with the Germans. One wretched schoolmate was half-French, and we surrounded him with taunts and reproaches. Unlike us, he had heard of Verdun, and protested violently that we had got it wrong: it must be the dirty politician Reynaud who was in favour of surrender, and Pétain who would again rescue France. I am afraid that he had a bad day.

For us at Twyford the war meant mainly air raids. In September 1940 we returned to school from the summer holidays and were indignant to be sent at once down to the shelter while the masters were allowed to follow in the sky the latest instalment of the Battle of Britain. In the months which followed the raids turned from day to night.

November 24 1940

Dear Mother,
Air raid after air raid. We've had 37 solid hours of raid this week. On Sunday night 50 incendiaries were dropped in the face of a terrific barrage. Fields were blazing – that raid lasted 10 hours. Tuesday and Wednesday there were 6-hour night raids. On Friday the raid caught us in our clothes, so we had to stay in them till <u>6 am</u> when the 'All clear' sounded – that was our longest – 11½ hours. Last night the electricity failed (it isn't on again yet: I think the line was hit) and 5 minutes later the warning went . . . Twyford won its first match yesterday – I'm afraid I wasn't playing – against Beechborough 2–0. You may remember that 3 weeks ago they beat us 1–0. Now the Greek campaign is on could you please see if you could buy us a little Xmas

gift – some flags for my map? If you can't obtain them I'll have to make them when I get home. Only 3 more weeks you know – we break up Monday Dec. 16 . . .

The different elements are there much as I remember them: strong interest in what was going on, a tendency to measure and record, a certain fatigue . . . We had not enough imagination to feel any fear at being bombarded, which would in any case have entirely contradicted the mood of the time. The masters achieved the target of clearing the dormitories within two and a half minutes of the siren sounding. Half-awake boys had to be deterred from falling back into bed and escorted down to the shelter, which I thoroughly disliked. It was warm, stuffy, made even less endurable by the record of George Formby played over and over by one of the masters on his portable gramophone. I remember an endless ditty about little fishes swimming over a dam. The thin, clear note of the siren sounding the all clear became for me the most treasured single note of the war.

> June 22 1941
>
> Last night there was a lot of activity and 2 landmines sent us down to the shelter and sent some plaster from the ceiling down to our beds. We went down at 2 am and came up at 4.45. There have been two matches this week – both lost . . . there was a huge tea and a conjurer who was very good . . . I can swim 8 lengths now in 3½ minutes. Mr Bartlett has left for a munitions job . . .
> P.S. Vive (?) A bas (?) les Russes! Nous apercevrons.

The grammar of the postscript (written the day after Hitler invaded Russia) suggests that Mr Davies and his silver pencil still had work to do.

All three Hurd boys worked well at Twyford and received good reports. There were two of these reports each term, meticulously prepared. This fairly consistent stream of praise descending on Rainscombe stirred my parents to protest. They asked whether Bob Wickham and his colleagues ever wrote a bad report. In reply they were sent a specimen of stinging criticism sent to other parents with the name of the boy removed.

Looking back on my time at Twyford, I have one dissatisfying memory. At the beginning of one term we were assembled in hall to hear various administrative details, including the list of those who were inscribed for the carpentry class. My name was on the list, though I had not volunteered. When I pointed this out, I was told that my parents had asked that I should do carpentry. So I dutifully produced a number of objects, in particular a misshapen toast rack with glue oozing out of the joins, such as I have enthusiastically received from more than one of my own children over the years. I did not stay long with carpentry. This reluctance ties in with Miss Kinder's earlier strictures on the raffia work and woollen ball. I am by nature clumsy with my hands, and out of sympathy with tools and machinery. I was never really persuaded or pushed to correct this failing, and am therefore incompetent to tackle small tasks about the home, and most things to do with a car.

The same is true of sport. My clumsiness and short sight were impediments, but not so serious that they could not be overcome. I am physically strong, and enjoy the feeling of a well-exercised body. But though at different times of my life I have dabbled under mild pressure from family, schools, my peers and two wives, I have never broken through into real satisfaction with any sport. Cricket, tennis, skiing, shooting, dancing, swimming the crawl – the experience of effort begun but not sustained is common to them all. Because I was exceptionally good at passing exams and after that reasonably good at getting on in work of most kinds no one really pulled me up short and told me that my lifestyle was several annas short of a rupee. My most striking athletic achievement was a score of 32 not out at a Twyford cricket match sixty years ago, the joy of which I still remember. I am left with swimming the breaststroke and walking quite long distances; neither activity requires any skill. I mildly blame for this failure those responsible for my upbringing, but mainly I blame myself. I have keenly attended my children's sports days, and applauded with envy their achievements at football, cricket, tennis and even lacrosse.

I left Twyford with a handsome prize edition of Shakespeare, the golden binding of which has just been restored to glory by a bookbinder in Oxford. But I knew that the small successes of Twyford would be insignificant and soon forgotten among what seemed the formidable mysteries of a public school.

2

ETON

On the morning of a.d.XV kal.Oct MDCCCCXLII, vulgarly known as 17 September 1942, I knelt in front of Lord Quickswood, formerly Lord Hugh Cecil, now provost of Eton, and clasped three of his fingers. His other fingers were allocated to the boys who knelt beside me. In a high, reedy voice he addressed us as follows: '*Ego Hugo Baro de Quickswood, praepositus huicusce Collegii . . . admitto te*', and so on into a long exhortation. This translated as: 'Be a good boy, obedient and respectful, so that you may grow up in purity and honesty among your fellows, and eventually leave the discipline of school as an honourable citizen useful to your country, to the greater glory of God, through Jesus Christ our Lord . . .'

I had already explained the significance of the ceremony in my first letter from Eton to my parents.

September 17 1942

Dear Mummy,

Life here is very exciting but so far everything has turned out all right. After I left you I walked up town. I met Mr Hamilton who invited me to tea – I felt I was justified in accepting, having only had one piece of bread-and-butter before. So I had tea with an Australian admiral and his wife and the Bishop of Salisbury's grandson.

After that I met Mrs Willink and Charles. At 6 my voice had to be tested – but that was soon over. Supper at 7.30 – prayers at 9 – bed at 9.30. This morning we got up at 7.30 and put on all our paraphernalia – except the gown, for we are not allowed to wear that until we are 'gowned' by the Provost this afternoon. (We kneel before him in an attitude of prayer, he murmurs a Latin blessing and then we retire with a bow – we are members of Eton when we have signed the book but we do not become members of College until we have been 'gowned'.)

At 11 we saw Mr Butterwick, our classical master (I am in D1) and he told that there would be early school at 7.30.

Another event this afternoon is a swimming test – I don't know if I shall enter for it.

The only thing I am dreading is chamber-singing on Sunday – each new Colleger has to mount Ye Olde Round Table and sing something – very embarrassing.

Sometime soon I – or rather my election – will be examined on house-colours. I have bought a chart of these at W.V. Brown's.
More on Sunday
Yours with love
D.R.H. KS [King's Scholar]

My parents' decision to enter me for the Eton scholarship in 1942 was almost as bold as their decision four years earlier to send me to precarious Twyford. Two other choices would have been more natural. My father, like his three brothers, had been to Marlborough and had kept in touch with the college and its masters. Since we lived only five miles away there would have been practical advantage in making me a Marlburian. Twyford, on the other hand, had for long been one of the cluster of prep schools which fed Winchester; its curriculum pointed towards the regular Winchester entry exam and, for really bright boys, the formidable Winchester scholarship. But my parents had it clearly in their minds that the three of us, being only three years apart in age, should go to three different public schools. They worried that if we all continued to go to the same school life might be difficult for whichever of us fell behind his siblings in work or general esteem. Whether this arose from my father's experience with his brothers at Marlborough I am not sure; certainly no particular difficulty had arisen for the three of us together at Twyford. Looking back, I think the decision was probably a mistake and I have not followed it with my own children. Stephen, Julian and I all did pretty well at school, so there could have been no real embarrassment. Although we often wrote to each other, and later travelled abroad together with and without our parents, the separation meant that we were not as close as we might have been otherwise.

Eton was wholly unknown to me. There was not a single Twyfordian there when I arrived. Indeed, I don't think I had ever met an Etonian anywhere, and certainly I did not know a single boy in the school when I started. I took the scholarship just three months after my twelfth birthday. This meant that I had a year in hand, and if I failed could resit the exam. But it also meant that I was not fully prepared, particularly in Greek, and no match for the massed candidates of Summerfields, Sunningdale and the Dragon, prep schools which focused their energies on Eton and studied every detail and quirk of the scholarship examinations. In the event I emerged thirteenth in the list, on the borderline. In those less regimented days boys at the top of the school left at Christmas or Easter as well as July. The number of Eton scholars living together in college had been irrevocably fixed at seventy by King Henry VI in 1440. As a result, small boys in my position at the edge of the scholarship list might be asked to wait one half or two before joining the rest of their election in college. (Half is the Etonian word for term: there are three halves in one year.) This would have been a disadvantage, but luckily I was squeezed in for the first half, and entered college as a King's Scholar in September 1942.

Eton has been part of my existence ever since. There have been gaps of several years, and recently the link has weakened, but as a scholar for six years, a fellow of the college for fifteen, and a parent of four Etonians, I have watched and been influenced by Eton in many phases of the school's life and my own. I revisit Eton with a mixture of amusement, loyalty and affection stirred by strong memories. Eton now is glossy with success. The reality is different from the tabloid reputation of snobbery and foolish exclusivism. Some people, including the headmaster, have to worry about this gap, but it is not of huge concern to most.

Thanks to King Henry's pious generosity, Eton has had the money to change, to modernise boarding houses and classrooms and to stay well ahead in ideas and equipment. Eton has restored to perfection the elegant yet homely beauty of its ancient centre – school, yard, chapel, cloisters, playing fields, river. I find it hard now to imagine the shabbiness of 1942. In 1940 incendiary bombs had destroyed half of Upper School and the whole of Savile House, shattering the chapel windows. During the whole of my time there these wounds remained. Willowherb grew in the fenced-off gap thus created in School Yard. As at Twyford, air raids became part of the curriculum. We collegers trooped down across Weston's Yard to the shelter in the ruins of Savile House.

For my first four years I accepted Eton without any particular emotion, just as I had accepted Twyford. I do not think I was singular. This acceptance of what existed is the main difference between my generation of schoolboys and our successors now. There was no television, of course, no girls in school, no drugs. Rules or (more often) conventions governed most aspects of behaviour. There was little scope in wartime for spending money and thus there was small visible difference between those whose parents were rich and the rest. It sounds today like a narrow and restricted regime; to most of us it seemed normal. Work and games, games and work, spiced with traditional festivals and news of the war, filled the first years. Then personal relationships thrust themselves to the fore, and what had been accepted without emotion quite suddenly became highly stimulating, sometimes tense with rivalry, but on the whole enjoyable.

The seventy King's Scholars lived at the heart of Eton, in the cluster of buildings which separates School Yard from Weston's Yard. In those days new boys started life in the ancient Long Chamber, notorious for bullying in the eighteenth century. Long Chamber in my time was a compromise between a dormitory and separate rooms. Each of us had a cubicle, or stall, defined by wooden partitions about ten feet high and by curtains opening on to the main common area. Privacy was secured by convention. If you wanted to keep Jones out of your stall you proclaimed a loud 'stall curtains, stall curtains, Jones', and public opinion did the rest. Mild cheerful disorder was commonplace, kept within bounds partly by the captain of chamber, who had the power to beat boys with a rubber siphon (not very painful) but mainly by the fact that we all had to work hard at our desks in our stalls preparing for the next day's classes or the end-of-term trials. We learned quickly to organise our time to accommodate the pressure of preparation, overwhelmingly at first in Latin and Greek. 'Work crisis' was a recognised condition; once proclaimed it earned the sufferer quiet for an hour or so. No one regarded a work crisis as undesirable or called it stress. But there was time enough for indoor games which were a matter of fashion – Monopoly in one half, then Totopoly, Tritactics, Invasion or fiendish tribal contests which we invented ourselves, dividing chamber into Athenians, Spartans and Thebans.

There were two unforgettable characters who dominated the lives of young Collegers. I do not know how they would fare in, or enjoy, the blander, more bureaucratic world of today. Elsie Iredale-Smith, matron in college, was small, bun-shaped and fierce. She had the formidable responsibility for keeping us fit and fed in the middle of a war. How she did this we never knew; some explanations verged on the slanderous. Our meals in College Hall were simple but generous throughout. By convention (it is hard to overstate the power of convention in our lives) this powerful lady was not allowed to set foot in College Hall, though she ruled almost everything that happened there. She watched us eat from the Minstrels' Gallery, her head just visible above the parapet. Her eyes were keen to detect below her a plate left with food still on it, a mini-riot at a junior table. On the occasions when one could choose where to sit, there was a rush for places right under the gallery, screened from this disciplinary gaze. Impossible to avoid were her nightly inspections in chamber. The usual noise died down as we strained to hear over the stall partitions what she was saying to the occupant of each stall. One boy was notorious, at least in her eyes, for not showering properly after the Field Game. 'Knees Williams, feet Williams' we would hear as she summoned each limb for inspection.

The Airedale, as we called her at this stage of our lives, was brisk and decisive in dealing with ailments. In January 1943 I returned to Eton from the Christmas holidays with a swollen gland in my neck. She and the doctor took one look and packed me off by bus to my grandmother in Beaconsfield. My lump was removed in a nursing home near Newbury, and I spent the whole of what should have been my second Eton half convalescing at Rainscombe, cutting kale and painting blackout signs. This was the only event in these early Eton years which really depressed me. Good teaching afterwards enabled me to catch up the lost ground. Later Elsie became a friend to most senior boys. We were addressed as 'dear'. She invited us to listen to music on her gramophone in the evenings, but her tastes were decidedly conservative: 'Bliss, dear, who could want to listen to Bliss?'

Years later, after her retirement, Elsie was left a large sum of money. She used part of this, in secrecy, to help a number of her former charges, including once myself, who might not otherwise have been able to afford the Eton fees for their sons. She spent her last years in a flat at the top of Swan Court in Chelsea, shopping by telephone exclusively from Harrods, and reading books from Harrods' Library on the French monarchy, which was her special subject. Judy and I and many others used to visit her, and she became a stock exchange of all kinds of Eton gossip and history. She remained entirely loyal to the school, and we came to realise how often she had been the champion of the small collegers against Eton rules and restrictions which she thought unreasonable.

Our other nightly caller, Walter Hamilton, Master in College, was at first more difficult to deal with. Walter was near the beginning of an academic career which led him to be headmaster of Westminster and Rugby and master of Magdalene College, Cambridge. He was, I suppose, one of the last of those talented men whose early mastery of Latin and Greek and skill as schoolmasters brought them to the top of their career, bypassing the usual complicated barriers of English life. He did not achieve his success by easy speech, being a man of many moods but few words, and those often uttered in a deep, melancholy voice. 'Well?' he would begin his evening visits, having stationed himself awkwardly in the doorway. The monosyllable without follow-up on his part was apt to stifle any possible conversation, while we tried to calculate whether that evening the melancholy was the result of real gloom or just his normal protection against trivial chatter. It is rumoured that his proposal of marriage some years later was couched in the form of a characteristic question: 'Would you like to see my name on your tombstone?' He knew his own problem, and in one of my reports thanked me for my efforts at conversation during these visits.

Walter Hamilton was a deeply serious and straightforward man. He was himself a scholar, translator of Plato, and he never belittled the importance of hard work. But it is striking how in his letters to my parents and no doubt to others he concentrated on analysing character. His published letters to his friend James Duff, then at Durham, showed that during the war he thought seriously about taking holy orders. But he disliked anything which smacked of affectation or exaggerated feeling, and clerical sermons were a frequent target. For example, although deeply patriotic, he had little time for the hymn 'O Valiant Hearts', often sung on Armistice Day because (he thought) of its romanticisation of war. One sermon of his powerfully exposed the pretence that happiness is a right to which we are all entitled.*

Most, though not all, Collegers learned before the end of their time at Eton to penetrate the mask of Walter's melancholy, to appreciate the help which he could give, and even to convert the respect which was his due into affection and friendship. This process was much easier as we began to share his adult sense of humour. In so-called 'private' sessions a dozen or so of us sat on the sofa or on the floor in his study while he read aloud. One of his reports commends my understanding of *Wuthering Heights*; I do not remember this and have always found the book intractable. What I do remember, narrated in Walter's baritone, are Mrs Proudie and Mr Slope and the gradual unfolding of Trollope's Barchester. Thanks to him, I read again and again the great scene full of Homeric imagery when the slanting sofa tears a great rent in Mrs Proudie's dress and she thrice rebukes the offender, 'Unhand it, Sir.'

The early teens are the right time to imprint such pleasures on the memory. Behind Trollope lurked another master. I doubt if in 1943 and 1944 Walter would have read much P.G. Wodehouse to us, not because of the author's alleged lack of wartime patriotism but because Eton under the headmastership of Claude Elliott might have suspected frivolity. But Walter's conversation, as we matured, frequently flowed into Wodehousian channels. We were expected to catch the allusion. It is through Walter that I came to know, and constantly renew acquaintance with, Jeeves and more particularly Lord Emsworth, his sisters and Beach the butler of Blandings.

_____

*This sermon is preserved as an annexe to Donald Wright's *Collection of Essays – Walter Hamilton 1908–1988: A Portrait* (James & James, 1992). The book is an admirable summary of a remarkable life.

It is intelligent of Harrow to have understood that even tuneless boys like to sing, and the annual Harrow Songs are a rock of strength. Eton has two perfectly good songs, the 'Boating Song' and the 'Vale', but no longer makes full use of them or of others which lie dusty in the archives. But we scholars gathered regularly for what we called Secular Singing. Structured like so much by popular convention, this was an hour or more of rumbustious ditties with a strong emphasis of tongue in cheek. The climax came with the solo of Walter Hamilton (as the Master in College), his voice tuneless and funereal. I can hear it now. It might be the 'Earl of Murray':

Now woe be to thee Huntly! And wherefore did ye sae!
He was a braw gallant and he rid at the ring;
I bade you bring him wi' you, but forbade you him to slay.
And the bonny Earl of Murray, Oh! he might hae been a king. [. . .]
Oh! lang will his lady look owre the Castle doun,
Ere she see the Earl of Murray come sounding thro' the toun.

But his favourite, sung slowly in total gloom, was a lilting Victorian ballad:

If those lips could only speak,
If those eyes could only see,
If those beautiful golden tresses
Were there in realiteee,
Could I only take your hand,
As I did when you took my name,
But it's only a beautiful picture,
In a beautiful golden frame.

I kept a friendship with Walter in his later life through his headship of famous schools and colleges, through his happy marriage to Jane, through their house in Mull and finally back to Cambridge. That was my good fortune. It is hard to work out what I learned from him because he rarely 'taught' in the narrow sense of that word. His dislike of pretence or posturing made him reluctant to mount a pulpit of any kind. But the mixture in his personality of melancholy, humour and straightforward honourableness left a deep impression on many, and certainly on myself.

Services in College Chapel were of course compulsory; we spent a good deal of time there. The chapel did not shine physically as it does now. The windows broken by the bomb blast of 1940 were patched with black, to ward off the return of the Luftwaffe. The wall paintings were still hidden behind dark panelling, and the roof, also of dark wood, had none of the splendour of the present vaulting. The words of the Authorised Version and the Book of Common Prayer, the tunes of the hymns, and the chants of psalms and canticles were drummed into us morning by morning, a gift for which I am deeply grateful. In my early years the precentor was Henry Ley, known to the world as a composer for the organ, and to us for the immense volume of noise which he could summon from that instrument. All Saints' Day each year was notable. Many old hymns end with a quiet verse (marked *p* in the traditional Ancient and Modern hymnal) followed by a final loud verse (*mf* leading to *f*). But the hymn 'For All the Saints' ends, after its quiet verse 'The golden evening brightens in the west' with *two* loud verses, 'And yet there breaks a yet more glorious day' and finally, and beyond any doubt, *fortissimo* (*ff*):

> *From earth's wide bounds, from ocean's furthest coast,*
> *Through gates of pearl streams in the countless host.*

Dr Ley accepted this as his annual challenge, and led us in a great charge of triumph and acclamation.

Each Sunday at evensong during the war we heard read out the names of Etonians killed in action. That ritual chimed with one aspect of Eton which most impresses visitors. The cloisters beyond Lupton's Tower are crowded with memorial tablets from the Great War – not organised in any orderly way, not following a uniform pattern, but mixed up individual by individual, family by family. Each chose its own materials and inscriptions, a few still in Latin, most in simple English – seven Grenfells on one plaque, three Tennant brothers killed in 1915, 1916 and 1917, three grandsons of old Provost Goodford. They fill the four sides of the cloister. By their variety these memorials emphasise the share of suffering borne by those who some years before had thronged the same houses, fields and classrooms which we knew. Now a new list was growing, and would require in time new memorials. To me at least, having no one close to me at risk in the front line, there seemed little connection between these battlefields and our own experience of war, which consisted once again of air raids and shelters. Two letters from summer 1944, the era of the flying bomb or doodlebug, perhaps convey the flavour.

Tuesday morning

Dear Mummy,
Thank you very much for the ties – yes, we do need them. We are allowed to go to afternoon schools and supper in white flannel shirts and grey flannel trousers <u>provided that</u> we wear a tie. I shall look around for some bathing shorts but shan't buy them till I'm sure there will be bathing this half at all.

We still live in an atmosphere of sirens and shelters. Friday and Saturday nights were fairly quiet and we did not have to go down.

Sunday night however we went down no less than three times
(9.50–10.30, 11.10–11.45, 12.15–5.50) and finally emerged into
broad daylight. We slept from 6 till 9 and again in the afternoon
from 2.30 to 4.30 getting off two schools. Last night they decided
to keep us down there when once the sirens had sounded so we
spent from 10.30–6.00 in the shelters.

There is now much more chance of getting to sleep – by putting
mattresses on the floor they have created a few new bunks so that we
don't have to share. The atmosphere is terribly stuffy at first but gets
cooler later. Biscuits are served at regular intervals! Several 'flying bombs'
have crashed nearby but none on the College grounds. We represent the
150-mile-range limit, so that any of them flying in this direction are
bound to come down near here if they get through unscathed.

Yes, we beat the Army soundly on Saturday – Rudd mi, who was
15 last April making 88 not out in an incredibly short time. Today we
are playing the MCC who are batting now.

Wednesday morning

We were down the shelter again for nearly ten hours last night, not
coming out till after eight. There is still an alert on so I don't expect
there will be chapel at 10.

Wednesday evening

This letter seems to be getting more like a diary! A notice has just gone
up with the most detailed instructions for daylight raids – when the light
in the bomb goes out hurl yourself on the ground and hope for the best.

As you will realise the timetable is very much out of gear. We have
missed seven schools so far and there is talk of completely rearranging
the whole routine. But then there is talk of everything – one minute
rumour has it that we are all going home, the next that we are to be
evacuated to North Wales!
Much love
Douglas

Saturday July 8 1944

Dear Mummy,
Thank you very much for the gooseberries, which arrived safely in the
best condition on Thursday. They are very good indeed.

The Boche has stopped his night attacks here and started daylight
ones. What we thought was the military firing mortars during the
Winchester match was really a flying bomb – which landed on the
incinerator by the side of the neighbouring racecourse. Boys who were
on the river, about a mile nearer the explosion than I was on Agar's,

saw a column of smoke rise into the air after the explosion. A loudspeaker told the race-goers to take cover but afterwards the race went on as usual. The Headmaster is reported by Mr Hamilton to have longed to tell the fashionable crowds on Agar's to hurl themselves to the ground in the approved style.

On Sunday the siren went while we were in chapel – so the Provost got up and asked us to go back to our houses while he and the choirboys continued the service – they are terribly afraid of all the glass in chapel being blown on top of us.

On Monday a new type of warning was introduced – a 10-minute ring on the electric bells which are situated in every house and block of schoolrooms. This means 'Get to cover immediately – hurl yourself on the ground – cover your ears with your hands – lungs three-quarters full – handkerchief in your mouth. Don't get up till you hear the explosion or if nothing happens after 2 minutes.' Since then this alarm has been sounded nine times – once on Tuesday, four times on Wednesday and four times yesterday. Five times it found me in College, twice in school, once in the street and once cricketing. It was really very peculiar to see the whole street suddenly bow down to the ground! Each time there have been far-off explosions except yesterday evening when I was playing cricket. We were having the 1st innings of the 1942 Election Drybobs v Wetbobs on a remote pitch so that we could hear no bells. So we only took cover when we heard the explosion which sounded very near – they say the actual bomb crashed in the Great Park.

I am glad you did not think it necessary to keep me down in the shelter every night – only poor Elmsley has to do that, though several others kept him company until their parents sent replies.

How is the flax? From Daddy's article in *Country Life* this week it would seem to be rather mouldy.

Much love
Douglas.

Looking at my diary and letters home, I am surprised at the amount of space I gave to facts and figures about cricket and different kinds of football. These records resemble the passages in the Old Testament which record without elaboration the reigns and deaths of the kings of Israel and Judah. My heart was not in the scores thus recorded. I continued as a clumsy and somewhat reluctant performer of most games, made a hash of rowing in my first summer half, and never made a successful transition to cricket. Indeed, I still sometimes catch myself looking through a window at the gathering rain of an English summer morning and recall the hope that it would last long enough to prevent cricket that afternoon. The winter was better. I enjoyed playing as an average performer at the Eton Field Game and positively relished what is perhaps the most misunderstood of public school sports, the Wall Game – so little understood that it is perhaps worth a few self-indulgent paragraphs of its own.

The Wall Game has never appealed much to spectators. Dean Inge ('the gloomy Dean'), who commented on most matters human and divine in England between the two wars, described it as a relic of barbarism. But for scholars in College it was cloaked in myths of loyalty and superhuman prowess. The Oppidans – that is, the rest of the school – put together a light-hearted team each year of athletic youths who had some time on their hands and wanted to gain extra colours. But it was our game, not theirs. The annual climax of the Wall Game came on St Andrew's Day at the end of November, when College Wall, recruited from the seventy scholars, played Oppidan Wall, recruited from a thousand Oppidans. By then the mud and often the fog were at their thickest. We had prepared ourselves intensively week by week, aiming to overcome by subtle tactics the greater brawn of our opponents, usually described as 'elephantine' by the meticulous College scribes. Each side defends a specific area called 'calx' at its end of the wall, one marked by a door, the other by a tree. Once you have forced your opponents back into their area, you can score a shy by lifting the ball against the rough, uneven side of the wall and touching it. Of course, it is not as simple as that; I pass over much technical detail. Foolish or bored critics allege that it is impossible to score anything at the Wall Game. But shies are not rare; what happens only by miracle is the conversion of a shy into a goal by hurling the ball to hit a marked segment of the door and tree, respectively.

The rules of the game have been softened since the 1940s and as a result the garments worn by the players are less formidable. Those of us who played closest to the wall itself in the forties wore padded helmets of violet and white, thick gloves, heavy sacks of white canvas, shin pads, and coarse chocolate-coloured trousers dating from the Boer War and bequeathed to us by the Corps after its conversion to khaki. The main but unenforceable rule of combat was that you were permitted to 'knuckle' your opponent by *placing* your gloved hand against any part of his face or body and twisting; you were forbidden to *strike* him. The distinction was scholastic because the offence was usually invisible. Loud accusations of 'Striking', emerging from the cloud of steam and mud round the struggling bodies at the wall, were hard to adjudicate, even though two umpires and a referee were provided. The only cry on which action was immediate was 'Air', when the bullies or scrums would rapidly break up into individual parts so that the suffocating player could survive. Sometimes long minutes would pass with an equilibrium of force in the scrum, much shoving and knuckling but no movement. Indeed, a college side, conscious that the Oppidans would kick more strongly once the ball was free of the scrum, might well decide to play a static defence game, keeping the ball against the Wall. Oliver Leese, though an Oppidan, knelt on the ball for twenty minutes, twenty seconds in 1911. His later exploits – for example, commanding the 8th Army in the Western Desert during the Second World War – were regarded by us as modest by comparison.

The whole of College was mobilised for St Andrew's Day. On the eve small Collegers were invited to stand in groups on a table and practise the roar of encouragement with which they would support College Wall from the touchline next morning. 'Coll-eg-ers' 'Louder!' 'COLL-EG-ERS!' until the volume was judged sufficiently loyal. Kedgeree was served at breakfast. The rituals of the day, like most in English public schools, were in origin Victorian. (The game, in a fierce, chaotic way, took shape at the beginning of that reign but was codified in 1877 under the leadership of J.K. Stephen, who beat the Oppidan by ten shies to nil, and established the supremacy of the game in College for a generation.) I played for College on St Andrew's Day in 1946 and 1947. On the second occasion we lost 2–0. In a letter home I lamented, 'College had not enough skill to balance their superior weight and power. It was a cruel heartbreaking game. I was terribly set upon in the third bully and my face was damaged. It went on and on and was horrible.' Strong men wept; we washed off the mud, rallied for the necessary feast in College Hall, filled with medieval smoke from the three great fireplaces, whose chimneys were never swept. We drank one toast, '*In piam memoriam JKS*,' in a loving cup. Tony Lloyd, keeper of College Wall, and I as second keeper sang the traditional duet 'A policeman's lot is not a happy one'. Then the final toast, '*Floreat gens togata et hic noster ludus muralis esto perpetuus*' ('May the tribe of gowned scholars flourish, and this our wall game last for ever').

The conservatism of schoolboys is well documented; it was particularly marked in my generation. This had nothing to do with party politics, something to do with the patriotic solidarity of wartime Britain. We read *Enemies of Promise* by Cyril Connolly, in which he described the radicalism of young collegers after 1918 and their clashes with authority, but there was no echo of this discontent in our lives. One or two boys were critics of College and Eton; they were neither persecuted nor admired for this dissent. The 1942 election of Collegers to which I belonged was perhaps particularly self-assured. On one occasion we were summoned *en bloc* by the captain of the school, the alleged offence being 'general attitude'. We were rebuked for behaving like little tin gods, a phrase which stuck. On the whole we worked contentedly within the settled feasts and challenges of the Eton calendar, accepting the rules which went with it: early school at seven-thirty; tails for the tall, bum-freezing jackets for the rest; coloured waistcoats for Pop, stick-up collars for sixth form, top hats if you crossed the Bridge into Windsor; 'ticking' a master with a one-finger salute when passed in the street; school concert with the 'Vale' and the 'Boating Song'; the Fourth of June with proper fireworks; prayers in Latin in college on Sunday evening – '*Rex Henricus, sis amicus*'. Much of this has gone, no longer acceptable to boys or (perhaps more often) masters. The buildings remain, and the excellent teaching; for better or for worse the self-confidence which held us together sixty years ago has largely dissolved.

For Collegers the core of our lives at Eton was hard work, enforced less by authority than by competition. I do not think I was more ambitious or competitive than most in my election, but the cramped daily entries in my diaries are full of marks received, percentages of perfection, and position in this or that order table. At this early stage we were educated across the board – including science, maths, history and French – but the heart and glory lay in the classics. These were the masters I remember, because we feared, admired, respected or laughed at them. Much of the classical work was mechanical, but looking back I do not use that as a term of reproach. It is extraordinary now to recall the gymnastics to which our teenage minds were put. To learn long Greek and Roman speeches by heart is one thing. To translate them into English is another. We did both. But we spent hour after hour on a third traditional, but now almost incredible, manoeuvre: we turned huge quantities of English poetry and prose into Greek iambics as perfected by the tragedians of Athens, and Latin elegiacs as perfected by Ovid, or Ciceronian or Thucydidean prose. ('His iambics were exceedingly promising, and some of his Greek proses were good. His Latin verses varied greatly. His critical papers were just like those of the others – that is he had learned the set pages, but was defeated by the more recondite questions. He construed well, and seemed friendly' (Richard Martineau's report, Michaelmas 1945).)

Every now and then, when reading or at the theatre, I come unplanned on a passage of English literature which sets me tingling. This is not the same as the shiver inspired by intrinsic beauty, pity or terror. It is more like finding oneself unexpectedly on a familiar highway with remembered clumps of trees or sudden slopes, where I went and cannot come again. 'Stop thy unhallowed toil, vile Montagu. Can vengeance be pursued further than death?' I cannot remember now how I turned Tybalt and Romeo into Greek iambics but I am closer today to Shakespeare because I did so. Nothing remains, I am glad to say, of the mass of Hurd-produced Greek and Latin, though in pride I cannot forbear quoting the only scrap in my memory, kept there because its artificial reference to the bosom of Neptune was at the time highly commended. Swinburne wrote:

And even the weariest river
winds some where safe to sea

Hurd rendered:

Quamvis longissimus amnis
*Denique Neptuni pervenit ad gremium**

It may be argued that this was really a higher form of crossword puzzle. But relentless exercises drummed into us an intimate sense of three languages, their structures and harmonies. I learned more about the English language from studying the classics than from any number of English lessons.

This was a ladder which I found quite easy to climb. But those who taught us classics were also in charge of drawing out our ability to form and express ideas. ('The only criticism which I could possibly make of him is that he expresses his ideas so downrightly that sometimes a stranger might almost think him rude' (Walter Hamilton's report, December 1945).) Once about this time, when I was given a message to take to the Headmaster, I broke into a meeting he was holding in his study and delivered the message so abruptly that he complained to Walter. This occasional roughness, born of shyness, has stayed with me. So perhaps has another failing noted by the sardonic Richard Martineau: 'He gave me full measure in his essays, having developed a curiously clerical rhetoric. He tried to tone it down to my lay taste' (Michaelmas report, 1945). Martineau next half described me (I was sixteen) as 'a simple and very likeable boy'. Walter commented, in that dialogue between teachers which distinguishes Eton reports, 'He certainly isn't simple in some senses of the word, but he has a very direct mind, which goes straight to the point, and a great intolerance of shams.' As is apparent, by this time Walter was a committed champion on my side.

On a Monday evening in May 1945 bugles sounded from Windsor Castle, and we could hear that special rumble of a crowd cheering in the street. The war in Europe was over. Walter Hamilton threw an impromptu party, with beer, singing and three cheers for Elsie Iredale-Smith as she passed through School Yard beneath his window. Henry VI standing serene in the centre of the yard was crowned with Union Flags,

---

*The pedant will immediately denounce an error. Ovid insisted that the pentameter (second half of each elegiac couplet) should end with a word of two syllables. But in this exercise we were copying Propertius, who, kindly man, allowed three syllables, hence '*gremium*'.

and we swung round him chorusing the 'Boating Song'. There was a great thunderstorm as we went to bed. The next day, the official VE Day, was seriously riotous: the headmaster's appeal for calm was greeted with loud cheers and disobedience. Quiet returned temporarily so that we could hear Churchill's broadcast on a wireless rigged up on Lupton's Tower. In the evening, characteristically, there was a college treasure hunt with Latin clues. Later the Provost, Vice-Provost, Headmaster and Lower Master lit a huge bonfire on Fellow's Eyot by the Thames; the effigy of Hitler disappeared in sheets of flame. For an hour that night the chapel was floodlit, an event itself after the years of darkness. Only a few weeks earlier air-raid precautions had been tightened and we had been told to stand by for a new V weapon, erroneous details of which I had passed on to my mother on 4 March: 'The Captain of the School told me last night that he thought it was a new jet plane which flies at an incredible speed.' On VE Day schoolboys were excited and triumphant, feelings to which masters added a deep relief that the killing was almost over.

One result of the victory in Europe was the holding of the delayed General Election. Because of the need to count service votes from all over the world, there was a gap of three weeks between polling day and the declaration of the result on 26 July, which happened to be the day when the Eton summer holidays began. My father was standing for Newbury. For the first time I felt that partisan excitement about the detailed outcome of an election which has never left me. I reported to my grandmother in Beaconsfield on events:

Dear Granny,
We're in! In with a solid majority over all the other candidates. In with our neighbours Reading and Slough fallen into the hands of the enemy!
   I arrived on the train from Windsor about 10 a.m. Mummy and Daddy were already in the Corn Exchange, where the votes were being counted. At first the Conservative and Labour piles were about level, but then as more and more of the village votes were counted our pile rose and rose. Mummy apparently sat knitting with an outward show of calm, but she found she had to undo every second row! No smoking was allowed inside, so the poor Labour candidate, when she saw the tide turning against her, dashed outside and had a cigarette there. Meanwhile outside in the Market Place a small crowd collected, including myself and our supporters from the Conservative Club, all sporting cornflowers. At 11.30 we heard Labour had already made 20 gains and that London was sliding fast. At 11.40 the Press were allowed in; five minutes later the Returning Officer appeared on the steps with Daddy close behind him, followed by the other candidates. He read the names out in alphabetical order: 'Mrs Brook 15,754 (a

murmur of 'she's got it') A.R. Hurd 24,463 (cheers), Sugget (Common Wealth) 424, Vane (Liberal) 6,052. I hereby declare Mr Anthony Hurd of Rainscombe Farm, Marlborough duly elected member of this division.' Daddy came forward and thanked everyone, promising to do his best in Westminster. A huge red, white and blue bouquet was handed to Mummy and we walked back to the Conservative Club. Various local notables came in and congratulated Daddy. The news came in 'Government 25, Opposition 99' – glum looks all round. Then we went into the Chequers for lunch with Daddy's agent. Then Daddy had to go to give prizes at Bradfield Grammar School where he was first introduced as 'Mr Anthony Hurd M.P.' – Mummy and I went to a cinema and saw a crazy Hollywood concoction. At 4 we went back to the Club and saw the *Evening Standard* – '5 Ministers out. Big Socialist gains.' We rejoiced over Beveridge's fall at Berwick but could find little else to comfort us. No one was very sorry to see Mr Brendan Bracken out, but everyone was badly shaken by the collapse of Buckingham, and the capture of Reading by Mr Mikardo who is apparently the worst of the worst. However Devizes, you at Aylesbury and Windsor were held, and we still hoped for a revival somewhere. We motored back and found telegrams of congratulation already showering on us; we were finally convinced by the 6 news that we were in for a Labour Government – alas, alas!

Much love and best wishes to you both

Douglas

The *Newbury Weekly News* analysed the local result: 'Mr Hurd and his agent refused absolutely to stress the Laski and the Gestapo stunts* which, although they may have appealed to the rabid party man whose vote is always safe, cut no ice at all with the more thinking elector . . . We think Mr Hurd scored distinctly in framing his campaign on more dignified and positive lines, and secured much support which in some other constituencies was lost to the Conservatives.' That is, and remained, accurate. My father's calm political style in nineteen years as a backbencher flowed from character, not calculation. He never pontificated about it; but the example was important to me.

My parents at once began to look for a house in the South Berks constituency. The Winterbourne stream creates a quiet hidden valley as it flows south into the Kennet. Winterbourne village, three miles north of

---

*During the campaign Winston Churchill had fastened on the chairman of the Labour Party, Harold Laski, and given the impression that a Labour Government might be tempted into Gestapo-like methods of control.

Newbury, is built largely in the hard red brick of the county, and claims no particular elegance. The slopes to the east of the stream are heavily wooded, stretching along the ridge across Snelsmore Common to Donnington Castle, held stoutly for King Charles in both Battles of Newbury. A generation after the Civil War, the countryside being by then a place of peaceful prosperity, a successful farmer built a box of a brick house on the edge of the common, four square rooms downstairs, four square rooms upstairs, to which in later centuries were added an attic storey and a Victorian wing in harsher brick for domestic staff. Winterbourne Holt looks west across the Winterbourne valley to the plain parish church with the eighteenth-century tower on the opposite slope, where my mother and brother Julian lie buried. The house and garden at Winterbourne were older and more traditional than anything at Rainscombe Farm. There was no clutter of farm buildings, but on the lawn a cherry tree and a fallen mulberry, both ancient and prolific. The front of the house is open to the narrow road which curves down to the valley. The visitor happens on it suddenly as he emerges from the wooded common; in spring he finds an army of daffodils occupying the front lawn. The valley looks secluded and empty, and in our time was so. Soon after we left the M4 was built towards the northern horizon and years later the Newbury bypass sliced through the common between Winterbourne Holt and Donnington. Our house and the village below it are now caught between pincers of modern traffic. Secretly I sympathised with the objectors to the Newbury bypass. I do not feel strongly about the habitat of butterflies or frogs. There was no logic in my resentment. Nothing of exceptional splendour was lost. It is just that what used to be a quiet and private corner of southern England is now imprisoned in tarmac.

This was the house which my father bought for £8,700 in 1947, together with the three fields which adjoined it. He was forty-six. For the first time in his life he owned the house he occupied. He farmed the fields in conjunction with a similar small acreage belonging to our neighbour Godfrey Nicolson, also a Conservative MP. My father's instinct for Wiltshire downland and his experience in running a bigger farm were satisfied when about this time he became a director of a private farming company called English Farms. This company bought with City finance a tract of wild downland north of Marlborough, towards the Ridgeway and Barbury Camp, about half an hour from Winterbourne by car. To these downs we boys often went, either ourselves in search of rabbits, or as beaters alongside the farm hands to propel the partridges in biting wind and rain over the line of guns in the valley.

More than fifty years later, having a day to myself, I revisited these downs with our terrier. Barbury Camp is now bureaucratised, with toilets and painstaking diagrams devised by Wiltshire County Council. The sheep, too, appear to be employed on the rates for decorative purposes. Pressing along the Ridgeway in search of wildness, I turned downhill back towards my car, but soon cursed myself for having made a fundamental mistake of map reading. For there, instead of the empty combe I remembered (empty of everything except rabbits, partridges, wind and rain) stood lines of well-planted trees and a new Georgian country house, with sleek horses grazing in a neat paddock. Senile and stupid, I thought I had lost my sense of direction. I stumbled down the path, which soon became tarmac. Heavy, overfed pheasants hardly bothered to evade the terrier or myself. But ten minutes later I recognised, beside the polished new mansion, the old farmhouse off whose walls we had scraped ivy when English Farm restored it from a ruin half a century before. Fifty years had been enough to tame a wilderness. Once again nature had been domesticated; once again something had been lost.

Winterbourne Holt was, apart from one disaster, to a house of unexciting and enjoyable rest and recreation for the next nineteen years – not a place of origin and roots as Rainscombe had been, but the home to which I naturally went on holiday from school and university, and then on leave from work. But at the beginning in 1947 and 1948 my excitement did not lie in moving house but in the opening up of my life at Eton.

Perhaps I am not alone in finding the change from junior schoolboy to adolescent easy to remember but hard to describe. I ceased to be just a machine for passing exams, or at other times a less successful machine for kicking a football. In my diary my contemporaries were no longer described by surnames or initials, but by Christian names. Friendships blossomed, became intense though sexually innocent, were disrupted, blossomed again. Schoolwork and games remained important, but all kinds of other activity flourished in the cracks between them.

Walter Hamilton left at this time to return to Cambridge. His place as Master in College was taken by Freddie Coleridge, a large and deeply orthodox schoolmaster, whose natural kindliness was sometimes overshadowed by suspicion of what the clever Collegers under his roof might be up to when they should be playing games: 'He has a passion for putting up notices and making announcements – and in his search for material sometimes trespasses on our property.' Fortunately at this time, no thanks to me, Collegers were high in the repute of the Oppidan world outside our walls, as measured, for example, by the number of Collegers elevated to the select paradise of the Eton Society, or Pop. A club of about twenty senior boys, Pop was then still self-elected, without the guidance on which headmasters have since insisted. The gorgeous waistcoats of its members symbolised limited powers but high prestige. It was a good moment to be a Colleger, and relatively easy to make Oppidan friends.

But our main concerns were still within College and they were still about competition. Our final order in College was fixed by the last examination which we all took in common before we separated into different specialisations. In this examination I came fourth in my election and there I remained. The contest from then on was now for prizes, of which there were many for classical specialists, rather than for a higher place in the pecking order. The three boys ahead of me were formidable competitors. Indeed, the first, Charles Willink, was hardly a competitor at all. In a carefree manner, without any signs of exceptional study, he swept the board in every classical examination continuously through his five years in College. It was impossible to catch him – or to be maddened by his superiority. He was not ambitious in other spheres, never boasted, never sought fame, was always good tempered. His mind was totally attuned to the curriculum of our time, and to playing bridge. He later returned to Eton as a housemaster. So did the second in order, Raef Payne. Raef was quiet, plump and calm. He acquired from Wilfred Blunt an aptitude for painting. Antony Acland, when provost, hung outside the downstairs loo in the Provost's Lodge a pair of rather good portraits painted by Raef, of himself and of me. Raef's shrewdness and good humour led me to send my two eldest sons to his house, something they remember with pleasure. My main competitor was third in order, Tony Lloyd. We had a relationship of affectionate rivalry, with frequent ructions in the early years. Though he might still contest this, I became modestly superior to him in the narrow world of classical examinations and well ahead in such peripheral subjects as French and history. But Tony was an athlete and a charmer, with a range of accomplishments and friendships much wider than my own. I sometimes found this hard to bear though impossible to contest. One week he beat me to win the Loder Declamation Prize; next week I scooped the prize for Greek iambics. After Eton we were neighbours on the Great Court of Trinity, Cambridge, and the competition continued. In later years we kept in touch by letter and frequent meetings. We were married within two months of each other in 1960, each acting as the other's best man. Friendship remained when rivalry faded, or rather became a very English game; we continued to measure each other's social and intellectual standing by awards gained or even invitations received. A few months ago I was standing under the porch of the House of Lords waiting for a taxi. It was late, wet, cold; the taxis were reluctant. A large limousine drew up, provided by the Salter's Company for its master, who stepped out, warm, dry and in evening dress. We each felt a flicker from the past as we greeted each other and contrasted our positions. Lloyd KS had scored again.

Even immediately after the war, Eton provided an amazing range of activities outside the schoolroom. A boy would be very unlucky not to find something which caught his interest and unwrapped a talent. Not all such activity was congenial. Membership of the Corps was compulsory, and it soon became clear that I was not one of nature's soldiers. 'The Corps this half has plumbed new depths of lunacy; has issued us with greatcoats which transform us from a respectable battalion into survivors of the retreat from Moscow, with new waterbottles which are never used, and with gingerbeer on Field Days; a drink at once degrading and disgusting' (letter to Walter Hamilton, 25 October 1946). The scorn was mutual; one officer commented that on parade I carried myself like a butler. On another occasion I was taken to task for tarnished buttons just before inspection by the visiting Labour minister Emmanuel Shinwell. Yet I always enjoyed military music. At the end of a field day as we marched up Eton High Street the band broke into a particularly jolly tune, the march of the Ox and Bucks Light Infantry. We broke step in approved manner as we crossed Barnes Bridge, knowing that a bath and tea were close at hand.

More spontaneous was enjoyment from the different societies which held evening sessions with a visiting speaker. The chief was the Political Society, where I listened in turn to Anthony Eden, Lord Woolton and Ernest Bevin (of whom we highly approved). Speakers came thick and fast. A letter home from 1947 gives a fairly typical itinerary:

Yesterday in the afternoon Lord Templewood (formerly Sir Samuel Hoare) addressed all specialists on Spain. He told us absolutely nothing but got tremendous applause because he stopped ten minutes before school would normally have ended. Yesterday evening I put on the stiffest of stiff shirts and a beautifully creased dinner jacket to dine with the Provost. Tony and I were the reception committee for Walter Elliot, and so we were invited to dine with him, the Provost and Miss Marten [formidable sister of Sir Henry Marten, who had by then succeeded Lord Quickswood in the Provost's Lodge]. I liked him very much – he kept the conversation sparkling and was a great success. He raised more chuckles with his Scotch humour than any speaker I can remember. His imitations had a great reception.

I hope I have not up to now given the impression of a gilded blasé young Etonian of the kind often caricatured. But I must admit that this regular access to the famous of the world gave (and still gives) Etonians an extraordinary privilege. I am not proud of an entry in my diary in October 1947, which reads, in full, 'Dine with Archbishop of Canterbury – a good man.'

I became editor of the *Eton College Chronicle*, then a staid narrative of events, with little of the colour and boldness of today's publication.

In turn I worked with two Oppidan fellow-editors, Nigel Leigh Pemberton (now as Nigel Douglas a distinguished singer and producer of opera) and Tom Stacey (now a successful novelist and publisher). Both of these were ambitious reformers, Nigel hard headed and practical, Tom romantic and eloquent. In one leader I wrote wistfully, 'The House of Lords is menaced today: why should the *Eton College Chronicle* be spared tomorrow?' Sandwiched between the excited proposals of my co-editors and the ever anxious eye of authority, I had to devise accommodations and draft compromises, a role which as I learned again later in life earns little applause, even when essential.

So we listened, we wrote – but we spent increasing time speaking. There was a debating society for the clash of opinion on traditional subjects, but overwhelmingly speaking meant declaiming the words of others. We had done this throughout our time in the classroom, but it was one thing to stumble through a saying lesson for a classical beak and quite another to put on a gown and declaim from a platform in the Music School to a wider audience on 4 June. The piece could be a solemn solo effort, some of my examples being Agamemnon slaughtering his daughter Iphigenia, Lord Randolph Churchill slaughtering Gladstone, or Tamburlaine slaughtering almost everyone in sight. Or it could be a comic piece by several of us from Sheridan's *The Critic*, or the playlet in *A Midsummer Night's Dream*, or Housman's masterly parody of those Athenian tragedians with whom we lived in such exhausting intimacy:

> *O suitably attired in leather boots,*
> *Head of a traveller, wherefore, seeking whom,*
> *Whence, by what way, how purposed art thou came*
> *To this well-nightingaled vicinity?*
> *My purpose in enquiring is to know,*
> *But if you happen to be deaf and dumb,*
> *Pray, raise your hand to signify as much.*

Then there was the Shakespeare Society, dourly run by a housemaster, Mr Prescott. The steps down from College Hall into the cloisters fan out into a semicircle, near the tablet later erected after the Falklands War to remember Colonel H. Jones VC. Here, without costumes or props, Mr Prescott practised us in his perfectionism, calculating out of long experience the point when we would begin to enjoy ourselves. My harsh voice made me a natural Shylock, and odd phrases recur at odd times: 'It was my turquoise. I had it of Leah when I was a bachelor'; 'I would not have given it for a wilderness of monkeys'. 'Wilderness' has to be an agonised shout.

But something more substantial was in the offing. Nowadays school plays and house plays are two a penny, at Eton and throughout English schools of all sorts. But a school play at Eton in 1947 was a formidable innovation, watched with anxiety and suspicion by the headmaster Claude Elliott, for whom enthusiasm was not a virtue. He was reported to believe that playacting was at best a grievous expense of time; where boys were required to take female parts the consequences might be horrendous. That *Henry IV Part I* took shape and was performed in School Hall in November 1947 was the result of one boy's unstoppable enthusiasm. None of us who worked with John Barton at that time were surprised at his brilliant later career in the theatre. Funny, temperamental, generous, wholly determined, for some months he dominated a large chunk of my life. My own minor part in the play suited my wooden style of acting. The Earl of Worcester is one of those rebellious and not very interesting barons with whom Shakespeare peoples the history plays. My mother hugely enjoyed the play ('I could not have believed that I should be so entertained') but wrote in her diary that I was inclined to talk too villainously through my teeth. Tim Raison, by then a close friend in College, played King Henry and occasionally still addresses me as he did then: 'Worcester, get thee gone for I do see/Danger and disobedience in thine eye.' I am not sure that Julian Slade, later famous for the musical *Salad Days* and much else, was ideally cast as Prince Hal. The stars were John Barton as Hotspur and Raef Payne as Falstaff. Raef was just himself, with the help of a cushion or two; though I have seen many Falstaffs, his is the chuckle I remember. John, director as well as star, worked himself into illness, hurled himself about the stage, fell from a considerable height in full armour, became the full embodiment of chivalrous scorn. For a year or two after the play, I was enchanted by John's enchantment with the theatre. More than once I stayed with him in his family flat in Baker Street, from which we sallied afternoon and evening to savour Guinness, Richardson, Olivier and Gielgud in the great post-war rebirth of the English theatre.

By this time I had won a classical scholarship to Trinity, Cambridge. That was a jolly expedition, which included sitting next to the master, G.M. Trevelyan, in hall, savouring for the first time the grapes, port, coffee and snuff which followed dinner. Food rationing was still severe; magnificent silver boxes contained hard black biscuits of the kind normally associated with large dogs. In the room allocated to me in Whewell's Court a single-bar electric fire hardly kept the Cambridge December at bay. A party of us, guided by Walter Hamilton, climbed the tower of Ely Cathedral, went one evening to the cinema, and another to evensong in King's College Chapel, lit only by hundreds of candles. Despite long papers ('2½ hrs of Greek verse this morning and 3 hrs of classical prose this afternoon') my diary and letters are light-hearted. There is none of the anxiety which normally went with important examinations. This must be because I had a year in hand. A miss in 1946 could be repaired a year later. By winning in 1946 I gave myself time for manoeuvre but had to decide how to use it.

The next step certainly was to tackle Everest, in the form of the Newcastle Scholarship. What was for us and for our teachers the peak of classical effort at Eton has now been fragmented and levelled, and is no longer treated with awe. In 1947 the Newcastle was certainly Victorian in its intensity. It consisted of the usual Greek and Latin papers, namely construing hitherto unseen Greek and Latin prose and composing Greek and Latin verse. These were similar to the papers I had tackled at Cambridge four months earlier. But to them were added a general divinity paper, and most important of all detailed examinations on St Matthew's Gospel and the Acts of the Apostles in the original Greek. These last two required intense preparation in our spare time, on top of the ordinary school curriculum. I would have had no hope of winning the Newcastle in 1947 had Charles Willink still been in the fray – but having as usual swept the board the year before he was out of contention.

Nature asserted herself that winter. It snowed hard, thawed, snowed again. Coal began to run out. The Labour Government imposed power cuts. Like the Government, we floundered in a muddy slush, revealed in a letter to Walter Hamilton:

> School clock, which has not kept any sort of time this half, gave up the unequal struggle this morning, and is firmly fixed at quarter past ten. Although our electricity has been on all day we are apparently put on our honour not to use it, the result being that the chapel service this morning took place in a gloomy twilight with the two candles on the altar as the only other illumination. Dr W. [Watson, precentor] had a piano up by the north entrance on which he performed a funeral march, as the Ram [the daily sixth-form procession, now abolished] crept in through the dusk at about half the usual speed. My Oppidan counterpart murmured as we went in, 'We are in mourning for England' which is possibly quite true.

Matters worsened. I was gloomily working hard, but a certain journalistic instinct prevailed: 'A torrent of brown water is pouring under the bridge that separates the College from the Town and has covered the whole of Luxmoore's Garden and Fellow's Eyot . . . Miss Iredale-Smith has evacuated her stores from the cellars – you may see us home before our time.' The day after that letter home, the situation had clearly deteriorated, as a sucession of diary entries reveals: 'Have just come down from College Chapel roof. Eton is surrounded by floods, which are still rising. Our last links with civilisation are the High Street and the main road to Slough – water highest since 1894. Telephone system broken down (12.30 p.m., 16 March). High Street is now covered for a hundred yards. The Slough road is also reported flooded. Housemasters are meeting at this moment (3.30 p.m., 16 March) . . . We are staying put. There is not enough room in the drains, so no baths till further notice. No water to be drunk unless boiled (9 a.m., 17 March).'

But that day the authorities gave up the struggle and issued the order that we should all go home. *The Times* published a leader *Exeat Etona*. My immediate difficulty was that I had no home, or rather two homes. My parents were in the throes of moving house from Rainscombe to Winterbourne, and neither was in a good state. Quickly both were ruled out, when my brother Julian came home from Marlborough in quarantine for scarlet fever. (The quarantine rules were strictly observed in those days.) As so often, the kindly aunts came to the rescue and I was packed off to Bennetts, their cottage in Oare. My concern was with the Newcastle exam, still due to begin in flooded Eton on Tuesday, 25 March. I walked over the downs in the rain, listened to Schubert, finished revising the Acts of the Apostles, and finally in exasperation sent a telegram to Fred Coleridge, the Master in College, asking if I could return to Eton before the weekend. He agreed and I arrived on Saturday to find the floods subsiding. A fairly idle weekend, and the Newcastle exam began on Tuesday as planned. Life seemed to be back on the rails – for four days. By Saturday the rumour was that the Newcastle was going to be a close-run thing, with two papers still to go. I felt out of sorts. With Jonathan Crawshay Williams, another genial companion from my election, I bicycled to Beaconsfield for tea with my grandmother. This was a great success, though it rained on us as we cycled back through Maidenhead. I did not sleep that night, and woke covered with spots. Miss Iredale-Smith at once diagnosed chicken pox. My diary entry was despairing: 'The ultimate BLIGHT following and dwarfing all others. May wreck Newcastle, holidays, everything.' But Miss Iredale-Smith showed her greatness. Ignoring (I imagine) a number of medical and school rules, she ensured that I took the last two Newcastle papers, sitting up in bed with a high temperature in the College sickroom, before being transferred to the sanatorium. One of these papers was always the most difficult, turning English verse into Greek iambics. The chicken pox gave wings to my muse. Raef Payne rang up the sanatorium at ten-thirty on Tuesday morning to say that I had won the Newcastle. Visitors, telegrams and a letter from the Headmaster followed. My temperature fell, scabs began to form on my spots, anticlimax followed triumph. I spent the next fortnight in quarantine in Beaconsfield with my long-suffering but understanding grandmother. Her bicycle broke down quite often, but it carried me to Hughenden to visit the shades of Disraeli, and a few days later to Stoke Poges, as a result of which I learned Gray's 'Elegy' by heart – yes, all of it, though it has gone now.

About this time I had to make a number of thorny choices. It would be tedious to rehearse the pros and cons of each. I felt that I had exhausted my own interest in the classics. I decided to take advantage of the fact that I was the youngest in my election to spend a full year at Eton as a history specialist, including a final summer as captain of the school, by which time I would be just over eighteen. I would then after National Service read history at Cambridge, even though I had got there on a classical scholarship. There was a gamble in this. The Cold War was under way, there was trouble with the Russians in Berlin and the Government made uncertain noises about the likely length of the obligation to National Service. The gamble was that if I plunged into the army immediately after leaving Eton in July 1948 I would be demobilised in time to go up to Cambridge in October 1949. My timetable depended on Stalin.

The decision to convert to history disappointed Walter Hamilton at Trinity and those who still taught me classics at Eton; but they were magnanimous. I was particularly grateful to Richard Martineau, the senior classics master. Richard belonged to a generation of schoolmasters which has passed away and will not be repeated. His bald head with a brown patch on top, mild voice, quick walk, flowing gown, and disinterest in games disqualified him from making much impression on small boys, though those in his own house were deeply loyal. Most of his remarks were incomprehensible to them, and he disdained the cruder techniques of authority. But as one grew older, his civilised and subtle mastery of his own subjects, and his voice spiced with harmless malice over a much wider range, gained him many adherents. Later, like many others, I was asked to stay in his retirement home at Droxford in the Meon valley north of Portsmouth, where he lived at ease, puzzling the retired naval officers who throng that valley rather as he had puzzled lower boys at Eton. That summer of 1947 when I was still doing classics but inclining towards history, Richard, though a classics beak, suggested that I should spend time sitting in his garden reading Macaulay's *History of England*. I recoiled, being already hostile in a shallow sort of way to the Whig interpretation of history and fearing that Macaulay would be a bore. Richard gently insisted, his deckchair was comfortable, the summer warm and I entered the study of history by a good door.

History at Eton was a gentlemanly pursuit, presided over by C.R.N. Routh, a housemaster of great experience, whose handsome handwriting on the reports before me bring back his rich voice and orotund phrasing. His secret was to treat intelligent youths as adults. His example was followed by two young history beaks who lived in bachelor apartments in 2 Common Lane: Giles St Aubyn, author of what I regard as the best biography of Queen Victoria, and Alan Barker, later headmaster of the Leys School, Cambridge, and husband of my celebrated colleague in the House of Lords Jean Trumpington. These were smart, rather fashionable young masters who enjoyed putting forward extravagant opinions. In 2 Common Lane you could be sure of a glass of sherry and an argument. Alan Barker was, for example, a strong advocate of Strafford's policy in the run-up to the English Civil War. My parents may have been slightly baffled by his report, 'I shall be satisfied if I have taught him no more than the case for "Thorough" truly stated', but it was a step nearer to real life than Greek iambics.

The scholarly peak for history specialists was the Rosebery Prize. This peak was not in my eyes as high as the Newcastle; but there was no precedent for a boy winning both. It was worth a go. I set my hand to the task in March 1948. The result is best conveyed in Routh's generous but typically long-winded prose:

> He came within an ace of winning the Rosebery and accomplishing his object. A difference of five marks between himself and the winner is so small a difference that the examiner would have been justified by splitting the prize. He very nearly decided to do this, and I could have wished that he had done so, for Douglas had done such good papers that a tie would have justly represented the result. But the examiner in the end gave the prize to Barrington-Ward on one ground only, that in his opinion Barrington-Ward was the more natural historian who wrote the best kind of history, while Douglas brought a wonderfully competent and clear mind to bear on a series of historical problems, but with less feeling and imagination. The examiner's actual words in his Reading Over were, 'I read Hurd with admiration, but I read Barrington-Ward with excitement.' That is perhaps another way of saying what I wrote last Half, that there is not yet much poetry in Douglas' historical writing.

> The decision was, I believe, a just and sound decision, but it is a measure of the high opinion I have of Douglas as a historian and of my great liking for him that I found myself saying to him, 'I wish you could have won,' although Barrington-Ward is in my own House. I had to add that I could not wish that Barrington-Ward had not won. Both my liking and my high opinion of Douglas were enhanced by his answer, 'It was quite right that

Barrington-Ward should have it, and I am very glad about it.'

But I do not suppose for a moment that he is mainly interested in material success. He has a mind a long way above that, and the secret, or part of the secret, of his success is that he is more interested in the subjects and the study of this and that subject than he is in his own success.

Routh is right that I had no jealousy; Simon Barrington-Ward is one of those people against whom it is impossible to feel resentment. Routh does not record another remark attributed to the Rosebery examiner: that he thought I would make an excellent civil servant, but that a higher future was reserved for Barrington-Ward. Others reached a similar verdict over the years. Simon later became Bishop of Coventry and a chief architect of the difficult reconciliation between Coventry and Dresden.

And so my time at Eton wound down in an atmosphere of hazy well-being. Gone were the struggles for prizes and the tense personal rivalries. John Maude, MP for Exeter, spoke to the Political Society for sixty-five minutes and enthused me more than anyone else about the importance of politics. Roy Campbell came to the Literary Society ('looks exactly like a comfortable country station master . . . read his own poetry as if he didn't understand a word of it'). I was summoned to Windsor Castle to meet the Australian cricketers and show them around Eton ('I attached myself firmly to Bradman, as he was one of the few who could or would talk'). For the Fourth of June speeches I selected a piece of *Caesar and Cleopatra* and was commended in *The Times*, which in those days followed all important cultural events. The captain of the school takes a dangerous part in the Procession of Boats that evening. Fortunately, the crew in which he, the captain of the cricket first eleven and the captain of the Oppidans row is not required to stand with oars upright when passing Fellow's Eyot, as is the case in the boats manned by experienced Wetbobs. I had been elected to Pop six months earlier, and sported a blue brocade waistcoat.

In 1948 Easter was in March and Holy Week fell in term time. Each evening an address was given in College Chapel by Cyril Alington, former Headmaster of Eton and by then Dean of Durham. These services were voluntary; the chapel was packed. The Dean proceeded up the nave behind the verger, climbed into the pulpit, and the lights were turned out. College Chapel lay in total darkness except for two candles on the pulpit which framed his leonine head, ennobled with silver hair. He was a master of language, and portrayed each night in a deep, musical voice one character of the Passion story – Judas, Peter, and, on Maundy Thursday, Pilate. The last paragraph of each address was dramatic and carefully crafted. The Dean paused for a second after pronouncing it, leaned forward and slowly in turn blew out each candle. We spent a second in total darkness with the Dean, Pilate and Christ before the chapel lights returned us to 1948. Walter Hamilton disliked the theatricality of the performance; most of us disagreed.

My final reports glowed more warmly than anything ever written by later political commentators; I always managed to please schoolmasters. On 24 July in accordance with custom, I sang in School Concert in a cracked voice the first verse of the 'Vale' to its memorable tune, part fast waltz, part slow melancholy:

> *Time ever flowing bids us be going*
> *Dear Mother Eton, far from thee*
> *Hearts growing older, love never colder,*
> *Never forgotten, shalt thou be.*

That was Saturday night; Sunday was for farewells – the hymn at evening prayer was 'Lord thou has brought us to our journey's end'; by eight o'clock on Monday morning I was gone.

These were years of egotism, without doubt. I do not know if I was more self-centred than most teenagers. To the reader, the description will have placed my life at Eton firmly in a distant age. It comes vividly alive again as I reread the material, but then it has never faded far from my memory. My life has seen a complete turnaround in the general perception of the practical usefulness of being an Etonian. In my youth the criticism was that it was *too* useful. Claude Elliott's only improper joke was to warn us as we took leave against fornicating in Old Etonian braces. But it was part of the left-wing legend of the time that an Old Etonian tie provided a fast track to every kind of worldly success. Now universities, it is said, discriminate against talented Etonians in the cause of political correctness, and my daughter believes that if I had not gone to Eton I would have become Prime Minister in 1990. Both ends of the story are exaggerated, and we have probably now reached a reasonable equilibrium. So far as I can judge, my Etonian past neither helped nor hindered me decisively at any of the turning points in my life.

Did Eton give me anything which I could not have gained elsewhere? Yes, certainly: a sense of beauty allied to history, of ancient buildings in sun, fog and rain, of trees, field and river – a richness not to be despised because it crops up in every memoir. Add to that some understanding of the structures and harmonies of language, in particular our own, a grasp imperfect but important because it has led me throughout my life actively to enjoy reading, writing and speaking to an extent which I see others do not. Add friends, not as a means of influence, just friends. I suppose I have ten or twelve close friends of my own sex. Half of these friendships were formed at Eton sixty years ago. These are people with whom I have stayed, travelled, enjoyed food and drink, shared many ups and downs at irregular intervals through these years. Their wives and mine have joined the friendships. They know so much about me, and I about them, that there is nothing important to explain or excuse. These friendships are unalloyed pleasure, an essential part of the structure of life. Next, the importance of time. At Eton there was always more to do than time to do it. Collegers in particular were constantly trying to squeeze a quart into a pint pot. For better or worse, I have always been ill at ease when I have nothing to do. An article or book with a deadline, a journey, a red box of ministerial work, the prospect of a dinner party with friends – these have tended to lift my spirits, which an empty day can quickly depress.

What remains to be listed is, I think, an insistence, classical in origin, on the best. It sounds pompous, and performance often fell far short; but the standards were set and on the whole accepted. Rebellion was rare, and cynicism was kept at bay. The scene nowadays is very different. Eton has fended off the worries which in the post-war years vexed those who thought about its future. No socialist government is now likely to nationalise it, or even abolish its charitable status. The financial position is secure. Eton will not run out of talented boys pressing to enter. The difficulty lies elsewhere, in the extraordinary variety of temptations and dangers which beset the middle-class British teenager today. We were a simple, uncomplicated lot by comparison. Money made little difference to us in the years of war or post-war austerity. Drink meant beer, not vodka. There were no drugs to abuse.

The job of a housemaster today, at Eton or any other school, is formidable and exhausting. The new computers and language laboratories weigh light in the positive scale by comparison with the negatives on the other side. The search for excellence has never been more difficult, or more necessary.

I shall desert chronology for the moment, and bring together several decades with a diversion into Scotland. Mark Stuart, the brisk young lecturer (himself a Scot) who wrote a biography of me five years ago, records that my private secretaries at the Foreign Office got rather tired of learning from me that I had two Scottish grandmothers. So, as Cicero would say, I will pass over that fact and forbear from mentioning it on this occasion. In any case, it was neither of my grandmothers who introduced me to Scotland, but my father's younger brother Robert, a successful architect in Edinburgh.

I remember Uncle Bob as a good-looking bachelor with silver hair, a kilt and a great variety of friends. The kilt was plain tweed and thus a statement of culture, not of ancestry. He inherited a spice of mischief from his father, but with him it had become sophisticated. He was regarded, on no very solid ground, as the radical of the family. As evidence it was recalled that as soon as he was legally able he had gone out and changed his first name from Philip to Robert. There was occasional grown-up speculation as to what Bob might do next to surprise us. He might, it was said, turn Roman Catholic; he might, alternatively or in addition, marry Edith Evans. It was not clear why either deed would be scandalous; in the event neither was accomplished. Uncle Bob had become a Scottish nationalist, but was not politically active. His patriotism found a channel in the early years of the Scottish National Trust, about which he wrote the first authoritative account, and the Saltire Society, whose stylish headquarters in Gladstones Land, just downhill from Edinburgh Castle, he rescued and restored. He did the same for several other of the forbidding courtyards on Canongate and the rest of the Royal Mile; and for castles such as Culross in Fife and Cuilzean in Ayrshire, specialising in the Scottish vernacular style. He enjoyed music, the theatre, Scandinavian design and the entertaining eccentricities of life in both Edinburgh and the Highlands. He acquired a mild Scots accent, which lent point to his anecdotes. He was a generous and happy uncle.

On my first visit to Edinburgh at the age of eight, my mother and I stayed with Uncle Bob in his flat in George Square, not yet vandalised by the university. We saw the sights by day and by night played Monopoly, then newly arrived in Britain. So deep was my passion that one Sunday we played the board game instead of going as planned to evening service at St Giles. The next day Uncle Bob was late in saying goodbye to us on the platform at Waverley Station. As the *Flying Scotsman* was about to leave he dashed up the platform and thrust a brown paper parcel through the carriage window. A set of Monopoly, of course; a gift never forgotten.

On the night of my next arrival in August 1945 Uncle Bob took me to a party with a poetess. Mr Attlee broadcast, the castle uttered a salvo, the bells of the city pealed and the war against Japan was over. Uncle Bob had kindly undertaken to show his solemn fifteen-year-old nephew something of the West Highlands. Sadly I have lost my 1945 diary. My memory is of twisting roads and malt whisky administered in large houses by welcoming eccentric old ladies, each delighted to see Bob and hear the latest gossip. One such was Wilhelmina Macrae, hostess of the inn at Loch Ailort. It was said that a year or two earlier, when Free French forces were training in the area, she had received General de Gaulle with two goslings sheltered for warmth within the generous curtilage of her bosom. Our furthest objective was the modest hydroelectric station which Uncle Bob had designed on the short span of river down which the water of Loch Morar tumbles to the sea. His salmon ladder was original for that time. I cannot remember whether on that visit in 1945 we made contact with my contemporary in college Jacky Shaw Stewart, then living a mile away at Morar Lodge. Certainly the next year I was invited to stay with the Shaw Stewarts and a new window in my life was opened.

Morar Lodge stands above the road which runs along the western shore of the loch of that name, its privacy protected by an army of rhododendron. Jacky's mother at that time rented the lodge from Lord Lovat, and lived there with her mother and two sons. A year or so after I first knew the family she moved to Traigh, a distance of about two miles, thus giving up a view of Loch Morar held in the grip of harsh mountains, but receiving in return one of the great views of this kingdom. At Traigh you breakfast, lunch and in summer dine in a bow window looking across the lawn, then across a beach of rocks and silver sand, and across a blue or grey sea – to a dramatic theatre of islands, each with its individual character. To the right the southern end of Skye, a ridge of low hills behind which loom the jagged peaks of the Cuillins. In centre stage the romantic mountains of Rhum, rarely without a cloud, and to their left Eigg, and its Sgurr, a steep hill which from this misleading distance seems to dominate the island with a high, sharply marked plateau. Further to the left the small island of Muck, and left again the mainland reasserts itself with the rough promontory of Ardnamurchan. If the weather is particularly clear you can see right across the Minch beyond Rhum to the indistinct blue shape of South Uist. Sometimes rain and mist close in, hiding all the islands. You are conscious of them there behind the murk, waiting for the command from the director which will bring them back on stage.

To Morar and then Traigh I have for nearly sixty years brought myself, my first wife Tatiana and now Judy, two batches of children, red boxes, protecting police officers, and whatever was on my mind at the time. I have sometimes arrived tired and wondering how to cope with life outside that theatre of sky, sea and islands. I have always gone away refreshed. It is the only place to which I have many times invited myself, something made possible by the understanding and unvarying generosity of Jacky and his family.

The Shaw Stewart way of life was transplanted from Morar Lodge to Traigh, though its eccentricities have smoothed themselves out over the years. One dominant principle was that nothing was thrown away. Each room according to its character was piled high with magazines, musical scores, framed photographs, albums, games, indeterminate textiles, boots and opened bottles. No rods, rifles or shotguns, but a great array of books – classics, serious and comic – in shelves or stacked on the floor, as befitted a family which provided three generations of Eton Collegers. In summer 2002, after many changes, the *Oban Times* of 1931 was still conveniently stacked beside the back door. Gavin Maxwell in his book *Harpoon at a Venture* had a shot at capturing the flavour of the Lodge about the time I knew it.

> Probably it is impossible to describe Morar Lodge to anyone who did not know it . . . In fiction perhaps, old Mrs Knox's house, as described in *The Experiences of an Irish RM*, approached it most nearly: its atmosphere of comfort, kindness, but, above all, its animals. The living-rooms were occupied by a numerous, indeterminate, and largely floating population of animals and dogs and the noise of their disagreements, and harsh protests, was one of the more characteristic sounds of the house.
>
> Whereas there was definitely traceable farming activity at Morar Lodge, the pursuit of which occupied much of the family's waking hours, it was for their charm or pathos that the livestock was mainly selected . . . Only one obvious animal was missing from that house, but there was evidence of its existence in the past, for on the shelf in the bathroom there stood for a long time a bottle labelled in faded ink 'Donkey's eye lotion – I think'.

In his early or shark-fishing period, before the otters dominated his life, Gavin Maxwell came often to Morar, and kept his ex-torpedo boat *Sea Leopard* up the road in Mallaig's harbour. His charm was formidable, his arrangements impossible to predict. One evening he appeared late at Morar Lodge and invited one or two of us on an immediate hunting expedition. The Minch was rough, and the provisions on the *Sea Leopard* consisted mainly of lobster and sherry. By the time we reached South Uist I had been considerably sick. Next day we cruised round Rhum, spotted shark fins in the distance but never came within harpoon range.

Traigh does not offer the entertainment traditional in the Highlands for visiting Englishmen of a certain background. Grouse are not shot, nor salmon fished. There is no settled pattern of activity. Breakfast, which includes home-laid eggs and is served late, provides for a debate, often long, on the best way of using the day. The morning weather may dramatically change for better or indeed for worse, and both possibilities have to be carefully weighed. In early days sailing was an option. Even when rain is relentless a picnic is discussed. Should it be on the beach, accompanied if children are there with elaborate contests of hop, skip and jump or sandcastle building, followed by happy squeaking invasions of the cold sea? Or should it be on Loch Morar, taking a boat to one or other of its islands? In which case the enemy will be the mosquitoes and there will be detailed discussion of the latest repellent on the market. Or golf? In early days the golf course alongside Traigh was a purely local affair, possessed jointly by a small number of club members and the Shaw Stewart cows. The effect on play of bog, tidal streams and cowpats paradoxically encouraged the beginner, since these handicaps afflicted the expert as severely as himself. Latterly Jacky has invested thousands in expansion and drainage, so that the course is technically advanced and much more widely used. But because it too looks out on the islands one of its many commendations is as the golf course with the best view in Scotland.

In my early schoolboy years Traigh carried a flavour from Eton. Walter Hamilton came often with his dog Sam, before he married and set up his own Scottish home on Mull. I remember a testing academic walk with three distinguished dons in the hills above Loch Ailort. A few years later the house began to fill with girls. They were all beautiful, and some gradually became approachable. One year I danced reels through two nights at the Portree Gathering on Skye. Hospitality at Traigh was both simple and luxurious. Lobsters (which in 1946 I had no idea how to tackle on the plate) and fish in abundance came from the warehouse on the harbourside at Mallaig. Jacky's grandfather had formed the view at an advanced age that Chateau Yquem offered the secret of long life. He ordered a large quantity, and died soon after. This sweet and expensive wine flowed freely at Traigh for several decades at many hours of day or night and only recently came to a lamented end.

Every visit to Scotland has for me a special flavour: watching Judy (more skilled than myself) pull salmon from the Brora, or shoot a stag on a Perthshire hillside; canvassing in Perth, a city by temperament deeply conservative, in a by-election disastrous for the Conservatives; researching for *The Arrow War* among the Victorian trunks of Lord Elgin's home at Broomhall; returning repeatedly to Edinburgh on almost any pretext, as, for me, it is the most exciting city in the kingdom. I like to travel north by train on the eastern route because of the mounting schoolboy excitement of the sights from the window: Grantham has a big church, Peterborough a cathedral, York its great minster, Durham is nobler still, then the bridges over Tyne and Tweed, and the sudden slipping into Waverley Station under the lee of Edinburgh Castle, rediscovering a country which is infinitely varied, always special without being strange. But out of familiarity, affection and gratitude the Scottish image which returns most readily to my mind is of the slow, many-coloured sunset, escorted by clouds, over that gathering of islands across the lawn from Traigh.

3

THE ARMY

To Park Hall Camp, a wide desert of red brick, concrete and asphalt, two miles outside Oswestry in Shropshire, were sent the young men who, facing the requirement of National Service, had chosen for that service the Royal Regiment of Artillery. At Park Hall arrived late on 26 July 1948 22052418 Gunner D.R. Hurd, who the previous day had been captain of the school at Eton. Like many others, I had struck, I hoped, half a bargain with the army. If I moved immediately within hours from school to the military then there would be a reasonable chance that I would be demobilised within fourteen months, in time to take up my scholarship at Cambridge in October 1949. This bargain, entirely unenforceable on my part, made the change of culture exceptionally abrupt, though from the experience of friends I knew broadly what to expect. My first letter home, scribbled on paper specked with boot polish, illustrates the contrast:

> Could you please dispatch a piece of soap – quality no object?
> As we are only here for 3 weeks, we have to wash all our clothes,
> and the soap ration issued at the NAAFI is quite inadequate to do
> that and keep us clean . . . keeping clean is perhaps the most difficult
> thing – blanco and boot polish work themselves into the skin. I
> would also like a pair of pyjamas which will stand up to my
> attempts to wash them – the present pair has a great rent in the
> shoulder. Otherwise I seem to be well equipped.

After Eton there was nothing particularly barbarous to me about sharing a wooden hut with twenty other conscripts, or about the food or other physical conditions. But I disliked being woken at five-thirty by the raucous voice of the sergeant and the bang of his stick at the end of the bed. I disliked being marched to meals, and even more the assumption that leisure time was properly spent cleaning one's equipment ('I must now go back to my boots – I spent 3 hrs on them this morning without any visible effect'). I do not think I am by nature particularly dirty or untidy, but throughout my army career I failed to master the art of achieving that extra-deep glow on black boots, that particular sparkle on buckles on belt and epaulettes, which could alone guarantee against public humiliation and even relegation. I am physically clumsy, and by nature and my own past failures pessimistic about all mechanical tasks. As a result, assault courses, PT classes and tests involving electrical equipment or vehicle engines filled me with gloom before, during and usually after my performance. Barrack square drill, the regimental tug-of-war, surveying, map reading, the loading and firing of a 25-pounder gun were less awesome. The first few weeks at Oswestry were exceptionally hot and I was not fit. I sweated hard, and as we were hustled and shouted at I was always looking for a tap and a minute or two to drink water from my mess tin. Within days one hand blew up with poison and needed a large bandage.

We soon realised that the army had gained nothing by forcing us so quickly into its embrace. We had been scooped up between the usual dates for the intake of recruits, with the result that those in charge at Oswestry had no notion of what to do with us until the next intake arrived. We expected little of the army, but quickly found that the army expected even less of us.

My diaries at the time were written each night in a tiny pocket volume, just four or five lines to a day. From the beginning at Oswestry, like a homesick schoolboy half my age, I recorded in a corner of each day's entry the fraction of my expected time in the army which I had accomplished. Thus on the first day I wrote 1/456, on the second 1/228, and by the first weekend 1/91.

Gradually, as army life developed a pattern, it became easier to handle. Once our uniforms were fitted we were allowed to leave camp. We discovered the NAAFI Club in Oswestry, a large extended Georgian house, furnished to a high degree of comfort. I developed a taste for beer, though on pay of twenty-eight shillings a week there was not much opportunity for drunkenness. The army was particularly proud of this NAAFI and a lieutenant general wrote a glowing piece in the *Daily Telegraph* about the care which its customers took to keep it clean and tidy. I added a gloss in a letter home: 'The reason why there are no cigarette burns in the carpet is that the ordinary gunner is scared away by the padded armchairs, polished tables and the near-Athenaeum atmosphere created by the rows of sleeping figures on the sofas and the carefully bound copies of *The Times* and the *Tatler*.' Later I discovered Chester and later still Llangollen (forty-five minutes by bus from Oswestry) and the abbey two miles beyond it in the Welsh hills. When I could, I went to Sunday evensong in the little village of Whittington, to a hideous brick church with a nice Welsh parson and a lusty choir, followed by beer and sandwiches at the White Lion. And not alone, for I had made a new friend in James Bennett.

James, a Wykehamist, slight in figure with clipped speech and a sophisticated sense of humour, could claim to be an even less military figure than myself; his lamentations were certainly louder. Four years later he joined the Foreign Office at the same time as myself. I lodged with him briefly at the British Embassy in Moscow in 1956, and we stayed close friends by post and occasionally in London until his tragically early death a few years later.

At the end of August I began to run a fever and spent a bloody few days sometimes in bed, sometimes peeling potatoes, sleeping, writing gloomy letters while my temperature went up to 102, fell, rose again. I seemed a long way from anything that gave pleasure or was worthwhile. After a week of this I was sent suddenly and without explanation to the Moston Hall Hospital in Chester. An X-ray had shown a patch of pneumonia on one lung. It was a relief to know that I was legitimately ill; it was in order to sleep heavily and not worry about boots and the next parade. Fruit came, as did visitors, including Tony Lloyd, and books; I read *Cranford*, *The Young Melbourne* by David Cecil, *The Return of the Native* and *Hard Times*, the last of which I disliked. The colonel and the matron squabbled amiably up and down the ward, and a giggling orderly swapped views with me about Tudor architecture. Letters flowed in and out. It was a great letter-writing time. My Eton friends were scattered in military establishments up and down the kingdom – and beyond, for Jacky Shaw Stewart was a Royal Engineer in Kenya. At last I was released and given my first forty-eight-hour leave in two months. I hitch-hiked home to Winterbourne; in those days a uniformed figure signalling at the roadside could be pretty sure of a lift. Breakfast in bed, the Newbury Agricultural Show, blackberries to pick, a glorious September Sunday in Wiltshire, traditional tea with Aunt I at Bennetts, and back to Oswestry at 6.15 a.m. on Monday. Next came a training exercise in the bleak Welsh mountains around Trawsfynydd with our 25-pounders. Our return to Oswestry was delayed while the police investigated an overnight theft from the NAAFI till by one of our number. I had, a few weeks earlier, written home:

The stealing in this regiment is on a quite fantastic scale. The other night the chap in the bed next to me hung his belt out to dry. Suddenly there was a click, and we looked up to see it disappearing, and a figure vanishing into the shadows. We rushed out, but there was nothing to be seen. Tonight I only just escaped being one of what is called the Prowler Picket. This picket of 6 men solemnly patrols the regimental orchard every night from 8 p.m. to 6 a.m. to stop the starving soldiers stealing apples.

Many years later my Conservative constituents in Oxfordshire used to ask me to support their view that what modern youth needed was a return to conscription. I used to reply, truthfully referring to the French experience in Algeria and the American in Vietnam, that a conscript army would not be able to cope with the problems British soldiers were skilfully handling in Northern Ireland or Bosnia. I did not add that my recollections of National Service must be different from theirs. There was nothing disastrous for me to remember, and no serious complaints to relate. But petty dishonesty and wasted time were too high on the list of these recollections for me to see conscription as any cure for social malaise.

I admire our modern regular army. It is far removed from the clumsy post-war version swollen with conscripts which I experienced during the summer and autumn of 1948. My own parallel is with the army which Evelyn Waugh loved and hated in *Brideshead* and in the trilogy *Sword of Honour*. He began to write these books about the time I was at Oswestry. Waugh shows wickedly how the discipline and hierarchical authority of a military system are brought to bear, not on defeating the enemy but on solving or failing to solve some problem so small that the effort becomes ridiculous. By 1948 the old threat had gone, and though a possible new Soviet enemy was grumbling dangerously around Berlin, there was no great sense of fear or outrage against Stalin. But the military machine ground on regardless. Two stories give the flavour. We were set one day to pull a weed called 'fat hen' out of a crop of potatoes, a task familiar from Rainscombe days. The gunners became bored, and one of them brought work to a halt by discovering an insect which he declared to be the pestilent Colorado beetle, whose picture was then familiar on every railway station. The insect was passed up the hierarchy from NCO to NCO until it finally reached the regimental sergeant-major, who pronounced that it was an anaemic ladybird, and we should resume work. In Waugh's hands Captain Guy Crouchback would surely have been the arbiter of this decision. The same is true of a second Oswestry occasion. A group was set to plant blackcurrant bushes around the barrack rooms. The sergeant told them to douse the bushes in *cold* water after planting. Along came Sergeant Smith, more senior and feared throughout the regiment. 'Nonsense,' he barked, 'you must put on *hot* water.' But the first sergeant was proved right: the bushes treated with hot water died at least twelve hours sooner than the others.

The best path out of Oswestry lay through the War Office Selection Board, which would decide whether I was suitable to become an officer. I had warned my parents and myself that only a small minority of those who put themselves forward received a commission. I had no illusions. My new friend James Bennett had failed. This was quite a different sort of examination from those that I had found quite easy at school. The tests were held at Catterick in Yorkshire in the last days of October, where it was already cold. They comprised an exhausting mix of obstacle races, intelligence tests and discussion groups, mitigated by much beer in the Richmond pubs and a miraculous coal fire in the officers' mess.

On Saturday around lunchtime I heard that I had passed, so I treated myself to a civilian weekend. My standards of pleasure were not dramatic. I have ever since felt strong affection for the Royal Station Hotel at York, in gratitude for a hot bath fifty-five years ago, an expensive dinner, sheets on the bed and a late Sunday breakfast. On Monday life at Oswestry resumed its pattern: namely, hours of empty uncertainty followed by sudden action. After escorting the regiment's laundry to Shrewsbury on 4 November I was ordered to proceed immediately to the Mons Officer Cadet School at Aldershot.

My four winter months at Mons were unremarkable. There was less idleness and uncertainty than at Oswestry. The pressures of rising before 6 a.m., inspection of equipment, tests and exercises of all kinds were more intense; but we officer cadets were by now used to being hard driven. We learned to march at 180 paces a minute instead of 120. We could be put on a charge if a piece of fluff was found under a bed. We were proud, although also frightened, of the furious figure of Regimental Sergeant-Major Brittan, 'a vast Coldstreamer who looms formidably through the fog'. On ceremonial occasions we drilled to music and the adjutant rode up the steps of the square on a fine black horse. Some familiar themes persisted: 'When I shut my eyes I see both polished and unpolished boots, but always boots.' We returned in a wet blizzard from Christmas leave to find all our lockers broken into and possessions scattered on the floor. An infected rash on my neck resisted the efforts of penicillin.

Oswestry, despite its attractive countryside, had seemed dismally remote. From Aldershot, it was easier to reach Winterbourne, Eton and indeed Cambridge. I played the Wall Game at Eton, but found it awkward to fit in with the next generation of collegers. Elsie Iredale-Smith, a staunch Tory, assumed that I and all her former charges were being starved in the army by the wicked Labour Government, and provided us with a huge, life-saving tea.

Politics were also on the menu at Trinity, where I dined one Saturday night. The Lynskey Tribunal had just reported on the first post-war outbreak of ministerial sleaze. Some of the dons had learned part of its findings by heart and recited them to one another like a catechism across the table. Question: 'Were you at that time transacting business under the name of E.J. Watkins?' Correct answer: 'I do not remember.' I rediscovered the London theatre with John Barton – one night absent without leave to Hermione Gingold's revue *Slings and Arrows*, another more respectably to Laurence Olivier's *Richard III*, which John found disappointing. On 3 March 1949, after a wet, misty artillery exercise in Wales and a final ugly dispute that morning with a sergeant about alleged dirt on my rifle, it was my turn to march off the parade ground to the tune of 'Auld Lang Syne' and wake up next morning a second lieutenant posted to the 5th Regiment of the Royal Home Artillery.

This meant Larkhill and a summer on Salisbury Plain. The officers' mess, a massive building after the fashion of Lutyens, looked across a nondescript stretch of downland to Stonehenge, rather as an eighteenth-century mansion looks out to a Grecian temple erected to close the vista and focus the gaze of the cultured visitor. I lived in a hut to the side of the main mess. The immediate problem was social. Neither Oswestry nor Mons had taught me much about how army officers behave in one another's company. I knew little about toasts at guest nights, safe quantities of wine, the manner of addressing the commanding officer, the diplomacy required in the sergeants' mess, the psychology of returning a salute, the mixture of friendliness and formality required in coping with a batman. I was helped over these first hurdles by one old friend and one new. Antony Acland and I had been together at Eton. He was much more adept than I as a soldier and enjoyed himself. I have watched and respected him as Her Majesty's Ambassador in Washington, as a permanent under-secretary at the Foreign Office, as Provost of Eton; but my most vivid memory is of him standing on a table, fair hair flopping over his forehead, leading an intoxicated group in songs from the musical *Oklahoma*, including with particular verve 'Surrey with the Fringe on Top'. Guy Wilkin, pale faced, shrewd and gentle, belonged to the same troop as myself and so was closer to me day by day. It was Guy who learned in advance and tipped me off that we were going to camp, that the commanding officer was angry about the state of the vehicle park, or that I was to be duty officer when the rest of the regiment went on Easter leave.

The main task of the 5th Regiment RHA was to deploy mounted, self-propelled 25-pounder guns on artillery exercises in order to sustain our own skills and entertain distinguished visitors, British and foreign. Acting as safety officer on these occasions, or commanding three of the guns oneself behind a fold of Wiltshire downs, was not a bad way of spending a summer day; particularly for me, who had passed my childhood fifteen miles to the north, listening often to the salvoes fired by our predecessors on the plain. In the intervals between commands to fire from the observation post it was possible to lie, though unsafe to doze, in the long grass, uncropped by sheep; and in those days there were plenty of skylarks overhead. A typical exercise was described in a letter home on 10 May:

> All day resplendent staff cars with pennants flying have been stirring up great clouds of dust on the tracks over the Plain on their way to the stand for the Scapa Artillery demonstration. It looked like a race meeting – car parks and refreshment tents and immaculate military policemen with their red caps and white belts ushering the great ones this way and that . . . We did our little piece satisfactorily. I was absolutely baked, as we had to wear tank suits over battle dress.
> We have to do the same again on Thursday for a batch of grandees.

There were expeditions on duty, for example escorting 56 gunners to Dover via London on their way to Hong Kong and counting only 55 of them on the platform at Charing Cross. Or leading a particularly chaotic exercise near Marlborough, and returning in my self-propelled gun down through Oare, where I accidentally collided with part of my earlier life. The incident was described by Aunt I, by then at least eighty, on a hurried postcard to my mother in her sloping Victorian hand: 'Had just posted parcel and flattened myself against the wall to avoid being crushed by an appalling enormous War Machine lumbering down. It stopped at my feet – so to speak – and off jumped such a smart person in uniform, saluting his Aunt I. He looks awfully well. They had stuck on Oare Hill. My wits didn't rise to asking them all into tea – but he said he was coming soon – I've not got over it yet.'

I managed the military summer not brilliantly but without disaster. Larkhill was close to tea at Bennetts, the swimming pool at Oare House, and my brothers at school at Winchester and Marlborough. I got to know the Wilts and Dorset bus timetables quite well. Near the barracks were the cinemas and the Arts Theatre at Salisbury, to which I went often with one or other Larkhill colleague. *Murder in the Cathedral* impressed me particularly: I wrote a long review for my own satisfaction on the back of Royal Corps of Signals forms marked 'secret'. My colonel, a snob, gave me a lift to Newbury races and could not understand why I, the son of the local MP, preferred to pay my own way at Tattersalls rather than go with him to the Members' Enclosure.

I had long since stopped writing the fraction of military service accomplished in the corner of my daily diary. Anticipatory letters began to arrive from Cambridge; the Ministry of Defence was honouring its bargain. A course at Warminster with Guy Wilkin, a final camp under canvas at Tilshead, and I was demobilised on 9 September: 'Home 3.15. That's over at last. But no rejoicings – a few regrets, but haven't done too badly.'

4

CAMBRIDGE

For me, when I revisit, Eton is full of memories and Cambridge almost empty. I do not understand why. I enjoy going to Cambridge, and take any opportunity to do so, whether as a member of the university's fund-raising Foundation or as a speaker to one of its innumerable societies. A walk on the Backs, a visit to the Fitzwilliam, dining in any college hall and in particular my own college, Trinity – these are substantial pleasures in their own right, but they do not evoke a memorable past.

Perhaps this is because, after the army, in three years as a Trinity undergraduate my life reverted to a pattern largely indistinguishable from that at Eton. A river, ancient and beautiful buildings set among magnificent trees, the flow of the academic year, the conventions and eccentricities which give character to a college, these were already familiar. As a scholar of Trinity I was privileged to live, if not comfortably by modern standards, in some style – the first year in the early nineteenth-century neo-Gothic of New Court, then two years in Great Court, the best academic space in the world. There is nothing pretentious about any one of its components: hall, chapel, Master's Lodge or even the tower of our flamboyant founder, Henry VIII. Because there is so much space, none of the buildings in Great Court overbears its neighbours. They live together through the centuries, their peaceful coexistence ratified by the sound of the fountain in the centre. The total is splendid. To work in such surroundings, to walk to lectures, to argue with friends, this was familiar enjoyable stuff too much taken for granted. To cross the Cam and read for hours in the Fellows' Garden was not so different from crossing the wooden bridge into Luxmoore's Garden at Eton and reading on Fellows' Eyot beside the Thames.

Particularly as I would be accompanied or interrupted in these things by well-known voices. There was a batch of friends a few hundred yards away at Kings, notably Jacky Shaw Stewart. At Trinity were gathered three of my closest earlier companions: Raef Payne, Tony Lloyd (the arguments in his room or mine in Great Court were just as frequent but less fierce than at Eton) and at the beginning Walter Hamilton, before he left Trinity to become headmaster of Westminster. Others now enriched my life: for example, Dennis Robertson. In appearance resembling a wise and friendly tortoise, Dennis wore his fame as an international economist with a modesty which went beyond understanding.

In *Decline and Fall*, and later, more indulgently, in *Brideshead Revisited*, Evelyn Waugh describes two ways of undergraduate life in pre-war Oxford, between which in both books his hero is torn. On the one hand, there were tea parties at which the League of Nations and the Polish plebiscite could be discussed, from which the undergraduate could pass to serious debate at the Oxford Union. Or there was the Bullingdon, much drink leading through laughter to vomit, and in a deservedly immortal phrase, 'the sound of English county families baying for broken glass'. My life at Trinity, Cambridge, was passed in the first of these styles, with gradually increasing hints of the second. Certainly there were earnest tea parties. The League of Nations had passed away, but it was important to discuss modern Christianity and the right means of helping the poor countries of the world. My diary records in the first two years an amazing abundance of tea parties, mostly social and without message. But subtly my life evolved: beer in pubs and gin in clubs began to take the place of tea in college rooms. I joined the Pitt Club, and within it dined with the True Blue Club. I still went to Eton to play the Wall Game, but the greater social excitement now lay in forays to Oxford, reached by train via Bletchley. Of course, in Oxford they too worked, worried over examinations, and perhaps even had tea parties. But they pretended otherwise. The face which Tim Raison, Antony Acland and other Oxford friends presented to visitors from Cambridge was impressive. They suggested to us lives of continuous jollity inspired by wine and stylish company. About once a term I took advantage of this, then tumbled full of port into bed in some cobwebbed corner of Christ Church, and woke blearily in the morning to rediscover Bletchley.

John Barton had brought to Kings from Eton his passion for the theatre, and also a mistaken belief that he could make me a passable actor. My part in his play *It's All One* was modest and villainous. To it was added a silent part as First Rustic. We performed for a week at the ADC. A bucket of cold water was poured over me in my chain mail during each performance. I disliked the first few evenings but cheered up when my main problem was solved, courtesy of a new and more stable moustache.

In the background my historical studies progressed. I did not regret rejecting Walter Hamilton's advice and turning away from the classics. At Eton I had gained a taste for history; at Cambridge I began to recognise scholarship. At Eton the beaks stimulated a broad sweep of ideas; at Cambridge I learned that these had to be based on sources, on references which needed to be checked, on rival versions of an event which had to be disentangled. My special study was the Second French Republic (1848–51), several of whose leaders wrote voluminous accounts of their own eloquence and heroism. At hand in Great Court was the elderly, shortsighted F.A. Simpson, whose two volumes on the rise of Louis Napoleon remain a model of scholarship presented in elegant, educated prose. I took my essays to Professor Kitson Clark, in the tower alongside Great Gate. Sir Robert Peel was his favourite subject. I suspect that, had he taught at the time, he would have defended the Corn Laws and perhaps even opposed Catholic emancipation, for he was ripe in both complexion and views. At that stage I thought Peel dull and was all for Disraeli, *Coningsby* and Young England. At the other extreme, a bicycle ride away, Professor Ullman, the great medievalist and refugee from Austria, led me through popes and Holy Roman Emperors with the help of heavy books translated into strange English from the German. There were plenty of able lecturers and I enjoyed reading in the Seely or the University Library. I agreed with Butterfield on Christianity and history, and his demolition of the Whig interpretation; my copies of his slim, very English books are well thumbed.

But somehow none of this inspired. It was not in my nature to be slack, but I certainly did not soar, and my preliminary exams in the summer of 1950 yielded only a 2:1. There was no rebuke, but a scholar of Trinity should do better. The mood was caught in a letter to my mother during my last year:

> Have been reading Roy Harrod's Life of Keynes – the Cambridge bits very interesting, and made me feel how very insignificant present generation is – no intelligent little clubs meeting round a don's fire once a week and settling all the world's problems, no sparkling conversation – decide it's mainly the dons' fault, they're so caught up in the routine of teaching and administration that they have no time or energy for putting into our heads anything except what's in the Tripos papers, grimly conscious that even that will fall out once the examination's over.

This critique would be more accurate today than it was fifty years ago. The problem for me was not the dons, but a distraction: not yet girls, but party politics.

At the outset I warned myself in my diary against too much involvement in politics. Perhaps I might have listened to my own advice had it not been for the General Elections of 1950 and 1951. The Cambridge University Conservative Association was a formidable force, with more than a thousand undergraduate members. Nowadays students are still interested in political issues, but not in the political parties. In those days the two amounted to the same thing. We were kept informed in a steady stream of meetings with first-class visiting speakers. The Conservatives maintained a fairly consistent majority in political debates in the Union. Gone was the left-wing pacifism of the thirties. There were Labour enthusiasts such as Jack Ashley, and such witty satirists of the left as Percy Cradock, later a most sober and traditional foreign affairs adviser to Margaret Thatcher and John Major. But the general mood was one of boisterous contempt for what felt like a failed and exhausted Labour Government. Clement Attlee's administration of 1945–51 gets a better press now from commentators and historians than is justified. It set Britain firmly on the wrong post-war path of restriction, nationalisation and trade union power. It put us at a competitive disadvantage compared to our continental neighbours from which we took decades to recover, and frittered away the radical idealism which elected it in 1945. This may be an unfair summary, but it was certainly the general feeling at the university during my time.

Conservative Central Office, then in one of its efficient periods under the great Lord Woolton (known to us as Uncle Fred), made good use of our enthusiasm. A formidable lady called Mrs Thirlby trained us to speak. The party organised speaking tours, sending us out in teams of three or four to orate from a soapbox at factory gates and in market places in marginal constituencies. For me that meant Stroud in 1950 and Carlisle in 1951. The sight of young Tory students in ties, tweed jackets and grey flannels going through their repertoire in a public place produced a crowd quite quickly. We learned to deal with hecklers, to distinguish between the rude shout which could be turned aside with a joke and the heartfelt hostility probably derived from personal experience of unemployment in the thirties. Because we were young, keen and enjoying ourselves, we looked and sounded different from what the audience at a factory gate expected of Tories. We gave heart to the regiment of elderly local supporters, who fed and mothered us generously.

Once an election was called our cohorts were deployed night after night into market towns and villages. In 1950 both the town of

Cambridge and the county of Cambridgeshire were being defended by Labour. That year I was sent out with others to cover Labour meetings in the two seats, and into Norfolk to ask awkward questions and report on subjects covered. The Labour MP for the county, Alderman Stubbs, had come up through the National Union of Agricultural Workers many years earlier. He was a turkey cock of a man, easily flustered as we pursued him from village hall to village hall. We found the best technique was to shake our heads vigorously but silently at most of the alderman's statements, so that he was drawn to address himself exclusively to us. He lost. The next year Labour attempted to regain the seat with a wealthy landowner, Harry Walston. We used to ask him from the back of the hall how his butler intended to vote. Cambridge Town also changed to Conservative in 1950 and had to be defended in 1951. I did not respect our candidate, Hamilton Kerr. He lived in a sumptuous flat, was waited on hand and foot, and an orchid was laid out for him every evening. He was a good-looking bachelor, and faithful ladies twittered about him, complimenting him on each performance. I preferred Denis Bullard in South-west Norfolk, who campaigned with a broad local accent and lots of common sense.

In those elections candidates held four or more meetings every night. They were driven dozens of miles over dark roads through the scattered East Anglian constituencies. It was impossible to keep to an exact timetable, so the candidate would use us as fill-in speakers for ten, fifteen, twenty minutes, until he arrived from his last meeting. We usually operated in pairs. The quality of our speeches was not important, provided only that we did not provoke an uproar and that we kept going until but not beyond the blessed moment when the candidate appeared in the doorway. By modern standards, audiences were big: nervously I addressed seven hundred people in the Guildhall at Thetford in February 1950. My most memorable evening was at Ampthill in Bedfordshire, supporting Alan Lennox Boyd, soon to be Colonial Secretary. A big, dark, handsome man, he arrived late. It was not a safe seat, and the hall was full of workers from the local brickyards, beginning to show mild irritation with our undergraduate sallies. Lennox Boyd had lost his voice, which was hardly surprising as it was his sixth meeting of the night. But within seconds he mastered and soothed the meeting in a husky whisper. He had been there twenty years and they all knew him. I have never seen personal charm so effectively deployed at a meeting.

On the last day of both election campaigns I went back to Newbury, in 1950 taking Tony Lloyd with me. I had just passed my driving test and my job on polling day was to drive my mother round half the Conservative committee rooms in a car decked in blue while my father covered the other half. We had to remember to hang the right way up in his car the horseshoe given to him for luck by the Lambourn horseracing trainers. This style of campaigning, entirely local, good humoured, with cheerful noise and plenty of posters in fields and windows, was very attractive. Each candidate used the arguments which suited him or her best, generating real enthusiasm in hundreds of active supporters. I tried to sustain this approach as closely as was practicable in Oxfordshire twenty-five years later.

Two memories stay vivid from the aftermath of the 1951 election, which returned Winston Churchill to Downing Street.

Our parents came to visit Stephen and myself in Cambridge. Delayed by a boiling radiator, they arrived at the Garden House Hotel at teatime to find the lady at the reception desk consumed with excitement. Downing Street had been ringing for Mr Hurd all afternoon; he must call them at once. My father borrowed sixpence from the porter and was wedged (he was already a bulky man) into the small telephone kiosk in the hall. In those days there was a complicated procedure involved in making a call, culminating in the need to press button A. Having mastered this task, my father was invited by Winston Churchill to join the new Government as a junior minister at Agriculture. He declined. To accept would have involved giving up his farming, which meant more to him than anything in politics. It was not an easy conversation, and would be inconceivable in the present Commons, packed as it is with professional politicians who see it as their *raison d'être* to receive and say yes to such a telephone call.

My second memory is of Churchill broadcasting on the wireless as Prime Minister at the death of King George VI early in 1952. As a sentimental amateur historian I was moved by the last words of his broadcast and wrote it out in my diary. It still seems, in harmony and aptness, an ideally constructed English oratorical sentence, delivered by the veteran master of the language with the skill it deserved: 'And I, who spent my youth amid the august, unchallenged and tranquil glories of the Victorian era may feel a thrill to raise again the prayer and the anthem,' then, very loud, 'God save the Queen.'

The other and at that time less exciting ladder of university politics was the Cambridge Union. Gradually I climbed the rungs: a speech from the back of the hall, a speech 'on the paper', equivalent to the front bench, the Committee, secretary (won by one vote), vice-president, president. The debates were well attended. Those of us who were active in them learned how to construct a speech and deal with interruptions in a heightened atmosphere. Geoffrey Howe, Norman St John Stevas and Julian Williams helped to show me the way. I enjoyed debating in Dublin with Greville Janner, later a Labour MP and peer, who was president the term before me. Greville, unstoppable then as now, was an opponent impossible to dislike.

There was a great deal of time-consuming intrigue and domestic jockeying in the Union, together with worry about its finances. I did not particularly relish hours spent in the dark red Union building behind the Round Church, designed by Waterhouse in a gloomy mood. But a rather narrow ambition drove me on. The job of arranging debates was something of a nightmare. Indeed, one of my recurring bad dreams is still that the outside speakers for a debate, having accepted my invitation, pull out at the last minute, leaving me staring at disaster. My diary shows that more than once this almost happened.

The university timetable provides long holidays, and I made good use of them, in particular by exploring Europe on train and bus. In the spring of 1950 Tim Raison and I made a first trip to Paris, then on to Florence, Siena, Venice and Milan. That summer I spent rainy weeks learning some Spanish in Santander, then broke away to Burgos, Madrid and Toledo. It was a distant age: on return I wrote to Antony Acland, 'The great thing about Spain is that there are comparatively few tourists.' The next summer my brother Stephen and I travelled around Burgundy and I took a course at the summer school in Tours.

Most notable was an expedition to Greece with Tony Lloyd and Antony Acland in April 1951. Greece was not, to put it mildly, organised for tourism. The Civil War had just ended, bridges were destroyed, public transport impossible to predict, roads impassable. We had a marvellous time. Our base was the Hotel Kentrikon in Athens, which charged one pound a night for a room with three beds and occasional hot water. A steamer took ten hours to reach Delos, where we were marooned by a storm. Soaked to the skin, we spent most of a day in bed in the hostel run by the French School of Archaeology while our clothes dried on the veranda. As everywhere in Greece, the diet was limited; we ate eight eggs apiece during those two days on Delos. The next day the storm had abated, but the waves ran high, and the ferry to Mikonos was cancelled. After exploring the temples and villas, we sat on stones on the beach and bargained with the local fishermen as they mended their nets among the sea lavender and banks of red poppies. The tiny motorboat which they eventually provided was tossed mercilessly by the billows of the Aegean. We lay under hatches, trying not to be sick or anxious. We reached Mikonos safely, but had missed the Athens steamer and run out of money. A tall, cadaverous Englishman appeared to rescue us, explaining that he had been a spy during the war, but had settled on Mikonos with a vineyard and a Greek girl. We found the one hotel which the island then boasted and spent Easter Day swimming in the cold sea, toasting Greek

Independence Day in cognac with the local grocer, and watching a procession of schoolchildren in white kilts and tasselled caps singing their way through the tiny houses on the harbour, each flying its blue-and-white flag.

From Athens we invaded the Peloponnese by bus, declaimed from the amphitheatre at Epidaurus, and hitched a ride in a fragrant onion lorry to Mycenae, a village rich in hostile dogs. There we stayed at La Belle Hélène, an inn boasting Goering as a comparatively recent guest. Bus services came to an end after that, so we spent time in the back of a lorry with a goat. We trudged west across the Peloponnese to the great temple at Bassae, then three hours' walk from the nearest village. I am glad that we found Bassae, perched on a crag in remote wilderness, before the amenities of civilisation closed in on it. West again towards Olympia, relying on hospitable omelettes and a spare bedroom in a village on the way, offered after much discussion among the whole population in the square about our best route. The River Alpheus was flowing high and fast, the bridge was down. Hercules had diverted the Alpheus to cleanse the Augean stables. Lacking his strength, we crammed trousers, socks and shoes into our packs, tucked our shirts up to our shoulders, and waded waist deep over sharp stones. Olympia was a place of simple comfort as well as beauty. We noted that our knowledge of ancient Greek was useless, that elderly Greeks in each village who claimed to speak English were incomprehensible, that as a nation they seemed strongly royalist, generous, pro-British and apt to be sick in their own buses. We paid our respects to the Oracle of Delphi, and finally to Knossos in Crete, where I passed out in a restaurant after too many hours on the beach. To modern students accustomed to bestride the world, all this would seem tame stuff – Leigh-Fermor on a dull day. To us, it was magic.

During vacations I spent occasional weeks at Winterbourne and at Ashens, a farm on Kintyre bought by the company which my father now chaired. The old-fashioned steamer proceeded slowly down the Clyde, past down-at-heel holiday towns like Dunoon, crossed Loch Fyne and docked at Tarbert. Ashens was a plain farmhouse halfway up a hill a few miles to the north. My parents were very fond of it, perhaps because of its simplicity. The long walks with a birdglass, the talk of shearing, markets and weather reminded them of the life of daily farming which they had left behind when they moved from Rainscombe. There was a loch up the hill with small trout, and we three boys chased a very few grouse round the slopes of heather and bracken.

In these years my diary refers often to days out with a gun: those grouse at Ashens, rabbits and squirrels at Winterbourne, partridges at Temple in Wiltshire, and rare organised pheasant shoots with friends.

I bought plus fours, indestructible and the colour of bright rust. Many of the diary entries record that I shot poorly; yet I enjoyed it. When I lived abroad I never shot, and only rarely after I returned to England in 1966. I stopped after I was allotted police protection in 1984, finding it awkward to shoot with a police officer at my side saying, 'Bad luck, sir,' or, 'A bit behind, Secretary of State.' I meant to resume later, but never did. Poor eyesight, slow reactions and lack of practice combined against it. The shoots I most enjoyed were small and informal: for example, at my brother Stephen's downland farm in Wiltshire on Boxing Day. I relished the local gossip at lunch sitting on straw bales in a barn, and the last drive of the day. The sun sets red, picking out the profile of the beeches ahead, the cold hardens with frost around you, but for the moment you feel warm and pleasantly exercised. The next gun is too far off to intrude on your solitude. You think of imminent tea and perhaps fruit cake. For ten minutes, waiting for the beaters, you enjoy the subtle sounds and movements of an English wood in winter.

But what to do after Cambridge? My father wisely warned me against plunging from undergraduate politics to the relatively grown-up version at Westminster. Indeed, in those days there were no jobs for passionate, ambitious politicians in their twenties. Now the Palace of Westminster is full of important young men and women, hurrying from one meeting to another, clutching their files and laptops, as they ply their trade as research assistants, political consultants or special advisers. The House of Commons is increasingly composed of Members with that background. Such apparatus hardly existed fifty years ago. There were no bottom rungs on the political ladder. My mind had for some time turned to the Foreign Service, partly because it fitted my interests, partly because it was difficult to enter and thus provided a natural sequel to my earlier assaults on scholarships and prizes. I do not think that any of us worried that we would not find a job. We were willing to work hard, and the demand for graduates with reasonable degrees seemed infinite.

In March 1951 I had been approached quietly by an admiral who asked if I would be interested in joining the Secret Service. I attended a selection board in London, but before matters proceeded further was brought up against a fundamental question. It was pointed out that I should go forward only if I was ready to accept a career in which anything I achieved would remain hidden. Having examined myself, I pulled back. I do not think I have on the whole been consumed by a lust for publicity; but I thought it reasonable to expect some modest recognition of hard work, and I suppose I was already beginning to enjoy the sound of my own voice.

So I applied for the Diplomatic Service in the usual way. The first day of the written exam started badly: I cut myself shaving and lost a gold cufflink down the plughole of the sink. The group tests two months later in March 1952 involved concocting a scheme for developing a new town in North-east England and dealing with juvenile hooliganism. I wrote to Antony Acland, who was preparing for the same experience:

> Quite fun in a rather pompous way. You don't have to know anything about drains or Urban District Councils – just our old friend common sense. The atmosphere is fairly civilised, cups of tea and cake and a carefully calculated geniality. Chairman: 'It makes me feel very old, but I find I was at school with your father – in C2, wasn't he?' The trouble is, you haven't the faintest idea how well you've done at the end – they are all smiling and inscrutable, and wish you luck with every appearance of good will.

I was cross-examined portentously about a silly phrase I had used in discussion that the law was an immoral profession. It was a point I often hurled at Tony Lloyd in our Great Court arguments (he studied law), but it was unwise to expose it to senior officials who had no taste for undergraduate banter. Nevertheless, I moved on to the Final Board in April, stately across a highly polished table in Burlington Gardens.

No one, I hope, will be reading this book in expectation of detailed romance, let alone bedroom excitements. But the sympathetic reader may have worried that I seemed hitherto to have lived in an entirely masculine world: two brothers, two single-sex schools, a set of male friends and a university where girls, though permitted, indeed encouraged, did not yet loom large. It is therefore with pleasure that I record – late certainly, tame perhaps, but authentic – the following entry from my diary for 6 June 1952: 'Supper in my room and midnight matinee of Footlights with Jane Toynbee and the delectable Diana Lewis – a most admirable party – my really successful social idea – salmon and hock and strawberries and funny jokes and beautiful girls laughing.' From then on my memories and diary jottings include, if not a rush of beautiful girls, for I remained shy and abrupt, at least enough to keep life busy and nervous.

June 1952 should have been a great month. In the space of a fortnight, which included this modest dinner party, I held my presidential debate in full evening dress at the Union, achieved a first in history, and passed top into the Foreign Office. The days passed in a haze of summer parties. The Trinity May Ball ended with breakfast at Newmarket. The necessary nostalgia was provided by the catchy tunes of Julian Slade's *Salad Days*, playing at the ADC:

If I once start looking behind me
And begin retracing my steps,
I remind you to remind me,
We said we'd never look back.

By the end of June Cambridge was over, I was haymaking at Winterbourne and being given what I described as a 'salutary jolt' by Tony Lloyd, in the form of a rocket for complacency and misdirected effort. But a cloud had not yet lifted, a cloud from the disaster which had struck our family a year earlier.

I have written little so far about my brother Julian, two years younger than myself. In August 1945 Bob Wickham, headmaster of Twyford School, wrote to my parents:

> Just a note to say how sorry we are going to be to be without Julian – one more milestone passed! We must not regret these things because these lads have to grow up, and Julian is quite ready to go on. In fact we should spoil him if we kept him on here. As you know we were more than ordinarily fond of Douglas, and Julian is even easier to be fond of, as he is really such an extraordinarily easy boy in the way he gets on with people. I have never seen him anything but good tempered and anxious to do the kind thing.

Julian was thirteen when these words were written as he left Twyford for Marlborough College. Over the next few years he developed new qualities. He was by a mile the most high spirited and imaginative of the three of us. He fed his imagination from voracious reading, from a network of friends, and from a keen enjoyment of life at home, both at Rainscombe and at Winterbourne. He bound these interests together by writing – letters, diaries, articles, snippets of all kinds. It was Julian who edited the *Winterbourne News*, an irregular family magazine of typed sheets pasted on cardboard. The articles were unsigned and I cannot now work out who wrote what. But it must have been Julian who denounced a proposal to ban hunting and rebuked the local curate for conducting the carol service dressed as a boy scout.

He and I, as already noted, spent days together in Normandy in the summer of 1949 and kept a joint diary; Julian's entries are more lively and colourful than my own. I have an essay of his (marked 20 out of 20 by the Marlborough master) in which at the age of fifteen he records listening to Winston Churchill speaking to a Conservative rally at Blenheim in 1947. When the great man appeared 'there rose a tremendous shout. I shall never forget that moment. It was one of the finest in my life. Round me men who were usually so silent and taciturn shouted themselves hoarse, women hoisted their children onto their shoulders better to see "him" and old people wept, they knew not why.' But Churchill, so Julian thought, let them down, by talking about the Conservative Industrial Charter and other matters of no interest to them: 'Now he must give up his place as king of orators to another who may use this "power of speech to stir men's blood" in less worthy causes.' Julian was often critical of the powers that be, but from a traditional, even romantic, point of view. He was becoming a radical in the sense that Chesterton, Belloc and Kipling were radicals. He preferred country sports to the more organised routines of cricket and football. Most days when we were at home the three of us roamed the woods with our Hungerford terrier in search of rabbits and squirrels. In one of his last letters to me Julian explored jokingly the possibility of starting a pack of beagles at Winterbourne. Characteristically his membership card of the British Field Sports Society (found in his wallet) is scribbled all over with jotted quotations from Disraeli, Kipling, Pascal and others. It must have been the only piece of paper available when he came across sayings he wanted to remember.

Julian enjoyed Marlborough and did well there, becoming head of his house. Returning from a visit to Stephen at Winchester, he once wrote to me, 'Of the place as an institution I think I approved; and of its inmates, judging solely by faces and mannerisms, I did not. Of Marlborough my judgement would be exactly the reverse.' His masters at Marlborough wrote warmly of his lively imagination and thoughtfulness for others. He did not succeed in winning a scholarship to Cambridge, but he did well enough to secure a place there, at my father's old college, Pembroke.

But first he had to perform his National Service. No one supposed that he would enjoy it. After he joined the army in January 1951 he asked me to write to him often from Cambridge. His letters in reply from the St Lucia Barracks at Bordon in Hampshire were similar to the letters I had written home from Oswestry two years earlier. He was plunged into a world of dirt, noisy music, bullying NCOs, and fellow conscripts who made fun of his public school voice but were generous with the contents of their massive food parcels from home: 'brandy butter, crackers, rich fruitcakes, filled cakelets, dates, Brazil nuts, and so on'. They had no respect for the King or the Royal Family: 'Out of 13 in the room one is RC, one Methodist; of the rest I gather 8 do not go to church, and the last 3 when they can expect good hymns. I did not tell them it was like eating All Bran and expecting nutritional value.' Julian's voyage of discovery was told in exactly the tone of voice I expected. He neither confirmed nor denied the rumour in the barrack room that his father was a general. He was selected for the company darts team. After a couple of months he passed the necessary selection board for a commission and was transferred, as I had been, to the Mons Officer Cadet School at Aldershot. As a result, he was in good form when we were both at home for a weekend after Easter. We split the trunk of an oak tree in the wood on Sunday afternoon, 15 April, and I drove him to Newbury to catch his bus back to barracks. That was the last time I saw him.

Six weeks later Julian went home for another forty-eight-hour leave to celebrate my mother's birthday. What followed can best be described in the words from her diary. I think she would have wished that.

June 1, Friday
J rang up about 8.30 o'clock from Newbury – went down to fetch him – came in mufti – no luggage – just his small writing case.

June 2, Saturday
<u>My birthday</u> and a lovely morning – all rather late getting up – J decorated my chair with a charming bunch of flowers – a leather car keyring from him and a box of chocolates and a charming card a regular library of books – a merry read – then I bustled around and was haymaking in the orchard when they heard the ice cream van – so J went and got us ice creams. He and I and Da licked them on the terrace together. We had our early lunch – and then went off to Temple – left the car up by the White Horse and walked over down to Wick Bottom – Ranger distinguished himself by killing 2 rats – had tea and looked over Sharpridge. From there we drove to Hackpen – then over to Huish Church to see about the Memorial Stone to Father and Mother Hurd – I called J to the gate to look at that lovely view of the Pewsey Vale from under the laburnum bush – Mary Harrison Smith came home and we talked with her and went into her garden and then home by Geoffrey's Woods and up Oare Hill and then quite exhausted by so much loveliness J and I both slept on the way home – dinner almost straight away – asparagus and chicken and banana cream and Yugoslav wine – J talked quite a bit then went rather early to bed – he read late. I heard him moving about upstairs.

June 3, Sunday
My day to fetch the organist so left early. Anthony and Julian walked down to church together – we were all early and went out and stood beneath the big tree and looked out over the valley – it was looking so beautiful – a rather feeble service, no sermon,

merely a talk on coming visit of evangelists – went and had a drink at Godfrey's altogether again.

Julian shot himself in the wood this afternoon after lunch. Anthony in the garden and myself at my desk quite unconscious of anything wrong and only when he did not come in to tea – began to feel uneasy about him and I ran upstairs to his room and found his Red Book – his anthology open on his desk at a quotation from Sophocles.

A frightful certainty filled me – I ran down to the gun room – the gun case lay on the table closed. I opened it and it was empty – I ran to Anthony – I could not speak what I knew – we called Peter and went into the wood and found him down in the most lovely corner – stretched out with the filtering sunlight playing over him – Peter was quite wonderful – after those first moments neither Anthony nor I went back – but Peter sat with him until the police took his body away – we were so fortunate in all who helped us, the police officer and the coroner. Godfrey came in all unknowing of what had happened and proved his great kindliness and love.*

June 5, Tuesday

I try to remember the wonderful feeling of beauty and peace as I knelt beside Julian among the bluebells – a great uncalled for thankfulness before I knew anything of grief.

We drove down to Winchester Sunday evening to tell Stephen ourselves and I remember saying to Anthony then that we must hang on to what we know now, that Julian died from what might be called an overdose of beauty after having been starved of it so long – it was as if I knew all the doubts and uncertainties of 'if only' were bound to crowd in as soon as the stunned and enchanted moment had worn away.

We had had a very lovely weekend. We could not have planned a more beautiful farewell time had we tried – was it mere coincidence? – and I remember particularly leaning on the gate by the Rectory at Wilcot looking out across the Pewsey Vale from under an arch of golden laburnum – we leant on the gate together and just looked and felt.

This feeling of consciousness in beauty and peace in the loveliness of God's world lasted for days and there was a great

---

*Peter Hiscock, a few years older than myself, had come with us from Wiltshire to help run our garden and fields. He was and remains a firm friend. Godfrey Nicolson MP was our friend and neighbour.

slowing down of time so that one slipped back almost into childhood days. Nothing that used to worry worried any more, no erstwhile urges moved one any more – although lost later in a maze of thoughts and doubt and 'if onlys' later and sunk at times in self-pity – I do really think that I got nearer to having a peep into the infinite than ever before.

There cannot be much to add. That morning, writing firmly and tidily on two sheets of Winterbourne paper, Julian had made a dated will leaving his property to Stephen and myself, and asking us to remember from it four named friends.

My mother telephoned me at Cambridge on the Monday morning. I spent the day in a daze, walked to Grantchester, sat in the church there, and read *Howards End*. The next day I went home. The *Evening Standard* being read by my neighbour in the train carriage carried on its front page a full and accurate account of what had happened. Stephen and I visited the place in the wood where Julian had lain. We buried him in Winterbourne churchyard on the Thursday. Although a hedge has grown up now which partly obscures the view, one can still look from his grave across the quiet little river valley to our house and the surrounding woods. Thirty-four years later we added to the grave my mother's ashes.

My own recollection of the days and weeks which followed is of continuous high summer: my bedroom at Winterbourne looked west to the wood, and a great isolated oak tree in the adjoining field, behind which the sun set evening after evening in relentless beauty. Neither Stephen nor I can now find the red notebook, though we remember being shown it after Julian's death. But the quotation from Sophocles at which it lay open is as follows: 'That I must die some time I knew, edict or no edict, and if I am to die before my time that I count a gain. When one lives as I do in the midst of a sorrow surely one were better dead.' Antigone is justifying her decision to risk death by defying King Creon's decree, and going out to perform funeral rites for her brother.

I have one other literary clue. During the short time he was at Aldershot Julian bought the *Collected Poems* of A.E. Housman, the green hardback edition published by Jonathan Cape. I have it in front of me; it is in excellent condition. Interleaved is a mauve eightpenny bus ticket issued at Aldershot on 28 May 1951. I suppose that Julian bought the book on that day and read it when he came home for the last time the following weekend. Housman's repeated messages of despair addressed to young men in language of powerful, carefully contrived simplicity fitted exactly Julian's mood.

Most casual friends on learning the news naturally assumed that some extraordinary external pressure must have pushed Julian over the brink. Our parents, Stephen and I did not agree. The future for Julian was bright; he certainly looked forward to taking his place at Cambridge. There was no evidence from him or later from his friends who wrote to us of a breakdown in any of his human relationships. As we tossed the tragedy round and round in thought and conversation we came back again to the same conclusion, and I can still think of no other. The damage was done by the immediate contrast between the beauty and loving kindness of a weekend spent at home and the ugly misery of army life to which he had to return that Sunday night. This contrast played on the strong emotions of a romantic nineteen-year-old keyed up by a sentimental education. Deep down in Julian's nature must have been a strain of sadness which suddenly overpowered him.

Why did he find army life so miserable? Remembering my own feelings two years earlier, I could glimpse the answer, though my own nature is more prosaic and accepting. It was certainly not the physical hardship or any failure in his military life. He had laughed at the hardship, and by passing into Mons had overcome the main obstacle. There was nothing in the army to attract or interest him, but most people can live with boredom for a few months without disaster. My parents felt, and were probably right, that Julian detested the purpose of it all: the training to kill. When, after the first few days, we reached what my mother called the 'what if' stage, they speculated whether Julian should have been encouraged to become a Roman Catholic or to declare himself a pacifist. No one would have stood in his way for a moment if he had done either. But I believe that he had not rationalised his dislike of the army until it suddenly overflowed and destroyed him.

My father reacted in a characteristic way. Quietly, but persistently and firmly, he pursued in writing a number of questions with Julian's commanding officer at Mons, Colonel Wood, and then with the chaplain general of the forces. The course for officer cadets at Mons was so compressed that there was no time for the young men to discuss the moral and intellectual reasons for compulsory military service. A perfunctory meeting with the chaplain had not been followed up as promised. Why, my father asked, was this allowed to happen? Since conscription was bound to bring into the forces young men not suited for military life, what steps were taken to identify and help such individuals? 'It was the grim atmosphere and the systematic preparation for killing his fellow men that he felt he could not bear,' my father wrote to the colonel on 10 June. 'The climax came when he was home last Sunday and the peace, happiness of a June day overwhelmed him . . . There are boys who find it impossible to express these inner feelings. They will not make themselves different from their fellows by claiming exemption from combatant service, and unless they are helped to find a link between their home and school life and army life they may come to feel, as Julian did, that life is not really worth living.' Colonel Wood replied at once that my father's letter had hit him where he was most vulnerable. He had recently lost a child of his own. He explained what he had tried to do to reduce the impersonal pressures at Mons, acknowledged that the course was too short and intense, and invited my father to visit the school. My father, rightly judging that this would simply turn into a routine visit by a Conservative MP, suggested instead a meeting over dinner. He asked me to join Colonel Wood and himself at his club, the United University, on 10 July, and afterwards wrote a careful summary of five particular suggestions which the colonel (who was leaving Mons) undertook to hand on to his successor. A particular effort should be made in the first few weeks of training to set the course in proportion and explain that it would be no disgrace to a cadet if in the end he did not pass; school reports should be available to platoon and company commanders; there should be a structured discussion among cadets of the implications of National Service; there should be time for the chaplain to meet small groups of cadets informally; the Treasury should be pressed to agree that the course should be extended by a fortnight. 'If these changes are made at Mons,' my father concluded, 'life may be made easier and more tolerable for some boys who have been caught up in the military machine and who mean to do their duty, but whose hearts will never be in the army.' I do not know how far this trail led to actual improvement. I have followed with pain the story of the recent deaths of young soldiers of roughly Julian's age.

The rest of that summer of 1951 became a bustle, as we returned to the banalities of ordinary life. For me, one such banality was a compulsory fortnight with the Royal Artillery on Salisbury Plain as a reservist. The *Spectator* paid me eight guineas for an article on this experience; it still reads quite well. A little later I took a decision which surprised myself: to volunteer for yet another military fortnight at Larkhill the following summer, almost immediately after leaving Cambridge. It was hard to argue that my country needed me. I did not expect to enjoy deploying a gun troop again, nor to discover that I was good at it. I found myself under the command of a sarcastic gauleiter. 'Why have I come on this curious affair? Terrified by day, depressed by night. Is it an exercise in humility (because really I'm a bit incompetent) or masochism, or what?' A bit of both, probably. But certainly I wanted to test the army again and so live as close as I could to the final experience of Julian's life.

So there it is. I look again at his letters, and those of his friends, the sparkling leaders in the *Winterbourne News*, the diary of our Normandy holiday, and a photograph of Julian walking fast towards the camera, tweed jacket open over Fair Isle sweater, unruly hair, a smile of welcome. The sadness is of course that fifty years is too long. Even with the help of these things I cannot reconstruct what we then lost, or imagine what Julian would have achieved up to today. Except to be sure that it would not have been ordinary.

It goes without saying that the pain of that June day never entirely left my parents. My mother's diary shows that it returned to hit her suddenly and hard several times during the months which followed. My father was a man of few but good words. On 18 March the following year, the eve of what would have been Julian's twentieth birthday, he wrote to my mother:

> Dearest
> This birthday is a day of memories for us. I know you will be feeling sad – not too sad I hope – and wishing as I do every day that we could have read Julian's feelings more clearly and helped him more in his struggle.
>   But let's cherish the happiness he had in his time and gave in our family. He decided for himself when to go on ahead and that was his right which no one, not even Christ, can deny.
> My love to you today and always.
> Anthony

Without forgetting, they settled to enjoy fifteen years together at Winterbourne Holt. Sitting up in bed and discussing their twenty-third wedding anniversary over morning tea, they wished (but only mildly, my mother wrote) that they had had more children and that they had never moved from Wiltshire.

Theirs was an abundantly happy marriage. I cannot remember any serious upset between them. My father was by nature practical, unpretentious and a peacemaker. Village by village, town by town, he built up a reputation for trustworthiness and hard work in the South Berkshire constituency, which he won in five successive elections without difficulty. Local people of all parties were pleased when he was made a life peer in 1964 and took the title Lord Hurd of Newbury. Before that in the Commons he took an interest in the general gossipy flow of politics, and held on almost every occasion a central position in the spectrum of Conservative Party ideas. He wished that Churchill would retire earlier than he did, was clear that Rab Butler was not the right man to lead the party, and showed more interest in the Commonwealth than in Europe. In the House he spoke almost exclusively on agriculture and for twenty years chaired the backbench Agriculture Committee, thus acquiring a quiet, substantial influence over successive ministers during those long years of Conservative rule. His business interests gradually increased, all focused on farming. He had a circle of friends like himself – calm, sensible, occasionally humorous, with a strong sense of service. As he grew older his wide chest and shoulders became rather too much for legs weakened by polio in early youth. He walked less often across our fields at Winterbourne and over the Wiltshire downs, and used a shooting stick while waiting for the partridges and pheasants. But I picture him most clearly moving briskly with the help of a stick down the corridor into the Central Lobby of the House of Commons where I would be waiting. He would be wearing a stiff white collar, a well-cut double-breasted suit neatly pressed, and black shoes highly polished by the porter or valet at the United University Club, where he had stayed the night. He would be exactly on time, holding that it was as rude to arrive early as to be late. He would give me a good plain lunch and listen carefully to all I said about my own comings and goings. He would slip in a comment or two, not usually presented as advice, but always worth remembering.

My mother was a person of stronger feelings which she rarely revealed, even in the privacy of her diary. In early days she suffered from migraine, which would disable her for one or two days at a time. Later this wore off, and until old age she enjoyed robust health. She came from a family and married into a family which never questioned that the men took the important decisions, but only after listening with respect to the opinions of the clear-minded women whom they had married. My mother disliked show and was not interested in attempting a glamorous appearance. She despised vehemence and bitterness in politics or anywhere else, and helped to keep my father on the path of broad-minded toleration which the local paper had praised at his first election in 1945. She sat as a Newbury district councillor, always, I think, unopposed and certainly not as any kind of partisan. She was the peacemaker of her own side of the family, particularly in trying to reconcile the disputes of her brother John Corner with his wife and children. Her main interests were her children, and later grandchildren, the wider family, her home and all the activities of farm and garden which revolved round it.

Both my parents were skilled at words. My father spoke and wrote with ease, aiming at all times to be brief, simple and clear. A letter of a dozen sentences from him was long. My mother spoke a few words in public only when she had to, but her letters and diary overflow with vivid descriptions of scenery and occasions.

They were both enthusiastic travellers. Of their many destinations, the most unusual and for them the most enjoyable were the Falkland

Islands. My father became a director of the chartered Falkland Islands Company, which then owned most of the sheep farms in the colony. They went out several times during the fifties and sixties, flying to Montevideo and then bucketing across to Port Stanley on the steamship *Darwin*. My mother was a poor sailor, but she was recompensed by the welcome they received in the islands. My father was keen on improving the quality of the pasture, for example by introducing a grass seed called Yorkshire fog. He discussed sheep with the farmers out in the camp (the islanders' name for everything that is not Port Stanley) while my mother marvelled at the sea birds, the wind driving the clouds, the difficulty of manoeuvring jeeps down rough tracks, the generous hospitality, the impossibility of man and wife finding a bedroom big enough to share in Government House. Despite this technical difficulty, they managed somehow to have morning tea together, a ceremony which my mother described as the most important occasion of married life. Her letters are so vivid that I have sent most of them to be part of the archive in the admirable museum in Port Stanley.

Much later, after we had recaptured the islands from the Argentinians in 1982, I visited my mother, expecting to find her overjoyed at the news. But she was sad, believing the war would have destroyed the simple way of life which she had found attractive. Going there myself twelve years after that, I think she had been too gloomy. There are roads now instead of tracks, a big new school at Stanley, a garrison, and relics of war littering the islands. But the wind, the birds and the feeling of friendly remoteness are as compelling as ever.

PART II

DIPLOMACY

5

LONDON

THE FOREIGN OFFICE

The morning walk from my flat in Tufton Street to the Foreign Office became a satisfying ritual. Past the ecclesiastical outfitters into Dean's Yard, avoid an onrush of Westminster schoolboys, clip the edge of St James's Park, up the Clive Steps, and into the Foreign Office courtyard. I had bought a bowler hat at Locks that summer of 1952, but was not sure if it made me look professional or just ridiculous. (I used it again, during my next spell in London between 1960 and 1963, but by the time I returned in 1966 fashion had changed.) I learned to furl my umbrella tightly; this took so long to perfect that it was clearly frivolous to unfurl the umbrella simply because it had started to rain. To reach my first office in the Economic Relations Department (the ERD) I climbed the great double staircase at the heart of the Foreign Office building, past the preposterous mural paintings of Britannia waging war and peace while around her languid youths push boats about or drape themselves on spears. The staircase now glows again with the original colours, gold predominating; but fifty years ago its magnificence was dark and decaying. Those were the years of the last great London fogs before the Clean Air Act. Some of these Victorian public interiors (the Reform Club in Pall Mall is another example) feel as if they were designed with fog in mind. Certainly the Foreign office was at its most suggestive on a November afternoon, when the light retreated and winter pressed in on the windows. Occasional wisps of fog were granted admission to the heart of the building to remind us of the vanity of any efforts to spread light in the world.

The Economic Relations Department worked in part of the huge Locarno Room at the top of the grand staircase. The room was divided into cubicles with plaster walls, so that its splendour was obscured. Glancing up from my desk, I could see part of a dingy gilt cornice of the Corinthian order. We were part of a lesser civilisation which scurried about ignominiously on our insignificant tasks in a palace where once the great Lord Salisbury held sway. Colleagues in other departments were even less fortunate. Some were issued with buckets to cope with rain dripping through the ceiling. Ladies fed coal fires in the more important offices. Pigeons defied all efforts to clear the shit from the window sills. Along the passage the Durbar Court, built at great expense to embody the majesty of the Raj, was still smothered in wartime blackout, under which dwelt a communications unit.

It was generally agreed that, once we could afford it, all this grubby history should be swept away and the Foreign Office demolished and replaced with a modern building of glass and concrete. I remember walking in St James's Park one lunchtime with Humphrey Maud, a contemporary in the office. We paused on the old iron bridge across the lake, now replaced, and I passed some admiring remark on the Foreign Office façade in the distance, and hoped it would be spared. 'If I thought you really believed that,' he gravely replied, 'I would have serious doubts of your intelligence.'

There was no training for new entrants to the Foreign Service, except for those who were to learn one of the specialist languages. Generalists such as myself were simply allocated to a department and expected to learn the trade. I was lucky to share an office with Peter Ramsbotham, eleven years my senior. Peter was wrestling with the tail end of the long crisis over the nationalisation of the Anglo-Iranian Oil Company. When I arrived in the morning he would be barking harshly into the telephone; when I left in the evening he would be doing the same. I watched how policy papers and telegrams of instruction to our overseas embassies would be conceived in his fertile brain, meticulously translated on to paper, and then presented in meetings and telephone calls to his superiors in the department, to under-secretaries further up, to ministers, to the Treasury, to the bereaved executives of the oil company, to the Americans.

In the intervals of handling the crisis Peter took time to educate me about paper, the handling of which was in 1952 the essence of Foreign Office life. Before the days of rapid copying, each substantial paper had a dignity of its own. It was clothed in a jacket, on which was marked a record of its coming and going. Occasionally some particularly glorious paper would be initialled AE in red ink, or a shade less gloriously R in green, to show that it had passed through the hands of the Foreign

Secretary, Anthony Eden, or the Minister of State who supervised our work, Lord Reading. Jackets on the same subject would be bundled together with lengths of white or pink tape. Twice a day there would be a circulation of telegrams, differently coloured as between incoming (white) and outgoing (pink). I have a copy of the first pink telegram which I authorised myself, three days after joining the department: 'Foreign Office to Bangkok No 228 En clair. We regret that there will be no United Kingdom participants Agricultural Statistical Sampling Centre September 16 despite travel expenses offer'. It somehow lacks the pulsing drama of high diplomacy.

As the junior of the department I was allocated the handling of our economic relations with Latin America. Then, as now, these relations were full of happy potential, always about to explode into something magnificent which never quite materialised. My main concern at first was the negotiation with Argentina for the bulk purchase of meat by the British Government. The Ministry of Agriculture conducted the negotiation but in ERD we regarded ourselves as the pilot who would save it from the rocks. There was nothing trivial about this negotiation, for on it (seven years after the end of the war) depended the weekly ration of ten ounces of meat on which the British people survived. Like many good negotiations, it reached its climax in the Christmas break. On Christmas Eve 1952 I was 'Up 6.30 in the pitch black and rain. To FO to find a flood of confused interlocking telegrams – I become flustered, evasive and unreliable. Gradually recover, compile text, write it for John Simpson (Legal Adviser) to vet in Queens Gate, then send off classified unifying telegrams.' Then, six days later, 'Argentine cracks appear in accord, busy days, buy plus fours after lunch.' Finally, on New Year's Eve, gloomy resolution: 'Argentine minutiae become ever minuter, and we wait hourly but in vain for news of signature. Life neither desperate nor inspired . . . ARGENTINE AGREEMENT SIGNED.'

In this way I learned the rollercoaster nature of such negotiations, and the ins and outs of Whitehall. The head of my department, Denis Wright, was encouraging, watchful and shrewd. When I had to be deflated he performed the task without leaving a scar. Almost all our direct dealings were with other Whitehall departments, hardly ever with foreigners. But once a French economic delegation hove into view. I was confident that my hours with Mr Davies at Twyford plus my acquaintance at Eton with Victor Hugo and Lamartine would enable me to take the record of this meeting with no need for a professional interpreter, and I volunteered. But my French was rusty, the delegation spoke fast, and the technical subject matter would have been as alien to Victor Hugo and Lamartine as it was to myself. Denis Wright complained gently next morning of the scanty result. I never again pretended to unreal linguistic skills.

The ways of the Foreign Office were, and to some extent remain, a paradox. In those days, much more than now, the hierarchy of decision-taking on paper was rigid. Submissions moved up the pyramid of authority until they reached a level whose occupant felt able to take the decision. But the social habits of the office were different, and in some ways discouraged formality. For example, we learned never to knock on a Foreign Office door, and not to call anyone 'sir'. But, as often happens, these apparent informalities solved nothing, and indeed created problems. It required more courage to enter the grand room of an under-secretary without knocking, and once in the room what on earth were you to call the great man if not 'sir'? But gradually faces met in corridors and at meetings became familiar, even friendly, and the concept of the Foreign Office as a family began to take hold.

I could not decide if I was over- or underworked. The office usually required me on Saturday mornings, and that was a nuisance. But the hours were not long and there were few hectic moments. I had passed out of the world of examination scholarships and prizes, and there was no measurable objective in view. Looking back, I can see it as a necessary but uninteresting period. Nine months into the job, my diary records that one day I was 'Saved from complete inaction by the devaluation of the boliviano.' That about sums it up.

At this stage living for the first time in London was much more interesting than work at the Foreign Office. Jacky Shaw Stewart, Tim Raison and I shared a flat at the south end of Tufton Street in Westminster, close to its junction with Horseferry Road. The shop below the flat was a dairy-cum-village grocer's in the heart of London, owned and kept by two friendly sisters, the Misses Howell Davies. They sold us milk at all hours, and let us into our separate staircase when we had forgotten the key to the outside door. There were only two bedrooms, so by rote one of us slept in the dining room. Conditions were austere, but we got used to them. There was trouble over a refrigerator, and once at least food parcels were sent from Selfridges. But before long we began to entertain, even cook in a primitive way, and 78a Tufton Street became a convenient centre for friends to drop in for gossip, or for us to feed girls before or after theatre and cinema. After one such event Antonia Pakenham (now Fraser) congratulated us in her thank-you letter for having bought such an attractive milk bar and converted it into a flat.

Since the three of us were already friends we often explored London together, paying first visits to Ham House, Kenwood, Covent Garden, Sadler's Wells, Apsley House, the Boat Race, the Chelsea Flower Show. There was a certain amount of religious tourism. We listened to Canon Reindorp preach to hundreds in St Stephen's Rochester Row; on another

Sunday we favoured St Bartholomew's Smithfield; and on Ash Wednesday were sprinkled with ashes in St Matthew's Great Peter Street.

Unlike other European cities, London had wrapped itself in frozen austerity for six years after the war. In 1952 there were still plenty of gaps in streets and squares untouched since the Luftwaffe had struck ten years earlier. While the planners wrangled, the willowherb and buddleia flourished on neglected sites. But there was no neglect of theatre, cinema or music. Wolfit as Lear, Richard Burton as Coriolanus, Gielgud in *Venice Preserved*, repeated visits to the magical French film *Les Jeux Interdits* are memorable examples taken from the long list in my diary.

The young Queen and the return of Winston Churchill to Downing Street suggested traditional change within strong institutions. The climax of this line of thought came with the Queen's Coronation in summer 1953, as a series of diary entries indicate:

28 May
Sunny. Gay crowds and emblems up and down the Mall. Last banners and devices being hoisted into place. A splash of uniforms and a swish of Bentleys. The annexe to the Abbey now complete – looks like a magnificent bathroom. Parliament Square transformed with tiers and billowing roofs. Gilded crowns suspended handsomely over the Mall. Hideous pink waterproof roses in Regent Street. General effect uplifting.

2 June
Stephen and I in seats in Parliament Square 6.15. Grey showery day. Emerge from lunch on House of Commons Terrace into temporarily sunlit square and Zadok the Priest – service most impressive even relayed. Procession back almost but not quite spoilt by cloudburst – our stand leaks. [We were exactly under a dip in the canvas where the rain collected and formed a thin, cold waterfall down on to loyal spectators.] But magnificent, esp. Q of Tonga, Sir Winston Churchill and the Royal Family. Feel almost ill with emotion and too much drink.

3 June
Back to work with a bump, and perhaps a greater sense of service.

It was not generally supposed by his friends that Jacky Shaw Stewart would settle easily into the grind of becoming a chartered accountant in London. His heart was emphatically Highland. Tim Raison and I were sad but not surprised when he abandoned Tufton Street for his native Scotland in 1953. In his place we chose Philip Ziegler, whom we had both known as an Oppidan at Eton, and who quickly became a close friend. The bundle of Philip's letters written over twenty years and now in front of me is as entertaining a collection as anyone could have received in the twentieth century. Philip's home with his father was near Ringwood in the New Forest. I associate my weekends there with long, damp walks through autumn bracken and (since all Zieglers are argumentative) with discussions at his fireside about such matters as the Immaculate Conception. Tim Raison, dark, easy tempered and quiet, was quickly evolving into a serious journalist. Philip, like me, was in the Foreign Office, but markedly less orthodox than Tim and myself. He remembers how we used to drag him late at night after a cinema into the empty gallery of the House of Commons where he marvelled as we listened with rapt attention to some abstruse and boring debate.

Tony Lloyd had returned from a year at Harvard to take up a fellowship at Peterhouse, and I went more than once to stay with him in Cambridge. For purposes of our long-running debate about ourselves (now ten years old), I disapproved of this move and accused him of avoiding the dust of the arena. In reality I envied the intelligent conviviality of his life, and wondered how on earth we could achieve in crowded little Tufton Street the aloof handsomeness of Tony's rooms in Peterhouse. I did not yet feel fully committed to the Foreign Office and played occasionally with ideas of returning to academic life, or even of taking orders in the Church of England.

Few of my friends had married by this stage, but all seemed more at ease than I did with the array of attractive and intelligent girls who thronged London. I learned from them – for example, gradually overcoming my dislike of dances – but I was still some way behind. This was a worry because I expected any minute to be posted abroad, and might not be back in London for six years, by when I would have reached the horrendous age of thirty. What chance would I have then of finding a nice wife? Unconsciously I began to work at falling in love. Fortunately, the girls concerned were too sensible to take this seriously, and too nice to hurt me when putting me aside.

In those days young diplomats had no say whatever in their postings and in November 1953 I was told that I was posted to Peking, then as distant and monastic a post as one could conceive.* The girl to whom I then proposed gently turned me down on the accurate ground that I was too young. That proved to be the beginning not the end of friendship. In the next weeks I took her to Redgrave and Ashcroft as

---

*I use the Wade Anglicisation of Chinese and other familiar names as these were current in this period. Hence, Peking, Tientsin, Canton, Mao Tse-Tung, etc.

Antony and Cleopatra, to the Spanish dancer Antonio, to the Pitt Club Ball in Cambridge, and on a 29 bus through rainy streets to the evangelist Billy Graham at Haringey Arena. To my relief, she did not insist that we went forward to present our sins. She lived in SW5, and in spring 1954 I predicted, 'Earls Court Station will always for me be associated with self-pity of the most maudlin kind.' I still often feel self-pity at Earls Court, but this is now associated with the chaos of London Transport rather than spurned affection.

There was not much time for moping. Preparation for China covered a wide range. I read extensively on Chinese communism. A retired ambassadress told me that Proust and Dostoevsky would be essential companions, so they were enlisted.

More practically I had to amass large quantities of wine, toothpaste and razor blades, since none of these were said to be obtainable in the People's Republic. I had bought a larger, though still small, diary for 1954, 'in the hope of greater events, but hardly likely'. I was not sure about great events, but I had no difficulty in filling it.

6

PEKING

The British Embassy in Peking was in no particular hurry to welcome their latest recruit, and to my surprise the Foreign Office agreed that I should travel east by boat – and on a French liner. This involved a scramble by train across France to Marseille and then a month on the SS *Cambodge*, trim, white and modern. I found myself in a luxurious capsule, in places and among people unrelated to my past or my future.

At the forefront of the minds of most of my fellow passengers was the war in Indo-China, which the French were losing. Below decks the *Cambodge* was carrying troops destined for that war; in first class were officers, wives and a batch of nuns heading the same way. The nuns moved in formation, and were embarrassing to meet in a narrow corridor or on a companionway. The noticeboard carried each day news of the tightening grip of the communist Vietminh troops on the besieged French fortress of Dien Bien Phu. The future, not just of Vietnam and the rest of Indo-China, but even of Asia and the French Fourth Republic, seemed at times to hang on the outcome of that battle.

At the beginning, in the Mediterranean and the Red Sea, it did not weigh on us too much. I was seasick to the south of Sicily, and found myself getting through my books too fast. *The Duke's Children* (Trollope), *The Nigger of the Narcissus* and *Youth* (Conrad), Burke on the French Revolution alternated with books on Confucius and Mao. At sea I sank into a passive overfed existence, made more difficult by a rash Lenten vow to abstain from all alcohol. I could have asked one of the nuns whether the vow could be abandoned, on the grounds that to remain without wine during a month on SS *Cambodge* was a higher hurdle than I had originally proposed to the Almighty, but she would have rejected the plea and perhaps declined to play ping-pong again with such a weak Christian. Being in the hands of the French, we stopped at Djibouti rather than Aden, and dined at a restaurant on the sea to the sound of Beethoven's Violin Concerto. The *Cambodge* provided little organised entertainment, but there were films as well as table tennis, and protracted conversation, nine-tenths in French. Personal likes and dislikes faded as quickly as they had sprung up. A harsh young Spanish intellectual worried in the Mediterranean about Aldous Huxley and the unreceptiveness of Western science to philosophical thought; by the time we reached the Indian Ocean, his anxieties had shifted, and he consulted the ship's doctor because the heat was sapping his energy and he was no longer thinking of his girlfriend. Air-mail copies of *The Times* reached me at every port, organised by my father. When my books ran out a charming elderly French lady lent me a life of Victor Hugo by Maurois. The extracts from his letters began to influence my own style in the many letters I wrote to friends. We became bloated and unfit. The magnificence of the cuisine began to pall, and after Djibouti most passengers adopted a strict 'regime', which meant five courses at dinner instead of six, accompanied by copious discussion at table of our small afflictions.

We found the Queen visiting Colombo on the liner *Gothic*, and the city garnished with bizarre arches and flags. I was much impressed by Singapore. The news bulletins on the ship's board became more significant as we headed east, nearer to the fighting which they described. Eventually, on 25 April, eighteen days after leaving Marseille, the *Cambodge* worked her way up to Saigon, her wash lapping the tree trunks and the poles supporting the watchtowers along the banks of the Mekong. The troops below us filed ashore in the boiling sun. On deck the ladies wept into their embroidered handkerchiefs as the band played the 'Marseillaise' under the tricolour on the quayside. By then I had become fond of my fellow voyagers and shared some of their emotion ('What nonsense that the bogus Vietnamese should reap the fruit of so much French endeavour and torment'). The *Cambodge* stayed three days in Saigon, during which I was entertained by the British Embassy. They kindly arranged meals, swimming parties and much talk. There were thunderstorms, and in the heat it was hard to sleep under the mosquito net. The city showed no signs of war, but at night I could hear the thud of artillery beyond its outskirts.

In these days, and previously on the *Cambodge*, I was immersed in the total pessimism with which all the French viewed their future in Vietnam. They had made their effort over eight years since the war. It was failing, they could not afford to sustain it, and the sooner the peace talks in Geneva provided an excuse for withdrawal, the better. The

Americans with whom I spoke thought differently. The USA was already paying for 68 per cent of the war, the French troops were volunteers, not conscripts, if Vietnam fell the rest of Indo-China would follow, then Thailand and perhaps Malaysia. One elderly American on the *Cambodge* favoured dropping a few atomic bombs here and there in Asia to shake the place up a bit. I sympathised with the French.

After a brief stop in Manila ('an almost unbroken vulgarity') we approached Hong Kong and I ate my twenty-third and last excellent dinner on the *Cambodge*. I hardly knew what to expect. I was about to leave my capsule.

'Entranced by Hong Kong, rising almost vertically across the water, I think the most spectacular place I have ever seen.' So I wrote on 2 May 1954, and so it remains. I missed out in the sixties, but in every decade since then I have revisited Hong Kong several times, and long may it continue. There are many parts of the world where the balance between man and nature is uneven and unattractive. In some (Siberia, Patagonia) man is still outmanoeuvred, often defeated by the forces of nature, and one still wishes him all success in staking out his claim. In other places (almost all of England) nature is a captive confined in a cage, and one longs to help her escape. In Hong Kong in 1954 the struggle between man and nature was a draw. The barren rocks of Victoria Island, once refuge for a few fishermen and smugglers, together with the Kowloon peninsula opposite, were already transformed into an energetic and orderly city. Colonial and merchant citadels on the waterside were backed by miles of Chinese streets, running up into hillsides of shacks and tents. In recent years prosperity has shifted the balance against nature. The island of Lantau is no longer mysterious now that it houses the new airport. The New Territories stretching north from the harbour to the 1899 frontier with China have become largely suburban. The golf courses, the new racecourse, signposted walks, nests of new skyscrapers have replaced duck farms and paddy fields. But the magic remains.

The harbour of Hong Kong was and still is the focus. Over the decades I have watched it and Singapore's harbour evolve in different directions. In antiseptic Singapore the computer imposes a regime of regulated order; every movement of every boat is efficiently controlled. In Hong Kong there is still space for an old painted junk crowded with household washing to cross the path of a huge container ship, and for the tireless bustle of the Star ferries.

Part of the city's magic lay in the successful mix of traditional British order and Chinese energy. The British aspect was well to the fore in the week I spent there after leaving the *Cambodge*. I was placed in the Harbour View Hotel, which reminded me of Bournemouth. The cooking was sternly British, consumed in silence by British families off plates decorated with pictures of Edinburgh Castle and Holyrood House. Withered daisies stood on the tables. On my first evening I found St Andrew's Church in time to join in the Old Hundredth, and receive a blessing. I crossed the harbour two days later to dine at Government House. The Governor, Sir Alexander Grantham, believed in keeping full state. It was a more portentous occasion than any I had attended in London, Eton or Cambridge and I thoroughly enjoyed the pomp. We ate roast beef and Yorkshire pudding by candlelight, served by footmen in scarlet waistcoats, at tables flanked by banks of gladioli and gardenia. I arrived far too early; my taxi was saluted at the gate. A friendly aide briefed me in precise detail: after dinner, at seven minutes past nine, I would sit next to the wife of the Korean Consul-General; exactly ten minutes later he would escort me to talk to the wife of the admiral commanding the US 7th Fleet. Over whisky Sir Alexander discoursed amiably on the lessons of the French Revolution, then on the corruption and unpopularity in China of Chiang Kai Shek's Nationalist Government before 1949. In those days Government House had not been visually swamped by the skyscrapers of free enterprise; it still dominated the harbour and the colony which Britons and Chinese had made. By then I knew the dark side of that story: the Opium Wars and unequal treaties. But I also knew that the Chinese who lived in the shacks on those hillsides were not a subject race longing to be free. They had fled there within the last five years, escaping from upheaval and persecution in China, seeking order and the rule of law as administered by Sir Alexander. The toast to the Queen at his table was more than an empty formality.

The great men of Jardine Matheson, who had themselves been persecuted in Shanghai, acted generously on my letter of introduction and took me to the Derby at the Happy Valley racecourse. I was welcomed there, though not quite so enthusiastically as had been the Duchess of Kent a few months earlier. All the horses backed by Her Royal Highness had won, except in one race when she changed her bet at the last minute. I enjoyed a day in Macau, and another driving up to the frontier in the New Territories. I had a suit made, and worried about money and about several requests from the British Embassy in Peking to bring up quantities of sherry and Indian tea. I bought paperbacks for the last leg of my journey, which would be on an elderly black-funnelled merchant ship, the *Human*. On board I read *Crime and Punishment* and several thrillers, drank much gin and lime, and talked politics with the ship's officers as very slowly we steamed north to Tientsin. Finally, five weeks after leaving London, I set foot in the People's Republic of China and was escorted by the embassy's administration officer on a hard-seat train to Peking.

From Coal Hill at the centre of Peking, just north of the Imperial Palace, I could see spread around me the greatest walled city in the world. On the east flank of the hill stood a locust tree from which the last Ming Emperor hanged himself as the Manchus poured into Peking in 1644. The city walls themselves, the pavilioned towers which marked each gate out of the city, and at its heart the many courtyards of the Imperial Palace (or Forbidden City) dominated the scene below me. It was easy to pick out a handful of temples, notably the blue-roofed Temple of Heaven in its park to the south, and the broad avenues decorated with arches which linked the city gates in a series of rectangular patterns. A few early twentieth-century buildings obtruded, mostly banks or European embassies in the Legation Quarter, and closer at hand the ungracious bulk of the Peking Hotel.

When I walked through Peking, or was pulled in a pedicab behind a bicycle down the city's innumerable lanes, the prevailing colour was grey. The family courtyards threaded by these lanes were of one storey only, dominated by the trees which gave them their character. So in July 1954 this grey city when seen from above was overwhelmingly green. It was hard to imagine the bustle of running, walking and bicycling, making and mending, buying and selling, banging and shouting, which was taking place in this urban forest below.

In 1919 an American lady, Juliet Bredon, wrote a massive guide to Peking which was my bible during my time there. In her old-fashioned prose she did justice to the city walls.

> Towering forty feet above the Manchen–Tartar City, higher than a two-storied building, broader than Fifth Avenue, these noble battlements encircle the capital with a circumference of fourteen miles. The moral effect on those who dwell within them is curious. Strangers they impress painfully at first with a sense of imprisonment, even of suffocation. The feeling of being shut up in a fortress is very strong and generally disagreeable. But in time this changes to a soothing sense of security – to the comfortable sensation that the massive gray arms can keep out the rush and worries of the outer world.

All that has gone. European cities long before had set the example of destruction; but no recent act of vandalism in the world over the last fifty years has been so complete. The walls and arches of Peking have been pulled down. The lanes are being bulldozed out of existence. Office blocks and hotels, high, assertive and undistinguished, take their place. The city has spilled its new ugliness out on to the plains which surround it. The climate too has been modernised. Gone or almost gone are the cold, brilliant days of autumn, when the sky shone a hard blue week after week until the first snows appeared on the further Western Hills and skating began at lunchtime on the moat of the Forbidden City. Now the seasons alter the temperature but do not touch the grey pollution which hangs over Peking, ugly sky over ugly city. The Forbidden City, the Temple of Heaven and some of the old gates are preserved, but their relationship with the rest has changed. They have shrunk. They no longer dictate the imperial character of the whole. They are oddities, anachronistic extravagances preserved to please tourists who care for such stuff.

This process is, of course, part of a deliberate bargain. In return for the destruction of their city, the citizens of Peking are better fed, better housed, more colourfully clothed, more knowledgeable than ever before. Once, during my time there in the 1950s, the Swedish Ambassador invited Chou En-lai to dinner. The ambassador began to admonish the Prime Minister on plans already being discussed to demolish the walls of Peking. Above his mantelpiece hung a print of medieval Stockholm. 'And where', gently asked Chou En-lai, 'are the walls of Stockholm?'

During the Cultural Revolution from 1966 to 1972 Mao encouraged the Red Guards to turn against the past and actively destroy what survived from it. That destruction was too much for most Chinese, including Chou En-lai, who stationed a whole division of troops in the Forbidden City to prevent vandalism. When, much later, I visited the temple and tomb of Confucius at Chufu I learned that Chou En-lai, then at the end of his life, had sent a message to its guardians warning them to close the gates and defend the temple, for the Red Guards were on their way. A few months later the huge unplanned demonstration of grief in Peking at Chou En-lai's death showed that people had had enough of the Cultural Revolution, including its destruction of the past.

After the Cultural Revolution such destruction stopped being an end in itself. But still today, when the choice is between preservation and immediate enrichment, money wins. In Peking the price has been high. Civilisation has been diminished. It is a city best avoided by old-fashioned folk who knew its former spendour.

The British compound in which we lived and worked was the outcome of more than a century of wrangling. The traditional Chinese view at the time of their empire, tenaciously held for good, practical reasons, was that foreigners, who were by definition barbarians, should not be allowed to live in Peking, the centre of imperial power. From time to time they could bring tribute, as George III's envoy Lord Macartney did in 1793. But there could be no question of diplomats residing in the capital, or of tolerating any pretence by the barbarians that their rulers were on an equal footing to the Emperor. As trade, legal and illegal, multiplied between the Chinese Empire and the West, contact became necessary on practical matters. The Chinese Government insisted that this should be conducted exclusively through the Viceroy of the two Kwangs, who was the Emperor's representative in the south at Canton, the most important of the trading posts. The manoeuvres and affrays which led to both the first and second China Wars (1838–40 and 1856–60) originated in the Pearl River which runs between Canton and Hong Kong. Lord Elgin, who led the British effort in the second China War, shrewdly judged that there could be no sound foundation for relations between the West and China until Western governments could have access to the Chinese Government in its capital. Brushing aside the narrow concern of the Hong Kong merchants with Canton, he twice with his French allies sailed north, and finally in 1860 established by force the right to appoint resident government representatives to live and work in Peking. Thus equality between nations was imposed through superiority on the battlefield. The Western powers created a Legation Quarter just to the south of the Forbidden City in which each of them maintained a compound, the British being the largest. These were the compounds which the Boxers unsuccessfully besieged in 1900. In 1927 Chiang Kai Shek moved the Chinese capital to Nanking. After the triumphant communists had in 1949 restored the capital to Peking, the British, rather surprisingly, were allowed to return to their old compound.

We knew that we were there on sufferance. Our predecessors had already allowed to fade away the legend 'Lest We Forget', which had been painted on the compound wall to remind everyone of the Boxer attack and its failure. It was most unlikely that the Chinese would allow us indefinitely to occupy several dozen acres close to the heart of their city on a site which reminded everyone of those humiliating years. Eventually, in 1958, after I had left, they did indeed move the British Legation to the new diplomatic quarter outside the eastern wall. It was this new and much smaller compound which was attacked during the Cultural Revolution in 1967, and which Britain still retains.

So in 1954 our small staff lived, comfortably but precariously, in huge premises designed for a semi-imperial presence. Because British policy was too closely allied to the Americans', we were given a humble status. Our documents did not describe us as diplomats; we were not invited to the round of official diplomatic occasions; there was no ambassador. The rambling No. 1 House in the compound stood empty. There were two large neo-Georgian houses for senior staff; a charming two-storey white house, at one time the Prussian Legation, where Anne Bridge in the thirties had written her silly but evocative novel *Peking Picnic*; a chapel where we held Sunday services, but no communion, for there was no chaplain; a range of administrative buildings in the style of the barracks of the Indian Empire; and seven or eight grey bungalows with verandas, redeemed from dullness by the scarlet paint of their eaves and pillars and the salvias of the same colour which dominated our flower beds. In one of these bungalows, No. 3, just past the Chinese sentry on the left of the main gate into the compound, I lived for two years, sustained by three servants. We enjoyed lawns, a tennis court, a small swimming pool, and a splendid variety of trees sheltering hoopoes, sometimes a golden oriole, and a cuckoo with a song which was construed, rather too aptly, as 'one more bottle'.

And sparrows, which caused us trouble. The Peking authorities, always anxious to assert new civic duties, decided that sparrows were responsible for stealing huge quantities of grain. A crusade was launched. Sparrows were to be lured into false nesting boxes. Drums and gongs were to be beaten at all hours until the birds, unable to alight, fell exhausted to the ground. Sparrows, as 'enemies of the people', were to be pursued on all occasions. The sparrows of Peking quickly concluded that the British trees were a useful haven. The Young Pioneers in their red scarves requested access with their drums and gongs (and sticks and air rifles). After anxious deliberations, they were refused. We held our collective breath; but no more was heard of the matter. The sparrows flourished.

We felt that we lived at the end of the world. At the beginning there were virtually no visitors. Letters took ten days or more. The diplomatic bags brought by Queen's Messengers by boat from Hong Kong to Tientsin were erratic. We relied on a fragile lifeline from the merchants Lane Crawford in Hong Kong for many of the conventional needs of European life – coffee, wine and spirits, toiletries. Our contacts with the rulers of the new China were confined to bureaucratic and often bad-tempered exchanges with junior officials in charge of travel and customs permits. There were one or two lingering survivors from the raffish British pre-war community made famous by Harold Acton and Osbert Sitwell. One old couple, Mr and Mrs Hemmings, still entertained in the house they had built out towards the Summer Palace. He was a retired merchant. Their prized herbaceous border, and the poplars they had planted on arrival in 1903, were already dwarfed by new, grey, multistorey flats. They had no children, nothing to do, nowhere to go, as their savings dribbled away. Eventually they were given exit permits which amounted to exit commands, and left sadly for an austere England with which they had lost all contact.

Cut off from any meaningful contact with the Chinese, the diplomatic community revolved feverishly around itself. It was quite small. There were no Americans, no white Commonwealth, no Catholic Europeans, no Japanese or Latin Americans, no one from the many Third World countries who recognised the Chinese Nationalist government in Taiwan. New countries rented the compounds of absentees in the Legation Quarter: the Indians were tenants of France, the Burmese of Belgium. There was little social, national or racial distinction between foreigners, for regardless of rank or origin we shared the same isolation. We went to great pains to entertain one another. The British brought in old film prints of Ealing comedies to show in our club room. We taught our colleagues Scottish dancing; the Indonesian eightsome reel was a formidable sight. At Christmas we sang carols in the lanes of Peking, to the bafflement of its citizens. Because of an unobtainable note in the 'First Noël', I found myself degraded from tenor to bass.

I complained to Walter Hamilton of 'endless amiable diplomatic buffet dinners, night after night balancing lukewarm curry on one's knees, dancing to the same records with the same nice women, drinking a little too much, staying a little late, rising limp and fragile the next day'. Compared to what I remember, this was an understatement, suitable for a letter to my former tutor, by then headmaster of Westminster. There was a crescendo of party-giving around Christmas. Late nights, hangovers, small feuds leading to shouting matches reached their peak in the season of goodwill. I wrote disconsolately to Tony Lloyd soon after my arrival that, despite all the chatter, there was no one really to talk to or to fall in love with. I would therefore be compelled to study either Marxism or porcelain.

Most of us looked for a way through frustration by breaking into Chinese life in one form or another, despite the efforts of the authorities to keep us isolated. I began to learn the language. A pretty girl called Miss Yu came to teach me on my veranda at lunchtime. She always wore a blue Mao jacket and trousers, but told me that at home she kept a camphorwood chest full of her old colourful clothes. She took these out from time to time, hoping that she might one day be able to wear them. I still have the small square cards, one for each character, which contain Miss Yu's firm, handsome calligraphy. On the back of each card I wrote the phonetic pronunciation and meaning of each character. Mastering the written language is, of course, a separate exercise from listening and speaking when the alphabet is not phonetic. My efforts in that direction stuttered and failed, not least because of the reforms then under way. I would struggle to imitate Miss Yu's brushwork and painstakingly reproduce, say, six or seven characters composed of ten or fifteen strokes each. Then Miss Yu would arrive and announce with a smile that in the *People's Daily* that day it had been announced that the number of strokes in these particular characters had been reduced by half. What was intended as simplification was, to me, a deep discouragement. But

I learned enough Mandarin to travel by myself in a land where very little English was spoken. This proved invaluable.

In my first months in Peking the office work was intense without being stimulating. We were a small staff, and everyone took turns with everything. I learned how to issue a visa and a passport. Some of the routine tasks were bizarre. For example, there was a small permitted flow of White Russian refugees from China to Australia. Because we represented Australia in Peking, it was our duty in accordance with Australian law to examine each applicant for any signs of tuberculosis. These forlorn Russians came to the embassy with X-rays which we held briefly to the light. None of us had any medical knowledge. If the X-ray showed a blur around the ribs we occasionally rejected the applicant. Almost always he or she returned a few days later with an X-ray which showed no blur, and was given the permit which led to a brighter future. We never received any complaint from Canberra about the thoroughness of our procedures.

Deciphering telegrams was the main chore, particularly in the summer months of 1954 immediately after I arrived. Only very rarely did our work in Peking throw up anything urgent and confidential which had to go to the Foreign Office by telegram. Nor did the Foreign Office send us much in the way of urgent confidential instructions. But they and all major British posts had us on the list to receive repetitions of telegrams on the Far East which they exchanged with one another. Those noticeboards on the SS *Cambodge* had carried, in addition to the news of Dien Bien Phu, reports from the international conference at Geneva at which Anthony Eden and his fellow foreign ministers struggled manfully and in the end with success to bring the Indo-China War to an end. Copious reports and comments on each twist of that conference were repeated to us as telegrams by posts which already had cypher machines. The same thing happened with each crisis over the next few years. We had no machines; we just received sheets of numbers. Our job, with the help of special notepads and tables, was to convert these numbers into words. The pads and tables could not leave the embassy's high-security room. When it was our turn on the roster we were imprisoned there for hour after hour of hot days and nights, without air conditioning, just a slow, ineffectual fan. We fortified ourselves with the excellent Tsingtao beer, which cooled the body for a second or two before producing a stream of sweat. Of course, it was gratifying to feel that we were in the loop of great events; but we cursed the prolix draftsmen in the Foreign Office and the well-staffed posts who produced a deluge of detail about what Sir Roger said to Sir Pierson and how Mr Molotov kept looking at his watch.

The prospect steadily improved after the return to Peking of the head of the mission, Humphrey Trevelyan. (He was not strictly our ambassador, but because of our lowly status, a chargé d'affaires.) He had been present at the Geneva Conference, where he had helped Eden to make the first contact with Chou En-lai and secure agreement for a slow upgrading of our position. The first manifestation of this was an invitation for all our staff to a performance by a state circus. Soon the colour of our identity cards was changed. Decisions of this kind were the currency of Chinese diplomacy, under the communists as under the empire before them – trivial in substance, rich in inner meaning.

I was lucky in both the heads of mission whom I served in Peking. Neither Humphrey Trevelyan nor Con O'Neill was a traditional diplomat. The former had started in the Indian Civil Service. He brought to each post he held in public life the charm and intellectual self-confidence inherited from his clan. In Northumberland, Cambridge, India and across the world, Trevelyans were radical, brisk, highly literate and successful. Humphrey, with his large head, sallow complexion and prominent ears, looked plain to the point of ugliness until he smiled, when everything lit up. He was generous in spirit but impatient, and not an easy companion unless his wife Peggy was with him. We owed much to her tempering authority. In India disease had weakened his kneecaps. This meant that on hill walks he was always testing himself, and therefore us as well. Pointing to a temple nestling under some distant crag, he would say, 'First stop there,' and stride off. He would then stand at the threshold of the temple and time the arrival of each of us against his own: 'Not bad, not bad at all'. He was always on the move. He believed that further down any train there would be an empty carriage. He knew about Chinese porcelain, painting and architecture because those were obvious interests for an educated Englishman to pick up when sent to China. But his main concern was with the present, and the possibilities of building workmanlike links with the communist regime. He was not blind to its cruelties, but judged correctly that at that early stage most Chinese preferred the order which it brought to the chaos, inflation and corruption of civil war and Chiang Kai Shek's Nationalist Government. He thus had no patience with the ideological hostility of the Eisenhower administration to Red China – just as two years later, when ambassador in Cairo, he disagreed with Anthony Eden's ideological hostility to Nasser.

Trevelyan loved debate. He assailed anyone who disagreed with him with a relentless barrage of arguments, but at the same time listened to the counter-arguments without appearing to do so. We learned to leave a gap of a few hours before carrying out one of his firm instructions, because an equally firm instruction in another direction might soon follow.

He did not want his newest young diplomat immersed in issuing visas and scanning X-rays. The chores continued, but were varied with other, more interesting jobs. One of these Trevelyan knew was necessary, though it did not attract his own sympathy. In Tientsin there lingered a small British community and further south in Shanghai a large one. They were a rum lot, irrelevant to modern China, but their British nationality gave them the right to bring their problems to British official attention. And problems they certainly had in abundance. The Chinese played a cat-and-mouse game with the great British companies who had once stood proud in all the ports identified in the Victorian treaties for Western trade with China. Hardly any business was put in their path by the new state authorities; but nor were they allowed to close. ICI, Shell, Jardines, the great banks and a dozen others had to maintain a 'responsible person' in their Chinese office. They could not sell property or sack their staff; they were stuck. The companies reacted by withdrawing as many of their British employees as they could, each time nominating as the 'responsible person' someone lower, then lower again, in the scale of usefulness. The barrel thus scraped produced some odd personalities. Those managers in Shanghai with nothing to manage moved into the homes of their departed superiors. Typically these were huge mock-Tudor mansions, pre-war Beaconsfield on a giant scale, with cellars full of gin and an army of gardeners who cut the sweeping lawns with scissors. The managers drank and dined, danced, gossiped, swapped ladies – and fell into all kinds of trouble with the authorities.

These British citizens provided bizarre entertainment at the tail end of the treaty port system. After the strictness and uniformity of Peking, my pastoral duties were quite fun – at least in Shanghai, for Tientsin was deeply unattractive. In Shanghai the Bund and the streets behind it, though they badly needed paint, conveyed a flavour of Europe and of a buccaneering past which had its charms. Eventually the Chinese tired of the game, and graciously allowed the companies to close, and hand over all their property to the state without compensation. A few years later the same companies were back on a new basis, hanging about in bleak hotels for contracts which were slow to come. By the time I visited Shanghai in the seventies the era of Tudor mansions, gin and nightclubs was over.

Not all British subjects were so fortunate. From others scattered across China we learned about the ruthlessness of the regime to all who did not fit the pattern of the new China. A toothless old woman, half Chinese, came each month for her allowance as a DBS (Distressed British Subject). She was breaking the law by not registering with the police as an alien, and I urged her to do so. 'Why I bring trouble on myself? I Catholic, you know what they did that Italian priest, shot him. Now they think I Chinese. If I go say I British they say why you no tell us? They shoot me too. I old woman, not live long, my head bad goes bang bang at night when I think they shoot me.' I had no answer.

One proof of the unfreezing relationship between Britain and China as a result of Eden's efforts was the trickle, broadening into a substantial stream, of British visitors. Since most of them at this stage were left-wing critics of the Conservative British Government which we served, our role in these visits was not entirely self-evident. But we saw just about all of them, and from them heard something extra about China. Carefully tutored by the authorities, they visited parts of China from which we were excluded. We also learned much about the variety and eccentricity of intellectual life in Britain. The most impressive delegation was the first. In August 1954 we welcomed Clement Attlee, the Leader of the Opposition, Aneurin Bevan, leader of the Labour left, Dr Edith Summerskill, tall and dogmatic in an angular hat, the Durham miner Sam Watson and Secretary of the Party Morgan Phillips. Their journey across Siberia had not been without incident; in Irkutsk Mr Attlee and Dr Summerskill had been offered a double bed. The Chinese set out to entertain and impress with banquets, Peking opera, and many speeches. The delegation acquitted itself well. They refused to drink the toast to Chairman Mao unless Chou En-lai proposed the health of the Queen, something which had never happened before. They asked their hosts searching questions. Sam Watson told us that he had cut short a long lecture about religious freedom in the new China: 'So I said to the bloody bishop, "Where's your loyalty lie, man, to Jesus or to this lot here?"' Morgan Phillips, after touring a housing estate, remarked that he never thought he would see Gorbals tenements built with a sense of pride. Attlee himself seemed tired but told the Chinese People's Consultative Conference that the object of government was the happiness of the individual, not the power of the state. He also (we heard) advised the authorities that it was not seemly to cart night soil through the streets to the vegetable plots outside the walls. Bevan argued at great length that it was possible to achieve socialism by parliamentary democracy as well as by revolution. I did not think that the Chinese audience followed this argument, but they clapped loudly whenever they heard the word 'peace'.

At the end of an exhausting tour the delegation came to the British compound, straw-hatted and in open-necked shirts, for final refreshment. It was very hot. Aneurin Bevan wore one of those uncomfortable nylon shirts, then state of the art, which did not absorb sweat but allowed it to gather visibly between fabric and skin. He

informed us at length about the state of China as though we were the
visitors. My verdict two months later was gloomy when I wrote to
Dennis Robertson: 'Any disappointment the Chinese may have felt while
the Labour circus were here has, I am sure, been removed by the fatuity
of nearly all their statements since they left.'

Attlee and his colleagues were robust compared to most of those who
followed. I exclude some of the journalists, who brought their professional cynicism to bear on targets which deserved it. But the real
left-wingers were hard to handle. They came to the compound for
whisky, home news, and the sound of an English voice. They plied us
with requests, reasonable and unreasonable. For example, Barbara
Castle asked us to arrange an exclusive interview for her with Prime
Minister Nehru, then in town, which had to be kept secret from the
fellow Bevanites in her delegation. Like Bevan, they dispensed a lot of
superficial information about China. One thing they did not want was
any disruption of their idyll. They were visiting as guests (all expenses
paid) a remarkable and highly efficient dictatorship and wanted to
believe that it was a gate to Paradise. It suited them to believe the
assurances given to them, as they ate and toasted their way through
China, that they were building mutual understanding. There was
nothing mutual about it. The Chinese were not at that stage interested
in understanding the West. They had chosen a different model. The
Soviet Union would supply them with the technology they needed, and
as for political and social philosophy the Chinese system was in their
eyes clearly superior to anything we could offer. The dogmatism of the
Marxist–Leninist creed, piled on top of the traditional Chinese belief
that all foreigners were barbarians, created a sense of superiority
formidable to behold, particularly among young officials. It was painful
to watch our progressive thinkers such as D.N. Pritt and Kingsley
Martin crouching before this performance, just as their predecessors had
crouched before Stalin.

I wrote angrily to Tony Lloyd in November 1954.

A French journalist wrote that he had come to the definite conclusion
that there were no concentration camps or evil practices in Chinese
prisons. Words probably written within a few hundred yards of the
prison where the recalcitrant Americans eat their food off the floor
with their hands chained behind their backs. Of the facts there is no
doubt because the many prisoners recently departed have been
carefully and thoroughly interviewed in Hong Kong. But the people
who came here are not in a mood for that particular brand of fact,
which they consider old fashioned and unreal when they see the
smiling charming faces of their hosts.

It is true that the Chinese Revolution was still young; the horrors of the Great Leap Forward and the Cultural Revolution were yet to come. Nothing was inevitable; the short experiment of allowing a hundred flowers to bloom began just as I was leaving China. But the ominous signs were there, and in 1956 the rush to collectivise the farms began. We had on each visit an hour or two, while they sipped our whisky, to suggest to a British delegation that infant crèches, model prisons and the songs of Young Pioneers were inadequate as evidence of the new China.

As the months passed we began to see more of the Chinese leaders, though Mao himself was remote. Like others, I was fascinated by the personality of Chou En-lai, Prime Minister and Foreign Minister, who turned up quite often on diplomatic occasions. His thick, dark eyebrows and mobile, half-humorous mouth made me think of a French priest. Unlike Mao, and wholly unlike the Soviet leaders, he seemed to have no worries about personal security. I watched him once passing in an open car through huge crowds beside the Indian Prime Minister Nehru. They were both strikingly handsome: Nehru in brown frock coat, hanging straight from shoulder to knee, white cap, rose in buttonhole; and Chou in black cap, black, beautifully cut Mao jacket, black trousers. At an Indian evening party, set in a garden with many lanterns, I saw Chou advancing, surrounded by a smiling entourage, towards the table where I sat with some senior Indian officials. I rose to move out of the way so that he could talk to them undisturbed. Characteristically, I knocked over a chair, then found that everyone was laughing at my embarrassment, because it was with me that the Prime Minister wished to talk. The conversation was an anticlimax: Chou complimented me on my Chinese, which then of course dried up.

On May Day and on 1 October each year the regime paraded its authority before the city and the world. It is a vulgar confession, but I have always enjoyed parades. The two examples which I have seen repeatedly are Trooping the Colour to celebrate the Queen's Birthday on the Horse Guards in London, and these twice-yearly performances in Peking in front of the Gate of Heavenly Peace, the much-photographed entrance to the Forbidden City. The two events are at opposite ends of the spectrum. Both depend on a historic architectural setting, and on the central presence of a ruler who attracts personal loyalty. Trooping the Colour is based on the intricate, colourful manoeuvring of a small number of perfectly trained men and horses in a confined space. The bands play; the soldiers and the audience are silent. The Peking parades are based on huge numbers, a vast space and the orchestrated enthusiasm of the participants. May Day is for the workers; 1 October, the anniversary of the proclamation of the People's Republic in 1949, for

workers and the armed services combined. In a letter to my mother I
described the first of these which I witnessed, in October 1954.

In the old days the Emperor proceeded at midwinter and midsummer
from the Forbidden City to the Temple of Heaven to do sacrifice.
Likewise Mao, the peasant's son, emerges from his fastness twice a
year, on 1 May and 1 October, and shows himself to his faithful
people. By 10 a.m. we were all in our stands in Red Square, diplomats,
delegates, massed bands, workers, children. The bands played the slow
solemn 'Hymn of Praise' and as they ended the burly fatherly figure in
grey worker's cap and uniform appeared on the long balcony of the
First Gate leading to the Forbidden City. The guns in the nearby park
fired their salute, the bands played the rousing National Anthem, the
people shouted, and the rest of the party of honour followed Mao
onto the balcony – the top Russians (headed by Khrushchev, who is
second only to Malenkov) looking like successful commercial
travellers in their floppy suits and grey trilbies, except for Bulganin in
a resplendent Marshal's uniform; Chou En-lai and the rest of the
Government; the President of Poland and other satellites; and at one
end of the balcony, in a long purple robe, the Dalai Lama of Tibet –
alas, an unprepossessing young man with a shaved head and a rather
foolish melancholy face.
    Then followed a military parade, efficient but not extraordinary –
smart goosestepping, cavalry trotting by very fast on attractive
Mongolian ponies, MiG jets overhead, tanks and guns. Then came the
People, and that is where the affair became quite unlike anything I
have ever seen before. For three hours 3,000 people passed the stands
every minute, jammed in a tight quick-moving mass, half a million
people in all. It was a fantastic sight – the wide street as far as the eye
could see blocked with bodies carrying banners, portraits of everyone
from Marx to Harry Pollitt, giant cardboard production graphs,
models of locomotives, maps of Formosa. The most terrifying thing
was the great multitude of children, brightly and charmingly dressed,
almost hysterical with excitement as they shouted their way past
Mao's balcony, some waving large posies of paper roses, some
releasing flocks of pigeons (peace doves of course).

Once the people had filed past, they turned and massed in the huge
expanse of Tienanmen Square, shouting the patriotic slogans of the
moment. In front of them, high above on the balcony which stretched
the whole length of the Gate of Heavenly Peace, stood the line of their
leaders and their leaders' friends. The leaders applauded the people as
the people applauded them. But one man in the centre of the group was

the Leader, tiny in comparison with the great portrait of himself above which he stood. Slowly Mao walked to the west end of the balcony, doffed his grey cap and presented himself to the people. Then to the east, the same ceremony. Then back to the centre for a final great roar of applause.

The impact of this ritual was formidable. It was a celebration of revolution. Six or seven years before, this country had been split into warring factions, humiliated throughout a century, corrupt, defeated, hopeless. Now everyone could see that it was orderly, powerful, with one opinion held everywhere on every subject, with one universally popular leader. 'China has stood up' had been Mao's famous statement from that balcony at the moment of triumph in 1949. The Leader had his own anthem: 'The East is red; the sun has risen.'

But there was another layer to the celebration. Mao was the heir to the empire from whose palace he presented himself to the people. The Mandate of Heaven had descended on him. He ruled the people whose name meant that they lived at the centre of the world. The others, whether Bulganin and Khrushchev or the Dalai Lama, were there as barbarians bearing tribute. They might not know it. They might even think themselves superior. But Mao knew it and so did the people in the square.

Although I grew more fond of Peking itself as I knew it better, a greater pleasure for a sizeable handful of us lay in the hills to the north and the west. Less than an hour in our old RAF wagon took us to one of several possible starting points for a day's walk. In summer it was too hot, in winter too cold, but for two months in spring and two months in autumn the walking was ideal. The Western Hills contained several dozen Buddhist and Taoist temples, each with a spectacular view, linked by easy ancient stone paths. No modern maps were available, so we had to rely on old-fashioned guidebooks in florid English. These told us the traditional names of the temples – and their translations, Monastery of the Wild Mulberry, Temple of the Azure Cloud – and of the hills and passes. What they did not tell us was the present use of the temples. One turned out to be a railway school, another a military barracks, a third was still a monastery where a decrepit monk gladly gave us hot water to drink and a towel to wipe away our sweat. This gap in knowledge gave an attractive whiff of uncertainty to each expedition. We never knew when we might be stopped, questioned and prevented from reaching the point where we had asked our drivers to collect us at evening. It was no use asking the Ministry of Foreign Affairs for guidance; the result would have been a clampdown on these irregular activities.

I have a photograph of Teddy Youde, then First Secretary, later

Governor of Hong Kong, sitting in a little square, writing us a letter of introduction, the village elders crowding round. On another day we were barred from our objective by soldiers, and told to catch a train from a station four miles away. We missed that train, and sat late into the night at a tavern until our drivers found us.

Each weekend during spring and autumn a group of congenial people of many nationalities and all ranks would set out. I fell often into company for this purpose with three young Swedes: Margaretha Holstad, Barbro Sonander (who later married Francis Noel-Baker MP) and Peder Hammarskjöld (nephew of the UN Secretary-General). Towards the end of 1955 three language students arrived at the mission: John Fretwell, Richard Evans and Alan Donald. They transformed my social scene; I had lacked companions of my own age and interests. It was agreeable to introduce the newcomers to temples, paths, peaks and valleys which I had already discovered. The Western Hills concealed several such valleys, which in spring shone with white blossom, though then there was also dust to catch in the throat. Later it was warm enough to strip and bathe in river pools. In one such valley we came upon the ruins of a bungalow built by Sir Reginald Johnston, the tutor of the last Emperor, Pu Yi, and wondered unrealistically whether we could restore it as a weekend retreat for ourselves.

But my favourite was the valley of the Ming Tombs. The Ming emperors lie in separate tombs at the foot of a semicircle of hills, approached up an avenue lined with stone warriors and heraldic beasts. The Ming, a purely Chinese dynasty, ruled in what were for us Tudor and Stuart times. Each of the thirteen tombs was a mile or half a mile from its neighbour; they were already derelict. Trees grew out of the walls and carved sacrificial vessels lay in long grass. Each had the same pattern: a hall with a yellow tiled roof supported by carved pillars, a courtyard with a sacrificial altar, then a memorial tablet mounted on a stone tortoise signifying long life, and finally a tree-covered mound where the emperor lies. In the late autumn sunshine donkeys carried maize to the threshing floors in the valley, and persimmons glowed red on trees already bare. The peasants worked hard until the frost began to bite through their quilted jackets. The crests and ridges of the mountains towards the Great Wall stood out jagged against the yellow evening light. We would have picnicked perhaps in the courtyard of the biggest tomb, that of Yung Loh, and walked several miles round the valley, ending in the Avenue of Beasts where the faithful wagon waited. In the gathering dusk the stone animals grimaced; the warriors gripped their swords. It was a magical place, similar in purpose to the tombs of the Pharaohs in the Valley of the Kings opposite Luxor, but more human in scale, less frightening in concept, and to my eyes more beautiful both in design and setting. We returned to Peking, pleasantly tired, to hot bath, gin and lime, early bed.

The Red Guards twenty years later attacked the Ming Tombs which were protected by villagers. One tomb was later rescued and jazzed up with scarlet paint and crude explanatory posters. As the new slogans and colours have faded, I am told that the spirit of the place has returned. I would like to see it once more.

At any given time most of us were hatching some plan to escape from Peking into the rest of China. Life in the capital was perfectly tolerable, a mix of extraordinary and banal, but it was maddening to be surrounded by hundreds of millions of Chinese whose lives were being transformed by revolution and yet to rely for news of this on the doctored state press and radio tempered by occasional rumours and anecdotes from the real world. Travelling in China in the mid-fifties was a game of negotiation with unwritten rules. Permits to visit Tientsin and Shanghai were easy to secure. We could leave the fierce summer heat of Peking for a week or weekend in the seaside resort of Peitaho, which looked and felt like Italy and was frequented by model workers and, secretly, by the Chinese leadership. Before the war Peitaho had been the main holiday resort of Europeans in north China. For decades a Swiss ice-cream shop lingered on. We had managed to hang on to at least one of our bungalows there, thanks to a shrewd policy of leasing to Asian ambassadors whom the Chinese did not wish to offend.

At the end of my first summer I took a conventional holiday with three friends at Hangchow, the inspiration for much Chinese landscape painting. We explored temples day by day or relaxed with wine and books on a boat moored under willows on a haven of the West Lake. At the end of the holiday I experienced one of the paradoxes of the new China. The authorities who confiscated land and business without compensation on a huge scale were meticulous about small items of private property. I threw away a soiled napkin and a rusty bottle opener in my hotel room at Hangchow. As our train drew out of the station the hotel manager sprinted down the platform and thrust these objects, carefully wrapped, into our carriage, with the words, 'These are your property, Comrade.' Tips were immoral. Once, through lack of small change, I left a railway porter having slightly overpaid him. After much rushing to and fro he found me and gave me my due, a dirty note worth rather less than a penny.

In 1955 I was sent to Hong Kong to meet and bring back to Peking by train Trevelyan's successor as our head of mission. Con O'Neill and his wife, a German baroness, became reconciled to the ceaseless bustle of Chinese train life. The train itself moved slowly, but there was nothing languid about the life of the passenger. Our mugs of green tea were constantly refilled from a big Thermos of flowery design. Carriages were swept several times a day, the passengers required each time to lift their legs so that the broom could catch every particle of dust. Through the day the loudspeakers broadcast patriotic and party songs, interspersed with advice on personal cleanliness and the need to liberate Taiwan. The smash hit of the time was a lament from the film *The White Haired Girl*. The heroine's hair had turned white following her rape, though whether by a feudal landlord or a Chiang Kai Shek bandit I cannot now recall. Years later, when asked to choose music for the BBC programme *Desert Island Discs*, I tested their thoroughness by asking for the theme tune from *The White Haired Girl*. With some difficulty they found it, though in a Westernised orchestration which lost some of the haunting quality of the original.

Gradually China began to open up. In November 1955 the authorities surprised me by granting my application to visit the British consular buildings in Kunming, Chungking and Hankow. No British official had been allowed to visit our properties since 1951. We could not sell them. We employed in each a caretaker and staff whom we did not see and could not sack. The Treasury at home was restless at the outflow of public money on buildings which we did not use and salaries for services which we did not receive. It was agreed that I should go and have a look.

My official reason for the visit, though genuine, covered a quite separate enthusiasm for seeing something of the hidden centre and south of China. I was away for a fortnight. Kunming, in the far south-west, was cold and wet, and my hotel room was bleak. I read *The Wind in the Willows* and *The Brothers Karamazov*. The local authorities were wholly unused to the presence of foreigners, but fed me well, rented me a British Vanguard car, and allowed me to visit a new agricultural cooperative, and the spa further south at Anning. I bathed in the health-giving water rather apprehensively, since most of the villagers I had met seemed to be suffering either from goitre or mental illness. This was the only time in China when I was followed. Europeans were so conspicuous in China, and in the cities the control of the population so complete, that the authorities knew they could trace us without much difficulty at any time. In any street we would rapidly find ourselves the centre of a small crowd of children, who would shout to each other, 'Soviet person, Soviet person.' The only white people they knew of were Russians and Americans, and it could not be an American in the street because Americans were easily recognised as devils in tall hats who carried bombs and spread poisonous germs.

Kunming, a city of yellow stone buildings and (on my first visit) yellow mud, had been the high water mark of French influence which spread along the railway into China from French Indo-China. Before the Second World War a Hotel de la Gare had competed with a Hotel Terminus. In my hotel one bath tap was labelled 'Froid', the other 'Cold'. Both were accurate.

Everywhere in China morning arrived at six-thirty precisely with the crash of the national anthem on the loudspeaker, followed by about fifteen minutes of physical jerks, music and instructions through the same medium. All except the very young, the very old and ignorant foreigners were expected to stop whatever they were doing and join in. It was a striking illustration of the uniformity being fastened on the Chinese people. We became familiar with the commanding tone of voice in which every message was subliminally conveyed: 'You are one poor individual, but we are the Chinese people, led by Chairman Mao, and it is in the interest of all of us that you do as we say, up, down, in, out, touch your toes.'

In Chungking I found an antidote, the first Chinese I had met who was ready to criticise the regime. Mr K.C. Lu, our caretaker, listened to the BBC and was anxious about Princess Margaret's blighted romance with Group Captain Townsend. He criticised the extravagance of the Chungking Assembly Hall, and of the municipal tennis courts. Only the Vice-Mayor and the military commander could afford to pay for tennis balls imported from Hong Kong at nine shillings each. Unemployment was high, he said, and the peasants aggrieved at the low prices fixed for their produce. He himself had been persecuted for working for a foreign government, but he managed to keep the busybodies quiet by occasional purchases of government bonds and gifts of winter clothing for the poor.

The hills on which Chungking is built were wreathed in mist and drizzle. Mr Lu put me on an ancient steamer for the voyage of three days down the Yangtze to Hankow. The famous journey through the gorges took us six hours, the river fretting its way into eddies and whirlpools, past looming pinnacles and deep ravines. There were few signs of the new China here. The coolies trudged over the rocks and chanted rhythmically as they hauled their junks painfully upstream.

Our caretaker at Hankow had removed his nephews, nieces and cousins who (it became evident) normally lived in our Consulate General, and I stayed in the gaunt, chilly building alone. These symbols of the former British presence in the treaty ports of China were alike; I cannot now remember which consulate-general had the ornamental bandstand in the garden and in which (probably several) the portraits of King Edward VII and Queen Alexandra were about one and a half times life size. Once each had been the centre of a thinking and eccentric community. Later I found in the Foreign Office a file on the private lives of certain China consuls so sensational that it had to be kept in a special

My paternal grandparents Percy and Hannah at Hillside in 1933. (On the back of the photograph they describe it as 'rather a silly picture' – perhaps because my grandmother is smiling?)

Edred Corner, my maternal grandfather, at the height of his professional career as a surgeon, living at 37 Harley Street.

Henrietta, my maternal grandmother.

My father Anthony Hurd.

My mother Stephanie on
her engagement in 1928.

Dashing Uncle Bob in 1930,
aged 25.

Rainscombe Farm, where we lived for the first seventeen years of my life.

Early motoring.

Ready for the 1935
election campaign.

The family (from left to right, Julian, myself and Stephen), Easter 1936

The Hurds at Stratton End, the home of Edred and Henrietta (my maternal grandparents), with Mama's brother John and his son John.

The Aunts as I remember them: taking tea with my grandmother, Stephen and Mama at The Old Oxyard, Oare, in the sixties.

A 1938 portrait by Keith Henderson of Julian, Stephen and me.

Myself, Stephen and Julian on a Scottish holiday at Ashens, but not looking very sure about the day's sport.

Julian when seventeen years old.

The Eton Wall Game, St Andrew's Day, 1947. We lost.

Eton 1947 – the way we were then: myself, Antony Acland, John Barton, Nigel Leigh-Pemberton, Tony Lloyd, Raef Payne, Tim Raison, Jacky Shaw-Stewart, Philip Ziegler.

Winterbourne Holt, the house to which we moved in 1947.

Gunner Hurd (back row, fourth from left), Oswestry, August 1948.

safe outside the ordinary archives. But in 1955 these buildings were melancholy and pointless, poised between two eras. Eventually we were allowed to give them to the Chinese Government.

My last months in Peking passed quickly. The work had diversified. The British citizens in Tientsin and Shanghai no longer produced so many problems. We spent more time on citizens of other countries whom we represented. For example, Belgian and American deserters from the Korean War were cast off by the Chinese once their usefulness for propaganda had been exhausted. They drifted about, longing to return home but frightened of persecution. Jolly Ceylonese businessmen came to sell rubber in return for rice; they stayed late at night drinking whisky, and telling us the blue stories at which unaccountably their Chinese hosts had failed to smile. Our new chief, Con O'Neill, like Humphrey Trevelyan, brought a first-class unbureaucratic mind to bear on analysing China. His unprepossessing figure and bespectacled face so pale that it sometimes seemed almost green were mysteriously attractive to women. His quiet voice never lacked authority. He was more sardonic than Humphrey, more interested in ideas as such, less confident that imaginative effort would break down the barriers and build a modern relationship between our two countries. I wrote to Tony Lloyd, 'He is much easier to get on with than HT, no barks down the telephone, no despatches retyped time and time again, no overquick decisions later retracted. But perhaps a little less generous and lacking the sudden flash of perception. She is delightful, rather ugly, impulsive, aristocratic, indirect, and already very popular.'

One of the language students, John Fretwell, later our ambassador in Paris, moved in to share my bungalow; we lunched each day with the other two students, Alan Donald and Richard Evans. I quickly built a close friendship with Alan, just younger than me, with a gentle touch of Scots in his voice and a lopsided grin. We dipped superficially, but with much pleasure, into that store of customs, festivals, sayings and age-old assumptions which are the background of any civilisation and in which China is amazingly rich. In fur hats and overcoats we trudged the streets of Peking and found monuments and scraps of the past which had eluded me but yielded to Alan's knowledge of the written language.

We set our hearts on one project, to be accomplished before my posting in Peking came to an end. Taishan is one of the five Taoist holy mountains of China. It rises 4,500 feet above the plains of Shantung Province, south-east of Peking. In times of prosperity, when the granaries were full and the barbarians quiet, the emperor would gather together his court, climb the mountain, and make sacrifice in the temple on the summit. Also worshipped on the mountain were the goddesses who brought children to the childless and who cured ophthalmia. No

European had climbed the mountain for many years. We asked for permission, and the usual game began. Although the Korean War was over, tension was still high in the Taiwan Straits and just about every public building anywhere was, the Chinese thought, at risk from espionage. They had quickly learned how to shepherd foreign delegations round sights selected for the good light they cast on the new China. It was quite different to allow two young British diplomats, both of whom could converse in Chinese, to wander round Shantung and climb Taishan. On the other hand, to forbid us would be embarrassing. The result on this as on many other occasions was advice that the journey would be 'inconvenient' for us. That Chinese word became famous through repetition. In particular, they said, there was no hotel in Tai'an, the town at the foot of the mountain, from which we could make our climb. We knew from a Chinese member of the embassy staff that there was a hotel. We persevered, and at last permission was given.

Our arrival at Tai'an caused some consternation among the local officials, who passed us from one waiting room to another while they thought what to do. There was the same contradiction as before: yes, said official A, there was a hotel and he had sent for a car to take us there because it was rather far; no, said official B, he knew of no hotel and was very doubtful. We wrestled for almost an hour, when it emerged that the large grey building which we had been looking at all the time a hundred yards across the square was the hotel, and we moved in. Sanitation was negligible, but we were given two reasonable beds in a clean room.

We soon found the stone path which leads right from bottom to top of the mountain. Pilgrims were still using it – mostly old women in black, hobbling painfully upwards with bound feet, and occasionally in steep parts climbing on all fours. Important people or those in a hurry were transported over the lower, gentler slopes in squeaky wheel-barrows. They then transferred from these into stretchers carried by two bearers who took them up to the top. Every half-mile or so there was a rest-house, stone benches and a wooden table under a tree, where we were given hot water out of a teapot, an excellent drink for the exhausted traveller. Once we were given tea by a Taoist nun in a little monastery, who told us that there were only four nuns left now, and showed us photographs of a big Taoist gathering in Peking. After a picnic lunch the climb became steeper and we began to pass more shrines and inscriptions on the rock or stone pillars commemorating the solemn events of the past – for instance, the spot where the Emperor Ch'ien Lung's horse refused to go any higher, and the pine tree which was created in 219 BC a Grand Officer of the 5th Class by the grateful emperor who found shelter under it in a thunderstorm on his way down.

The last 500 feet or so of Taishan are an almost insolent challenge to the weary pilgrim – just a steep staircase going straight up the side of the mountain to the Southern Heavenly Gate at the top of the pass. We eventually reached our destination just after five in the afternoon. This is a plateau of perhaps seventy acres with many temples, including that of the Jade Emperor of the Summit, in which we had been told we might be able to spend the night. The monk-caretaker whom we found in charge ushered us into a room next to the main chamber with the image of the Jade Emperor. Red paper instead of glass filled the window; two large, raised brick platforms were covered with sheets of straw matting. One was occupied by a Chinese newspaperman, and we took possession of the other. The weather was becoming steadily worse. We ate a supper of omelette and noodles and retired to bed on our platform. With two quilts each (hired from the monk) and three sweaters on top of our normal clothes we passed the night comfortably while the wind raged fiercely about the temple roof.

At 4.30 a.m. there was much stirring and shouting because this was the moment when the sun should have risen – but the newspaperman who poked his nose out of the door assured us that the weather was so thick that nothing could be seen. At seven I went out and found the temple enveloped in thick white cloud moving at enormous speed. At eight, just as we had finished breakfast, a miracle occurred: the clouds broke, and the sun chased them away in a matter of minutes, revealing a view of valleys to the south and ranges of hills to the north and east.

We spent the morning wandering about the plateau. At the Temple of the Princess of Coloured Clouds we watched old ladies offering incense and bundles of prayers written on yellow paper to the image, and prostrating themselves while a monk beat a gong. We found the celebrated tablet which marks the spot where, around 500 BC, Confucius, having climbed Taishan, observed as he surveyed the scene from the top that 'the world was a small place'. About noon we left the plateau, having paid our monk the equivalent of fifteen shillings for our lodgings, and, out of courtesy, lit sticks of incense before our real host, the Jade Emperor. We went rapidly down the steps we had climbed so laboriously the day before, lunched on a knoll, and took a different and more westerly path down to Tai'an.

Thirty-five years later, in April 1991, the Foreign Secretary visited Peking to negotiate with the Chinese Government on the financing of the new Hong Kong airport: Sir Alan Donald was by then Her Majesty's Ambassador. Alan and I decided that we would use a weekend to revisit Shantung and climb Taishan. This time the authorities were most obliging. Certainly we would be welcome to visit Taishan, but there was no reason to weary ourselves by climbing. There was a road halfway up and then a cable car to the top. We explained that for old times' sake we wanted to walk. The Chinese were amazed, concurred, but had the last word: stretcher bearers were attached to our party in case these elderly gentlemen should be taken ill on their bizarre expedition.

We set out with our wives, and one or two volunteers from my party. As we had foreseen, the mood of the mountain had changed. Tourists not pilgrims bustled up and down, buying knick-knacks at stalls along the path. We were given a sumptuous lunch halfway up. But the last steep staircase remained formidable. Whether through protocol or slightly better fitness, the Foreign Secretary reached the summit a little before the British Ambassador, but we both panted. We found a brand-new hotel at the top, to which we were the first visitors. The fittings were lavish, and the staff decked out in Ivor Novello uniforms. There was no hot water or central heating, and it was a cold spring. The local mayor gave us a banquet there of well above-average standard, which we ate wearing sweaters and Chinese army overcoats. Despite or because of the fierce grain liquor (mao't'ai) in which the later toasts were celebrated, I got up at five-fifteen, and climbed as before through thick white cloud to the Jade Emperor. Here the past was more evident: bells tinkled in the cold wind, and worshippers still offered biscuits and money at the shrine. But this time there was no break in the clouds, and no sunrise. Back in Peking, the airport negotiations ended in deadlock.

In 1956 my departure from Peking after a posting of two years degenerated into farce. The usual exit was by way of Hong Kong, but I had resolved to be the first British official since the revolution to travel through Ulan Bator, capital of Mongolia, to join the Trans-Siberian Railway at Irkutsk, and thence to Moscow. This required the permission of the Mongolians (whom we did not at the time recognise) as well as the Russians and Chinese. It was thus an advanced or three-ring version of the bureaucratic travel game in which all would-be travellers in China were constantly engaged. Eventually all the necessary documents were assembled.

It was the custom for departing diplomats to be seen off by their friends. I was gratified to find a good turnout on the platform. I put two heavy suitcases on board the train, and returned for the necessary farewell kissing or shaking of hands. As the train showed signs of departing I realised that I did not have my passport. I had given it to our administrative officer, and was horrified to see that he was engaged in argument with a Chinese official at the entrance to the platform. Doors banged, a whistle blew, purposeful steam emerged from the engine – still no passport. The argument ended, the official flung my passport at the administration officer, and he ran towards me. As the train began to move I grasped the passport and tried to board. The train gathered speed faster than I did. I sprinted down the platform, past gaping counsellors, first and second secretaries, past language students, translators, security officers, friendly Swedish girls, the whole melange of Peking diplomatic life – towards Mongolia, Moscow and London. But I sprinted in vain – the train drew ahead and vanished. Utterly humiliated, I was rushed to the next station in an embassy jeep, and arrived just in time to see the train again disappearing. By then I understood what had happened. The Chinese exit visa in my passport specified that I intended to leave China by air. Here I was, attempting to leave by train. This grave irregularity required careful examination, which could not be rushed.

My suitcases came back at once, having been efficiently unloaded as the train passed the Great Wall. I skulked in the embassy compound for a day or two while all the documents were reworked; then, without further farewell, flew to Ulan Bator.

The Mongolian officials took me to the Lama Temple, and displayed the treasures of its library. The only English book was the proceedings of the 1952 Vienna Peace Conference. I was escorted to the round beehive tent to greet the highest lama of all, who was very old and very large. Motioned to a chair, I was given mare's milk and huge lumps of shortbread mixed with cubes of sugar. The lamas munched away and I did my best. The tent was lined with red silk, and furnished with red lacquer tables and a Buddha before whom light burned. The senior lama said that he understood that in Canterbelly in England there was a lama called Johnson.* I said there was. The senior lama said it was clear that this Johnson was a good lama. I said nothing. After we had assaulted the shortbread in silence for a while the senior lama presented me with a scarf of blue silk which I still have.

I was whisked round an agricultural cooperative, and wrote enthusiastically to Alan Donald of 'a splendid emptiness of rolling downs, here and there a horseman driving sheep in a cloudy dust, or horses bathing in a watercourse, an eagle or a sheep's skull or a big cluster of irises. In Mongolia they make the camels pull carts, and the camels do not like it.'

Because of the delay in Peking, my railway journey was limited to the forty hours from Ulan Bator to Irkutsk. Russian passengers on boarding immediately put on pyjamas over vest and pants. That was correct wear for platform and station buffet. I travelled with two professors and their wives, who fed me from huge picnic hampers. They were particularly enthused as we passed Lake Baikal. The radio played a solemn local tune, and the professors beat time with radishes on the end of forks.

---

*Dr Hewlett Johnson, the famous Red Dean of Canterbury, a consistent acolyte of Stalinism.

From Irkutsk I flew to Moscow, and stayed for a day or two in the British Embassy, the best spare bedroom which the British Diplomatic Service has to offer anywhere in the world. With the adjoining bathroom, it is fashioned of dark brown wood, which creaks at all hours. The light switches require the skill of a detective. But the windows open on to the river and, quite near on the far bank, to the unique towers, walls and domes of the Kremlin, at their most spectacular when there is snow on the ground and the gold cupolas dazzle in frosty sunshine.

I spent just long enough in the Soviet Union to note the contrast with Peking. 'Trains are late, basins have spiders, waitresses take tips, the great are obviously privileged, and the people look pasty and listless. Whereas in China I, and I think you [this is the same letter to Alan], sometimes felt that they've got something which is almost irresistible, and is sweeping away the ordinary obstacles of human nature, here there is no such feeling. The dynamo seems to be running down.'

THREE CHINESE PENDANTS

I

One of the least frequented ruins outside Peking was the oddest. As you left the road and trudged across open country, you seemed to be leaving China and going for a walk somewhere off the Appia Antica outside Rome. Corinthian pillars, broken pediments, baroque arches were the remnants of the old Summer Palace built at the beginning of the eighteenth century and developed to the designs of Jesuit priests in vague imitation of Versailles. It became the favourite pleasure dome of successive emperors, and for that reason was destroyed by the Anglo-French forces in 1860. The Chinese had killed four European and several Sikh prisoners whom they had captured by violating the terms of a truce. Lord Elgin looked for a means of retribution which would be painful to Emperor Hsien Feng, rather than to his people – what in modern diplomatic jargon is called a 'smart sanction'. The old Summer Palace had already been occupied by the British and French soldiery; fruits of their hectic looting can be found in several of our stately homes.

I tramped through this strange desolation, and back in our compound read the story of the Second Chinese War (1856–60), of which this was almost the last deed. Slowly the idea of writing a book about that war grew in my mind. The Arrow War (called after the small craft of that name from which Chinese officials seized two suspects even though it was flying the British flag) had been a cause célèbre in Britain. Both Houses of Parliament debated the decision to go to war. In one of the great set-pieces of Victorian oratory Gladstone, Disraeli and Bright spoke on the same side against Prime Minister Palmerston, and the Government lost. Palmerston, who was seventy-two, dissolved Parliament, launched an election campaign on patriotic slogans and won handsomely.

But what was it all about? Did the British and French want to conquer China and ram opium down Chinese throats? Or were they sincere in saying that they simply wanted equality of status and free trade? What was certain was mutual ignorance; during four years each side repeatedly misunderstood and mishandled the other.

It became clear that the central character was the commander of the Anglo-French expedition both in 1857 and 1860, the eighth Earl of Elgin, son of the man who brought the Elgin Marbles to Britain. Independent-minded and humane but suspicious and irritable, he was a complicated character. Had he written anything besides official despatches? I wrote to Uncle Bob, the Edinburgh architect, knowing that this was the world in which he moved. Uncle Bob replied at once. Yes, he knew the present Lord Elgin, had indeed designed a house for him at Culross. Yes, he knew the Earl's son, Lord Bruce, who by then had moved into the big house at Broomhall, overlooking the north shore of the Firth of Forth not far from Dunfermline, where the family papers were kept. It would be tactful to approach the Earl first. Yes, he would pave the way.

All this moved very smoothly. For a week in August 1961 I made daily journeys from Edinburgh to Broomhall. Andrew and Victoria Bruce were enthusiastic and hospitable. They made that week great fun. 'No Bruce has thrown anything away,' I wrote in my diary, 'from the Sword of the Bruce via the Marbles and Summer Palace silks to the last Minutes of the Fife County Council.' My prize was in the basement, a set of black tin trunks containing the eighth Earl's papers. They were in ideal condition for an amateur historian, bound in logical order, but never explored by anyone who was going to write about him.

James Elgin, the eighth Earl, had inherited part of the Fife coalfield from his father, but also the debts flowing from the saga of buying and shipping the Elgin Marbles. He could not afford to live at Broomhall as a Scottish country gentleman. He needed a government job. Before his mission to China he was Governor of Jamaica, then Governor-General of Canada; after China he became Viceroy of India, where he died. The papers on China were only a fraction of what lay in those trunks, but enough to keep me busy and excited for a week.

Elgin kept two records of his actions and anxieties in China. There was nothing remarkable about the heavy Victorian prose of his formal despatches to the Foreign Secretary. More interesting was the diary which he wrote in the form of a running letter to his wife. When a suitable ship was going home he broke off the narrative, sealed what he had written and sent it off. In the diary Elgin released his frustrations and resentments – against the politicians whom he served, against Sir John Bowring, the unlucky and preposterous Governor of Hong Kong, against the British admiral, the French general, the greedy British merchants of Shanghai. Almost everyone was at one time or another his target, except the Chinese against whom he was fighting. He looked on them with a mixture of pity and despair.

At Broomhall I learned a lesson about diaries which I have remembered when reading the outpourings of our own time. Some diarists are simply entertainers of the moment who see no need to distinguish between truth and fiction. But even serious diarists like Cadogan, Alanbrooke, Tony Benn and Douglas Hurd cannot be taken entirely seriously. Like Elgin, they use the diary as a means to let off steam. What they write late at night in the diary is often what they stored up unsaid during the day. But it does not follow that what is in the diary is more valid than what they wrote and said to others at the time. The two sources have to be read together; the diary complements but does not replace the rest of the record. A man may be exhausted and angry when he scribbles late at night; it does not follow that he spent his time in exhaustion and anger.

In further search of the Arrow War I spent hours in the London Library in St James's Square; in the archives of the Quai d'Orsay in Paris; in Cambridge looking at the records of Jardine Matheson. But my main resource apart from Broomhall was the Public Record Office, still then housed in dark Victorian grandeur in Chancery Lane. My lunchtime from the Foreign Office in 1961 and 1962 could just be stretched long enough to buy a pork pie and a Kitkat, munch them on a No. 11 bus, and spend an hour or a bit more exploring the official papers.

Gradually the book took shape. If the Crimean War was the first in history to be photographed, the Arrow War must come second. Another stroke of luck was the discovery in the *Radio Times* Hulton Picture Library of a handful of dramatic pieces by the Italian photographer Beato. I was encouraged by Philip Ziegler, whose marriage to Sarah Collins had given him an entry into the world of publishing. More important, he had already published his first book, *The Duchess of Dino*, and was hard at work on a biography of Addington. He knew the craft. I might have become bogged down in my own researches had it not been for Philip's urging and teasing from afar.

In 1967 *The Arrow War* appeared, much improved by the advice of my editor at Collins, Richard Ollard. It was well received, and followed by an American edition. The only Chinese documents I had used were those which had previously been translated into English. That is a serious limitation, but I do not believe that there is a pro-Western bias in the account. The narrative is slow to get going for I was fascinated by the political crisis which the opening of the war caused in Britain: the arguments in Cabinet, the parliamentary debates, the General Election of 1857 are described at length. My mother at least, and probably others, longed to get on with the action in China itself. But as my first-born book, *The Arrow War* holds my affection; I think it still reads well.

II

Ted Heath had been invited to visit China as Prime Minister in the summer of 1974. The Chinese wanted to mark the fact that under his premiership Britain and China had at last exchanged ambassadors. But in March 1974 Ted Heath lost office and was again Leader of the Opposition. The Chinese said that they still wished to receive him. But how would this work? Could it be a success? Just elected as a backbench MP, I no longer had any formal position in Ted Heath's entourage, but he had liked *The Arrow War* and remembered that, long before, I had worked in China. On these sketchy grounds I was included in the party, along with Tim Kitson (his parliamentary private secretary) and his wife Sally, William Waldegrave, his doctor Brian Warren – and Maurice Trowbridge as press officer. As we left Heathrow on 23 May, the Chinese Ambassador whispered to me that he thought everything would be fine. But we had no programme, no idea what would happen. The job of Leader of the Opposition was not one with which the Chinese were familiar. My memory of the Attlee visit twenty years earlier did not fill me with total confidence. Strict adherence to protocol might create a visit well below the level which Ted and the British media would think acceptable. The next evening I looked out of the window of the Air France jet with some anxiety as we approached Peking airport. The nature of the initial reception would tell us accurately what would follow.

I need not have worried. In the evening sun 4,000 girls were assembled on the tarmac in bright summer dresses as we touched down. They danced and sang an enthusiastic welcome. This went on for more than half an hour. Ted passed slowly through their ranks. He made it a rule never to appear surprised by good fortune. This was exactly what he had expected. The Chinese had decided to break the rules and treat him as the head of government of an important power.

The rest followed. I noticed at once that 'the city I knew is destroyed – no gates, no walls, no sense of a city'. But that did not bother those who had not been there before. The Cultural Revolution was in its death throes, but we could not know this at the time. The actors of the old regime and their successors were for the moment on stage together. Our main interlocutor in several hours of talks during the next four days was Teng Hsiao Ping, small and chunky, quick of mind, direct of speech. The question in all minds was whether Ted would be received by Chairman Mao himself. The day after we arrived we were taken round the Forbidden City and then to a handicrafts exhibition. There was a scurry among our Chinese entourage, we were bustled back to the guesthouse to wait 'for a special event', and then in black limousines to the heart of the Chung Nan Hai quarter, across the lake west of the Forbidden City, from where modern China is now ruled.

There was no pomp or luxury about Mao's surroundings. We were all presented in turn. I remember the liver spots on his hands, and his peculiar voice, loud and pitched somewhere between a chant and a grunt. When Ted introduced his spokesman Maurice Trowbridge, Mao said, 'I hear you are a very dangerous man.' It was a joke, such as any politician might make when confronted with a press officer. But this was the mightiest single ruler in the world, with unparalleled power and much blood on his hands. There was a shiver in the room. The jokes of such men may be misunderstood.

The rest of us were ushered out; Ted Heath and Mao spoke at length, in the presence of the interpreter and the British Ambassador, John Addis. Ted Heath's memoirs give an account of what passed, but in addition, as Ted told us afterwards, the Chairman gave his visitor a frank account of the reasons underpinning the Cultural Revolution. If you left the Chinese people to themselves (he said), they would fall back into bourgeois capitalist ways. They would start having too many children and exploiting one another all over again. The vessel had to be broken and remade in every generation. It struck me then that the contrast between Mao and most successful revolutionary leaders was stark. Napoleon made his brothers kings and crowned himself Emperor in the presence of the Pope. Mao deliberately broke up the structures of power which he controlled.

We passed the week in a haze of banquets and sightseeing. Mao's wife, Madame Chiang Ch'ing, a Victorian governess in black from head to foot, took us to a long and dull concert with many solos and the Yellow River Symphony. She did not smile from beginning to end of the evening. She was still that evening an inspiring force behind the Cultural Revolution, but not far from her disgrace as a member of the Gang of Four. I have always found it difficult to believe the accusation then made that she spent secret hours giggling at blue movies. (Oddly, in Chinese these are called yellow movies.)

I shook hands with Chou En-lai for the last time. As compared with Teng Hsiao Ping's brisk, practical manner, Chou ranged philosophically across the world, as old men do towards the end of their lives. For the first time I saw Hsian, the old capital whose walls and gates still survived, and revisited Shanghai, Kunming and Canton. The slogan of these months was 'Dig tunnels deep, store grain everywhere, always oppose hegemony'. The Chinese were anxious to support European unity as a counter to American domination of the world, and exaggerated Ted Heath's readiness to play an anti-American role. In Shanghai thousands of citizens lined the streets, clapping him quietly under the trees. The food and drink were best in Kunming, Ted's best speech an impromptu one in Shanghai, the children most tuneful and charming in Canton. Mao had volunteered that at his departure for Hong Kong Ted would receive a military guard of honour, in addition to the civilian enthusiasm which was organised for us everywhere. Chancing his arm, Ted asked if the Chinese might possibly spare two pandas for London Zoo. This was organised in the small hours of 2 June, and his triumph was complete.

III

Attlee 1954, Heath 1974 – and I was to score a hat-trick of Leaders of the Opposition accompanied in China. In April 1977, two years before she became Prime Minister, Margaret Thatcher asked me to join her party on her first visit. We flew out slowly in a Chinese Boeing 707, the chatty presence of a basketball team from Surinam making sleep difficult. There was no repetition of the splendid airport pageant which had greeted Ted Heath and much else had changed too. Mao and Chou were dead, the Cultural Revolution over, the Gang of Four in prison. Soft-faced, gentle-voiced Hua Kuo-feng, who has left little trace on Chinese history, was in charge. Margaret Thatcher's main interlocutor was Vice-Premier Li Hsien-nien, 'like a melancholy but vigorous reptile, who gives a long grunt at the end of each sentence'. There were two main themes of Chinese conversation: the iniquities of the Gang of Four and the inevitability of war with the Soviet Union. They dismissed the usefulness of nuclear deterrence, then the prevailing doctrine in the West. Margaret Thatcher was of interest to them because of her stern opposition to the Russians, just as Ted Heath had been interesting because of his support for European unity.

Though the individuals and their themes had changed, the system had not, nor the components of a visit – banquets, speeches, acrobats, the

Great Wall and a tour of Soochow (a commune of ducks), Hangchow and Shanghai. Teddy Youde was now British Ambassador in Peking, and I managed to get him included in the talks. I broke away from the visit for a nostalgic drive through Peking with the Youdes 'mourning walls destroyed and vanished temples . . . The City has shed its old character without gaining a new.' The flow of official visitors was already making the small part of the Great Wall shown to visitors somewhat tatty.

This was the first time that I had worked closely with Margaret Thatcher. John Stanley, her parliamentary private secretary, and I briefed her before meetings and drafted speeches. I began to learn to live with her extraordinary mixture of qualities – physical energy, intellectual curiosity, a passion for detailed information, excellent social manners, strong opinions even on matters of which she knew little. These qualities sometimes came into conflict with one another, and the result could be hard pounding. She opened every discussion on China, in a plane or at night in a guesthouse, with a firm statement of her own views. If one of us answered with a view of our own, or some counteracting facts, we were swept aside. But that was not meant to be the end of the matter. What I wrote then I could have written at any time in the next thirteen years: 'If you contradict her [first statement] you find your information appearing in her next public remarks. But she was not drawing you out. She is simply burying her original judgement under greater and greater heaps of knowledge, which she accumulates at a notable speed.' In 1977 I added, 'What kind of PM this creates I do not know.' We were soon to find out.

Margaret Thatcher had not visited a communist country before, except briefly Romania. She asked the right penetrating questions. At the Shanghai shipyard she cross-examined the management about costs and profits, concepts which for them did not exist. A girl chemist at a Shanghai university acknowledged under persistent questioning that she had gained her place because her father was a party boss. An academic in Peking, asked for his view of Stalin, replied that Stalin was 60 per cent right and 40 per cent wrong. Our guide hundreds of miles away in the south replied to the same question that she had given the matter much thought and believed that Stalin was 60 per cent right and 40 per cent wrong. Margaret Thatcher was appalled at this efficiently imposed uniformity of thought. The more she heard, the more she disliked the Chinese system. This did not impair her courtesy to her hosts, but she took it out on me afterwards. Because I was the only member of the visiting party who had worked in China, I was treated by her as largely responsible for whatever aspects of the country she disliked. (This too became a familiar role for me. I later found myself held to account in turn for whatever displeased her in Ireland, the Metropolitan Police, the BBC and Europe.)

My role was exactly the opposite of that required from me during Ted Heath's visit. Then I had cast myself as the necessary cynic. I had to suggest to Ted that the expert on the works of Spenser who told us that he greatly preferred to academic study his new job as a tourist guide in a Peking hotel was simply mouthing the jargon of the Cultural Revolution. When posters appeared in Kunming criticising a local bigwig and printing his name-characters upside down, I suggested this was not a gentle exercise in free speech, but a warrant for his imprisonment or death. Someone had to damp down Ted Heath's unquestioning enthusiasm. Equally, someone had to put into Margaret Thatcher's mind that, repellent though the communist system was, most of the peasants in the Soochow commune and the shipyard workers in Shanghai probably preferred it to the brutalities of the Japanese or the chaotic corruption of Chiang Kai Shek in his last days.

It was quite a relief to move on to Japan, where I was as much of a newcomer as Margaret Thatcher. I had an example of her intellectual rigour in the plane from Shanghai to Tokyo. The CBI had provided her on behalf of British business with speaking notes for her use with Japanese ministers and businessmen. They wanted her to complain strongly of unfair Japanese competition. But in the plane she covered these notes with dismissive comments and crossings out: 'Rubbish!'; 'I can't say that'; 'What a rotten argument'. I was alarmed, not because she was wrong, but because at the rate she was going she would arrive at Tokyo with no speech at all for her imminent speaking engagement. I already knew what that would mean in terms of rushing to and fro and lost sleep.

All the domestic party-political calculations were in favour of criticising the Japanese, and winning applause from the business community at home; but Margaret Thatcher was not prepared to use an argument by which she herself was not convinced. The CBI produced the opposite to their intended effect, and Margaret Thatcher arrived hoping to find Japan a shining example of an advanced market economy. Despite the welding robots at the Nissan factory and the meritocratic school which she visited, I think she came away slightly disappointed. Minds did not meet as they should. The Keidanren (the senior organisation of Japanese employers) gave her a working breakfast. They were all very old. Several of them made long speeches of welcome, saying how sad it was that the time for the meeting was so short. Margaret Thatcher followed with a long reply of her own to the first question. Time for discussion there was minimal.

I was dismayed that during her speech so many of these powerful old gentlemen closed their eyes. But from repeated experience over the years I learned that in Japan this really can signify thought as opposed to sleep.

7

NEW YORK

Peking was amazing, but my two years there had little to do with modern diplomacy. It was at my next job in New York, at the British Mission to the United Nations, that I learned how the wheels of the world turn, jerkily, sometimes absurdly. Once again I was allowed by the Foreign Office to travel to my post by boat, this time on Cunard's *Queen Elizabeth* from Southampton.

This followed several weeks of wistful summer leave in England, revisiting scenes of my past and finding them changed. Tim Raison was happily married to Veldes Charrington deep in Dorset. After the wedding, full of champagne and self-examination, I drove the Morris Minor borrowed from my brother Stephen homeward across sunlit Wiltshire downs. My last weekend I spent in Cambridge, staying with Tony Lloyd in his rooms in Peterhouse, again admiring the elegance of the Ackerman prints on his walls. We bathed in a splendid cut near Cottenham fringed with bulrushes, very clear and deep, reflecting the clouds and pale washed Cambridgeshire sky. I argued at Westcott House, the low-church theological college, for most of one evening over the usual over-percolated coffee. Next morning, to redress the balance, I attended Little St Mary's where pale young men swung their censers with surprising vigour, and I found that I had forgotten to bob in the right places. There followed an immense lobster-and-champagne lunch in the Junior Parlour at Peterhouse with lots of pretty and intelligent girls who were afterwards duly punted to Magdalene and back. That night I dined with Dennis Robertson in the Combination Room at Trinity. It was as good a last weekend as I could have contrived.

All this was backward living. Not far ahead lay the first real international thunderstorm which soaked me, though as bystander, not actor. President Nasser had nationalised the Suez Canal on 26 July 1956, a month before I left England for New York. To Alan Donald in Peking I wrote, 'I am rather sick at heart about Suez, aren't you? There is tremendous argument going on here, in newspapers, in clubs and places where they drink of course, but also to an amazing extent among ordinary unpolitical people. A: We can't get what we want without force, which we can't use. B: If we don't get what we want, we are finished as a great power. A argues passionately against B, but I have a sick feeling that both are right.'

New York is not a welcoming city, nor is late August its best season. It particularly baffled a young man inexperienced in the art of hiring and furnishing an apartment, arranging laundry, fixing a cleaning lady, and buying the right number of electric plugs of the right shape – all this to be accomplished in the curt, monosyllabic vocabulary of that city. The administrative staff of the British Delegation helped me sort things out, but the senior members were already absorbed in the first skirmishes of Suez diplomacy. Peter Ramsbotham, Head of Chancery, with whom I had shared an office four years earlier, had little time to explain to me what was happening and how things worked, let alone what I might do to help. For several weeks I felt unhappily idle while those I was meant to support bustled furiously about me.

The geography of the British effort at the UN belonged to a more leisurely age. Our ambassador, Sir Pierson Dixon, whose private secretary I became, still lived north of Manhattan in stately Wave Hill, characteristically chosen for its grandeur by his predecessor, Gladwyn Jebb. Wave Hill was enriched by a collection of medieval armour and provided a notable view west over the Hudson River to the Palisades. But its occupant spent hours each day driving in a Rolls-Royce through hectic traffic to the UN Building or to our delegation office in midtown Manhattan.

My life in these early weeks was made tolerable by my immediate colleague in the British Delegation, Mary Galbraith. She had been posted to New York from Budapest just one month earlier, but had already mastered the geography and gained a shrewd understanding of the personalities. Her rocklike academic background in Oxford made her fear no man, though events could depress her. We became (and remain) close friends and allies. In the next hectic months and the calmer years which followed we found that we complemented each other well, each seeing things the other missed, rarely both downcast on the same day, each usually able to volunteer for a task which the other wanted to be rid of.

In early autumn 1956 British policy on Suez slithered to and fro, and it was not clear to us in New York how if at all the UN fitted in. Suddenly, on 22 September, the Foreign Office instructed us to appeal to the Security Council. The motive was unclear. We were not told whether we should aim at a resolution which the Soviet Union would veto, thus providing some pretext for British and French military action, or whether we were seriously interested in the kind of negotiating committee which Secretary-General Dag Hammarskjöld was already suggesting. We launched the necessary preliminaries, and on 2 October were joined by the Foreign Secretary, Selwyn Lloyd. We were following closely the angry debate in Britain. It was clear to us that Selwyn Lloyd had come out a few days earlier than necessary to escape from that debate and in particular to put an ocean between himself and the feverish anxieties of the Prime Minister, Anthony Eden.

'The debate starts tomorrow,' I wrote to Tony Lloyd on 4 October,

> but the characters have been playing their parts for some hours. Selwyn Lloyd in the Waldorf, in his shirtsleeves, looking fat and exhausted, with that awful sort of abrupt briskness which one learned in the army was a sign of a man who didn't know his own mind, and which occasionally becomes mere petulance – 'no one can call me a fussy man, but must I really have dinner with Pineau [French Foreign Minister] again?' – the French, bitter and very stubborn – Ambassador Cabot Lodge, Jr [of the USA] trim and well groomed and ready to sell everything for a Republican victory – Hammarskjöld, subtle and honest, but believing too much in negotiation for its own sake. And padding endlessly between them, infinitely patient and skilful, worried and sad, smoothing a difficulty here, proposing a compromise there, comes Sir Pierson and at his heels, clasping his despatch case, his private secretary . . . One gets so caught up in the machinery, in the tiny satisfactions of an amendment which is accepted, or an interview which goes well, that one forgets that the thing is tragic and intolerable. We do not know what terms we would accept; we do not know what we will do if acceptable terms are not forthcoming.

I had come across Selwyn Lloyd earlier when I was an undergraduate politician, and found him intelligent and approachable. I knew him quite well late in his life as Speaker of the House of Commons. At this stage in New York I was not alone in finding him disagreeable. He had a manner in private familiar to me later with Ted Heath, of treating officials in a way which they found impossible to handle. His jokes at their expense were not funny, and sometimes degenerated into unfair abuse. Unlike Ted Heath, he had not learned to signal at the same time to those who knew him that this was all meant as fun. Nor could officials cope with his monologues on domestic British politics. On the other hand, his legal training had made him a good advocate. His public speeches during the long Security Council debates that month were clear, reasonable and well delivered.

During these same weeks I saw Sir Pierson Dixon (Bob to his friends) at close quarters. His years in New York were the climax of a brilliant professional career, but I am not sure that he enjoyed them. His outlook on life was benevolent, cautious, mild and scholarly, based on a classical education which long before had led him to break out into a novel about Catullus. Having worked close to Ernest Bevin and Anthony Eden, he was not naïve about politics; indeed, if anything, his subtle mind led him to imagine conspiracies and even occasionally to devise them. He was concerned, perhaps over-concerned, with his own reputation. He hated noise and violence, and was an unimpressive public speaker – not an ideal successor to the rumbustious Gladwyn Jebb in the most talkative job open to a British diplomat. But Bob Dixon was praised throughout the United Nations and in much of the Foreign Office as the perfect professional, far sighted and ingenious, admired even by those who could not follow the complex workings of his mind. One such was Selwyn Lloyd. I sometimes felt that the ideal operator at the UN would have combined the virtues of these two very different men. If only Selwyn Lloyd could absorb some of Bob Dixon's courtesy and patience; if only Dixon could bring his labyrinthine arguments before too long to one of Selwyn Lloyd's workmanlike conclusions.

Dixon did not return Selwyn Lloyd's respect. Once, at the end of an evening spent listening at his own table to the Foreign Secretary rudely ragging Casey, Australian Foreign Minister, beyond the point which even an Australian would find acceptable, Dixon burst out to me that he loathed all politicians – characteristically adding, 'with respect of course to your own father'. But usually he kept silent. Though he was always considerate, I never had with him the informal, outspoken relationship which later I tried to create with my own private secretaries. I learned to guess his moods, guided partly by the way in which the back of his neck flushed when he was angry or perplexed. As time passed, I liked him more as a man, but became convinced that I did not want to end up as such a very professional diplomat.

The debate and negotiation on Suez at the UN in mid-October sputtered out with neither breakdown nor conclusion. In the last week of the month Russian tanks began to fill Hungary with blood as they crushed the popular uprising. We took the USSR to the Security Council and after the first round there on Sunday 28 October I wrote, 'Our action may have helped to make it impossible for Russians to put down revolt by force.' But in any case the British Prime Minister had by then hatched a plan for Suez, unknown to any of us in New York, which had the effect of leaving the Russians a free hand in Hungary.

Monday 29 October was the opening night of the New York Metropolitan Opera. Sir Pierson and Cabot Lodge, both handsome in tails and white tie as ornaments of New York society, were installed in separate boxes, listening to Maria Callas sing the title role of Norma. It was my duty to carry to Sir Pierson the news that Israel had moved against Egypt. I sat in his box sipping champagne and listening for the first time to the dramatic screech which made Callas famous. In an interval Sir Pierson began to scribble an immediate telegram to the Foreign Office. I encouraged him to write this on the opera programme for history's sake, but he dismissed the idea as unprofessional. His sensitive antennae, remembering perhaps something Selwyn Lloyd had let slip, led him to suspect that something was brewing, more serious than yet another skirmish between Israel and her neighbours.

The suspicion was increased by a short telegram from the Foreign Office, giving no background, but simply instructing us not to go along with any attempt to take the attacking country to the Security Council. During the interval Cabot Lodge appeared in the box, assuming that we would join the Americans in doing precisely that, as had been normal practice in previous flare-ups between Israel and an Arab state. Dixon, having no explanation to give for our refusal, prevaricated. Lodge left the box baffled and disturbed. On stage Callas resumed her own tragedy. It was the last time the two men spoke on friendly terms for several months.

The pace of events in the next three days amazed us all. The United Nations, widely regarded as slow and ineffective, gathered the speed of a hurricane to overwhelm us. On Tuesday Cabot Lodge called a meeting of the Security Council. Sir Pierson and his French colleague read out in the Council the text of the twelve-hour ultimatum which we had sent to both Israel and Egypt, threatening armed intervention unless they stopped their day-old war. The only people deceived by this manoeuvre were the servants of the Crown who were instructed to announce and defend it – and we were deceived only for a day or two. Anthony Eden had decided to deal with Nasser by force; the rest was pretext. The Americans, furious and deceived themselves, moved a resolution against us, backed by the Russians, who were that day preparing their final pounce on Hungary. At around seven on Tuesday evening there was a gasp in the public gallery as the British and French raised their hands against the American resolution. Sir Pierson cast the first British veto in history. My diary recorded: 'Voluble taxi-drivers [they were throughout our strongest supporters]. Bed 1 a.m. as the troops (presumably) move in.'

That last comment shows how far we had been kept from reality. There were no troops moving in next day, or for several days thereafter. Wednesday 30 October was 'if possible an even more disastrous day. The bombs began to fall on Egypt, no troops in yet, our unpopularity grows, everyone is against us. Afternoon bad for me personally, I get soaked in downpour, lose my keys, get barked at continuously by Peter [Ramsbotham, my immediate superior].' The majority of the UN did not allow the Anglo-French veto to stand for more than a few hours. Led by the Yugoslavs, inflexibly and mysteriously vindictive, they used a device called 'Uniting for Peace' by which the Security Council, in a procedural motion not subject to veto, requested the General Assembly to take over the handling of the crisis.* So on Thursday 1 November we were pitchforked into the General Assembly. The French Ambassador collapsed under the strain.

> Incredible. Morning spent largely with Peter [Ramsbotham] concocting speech for H.E. [His Excellency, i.e. Bob Dixon]. This comes out diffuse but not ineffective. We sit from 5 p.m. to <u>4.30 a.m.</u> in the General Assembly, hearing the world crumbling around us. Dulles [the American Secretary of State] very solemn and impressive and unscrupulous about Suez. Poisonous attacks on us by the Afro-Asian ranks – gallant worried attempts by Aust[ralia] and N.Z. . . . to come to our help. Louis de Guiringaud [the French No. 2] calm and euphonious. Ludicrously massive vote against us. Then Lester Pearson [Canadian Foreign Minister] brings the first ray of hope with his talk of a UN force, echoing the PM's wish. We pounce on this and recommend it. On and on and on.

So the pattern was set for the next few days. Night after night we were hunted through the General Assembly. Mary Galbraith and I took it in turns to sit behind the United Kingdom placard in that melancholy great chamber. We recorded briefly the abuse hurled at Britain from the podium by each speaker so that we could send the necessary reporting telegrams to the Foreign Office. The Arabs were venomous beyond belief and our former friends had turned overnight into sorrowful enemies. I wrote to Tony Lloyd:

---

*This device had been put together a year or two before as a theoretical means of circumventing a Soviet veto. 'Uniting for Peace' is not used nowadays because the Americans know its most likely use would be to circumvent American vetoes on behalf of Israel.

The crisis of each day's debate came about midnight, 5 a.m. in London, when we made or received telephone calls from Prime Minister or Secretary of State. They were always cheerful, even at that hour: 'Splendid, Bob, splendid. Do what you like. We're over the hump, had an excellent evening in the House, majority of 50.' Little men, whistling in the dark, not realising what they had done. Everyone quickly became tired for lack of sleep, and consequently over dramatic. One night [Sunday 4 November] an Australian took me aside – they had stood by us at great cost to themselves, not knowing what we were doing, but trusting us. They were fed up because there had till then been bombings and no invasion. So he asked me, 'When the hell is the real thing going to start?' I was able to look at my watch and say, 'In exactly seven minutes.' If the Assembly had still been in heated overnight session when the news came of the first British troops landing at Port Said they might have rushed straight into sanctions against us. We adjourned that night with about half an hour to spare. In the sober light of the next day there was no talk of sanctions.

In these few days our reputation and influence at the UN were destroyed. This was particularly hard on my superiors, particularly Sir Pierson and his deputy Moore Crosthwaite, who had spent years patiently and professionally building that influence. As new arrivals in junior positions Mary Galbraith and I had different perspectives. Mary was hit hard by the coincidence with the tragedy in Hungary. Budapest having been her previous post, she had many Hungarian friends. The final bombardment of the city began on 3 November, the day before British troops landed at Port Said. The Security Council met at 3 a.m. on Sunday and the General Assembly passed a noble, useless resolution on Hungary that afternoon. The Russians sent out Kuznetsov, who looked, I wrote in a letter to Alan Donald, 'like Cruikshank's drawing of one of Dickens' villains. I am not sure which? Silas Wegg. Stiff sandy hair, a red nose, and no lips, just a leering gap in his face, and a voice like a file. A terrible creature, very appropriate for his present job.' The pressure on the Soviet Union to call off their campaign was in no way comparable to the pressure on Britain to abandon hers.

Until that day, 3 November, I nursed in my mind a private hope that somehow, somewhere deep in Whitehall, there was a master plan which would make everything right. In the last resort, I had thought, our influence at the UN was expendable. In the last resort it did not matter if we were embarrassed, distressed and kept in the dark – provided that we were low cards being sacrificed until the moment came to play Britain's aces and trumps. I was a Tory with Tory instincts. I had never met Anthony Eden, but I had the highest respect for what he had achieved as Foreign Secretary, in Indo-China and in Europe, only two years before. Of all our active politicians he had the greatest experience of the world, and in particular of the Middle East. But on that day we heard that Anthony Nutting had resigned as Minister of State at the Foreign Office. Walking alone across Manhattan to the UN from our office at 99 Park Avenue, I tried to think this through. Nutting, whom I knew slightly, was a young, attractive, modern Conservative minister, with none of the bluster which discouraged me in Selwyn Lloyd. Moreover, Nutting was close to the Prime Minister, indeed his protégé. If there were a master plan he would have known it. Nutting had left; so there was no master plan, no aces, no trumps; just deception. Would deception now be followed by defeat?

On the same day Sir Pierson Dixon came to his own point of decision. A report reached us that British planes were bombing civilians in Egypt. Sir Pierson told me that he was considering resignation unless this was denied. He telephoned the Foreign Secretary. Selwyn Lloyd, as ever cheerful, emphasised that the bombers were instructed to attack only military targets. In my experience this is said at the beginning of every war, and is always wrong. In a crowded country like Egypt air attacks on any scale, using the haphazard technology available in 1956, were bound to kill civilians. Dixon, facing a hideous personal dilemma, believing that the British Government's policy was tragically mistaken, needed to find a test for that Government which would decide whether he continued in its service. In his diary he described this as 'the severest moral and physical strain I have ever experienced'.* Having been reassured, albeit on a secondary aspect, he stayed in his position and did his best, which was substantial, to minimise the damage to Britain of British policy. I agree with the verdict of the *Dictionary of National Biography*: 'He sustained his ordeal with great dignity and self-control, and his conduct during this crisis helped Britain to regain respect and influence in the UN in subsequent years.'

Under the British system an official is in a different ethical position from a minister. Even a senior official is not responsible to the electorate or indeed to posterity for the success or failure of policy in the same way as a minister is. His job is to advise, then carry out what ministers decide. Dixon was in a particularly exposed position, being the man who day by day was expounding British policy to the world. His resignation would have been a shattering disaster for the Government. By staying he

---

*Quoted by Edward Johnson, 'British Officials and the Suez Crisis', University of Central England, April 1997.

helped to rescue its policy. Nutting, an elected politician, was right to resign in November 1956; Dixon was right to stay.

During a lull I let out my own feelings in a letter to Peder Hammarskjöld.

> The only occasions on which I have begun to believe that Sir Anthony was right was when I sat night after night listening to the abuse and venom of our enemies. If the world were really fashioned in the image of Krishna Menon [India] and the poisonous Arabs, and if all Americans were as hypocritical as Dulles, then the sort of action we took would be inevitable. But the world is a bit better than that and therefore we were wrong.

The position of the US Delegation particularly baffled us. It was not simply that they frustrated what we were trying to do. They destroyed the intimacy of Anglo-American cooperation. They cut us out of their lives on all subjects for several months.* We spent humiliating hours trying to find out what had happened at meetings which they had called, from which we had been excluded. But their policy was essentially negative. They allowed the General Assembly to drift out of their control. They played little part in the constructive work which built a UN force in Egypt, thus providing us and eventually the Israelis with a ladder down which we could climb.

I have often pondered on this American ruthlessness towards us. Not long ago I read Robert Skidelsky's account of Lord Keynes's efforts in Washington in 1945 and 1946 to negotiate help which would save Britain from bankruptcy. For a short period, after the defeat of Japan but before Stalin's Russia was seen as a major threat, Britain was not particularly important to the United States. Keynes was treated by the Americans with the sort of ruthlessness which we experienced in 1956. No sentimental recollection of our lonely stand against Hitler, no rhetoric about a special relationship influenced on either occasion the chilly American calculation of US interests. Too often we British clothe the Anglo-US relationship in a warm, fuzzy haze. Its basis is the real usefulness of one country to the other. If that usefulness dries up, no amount of speech-making will prevent the relationship from withering.

---

*As this official cold-shouldering was perceived, friendly New Yorkers reacted against it. Just before Christmas one of these offered the British Delegation at two hours' notice tickets for the most sought-after show in town. With difficulty I managed to break away from the General Assembly to see Rex Harrison, Julie Andrews and Stanley Holloway in the unforgettable original of *My Fair Lady*.

Anthony Eden as early as 1 November in the House of Commons had referred to the possibility of the UN taking over the physical task of maintaining peace in the area. But this at the time was a pious hope, expressed to justify the task which he in practice believed only the British and French could carry through. Fortunately his phrase fitted the thoughts coming to the fore in two creative minds in New York. Lester Pearson, the Canadian Foreign Minister, and the Secretary-General Dag Hammarskjöld set to work with a handful of dedicated helpers to create a force and gain Egyptian as well as Anglo-French support for it. Sir Pierson, with the rest of us who helped draft his telegrams, did his best to pave the way for the success of this project. It took a form very different from what Eden originally had in mind. The British and French were excluded from membership of the UN Emergency Force, the emphasis being on replacing not reinforcing our invasion. Once a ceasefire was in place and our withdrawal agreed, discussions in New York moved on from the huge question of peace and war. Weary, exasperated men began to argue about secondary issues, for example the clearance of the Suez Canal and the treatment of our nationals in Egypt. The first of these was particularly intractable. One of the declared purposes of the Anglo-French operation was to keep the Canal open; one of the immediate effects was to close it. We organised a salvage fleet to clear away the wreckage, and the Royal Navy sent a pale, sad admiral to New York to explain to the UN how we would set about it. At lunch on 20 December I found him 'sweet and very dispirited'. Neither the admiral nor ministers at home understood why the Secretary-General could not contemplate any involvement in canal clearance by those countries which most of the UN regarded as aggressors. Hammarskjöld made his arrangements without the British. The argument became heated. I kept several of Hammarskjöld's pencilled scribbles of this time, including one to Sir Pierson dated 13 December following a tough statement on canal clearance by a minister in London. It is a good illustration of the Secretary-General's impenetrable style. 'A statement like Butler's settles the issue in a way which makes it only a question of time (perhaps hours) when I must define the UN hand. This is, possibly, in my view a policy too much in line with the action from which it originally derives. I hope that you are quite aware of what may be the end of this development for my part. I may feel that political casualties should be reserved for major issues.' What on earth did he mean? In the British Delegation we tried to construe the passage. I have our handwritten comments. I thought Hammarskjöld was hinting at his own resignation, not on the issue of canal clearance, but on the wider question of our lack of cooperation and respect for the Charter. Peter Ramsbotham wondered whether he was suggesting that the British

Government may be forced to resign. Sir Pierson refused to arbitrate between us. The paper with his comment has been torn, but certainly ends with the word 'maniac'. We owed Hammarskjöld a great deal, but by this time felt that 'the S/G with his moods and his obscurity and his pontifical outlook is really exasperating'.

The word 'pontifical' was not chosen at random in my diary. At this time many people began to comment on the change which had come over the Secretary-General. His predecessor, Trygve Lie from Norway, had been an untidy administrator, who quarrelled with the Russians without giving anyone else a particular sense of direction. Dag Hammarskjöld was chosen primarily by the British and French. They saw him as a sound, intelligent European, skilled in the niceties of bureaucratic life, doubtless a shade moralistic, like all Swedes, but unlikely to stir up anything too far – in short, a safe pair of hands. From 1956 to the last year of his life, 1960, Hammarskjöld increasingly displayed other qualities. Parallels with Thomas à Becket or with Sir Thomas More would not be exact, but, like them, Hammarskjöld began to place himself on a different moral plane to the representatives of temporal governments. He alone was the custodian of the United Nations Charter, and of the values and interests of the international community. Article 99 of the Charter, by his own liberal interpretation, gave him the right to intervene wherever he thought it necessary. Hammarskjöld possessed qualities which made this more than an empty pretension to papal power. These included a great capacity for hard work, a highly educated and sensitive mind, an interest in and commitment to the philosophical wisdom of different civilisations, and a personal dignity which required no buttressing with pomp and protocol. No trumpets sounded when the Secretary-General entered a room; there was no swarm of acolytes around him. Yet, despite his simplicity, he was a grander, more authoritative figure than any of his successors. When he talked you knew you were in the presence of an exceptional, perhaps a great, human being. More than any other individual then or later he established a set of expectations of the United Nations, an idea of what might be achieved. This idea has survived many disappointments, and is skilfully used, albeit in a more modest way, by the present incumbent, Kofi Annan.

I was lucky in my opportunities of watching Hammarskjöld. For practical reasons Sir Pierson found it convenient to take me with him when he called on the Secretary-General in the top (thirty-eighth) floor of the UN Building. Dag Hammarskjöld spoke quickly, in perfectly constructed English but with a strong Swedish accent. Knowing Sir Pierson to be a scholar like himself, he filled his conversation with classical, literary and philosophical allusions. His process of thought was in any case oblique and zigzag. He had a habit of suddenly providing a crucial document, say a message just received from the Egyptian Government, and thrusting it at Sir Pierson, but for a few seconds only, during which time he maintained the flow of his own discourse. It was not possible for a conscientious professional like Sir Pierson to store in his mind what the Secretary-General said, keep his end up in discussions, and somehow insert the points laid down in his own instructions from London. So I was required to sit on the sofa, a dumb junior presence, gazing at the surrounding Picassos, while I stored methodically in my mind the course of the conversation, so that I could construct an immediate reporting telegram to London as soon as we were back in our own office. Nowadays young diplomats scribble openly in pads on their knees when they attend such meetings as reporters. This decadent habit would have been regarded as unseemly by both Sir Pierson and Dag Hammarskjöld. I had to just fill my mind silently with what I was hearing; often I was close to bursting before I could relieve myself outside.

I summed up the end of the Suez Crisis for Tony Lloyd on 10 February 1957:

I act most of the time as Sir Pierson's shadow – he is now so tired and overworked that without a constant remembrancer he cannot always recall how the battle is going in any particular sector. It is just like a battle, Cyprus being discussed in one room, Israeli withdrawal, Kashmir, the Canal, Algeria in others, simultaneously, all matters in which we have great interest. We throw ourselves in wherever the fighting is thickest. About 6 or 7 each day it dies away, and we sit down to draft the telegrams giving an account of the day which will be read in the Foreign Office as we sleep, in time for fresh instructions if necessary to be on our desks next morning. Occasionally I act as remembrancer on other matters, as yesterday when Sir P was complaining to the French Ambassador: 'Hammarskjöld behaves as if he was . . . What was his name . . . the judge of the underworld?' 'Rhadamanthus, Sir,' breathed the shadow.

For three years after Suez my work at the UN settled into a predictable rhythm. There were certainly unpredictable events – for example, the revolution which killed the King in Iraq, American troop landings in Lebanon and British in Jordan, a stormy visit by Khrushchev. But each of these was handled without the river of UN life overflowing its banks as it had over Suez. Each autumn the General Assembly met, Selwyn Lloyd appeared, shouted at us in his suite at the Waldorf, and spoke competently in the general debate. After a few weeks he departed and his place was taken by the Minister of State, Allan Noble, a genial, strong-voiced naval commander, who once loaded carefully with the right speech and pointed in the right direction could fire an impressive salvo.

Each year there were set-piece debates on Kashmir, Cyprus, Algeria. These debates resembled performances of classical plays. The policies were known; the text and the actors hardly altered from year to year. The pleasure for the connoisseur, as of *Hamlet* or *Phèdre*, lay in detecting slight variations in the tactics or the eloquence of the performers, as they recited their familiar lines.

On Cyprus the two stars were the Greek Foreign Minister Averoff and his Turkish counterpart Zorlu. It was not much of a debate, since their arguments hardly met, but both were men of substance. Britain was still the sovereign power in Cyprus. One year, as I wrote to Alan Donald on 5 January 1958, 'The Greeks had badly mauled us . . . and we had to stop them getting a two-thirds majority for their resolution. Our full might was put forward for the first time since I have been here – emergency telegrams to capitals of the waverers to get their instructions changed, intensive arm-twisting in the corridors. My job was to flush the Latin American ambassadors out of their coverts in the committees and send them like rather ponderous pheasants over the Anglo-Turkish guns. The Minister of State bagged the Spanish vote with his first barrel – the firing continued through an afternoon and evening, and next day when the vote came the Greeks were discomfited.' But there were *longueurs* before these bouts of action. I could point out today the staircase in the lower ground floor under which our Cyprus expert John Thomson sat reading Thucydides in the original, while a few yards away in the committee room the repetitive oratory ebbed and flowed.

Kashmir debates had just one star, Krishna Menon of India. With his mountain of wiry grey hair, thick walking stick, eagle nose and glaring, furious eyes, Krishna was the bad fairy of the UN. His destructive influence was felt on many subjects. At the news that Krishna was interesting himself in their subject, peace-loving Norwegians, Canadians or Japanese abandoned whatever small, useful tasks they were attempting and shrank into a corner, scared lest his invective flay them alive. His years as a Labour borough councillor in North London had not been wasted. Usually his target was Britain. He belonged to that generation of Indians whom we had trained in the art of being beastly to ourselves. For hours on end he would denounce viceroy after viceroy, admitting only a reluctant admiration for Lord Curzon and for Her Imperial Majesty Queen Victoria. Because he was genuinely eloquent and yet preposterous, we listened to him with some pleasure. His thunder did not really hurt us. The fact that India, the champion of international morality, was accused of trampling on the people of Kashmir roused Krishna to heights of defensive fury. Once he attacked Sir Pierson in strong personal terms. A little later he collapsed while still speaking, after the manner of Lord Chatham in the House of Lords. While the photographers clicked and flashed Krishna was taken to a small room adjoining the Security Council, and laid on a couch, from which he asked to see Sir Pierson. My master went to him, through a chatter of Indian doctors and officials, expecting to receive some apology. 'I forgive you, Bob, I forgive you,' murmured the great man, and closed his eyes.

Our own delegation contained a less spectacular but, to Mary Galbraith and myself, equally memorable figure – Sir Pierson's deputy, Moore Crosthwaite. We both became fond of him, though he often chastised our errors. Moore, a bachelor with a close circle of women friends, was an old-fashioned perfectionist. We learned in New York that what was required was often not the best speech but the best speech that could be produced in thirty minutes. But Moore stood as a barrier against the sloppiness which goes with haste. Smoking each cigarette as if it were his first, noisily sucking in and expelling smoke with each breath, jabbing the butt into an overflowing ashtray, Moore corrected and re-corrected our drafts, or else cast them aside in despair and, puffing even more furiously, created within seconds an elegant version of his own. From him too I kept some scribbles, including this one, made during a Kashmir debate. Sir Pierson had wanted to adorn his own speech with a reference to Swift's *Gulliver's Travels*. Moore Crosthwaite demurred.

'Philosophy of the Laputians' is bound to annoy Krishna
(a)   because he won't know what it means;
(b)   because he will suspect it to be derogatory.
Also, it will puzzle the interpreters!
Douglas thinks it is LAPUTANS without an 'i'

On which Sir Pierson has scribbled: 'All right – drop it. Jokes always rebound. But I wd bet a $ on the "i". PD'.

I would have bet a dollar *against* the 'i', but I have checked, and I was wrong.

As the work at the UN became less frantic and more familiar there was more time for pleasure outside. One spring I bought an old Chevrolet for $350, and with three friends drove west by way of Charleston, New Orleans and the Grand Canyon. The Chevy broke down for the first time after half an hour on the New Jersey turnpike, and at intervals of forty-eight hours thereafter. Unluckily my one male companion was even less proficient than I at coping with ailing engines, and the girls simply mocked. Refreshed by constant investment the old slug eventually limped into San Francisco; I was glad to find a buyer at

$300 before returning by train. In every other respect the trip was fun. I took two other holidays, in Canada, and spoke for the English Speaking Union in wintry towns of upstate New York.

My midterm leave in 1958 included the by now usual whisk round old friends. I stayed with Walter Hamilton, by now headmaster of Rugby, swam again with Tony in the cut at Cottenham, entertained Alan Donald and his new wife at Winterbourne, and strolled with Raef Payne, now Master in College, through Luxmoore's Gardens at Eton. My parents, because of my father's connections with *The Times*, were invited to a weekend with its owner Lord Astor at Hever Castle and took me with them. I was still ill at ease on such occasions, made more difficult by the presence in the house of a number of malevolent hounds who had recently bitten a lady at lunch. Lord Reith was a fellow guest, in appearance and voice very like the comic actor Alastair Sim, and an enthusiastic player of Scrabble. On Easter Monday my diary reveals two contrasting examples of contemporary England.

> Drive to Reading in search of the Marchers to Aldermaston against nuclear weapons. Air in the villages exactly as when the hunt has passed or is about to – straggling youths on bicycles, curious groups in doorways. The procession, bannered but leaderless, is mild and out of place in the lanes, but quite impressive. After lunch to Lockinge (above Wantage) for the Old Berks point-to-point. A lovely course occasionally lit by sunshine. A big crowd of all classes and types, bigger and more democratic than Aldermaston. Lose a little money.

Philip Ziegler, now stationed in Paris, had planned with me an expedition to Vienna. I found myself staying with him in the rue Spontini listening to the death rattle of the Fourth Republic. No one knew what the French settlers in Algeria, or the army, or General de Gaulle would do. Armoured cars sat irresolute at street corners under the flowering chestnuts; police and rumours were everywhere. We managed our holiday unhindered, visiting Philip's ancestral home in Heidelberg, then Munich, Berchtesgaden, Salzburg, and friends in Vienna. Back in England I walked on a rainy June evening up the wet, overgrown path to Winterbourne churchyard, stood by Julian's grave and sat for a time in the church. His death exactly five years earlier seemed 'closer than most of the things (unimportant) which have happened since'. Next week I left Winterbourne and its roses, 'Albertine and Gloire de Dijon tuning up for their great annual performance', and flew back to New York for my second two years.

Now that I knew its ways I was fond of the place. I was established in a brash modern block of flats between Third Avenue and Second at 76th Street, within brisk walking distance of both Central Park and the UN in midtown Manhattan. I brought back from London a small Sunbeam Rapier Convertible with funny little fins, in two sickly shades of green. Like the old Chevy, the Rapier was constantly breaking down, and spent many days convalescing in an inconvenient workshop across the East River in Queens. But it greatly increased my social range. Though still shy, I found myself quite popular. It was easy to find good beaches on the south shore of Long Island, at other seasons to walk in the wooded hills of upstate New York or to lunch in a particular pub I found at Lumbersville on the Delaware River in Pennsylvania, and we could get back to Manhattan in good time for supper at a restaurant and a film or play. It had been slow in coming, but for the first time all my new friends were girls. The question whether I was in love posed itself at regular intervals. In short, life as a whole perked up. My letters to Tony, like his to me, kept the old tone of modest but unfailing competitiveness:

I like chatting to Hammarskjöld about King Hussein's plane, nodding to Aly Khan on the stairs, even being called 'Doug' by Cabot Lodge. I like going to the theatre twice a week, cheering among the class of '28 at the Harvard–Princeton game, tramping through New Jersey orchards red with apples, driving upstate in my Sunbeam to beagle through fields and woods white with premature snow, skating full of brandy in Central Park. I am nearly in love with a tall serious beautiful girl called Susan – but not quite, and she not at all, so expect to hear no more of it.

But he did.

She speaks what Piers [Dixon, Sir Pierson's son] calls 'Park Avenue Cockney', is really rather splendid. Nothing serious, though. She asked me out to a quiet family lunch the other Sunday, which proved to be quite otherwise. I was driven out there by Cabot Lodge who was so charming that I was persuaded he is almost a great man – and a familiar figure which emerged from the shrubbery proved to be Adlai Stevenson.* There is something very attractive about American upper-class life – the Manet in the drawing room, the hordes of guests for lunch, the strong

---

*Governor of Illinois. A cult figure of the time, widely admired for his wit and generous spirit, Stevenson had opposed the Republican Eisenhower unsuccessfully as Democratic presidential candidate in both 1952 and 1956.

Martinis, the intelligent talk, the beautiful-haired girls, the leafless woods stretching for miles and miles under the hard blue winter sky. Do you have memories of that kind?

In New York itself the most remarkable entertainment came unexpectedly. Rudolf Bing, director of the Metropolitan Opera, was a former British citizen, someone who loved Britain not as the place where he happened to be born but as the country which had welcomed him in distress. Each night of the season he occupied a box at the opera – or more accurately flitted to and fro, in intervals of wrestling with whatever backstage drama that evening had thrown up. He often invited me and other young members of the British Delegation to fill the other seats in the box, sometimes at a few hours' notice. I suppose I went eight or nine times each season. Rudolf Bing was an entertaining but melancholy host. He talked of retiring to a chicken farm in Sussex ('at least I can wring their necks') and of writing a book entitled 'Singers and Other Beasts'. Tony Lloyd in earlier days had done his best to form my musical taste, but could not educate me out of a certain vulgarity which is with me still. I adore the preposterousness of the mad scene of *Lucia di Lammermoor*. Maria Callas sounded like a steam train forcing its way through a tunnel – a slow train given to unexpected pauses. As this was happening, Bing explained to us in the box that the conductor had lost control and was simply waiting helpless for the train to emerge somehow, somewhere from the tunnel. I relished and often play the third act which follows: 'Parte esterna del Castello. Tombe dei Ravenswood, e notte'. It certainly is night. The tenor after long and juicy lamentation stabs himself on the tomb of his ancestors.

In October 1959 Lady Dixon, wife of my ambassador, acquired from England a new social secretary. It was not an entirely easy post. Ismene Dixon was a generous, tempestuous soul, deeply protective of her quiet husband. Her mother was Greek and in Mediterranean fashion she moved quickly from rejoicing to despair. From their big, rather gloomy apartment on Fifth Avenue at 66th Street the Dixons played a central part in the fashionable society of Manhattan, entertaining not just visiting British ministers but such celebrities as the Aly Khan and the Duke and Duchess of Windsor. Constantly revised guest lists, elaborate menus, and the handling of a storm-tossed staff became the responsibility of the new social secretary, Tatiana Eyre. She and I met over the spoons and forks about which Lady Dixon was particular; the inner spoon and fork had to be laid exactly thirteen inches apart, except when the Duke of Windsor was present, when the distance became twenty-one inches. Tatiana, then twenty-four, was new to New York and had never done anything like this before. She was brave throughout, but a little support from the ambassador's private secretary was welcome. The two of us fell in love. For my last eight months in New York my time, the Sunbeam Rapier, the beaches, hills, cinemas and restaurants were at her command. So was Bing's box, when Lisa della Casa unforgettably sang in *Der Rosenkavalier*. We went to Connecticut to stay with friends, a weekend prolonged because the Rapier once again broke down. We penetrated the secretive Barnes Collection of Impressionists in Philadelphia. In 1960 we spent Easter with hospitable cousins of mine outside Milwaukee. It was still cold, but the snow was disappearing and we walked well wrapped up by the glistening lake. By Easter Monday afternoon in our host's garden Tatiana and I were engaged.

In the summer of 1960 the crisis in the Congo began to poison once again the atmosphere of the United Nations. Eventually it was to cost Hammarskjöld his life. I never became closely involved, being preoccupied with farewell. Sir Pierson's long tour had come to an end, and he left New York a fortnight before we did. I sold the Rapier to Tim Rathbone, a young advertising executive, for £450 and happily our friendship survived. A last picnic on Tobay beach, a fond expedition to the Black Bass pub on the Delaware, a final dance at the Waldorf, and on 22 July Tatiana and I sailed on the *Mauretania* for Southampton.

8

LONDON

Privileged visitors enter the Foreign Office by the Ambassadors'
Entrance off St James's Park. Privilege, as sometimes happens in Britain,
is the opposite of splendour. A narrow door gives on to an insignificant
staircase, at the top of which most visitors step left into the main pillared
hall of the Foreign Office, past the memorial plaque to Foreign Service
officers killed by terrorism. One or two of the privileged may instead
walk straight on into a small rectangular anteroom with (in the 1960s)
a coal fire and a window on to the park. This anteroom leads into the
stately office of the permanent under-secretary of state. 'Permanent' does
not imply immortality or even life tenure: the occupant retires at the age
of sixty like every other Foreign Service officer. The title denotes
independence of the ebbs and flows of party politics. The permanent
under-secretary, as the head of the professional Foreign Service, remains
when governments change. He obeys ministers, but is not their creature.
The right relationship between him and the Foreign Secretary should be
one of wary affection based on mutual understanding.

   In that anteroom I worked from 1960 to 1963 as private secretary to
two permanent under-secretaries, Sir Frederick Hoyer Millar (later Lord
Inchyra) and Sir Harold Caccia (later Lord Caccia and provost of Eton).
No one asked me if I wanted the job, it just happened. But I was pleased
to be right at the centre of Foreign Office life. My two masters were
strikingly different, each illustrating one aspect of their office. Sir
Frederick (known to all as Sir Derrick) saw himself mainly as the
guardian of the Foreign Service. He took infinite trouble over postings,
welfare and the distribution of honours. Others with quicker intellects
and more intrusive temperaments could be left to handle policy, draft

instructions, and brief the Foreign Secretary. He kept an eye on these clever men, testing eccentricities for any trace of unsoundness. He seldom intervened in policy matters, but always shrewdly when he thought that intellectual or political excitement was crowding out common sense. At the height of a crisis on Laos he expostulated to me after a talk with the head of the relevant department, 'I could tell by the smell – fellow waltzes in here straight from a night club.' Fresh faced, large but not clumsy, tolerant and old fashioned, Sir Derrick enjoyed himself at the heart of the broad-minded establishment of the day. He would absent himself for hours to attend Ascot, a parade of the Scots Guards, or the annual service of the Order of St Michael and St George. He might leave the office about noon, taking his bowler hat and tightly furled umbrella from their peg in our outer office, and disappear we knew not where. He would return about three, his outdoor cheeks only slightly flushed, and reveal a triumph. He had persuaded Sir Burke Trend, head of the Civil Service, to accept a senior Foreign Office mandarin for some position at home, thus freeing a slot in the ever-crowded queue for Foreign Service promotions. Though he would never quite say this to us in the outer office, his smile would be broader if the person thus exported was not quite of the first quality, or perhaps a shade difficult to handle.

Sir Derrick was on the same wavelength as the new Foreign Secretary, Sir Alec Douglas Home. In late summer he gave us grouse from his Perthshire estate, at Christmas brandy for me and something stylish from Floris for Tatiana. When he left he was honoured with a great dinner at Boodles, fifty-two of the good and great gathered at table. His farewell present to me was a roll of Scottish tweed, the check emphatic but not loud. The jacket made from this material is handsome, indestructible and heavy. In these days of global warming and central heating it can be worn only on cold days between the months of November and March, and then out of doors.

On New Year's Day 1962 Sir Derrick was succeeded by Sir Harold Caccia. Four days later I thought that he would turn out 'a brisker, more interesting, more efficient, less lovable master'. In fact, by the end of my time with each master we had become friends. Caccia worked hard hours and immersed himself in policy. Whereas Sir Derrick was content to let the huge flow of inward and outward telegrams wash twice daily over his desk, Sir Harold constantly intervened. He hated any accumulation of paper, and forwarded it at once. If necessary he shoved it through the door at me within minutes of its arrival with a demand for more information. Physically small, he moved and spoke rapidly, as if every minute was of value.

Sir Harold was not easy in small matters. Like Sir Derrick, he was a man of some means, but unlike Sir Derrick, he was always agitating about money. He expected me, as his private secretary, to run private errands for him across London, to pick up this object and that, to give messages to solicitor or stockbroker. When I had to take a young relative of his to Heathrow to catch a plane to Paris, she urged me to swap her first-class ticket for economy and give her the cash balance. I declined, and felt a boor. Such are the trials of diplomacy. Sir Harold filled his room with heads of deer shot during his time in Vienna. Soon heads arriving from the Scottish Highlands began to crowd this forest. It seemed that the only solution would soon be to mount them on the ceiling, antlers pointing downwards. These same trophies were later displayed in Election Hall at Eton when Sir Harold became provost. There too they were, to put it charitably, a talking point.

But in greater matters Sir Harold was refreshing. His views had been strongly influenced by his time as British Ambassador in Washington. He understood the Americans, he had a clear grasp of political necessities, and was apt to side with ministers against the inherited orthodoxy of officials. For example, he made a stand against the habit of 'nannying', that is the sending of long, pious telegrams to our ambassadors instructing them to advise friendly governments on matters of which those governments knew more than we could.

It was sometimes supposed that mine was a prize job. Certainly it was central; I saw everything and learned a lot. But events and papers moved so fast that I had no time to master any of them. Whereas in New York my superiors had been interested in my advice on UN matters, now my input was not sought on anything. In general my task was that of a lubricator, to make sure that the machine ran smoothly, that the right people saw the necessary papers and were asked to the necessary meetings. My role in great events was procedural; the impressions I received were second hand. Sometimes side-issues flowing from some great matter fell to the PUS and then to me. For example, I watched the Cuba crisis in 1962 and formed at second hand the impression that Prime Minister Harold Macmillan had been irresolute at the crucial moment. The side-issue which I handled was the naïve but genuine attempt of our Berkshire neighbour Godfrey Nicolson MP to promote a dialogue with the Soviet naval attaché, Ivanov, who played a baleful part the following year in the Profumo scandal as one of Christine Keeler's lovers.

In January 1963 de Gaulle vetoed British entry into the European Community and threw into turmoil the main objective of British foreign policy. The tiny slice of the action which came my way concerned royal visits to France, in particular one planned for Princess Margaret. Should we display our solemn displeasure by cancelling the visit? My former master, Sir Pierson Dixon, now British Ambassador in Paris, worked himself up, I wrote, 'into a frenzy of nuances'. Princess Margaret did not go.

A number of small, bizarre matters fell to me as minor residue of the old eighteenth-century system of unaccountable use of public funds for secret purposes. The motives behind the small grants available to the permanent under-secretary tended to be chivalrous rather than sinister. We helped modestly the ancient and inactive representatives in London of Lithuania, Latvia and Estonia, the three Baltic States which had been swallowed up by the Soviet Union twenty years before. More troublesome was our charity towards an Ottoman prince whose family had been rescued from Istanbul by a British warship during the revolution at the end of the Great War. The fact that Lord Curzon had helped them once proved to the head of the family, Prince Samy, that we should help them for ever. His visits and telephone calls took up hours of my time. His Christmas cards were huge, his suits well cut though probably not paid for, his manner dignified, his demands incessant as he perched perpetually on the edge of financial catastrophe. The well-bred words 'Samy here' on the telephone struck gloom into my heart, as into those of my predecessors and successors.

Tatiana and I had been married in St Bartholomew's Smithfield in November 1960. After much casting around and several near misses, we bought 27 Cheyne Row, on the modest side of a modestly elegant Chelsea street. Cheyne Row had been made famous by the house fifty yards away from which Thomas Carlyle had glowered over the world. We were very happy in No. 27.

From Cheyne Row on 12 May 1962 we set off at 3.30 a.m. for the Westminster Hospital, ten days before the due date, after Tatiana had signed her will in the presence of hastily summoned neighbours.

> Sceptically received and sent out to shop disconsolate in the Horseferry Road. Grey cold morning. Eventually T goes in, no more contractions, gloom and almost tears. I (ditto) take car to Brews to charge battery. Back to the hospital where things are starting. Sit with T, first in the corridor, then beside her in the labour room, as dusk gathers and the pain. A bad chop near Victoria and things become tense. I watch Humphrey Bogart in the corridor, and read J Dickson Carr and look at the Vickers Tower and hear Gussie [much loved Norwich terrier] bark below, and T moan and cry. 12.15 a.m. 13/5 son born, 8lb 3oz.

My diary throughout, like most diaries, tends to dwell on mishaps, disagreements, the car breaking down, the pipes freezing. But in the weeks following Nicholas's birth it sounds a note of sustained happiness. Nappies were then of rough cotton with a soft linen strip placed within, secured by huge safety-pins. I changed them quite willingly and often pushed our first born across the bridge and round Battersea Park.

We divided most weekends between Winterbourne Holt and the home of Tatiana's father and stepmother in Sussex. West Burton House looks across a lawn flanked by Irish yews direct on to the South Downs as they rise towards Arundel. It is a place of quiet and beauty, then given a special flavour by the character of my father-in-law, Benedict Eyre. As a dashing young clerk at the Bank of England he had captured the heart of Evelyn Lee, the heiress of the big family house at Hartwell near Aylesbury. Tatiana, their only child, was born at Hartwell. Her parents struggled to make ends meet there, but were compelled to sell at the worst possible time, just before the Second World War. Soon after they moved to West Burton Tatiana's mother died, leaving a shadow over Benedict's life which never entirely lifted, despite his happy second marriage. He was about sixty when I married Tatiana. He had left the Bank of England to become a stockbroker, and was rising to become master of the Grocers Company. (Our wedding had been followed by a reception in Grocers Hall, the company presenting us with a sack of sugar.) Benedict was deeply traditional in his attitude to the City. He hated the changes sweeping through it as liberalisation took hold in the sixties and seventies. The phrase 'verbum meum pactum' was often on his lips. He regarded his clients as friends rather than sources of income, and spent hours advising old ladies on the wisdom of switching a hundred pounds in or out of gilts. Although Benedict's outlook on life, and in particular the future of Britain, was deeply pessimistic, that did not make him dreary. On the contrary, he was generous and hospitable, showing a particular zest for long and cheerful argument over the port with the husbands of his daughter and stepdaughters. We covered a wide agenda of matters sacred and profane. Everything was going downhill, but you could still pass a jolly evening. Throughout my marriage he was a rock of strength and good sense. When he died there was a rent in the lives of those who knew him.

No one of sense can resent being posted to the British Embassy in Rome. When early in 1963 Tatiana and I were told of this next step we were delighted. As a generous gesture Sir Harold Caccia took me in the last days of my service as his private secretary to the signing of the Test Ban Treaty in Moscow. Britain fielded, by our standards, a large delegation, though as usual insignificant compared to the Russians and Americans. I had nothing much to do in Moscow except eat and drink for my country. I enjoyed hobnobbing with the mighty in the Kremlin and the British Embassy across the river. Humphrey Trevelyan was our ambassador; he and his wife welcomed me as an old friend from Peking days. My diary jottings from 3 to 8 August give the flavour.

Caccia not exigent except for mineral water. Like the pinks and yellow of Moscow . . . Leave [the embassy] finally after midnight as Trevelyan and Heath play duets through the window . . . Service in the Ambassador's study looking out over sunny garden and hose playing. The Privy [Ted Heath, Lord Privy Seal] plays the harmonium, the S/State [Home] reads the lesson: a full and hearty congregation . . . with Caccia and Anthony Loehnis to Pasternak's village and grove – a thick storm, then sunny and a lovely gentle valley and church, with women preparing flowers for tomorrow's feast . . . Dinner, Anglo-American . . . By chance sit next to Rusk [US Secretary of State] who is most wise, impressive, and likeable . . . A disappointing day spent hanging about in hot Embassy office while the great shunt to and fro . . . Punctuated by bouts of vast eating . . . Kremlin reception in St George's Hall. This is magnificent white with gold chandeliers and the uncouth crowd of guzzling Soviets underneath . . . Test treaty is signed, Khrushchev speaking small and pink with China in back of his mind, and Rusk and Home like tutelary angels behind him . . . Visit S/State upstairs, naked to waist, unconcerned in blue pyjamas . . . Worried at haphazard way business is done away from home – with Caccia round Tretyakov [museum famous for its icons] esp 3 Rublev angels announcing to Abraham. Excellent Anglo-Russian dinner – talk to Mme Gromyko who is fun [about the modern generation]. 'At her age I was knitting, praying and going with my grandmother, and now my daughter . . .' We left after breakfast on 8 August, seen off by Gromyko in a purple suit.

9

ROME

After my first hour of Roman traffic I surrendered. I parked my green Vauxhall illegally in a square with a big church and sat defeated at the wheel. I had lost all sense of direction and was certain only that I could not contend any longer with that roaring confusion. Fortunately the church was St John in Lateran, and I was quite close to my destination, the British Embassy. That afternoon in September 1963 I learned what no one in London had revealed: that, with all its splendour, Rome, like New York, was uncomfortable for the newcomer.

Practical decisions were elusive. My first task was to find somewhere to live; Tatiana, who had been ill, was to follow with Nicholas three weeks later. On the one hand stood the regulations and the cost ceilings of the Foreign Service; on the other a bevy of fierce Italian countesses and baronesses with apartments to let. On the whole the ladies were harsher than the British regulations. They were eager to show the marble steps, the gilt mirrors and the elegant balcony, but less revealing of the squalid kitchen and tiny lift. Their horror at the thought of a baby and a terrier could only be assuaged by many extra million lira of rent.

The weeks passed vainly. Tatiana, Nicholas and the Norfolk terrier Gussie arrived; we were crowded into a desperate English-owned *pensione* near the Colosseum. Family morale was sinking fast when we finally achieved a smart modern apartment in Parioli, the residential suburb north of the Borghese Park. From time to time, particularly when languishing in traffic, we lamented that we were not living in old Rome, say near the Pantheon or the Piazza Navona, but probably we were wise. Tatiana bought a tiny white Fiat Cinquecento, and learned to fill her eyes with tears when rebuked by police for overambitious driving.

We inherited a notable domestic couple from our predecessors. Francesco, a native of Assisi, was small, quiet and loyal. Somehow he had married a large, well-educated Hungarian with a gaunt face and high pride. At her best Antonietta was affectionate and full of ideas; at other times she stormed and wept. Her aged mother lived at the top of an ancient palazzo across the Tiber in Trastevere. There at Christmas we were lavishly entertained with heavy Hungarian meats and great cakes. Antonietta was much concerned about her health, particularly her migraine and her liver. She introduced us to a health-giving liqueur, Fernet Branca, that I thought was disgusting. We came to dismiss her worries and headaches as the result of temperament. When she fell ill with cancer, of which she later died, we felt deeply sorry. She was marvellous with Nicholas, and with our second son Thomas.

It was my duty last thing at night to take out Gussie for a short walk. He had long ago won all our hearts. The winding, hilly streets of Parioli were quiet at night and routine had made me careless. On Sunday night Gussie was following me without a lead across the via Ximenes. It had been a golden day, spent watching cricket in the park of the Villa Doria. A sports car roared round the corner, up the hill, and Gussie lay inert in the gutter. He made no sound. I carried him up in the lift to Tatiana, heavily pregnant in bed; I could not believe that he was so suddenly gone. Next day I buried him with blanket and collar among the acanthus beside the aqueduct in the embassy garden. Later I placed a stone over him, so that he would not be outclassed by the ambassadorial dogs ornately remembered around him. But there was no space for more sadness. That day Tatiana's contractions began. I took her into the Salvator Mundi Hospital and in Italian style slept that night in a truckle bed by her side. Thomas, my Roman son, was born just before noon the next morning, 22 September 1964: 'I sit in labour room. All smooth and quick and T. eating a steak by 1. Sadness swallowed up.'

My work as first secretary had two main parts: I kept in touch with the Ministry of Foreign Affairs on a range of small matters of interest to both our countries in other parts of the world; and I followed the Italian political scene. I have kept ever since an interest in the labyrinth through which Italian politicians pursue one another. They were as a profession highly subtle and intelligent, to a degree which made most visiting British politicians sound like yokels. But survival, let alone success, required them to spend such a high proportion of their intelligence in internecine combat that not much was left for the problems of Italy. Throughout my time in Rome the Christian Democrat Aldo Moro was Prime Minister, a remarkably long tenture by Italian standards. His immense and convoluted sentences concealed, including perhaps from himself, any clear idea of his conviction or intentions at a particular

time. In general he believed in what is now called 'inclusion', which in
Italy took the form of the '*apertura alla sinistra*', a prolonged flirtation
between left and right. I had enough Italian to read the political
columnists and to gossip over lunches and dinners with the second rank
of politicians in each of the democratic parties, neo-Fascists and
Communists being forbidden fruit. Given a glass of wine, I can still wax
eloquent in Italian on the ideological space and orientation of this or that
Italian political faction. Practical shopping in Italy is best left to my wife.

The drawback of this specialisation in Italian domestic politics was
that no one in the Foreign Office was interested in the results. I would
draft a despatch, for example, on the outcome of the regional elections
in Sicily, ending with a rich analysis of the implication for the present
administration in Rome. My ambassador would initial, then 'sign' it,
and it would travel in due solemnity to the Foreign Office. There it
would be read and again initialled off by some assistant head of
department about my own age. He would rightly judge that a despatch
on that subject was hardly worth the attention of busy under-secretaries,
let alone a minister.

Very occasionally during the three years I spent in Rome I was
involved in something politically interesting. In April 1965 Prime
Minister Harold Wilson paid an official visit, and I went to his talks
with Moro.

> PM dim voiced, but entirely master, and never asks us a question.
> This even more obvious after lunch, on Europe (EEC/EFTA
> bridges) and economics. Moro also impressive and likeable.
> Tatiana invited at last minute to Embassy dinner ... Fidgeting
> about communiqué off and on, and dinner for 44. Moro, Nenni,
> Colombo, Fanfani, La Malfa, Tremelloni etc. Sit next to Oliver
> Wright (Wilson's Private Secretary) who enthuses on Wilson's
> professionalism. Lilac, and asparagus. A success and T. looks fine.

In short, nothing much happened.

In August 1964 the President of the Republic, Signor Segni, lay dying
in the Quirinale Palace. It was a very hot summer. Our ambassador, on
leave in England, was already fussing about arrangements for his return
to attend the funeral. The Segni family decided on one last move, and
sent for the London specialist Lord Brain. For reasons of Italian prestige
his involvement had to be kept secret. I met him at the airport late at
night and drove him in darkness to a side-door of the Quirinale, where
we were met by the President's son and a group of tired doctors. Lord
Brain left the next morning; the President lingered on for some weeks;
the secret was kept.

Although I did not have an interesting job in Rome, I thoroughly enjoyed the office in which I did it. At that time the embassy worked alongside the big Villa Wolkonsky in which the ambassador lived (and still lives). This house and big surrounding garden had belonged to the Germans. The swimming pool had been built on Hitler's orders, allegedly because the Führer was constantly irritated by his ambassador's summer absences. After the war the British seized the Wolkonsky; our own embassy two miles away near the Porta Pia had been blown up by Palestinian terrorists. Several of the huts in the grounds which we used as offices had been the Gestapo headquarters, in which it was said terrible things had been done. My own office was in the oldest house in this private park, built to embrace the Roman aqueduct which ran through the garden. Looking down the aqueduct over cypresses, olives, Roman sculptures and inscriptions, spring flowers and later roses and oranges, I found it was an ideal place to savour the Roman seasons.

My ambassador, Sir John Ward, holding his last post before retirement, was bored and exasperated with almost everything to do with diplomatic life. He could not be bothered with the comings and goings between governments which had once enthused him. Sometimes he ignored what was going on; at other times he threw himself and us into a confused tumult, calling unnecessary meetings on a Sunday, drafting and redrafting, failing to distinguish the important points from the insignificant. But once outside Rome, Sir John was a changed man. He knew Italy well; his love for her took the form of devoted knowledge. He used to take me with him on his perambulations. In a city like Lucca or Bologna (and there are dozens of such cities in Italy) he would hobnob with the prefect, understand exactly what to say in his calls on the archbishop and the mayor, tell the story of the local saint, visit the gallery, buy the wine, and enthuse knowledgeably over the city's history under Guelf or Ghibelline. In short he behaved like a perfect ambassador of the old school. Only when his steps turned perforce back towards Rome and the paperwork from all those pretentious asses in the Foreign Office did he resume the scowl which he used for the transaction of normal business. Tatiana and I became very fond of him and of his wife Daphne. They were at all times generous to us, and we came to relish their company.

One of my duties was to take the minutes of the Governing Body of the British Institute of Florence, a cultural body which jealously kept its independence from the British Council and was chaired by the British Ambassador. The meetings provided a fine amphitheatre for the British personalities of Tuscany. Sir Osbert Sitwell came down from his eyrie to attend, but was already painfully beset by Parkinson's disease. The institute's director, Ian Greenlees, handled us with the feline subtlety of a Renaissance politician; he liked his problems complicated. Here I first made the acquaintance of Harold Acton, who generously provided the institute with new premises on the Arno after we were displaced from the Palazzo Antinori. He entertained us at his home, the Villa Pietra, with anecdotes of Oxford and Peking. There was just a touch of malice lurking in these stories. They were pronounced in an Etonian voice of the 1920s with much emphasis on the consonants, so that Ravenna and Vienna each seemed to have three 'n's. Harold Acton showed us without boasting that a real Italian garden was noted for its shapes and architecture rather than for vulgar colours. There could be no herbaceous border in the Villa Pietra.

The festivals of Rome became familiar. Tatiana particularly enjoyed the Horse Show in the Borghese Gardens, azaleas full out around the ring, the British and Italians in civilised contest, the sun pleasantly warm on glossy coats and trim uniforms. Opera in Rome was not famous, but I kept Tony Lloyd informed as my musical mentor:

Rome is on the up and up . . . This year the Embassy box has been for Sunday afternoons, a hopeless time. I have only seen three, of which one Italian – a mediocre *Fidelio*, admirable *Boris G[odunov]* with Christoff, and a splendid early Verdi, *Attila*, hairy Huns thwarted by virtuous Roman maiden and aged Pope, the sort of stuff which when first done had the patriotic audience in an uproar of enthusiasm. There's one scene when Attila negotiates with the tenor, a Roman, for a territorial settlement and the tenor bangs the table and at the top of his voice 'Let Attila take the world, but leave Italy to me' – imagine the cheers, and the Austrian Governor glowering from his box.

For the general public the great operatic occasion each summer was *Aida* performed in the open before a huge audience at the Baths of Caracalla. A loud cheer was raised each evening at the sound of the lorries from the zoo as they arrived backstage to decant the necessary camels for the great parade.

In August for two summers running we moved some twenty miles to the bluff on the far shore of Lake Albano, looking across to the Pope summering at Castel Gandolfo. The English College, which trains English candidates for the Catholic priesthood, owned the big villa, and let out part of it and a gatehouse to fellow countrymen. We had some difficulty with Antonietta and Francesco, who were essentially urban characters. Antonietta particularly disliked the insects, up to the size of hornets, which despite window screens and scented coils blundered round the lamps in the evening. But the cool air, the sensational view, and the company of other children for Nicholas suited our needs. I commuted in to work each day. Much of the organisation around us was in the hands of Donald and Catherine Cape, from the British Embassy to the Holy See. The flavour of entertainment was not so much incense and candles as Scrabble and charades. As August wore on the weather began to break; massive stormclouds formed, lumbered towards us across the lake, and dissolved in thunder and lightning.

There seemed no end to pleasant escapes from the routines of Rome: Capri, still under the domination of Gracie Fields, Amalfi out of season with the frozen palm fronds rustling in the wind, the Cala Piccola, a comfortable hotel scattered in the rocks of the Argentario peninsula much beloved of Tatiana's father and stepmother. We took a seaside house on Elba for three weeks which began and ended stickily. Tatiana and I had gone ahead in her Fiat by the ferry from Piombino to make ready, leaving Francesco to drive Nicholas and Antonietta in the Vauxhall next day. They were due in the early afternoon. The villa had no telephone. I can still in my mind's eye see the white road curving round the rocky hillside towards us, visible for more than a mile from the villa terrace. I watched that empty road for hour after hour as the sunlight shifted, softened, began to fade. No Vauxhall, no Nicholas. Finally we drove to a public telephone in Porto Azzurro and rang the embassy. There had been a crash on the via Aurelia north of Rome. The Vauxhall had been put out of action, but no one was hurt. We reorganised ourselves and the holiday got under way. After it ended I fell into angry correspondence with the Englishwoman who owned the villa. She alleged that Nicholas aged two (who has led a blameless life throughout the years) had committed an indiscretion in his bed just before leaving. I denied this firmly. My stand was weakened by the fact that I had left behind in the villa a stiff brown notebook containing part of the manuscript of *The Arrow War*, which was at last almost ready for the publisher. I had no copy, but hoped the exigent landlady did not know this. Eventually she wearied of persecution and returned the notebook.

Our most successful holiday took place in a large white farmhouse at Nugola, a hamlet in gentle hills inland from Pisa. Those three weeks contained all that I like best of Italy: the lengthening shadows of cypresses across rough grass which an old man came to scythe very slowly; a fig tree from which the midday sun drew its distinctive smell; high-ceilinged white bedrooms with mosquito nets; long ropes of onions on the outside walls; shy red deer beyond the fence; Nicholas and Thomas healthily tanned; a spotted umbrella under which, with a small cigar, I read the proofs of *The Arrow War* and then *Hadrian the Seventh*, *Trilby* and *Memories of a Catholic Girlhood*. Much simple food and local wine; a stream of visitors; frequent alarms about the impending exhaustion of the bottled gas canister or 'bombola' on which cooker and hot water depended; expeditions to the beach, to San Gimignano, Volterra and the Leaning Tower. Sir John had asked me to deliver a case of whisky to the journalist and former Independent MP Vernon Bartlett who lived the other side of a mountain near Lucca. We drank copiously in the farmstead which he had bought and converted for his retirement – a house, La Cappellina, which became more familiar to me later in almost yearly holiday visits from England as the guests of Dennis and Bridgett Walters.

In 1965 our days were enlivened by the arrival at the embassy of Andrew Osmond and his American wife Stuart. The four of us quickly became close friends. Andrew, eight years younger than me, was in part of his nature a rebel, though he held no left-wing views. He had helped to found *Private Eye* at Oxford; among his friends were all the leading young satirists of the sixties, fast building their reputations. But Andrew was not essentially a critic; his instincts throughout his life were to create. He liked firm, witty speech, quick decisions, and clear-cut achievements. Neither the world of satire nor, as it turned out, the Foreign Office, filled his requirements. Meanwhile, he was excellent company. One August I walked with him up and down the corridors of the Blue Sisters' Hospital talking of life and death while a storm blew outside. Within, Stuart was in labour with their first born, Matthew. Next summer we shared a beach house with the Osmonds at Sabaudia.

By then Andrew and I had taken a decision which over the years gave us much pleasure. One evening we sat in the lobby of the Hotel Minerva in Florence waiting for Sir John Ward. This was not an unusual occupation, but Andrew found it (like most of diplomatic life) difficult to bear patiently. As we reflected that neither of us had enough to do, we stumbled on the idea of writing a thriller together. I already had a publisher, Andrew a zest for journalism. Out of that conversation emerged three joint political thrillers on the trot: *Send Him Victorious* (1968), *The Smile on the Face of the Tiger* (1969) and *Scotch on the Rocks* (1971); and eventually a fourth, *War without Frontiers* (1982).

Writing with Andrew was both a great amusement and a stern test of friendship. Our literary styles were different. My sentences were by nature about twice the length of his; he had never heard of the semicolon. He was stronger than I into sex and violence; I tried to conjure interest out of politicians and bureaucracies. We accepted the essential principle that each had the right to censor the other's work. We began each book by spending hours together working out a plot, and dividing the responsibility of writing the different sections. Inevitably that initial sketch changed as we went along. One of us might discover a hole in the plot; or we might find that our concepts of a crucial character were beginning to diverge. Although we both ended up living in Oxfordshire, there were times when we were separated by hundreds of miles. My cupboards contain boxes of notebooks and letters in Andrew's elegant hand, ingenious and impatient, sometimes exulting, sometimes in despair. The thrillers were more important to Andrew than to me as he developed into a full-time writer. But they were an exciting part of my life too, during years which otherwise had dreary patches. They are good to reread, and it is fun that each still has a select band of admirers.

Andrew died of a brain tumour in 2000. After we had stopped producing thrillers we saw less of each other, but were always in touch. Without his inspiration I would not have developed the taste for writing which has remained with me. There is always a danger that middle age will make someone like myself stodgy and humourless. To the extent that the danger was averted in the sixties and seventies, this was largely the result of my friendship with Andrew.

In February 1966 my parents flew to Antigua for a holiday. My father, then sixty-five, had for some time been wheezy and short of breath. On the flight he found it difficult to settle down and breathe normally and when they reached their hotel in St John he took to his bed. After a day or two the doctor broke the news to my mother that he was in serious danger. What had seemed a passing inconvenience at the start of a holiday became a mortal illness. He died on 12 February. My mother, alone on an unfamiliar island, had to make all the arrangements. My father is buried across the road from the Anglican Cathedral at St John.

I flew back from Rome to meet my mother at Heathrow and take her back to Winterbourne Holt. Over that spring and summer the lawyers and accountants were busy, and Winterbourne Holt was sold. Mamma spent the remaining nineteen years of her life in a medieval house in Oare Village, half a mile down the hill from our old home at Rainscombe. She and my father had bought the Old Oxyard from the historian G.M. Young as an eventual place of retirement for them both.

The sadness which she and all of us felt at my father's death was tempered by a sense of calm. The loss of his two brothers in the Great War and of Julian thirty-five years later were the tragedies in an otherwise ordered, peaceful and happy life. My father had no enemies. In an unpretentious way he had helped hundreds of people with advice and encouragement, and enjoyed himself along the way. He gave quiet, substantial service to British farming, to the House of Commons, and to the counties of Wiltshire and Berkshire, in a style which he himself would not have thought remarkable but which is now rare.

Without his advice I began to consider my own future path, as my time in Rome came to an end. If I was to change careers, now was the hour. I had no grievance against the Foreign Service: Peking, New York, Rome – there could be no ground of complaint against my postings. My seniors from time to time muttered encouragement about my prospects, and I supposed that before I retired at sixty I was likely to achieve one of the important embassies. But I was thirty-six, and immediately before me stretched an arid decade or two for most of which I would hold subordinate positions probably as in Rome with not quite enough to do. It began to look as if my posting would be to Santiago. I had nothing whatever against Chile, by all accounts a friendly and beautiful country, but it corresponded to no existing experience or interest of mine, and was a long way away. Tatiana had mastered in Rome the arts of a Foreign Office wife. But, having formed the impression that most ambassadresses became slightly dotty under the pressure of the job, she had no ambition to follow them.

I began to write letters and to talk quietly to those who might advise, including Warburgs in the City, and Lord Netherthorpe, chairman of Fisons. The General Election of 1966, though soundly lost by the Conservatives, reminded me of my old enthusiasm to enter Parliament. Though I had suppressed the political fever, it was still there. I wrote to Ted Heath, then Leader of the Opposition, whom I had met once or twice in my father's company and elsewhere, asking if he had anything to suggest. Whereas others replied to me by letter after a decent pause, Ted sent a peremptory telegram requesting me to meet Sir Michael Fraser, the senior mandarin in Conservative Central Office. I was impressed. '6–7 July. London – cool, green, welcoming. To see Tories – M. Fraser in Smith Square, Sewill [Brendan Sewill, head of Conservative Research Department] in Old Queen Street. All falls easily into place, pay, time, etc. – so I'm OFF and OUT. Much relieved. Stay with Tony and Jane [Lloyd] and walk the Strand at Chiswick.' I was offered and accepted the number-two job in the Foreign Affairs Section of the Research Department. There was no proper pay structure; Sir Michael simply matched my existing Foreign Office salary. Pensions could not be transferred in those days, but that consideration was remote. The Foreign Office tried to dissuade me from the leap. A senior under-secretary, Evelyn Shuckburgh, was about to succeed Sir John Ward in Rome and had grown a beard to celebrate his promotion. He took me aside and remonstrated solemnly. I liked and admired Shuckburgh but was not swayed. I was about to jump on to a lowly rung of the political ladder. I knew that this ladder swayed a good deal in the breeze; but it was the ladder I wanted to climb.

We spent a vivid last summer and autumn in Italy, usually in the company of the Osmonds. With them we watched the Palio in Siena, and swam often near Rome at Fregene and Sabaudia. The climax came in October with the British Week in Florence. Andrew was despatched in advance to help our consul, Christopher Pirie Gordon, with the mammoth task of organisation. They were completely opposite characters. Christopher, an experienced Arabist, was, in the logic of the Foreign Service, moving towards the end of his career in an agreeable house across the Arno in Florence. His main task was to keep the British community happy. This involved reading Trollope to the elderly, and at a higher social level keeping within limits the feuds between the rival English hostesses, each with her store of gossip and her villa on a hillside above the city. Christopher was a pipe-smoker, slow and gentle, a bringer of courtesies and goodwill. Andrew was much younger, quick and sometimes peremptory. The two men did not mesh. By the time I reached Florence for the week itself Andrew was pale with exhaustion. He hurried around Florence in a white mackintosh and dark glasses, looking like a French detective, snapping out tense instructions, sometimes close to despair.

The concept of a British Week was bizarre in its ambition. Every aspect and eccentricity of British life had to be included in the programme. The Manchester United football team, Henry Moore, the Duke of Bedford, the model Jean Shrimpton, a Pearly King and Queen, the Lord Provost of Edinburgh, a minister from the Board of Trade, an array of Scottish pipers – all of these regarded themselves as notable visitors who required individual programmes suited to their tastes and last-minute preferences. We stayed in a *pensione* near the Ponte Vecchio, full of dark furniture and Siamese cats. The main task of Tatiana and myself was to keep our ambassador calm and prevent him countermanding arrangements already made. We hugely enjoyed ourselves. A few weeks later the destructive floods swept through the city.

As soon as the Week was over I drove Tatiana and the two boys to Naples and put them on the P & O liner *Oriana* bound for home. I spent a final ten days clearing up in Rome. Inevitably I had a fierce argument with our landlady the countess, who sniffed her way round our flat, noting as a scandal every stain or scratch made over three years by us, two small children and a terrier, and demanding horrific damages. I stayed finally with the Osmonds in the Piazza di Spagna, taking pills to keep the noise of traffic at bay. Andrew too was about to leave the Foreign Service. Then on to the Wagon Lits and home: 'Not sorry to leave and start afresh.'

PART III

BACKROOM POLITICS

10

CONSERVATIVE RESEARCH DEPARTMENT

In 1966 the Conservative Research Department had not yet been swallowed up in the ungainly embrace of Central Office in Smith Square. Proud of its intellectual independence, the Research Department kept its distance in two elegant Georgian houses in Old Queen Street, from which the Cockpit Steps lead down into St James's Park. I was allocated an office in No. 38, where a small section handled foreign affairs and defence. Traditionally, when the Conservative Party was in opposition, the Research Department exercised important influence over strategy and policy-making. In practice our output from No. 38 was pretty dreary. We serviced the weekly meetings of the Parliamentary Foreign Affairs Committee; there I began a long friendship with its secretary, the MP for Westbury, Dennis Walters. We produced a dull little review of world affairs, and briefing papers as needed by our front bench.

The department operated as an autonomous satrapy under the benign and powerful protection of Sir Michael Fraser, respected by all during these years as the Grand Vizier of the Conservative Party. An expert on wine, opera and Tory Party history, Michael would have made a first-class permanent secretary of a Whitehall department. He was not innovative but tolerant, even encouraging of the ideas of others. He believed in political integrity, order and unity. His tall, military frame and quietly authoritative voice helped him to achieve these in the enterprises which he conducted. Intellectually the Research Department was on a plateau, not soaring as in the past when Enoch Powell, Ian Macleod and Reggie Maudling had worked there, or as in the future when Chris Patten was to take control. In 1966 Ted Heath preferred to operate with his own teams, rather than use the formal structure of the department.

Sir Michael had implied when I was recruited that I was to be part of Ted Heath's team. It was characteristic of the way the party worked that my position was never spelled out. This was embarrassing for me in the hierarchy of Old Queen Street. Unlike others senior to me, I was summoned at irregular intervals to Ted's apartment at Albany, where I found his speech writer, Michael Wolff, and the young economist Brian Reading. Our first meeting in December 1966 consisted mainly of coffee, chocolate biscuits and silences. It gradually emerged that Ted regarded us as his inner cabinet in continental style, alongside the head of his office, John Macgregor. We were there to make original comments on the events of the day, to bat ideas to and fro in his presence, and to comment frankly on his own thoughts about the future as they struggled to birth. In preparation for these sessions at Albany we three used to meet at the Italian restaurant Vitello d'Oro at the side of Church House in Westminster.

Brian Reading was intellectually unconventional. He analysed each economic question from its origins up, not bothering with whatever conventional wisdom had gathered round it before it caught his attention. Brian was not at ease when required to adjust his ideas to the political needs of the day; it was precisely the freshness of his approach which had caught Ted's attention. Michael Wolff had known Ted for several years already, and educated me into his ways. After a few months I came to share exactly Michael's attitude to Ted. We were alternately exasperated and entertained, but inwardly admiring and for that reason firmly loyal. Michael, by profession a journalist, had acquired a benevolent but weary knowledge of the world of politics and the media which far surpassed mine. Whereas I started on every task almost as soon as I was set it, Michael waited to be stimulated by the close approach of a deadline. Whereas I was in those days of apprenticeship easily agitated by bad news or the approach of a crisis, Michael taught me the advantages of a philosophic mind. Whereas I was somewhat puritan in my personal tastes, Michael believed that much good could come from dinner at Pruniers with a large cigar.

Sometimes we were called as a group to Ted's family home at Broadstairs, shared by his father and stepmother. We would walk round the harbour, inspect the boats and visit the pubs. Ted, in jeans and polo-neck sweater, would tease us for our city suits and black briefcases. We might dine at the Albion Hotel before catching the last train back to Charing Cross. Ted speculated about de Gaulle's intentions, reminisced about cabinet meetings in the past, or posed fundamental questions: what, for example, in terms of the domestic well-being of the citizen, would follow the washing machine?

But mainly we wrestled with the embarrassments which beset Ted during this period. He had been chosen to lead the party in 1965 because of his reputation as a tough negotiator and his thoroughly professional approach to politics. Although he had lost the General Election of March 1966, it had seemed almost inevitable then that Harold Wilson would be given a clear majority after his narrow win in 1964, and Ted was credited with fighting a good campaign. But his leadership of the party was slow to take off. He was quickly criticised for being socially difficult, monosyllabic, dull, aloof. Europe was not a big issue in 1966 and 1967, but the party was bitterly divided on Rhodesia. The Conservatives began to do well in by-elections, but Ted's personal ratings were stubbornly low.

Each party conference became for him a test, not of success but of survival. The test passed, he enjoyed a good press for a few weeks until the carping started again. This unhappy cycle depressed us more than it did him. He did not allow the tactical needs of the moment to smother his preparation for the premiership which he was determined to achieve.

In April 1968 Enoch Powell, then handling defence in the Shadow Cabinet, made his dramatic speech about immigration. Looking back, I find that my views were then less liberal than they later became. On 22 April: 'Storm in the Party. EH sacks Powell for race speech. A pity, tho' justified by his lurid language and general obstinacy . . . Pity because EH and leadership were just beginning to realise hollowness of liberal opinion-forming consensus and ready to break away from it. Telegrams, letters etc. pour in, all pro-Powell, have angry telephone call in the same sense from Benedict [my father-in-law, to whom I was devoted].' Then, the next day: 'Storm on. 3,000 letters litter EH's desk. All for Powell. Efforts to whip in the left . . . EH relaxed, tired.'

John Macgregor had before this decided to leave the job of running the Leader of the Opposition's office for a position in the City. The job was offered to me by Jim Prior, who, as his parliamentary private secretary and firm friend, exercised more influence on Ted at this time than any other individual. Jim combined the bluff straightforwardness of a Suffolk farmer with considerable political guile. He had been encouraged in his early days in the Commons by my father, and found it natural in turn to encourage me. In the years which followed I could always rely on him for unflustered advice. In April 1968 John Macgregor was away and I handled the job temporarily while I (and presumably Ted) considered whether I should commit myself for two or three years up to the next General Election. My immediate task was to go with Ted on a long-planned tour of the West Midlands, Enoch Powell's home territory. The tour began three days after Powell's dismissal, and was fraught. Throughout I felt clumsy and gauche. I blamed myself for the fact that we caught the train at Euston by only one minute. I realised later that Ted liked to tease trains (which he regarded as old fashioned) by daring them to leave before he arrived. I lost necessary papers, often felt that I was saying the wrong thing in the wrong place at the wrong time, and on the first evening wrote that I was almost sure that I didn't want the job and wouldn't do it well. Rugby, Birmingham, Gloucester, Kidderminster, Dudley, Birmingham again – at least a dozen functions were packed into three days. We were followed by massive cohorts of press and television.

The tour was supervised by two remarkable local potentates, using power which their successors do not possess now in this age of rather ineffective political centralisation. Jack Galloway, the Central Office agent for the West Midlands, operating from a humble office in Leamington, ruled through force of character over every Conservative manifestation in his area. Not a parliamentary candidate was selected, not a local by-election arranged, hardly a mouse stirred in the West Midlands without Jack's sardonic approval. That week he organised a meeting for Ted with local government leaders from across the West Midlands in the City Hall, Birmingham. We met under the solemn gaze of the three Chamberlains – Joe, Austen and Neville – who had transformed the city into a fortress of local enterprise The influence of the portraits perhaps helped the masterly chairmanship of Alderman Griffin, who as Conservative Leader of the Council ruled Birmingham with an authority now vanished from city halls across the land. I got to know him and other city leaders well over the next few years; they were still an important part of the body politic. Alderman Griffin was of modest height, and walked with a stick. I never heard him raise his voice; he had no need.

In Dudley we set up camp in the Station Hotel. A big crowd of Powell's supporters gathered outside the meeting hall. They shouted and jostled the police, but in the hall itself we were helped by an extremist who shouted so offensively that the audience rallied to Ted. That Saturday afternoon, and throughout the tour, Ted rarely rose to eloquence. He doggedly ploughed through figures of schools and hospitals, and dealt only defensively with immigration. He thoroughly disliked the subject, at this stage was not clear about the right course, and refused to make policy on the hoof. After two tea parties in Dudley, we spent an hour and a half consuming gin and crisps in the ghastly Bull Ring at Birmingham. Everywhere there was tension, but except at Dudley it never broke into the open. Ted's persistence and hard work with party members was beginning to have its effect. 'Back in train . . . drop him dead tired at Albany. I think he's scotched Enoch for the moment.'

I came home from that first tour undecided whether to accept the job of running the Leader of the Opposition's office. It would certainly be fascinating, and I already liked and respected Ted. But what I really wanted was a parliamentary seat. I was on the list of candidates approved by Central Office, and had been interviewed unsuccessfully for the by-elections at Meriden and New Forest. If I took the job with Ted, I would have to give up that ambition until after the General Election, since he needed someone who would stay at his side through that campaign. It seemed sensible to try my hand once more for a seat before deciding. I reached the semi-finals of the selection process at Hendon South, a reasonably safe Conservative seat in North London. At the end of June 1968 I sallied forth with Tatiana to the ballroom of the Brent Bridge Hotel, just beyond the North Circular Road. The Conservative activists, predominantly Jewish in character, were very friendly. They laughed and clapped at my sallies against the Government; we drove back to Cheyne Row with high hopes. Just before eleven in the evening the association chairman rang to say sorry, the seat had gone to the ex-MP and future Party Chairman, Peter Thomas. That clinched it; on 25 June I told Jim Prior that I accepted the job with Ted. 'Still dislike the hecticness and administration, but will be reconciled. Can't afford to sit about waiting for seat which won't come. So, long evenings again.'

The workload did indeed prove daunting. On one day when I was still overlapping with John Macgregor I looked through the first incoming post and threw into the wastepaper basket a lot of paper which seemed to me pointless. When I returned from lunch I found that John had rescued these crumpled rejects and carefully smoothed them out for further consideration. I learned from his meticulous care, at least until I could make my own judgements out of experience.

By mid-July 'am partly scared of the immense weight of administration falling on me. Meetings all day, and the night left for dictating letters. E.g. Friday, when I get [home] at 11, spoiled dinner, furious wife, having been two and a half hours with EH at YC leaders, and leaving a mass of work undone . . . There must be an adjutant, like unpopular whizzkid Jeffrey Archer.' I had already given Jeffrey Archer lunch at the Travellers, and came away thinking that he could be a lot of help. I realise now that he would not have been content with the job of my adjutant, answering letters and handling routine. I was saved from what would have been a bumpy ride by a message from the Party Chairman, Lord Carrington, that I was to proceed no further with this idea. Eventually I chose Cyril Townsend, just out of the army, who did the job admirably and later became MP for Bexleyheath. Jeffrey Archer followed a different career.

The routine of handling correspondence, composing Ted Heath's diary and organising shadow cabinet meetings was shared among a small team, squashed into a small anteroom to a House of Commons office. There were welcome variations in the form of trips abroad, and Ted's increasing emphasis on preparation for government. The informal chats at Albany with Michael Wolff and Brian Reading continued, but the main breaks in London routine were forays into the constituencies. Ted was making himself known in an almost continuous and countrywide campaign. For the first time I was educated into the character of my own country, city by city, county by county. We visited an oil rig in Aberdeen: 'Usual worries, leave black bag behind, too many press officers etc. Rig is incomprehensible, white overalls, helmets, misty sun, in and out of machinery.'

Through these years I developed a wry affection for the notables of the Scottish Conservative Party, who referred to themselves as 'office bearers'. Nice men with an excessive regard for hierarchy, they presided over a declining party with scant regard for what was happening in Scotland outside their own playground. In May 1968 Ted had committed the party to a Scottish Assembly in the Declaration of Perth. In September he visited them again. 'Dinner for the notables to sound off against the Assembly notion. This they do feebly, a poor lot, as the malt goes round.' They had an alternative vision: 'Relieve surtax and appeal to the common man.'

A week later we were in the Hull fishdock at dawn, followed by an immense speech on immigration in York. The audience listened in amazed silence as Ted took them through a detailed policy statement which led three years later to the Immigration Act 1971. Later that autumn I record a wet Saturday in Swansea, a trip to Manchester, Oldham, Preston and the ancient splendours of the Adelphi Hotel, Liverpool, now sadly devalued. Ted spoke in St George's Hall near by. I had already learned that speeches were more likely to succeed in huge Victorian halls than in modern centres with dull acoustics calculated for music not resonant human speech. Thirty years ago the audiences were still there for mass meetings. In St George's Hall that evening they sang 'Land of Hope and Glory', standing to attention. Next day we watched Manchester City beat Burnley 7–0, then 'a round of very cheerful and alcoholic progresses, Macclesfield (2), Stockport and Wilmslow. EH on and on and on, never superb, always adequate, sometimes good. Sleeper 0025.'

At the other end of England, the tone was different. In June 1969 we spent a night at Fonthill in Wiltshire with Lord Margadale, a former chairman of the 1922 Committee and a Tory grandee, who displayed his wisdom in monosyllables and many chuckles. We drank too much whisky from his Scottish island Islay, and set out with a slight hangover around noon next day. Michael Wolff had by then worked out a speech for the afternoon among the racing papers in Lord Margadale's study. We drank sherry some two miles further on with Anthony Eden (by then Lord Avon), admired his Monet and his Corot, and arrived in reasonable time for the Conservative fête at Crichel Down. Our hostess, Mrs Marten, dominant in emeralds, entertained us to lunch while the park and garden filled with the faithful, 4,500 of whom were brought in by bus and car from all over Dorset. Clouds began to threaten, then miraculously dispersed. A band played under the portico; it seemed that the house itself was broadcasting a martial message of encouragement to cedars, chapel and lake. Ted gave the crowd a solid fifty minutes in the sunshine, after which there were long queues for tea. This was the kind of Conservative occasion familiar to me on a smaller scale from my childhood, and I was enthusiastic.

Everyone who knew Ted understood that one of his main aims was to lead Britain into the European Community. The veto with which de Gaulle in 1963 frustrated the entry negotiations that Ted had conducted had strengthened his determination. As Leader of the Opposition, he kept in close touch with European politicians and in particular Jean Monnet, who from time to time held court, apple-cheeked and friendly, in the Hyde Park Hotel. In January 1969 'dozens of oysters with Monnet at Albany. A wise and nice old man powered by optimism, but not in the fairyland inhabited by the F.O. etc. of new communities conjured up by resolution.'

This sour note reflected a sharp disagreement between Ted and the Foreign Office about tactics that had already been brewing for two years. Labour ministers had been persuaded to lodge a proposal for British membership. Ted was sure that Britain could enter the EEC only by persuading the French and this was the tactic which eventually succeeded in 1971. But the Foreign Office under Labour believed that we could succeed by rallying the other five existing members against France. The five, it was thought, could in the end force de Gaulle or his successor to lift the French veto. The view was urged on me at a series of private lunches with John Robinson, then in the middle rank of Foreign Office officials, and outstanding for wit, forceful opinion, and total resolve on behalf of a united Europe. We met at the Colombina d'Oro in Soho. I always ordered *penne alla rustica*, a spicy dish apt for the mixture of gossip and eloquence which made up John's conversation. He was superb in that job, but he was not a conciliator, and his later appointments as British Ambassador to Algiers and then Tel Aviv seemed exactly unsuited to his talents. This tactical dispute broke into the open at a big European conference in the Hague in November 1968, at which both Ted and the Foreign Secretary, George Brown, made speeches. Ted declared that it was pointless to try to isolate France, since there could be no Europe without France. This was a politically incorrect view. I was furiously rebuked in the conference foyer by Nicholas Barrington of the Foreign Office. Peter Kirk, Duncan Sandys and other Conservative pro-European stalwarts were also sad – and wrong.

My main recollection of that conference was of Harold Macmillan, then thoroughly enjoying his long Indian summer. He travelled out in the plane with us and a delegation of MPs, but did not enjoy their company. Eventually he was given a good lunch at the Hotel des Indes, surrounded by a crowd of young admirers. He chatted for an hour, regaling us with anecdotes about Churchill, soon to appear in the volume of his autobiography on which he was working. He liked to mix gossipy epigrams with philosophical questions. One minute in the context of the then Duke of Montrose's opinions on Rhodesia, he told us that Lowland dukes were well known to be the lowest form of intellectual life. The next moment we were asked to consider whether the Russians had for ever abandoned the age of faith. Throughout this discourse, Ted Heath, though leader of his party and surrounded by young people whom he needed to impress, acted entirely as a disciple, prompting Macmillan and urging him on, without intruding opinions of his own. The two men were wholly different in character and background. Ted sometimes criticised Macmillan in private – for example, on the way he had handled the Cuba crisis or the discussion with Kennedy at Nassau about the nuclear deterrent. But Macmillan had given Ted his chance to rise, and that was not forgotten. Anyway, Ted relished the old gentleman's company, and there was a genuine affection between them.

In 1968 the Labour Government announced a firm date for the withdrawal of the British military presence east of Suez. There were no particular local pressures on us to withdraw; the reasoning was economic. The Raj was long gone and the British Empire mutated into a commonwealth of independent states. Our economy was in continuous difficulty. It made no sense, so it was argued, to maintain in the Gulf and in Singapore a military presence designed to protect assets which were no longer ours and trade routes which were not at risk. The official world in London, like the economists and most politicians, accepted this analysis. Enoch Powell, until 1968 shadow spokesman on defence, strongly agreed. One might have expected Ted to do the same, given his belief in Britain's European vocation. Instead he reacted violently and spent much energy in opposition trying to frustrate the planned withdrawal. His reasoning was best set out at Bristol on 16 January 1970, in a speech in which I had a hand. Indeed, I was strongly and sentimentally attached to the far-flung deployment of British troops. I believed that we should continue in this way to serve our own interests and the stability of the Middle East and South East Asia.

Ted's efforts to keep the British military presence east of Suez were not restricted to speeches at home. He took me with him on two massive overseas tours with this as the central cause. I thoroughly enjoyed in particular the visit to the Gulf in March 1969, which gave me rich experience for later use.

A briefing session before we left London was a disaster. Ted exploded in the face of Geoffrey Arthur, a senior Foreign Office official with much experience and a reputation for plain speech. The Foreign Office was accused of feebleness and bad faith. We were clearly set for a stormy ride. The advance planning of the practical arrangements became a nightmare. Even with the help of a plane from British Petroleum for part of the journey it was almost impossible to produce a credible piece of paper showing how in thirteen days we could get to grips with Iran, Kuwait, Bahrain, Oman, all the main Trucial States of the Gulf, Saudi Arabia, Egypt and Israel. Yet somehow we did.

The paper travel plan was destroyed at the outset. We were sitting in a plane at Heathrow waiting for take-off when the Iranian Ambassador bustled aboard to say that the Shah was going to Washington for General Eisenhower's funeral and would thus be out of the country while we were in it. It was a bad blow, for it had seemed essential to know the Shah's mind before we set off round the Gulf. But it was too late to change plans. In Tehran my head became rapidly congested with spring dust, and I felt low and inadequate. We were lavishly entertained by the Foreign Minister and despatched for similar treatment in Shiraz and Isfahan, including a trip by helicopter to Persepolis. Then we flew to the south coast and Kharg Island – 'formerly convicts and gazelles, now a vast jetty and tankers and a supermarket and computers and hideousness, plus the Prime Minister, who turns out unexpectedly to have chosen the island for his holiday home and gives us all buffet lunch, sailors patrolling the scrub outside'. Then Prime Minister Hoveyda was cheerful and friendly, like all the Iranians who received us, but there was no way, in the absence of the Shah, of pinning them down to a clear view of Britain's role in the Gulf.

Two days in Kuwait followed. The members of the ruling family were soft in manner, intelligent and sceptical. Conscious that they ruled a rich, tiny and vulnerable country, they above all wanted to avoid fuss. They would have liked Britain to stay, but since she had announced that she was going, only fuss was likely to result if she again changed her mind.

Ted was at his best during the next crowded week of interviews with Arab rulers, punctuated by disagreeable meals and short, bumpy rides in a small plane. He was courteous and patient. He remembered the particular interests, history and idiosyncrasies of each ruler. He set out his own position with the right blend of deference and firmness. He enjoyed the company of these subtle men, and conveyed that enjoyment to them. His moments of brusqueness and impatience were reserved for occasional British officials or businessmen.

We spent the morning of 3 April on the island of Masirah off Oman, where Britain had an air base. Ted spent some time looking for flat land where a new runway could be built for the Royal Air Force. The donkeys on Masirah subsisted on a diet of cardboard boxes. Then we flew to Salalah, the palace of the Sultan of Muscat and Oman. The old Sultan rarely left Salalah, except for the Dorchester Hotel in London. He never visited his capital, Muscat, and hardly ever the rest of the kingdom. He ruled with absolute power, and did not like spending, let alone borrowing, money. He was thus the despair of all progressive persons.

There was a small RAF airstrip at Salalah, where a ragged guard fired a salute in our honour. Beyond lay the range of barren mountains of Dhofar in which the Sultan's forces under British officers fought their small, fierce and apparently endless war against rebels financed and armed from South Yemen. We were met by the melancholy Crown Prince, who later took his father's place as Sultan and rules the country today. He conducted us silently in a Land-Rover to the white inner courtyard of the palace. The Sultan waited on the steps to greet us, a small round figure, dignified by his great white beard, softened by large eyes with long lashes. The Crown Prince was excluded and the Sultan lunched alone in our company. He had just bought, from Harrods I think, a large and hideous revolving table with which he was greatly pleased. It was in effect a huge dumb waiter. He could thus eat his meals without the presence of a servant to bring and remove dishes. The menu was not elaborate. There was soup, lamb with rice, and tinned jelly from Australia, with little cubes of tasteless fruit imprisoned in it. A photographer darted in and out taking innumerable snaps. The Sultan spoke freely and with a twinkle. His English, very soft, was better than and different from that of the Arab rulers of the Gulf proper, for through the quirks of empire he had been educated and trained as an Indian prince. Things, he said, were going really rather well. There were still rebels in the hills, but the situation was better than it had been. For the first time in his life he had a good income from growing oil revenues. People were always urging him to spend it. Of course, he intended to: there were so many projects he had dreamed of achieving for his people; now he could begin to do them. But the great thing was not to be in too much of a hurry. The Americans were always urging him to spend money on great hospitals and schools, not at all what his people needed. Even some of his British advisers were giving odd advice nowadays. They did not seem to realise that if you brought change too quickly, much trouble came with it. The Crown Prince? Yes, one day perhaps, some kind of responsibility could be found for him, but meanwhile he was immature. As for himself, he was glad to say that he had never felt younger or more energetic. Visit his capital Muscat? Yes, why not, but of course a step like that would need careful thought. It was not the sort of decision to be taken in a rush.

And so on for a fascinating hour. For me the idea of total conservatism will always be linked with the old Sultan of Muscat and Oman, softly conversing while, through the embrasure, the spring wind drove the waves up to the beach towards his palace wall.

During the next three days we travelled at breakneck speed up the Gulf to Bahrain, eating and talking with five rulers in their different capitals, arguing with our diplomatic representatives, drinking with businessmen and soldiers. At Sharjah the last licks of paint were being administered to the brand-new military base established by Mr Healey three years earlier, now to be abandoned. Each ruler displayed his individual brand of subtlety, but basically their reaction was the same: the British and their funny ways were familiar; but the notion of a Leader of the Opposition telling them of a policy different to that of the British Government was new and puzzling.

The policy proffered by Ted was in many ways attractive. He told them that, after all, the British might stay. Neither the rulers nor their subjects had much desire to be rid of the British, whose presence had enabled them to come to terms with their new oil riches in an atmosphere of calm, marred only by their traditional, almost affectionate disputes with one another. But the British Government had announced a firm date for withdrawal. Was it really feasible that another British Government would or could reverse that decision? Were they to believe this forceful, knowledgeable man, or was it more prudent to believe the representatives of the British Foreign Office, who were more evidently in tune with the spirit of the age? The rulers were not themselves keen on the spirit of the age, but they felt it was there. Each conversation ended on a note of enthusiastic yet vague friendship.

The Shah had by now returned from President Eisenhower's funeral, and sent a Fokker Friendship to Dahran on Easter Saturday to pick us up. At Tehran airport in my capacity as baggage master I spent the small hours searching for some missing suitcases. Easter morning was peaceful. While Ted saw the Shah alone, Tony Kershaw, his parliamentary private secretary, and I at the British Embassy admired the almond blossom, the wisteria, and the caricature of Lord Curzon in the gents' lavatory. As can happen when high personages meet alone, there was a dispute afterwards about what had been said. The account of the Shah's attitude which Ted gave us in the plane that afternoon, and which appeared later in more general form in *The Times*, was more forthcoming than the Iranians would accept.

Slightly weary now, we turned homewards. Saudi Arabia, Egypt and Israel, King Faisal, President Nasser and Mrs Meir were hardly dull fare, but they lacked the drama of the Gulf. We reached home on 11 April, after an expedition of thirteen days which felt like thirteen weeks.

The second east of Suez expedition followed immediately on Ted's triumph over New Year 1970 in winning the Sydney–Hobart yacht race in *Morning Cloud*. During the six years that I worked for Ted, there were three *Morning Clouds*. I never set foot on any of them. He kept that side of his life as separate as possible. Anyway, I would certainly have fallen overboard or performed some other clumsy folly. But I listened often enough to his sailing comrades and competitors to understand how amazing they found his performance, not just in the Sydney–Hobart, but throughout his sailing years. While he was at sea I flew out to Sydney, passing over the smoke from the burning forests of Vietnam. Tony Kershaw and I had to deal with a flood of congratulations, and many parties.

Eventually we set off for Jakarta. Suharto, now reviled as a corrupt tyrant, had recently taken over as President from Sukarno, now revered as the father of Indonesia. In 1970 it was Sukarno who was denounced as the corrupt tyrant who had attacked us unsuccessfully in Sarawak and Borneo, and bequeathed to his capital city a desolate array of half-finished skyscrapers. Suharto, by contrast, was at this stage clean and efficient though ruthless. Such was the cycle of Asian rule. We called on Suharto in a modest villa, with cocks in a cage, two tigers, and gaudy fish darting about a tank. He was reserved but friendly as Ted made the case for a continuing British presence in Singapore.

In Kuala Lumpur we dined with the Tunku, Abdul Rahman, the father of *his* nation, but genial and relaxed. The Tunku availed himself ruthlessly of the privileges of old age. Every attempt to start a serious discussion was diverted into an anecdote or a joke. His ministers and English visitors were treated affectionately as children, only slightly more grown up than his granddaughter playing with the tiger's head on the floor. We ate sizzling steaks and crêpes Suzette, and drank wild honey in our coffee.

The contrast with the next two days in Singapore was striking. It was my first meeting with Lee Kuan Yew. Over the years I came to relish his sharp debating style. He explained to us without undue modesty how he planned to shape his country. We British had created the main ports of Asia, first as coaling stations, then as bases: Suez, Aden, Colombo, Singapore, Hong Kong – but in the long run Singapore would be the winner. He and Ted had much in common. They were determined patriots, sharing an appetite for facts and work. They both disliked the kind of short-term politics dominated by what is now called spin, then represented by the artful tactics of Harold Wilson. But whereas Ted believed that Britain had a strong future, Lee Kuan Yew did not trouble to hide his belief that our decay had gone too far for remedy.

The reaction to Ted's message was much the same in both the Gulf and South East Asia. No one was pressing us to go, but we had decided to go, and no one was pressing us to stay. The real problem was at home. We had lost the will to continue the effort. I wrote at the time, 'We are isolated from everyone on this, and can only persevere if there is a real change of nerve over the next few years – dubious.' So it proved. By the time Ted became Prime Minister the withdrawal from the Gulf had gone too far to be reversed. In Singapore Peter Carrington, as Secretary for Defence, put together a five-power arrangement which kept a modest British presence there in collaboration with our local partners. The east of Suez controversy was forgotten as if it had never been.

Meanwhile, Tatiana coped gallantly with the unrewarding task of being married to the man who ran Ted Heath's office. Having returned from Rome with two fast-growing boys, we soon bulged out of 27 Cheyne Row. We were sad to sell and move; it had been a happy house. Tatiana found a new home in Roehampton Gate, just a few yards from the entrance into Richmond Park. Comfortable, unexciting, it had been built in the 1930s, with several dozen companions in two streets, some mock-Tudor, some neo-Georgian. It suited us well for four years. Its best asset was Richmond Park itself. The oaks and bracken were admirable for the battles of small boys. The slopes above Robin Hood Gate were steep enough for toboggans. Coming back full of wine and cheap cigar smoke (this, alas, was my Hamlet era) from some political dinner, I used to take our black Labrador through the gate. On an autumn night rutting stags barked in the gathering mists; I sucked in fresh cold air to replace whatever fumes had gathered in my lungs.

To Roehampton Gate Tatiana returned from Queen Charlotte's Hospital in June 1969, having been delivered exactly at the hour planned of our third son, Alexander. 'That's the lot,' I wrote, not being gifted with second sight. 'We'll have to sell the Devises,' said my father-in-law Benedict, thinking of school fees. Several years earlier, when I was leaving the Foreign Service with its guarantee of school fees paid by the taxpayer, he had taken me aside with unusual solemnity. He knew, he said, that I would like Nicholas to follow me to Eton, but I ought really to sit down and work out the likely total of fees allowing for inflation, and ponder this against the modest salary of a politician. If I had followed Benedict's advice, I would not have educated one Etonian son, let alone four. Instead I did sums several times a year on the back of an envelope, and somehow with squeezing always found what was needed for the next term's fees. I do not regret it.

Despite financial worries, we wanted to be able to spend weekends in the country with the boys without always going to Tatiana's family in Sussex or to my mother, now back in Oare after my father's death. We rented a thatched cottage in Blewbury, on the edge of the Berkshire downs. The thatch disintegrated fast in the wind, and the cottage was remarkably cold. We survived the winter with the help of a mobile patrol of ancient electric fires, deployed from room to room as need arose. But with the spring discomfort turned to pleasure. For Nick and Tom this was the age of bike rides and grazed knees. I started a vegetable garden and walked the boys for hours round the empty quarter of downland, across racing gallops and a dead railway line, while the dogs chased hares and on the map we found old English names: Saltbox, Churn, Upper and Lower Chance, Superity.

Another big advantage of Blewbury at weekends was its nearness to my fellow author. Andrew and Stuart Osmond had begun the wander round various houses in Oxfordshire which occupied several of their years after we had served together in Rome. At this time they were at Wootton, the other side of Oxford from Blewbury, but well within reach. There were several good pubs in between where the four of us could meet, the wives joining to tease yet support our literary efforts. I suppose this was the high point of our cooperation. We were finishing our second thriller, *The Smile on the Face of the Tiger*, which drew on Andrew's experience as a Gurkha officer in Malaya, and my own in Peking and Hong Kong. Our thoughts moved on to the next, *Scotch on the Rocks*. Andrew's imagination carried more sail than mine, and he had more time available for writing and other adventures; but I think he needed me as ballast and occasionally as pilot. We both enjoyed ourselves enormously, and except at one difficult moment our publisher Collins was pleased.

The problem arose when in 1968 we felt that we needed a literary agent to negotiate with Collins on our behalf. Sir William Collins, tall, bony, magisterial, summoned us to his office in St James's Place. The usual twinkle had vanished from his eye. Standing in front of the mantelpiece like a headmaster, he reminded us that the firm had encouraged us and brought us on. We had made no complaints. Why were we now treating our relationship as a purely commercial affair? He was hurt and asked us to reconsider. Shaken, we surrendered to the headmaster, and a reasonably fatted calf was provided in the form of an advance for *Scotch on the Rocks*.

Although Tatiana would one day have money of her own and we led a fairly comfortable life, I worried about our finances. One Sunday at the beginning of 1968 I worked out that my salary stood at £2,500 per annum, my expenses at £4,100 – 'not good'. The next year I earned £4,000 from writing, which seemed splendid, were it not that I had spent the money but not yet paid the tax due on it. Most writers know the feeling.

On 30 January 1970 the inner group of Ted's advisers met at Albany to plan the conference of the Shadow Cabinet in the Selsdon Park Hotel which was to finalise our policies for the coming election. Ted was in glowing form, and served us caviar presented by the Shah. His grand piano hosted an array of silver cups and medals from the triumph of the Sydney–Hobart race. He teased us for our cautious gloom.

The hotel near Croydon where we gathered later that week was hideous and comfortable. 'Historic conclave, as they say. The Shadow Cabinet, a basically frivolous body designed to discuss ephemeral H of C [House of Commons] business is taken in 4 long sessions over the whole range of British Politics. They are exhausted and enjoy it. Wrestlings a.m. over the tax package.' This perhaps gives the flavour of earnest policy work. Later the Selsdon Park conference passed into history as something quite different from its reality. Harold Wilson, always searching for the cutting phrase, christened Ted as Selsdon man: a primitive caveman bent on restoring crude capitalism and destroying the welfare state. That was never Ted's caste of mind. He believed in policy, not philosophy. He had already worked out in detail his policy on reforming the trade unions. He had been forced by Enoch Powell's speech to elaborate a policy on immigration. He wanted plans almost as precise on the other main areas of policy.

From 1974 onwards Keith Joseph, followed by Margaret Thatcher, shifted the Conservative Party to an attitude of scepticism about the usefulness of state action. Although Ted in opposition used fierce anti-socialist phrases he was by temperament inclined to strong govern-ment action when necessary. What he detested about the Wilson Government was its essential frivolity, lack of long-term thought, and devotion to tomorrow's headline. On the edge of the 1970 election I drafted him a personal foreword to our manifesto to embody the scorn which I had heard from him so often. In plain, strong words it denounced government by gimmick and promised a new style of sound and honest government aimed at the long term. His thought, my words – it caught the mood. Having just read Trollope's novel, I christened it 'The Way We Live Now' foreword.

But if the government machine was to be an effective instrument of a Conservative government, it had to be reformed. I was not deeply involved in the elaborate work carried out for Ted by a team of young radicals, including in particular David Howell and Mark Schreiber, or with the parallel team of businessmen whom he hoped to bring into government. My job was to read and comment on their papers, and make sure that they had the access to Ted which they needed, since their work depended on him personally rather than on the party.

Preparation for government was all very well, but pointless unless we won the election. Planning the election campaign of 1970 involved two very different sets of supporters. On the one hand was the party machine, notably more robust than it is today. On the other hand were the advisers of the television age, the makers of party political broadcasts, the designers of stage sets, the shapers of political image. For all their modern skills they were baffled newcomers to the world of politics. They survived and mostly flourished under the wing of the director of publicity, Geoffrey Tucker, recruited from the agency Young & Rubican. Geoffrey's great talent was persistence; it was impossible to close a door in his face. Rebuffed at one meeting, he would raise the same point at the next, until he got his way. He was usually right. The stalwarts of the party and the dynamic young adviser came from different civilisations, and hardly spoke the same language. It was my task to keep them in harmony, to smooth away vanities, settle small disputes before Ted heard of them, forge a plan for his election campaign. I relied greatly on the benevolent and civilised authority of Sir Michael Fraser, Deputy Party Chairman. He knew a little but enough of every issue; his strength was the judgement of men.

So as the spring of 1970 wore on, we waited for Harold Wilson to announce an election date. The Conservative lead in the polls began to shrink; on 22 April Labour moved ahead. 'We must just pound away – steady not shrill.' Meeting followed meeting – 'big and vague and useless. Rumour of even bigger Labour lead in offing.' We were marking time; our preparations were made; there was little more we could do. I went with Ted to Paris, where he made a speech, to the Chamber of Commerce in the Bois de Boulogne: 'Lake and ducks and chestnuts in flower. A boring bad lunch, but EH speech on Europe reads well, and should deal with the Common Market issue for the present.' But only for the immediate present. Ted was thinking of the negotiation ahead when he became Prime Minister, as well as of opinion at home. He did not want the French to believe he would be a pushover, so he warned them that entry to the EEC would need 'the full-hearted consent of Parliament and people' in Britain. The phrase returned to vex him two years later. Ted never had in mind a referendum. He was thinking ahead to the battle in the House of Commons and the decision on the negotiation which Members of Parliament would have to take on behalf of the British people.

Our next stop was Bonn, where we heard news of bad local elections at home. A few days later Harold Wilson announced that the General Election would be held on 18 June. Our machinery clanked into action, with yet more meetings: 'A wet day of sane and decent men endlessly taking their own political temperatures, discussing everything, doing nothing.' On May 12: 'Gallup tumbles to 7½ points against us, which is almost incredibly bad. In defeat defiance, mumbles Reggie [Maudling] over the whisky. A cheerful chattering among Labour men in the corridor.'

The Conservative army moved soberly to fight the campaign which had been planned. Although Michael Wolff and I were inwardly gloomy, we felt strongly on the central point. After our years of education with Ted Heath we were clear that he was the right man to run the country. 'Determination' is an overused word in the political vocabulary. It is the just word to describe that moment. We were determined to do everything we possibly could to get him to Number Ten.

The campaign was planned, like all campaigns, to avoid the mistakes of the immediate past. In 1964 Sir Alec Douglas Home had been shouted down in the Bull Ring at Birmingham. We novices were often regaled by the veterans with tales of the damage which this had done. There was some evidence that there would be violence again in 1970, particularly if the election was held when the universities were up. So Ted must be kept at arm's length from violence. Moreover, Geoffrey Tucker had drummed into all of us his conviction that the election would be won or lost on television.

Out of all these considerations the election plan was concocted. Each morning there was to be the press conference at Central Office in London, immediately after Harold Wilson had finished his own press conference on the other side of Smith Square. The middle of the day was to be set aside for television and for thought. Our own party political broadcasts had to be composed and contributions recorded for the regular television programmes. In the afternoon Ted was to depart to his evening rally outside London, usually in the Dart Herald aeroplane which we had hired for the campaign. To avert violence, these rallies were to be for ticket-holders only, and there were to be no questions, except in his own constituency of Bexley. The extracts taken by television from these rally speeches were crucial, and each hall was thoroughly reconnoitred on Geoffrey Tucker's instructions to establish the correct positions for cameras, lights and microphones.

The briefings upstairs in Central Office before each press conference were my particular despair. Because they were the first event of the day they set the tone for everything which followed. They were held in a tiny room on the first floor at 32 Smith Square, into which too many people pushed and jostled with their particular titbit for Ted. No one had the authority to slam the door in the face of the dignitaries of the Shadow Cabinet or the party. In the end we provided a half-bottle of champagne each morning so that Ted had at least some antidote to this flow of well-meant advice before he faced the press downstairs.

The campaign plane was a mistake. It is not sensible to fly from London to Norwich or Southampton or Cardiff. I do not think we would have ventured on these follies had it not been for Ted's distaste for trains. On 8 June we sat miserable in fierce sunshine on the tarmac at Heathrow while the pilot waited in vain for the appearance of the packed lunches, on which we and all the accompanying journalists had relied. Those cross, hot and hungry moments were a low point of the campaign.

It was unnerving to travel through this campaign in the company of highly intelligent journalists who were convinced that we had already lost. They were polite, even sympathetic, but they knew the answer, and it was not ours. Two of them were already writing a book during the campaign to explain how we had lost. Their starting point was the evidence of the polls. They sought diligently for incidents and anecdotes to reinforce their evidence, discarding other information which pointed in the direction to which they were not looking.

The set-piece evening rallies varied in quality. One, at Portsmouth, was a complete failure. It was a modern hall, seats too comfortable, acoustics too perfect. The meetings at Birmingham and Manchester were the best of the campaign. As fears of violence receded, the local organisers were instructed to relax the ticket-only rule, people were admitted freely at the door, and we began to come across the hecklers who give spice to any mass meeting.

It quickly became clear, however, that more was needed. Harold Wilson was making few set speeches. He was darting up and down the country by train, often late, always cheerful, chatting to small groups of supporters, making little speeches out of first-floor windows, shaking innumerable hands in the sunshine. The press and television quickly began to paint a damaging contrast between this folksy campaign and our aeroplane and solitary set speeches. Towards the end of the first week an important change was made. Conservative area agents were told that when Ted came to their town or city he would walk round a shopping centre or a market place before or after his meeting.

The new tactic worked well with Peggy Fenner in the crowded Saturday afternoon streets of Chatham on 6 June. It worked even better at Exeter two days later. A Conservative leader rarely sees the rural strongholds of his party in a General Election, because it is in the cities that the outcome will be decided. But the airfield for Exeter lies in the Honiton division of Devon, and when we arrived the ladies of Honiton were ranged in formidable strength outside the perimeter fence, like spectators at an outdoor zoo. As Ted shook hands through the wire there was much jumping up and down and cheering. An aunt by marriage of my wife shouted, 'Tell him many a good horse has won at thirty-three to one.' There was a roaring mass of people in the Civic Hall of Exeter and crowds in the streets. Later the same day on the outskirts of Bristol one of the Conservative candidates, David Hunt, lined up a regiment of tiny tots in a thunderstorm, all wearing the slogan 'I trust Ted'. The crowd in the pub at Bristol that night was also cheerful, and for the first time the campaign itself began to provide an antidote to the bad news from the polls and the journalists.

This new pattern continued, and the walkabouts were a success. The sceptics were confounded on two points. First, they had failed to understand that, compared to 1966, Ted was in 1970 a well-known figure, whom people liked to see in the streets of their town regardless of their politics. Second, he actively enjoyed electioneering and meeting people, and this showed. The well-worn argument about his lack of the common touch applied to a different part of his life. He felt far more at home in a crowded street than at a dull lunch party or a difficult press interview.

But the Conservative message was not getting through. On Sunday 31 May, at the outset of the formal campaign, I had written, 'We now have an even chance, though HW has tricks in his locker and we have none.' By Saturday 6 June, after a week of campaigning, 'Polls bad again, and a general edgy weariness all round.'

The next day was set aside for stock-taking and refreshment. Ted's flat in the Albany Chambers had a large drawing room where the great men of the party gathered that morning for coffee. Alongside was the small study where Michael Wolff and I pored over drafts and urgent letters. As far as I can remember, there was no serious suggestion from anyone that the course of the campaign should be changed.

The next week, the last full week of the campaign, was worse still. Campaign reports from the constituencies were good; everything else was bad. The opinion polls were hypnotic. On the evening of 12 June, after Ted's speech at Manchester, I was standing at the back of the Free Trade Hall watching the crowds jostle their way out when a party official told me that the *Daily Mail* next morning would carry an NOP poll showing us 12.4 points behind. It was the worst yet. There were only six days to go. I went to warn Ted, but he had already left for the hotel. I hurried after him, but was too late. On his way up the stairs from the public lounge to his room a journalist gave him the news and asked for his reaction. I cannot remember his reply, but I can remember the stony look on his face.

This was the week in which Enoch Powell put forward his full strength. None of us doubted the hold which he then had over the media and over the popular imagination as a result of his attitude on immigration in 1968. He was standing again as the official Conservative candidate in Wolverhampton South West, and in his final speech he urged the country to vote Conservative. But in his previous speeches in the campaign he concentrated on immigration and spoke darkly of 'the enemy within'. The impression was of a solitary prophet, filled with scorn for his former friends and colleagues, waiting for the nation to turn to himself as its real leader. Despite recent academic studies, it is impossible to judge what effect he had on the outcome of the election. It would be impertinent to enquire into his motives. What is certain is that he thoroughly disrupted the campaign of his own party. In particular Ted's press conferences that week were dominated by questions about Powell. Late in the evening of the Manchester meeting and the terrible opinion poll, we saw the advance text of Powell's speech for the next day. He seemed determined that we should lose, and lose badly. It was a dramatic and unsettling moment. I slept at the Travellers Club that night because it was too late to go home to Roehampton. I got up at six-thirty next morning, sat in the splendid library, and composed a powerful piece to rebut Powell, the cleaning ladies bustling around me. The piece was never used, but it eased my mind.

The last Sunday of the campaign provided the chance for a final stocktaking. This time there was a meeting of colleagues at Tony Barber's house in Montpelier Square. The Conservative Party owed a great deal in those weeks to the good sense of its chairman. Tony Barber was campaigning hard himself in the constituencies, but his cheerful steadiness also helped to prevent backbiting or panic at Central Office. His deputy, Sir Michael Fraser, used his long experience of General Elections to the same effect. I do not know how many of those drinking coffee in the sunny upstairs drawing room in Montpelier Square on Sunday 14 June expected their party to win the election. If they despaired they were too professional to show it. It was too late to change the content of the campaign, and no one suggested that we should. The discussion was almost entirely on the best way of coping with the challenge from Powell. The colleagues agreed on a short, mild and statesmanlike pronouncement, and issued it at once. They then dispersed and Ted went off to record his last television broadcast.

On Monday 15 June the atmosphere began to lift. At his morning press conference Ted finally threw off the incubus of Enoch by saying that he would take no more questions on the subject. He set off in a Land-Rover to tour the London suburbs. In the crowded constituency office at Putney we handed him the unexpectedly bad trade figures in time for him to use them for the rest of the afternoon. There seemed then just a fleeting chance of success.

On Tuesday morning, 16 June, the polls were still bad. Ted and the rest of us were in Bradford for the last big speech of the campaign. Everyone was tired. There was a row at the Yorkshire TV studio over some trifle. The stewards at the rally excluded, because he did not have a ticket, a leading member of the Pakistani community, who later had to be invited and placated at great length by Ted. Finally we got away. There was champagne for everyone on the return trip so that we could say goodbye to the campaign plane in style. It was a relief to be rid of it.

On Wednesday and Thursday we went to Ted's constituency in Bexley. It was a different world. The opinion polls and the television studios were far away. The seat was by no means safe, and the experienced agent Reg Pye organised matters accordingly with an immense army of eager helpers. The King's Head in Bexley High Street was thronged at all legal times with cohorts of Young Conservatives resting briefly from their labours. There were no more speeches to be drafted, reports to be analysed, or letters answered. We stopped speculating about the outcome. We re-enlisted as private soldiers in Mr Pye's army. We canvassed, ran messages, delivered literature. Bobbie Allan, a distinguished former Member of Parliament, had acted as Mr Heath's personal aide through the campaign, dealing with the inevitable rubs and irritations. He and I were given a special task on polling day. There was a maverick independent candidate in Bexley, who had no known views on any subject, but relied on the fact that having changed his name to E. Heath by deed poll, he appeared as such on the ballot paper. Bobbie Allan and I were issued with large placards which read: 'To vote for the real Edward Heath put your X against the BOTTOM name on the ballot paper'. We spent much of polling day patrolling with these in the sunshine outside the polling station at Uplands Primary School. That morning Peter Carrington had driven Bobbie Allan and me down to Bexley in his Jensen sports car ('All three of us think in our hearts that we are beat'). Upstairs in the King's Head he advised Ted that he should resign if the Labour majority was over twenty-five.

The count at Bexley took place in the Drill Hall. The Young Conservatives had a radio in an adjoining room. By the time the Bexley result was announced, we had a glimmering of what might have occurred. Because of the way we had spent the last two days, what seemed to matter most was Bexley. When Ted's majority of 8,000 was announced we realised for the first time what was afoot. There was cheerful pandemonium afterwards at the tiny constituency office at Crook Log. It was clearly right to return to London at once. The car radio persisted in telling us extraordinary good news. The Conservatives were winning the election handsomely. Extraordinary news to me, but not to Ted. To him, it was simply the logical result of the long years of preparation, and of the fact that the people of Britain, like the people of Bexley, were at bottom a sensible lot.

There was a large crowd in Smith Square outside Conservative Central Office, through which Ted had to thrust his way without police protection. One disappointed citizen stubbed out a lighted cigarette on his neck, burning him painfully. It was now well past midnight. Central Office was full of party workers and others in dinner jackets. It was not possible to distinguish clearly between those who had borne the heat and burden of the day and those who had come into the vineyard only during the last triumphant hour. It was a relief to go to Ted's flat at Albany and talk briefly about the morrow. At 4.30 a.m. it was nearly light, and I finally reached home.

At moments of exhaustion one's emotions are odd. Certainly that night I felt glad for the Conservative Party and for Ted, but little sense of triumph against the Labour Party. My strongest feeling was satisfaction that the experts, the know-alls and the trend-setters had been confounded.

11

NUMBER TEN

On Friday 19 June, after a late night of celebration, Ted Heath's team gathered in his flat to listen to the final election results from far-flung constituencies. He discussed on the telephone the hour at which he should go to Buckingham Palace and receive the Queen's commission to form a government. Then, turning to me, he observed that it was time for me to go to Number Ten. I asked how I should announce myself. 'It's perfectly simple. Tell them you are my political secretary.' Ted spoke as if reminding me of something which I had forgotten. But we had never discussed what, if anything, I would do for him if he won the election. It had seemed to me wrong to tempt Providence on the subject at a time when Providence seemed in a dodgy mood about our prospects. Ted, I suppose, preferred to postpone any discussion until he could confront me with an accomplished fact. It never occurred to me to refuse his offer, characteristically couched as an instruction.

At Number Ten I was welcomed by Sandy Isserlis, who that morning had been Harold Wilson's principal private secretary. On such occasions the wheels turn quickly; within two hours the staff of Number Ten lined the corridor leading from the front door to the Cabinet Room and welcomed the new Prime Minister with enthusiastic applause. (Each Prime Minister regards this enthusiasm as a tribute to his or her special popularity; the press is briefed accordingly. It is in fact a courteous and well-established ritual for every new arrival.) I joined that evening in completing the jigsaw puzzle of ministerial appointments. The prime mover in this task was the Chief Whip, Willie Whitelaw. The choice of cabinet ministers caused no particular difficulty, but Willie was shocked by the arrival of beer and pork pies as the evening's refreshment. Much, he felt, had gone amiss with the standards of public life since Sir Alec Douglas Home had left office six years earlier.

For nearly four years I worked as the Prime Minister's political secretary in the small, irregular room with two big windows which overlooks the garden of Number Ten and adjoins the Cabinet Room. The door which connected my office to the Cabinet Room was, with my agreement, kept locked. This symbolised the end of the battles which my Labour predecessor had waged against the civil servants. Marcia Falkender had campaigned for access to her Prime Minister and control over large chunks of his time. I was content to work with and through his official private secretaries; my way into the Cabinet Room lay past their desks. But that did not mean that I was absorbed into the machine. My office was a place of refuge for all kinds of visitors to Number Ten, particularly those who wanted a smoke or a good grumble. I usually kept my other door open into the Cabinet Waiting Room. Ministers passing it on the way to the loo would drop in for a short chat. Ted had forbidden smoking in cabinet, though in a very English way it was several years before the large square glass ashtrays were removed from the cabinet table. Ministers in desperate need of a cigarette left cabinet meetings on some excuse and came to gossip with me. Chief of these refugees was Tony Barber, who became Chancellor of the Exchequer after Ian Macleod's sudden death in the late summer of 1970.

My salary as political secretary was paid by the Conservative Party, not by the taxpayer as special advisers are paid today. This fact defined the core of my responsibility: I looked after what Ted did as leader of the Conservative Party. This means continuing to organise party tours, and with Michael Wolff trying to draft what he might say on these occasions and at the party conference each October.

In July 1970 there were two massive summer fêtes, at the Duke of Northumberland's Alnwick Castle, and at Felbrigg in Norfolk. Ted Heath was greeted as a conquering hero by large crowds of the faithful and after Felbrigg I wrote that he would be hard to shift. But drafting speeches for him became even more difficult now that the drafts which Michael or I produced had to compete with red boxes of government work and the demands of *Morning Cloud*. I spent a great deal of my early working life drafting speeches for other people, and I have always hated it. Later I disliked almost equally digesting other people's drafts for speeches of my own. The ideas of others should always be welcome. On trivial occasions, where a sprinkling of compliments and courtesies is all that is required, the words of others were fine. Otherwise, they did not fit my mind and came clumsily off my tongue. I always tried to write my own. So I do not now blame Ted for his cavalier way with our drafts; but our lives would have been happier if he had given us a clearer direction at the outset. Nine months into my new job, my diary revealed a degree of exasperation. 'Dictated a bad speech for Newcastle: It is really impossible to do these things without any inkling of what he wants to say.'

With the encouragement of the civil servants, I found that my purely party role extended naturally into the whole area of the Prime Minister's communication with Parliament and the public. This meant, for example, helping to brief Ted when Parliament was sitting for his twice-weekly bout of Prime Minister's Questions. Sitting on the sofa or the floor in Ted's flat at the top of Number Ten, I learned not to talk too much. From these sessions I gathered much inside knowledge of the workings of the government machine.

Ted's choice of his closest official advisers was impeccable. The two senior private secretaries, Robert Armstrong and Robin Butler, along with the chief press officer, Donald Maitland, were by nature calm, shrewd and genial. They enjoyed working with the Prime Minister because his instinct when faced with a problem was to find the right answer, even if it was not the most convenient politically. Substance first, then tactics and communication – that was the way he worked.

But of course communication remained essential. I had to keep in touch with the team of outside help, led by Geoffrey Tucker, who had helped Ted win the election. Ten days after the election victory Ted gave the team dinner at Chequers. There were no pork pies or beer on this occasion. Over the champagne we swore mightily that we would not allow the constraints of government to stifle energetic and imaginative communication. I am sure that every victorious party makes the same resolve. Geoffrey Tucker, driving me back to London in his Ghia Sprint, got lost quite quickly. We took a wrong turning and found ourselves smothered in a Chequers haystack. It was an omen. I spent much time thereafter warding off complaints from the team that they never saw the Prime Minister, and that we were lost in a bureaucratic haystack. They wanted to continue as a central part of the action, and were not consoled by Ted's generous social invitations to this or that concert or dinner party. Ted, for his part, became impatient of repeated advice from people who did not share with him the responsibility of government – and from many who did. He disliked stationary minds. Though not intellectually an innovator himself, he was always looking for new ideas from others. He wanted to move on from the ideas of opposition, and work out a new unbureaucratic language of government. He wanted to cut out superfluities and move straight to the rational answer to a problem. There was nothing unreasonable in this, but he was often disappointed.

I was by no means the most influential of the Prime Minister's close circle. Tim Kitson, MP for Richmond, was an inspired choice as parliamentary private secretary. He was expert on racing, Yorkshire business and human nature. He loved politics precisely because of the curious personalities and mixed motives in which the profession abounded, but was not personally ambitious. His predecessor in that job, Jim Prior, was now Minister of Agriculture, but kept close alongside. Willie Whitelaw, who became Lord President and Leader of the House of Commons, had the gift of speaking robustly without leaving a wound. Sometimes he did this with a joke, sometimes by contriving a great explosion within himself. No one could take offence at his eruptions of wrath or dismay, half genuine, half humorous, and they conveyed the necessary message. These three, unlike myself, were linked to Ted by the fact of being Members of Parliament. The freemasonry of the elected person is a special bond, hard to define but strong. Those personal friendships based on banter and total trust were a huge asset to the Prime Minister. About once a month, Tim Kitson would spot a gap in Ted's timetable and organise at a few hours' notice five or six of us to dine and drive away care at Pruniers or Wiltons or Scotts.

Within six months of the election victory of 1970 there was a serious industrial dispute in the nationalised electricity industry. The handling of that dispute established attitudes and reactions which persisted with variations through all the public sector disputes which weakened and finally destroyed Ted's government. My reaction was one of exasperation. The following jottings from my diary of 1970 on the electricity dispute were repeated with different names during the disputes with the coal miners in 1972 and again in 1973/4: 'Cold, and the electricity go slow hits harder and quicker than expected' (7 December); 'A bad day. It is clear that all the weeks of planning in the civil service have totally failed to cope with what is happening in the electricity dispute: and all the pressures are to surrender. Write EH a note' (8 December); 'With Tim [Kitson] and Donald Maitland [chief press officer] to EH in his dressing gown and tell him the whole machine moving too slowly, far behind events. If the Government treats the electricity [dispute] as a crisis it has the chance of a victory, not otherwise. Slowly and with many promptings this lesson soaks in through the day against all the weary platitudes of the electricity authorities. But still no deterrent to the men. EH takes over effectively from RM [Maudling] who is hopeless' (9 December); 'Throughout the day put in such small hawkish pressure as I can on the electricity dispute. RC [Robert Carr] and the DTI not robust enough, though RC handles the Commons well at 3.30' (10 December); 'The telegrams pour in urging steadfastness, and Ministers continue to wobble and be ineffective. And still no deterrent of any kind. Get v. tired and cross with making the same point' (11 December); 'A quiet Sunday while Carr etc.

wrestle over a Court of Inquiry. It's a tightrope and they are apt to slip towards surrender' (13 December); 'The unions cave in and agree to a Court on RC's terms' (14 December).

These comments strike me now as presumptuous, and the outcome of this particular dispute was not bad. My own experience of industrial relations was nil. But some disquieting truths emerged, and made a hawk of me. In opposition we had hoped that one massive, carefully prepared piece of new legislation would sort out the problem. The resulting Industrial Relations Bill was already on its way through Parliament but proved largely irrelevant to public sector disputes. The leaders of the nationalised industries were hopeless in handling such disputes; inevitably ministers were drawn in. But both ministers and industry leaders were reluctant to take any actions which raised the temperature, even though without such action there was little incentive to the men to return to normal working. The pattern was set early for repeated setbacks and the eventual collapse of the Government.

There were many fields of policy into which I never strayed, but I was expected to keep a close eye on foreign affairs. The first big row on that front concerned the Government's announced intention to sell arms for external defence to the apartheid government in South Africa. There was a strong reaction at home and abroad. Ted took me with him to the General Assembly in New York in October 1970, and to the Commonwealth Conference in January 1971. He travelled east, by way of Cyprus, Pakistan and India, to a vast hotel on a traffic roundabout in Singapore. The pace of diplomacy was slower then: that Commonwealth Conference lasted ten days. Foreign Office officials were not quite sure what to make of my presence in the delegation. Some of them, I suspect, believed I was helping to sustain the policy of arms sales which they disliked. This was not a worry for the Foreign Secretary, Sir Alec Douglas Home, who knew me well and used me occasionally as a conduit for informal thoughts not suitable for official channels. As sometimes happens with noisy disputes, when examined clinically the problem began to melt away. Neither South Africa nor Britain had any strong practical interest in an arms deal, but politically the British Government could not renounce under pressure the right to sell to South Africa. A strong anti-racist declaration was drawn up for all Commonwealth countries to sign, and a soothing study group established. I watched the cabinet secretary, Sir Burke Trend, and the permanent secretary of the Foreign Office, Sir Denis Greenhill, spend hours altering phrases and refining punctuation. The two great mandarins of Britain were rediscovering the skills and pleasures of their desk-bound youth.

But, for me, the memorable moment at Singapore had nothing to do with the conference. Peter Carrington, as Defence Secretary, had done his best to honour the Conservative commitment to remain east of Suez by negotiating a five-power arrangement with Australia, New Zealand, Malaysia and Singapore. This new pact was celebrated at a dinner on HMS *Intrepid* for the five prime ministers. It was easy to bang your head when entering the wardroom, but the meal was excellent. The Royal Navy took particular pride in the red roses on the table and the silver commemorative ashtrays. After dinner the Marines beat the retreat on deck in cloudy moonlight. The White Ensign was slowly lowered against the background of the low black hills of Johor. In theory we were saluting the start of a new venture. In reality the evening was a calm, good-humoured elegy for empire.

It was not easy to reconcile a hectic life alongside the Prime Minister with helping Tatiana to bring up three small boys. Tatiana got on well with Ted and enjoyed the elaborate dinners and concerts at Chequers and Number Ten at which he excelled. I began a new novel, this time by myself, and christened it *Truth Game*. It brought together my experience east of Suez with Ted and my growing cynicism with the media. Nicholas started at Sunningdale Prep School where he was happy and successful. We took two wet but not disastrous August holidays in Cornwall.

Some strains began to show. A few arose from my consistent failure in household chores at Roehampton Gate. The litany was endless, for example, through the autumn of 1971: 'All the mechanics of life crumbling around us – heating, cars, telephone etc.'; 'Telephone mended, light fuses blow. No progress on cars or heating'; 'Rescue ailing car with a twist of pliers in Richmond'; 'Demented by no progress at all on selling car or repairing heating'; 'The bloody paper fails to insert my ad'; 'Sell the bad Austin finally for a pittance in Castelnau'; 'Still getting nowhere on central heating'; 'Finally we have two cars which work, and boilers, taps and radiators ditto. This has taken 3 months'.

Even more stressful was the search for a constituency. Now that the General Election was over I was free from my undertaking to stay with Ted, and able to look for a seat. I was forty-one, and impatient. In a very small way I was now a political figure because of my job with Ted. Acquaintances who knew nothing of politics supposed that this gave me an advantage with selection committees in constituencies looking for a candidate. The opposite was true. I never asked Ted or Central Office to intervene in any contest on my behalf and it would have been fatal for them to do so. Patronage was dead. The one privilege active Conservative volunteers expected in 1971, and still expect now, is the right in return for all their efforts to choose a candidate whom they themselves like without being chivvied from headquarters. When I put my name in for a seat, little paragraphs appeared in the gossip columns connecting me with Ted, sometimes describing me as the front runner. Nothing could be more harmful. Even though Ted was at this stage hugely respected in the party for having won them an election they expected to lose, this did not extend to choosing for their next Member of Parliament a bespectacled Old Etonian ex-diplomat known only for his position at Number Ten.

I never expected to win selection in the Marylebone by-election of September 1970; Ken Baker, a young, well-known ex-MP was better qualified. But I had high hopes of Arundel and Shoreham in February 1971. This was a safe Sussex seat; I was the favourite; the local omens were promising. Tatiana and I set off in reasonably high spirits for the Beach Hotel at Littlehampton. Because feminists were at the time campaigning against wives being involved in these selection procedures, we were greeted outside the hotel by banners proclaiming: 'Mrs Hurd Go Home'. Inside a fork lunch lasted more than two hours, spent in resolutely affable exchanges with an exhausting number of selectors. Smiles wear thin on such occasions. Then the candidates were interviewed in turn, each making a speech and answering questions. I thought I did quite well; as always, everyone was friendly. At five-fifteen it was announced that Richard Luce had won the nomination. We drove away from the Beach Hotel as quickly and quietly as we could. Tatiana, who carried herself with great spirit through the day, made the necessary telephone calls from a public box on the way home. The Prime Minister rang that evening to commiserate, remarking that he who perseveres shall be saved. He added that he would quite understand if I decided to work in the City and look for a seat from there, thus escaping from the searchlight which was clearly damaging me while I remained at Number Ten. Central Office told me later that the Sussex Conservatives found me too quiet and conversational in my presentation.

I did persevere, but the next test proved even trickier. Two months after Arundel and Shoreham, the Macclesfield constituency in Cheshire, another safe Conservative seat, became vacant. I went there to reconnoitre; once again the local omens were good, but I had no faith in the prospect. Money was short, Tatiana was tense and unenthusiastic. If I succeeded it would mean uprooting the family to live in Cheshire. On the other hand, it seemed feeble not to try. I asked advice from Tony Lloyd, Tim Raison and several others, and put forward my name.

At this point my tiny concerns became linked with Ted's overwhelming ambition: to bring about British entry into the European Community. On 13 May the Prime Minister asked me to involve myself in preparing his

crucial visit to President Pompidou in Paris. That afternoon he sat under
the cherry tree in the garden of Number Ten, dunking digestive biscuits
in his teacup, while senior officials briefed him on the issues in the
negotiations – sugar, butter, sterling, many others. Ducks from the
nearby lake waddled amorously across the lawn; workmen noisily
erected stands on the Horse Guards for the Trooping of the Colour
parade. The next day Ted was travelling to Aberdeen for the Scottish
party conference. I went to Chequers in the morning with a packed
suitcase, not knowing whether I would unpack in Aberdeen with the
Prime Minister or in Paris as one of the advance party who were to
explore the French position. Ted greatly admired the Foreign Office, but
that morning he spoke critically of their anti-French mutterings, recalling
in my mind the fierce argument we had had with Foreign Office officials
at the Hague conference in 1968. Probably because the Foreign Office
associated me with these criticisms, Christopher Soames, British
Ambassador in Paris, did not want me to be part of the advance team.
Ted overruled the objection, and I flew to Paris that afternoon with his
senior private secretary, Robert Armstrong, and an experienced civil
servant, Peter Thornton. We dined light-heartedly with Christopher
Soames, who from then on treated me as an ally. Sterling, he was sure
that evening, would be the Becher's Brook of the negotiation.

Next morning an unhelpful piece of gossip about the Macclesfield
selection appeared in a London paper. The old story was repeating itself.
Quite apart from any political issues, no selection committee was likely
to choose someone who was being mentioned as the favourite simply
because he worked at Number Ten. I was depressed and tempted to
abandon the attempt. But there was no time to brood over that. We
spent the morning of 15 May going through the agenda in the Elysée
with the President's chef de cabinet, Michel Jobert. Small, dark and
witty, Jobert had not yet developed, or at least did not express, the
abrasive Gaullist views for which he later became famous as Foreign
Minister. The French were friendly, cautious and evidently determined
that there should be a precise and detailed discussion between the Prime
Minister and the President before the French veto could be lifted.
Because our visit was secret, we had to avoid being spotted by the BBC
Panorama team which was interviewing Pompidou a few yards away in
the gardens of the Elysée. The following days were spent in further
intensive briefings in London. In my few spare moments I worried about
Macclesfield.

Advice on Europe poured in to the Prime Minister from many sides.
The Italian Ambassador in London told me that we must cosset
Madame Pompidou because of her influence over the President –
'separate beds but no secrets'. On 19 May the Prime Minister flew to

Paris with an imposing team of senior negotiators. I tagged along, enjoying my small walk-on part. We dined again with Christopher Soames ('gold and white [dining room] and lobster and windows open to the lighted trees. The Knights in full cry, especially on sterling'). The crucial discussions took place during the next few days, but the advisers on both sides had little to do except wait while the Prime Minister and the President tested each other. The two men strolled and talked in the garden, and talked and strolled again. The news which reached us on the first evening was scant and slightly disturbing: 'It emerges that the great men have got through the agenda in high good humour without settling anything of importance. As C Soames said "this won't do".' After dinner at the Elysée the Jobert/Armstrong group met upstairs among the tapestries; we were dismayed how little had been finally decided. We mistook the process. The two men both liked detail, and were briefed to the eyebrows. But the outcome depended on trust, which was built gradually through the two days. The answer came as a whole at the end, not piecemeal problem by problem. On 21 May, a grey, wet day, President Pompidou was ready. He bravely chose the Salon des Fêtes, where de Gaulle had pronounced his British veto, to tell the world that he had reversed it. Ted took his triumph quietly, as he had taken the election victory a year before. These successes, which he regarded as the logical result of his own hard work and determination, came as no surprise to him. He knew that he had a further struggle ahead to secure the consent of the House of Commons, but the winning round of President Pompidou was probably the greatest personal feat of his premiership.

After a weekend at home I went to Macclesfield for the first round of interviews by the selection committee. One of my fellow competitors was Nigel Lawson. Most of the questions put to me were either personal or anti-European. No decisions were announced that day, and Nigel and I travelled back to London by train. We hardly knew each other at that time, but Nigel took the initiative and together we bewailed our plight. We both seemed doomed to travel the country from one non-selection to another. Was it really worthwhile? As we rattled south through wet, misty England and one miniature whisky followed another we became quite cheerful in our despair.

On 26 May I was told that I was on the shortlist for Macclesfield ('So further into the trap; some excitement of danger and fear . . . T bears all these uncertainties well'). During the next few days the situation in Macclesfield deteriorated fast from my point of view. The Government had not yet launched its campaign to justify British entry into the EEC. There was a good deal of hostility to Ted's achievement in Paris, and the Macclesfield selection process began to be seen as a test for him, as well as for me. Much in my mind depended on the outcome of the by-election being held at Bromsgrove in the Midlands on 27 May. This would be an early measurement of public reaction on Europe. If Hal Miller, who had been my contemporary at Eton, held on to the seat, then it would be right for me to persevere at Macclesfield. If we lost Bromsgrove, my chances as a pro-European candidate of being selected would be dismal, and it might be better to withdraw.

Hal lost. I received much contradictory advice. On 3 June Ted telephoned, genuinely angry at the turn of events, but giving no clear view. That evening Richard Webster, who was my main ally at Central Office and had urged me to persevere, rang to say that the news from Macclesfield was very bad. So, 'I decide to pull out. Hell either way . . . Crawl out of the Macclesfield trap. The burden of risks was too great.' It was one of those decisions which are difficult to take, but which once taken immediately feel right. Nicholas Winterton, a strong anti-Market Conservative, was selected and held on to Macclesfield, which he still represents.

On 23 August Tatiana and I enjoyed a characteristic example of Ted's hospitality. His guest list was uncalculating: he invited people whom he liked and who liked him. He mixed sociable politicians (without regard for their political usefulness) with talent from the stage and concert platform.

> To Chequers dinner for Olivia De Havilland and her rainbow Dior dress about which enormous trumpetings in the press. We pass her white Rolls hull down on the verge as we speed up the drive. [Because Chequers was notoriously hard to find, guests tended to allow too much time for the journey, and waited outside the gates rather than arriving early.] A very successful party. Sit between Nanette Newman and Mia Farrow with specs and an earnest chin and flat chest explaining about youth and Nixon and meditation and why the twins get soya milk not cow's.

Things had by then begun to look up. A massive campaign to persuade public opinion about the EEC was launched in early July. One diary entry from that time gives an idea of how my life was composed.

> Meetings at CO [Central Office] most of a.m. This is eve of European battle. It has a satisfactory feel, as if an army well prepared and planned with its charges and cannonades, now impatient for action against odds. Whereas the G[eneral] E[lection] was a defensive battle, won, but fought defensively in fog at a time and place of the enemy's choosing. Tonic with JP [Jim Prior] on my own affairs. Buy EH a birthday book. A vacant Question Time [I

always sat in the official box at the Commons for Prime Minister's Questions, then held twice a week]. Barry Day [star of advertising and a prominent member of the PM's unofficial help] produces an excellent script for the Ministerial [broadcast, on 8 July]. Dine at the Carlton with RMF's [Sir Michael Fraser's] group, with Keith Joseph, whom RMF wants rightly to launch as the Minister of next year. But he is diffident and uncommunicative except to the needy and the opinion formers. A good evening. St James's Park splendid in summer dress.

The Europe campaign of public persuasion went well, but it had been decided not to attempt the crucial test in the House of Commons until the autumn. Politicians began to discuss whether the Government should allow Conservative MPs a free vote on the issue, with no request for support from the whips. If the Conservatives allowed a free vote, it would be hard for the Labour Opposition to whip its supporters. But no one knew how many anti-EEC rebels would surface on the Conservative side, nor how many pro-EEC rebels existed on the Labour side. The experts relished the discussion, arguing endlessly on technical and mathematical grounds; in fact it was a matter of human nature. Ted had been Government Chief Whip at the time of Suez. Although he had made a reputation then for tolerant understanding, he retained a whip's natural instinct for discipline and order. So did Willie Whitelaw, also a former Chief Whip. But the current Chief Whip, Francis Pym, though normally a traditional spirit, began to argue for a free vote, with strong support from skirmishers outside. Tim Kitson, Michael Wolff and myself urged the Prime Minister to announce the free vote in his big speech at the end of the party conference in Brighton. The argument rattled round the restaurants and hotel suites of the Metropole Hotel, keeping us up until three one night. We believed that a free vote would give the Government a marked advantage in public relations, and greatly encourage the Labour pro-Europeans, led by Roy Jenkins, to vote with us. We argued that such anti-EEC Conservatives as Neil Marten and Derek Walker Smith were honourably set in their ways, and would not be swayed by the issuing of a whip.

We did not prevail at Brighton: 'The great men let the free vote founder late last night, indecisively and in weariness. This is a shame, and at the very centre of a mounting worry about the 28th [of October, date set for the Commons vote], caused by the hard and sizeable core of our antis – say 33.' The annual drama of Ted's party conference speech on the Saturday was played out without an announcement of a free vote. True to form, he had taken no interest in the speech, apart from a vague worry, until Friday afternoon. 'So we are left with key-note and peroration by B Day – not my style – economic and social by Tony Newton OK – Ireland by me, definitely good – and the muted tocsin about rough winds, which is OK . . . The usual ritual after – champagne in the suite, lobster thermidor in the Primrose Room, sit between Messrs Whitelaw and Pym.'

Back in London two days later, on 18 October, the decision about whipping on Europe was changed, though no new factor had emerged. A free vote was announced: 'All conscious of a risk, but I'm sure it is the only way to get into Europe on the right note.' In the set-piece debate on 28 October the Prime Minister spoke well: 'An overcrowded House, great tension and an overwhelming majority of 112, the Labour pros having held very firm, and the free vote having paid off.'

At the end of January 1972 Ted began to reap the benefit. I went with him to Strasbourg to receive his award from the Council of Europe. There is evidence here of jealousy among speech writers: 'He delivers a typical Barry Day speech, antitheses and false simplicities. I took out a few dreams and visions.' Next day he signed the Treaty of Accession in Brussels, an occasion marred by the throwing of a bottle of ink, but redeemed by magnificent meals. At one of these, at the gilded British Embassy in the rue Ducale, Ted conferred the Companionship of Honour on Jean Monnet. The final lunch was held at Ted's favourite restaurant in Brussels, Comme Chez Soi, familiar to him from the 1962 negotiations. At the end of this Christopher Soames thanked him: 'I don't know if you had anything to do with getting us into Europe, but you've given us a bloody good lunch.'

Perhaps I should acknowledge here that my diary for these years bulges with accounts of meals, usually accompanied by champagne. I am by nature rather greedy, but anyway I remain defiant about this part of the Prime Minister's life. Puritanism has now descended on the subject of politicians' food, drink and travel. But my belief is that a Prime Minister should feel able to entertain others and himself in the best style. Ted was an excellent host. He relaxed at his own table in a way which he sometimes found difficult elsewhere. To the extent that his hospitality came from the public purse, the taxpayer got good value.

My own affairs were also looking up. My latest novel, *Truth Game*, was accepted by Collins. My time as an unsuccessful would-be candidate, the humblest form of political life, drew to a close. The Boundary Commission had created a number of new seats in England to reflect changes in population, and new Conservative associations in these seats began to choose candidates for the next election. Some sitting MPs began to announce that they would not stand again. I found myself at the same time in the final selections for Eastbourne in Sussex and for the new Mid-Oxfordshire seat. The latter, with its small market towns,

Oxford suburbs, attractive villages and gentle river valleys was a Wessex constituency not unlike those held by my grandfather and father in neighbouring counties. It sounded reasonably safe, though, because of the boundary changes, this could not be certain. In Mid-Oxfordshire Michael Heseltine, not I, was the favourite; he needed a new seat because his existing constituency in Tavistock had been shot under him by the Boundary Commission. Everyone already knew his name, but the rule held good that favourites did not win. Michael dropped out before the final round and I wrote on 14 January 1972, 'This is a real hope on which we must on no account rely.' Six days later Tatiana and I drove gloomily to the constituency. This time there had been no press publicity at all, but the memory of past failures hung heavy upon us both.

The four finalists were interviewed in the British Legion Hall at Yarnton, an undistinguished building sacred in my memory. In the intervals we hung around at the Grapes pub near by and in the small house of the chairman, Brian Wright. As always, everyone was most friendly; the chat seemed endless. At 10.45 p.m. Brian Wright announced that I had been chosen.

I had found it harder to become a candidate than it later proved to enter either Parliament or the Cabinet. For that reason the relief was more striking. The three processes are quite different in character. Ministerial appointments are made by a Prime Minister who has studied the men and women involved. At a General Election most votes are cast for a party not an individual. But in the selection of a candidate, those concerned compete as strangers to the audience. Almost everything depends on the immediate impact of their individual personalities on that audience. I suppose that was not something at which I obviously shone. In such a contest both failure and success, being personal, are more deeply felt. 'It is really a great load off both our minds. Hard work now, but straightforward.' That evening in Yarnton began a friendship with a group of English towns and villages which became for twenty-five years one of the pleasures of my life.

No one knew when the next General Election would be. I had two, maybe three, years to get to know the Mid-Oxfordshire constituency. Since it was a new creation hacked out of the Banbury and Henley seats, its active Conservatives had not worked as a group. We all learned together; there was no pretentiousness. Indeed, by nature, the Mid-Oxfordshire Conservatives were unpretentious, far removed from the caricature of the Tory activist. Our first chairman was an administrator at a government research institute, our second a working farmer. There were good existing branches in several villages, but also gaps, notably in our main town, Witney. Active Conservatives enjoyed themselves organising the new effort and did not worry their candidate much on political issues. They knew that I was against restoring capital punishment, but though most of them disagreed they did not chase me on the subject. Much later two questions, the poll tax and Europe, divided the association, but on the whole for a quarter of a century they trusted me with my own political views. For example, the larger part of the new constituency transferred their Conservative loyalty to me without difficulty from Neil Marten, MP for Banbury and, as mentioned earlier, one of the leading anti-EEC MPs. Neil himself was correct and courteous throughout the handover. That argument within the party as yet contained little poison.

There was not much in common between the suburbs of Oxford and the Cotswold villages bordering on Gloucestershire. I had to get round them all as quickly as possible. This meant visiting local Conservative branches, sometimes at their annual general meetings, sometimes at specially devised suppers in supporters' houses and village halls. This work, which may sound dreary, was for me huge fun, which I cannot entirely explain. I have always kept a territorial sense of politics. I had known on the ground the exact boundaries of my grandfather's and father's constituencies. As a schoolboy and undergraduate I could have given a pretty accurate account of the result in every constituency at the last election. Now I was entering into territory of my own, not grandly I hope, but after much trouble and with some pride.

This task had to be squeezed in alongside my work with the Prime Minister. Ted never openly challenged the Fridays and occasional Mondays which I spent in Oxfordshire. But in characteristic fashion he used to welcome me back elaborately to Number Ten after a three-day weekend as if from an absence of many weeks, showing obliquely that he had not reduced his own demands on my time.

Tatiana and I relied heavily in the early months on the hospitality of Andrew and Stuart Osmond. After a day spent in assorted visits and meetings, we would stumble gratefully full of sandwiches and Bulgarian red wine into their big Victorian Old Rectory at Asthall, on the River Windrush west of Witney. At a weekend with them we might watch the *Private Eye* cricket team perform on the ground at nearby Swinbrook, and listen to Stuart play the organ to a tiny congregation at evensong in Asthall Church.

But we badly needed a house of our own in Oxfordshire, and began house-hunting. We had other friends near by. I had met John Tilley first at an elaborate UN Assembly staged in Montreal twelve years earlier. He was then teaching at a college in New Jersey. At this UN Assembly he had represented Afghanistan, with a deep voice and flowing beard. John liked to dramatise his life. By 1972 he had crossed the Atlantic and established a college of his own at Alvescot, a village about seven miles

west of Witney.* Never shy in his ambitions, he had bought up much of
the village, establishing himself and his family hospitably in the Lodge
at one end, and converting the Old Rectory at the other into his
headquarters, for good measure adding a cloister of classrooms at one
side. As his finances ebbed and flowed, it became convenient to sell the
Old Rectory, and in June 1972 the Hurds bought it from him. I paid
£42,500, and spent about £25,000 restoring the house to a family home.
For the winter of 1972 we rented the nearby Rectory Farmhouse, from
which Tatiana could supervise the work of our vague though ingenious
architect. We moved into the Old Rectory, Alvescot, at the beginning of
May 1973.

Alvescot in the early seventies was served by an ancient church on a
knoll across the road from the Old Rectory, by a renowned church
school, two pubs and a village shop doubling as post office. That gives
some idea of its size and status. It is not a beautiful village, but is saved
from ugliness by the Cotswold stone of most of its houses. The Old
Rectory, L-shaped in stone in the plain elegance of the years around
1800, is separated from the road by a paddock and a short avenue. A
traditional lawn and walled garden back on to a beech wood, which was
largely destroyed by the drought of 1976, but has since been replanted.
Part of Tatiana's argument for buying the Old Rectory was that it was
'a happy house'. Our time there did not prove happy; but I quickly
became fond of both house and garden.

I am always sentimental about leaving houses. Our home in
Roehampton Gate on the edge of Richmond Park had served us well,
and I shed half a tear when I left it. 'Home by 8 and picnic of British Rail
sandwiches and gin. Label furniture, take down curtains, final walk in
the Park over the footbridge half way up to the pond. Oaks against
summer light, sheep calling up by White Lodge, willows in the mist . . .
A place for boys and dogs, that's what it's been these 4 years'; 'Final
farewell to 40 RG, looking sunny and empty. The garden is all that I
regret – mowing the lawn, the fruit trees, the march of spring along the
shrubs from the forsythia on the left.'

So a new pattern of life was established. My colleague at Number Ten
Sally Villiers let me use her spare bedroom in Sutherland Street in the
middle of each week. It was not difficult to commute by train from and

---

*Everyone now pronounces Alvescot with three syllables. When we moved
there a few of the local gentry gave it two – 'Awlscot', in the same way as they
called Cirencester 'Cissiter'. According to the *Oxford Dictionary of Placenames*,
the stationmaster used a third version, hailing each approaching train with a
monosyllable – 'Awlskt'. Sadly the station was defunct before we arrived.

to Oxfordshire at the beginning and end of each week. Tatiana and I had to fit in another element now that Nicholas and soon Thomas (ten and eight years old in 1972) were schoolboys at Sunningdale. We learned that happiness both at home and at school was quite compatible with tears on the gravel as the car was loaded at the end of each school holiday. The modern town of Bracknell boasts a large number of roundabouts, vivid in my memory for the speed with which I often took them in my hurry to deliver the boys back in time for Sunday evening chapel at Sunningdale. Then I used to drive to London, snatch a solitary supper at a Chinese restaurant in the Kings Road, and go to bed reasonably early in Sutherland Street, preparing in my mind for whatever problems might be thrust at me on Monday morning.

By now the scope of my job at Number Ten, though never precisely defined, was reasonably clear in practice. I had to handle the Prime Minister's dealings with several sets of people both inside and outside the government machine. All these groups were important to his success. All from time to time became impatient; they did not see him often enough or he did not follow their advice. Inside Whitehall there were the irregulars brought into Government as a result of policy work done in opposition, including a small team of businessmen. More frequent visitors to my room were our leading innovators, David Howell and Mark Schreiber, who laid before me anecdotes of their clashes with the cabinet secretary, Burke Trend, as he tried to hold off their restless ideas for reforming the machinery of government. Later I became a junior ally of Lord Rothschild and his youthful Central Policy Review Staff. The CPRS was set up to be the anointed rebel within the system, the grit in the Whitehall oyster designed to produce a harvest of pearls. It was one of Ted Heath's most striking innovations, the servant of the Cabinet, not the Prime Minister. If the CPRS had survived, it could have helped to prevent the recent dangerous erosion of responsible cabinet government. Margaret Thatcher and on a much more sweeping scale Tony Blair have preferred policy units of their own to do their personal bidding. It was fascinating to watch Ted Heath and his cabinet humble themselves at the regular reviews of strategy presented to them at Chequers by Victor Rothschild and his team. The Prime Minister's support for the CPRS even when they criticised the Government's performance must be counted as a strong point in his favour. Ted was more interested in getting the right answers than in his own power or a quiet life. I was glad to provide an extra channel of communication for the CPRS in times of trouble, and I took my reward in kind, by poaching young William Waldegrave from them. This was for William the beginning of a career which led him into the Cabinet. He served Ted with a total loyalty which came naturally from his traditional background. But Waldegraves through the centuries have been lively as well as loyal. William has a sharper mind than mine and a more philosophical education, along with a more sombre temperament. Anything I lent him originally in the form of experience he has repaid over the years with many shafts of light. He would have made an excellent Foreign Secretary.

I had no consistent role in shaping domestic policies in 1972/3. Sometimes I was pitched by accident into dramatic discussions, for example when ministers used my office next to the Cabinet Room for excited informal argument. One such occaison was when direct rule was imposed on Ulster on 23 March 1972. 'Faulkner comes again at evening, rejects, resigns, all smiles into direct rule. Dine with Tim [Kitson] and Michael [Wolff] at Steak House. My room soon fills with Reggie [Maudling], Peter [Carrington], Sir Alec, Francis [Pym] – cigars and my whisky. They mull endlessly with about 20 civil servants over statement drafted by Burke Trend. Then Willie [Whitelaw] is appointed S/State and [is] pleased inwardly . . . Reggie a bit sharp toned, and out of things. Bed 12.40.' Almost the only advice I had given on Ireland in previous months had been peripheral: that it was a mistake to keep Home Secretary Reggie Maudling in the dark about possible moves, since he still held the departmental responsibility. Although I liked and respected Willie Whitelaw and in 1972 knew nothing myself about Ireland, I worried about his approach. Six weeks after his appointment, on 12 May we shared an Andover plane to the Scottish party conference: 'WW says eventual answer in Ulster is the unmentionable one, i.e. unification, to which young moderates are rallying. With no knowledge, suspect he is wrong.'

Sometimes I was pitchforked into the centre of a crisis because the Prime Minister needed to make a speech or broadcast which either Michael Wolff or myself had to draft. This happened over the decision to admit the Asians expelled by President Amin of Uganda in 1972, and over the announcements on the different stages of incomes policy. At other times Ted simply sent for me and others at short notice to clear his mind. On one Saturday morning in January 1973:

About to leave house when PM rings and bids to lunch to discuss Phase 2 [of incomes policy]. Rally Jim Garrett [friend, and head of advertising agency, a leader of the outside help] and MW [Michael Wolff], placate T[atiana] and am there at 1. Orange juice, plaice and fruit salad. We are all in training for Admiral's Cup [sailing]. Effect spoilt by PM drinking Kummel and telephoning for more. Desultory talk on prices and presentation of it all, but it helps him get his thoughts straight. I am glad he is thinking so hard about it.

Cedar tree beyond the window in Hawtrey Rm softens in dusk.
His new portrait by Derek Hill is good.

More formally I set up and attended party strategy meetings, also at
Chequers, two months later, on a Sunday.

Two hours and lunch. Pym, Carrington, Prior, Fraser, Wolff. PM
v. genial and relaxed in yellow pullover, rest of us tweeds. Hazy
sun and endless coffee in yellow and white parlour. Champagne
before lunch and 3 wines at it. Tour the half-finished swimming
pool. Everyone calm and reasonably reflective over the 2 yr
prospects . . . If no horrors occur, autumn 1974 might be best [for
General Election]. Early, before students in full swing. But we need
to be more diligent on housing, more political on everything. [We
are] In good with old, in bad with young.

On most matters my involvement was haphazard and occasional. One
subject only I followed with care and foreboding. I have already
mentioned my worry about the electricity dispute in December 1970.
This episode ended without disaster, but revealed a problem to which we
had no answer: that of trade union power pressing wage claims in the
public sector which if met could create intolerable inflation. The first
disaster occurred with the miners in February 1972. The National Union
of Mineworkers pressed hard; there was violence on the picket lines and
power cuts were imposed. Lord Wilberforce was appointed to arbitrate,
a high settlement was awarded, and the miners only with great difficulty
dissuaded from pressing for more. I could not understand why ministers
set about disguising and trying to forget what had happened, which was
a public and disastrous defeat. My own approach, vehement repeatedly
in my diary, was narrow. It seemed to me that in the public sector the
equation of power was hopeless. The new procedures introduced by the
Industrial Relations Act made little difference. The leaders of the public
sector unions succumbed to the pressure of extremists and put forward
unaffordable claims. They could inflict real hardship on the public
during a dispute, for which the public would then be inclined to blame
the Government. The employer was not the Government, but the
nationalised industry. Those who ran those industries were anxious for
a quiet life. They conducted negotiations with a view to surrender. They
refused to contemplate any disciplinary action or moves to make
uncomfortable the lives of those who were paralysing the docks, the
railways or the mines. At the end of the day the livelihood of these
salaried chieftains was not at risk. With a mournful smile they passed on
the costs of their incompetence to the taxpayer or the consumer. For

their part, ministers tried to stay out of the dispute until they eventually had to step in to organise some face-saving mode of surrender. They refused, for example, to change the benefits system which protected those on strike from the consequences of their own actions, or to contemplate the withdrawal of existing pay offers. So long as this was the equation of power, the Government could not withstand wage-push inflation or indeed seriously claim to be running the country.

This hawkish point of view did not find general favour. On 23 June 1972 I had an argument with Lord Rothschild and the CPRS. They were 'hooked on the idea of poor wronged nationalised industries yearning to be free, and wicked interfering Ministers'. The CPRS was thus moving to what became orthodoxy: that the answer was not to withstand the unions, but to transfer the problem for the free market to solve.

That summer of 1972 I advised in vain that the Prime Minister should not visit Japan but concentrate on inflation at home. I was at first impressed by his handling of the dock strike that July: 'This particular crisis has seen EH at his best – calm, far sighted, tolerant, firm.' But next day the situation had deteriorated: 'Out into the air for a bit, then crash into another tunnel as dockers reject Jones-Aldington and strike. Clear now: we live under a chaotic tyranny of tyrants not knowing they are such, and vassals usurping the power of barons. Any govt will try to work towards Bosworth.' (A reference to the battle of Bosworth (1485), which brought to power the strong Tudor dynasty by ending the Wars of the Roses.) Next day I gave lunch to Chris Patten of the Conservative Research Department, who did not agree with my weary meanderings about chaotic tyranny. Nor did Party Chairman Peter Carrington, Tony Barber or the Prime Minister himself. Committed by temperament and political conviction to moderation, these men pinned their hopes on an elaborate and (it seemed) never-ending dialogue with TUC leaders. At the start of September I still felt that 'we need a plan in the bottom drawer to produce when Ministers are bewildered, about the turn of the month, to find themselves in the crunch which everyone was predicting, and for which neither they nor the mandarins will be adequately prepared'. I was more than a year out in the timing of the crunch. When it came at the end of 1973 there was still no plan in the bottom drawer.

Michael Wolff and I continued to share the task of accompanying Ted on party visits around the country and to the party conference each October at Brighton or Blackpool. I looked on each of these expeditions as an adventure. I thought the party conference in Blackpool in 1972 the best I had known: 'Ministers have stood up and talked like Ministers, not officials.' Robert Carr, the Home Secretary, showed what quiet and courteous courage could achieve when he defused the attack on the admission of the Ugandan Asians. I learned at this time from Willie

Whitelaw that a really good party conference speech contains one (but only one) argument with which the audience strongly disagrees.

The greatest drama came at the least dramatic of occasions, the Scottish party conference. In those days this was always held in the Assembly Rooms at Perth, the Prime Minister pitching his camp in the prosaic surroundings of the Station Hotel. In May 1973 the Scottish conference coincided with revelations about the murky activities of the Lonrho Company. The Prime Minister's irritation against Lonrho fused with his natural antipathy to the hierarchy of the Scottish Conservative Party. He knew that they concealed political weaknesses beneath portentous titles and procedures. Their speeches were longer and their meals included more courses than the equivalents in England. The president's dinner on the eve of the conference comprised six courses. The Prime Minister was seated between Baillie and Mrs Mutch, the Baillie being that year's party president. As Michael Wolff wrote to his wife Rosemary:

> Ted used it to launch a ferocious attack, first on British industry for being cowardly, inefficient and incompetent, then for what he described as the ugly face of capitalism (Lonrho) with which the Conservative Party did not wish to be associated, and finally on the Conservative Party for being smug, upper and middle class and spending its time debating self-congratulatory resolutions. Sara Morrison leapt from her chair. But everyone else felt they had had a slap in the face or six-of-the-best, and were still tingling from it 24 hours later.

My own impression was in one respect different: that the audience had been only half listening and did not grasp what had been said. 'Mutch gets up and talks about the sole and the sweet and tickets for the agents' dance at £2. The Lord Provost contributes 50p and rejoins the Party in emotional terms. EH presented with a bottle of N. Sea Oil. It is all an Evelyn Waugh occasion.' But my diary corroborates Michael's account of what followed.

> Ted was absolutely delighted to have produced the effect he did, but Douglas and I and Tim [Kitson] determined to pin him down there and then, took Sara [Morrison] up to his room, and the 5 of us sat talking till 12.45 discussing how to implement all these fine ideas into reorganising the Tory Party in England – now. Ted was in excellent form throughout, made a good speech [next day] which he worked on quite hard, and ordered champagne on the Queen's Flight back. Unfortunately of course the QF does not run to champagne so, as

Randolph [Churchill, an old friend of Michael] used to sing, they had
to make do with gin.

During 1972 and 1973 I considered from time to time leaving Number
Ten, and finding some part-time job which would give me more time for
Mid-Oxfordshire and also continue after the General Election. But this
effort was half-hearted and unfruitful. Neither a City bank nor an
Oxford college was interested in providing a haven for someone whose
real aim was political. In any case I felt now more closely tied to Ted. His
own demands if anything increased. One summer night in 1972 Michael
Wolff and I took him to dine at Wiltons. For once my diary omits the
menu: 'He is in aggressive form, attacks us for drawing huge salaries and
not using our influence. "Never in my experience has anyone from
outside had such great influence in Number Ten as Douglas" and yet I
don't use it to good effect. Etc., etc. Against this we battle rather
ineffectively.' By the close of 1973 there could be no question of leaving
an enterprise over which heavy clouds were gathering.

On Sunday 2 September 1973 Ted Heath and I sat in the sun on the
terrace at Chequers eating scones and tarts while Nick and Tom splashed
in the new swimming pool. As usual it was difficult to pin him down in
conversation. Ted talked about the Commonwealth Conference at
Ottawa, about Ulster, about possible ministerial changes. But we also
managed to discuss the coming tours: 'PM now prepared to give much
more energy to political matters – but not prepared to change his essential
concentration on what he thinks important, e.g. Ireland, Europe, even
though political gains are obscure.' Two days later we set off to his own
county of Kent, then to Dunfermline and East Lothian. At Port Seton at
lunchtime there was a ludicrous mishap. The Scots had been asked to
arrange a meeting of local businessmen, but when we arrived the audience
consisted almost entirely of old ladies. They endured philosophically and
with only slight puzzlement a heavy speech of economic analysis which
had already been released to the press. Somewhere along the line there had
been a lapse. I tried not very successfully to persuade the Prime Minister
that in Scotland because of their academic tradition old ladies expected
solid fare. He was soothed by Peter Pears singing *Death in Venice* at the
Edinburgh Festival that evening.

Some of the flavour of these expeditions emerges from my diary for
the following week.

A hot sunny day electioneering in Walsall, for reasons which in
retrospect are by no means clear. Garden room girl extensively sick
in helicopter. Hours 9.30–11.30 spent quickly and strenuously
putting speech in order. Day overshadowed by building societies

bashing up the rate to 11% despite Barber's concessions. Otherwise
v. successful. At lunch in the Town Hall he delivers heavyish stuff
very clearly and well – as he becomes accustomed to electioneering
again he gets better at it. A primary school – he conducts a calypso –
knots of waving women in sunny streets – a hospital – walk down
the main street in a big cheerful crowd – local editors and gin – party
workers and back to tea – another clear speech. Away by 7.30.

The reception was markedly friendly. That indeed was the main message
from these excursions. No one in the autumn of 1973 was thinking of an
early election. The aim was to keep the political race sufficiently open to
leave the Prime Minister a choice of dates. We could not afford to fall
hopelessly behind in the polls. On 3 October I put in the black box at
Number Ten an opinion poll to be published the next day: 'Labour 34,
Liberal 32, Conservative 31. I asked Central Office to check and they
find a similar position in March 1962, except that Liberals were then
narrowly ahead of Labour.' This was indeed an open race, outwardly bad
for us, but paradoxically full of hope. For it was reasonable to guess that,
as had happened before, the Liberal vote was swollen by Conservative
dissidents who would return to us in the General Election. Against this
background we knew from the tours and the reception which he received
that Ted remained a formidable and respected campaigner.

On Sunday 7 October he held a working dinner at Chequers. Because
historians tend to analyse one subject at a time, they sometimes lose
sight of the pell-mell of politics. Problems crowd in on top of one
another, competing for scarce time. The immediate topic often crowds
out something more important. The principal actors thrive for a time on
the excitement of this way of life. They do not notice the onset of
fatigue. But if they allow themselves no respite their pace slows, they
increasingly miss their stroke, they begin without realising it to move
through a fog of tiredness. This happened to ministers in the winter of
1973. Perhaps the first signs were apparent on that Sunday evening,
though I did not spot them. Certainly the events were already crowding
in. There had been a visit from Chancellor Brandt of West Germany.
There had been a ragged and difficult set of decisions to take on stage
three of the incomes policy, to be announced by the Prime Minister the
next day. Ministers had been for some days at odds, and almost for the
first time news of their dissensions had spread widely in Whitehall. Also
unsettling was the prospect of ministerial changes which were known to
be in the offing, but not yet decided. The annual party conference was
imminent and bound to be difficult. And on top of all, reducing
everything else to insignificance, Israelis and Arabs were again fighting
each other in the Middle East.

Not that we all understood as early as this the disaster which the Yom Kippur War of autumn 1973 would bring on us. Indeed, that Sunday I was peevish because the Prime Minister spent so much time thinking and talking about it. I fumed when I learned that Sheikh Zayed, the ruler of Abu Dhabi, was coming down to Chequers at once. Rulers from the Gulf were not men to be bowed in and out in ten minutes or even half an hour. They required coffee and much ceremonious chat. A large slice of precious time would be thrown away on a matter which, however fascinating, the Prime Minister could hardly hope to influence. Far better to concentrate on the business in hand, the statement on stage three of the incomes policy to be made at Lancaster House the next afternoon, the dangers in Ireland and the party conference with Ted's own vital speech only six days away and still unprepared. The hours were ticking by, there was so much to be done, no one was doing it. The feeling of frustrated impatience was by then very familiar. As a former member of the Foreign Service I should have known better. The party conference and even stage three were to be much less important to Britain in coming months than Sheikh Zayed and his fellow oil-producers.

During November 1973 the earth began to move under the Government's feet. Our oil supplies were going to be cut by the producers. There was an immense confusion of information and much hectic diplomacy, so no one could yet tell how harshly we would have to cut our consumption. At the same time the Government was being drawn into a struggle with the miners on incomes policy. The Conservative Party, its leader, its ministers, its backbenchers and its supporters in the country had already been beaten on this very ground in 1972. Most of us had dreaded, beyond anything else, a further engagement with the miners. Yet here we were being manoeuvred once again towards the same fatal field, still littered with relics of the last defeat.

But, of course, while these dangers gathered, ordinary political life went on. People do not stop doing small things because big events are impending. On 24 October the Prime Minister for the first time took part in a BBC phone-in programme. The same evening Princess Margaret dined at Number Ten with Duke Ellington. We had to extricate the Prime Minister from the meal to hear Sir Alec Douglas Home's account of a sudden new crisis which, according to Dr Kissinger, had blown up in the Middle East. The next day the reshuffle, pending for so long, was once again postponed because Willie Whitelaw needed a week or two more in Northern Ireland. That morning the Chief Whip was very gloomy about a vote in the Commons on the Channel Tunnel, but when the vote came in the evening there was a government majority of sixty. And so on and so on. Each day had for ministers its sequence of anxieties, of unexpected news, of urgent decisions on unrelated matters. At the heart of a real crisis for a few days this sequence is interrupted while everyone concentrates briefly on the central issue. But this interruption can only be temporary, otherwise the whole process of government will come to a halt. In November the situation had not yet reached that stage.

The discussions with the miners showed how little had been learned about the tactical handling of public sector disputes. Once again the crucial opening rounds were in the hands of the nationalised board. Once again the board decided to give away everything immediately. Once again the National Union of Mineworkers, accustomed to negotiation, rejected this first offer as wholly inadequate. Once again the trade union was tireless in putting its case to the public. On 12 November I minuted to the Prime Minister under the heading 'Miners – publicity': 'The party (and Jim Prior) are still deeply worried about this. The press is good. But on radio/TV the NUM have it mostly their own way.' I went on to make rude remarks about the information side of the Department of Trade and Industry. On 8 November the NUM executive had voted for an overtime ban. Five days later the Government, determined to avoid the delays which had done harm in 1972, declared a state of emergency, and introduced regulations to cut the use of electricity.

One odd thing about the weeks which followed was that every now and then by some silent agreement everyone forgot the crisis for a few days and thought of something else. This happened for Princess Anne's wedding in mid-November. 'A fine brisk day for the wedding, and all goes splendidly. Nip out to the Horse Guards to watch them drive back. Leaves and breastplates and a smiling Queen. After all the carping the magic works.'

By the middle of the month it was becoming clear that the situation was going badly wrong. The oil crisis and the coal crisis could not be kept distinct. Together they were shaking the whole strategy of economic expansion. This had become more cautious in September before either crisis had occurred. Now, under this double assault, it would have to be reversed. Exactly when and exactly how had still to be settled. The political advisers drew together to pool our information and clear our thoughts. From now on we met often in my office at Number Ten. Under an immense workload the Prime Minister remained calm and unfussed. He was kept going by his own gifts of humour and courage. He held to a plan to tour north-east Lancashire on 22 and 23 November. As usual this expedition out of London went reasonably well, and the contact with real life lifted his spirits. On the way back we had a long talk of a kind which was becoming increasingly difficult in London because of the pressures of time. I suggested that someone, somewhere should be charting all the possible courses of the coal dispute. Although the Government had acted early and well to conserve stocks, it was hard to see the way through to a tolerable conclusion. Ted was more concerned about oil. He felt that the Foreign Office might not be exerting its full diplomatic strength to safeguard supplies.

That weekend I went to the Christmas supper organised by the Forest Hill Conservatives. Forest Hill is a small village on the ridge above Oxford, and its Christmas supper was traditional and splendid. Because of the petrol shortage garages along the road were dark and shut. Perhaps impressed by this experience, I gave them after the turkey a short speech of unexampled gloom: everything was going wrong; the prospect had never been darker; great sacrifice would be required by all. This went extremely well, and seemed to cheer them immensely.

On 6 December the political advisers met informally to review the situation. At this time we were much strengthened by the arrival in the Political Office at Number Ten of William Waldegrave, who crossed into these stormier waters from the comparative calm of the Central Policy Review Staff. The main paper agreed by the political advisers looked at the possibility that the coal dispute would drag on after Christmas. We recorded our view that 'a settlement in manifest breach of Stage 3 would not be possible for this Government, because it would destroy its authority and break the morale of the Conservative Party beyond hope of restoration in the lifetime of this Parliament'. We went on to consider the economic measures which the Government might then have to take. Finally, we looked cautiously at the idea of an early General Election. The drafting here shows signs of more than one view, but it was prophetic.

> The practical difficulties of holding an Election in these circumstances would be great, but doubtless they could be overcome. It would be a highly charged and violent Election, and it would of course be impossible to confine it to any one issue. The Government's election campaign would be credible only if it included proposals which would bring an end to the industrial action. It is not easy to see what these would be. A situation in which the NUM could influence the result of an Election by saying they would return to work if Labour were elected would clearly be dangerous. There is an important distinction between an early election held in the middle of an industrial crisis, and an early election held soon after the immediate crisis had passed. For the reasons just given the latter would be greatly preferable.
>
> The general arguments for an Election fairly early next year are becoming very strong. In particular:

a) The important economic indicators are not likely to improve in time to have a political impact in the lifetime of this Parliament.

b) Both the Opposition Parties are now in trouble, but will make strenuous efforts to get out of it during 1974. The timing of the South Worcestershire by-election is important in this respect.

c) The authority of government will gradually diminish during 1974 as the natural end of the Parliament approaches. This is particularly important in the context of Stage 3, or its successor.

It would be wrong in these circumstances to take any action now which would make an early Election impossible. We need to work quietly but fast on the additional themes which would be required to fight such an Election, e.g. on industrial relations and on the conservation of energy as a long-term policy.

In December the coal dispute dragged on unsatisfactorily. Willie Whitelaw was at last brought back from Ulster to take over the Department of Employment. The deadlock in discussions with the miners was unbroken. A rush of other events prevented senior ministers from giving the coal crisis the attention which it needed. On Sunday 8 December, for example, the Prime Minister entertained the former Italian Prime Minister Mariano Rumor to dinner at Chequers. The meal was hardly over when Ted flew to Sunningdale by helicopter to preside over the last stage of the conference on the future of Northern Ireland. Three days later it was time for the state visit of President Mobutu of Zaire. Two days after that the European summit began in Copenhagen. These were four major events, two of them (Sunningdale and Copenhagen) of outstanding importance. Each was the kind of diplomatic event which in normal times Mr Heath would much enjoy and at which he would perform well. They all involved talks, travel, long meals, extensive briefing beforehand; yet none of them had much to do with the crisis which was swallowing us up.

Talk of an early election began to mount, but at this stage it was no more than speculation. Nigel Lawson had been asked to draft a manifesto which might be used in a crisis election. We all noted an opinion poll on 7 December which put the Conservatives five points ahead. But as far as I know no serious discussion of an early election occurred among senior ministers. Certainly the Prime Minister had not yet begun to address the idea. Those of us who knew his natural caution understood that he would take a lot of persuading. The decision to introduce a three-day week was not influenced by any thought of an election. It was decided simply to postpone the day when the country ran out of coal. On 18 December, 'Slowly the bandwagon for an early

General Election is beginning to roll – but EH, so far as one can gather, still unconvinced.'

Christmas provided another interlude, this time a long one. I spent six days in Oxfordshire and do not recall that the Prime Minister telephoned once – an experience unique, I think, in the six years that I worked for him. Because of the timely introduction of the three-day week there was no prospect of an early national breakdown. The miners were still operating an overtime ban, not a strike. There was therefore some time in hand, but no coherent plan for using it. The Government had so far resisted various compromise suggestions which would have amounted to a breach of stage three. In this they were strongly sustained by the Conservative Party in the country. But this stand had no future unless a new element was introduced into the situation. That element, so far lacking, was a means of pressure on the miners to suspend their action and accept something not too far ahead of the privileged position which was already assured them under the 'unsocial hours' clauses of stage three. Plain men, including myself, could think of several ways of introducing this pressure, for example by withdrawing the original Coal Board offer, by linking more clearly the future financing of the industry by the taxpayer to reasonable cooperation from the miners, or by ordering a ballot under the Industrial Relations Act. All those concerned with the industry were sure that any such plain action would be counter-productive, exacerbate the situation, and so forth.

Whatever happened in the rest of the country, there would have to be an election in South Worcestershire, because of the recent death of Sir Gerald Nabarro. The Prime Minister decided that he would go to Worcestershire and talk to party supporters before the campaign began. New Year's Eve, the date fixed for this visit, was a splendid winter day of mist, sun and frost. That afternoon I stood with a group of dignitaries waiting for the Prime Minister by the bridge at Upton-on-Severn. Michael Spicer, the Conservative candidate, and the officers of the South Worcestershire association had the patient, professional air of regimental officers awaiting briefing from their commander-in-chief on the eve of a particularly desperate battle. The sun declined, the mist on the Severn meadows thickened, the frost began to bite through our coats. The Prime Minister was late, not an unknown occurrence, though this time there was a reason. At last he arrived, almost too late to be photographed in daylight with Michael Spicer, and walked up the hill to the meeting hall past small but enthusiastic groups of people. In the hall he gave the party workers a calm, careful account of what had happened, and why we now had a three-day week.

It was in one way a remarkable occasion. Any other politician I have known would have seized and used the emotion hanging in the air. The country was tense, a struggle had begun on which our future seemed to rest. Here in this small market town the Prime Minister was talking to his supporters at the start of a crucial by-election. He had led them to unexpected victory in 1970, his courage and doggedness were respected. He could have whipped them up against the miners. He could have sent them excited and enthusiastic into the streets. It did not occur to him to do so. What mattered to him was that they should understand the complexities of the issue, the objective facts and figures. He saw it as his duty to educate and inform, not to inflame one part of the country against another. So in one sense the meeting was a missed opportunity; but to those who wished to notice (we were a dwindling minority) it showed a Prime Minister who wanted to tackle not the miners but inflation, the balance of payments and the desperate consequences for Britain of the oil crisis.

I had heard little of this. I was fussing to and fro between the hall and a tiny office with a telephone. It emerged that the Prime Minister had been late mainly because of a crisis in Ulster. The German Consul, Herr Niedermeyer, had been kidnapped, presumably by the IRA. The German Government had some information about the background to this, and was showing alarm. While the Prime Minister was speaking at Upton, word arrived that the German Ambassador in London had an urgent personal message from Chancellor Brandt which he was instructed to deliver to Mr Heath that night. I had a personal interest in this, for Mr Heath had said he would dine at our house in Oxfordshire that evening before returning to Chequers. It seemed clear to me that this plan would now founder. Outside, the mist was becoming fog. The Prime Minister had as usual an immense workload. If he consulted his own convenience, and that of the German Ambassador, he would go straight back to Chequers and receive the German message there. The private secretary on duty obviously thought this would be sensible. I rang Tatiana to warn her that almost certainly her preparations would be wasted. But when Ted emerged from answering questions he had quite other ideas. He had agreed to dine with the Hurds, people had been asked to meet him, dine with us he would. While I hurried home to pave the way, long and complicated instructions were telephoned to the German Embassy on the best means of finding the village of Alvescot. We sent Nick and Tom out on to the main road with lanterns and they waved in both Prime Minister and Ambassador through freezing fog. In our dining room, by candlelight, the poor, travel-worn ambassador handed over Herr Brandt's message, and then had a brisk argument with Ted about the delay in setting up the European Regional Fund. Later Ted was in admirable form over our mushroom soup and beef, and left for Chequers half an hour before the bells rang in 1974. For him, it was not to be a happy new year.

During the next five weeks, from 2 January until 7 February, only two topics were of any interest in the Political Office at Number Ten. Would we have an early election? And if we did, how could we win it? This is a decision which, under our conventions, is to be taken by the Prime Minister, not by Parliament or the Cabinet. The Prime Minister listened patiently at meeting after meeting. He read memorandum after memorandum. If he was exasperated that so much of the advice was contradictory, he gave no sign. Sometimes he conveyed one impression of his own views, sometimes another.

On 6 January Ted held a meeting of senior colleagues. I wrote, 'Hard to think of a PM who has such a decent likeable sane loyal core of colleagues.' The opinions expressed varied widely. Ted had dinner with some of us at Pruniers that evening and said that it was exciting to feel an election in the air. I took that as a simple statement of fact, not as a sign that he had made up his mind. On Wednesday 9 January the TUC Economic Committee suggested that unions other than the NUM should undertake not to use any coal settlement in excess of the stage three limits as an argument for breaking the incomes policy themselves. This struck me as a flimsy proposal. There was a good deal of private evidence that the TUC would not be able to hold back individual unions once the miners breached the policy. Nevertheless, the Prime Minister and Mr Whitelaw considered that the TUC offer had to be explored, and this was done at a meeting at Number Ten the next day. As political secretary, I had no standing to attend the meeting, but I hung about outside in the anteroom. When I learned that the meeting had been inconclusive and was to resume on Monday, I was much dismayed and showed it. The Prime Minister, emerging from the Cabinet Room, demanded that I explain my black looks. He was always quick to spot disapproval. I said that the issues were becoming blurred, that an election would probably be needed, that it could only succeed if the Government could keep its stand against inflation clear cut.

On Friday the Prime Minister went over the ground again with Lord Carrington and Jim Prior. He agreed at least that preparations should go ahead in case an early election was needed. That afternoon Humphrey Taylor of the Opinion Research Centre presented the latest private polls at Central Office. ORC, and Humphrey in particular, had a strong hold on our judgements because he alone had predicted victory in 1970. The evidence of his surveys was not conclusive, but Humphrey in his exposition deduced that we should win an early election.

The next day, Saturday 12 January, was the turn of the 'outside help'. We dined at Chequers, drawn there from many places and professions by personal loyalty. Without concerting beforehand, they all pressed for an early election. For the first time in my diary that night I drew a parallel which often occurred to me in the next few weeks – that of Queen Elizabeth fencing with her advisers over the decision to execute Mary, Queen of Scots. The advisers argued cogently for execution; the Queen's instinct was the other way. She led them a pretty dance before the deed was done.

The following day the debate started all over again with different participants. The Steering Committee of the Conservative Party met at Chequers in the evening to review election preparations. This committee, a body which was normally comatose, sprang to life at the prospect of an election. It consisted of senior members of the Cabinet and senior party officials. As they went over the familiar arguments from a party point of view it became fairly clear that the practical difficulties of fighting an election on 7 February would be enormous. The party officials departed at about 10.30 p.m., but the ministers stayed talking and drinking in the Long Gallery upstairs for an hour or so more. The discussion became diffuse and wandering: 'Unhappy evening. We are in a desperate plight. I long to get the election behind us.'

There were three more days of intense argument. The renewed meeting with the TUC on Monday ended in deadlock, so the Prime Minister's hands were again free: 'Characteristically he refuses to show how he will use this freedom, but he is much more alert and cheerful after this marathon than he was yesterday, and I feel more hopeful of an early election. It is not certain of course, but other ways are blocked.'

On Tuesday the Steering Committee met again, this time in the Cabinet Room, in an attempt to complete the key passages in the manifesto which would be necessary if an election was called. No doubt deliberately, the Prime Minister was slack in the chair, and we made slow progress. That evening there was a further ministerial meeting, and in different forms the discussion continued through Wednesday and Thursday until all were exhausted. By Thursday evening the battle for an election on 7 February was lost. There was no more time. Suddenly the controversy stopped. Those who had argued most strongly for that date threw in the towel. Nothing was settled except that this option was ruled out.

Though it cannot be proved, I believe we would have won an election on 7 February. It would have taken place against the background of an overtime ban, not a strike. The three weeks which we lost brought with them, as we predicted, a steady ebb of the Government's authority. The issues became blurred. Practical people began to long for a settlement which would put the lights on again and get the factories back to a full working week. The dangers of inflation began to seem less important. The Government found the initiative slipping from its hands. The Opposition parties had precious time to prepare themselves.

No one in a position to give advice believed that the Conservatives would be bound to win an election. Nor did we believe that an election could or should be confined to the single issue of 'Who governs?' On the contrary, part of the argument for an early election was that the Government needed a chance to discuss the charged economic situation with the electorate, and gain a new mandate for harsh measures. Nor did we believe or argue that an election victory would automatically solve the coal dispute. Enoch Powell in a baleful comment accused the party of dishonesty in making this pretence; he was wide of the mark. Obviously the miners would continue to press their case; but they would be faced with a Government with five years' authority ahead of it, in particular with authority over the future of the coal industry. At present the Government held a desperately weak hand. No one was proposing an alternative way of strengthening it. An election victory would give the Government strong new cards. It certainly needed them.

The Prime Minister, backed by two or three of his wisest colleagues, looked more widely and came to a different view. First of all, they saw what was at stake. We faced an Opposition under poor leadership. Mr Wilson appeared at this time to have no convictions of any kind. There was no point at which he could be relied on to resist the onset within the Labour Party of their peculiar and destructive blend of chauvinist Marxism. Our membership of the EEC was clearly at risk. So was the fragile Irish settlement painfully put together at Sunningdale. So were the prospects for the private sector of British industry in the aftermath of the oil crisis. The stakes were formidably high.

Second, Ted Heath did not believe that a modern Conservative Party should fight an election battle aimed mainly against the trade unions. However skilfully the leadership might define the campaign issues, that was what the election would, in his view, become. A party which repudiated the class struggle must not fight a class election. We must not treat the union leaders as enemies. Irrespective of whether that was the right way to win an election, it was certainly no way to run a country.

Finally, truth was great and might still prevail. Ted believed passionately in reason as the governing force in politics. He had given the party workers at Upton-on-Severn not a battle-cry but a thoughful lecture. Many times over the last two years the union leaders had come to Number Ten to negotiate with ministers. Sometimes ministers had come tantalisingly close to agreement with them. He would not despair of reason. One more meeting, one more initiative, one more exposition of the national interest – it must be right to persevere rather than despair.

The Prime Minister's decision was one which I regretted, but respected greatly. A lull followed. There were, of course, further talks with the miners, but they were by now in a thoroughly unhelpful mood.

Following an announcement from Peter Carrington (by now Secretary of State for Energy) that coal stocks might permit us to move from a three- to a four-day working week, they went straight for a ballot among their members for a strike. This transformed the situation. It was clear that reason was not going to prevail.

On 26 and 27 January, while we were waiting for the result of the miners' ballot, I spent a strange, unreal weekend in the comfort of Ditchley Park. At this beautiful house in the heart of Oxfordshire had assembled an Anglo-American conference which included a group of young American Congressmen. They had come to discuss problems of government in the broadest and most philosophical terms. With typical courtesy, they refrained from any comment on the extraordinary condition of the country which they were visiting. The British participants included Sir William Armstrong, the head of the Civil Service, who more than anyone else except the Prime Minister and Willie Whitelaw had carried the burden of the last few weeks. The atmosphere was Chekhovian. We sat on sofas in front of great log fires and discussed first principles while the rain lashed the windows. Sir William was full of notions, ordinary and extraordinary. On Sunday after lunch I went home with a notion of my own. It was clear that the miners would vote overwhelmingly for a strike. The Prime Minister had ruled out an immediate election. The Government could not for long withstand a strike. The best course might be to settle quickly with the miners and then go straight to the country for a new mandate, which would have to include a counter-attack on trade union power.

On Monday morning no one liked my idea at the Liaison Committee. During the next two days Ted made clear in several conversations how deeply he still disliked the idea of an immediate election, but he could no longer offer an alternative. An election was the only weapon left in the Government's arsenal. Preparations were quietly resumed. There were no more great arguments.

A week later the Prime Minister began, though still not vigorously, to interest himself in election planning. On Tuesday 5 February he dined at Pruniers with Tim Kitson and Francis Pym after a cabinet meeting. I joined them for a glass after dinner. Ted explained more clearly than ever before his desperate worry about the size of the stake on the table. Everything he had tried to accomplish seemed at risk. No one pressed him that evening. Events had already taken over the argument.

It seemed that we had lived for months with a hypothetical election, though it was only a few weeks. Early on the morning of Thursday 7 February the decision was taken. We were off. The relief was great, although there was an enormous amount to be done. There were parliamentary questions to be answered that afternoon. The Prime

Minister had to broadcast. The manifesto had to be completed, which was achieved briskly that afternoon with Peter Carrington in the chair. The Prime Minister's election programme had to be approved. We had been at work on these things for weeks, but they all came to the point of decision on the same day. 'All in all we are off the ground, in better shape than I dared to hope.'

In Mid-Oxfordshire I began, with a sense of liberation, to fight my first personal election. I planned the campaign on traditional lines, which I repeated in five later General Elections. I did not visit other constituencies, and other politicians did not visit us. I still know what I learned then: the exact frontiers of the constituency along each road. Most mornings were spent at home dealing with letters, interviews and telephone calls. After lunch in some popular pub we canvassed in shopping centres and high streets. At 3 p.m. we met mothers collecting their children from school, remembering not to set foot on the school premises themselves, which must be neutral. We drove with a loudspeaker through back streets of Witney or Kidlington, but only for an hour or so, stopping before there could be any question of disturbing children in bed. Then a short rest, followed by two or (in earlier years) three meetings each evening. This was just possible with a competent driver, given the modest distances between Oxfordshire towns and villages. In 1974 I had an audience of 45 at Alvescot, 100 in Burford, 70 at Forest Hill, 80 in Wheatley, and so on. These village meetings have since fallen out of fashion, but were well worthwhile, particularly if there was vigorous (but not too vigorous) opposition at the back of the hall. Supporters were invigorated by debate and by meeting their candidate. The whole village knew that the Conservative had been there, not just with a wave and smiling handshakes, but in traditional election combat in their own village hall.

I developed the slow or anecdotal method of canvassing – 'up innumerable garden paths between the crocuses, listening to slow but fascinating reminiscences, gauging the look in the eye and the hesitation in the voice'. Each evening Commander Charles Jenkins, formerly of the Royal Navy, used to put through my door a brisk analysis of the canvass returns reaching constituency headquarters from all our active branches, together with his cautious comments. As the days passed, these canvass returns indicated a result not as good as 1970, but good enough. I became enthusiastic about political colour – posters in windows and fields and stickers on cars. There were occasional outbursts of poster warfare between blue, red and orange in our village and town streets. Probably these displays give more encouragement to the candidate than to anyone else. But still, years later, when I see in some cottage garden an estate agent's notice of sale in vivid blue and white, my automatic reaction is 'Good – another Conservative'.

The nature of my campaign largely cut me off from national events. I rarely listened to radio or watched television. The Prime Minister, amid his own troubles, telephoned on the eve of polling day to wish me luck. But we were not rated a marginal seat and Central Office left us to ourselves. My Labour and Liberal opponents fought orthodox, good-humoured campaigns, none of us much bothering the others.

It was a strange, rather exhilarating feeling. I had left the world of opinion polls, national press, categories of socio-economic groups and other generalisations. For three weeks I lived in the world of individuals – eccentric, unpredictable, varied, refreshing.

It was still winter and 28 February was grey and cold, with sleet in the evening. Sheila Cole, my chief of staff, drove Nicholas (now eleven) and myself round every polling station and Conservative committee room from 9 a.m. until 9.30 p.m. Morale was high. We consumed huge quantities of tea and cakes, Nicholas being particularly useful in this task. My own count was held next morning in the Langdale Hall at Witney. I had predicted a majority of 5,000, but it came in at 7,900. Tatiana was with me at the count. My mother and the boys were outside when in front of the returning officer and the high sheriff I did my little speech of thanks. That night in my diary: 'MEMBER FOR MID-OXFORDSHIRE. The one really consistent aim of my working life realised, and I don't really want to go any higher.'

I spent that weekend at Alvescot, much of it on the telephone. Nationally we had gained more votes than Labour, but fewer seats. Ted told me we should have hung on without an election. He was wrestling forlornly to form an alliance with the Liberals and so continue in office.

On Monday 4 March I drove slowly to London to assist at the death of the Government. The talks with the Liberals had collapsed. Number Ten was full of spring flowers sent to Ted by sympathisers. Someone had already packed into paper sacks the scanty personal belongings from my desk, and I smuggled them out of the garden gate where there were no photographers. At about six as the spring dusk gathered outside, Ted called us all into the Cabinet Room for a drink to say thank-you and goodbye. Tears flowed into glasses; not his, but certainly mine. I had worked for him for almost six years. The Carringtons gave him and some of us dinner that night in Ovington Square. Ted, though exhausted, perked up and began to plan the future of the party.

PART IV

OPPOSITION

12

BACKBENCHER

The Palace of Westminster had been familiar to me from childhood. I knew the preposterous splendour of the Central Lobby, where courteous policemen operating under the mosaics of the patron saints of England, Scotland, Ireland and Wales cope day and night with the flow of citizens looking for their Member of Parliament. Through that lobby at two-thirty every afternoon processes the Speaker on his or her way to prayers, their passage celebrated by a deep-voiced policeman with the cry, 'Hats off, strangers.' I could even remember the days when there were hats to remove.

For more than seven years before my election I had busied about the Commons as an adviser, though debarred from its most sacred place, the Chamber itself. The boxes where civil servants and opposition advisers sit are physically part of the Chamber of the House of Commons. But the wooden pews which separated our boxes and advisers from the elected representatives of the people were psychologically impregnable. Or, to be more precise, they allowed for only a one-way flow of ideas and emotions. The reactions and atmosphere of MPs on the same level a few yards away washed over us. We knew exactly when our man had scored a hit or fallen flat. But we could convey nothing the other way, except by the slow imperfect means of a scribbled note which might be passed along the benches to him, surreptitiously so that the other side did not notice. Often we longed to shout, 'The answer to that is at Flag E of the brief,' or, 'Don't stress those figures, they're wobbly,' or, 'Skip the rest. Sit down now, for God's sake, while the going's good.' We could will our advice to transfer itself over these fateful yards, but somehow it did not always make the trip.

Now in March 1974 I had leapt over those wooden barriers, and found a modest place on the green leather benches as a Member of Parliament. But I did not carry with me the knowledge, the excitement, the anxieties which go with working for the Leader of the Opposition or the Prime Minister. My temperature had chilled; the nervous strain, particularly of the last six months, had disappeared. I was just one of a crowd of new backbenchers. Since this was what I had always wanted, I did not mind. I knew all our front bench personally, and many of my backbench colleagues. About a dozen of the new Conservative MPs had worked in one way or another for the party, mostly in the Research Department. For several years after 1974 we used to dine together every few weeks, usually at St Stephen's Club in Queen Anne's Gate. We called ourselves the 'office boys' after a contemptuous epithet flung at us by Alan Clark. He was like us, a new boy, but had already set himself apart by arrogance. We office boys were not all of one mind on the right future for our party, or indeed on its leadership, but we shared a sober way of looking at things on what we hoped were their merits. That was something we had learned from Ted Heath.

William Waldegrave (not yet in the Commons) had taken my place as the head of Ted Heath's office, and I no longer had any formal position with the Leader of the Opposition. But Ted often got in touch, and I never lost the habit of answering his questions frankly. He sent for me after I made an innocuous maiden speech, congratulated me on it, offered me a CBE for my services to his government, and advised me never again to speak to the Commons with the middle button on my coat unfastened. As already recorded, he took me with him to China in the summer of 1974. That December he stayed a weekend with us at Alvescot. We took him to the National Hunt meeting at Cheltenham and lunched in the Royal Box with 'plenty of shrewd pleasant Lords'. To Sunday lunch next day at the Old Rectory we invited a mixed bag of friends, including the Osmonds, Anne Fleming and William Waldegrave, and finished the last of the Dom Perignon which President Pompidou had surprisingly sent me after Ted's historic visit to Paris three years earlier. I was glad when he performed well in the Commons, for instance in the debate on Northern Ireland on 4 June: 'EH a bit long, but very good – constructive and vivid. He has regained an impetus now – vital he should keep it up.' It was clear through 1974 and in the first weeks of 1975 that he would not be able to avoid a fight for the leadership of the party. Keith Joseph issued the intellectual challenge, but Margaret Thatcher began to emerge strongly. When she came to speak to the office boys at St Stephen's Club on 18 July I found her 'admirable and philosophical and [she] carries us'. I never at heart believed that Ted Heath would again be Prime Minister, but my affection and loyalty remained. His one-nation view of Conservatism was closer to what I thought right than the free market doctrine preached by Keith Joseph and Margaret Thatcher, which was rapidly gaining ground.

The two main political parties were drifting further from each other. The Parliament elected in March 1974 gave no one a working majority, so a new election was inevitable, though no one was keen on it. I was strongly attracted by the idea that Ted as leader of the Conservative Party should campaign on a pledge that if elected he would try to form a National Government in coalition with others: 'Nasty salmon at Constitutional Club with Cormack, Amery, Ancram, Meyer, Banks to discuss national government. Nothing coherent'. Four days later, on 15 July, I discussed the idea with Ted, but he did not wish to commit himself: 'I think of it as a real need but with him at present it has to be argued as a tactical ploy.' My own analysis contained much wishful thinking. The nation had just suffered a severe upset from the miners' strike, the oil shocks and the hung Parliament after February's election. The threat of inflation was formidable. People were impatient with the traditional rigmarole of partisan party politics. Harold Wilson was a master of those tactics and that vocabulary. At moments of national crisis in 1916, 1931 and 1940 the nation had repudiated party politics in favour of a coalition. The atmosphere was again heavy with a sense of crisis. There was just a chance that Ted could trump Wilson's skills and catch the mood by stressing national unity. I knew that instinct chimed with Ted's own philosophy. Unfortunately, the electorate did not know that, seeing in Ted only the man who had tried to beat the miners, caused power cuts and the three-day week, and ultimately failed. He had come within a whisker of winning the election, but that was that. People would not give him a second chance.

The argument continued after Harold Wilson announced the October election. Our manifesto committed us to consult other parties and interests and invite them to join us in government: 'Election called. The odds are against us. We have an excellent case, but will not deploy it well enough.' My own campaign in Mid-Oxfordshire was thin compared to March, but I had enough confidence to lend a hand to my neighbour in Oxford City. I canvassed at dawn outside the Cowley gates of British Leyland, and was rewarded by a stately breakfast with our candidate, John Patten, at Hertford College. Michael Wolff and Sara Morrison told me on the telephone that Ted was pulling his punches on the question of a National Government because he had not made up his mind. I tackled him on the campaign bus from Oxford to Reading on 28 September but made no progress. On 6 October I tried again on the telephone but by then, with only four days to go before polling, it was too late: 'This is becoming unrealistic: we shall have to fight hard and be lucky to stay in the game at all. I say we might hang on to Oxford. He says, "Was there any danger?"'

There *was* danger: we lost Oxford, and the election; though my own majority was a satisfactory 7,300. Next day Ken and Mary Baker gave a dinner for Ted in Sussex Street. 'We discuss everything except the vital question of his own future. He looks well but is full of anger and reproach against the press lords, his advisers etc., etc. I urge relentless Opposition. But that is not the point and we all know it . . . I am afraid he will decide to sail on to shipwreck.' The following morning Nigel Lawson rang to say that he thought that Ted should stay for the time being, but should take in Keith Joseph as Shadow Chancellor. Disagreeing, I drafted a letter to Ted advising him to say at once that he would step down. The letter was not sent, for later the same day he telephoned and I gave him the same message, rather stumblingly. It was taken quite well, but he replied that this was the least attractive of the options open to him.

The division within the party began to deepen, and to collect the poison which has never since then entirely dissipated. I was no longer at the centre of the different manoeuvres, but occasionally shoved in an oar. So long as Ted was in the contest I would do my best to help him. Jim Prior talked to me on 30 October.

> He has shot his bolt telling Ted to stand down, and is upset and worried. Dinner of our group the office boys at St Stephen's Club. Nurse them to a reasonable consensus – delay but a quick declaration by Ted either of a committee on procedure [i.e. on the rules for electing the party leader], or of an election in the spring on existing rules. We range from Latham who is basically anti-Ted to Keith Hampson who thinks he should soldier on regardless. A useful occasion.

When I gave Ted an account of this meeting he was pleased and spoke more easily about a party election in the spring, which he obviously thought he could win. A fortnight later he chided Tony Newton, John Cope and myself for being wet and inactive in fighting our (i.e. his) corner, and talked of a special party meeting (including Conservatives outside the Commons) to clear up everything. We demurred and were further chidden.

Michael Wolff and Sara Morrison, two close comrades of mine, were now in positions of power in Conservative Central Office, but reported that the place was in turmoil because of doubts about the leadership. Michael and I had been close colleagues since 1967. A long career in journalism had given him preternatural calm. Having worked previously with Lord Beaverbrook and Randolph Churchill, he seemed immune to shock. The leader of the party usually has trouble with Conservative Central Office. Hothouse intrigues flourish unnaturally in that unattractive hulk at the corner of Smith Square. Ted sought to control the situation by appointing Michael as, in effect, chief executive. Sara Morrison was at the same time put in charge of the women's section of the party. There was nothing calm about Sara; she charged full tilt at every obstacle. She occasionally had to be rescued out of a thicket, or dissuaded from a scandalously witty remark about a party dignitary, but she was huge fun and a constant help to Ted at this time, and forever after. Neither Michael nor Sara was allowed long enough at Central Office to complete the overhaul which they planned.

Ted came to dine with the office boys on 12 December:

4½ hours of talk. He dozes at one stage, then revives sharply and stays till 12.45, ordering port and whisky. We range too wide to be decisive. He doubts whether we will pull out of the present dive, does not show his hand, if he has one, which I doubt . . . Spends too much time attacking the monetarists and defending the past, egged on by John Macgregor. But it is a success and no other possible leader would be so open and easy.

But the other side was stirring. I liked Airey Neave, who was my neighbour as MP for Abingdon. He was emerging as chief tactician among Ted's opponents, attracting more esteem among the un-committed than the sugary chairman of the 1922 Committee, Edward du Cann. On 19 December Airey discussed the situation privately with me. We agreed that if Ted won the forthcoming contest there would need to be a new chapter of his leadership in terms of personalities and policies. We had a similar talk six weeks later, by which time Airey was in a suppressed fever of excitement as Margaret Thatcher's campaign manager. I interpreted his willingness to talk of a 'new chapter' under Ted as a sign that he was uncertain of Margaret's prospects. I see now that it was part of his tactic of underplaying her prospects. He was trying to attract Conservatives who really wanted not a change of leadership but a stern warning administered to Ted. William Waldegrave and I discussed the content of the 'new chapter' with each other and with Ted. He accepted generally our advice about greater openness and conciliatory discourse within the party. We were pleased . . . until he remarked at the end that of course he did all this already. Undeterred, I drafted a statement on the 'new chapter' for Ted to use on 4 February 1975 the party leadership election day.

It was not needed. On the first ballot he trailed behind Margaret in a way no one had foreseen. A stream of friends flowed in and out of his room at the House of Commons telling him that the fight was over. There should be no question of hoping for better luck in the second ballot, which would be necessary. Lord Hailsham struck an individual note by arguing that Ted must stay around to stop Margaret winning, presumably by campaigning vigorously for a third candidate, likely to be Willie Whitelaw. 'I demur, saying he should stay out. This is accepted. I draft a few sentences of resignation. These are used, though he strikes out the sentence about his services remaining at the country's disposal. He is less stricken than in March.' That evening Willie Whitelaw and his friends canvassed for support in the second round. Willie indeed drove me home, in a Mini too small for him. I did not commit myself. I wrote that night: 'WW <u>much</u> nicer than MT, less effective technically and intellectually.' Two days later I committed myself to Jim Prior, who had thrown his hat belatedly into the ring. He was my closest friend in the Shadow Cabinet; I trusted his judgement and his powers of decision. I owed him much, and there was nothing on which we disagreed.

On 10 February I walked to Wilton Street and dined alone with Ted. It was the last night of his leadership of the Conservative Party. He was calm and looked ahead to the future, but without any lift of spirit. We talked about Europe and the big domestic issues; there was really nothing more to be said about the party contest. The next morning Margaret Thatcher was resoundingly elected leader. Sitting sad in the House of Commons Library, I could hear the applause from the 1922 Committee as the result was announced upstairs in Committee Room 14. I have always disliked the roars of sycophantic applause to which the party is addicted on such occasions. 'She is a practical lady', I wrote resignedly that night, 'and knows the traps.'

Before and after the leadership contest of 1975 the Conservative Party groped towards a new set of policies and a new philosophy. There were many meals and meetings of lively debate. A new backbencher had to work his way through the arguments. My own stance was, and remains, not far from the centre of politics: that is, towards the left of my own party but firmly within it. I have never contemplated leaving the Conservatives, let alone joining the Liberals or Liberal Democrats. But at this time I flirted with the idea of proportional representation, joined the Conservative Action Group for Electoral Reform, and went to a study conference on the subject at Swinton College in Yorkshire. My interest waned, partly because most enthusiasts favoured a form of PR which would abolish the single-member constituency to which I was devoted, and partly because as the years passed the dangers of the present system producing a far-right or far-left government seemed to evaporate. Capital punishment remained strong on the agenda of most party meetings, and on this I saw no room for compromise. At this time I recorded that 'To judge only from the postbag the main causes which impassion my constituents are that we should hang human beings and prevent animals from travelling by sea. I disappoint them on both.'

We argued hard about Scottish devolution. I was one of the few English MPs who thought we should stick to our 1970 pledge to set up a Scottish Assembly. The office boys discussed this over dinner several times, notably on 10 November 1975, when the Labour Government's doomed plans for devolution were taking shape. 'As usual Malcolm Rifkind is hemmed in.* We disagree all over the shop, but I suppose the issues become a little clearer each time. I think the Government will get a 2nd reading on its Bill, will blame us for its disappearance in Committee, and an incoming Conservative Government may well face a colonial situation in Scotland, disastrously.' Not, as it turned out, disastrously, but with growing difficulty, which could have been avoided with much benefit to the Union and to the Conservative Party if we had held to our 1970 pledge and set up an Assembly when we had the chance.

Not all my conclusions belonged to the progressive centre of politics. I enjoyed the company of Nigel Lawson, also a newcomer to the Commons. His mind, which runs more quickly than his tongue, impressed me with its clarity and independence. Nigel has never belonged to any political school except his own. Together we gave mischievous evidence to the relevant committees of inquiry against two progressive propositions: first, Public Lending Right, by which authors (such as myself) benefit at the taxpayers expense from loans of our books out of public libraries; and second, the funding of political parties at public expense.

The real contest within the party was not about specific policies but our essential character and appearance. Here I was certainly on the losing side. I felt no animus against Margaret Thatcher, but was sick and angry at the action of her new party chairman, Lord Thorneycroft, in sacking Michael Wolff from his position as director at Central Office in March 1975: 'spiteful and foolish. He and Sara [Morrison] and the others were starting a long slow process of humanising the Party. This has been scrapped and the Party handed over to 3 sour old men of proven incapacity. Write accordingly but with more tact to H Atkins

---

*Malcolm Rifkind, later Secretary of State for Scotland, Defence Secretary and Foreign Secretary, had been elected for Edinburgh Pentland in February 1974. He never disguised his support for a Scottish Assembly, even when the thought was unpopular in the party.

[Humphrey Atkins, the Chief Whip]'; 'The team of generous and farsighted men who ran the Party till a year ago is now dissipated and defeated through lack of political cunning.' Two snapshots from successive days in 1975 illustrate the choice as it appeared to me then in gloomy moments. On Sunday 23 November at a Conservative conference in Malvern, 'Listen to the talk by a typical Thatcherite – dark-suited, articulate, 55, accountant, full of sourness.' Next day to Cambridge, 'quick sandwich in Pembroke and talk on devolution to PEST [left-inclined Conservative students] – a lively and admirable group. These are the people who must win the party, not stiff-collared accountants from Stratford on Avon.'

During 1974 and 1975 I was at work on a novel based on my time at Ten Downing Street, which Collins published under the title *Vote to Kill*. A quiet, rather shabby young man, not a million miles from myself, serves as the Prime Minister's political secretary, and jousts with the Prime Minister's flamboyant son for the affection of Clarissa, another private secretary. To prevent this *mise-en-scène* from becoming dim and bureaucratic, I arranged for Clarissa to fire a crossbow concealed in a red ministerial box into the Prime Minister's side as his car was driven out of Oxford up Headington Hill towards the end of an election campaign. In the background a monstrous young demagogue is campaigning on the slogan 'Troops out of Ireland'. Ted Heath read *Vote to Kill* on a plane to Hong Kong and wrote a glowing review in *The Times*. Its modest success helped to temper my disappointment at the way the political scene had moved.

For me politically the bright spot in these years was Europe. Soon after the election of March 1974 I began to look around again for a part-time job which could supplement my parliamentary salary and help to meet the mortgage payments on the Old Rectory at Alvescot and the coming school fees for the three boys. I went to see Sir Kenneth Keith at Hambros in St James's Square. He was immensely affable, took me into his confidence on many matters, and gave me two paperweights – but no job.

At this time some far-sighted pro-Europeans in the Conservative Party were working on the need to construct some all-party mechanism to promote the cause of Britain in Europe. Harold Wilson had fought the election on a promise to renegotiate the terms on which Ted Heath had taken us into the EEC in 1973. This turned out, as everyone expected, to be an empty performance. Nothing of substance was changed by the renegotiation, and the talk turned increasingly to the prospect of a referendum on whether Britain should stay in the EEC.

My own views on Europe had become less fuzzy while working with Ted. I never shared his personal enthusiasm for complete European integration. Somewhere along the line, I believed, the progress towards ever closer union would come to a natural halt, leaving the nation states with their separate identities, but bound by rules and habits of cooperation which would in effect unify Europe without forcing into existence a United States of Europe. But we were not at or near that halting point in 1975. From the point of view of an amateur student of European history the EEC was an extraordinary change for the better and British membership was a brave and necessary step forward for us which it would be disastrous to reverse. For years a highly respectable and dull body called the European League for Economic Cooperation had discussed and promoted that subject in a somewhat academic fashion. Two leading Conservative MPs, Geoffrey Rippon and Anthony Royle, decided to bring the ELEC under their control and convert it into a meeting place for European enthusiasts. These were two highly effective organisers in different styles: Tony Royle brisk and military with a limp from the war; Geoffrey Rippon subtle in his perception of the weaknesses of human nature and kindly in finding ways of turning them to account. ELEC had a tiny office in Regency Street, off Vincent Square in Westminster. The promoters felt that it needed a part-time director with political contacts and in June 1974 offered the job to me with a salary of £5,000. There was generosity as well as calculation in this, and I have always been grateful to those concerned, including the treasurer, Alistair MacAlpine, who later split away and became strongly hostile to our camp. We used to meet genially for breakfast on the top floor of the Dorchester Hotel, looking out over the fountain designed by Oliver Messel towards the corner of Hyde Park and Apsley House.*

On 24 October Geoffrey Tucker and I flew to Brussels to sound out the two British Commissioners, George Thomson (Labour) and Christopher Soames (Conservative). George Thomson, a former cabinet minister, delighted us by promising to fight hard for a yes vote in a referendum. Christopher Soames was more cautious, though we knew his heart was European. The necessary campaign organisation took shape ponderously under the direction of Sir Con O'Neill, my former chief in Peking. Con, as he once exclaimed, was 'not an administrator but an old retired man of sixty-two'. We met for the first time on 8

---

*I associate these years of my life with many political breakfasts in London hotels on different European themes. The politician who gets up early, whether to broadcast or to confer with others, sets the agenda for the day and has a strong advantage. He can spoil the effect by overeating; too many worms weaken even the early bird's performance. Half a grapefruit and one croissant and coffee are sufficient, except in Scotland, where there are kippers.

January 1975 in the basement of the Royal Horseguards Hotel, and rapidly became immersed in deciding the names and membership of various committees. A majority of us had to resist the attempts of the European Movement under Ernest Wistrich to pin us to a federalist definition of Europe. Lord Drogheda, a difficult but entertaining treasurer, began to raise money. John Sainsbury on the Budget Committee sorted out the claims on our funds as between expenditure on television and work by parties in the constituencies. Shirley Williams, a cabinet minister and a heavy hitter, usually turned up late bowed down by a big, battered black despatch case with straps barely able to contain the bulging papers within. I worried at first that we were creating a verbose bureaucracy rather than a fighting machine.

On 3 March a group of Conservatives called on Margaret Thatcher to discuss Europe, three weeks after she had won the leadership election. The party officials Michael Fraser and Chris Patten (the new head of the Research Department) emerged dismayed after an hour and a half of talk, but I thought the outcome reasonable. Margaret did not at that time have definite views on the future of Europe. She was clear about the need for a yes vote, but understandably saw the immediate problem in party terms. Europe was Ted's theme, not hers. She did not want to quarrel with him, and was quite ready to praise his achievement in getting Britain into the EEC, but she was wary about the campaign itself. She did not want the party sidelined by an all-party group, and she knew she would have to campaign herself. Willie Whitelaw told me a few days later that some of her immediate entourage were warning her against our organisation Britain in Europe as essentially a plot against her leadership. The poisoners were already busy, carrying absurd stories of insult and conspiracy from Ted to Margaret and back again; but the two of them had at this stage the sense to keep the rumours in proportion.

Roy Jenkins, then Home Secretary, was emerging as the leader of the all-party effort. He gave me whisky in his room on 10 April and I found him 'most affable and perceptive, a joy to work with'. After my support a few months earlier for a National Government, I began to wonder whether this new alliance across party boundaries or the referendum could survive in other fields. 'It is greatly needed. But no. Because we are a majority of the nation, but a minority in each party, and the parties have enough vitality to prevail.' So it proved, and fortunately so. In 1974 there had been a strong case for a united effort to deal with the aftermath of the miners' strike and the oil shocks. By 1975, though the Labour Government was failing in many fields, there was no longer a genuine atmosphere of crisis. Coalition government is best reserved for crisis; as Burke said of revolutions, the extreme remedy of the constitution should not become its daily medicine.

Ted Heath and Margaret Thatcher chimed together admirably at a Conservative meeting on Europe in the St Ermin's Hotel on 16 April: 'They don't actually kiss, but compliment each other and the lights flash and she makes a good speech and we all drink happily ever after.'

Britain in Europe launched its campaign for a yes vote at a press conference on 13 May: 'Serve EH as in old days, carrying bag, and writing handout which is v. dull.' For several weeks before and after that my life was consumed by helping to plan and take part in the campaign. By 16 May I was taking the chair at the second BIE press conference: 'Shirley Williams arrives three quarters of an hour late, and dictates into a machine wh. turns out to be broken. So no handout. She and GR [Geoffrey Rippon] gobble lots of figures, she under question produces one good phrase about fighting dreams. The press ask a few questions – report nothing.' Three days later we met Margaret Thatcher again, and found her more sure and knowledgeable than in April.

I campaigned in the Isle of Wight, Coventry, Lincolnshire, and with John Wakeham and his wife Roberta in the Royal Corinthian Club at Burnham on Crouch. Audiences were thin, but there was no particular reason why more than a few dozen people should turn up to listen to a new backbench MP. The London breakfast meetings, now at the Waldorf Hotel, multiplied and overflowed the bounds of reason. Outside London Ted Heath performed brilliantly. The rest of us became jaded; I suffered ludicrously from an infected nose. It was not clear how things were going, and press coverage seemed meagre to the enthusiasts. I enjoyed most the last three days of the campaign in mid-Oxfordshire, charging round the villages in a decorated 'yes' bus with my Liberal opponent and my co-author Andrew Osmond. Finally, on 6 June, 'we are in the Community by 2–1, carrying Scotland, Wales and Northern Ireland – a v. remarkable result wh. wd. have been incredible 6 months back'.

The referendum campaign was at the same time exhausting and exhilarating. We believed in the cause, and enjoyed the pleasures of working alongside people who were usually our political opponents. As I had expected, we slipped back naturally enough afterwards into routine party warfare; but I never lost the habit of discussing any subject comfortably with men like Roy Jenkins, John Harris and Bill Rodgers, who had been fellow campaigners for a yes in 1975.

Myths have grown up round that campaign as round any extraordinary political event. It is normal at political meetings nowadays for elderly citizens to say, 'I voted in 1975 for a Common Market, not for all this political interference which comes out of Brussels nowadays.' True enough; we had acceded to the Treaty of Rome which created a common market. We did not campaign in 1975 about a single internal

European market, a common foreign policy or a common currency. These ideas came later; they were not current in 1975. When these proposals arrived over the years they were considered and accepted (or, in the case of the currency, set on one side) by the elected British Government responsible to the British Parliament, which then passed the necessary legislation. No important change in our obligations was or could be imposed on Britain from outside. We argued that in 1975, and it is still true.

The referendum campaign had some economic content – for example, an argument on prices illustrated by shopping baskets. Prices were on the whole higher on the continent than here, but I suggested a Norwegian shopping basket which showed that in that country outside the EEC they were higher still. But on the whole the argument was at a less childish level, and overwhelmingly political. Anyone listening to Ted Heath, Roy Jenkins or indeed Margaret Thatcher would know that they supported Britain's membership of the EEC overwhelmingly for political reasons. Peace and prosperity in a continent which thirty years earlier had been prostrate and torn apart; friendship and collaboration with democratic countries whose future was linked with ours – these were simple themes repeated by those politicians in all parties whom the electorate were most inclined to trust. Gradually enough doubters were won over. We are nowadays sometimes accused of having concealed the fundamental constitutional point: that even though the Treaty of Accession was then narrow in scope we had already conceded that where domestic law clashed with European law on matters which fell within the treaty, European law would prevail. Yes, indeed, that was an essential feature of accession. And this was the main argument of our opponents, both in Parliament in 1971/2 and in the referendum of 1975. Nothing that was known was concealed. The no campaign, led by eloquent men such as Tony Benn, Peter Shore and our Tory sceptics, put the criticism at the centre of the argument. The argument against giving European law this priority was fully paraded – and firmly rejected.

The next six months for me passed without political excitement. On 15 January 1976 I put down a challenging question in the Commons to the Home Secretary about police expenditure in Oxfordshire. Roy Jenkins reacted crossly and I was pleased: normal politics had returned. Immediately afterwards Margaret Thatcher sent for me and briskly offered me the job of frontbench spokesman on Europe under the Shadow Foreign Secretary, Reggie Maudling. I at once accepted. I had been a backbencher for not quite two years.

Margaret Thatcher knew that I had supported Ted throughout the leadership contest. She guessed that I was still in touch with him; for example, I dined with him alone that same week and helped him with a successful speech in Scotland. For several years to come she used to consult me on small matters relating to Ted, for instance asking whether I thought he would like to come to this occasion or that. She judged loyalty to be a virtue; I had been loyal to Ted, and she hoped that I would be loyal to her. She never supposed, even much later when we worked closely together and I saw her just about every day, that I was a suitable candidate for her inner circle. I was never 'one of us', nor would I have been comfortable in that group. Only rarely, usually when we were abroad together, was I given a glimpse of her innermost political thoughts. But in 1976 there was no dividing line of policy which prevented her from offering me a junior frontbench job, or me from accepting it. I had fought for Ted at his Culloden and we had been soundly beaten. But Ted was not Bonnie Prince Charlie, and there was no Jacobite movement. He made no attempt to keep a political bodyguard together. His occasional outbursts of opposition to Margaret were solitary. He never reproached me for serving under Margaret Thatcher. I could not have done so had she held then the views about Europe which she professes now; but there was no hint of that. Indeed, she stressed the continuity of Conservative policy on the subject. I was not a free market zealot and wrongly suspected that one day we might have to go back to some form of incomes policy. I disliked the tone struck by some of her victorious supporters, but on the rare occasions when I had met her I had been impressed – and sometimes charmed. The future was all to play for.

13

SHADOW MINISTER

On the day when Margaret Thatcher promoted me to the front bench I wrote, 'This is just what I wanted, and in happier circumstance I would be walking on air.' But the circumstances were not happy. A few weeks earlier Tatiana and I had decided to separate. Our marriage was coming to an end.

The strains had been there for some time, even in Rome ten years earlier. Friends of us both, such as Andrew and Stuart Osmond, had done their best, as had my mother and Tatiana's father. Many couples learn to hold together even though their ways of life have diverged. After a time we were no longer able to manage this. Tatiana did what she had to do in the constituency. She became fond of some of my political colleagues, in particular the Wolffs and the Priors. She was on good, though not close, terms with Ted Heath. But she never relished political life or entered into its arguments. She was a talented tennis player and in Oxfordshire formed a group of tennis friends from which I was, by my own incapacity, excluded. Putting down these sober facts a quarter of a century later, I see they do not add up to anything like an explanation of the storms which broke over our marriage. They were not continuous, there were patches of sunshine; but they were fierce and increasingly frequent. In January 1975, for example, I could bear the shouting no longer, drove for the night to the Bell at Tewkesbury and walked the Malvern Hills alone next morning. Although we disagreed on more and more, each recognised the other as a good parent of our three sons, and never argued over the division of time spent with them.

I began to enjoy holidays alone with Nick and Tom. From 1975 I have a particular memory of the Palazzo Ravizza, an old-fashioned *pensione* perched above the walls of Siena. In spirit the palazzo survived from the world of E.M. Forster's *A Room with a View*. The dark brown sitting rooms were lined with books by Dornford Yates, Hugh Walpole and Arnold Bennett. I read their copy of *The Way of All Flesh*. An aged lift, outrageously abused by Nick and Tom, creaked up and down between the floors. Storms swept across the valley beneath us, and caused the postponement of the Palio, the famous horserace round the central piazza of Siena, which we had come to see. But it was run the next evening, and from the Mayor's balcony we watched the charge of *carabinieri*, the crowd slowly filling the square with a buzz of anticipation, the parade of flag men, the white oxen, and eventually the quick, rough ride and the victor acclaimed under the colours of the orange tortoise. The boys were always excellent company.

A strange thing happened after Tatiana and I agreed on 2 November 1975 that we must separate: the angry arguments fell away at once. In the background during the coming months the lawyers argued over terms, but we never let this get out of hand. I felt a mixture of relief and exhausted sadness. That Christmas Day we were invited to lunch with the Tilleys in the Lodge at the other end of the village. My diary entry reads: 'It is well done, but as N[ick] says, not as good as a family lunch here, of which there will never be another.'

Partly perhaps because of the wrangles during three and a half years spent at Alvescot, my affection had diverted itself into the house itself and garden, even though it was Tatiana who had devised improvements to both. Neither of us could afford to go on living in the Old Rectory after separation, which caused me great sadness. In the summer of 1976 Tatiana moved to a house which she bought in the next village, Black Bourton, a traditional inn at the entrance to the churchyard. In the following few weeks I rattled about miserably in the Old Rectory, which I had already sold. Ginny Tilley generously took pity on my coming homelessness and gave me two rooms at the Lodge. I slept and breakfasted there when I was in Oxfordshire, but spent most week-ends at Black Bourton with Tatiana and whichever boys were at home from school. People who knew of our past travails found this puzzling, but to us it seemed natural. An angry marriage turned into a friendship based on shared parenthood. I helped to dig Tatiana's garden, and in 1976 spent a happier Christmas there than had seemed possible a year earlier.

I could not sleep indefinitely at the Lodge, of course, and had to find a proper roof of my own. The village of Westwell lies in a hidden valley just five miles north of Alvescot, in the direction of Burford, right on the western border of what was my constituency. The farmer there was Chris Fox, whom I knew, though not well. He quietly took my problem in hand and arranged for me to rent from his landlord the second of four paired cottages at the edge of the village. I moved my scanty possessions in May 1977, and have lived in Westwell ever since, albeit in three different houses.

No. 2 Mitford Cottages, Westwell, had, I found later, a depressing effect on my mother, my association chairman, my constituency agent and other ladies who took an interest in my welfare. Built by Lord Redesdale in the 1930s for his farm workers, the cottages have no particular style. A staircase leads steeply up from the front door to one and a half bedrooms and a bathroom; downstairs there is a sitting room and a kitchen; that's it. My agent, Margaret Jay, out of a generous heart provided many packages of cooked delicacies, with instructions on how long each needed heating. But at that stage Westwell provided what I most needed – privacy. I have always enjoyed moderate doses of solitude and this was particularly true in the cottage in those years. There was room for one boy at a time to lodge with me, and the youngest, Alexander, then eight, came often. I took all three of them fishing and swimming beside Loch Maree that summer. It slowly began to feel as if a nightmare had come to an end.

During the three years after 1976 I busied myself with a rush of political errands while privately my life stagnated. My job as Shadow Minister for Europe was not powerful, and did not include a seat in the Shadow Cabinet. But it was active and brought me into increasingly close touch with Margaret Thatcher. For example, I sometimes escorted visiting foreign politicians to see her. One such was the Spanish Foreign Minister José María de Areilza, who early in the conversation asked her if he might speak frankly. 'I had been told, madam, of your formidable intelligence, but no one had warned me of your beauty.' I was horrified, thinking the impertinence would annoy. I had a lot to learn.

My immediate chief was the Shadow Foreign Secretary; there were three during this period. The first, Reggie Maudling, was coming to the end of his political career. He never lost his geniality or his shrewdness, but he had reached the stage where every problem seemed familiar and none important. It was impossible to excite him with good news or bad, and difficult to persuade him into any action which involved argument. I labelled him 'the great non-possumus'. His successor John Davies was intelligent, courteous and hardworking, but unluckily a fish from another river. His successful career in industry had not equipped him to cope with the rapids of political life. He had difficulty in expressing himself with precision or force, yet this is the first requirement of a frontbencher in the Opposition. The bitter argument within the party on Rhodesia swallowed him up. Either Sir Alec Douglas Home or Peter

Carrington would have sailed through the debate on sanctions at the Brighton party conference in 1978. They knew how to use the rudder. I understood that day that John Davies was ill, though not how badly. As individuals, most of the delegates in the hall should have been able to see from his stumbling performance that something physical was wrong. Collectively, in the artificially heightened emotion of a debate, they mauled him unforgivably.

His successor Francis Pym is the most central of Conservative politicians. By background he belongs to traditional Britain, but his instinct is to lean his weight against the direction in which the party is tilting so as to keep it on an even keel. During Margaret Thatcher's time the tilt was to the right and he reacted accordingly. He was pessimistic by temperament or possibly by his earlier experiences as Chief Whip. That position seems to leave its holders with an excessively dark view of human nature. Throughout, Francis found his dealings with Margaret Thatcher difficult. Her habit of leading every discussion with a firm statement of her own views bumped up against his natural reluctance to argue with a woman. He tended to lapse into silence and grumble afterwards, rather than surmount the initial hurdle and launch into the discussion which the subject deserved. But his difficulties with Margaret did not obscure either his good sense or the loyalty which always constrained the depth and length of those occasional grumbles.

We were confronted as an opposition with a proposal for converting the European Parliament from a body of national Members of Parliament sent to Strasbourg by their parties into a body directly elected by the people. Direct elections had been agreed collectively by all governments of the EEC, but they required domestic legislation. The Conservative Party, including myself, were overwhelmingly in favour of the principle. It seemed a natural consequence of the division of power in the Community between the Council of Ministers and the European Commission. The ministers who attended the Council and took all major decisions were, and still are, responsible to national parliaments. The Commission, which alone could make proposals and hold the responsibility for carrying out decisions of the Council, was unelected, and so could not be held to account by national parliaments. I spoke of a democratic pincer effect. National parliaments kept the responsibility for controlling the Council of Ministers; the Commission would be responsible to a directly elected European Parliament, both having limited power.

Margaret Thatcher never challenged the principle of direct election, but she found it uncongenial. Through 1976 and 1977 I went to a series of meetings which she chaired, as we painfully cleared our policy through the bureaucracy of the party and defined our attitude to the

Labour Government's Bill. Margaret was concerned with her own authority over the new regiment of Conservatives in the European Parliament which would emerge from the change to direct elections. In private she was inclined to question their likely loyalty, given that the techniques of patronage and party discipline familiar at Westminster could not be applied to them in Strasbourg. She insisted – indeed this was the price of support from the party as a whole – that the new MEPs should be elected under our traditional first past the post system. We were able to impose this condition against the Government's own preference for a proportional system.

But Margaret's underlying reluctance went wider. She was moving slowly from the vague enthusiasm for the EEC which she had shown during the referendum campaign of 1975 to the almost total hostility to Europe which she has shown in recent years. On 2 December 1977 I spent a foggy day in Brussels with her doing the rounds of the European Commission. It was her first visit. As usual she was charming in individual discussions. I had already learned that she was willing in turn to be charmed by handsome men who knew their subject. The example that day was the Belgian Viscount Davignon, who talked to her passionately about steel. I experienced for the first time on that visit her damaging habit of giving a destructive press conference at the end of what had been a constructive day.

Christopher Tugendhat, the British Conservative Commissioner, gave a dinner that evening in her honour. Because of the fog, I left early to catch the Ostend ferry and be sure of meeting constituency commitments next day. As I left Margaret was telling Christopher that she would have no time to run the European policy of her Government, because for eighteen months she would have to concentrate entirely on the British economy. The following week I had a long talk with her alone. After our Chinese expedition that summer I found these tête-à-têtes easier to handle, but I was dismayed that her impressions of the day in Brussels had grown harsher over the weekend. Another motif, later familiar, emerged when she denounced the amount of money which she saw sloshing about in European activities.

After the Direct Election Bill passed through Parliament, constituency associations began to think about their candidates for the first of the new European elections. A tiny handful of Conservatives in each constituency were enthusiastic, another handful hostile, most bemused. In those days the Conservative Party still maintained in good order an amazing array of subsidiary bodies – area organisations, women's advisory committees, Young Conservatives, students, the Conservative Political Centre, trade unionists, local councillors, a Commonwealth and Overseas Council, the Conservative Group for Europe, the Bow Group and no doubt others. Many of these have since withered away as the appetite for party politics has dwindled; but between 1977 and 1979 all of these bodies required briefing on the new European requirement. I trundled round the country, usually addressing quite small groups, repeating myself interminably, trying to blow each flicker of interest into a flame. My missionary work extended beyond the Conservative Party. ELEC, of which I was still a director, organised well-attended non-party conferences in Belfast, Glasgow, Newcastle and elsewhere. In my diary I complained of all this grind, but in fact I enjoyed myself. I like the act of travel, even on grubby British trains. I like poking about in different parts of my own country, walking unknown streets, snatching half an hour in an unexpected museum. I even like hotels. As is the case with all politicians, I am not averse to the sound of my own voice, though I prefer to hear it answering questions rather than presenting monologues.

Looking back, I can see that my enthusiasm for direct European elections was exaggerated. The cause was not bad and my theoretical justification still seems sound. There is nothing to be said for going back to the old nominated system. But, although the European Parliament has grown since 1979 in size and power, it has not so far put down deep roots in the political life of Britain or indeed of other European countries. I have never felt at ease when visiting Strasbourg or replying to questions from its members. I had hoped that the Parliament might apply corrections based on common sense to the rhetorical platitudes of the European Commission and its itch to intervene in the nooks and crannies of the citizen's life. Instead the Parliament has multiplied the platitudes and encouraged the itch. These failings are not irreversible. Much talent and energy are deployed in the Parliament, and my mild prejudice against it may before long be outdated.

A separate task at this time involved plenty of travel on the continent. The British Labour Party was joined with the European left in the Socialist International. The Conservative Party was keen to negotiate an alliance with like-minded parties of the centre-right within the EEC, but also beyond it. This was not controversial within the party at home because it involved no sacrifice of independence. It was controversial within some Christian Democratic parties on the continent, particularly the Italians, who regarded us, the Conservatives, particularly in our new free market phase, as outside their tradition. The name 'Conservative' was itself an obstacle on the continent where it seemed to mean at best stick-in-the-mud and at worst semi-fascist. Gradually, with Margaret Thatcher's help, we wore down the difficulties and formed what we called the European Democratic Union. Much massaging and many journeys were required to achieve this. For us the leading spirit was

Diana Elles. She remained almost unknown at Westminster and in the party as a whole; she never sought publicity. But she had a sound link with Margaret Thatcher and won round the other potentates of the party, and after that the leaders of the centre-right in Europe, by low-voiced, unyielding persistence. The CDU in West Germany were the key; they were in opposition and Helmut Kohl had become their leader. He accepted an invitation to visit Margaret Thatcher in London on 8 July 1976 and we besieged him with meals and meetings all day.

> Kohl large and beefy, with a nice smile, verbose, confident, historical, a man who creates confidence. Two hours with him in MT's room, with a phalanx of shadows. He talks too much but there are insights on the Union and the young. He is very forthcoming about bilateral cooperation, seems to know little of EDU. We strive to correct this all day ... He makes a varied impression, wordy again, but the quality began to come through ... Dine at Dorchester for Kohl – MT does it very well, works very hard. Kohl makes a remarkable speech – very much Ted's philosophy of human nature and the desire for fulfilment.

It would have been well if Kohl and Margaret Thatcher had continued to work as hard together as they did that day.

The French were particularly difficult to pin down because of the rivalry of their different centre-right parties. On 29 April 1976 Diana Elles and I set out to woo the French Minister of the Interior in the Palais Beauvau. The chestnuts were in full bloom. Prince Poniatowski made the most of the occasion, helped in his stagecraft by the fact that minor demonstrations were occurring in several French cities during the afternoon of our visit. 'He sits at a magnificent desk, the garden behind him, a great hourglass at his side. A hound lopes to and fro. Prefects ring up on coloured telephones for instructions. P talks to us in perfect English. He looks like a pink pig, shrewd and unamiable. They are all reasonably friendly, and at least we have them in play.'

Diana Elles taught me the arts of short-range travel. There is less leg room in the front row of most planes than in the second. It is worth a struggle to sit near the front because of the minutes you save by leaving the plane early. Do not throw away that advantage by checking a case into the hold. It is perfectly possible to look presentable for one or two days of meetings out of a hand-case, and still leave room in it for duty-free purchases, in particular what as her travelling companion I once described as 'the purposeful chink of bottles'. So, compact but I hope still reasonably elegant, we criss-crossed Europe in our search for allies, finally achieving what we wanted on 24 April 1978. On a warm spring day at Salzburg Margaret Thatcher and the other leaders of the European centre-right signed the agreement setting up the European Democratic Union. The French Gaullist attitude had been ambivalent to the last. Their place was empty when the ceremony started, but finally the General's ancient, upright disciple Couve de Murville stalked unannounced into the room and signed. 'Margaret enjoys herself, insofar as she can enjoy anything European.'

These European preoccupations left little time for domestic politics. In December 1976 I was cross and thought of resigning my frontbench job when the party finally ditched its commitment to Scottish devolution. I had two angry arguments with Willie Whitelaw – one under a lamp-post, the other in the Commons car park – before coming round.

I kept in intermittent touch with Ted Heath during these years. In August 1976 Sara Morrison invited me to an ambush in her home at Fifield in Wiltshire. She lured Ted from his sailing, and the three of us dined together. The Conservative Party under Margaret Thatcher was about to issue a strategy document which we thought would be not too bad. We argued that if Ted wanted to influence events, the party was his only vehicle; but he must help it to win the next election. The new document would offer him a splendid chance to confound his enemies and come aboard again. He should endorse it as soon as it appeared. The advice was better received than I had expected. But we were soon bogged down in arguments about the loyalty or lack of it of the party's present leaders. Over several hours Ted and I drank a bottle of claret each and, not for the first time in such encounters, I went to bed thinking we had made real progress. I woke late with a hangover, and Sara's dog had stolen one of my socks. Ted had already left; Sara made me a lot of coffee; our quarry had in the end eluded us.

That was the last time I tried a frontal assault. In February 1977 I suggested that he might stand in the direct elections for the European Parliament. At the same time I had to tell him that I was going with Margaret Thatcher to China, a country to which he had taken me three years earlier and which he regarded as his bailiwick. He showed no resentment at the news, but equally no interest in my suggestion about direct elections.

When mustering arguments for that abortive ambush in 1976 I had drunk two stiff gins with Chris Patten, director of the Conservative Research Department. During this time I came to know Chris quite well. 'He is the only person of substance in the Party of whom no one says a nasty word, being wise, humorous, and honest. The sooner he gets a seat the better.' These were the qualities which had drawn me ten years earlier to Michael Wolff. Michael had died suddenly in May 1976. He was no older than me, and he would certainly have overcome the setback of his dismissal by Peter Thorneycroft from Central Office. What new career he would have built I am not sure, but it would have quietly reflected those same qualities. About this time, or perhaps rather later, I began to ask Chris Patten for occasional advice on the books I should read – novels, history, poetry, the lot – exactly as I had asked Michael Wolff. This is a symbol of a particular kind of friendship.

After *Vote to Kill* had described my time at Number Ten in fiction, I tried next a factual account in *End to Promises*. The book was explicitly modest, as there was a great deal which I did not know, and I said so. Richard Ollard, my editor at Collins, was unenthusiastic about the manuscript, and only a big shove from my agent Michael Sissons and much rewriting achieved its publication in 1979. The book was well received, and continues to be used as a helpful source by proper historians. It has its *longueurs* but also some vivid sketches. One reader who received it badly was Ted himself. He felt that my effort skimmed along the surface of events which required deep analysis. This was true, and I never pretended otherwise. *End to Promises* was based on my diaries and a few party papers I had kept, not on any wider interviews or research. The book was favourable to Ted at a time when fashionable opinion was vehemently against him and his other friends were silent. But since he cared not a jot for fashionable opinion, this was of little interest to him.

Three expeditions educated me to cope with different aspects of my own future. The New Zealand Government then ran a policy of inviting young British parliamentarians to visit, and I benefited from this in September 1977. No trouble was spared. A senior official escorted me round the North Island for one week, handing over to a younger colleague for a second week in the South, punctuated by a weekend break in the mountains round Queenstown. This being New Zealand not China, there was no attempt at indoctrination; I met all types, and drew my own conclusions. These are not complicated. I have been to New Zealand three times now, and the only dull moments have been on the planes to and fro. For beauty and friendliness New Zealand can hardly be matched. The politician becomes aware of a paradox. At one level the country seems deliberately old fashioned, with its modest houses, elderly cars and unemphatic speech. At another level New Zealand pioneered the welfare state at the beginning of the twentieth century and its demolition (by a modern Labour Government) at the end. New Zealand plunged into proportional representation. It was the first country to give women the vote. Almost uniquely it runs an agriculture without subsidy. New Zealand has pioneered what might be called the politics of apology in dealing with its own past and the Maori minority. Perhaps the small size of the country inclines it to adventures of policy. Anyone interested in politics needs to keep eyes and ears open there as he enjoys the peacefulness of grass, sheep and mountains.

Early in 1978 the BBC decided to send to Northern Ireland two newish MPs, one Conservative, one Labour, who knew nothing of the Province. The BBC would make a programme out of the first impressions of these novices. It was a foolish notion, the producers being themselves inexperienced in the pitfalls of politics across the water. The Labour MP pulled out at the last minute, and I flew alone to Belfast on Friday 13 January. I lunched with the army, and chatted clumsily to Fusiliers worried about their pay. Then to the Divi flats in West Belfast escorted by a troubled headmaster, tea in Turf Lodge with a group of mothers whose children, persuaded into the IRA, were either dead or in jail. That was the Catholic day. Saturday was for Unionists in Belfast and the RUC. On Sunday there was tourism in the glens of Antrim, where I was filmed beside a waterfall.

The programme began to fall apart in conflict between the London and Belfast broadcasters. The latter, keen for a hot story rather than a reflective piece, wanted to challenge me about one event (which they themselves had organised) on the Friday night. Before coming, I had checked both with the Secretary of State Roy Mason and with his shadow Airey Neave that they saw no harm in my seeing members of Sinn Féin; neither demurred. In a bleak, bare room in the Ballymurphy Community Centre I argued for an hour with a small group of Republicans. The discussion was pointless and ill tempered. The group was led by 'an intelligent young man with black beard and thick voice – Gerry? Adams'. When I became Secretary of State for Northern Ireland six years later, Gerry Adams tried to make something of this meeting. He meant to embarrass the Unionists, portraying it as a deadly secret in my past, but even Ian Paisley refused to be enraged for more than a day or two, and the story died. It was the security forces and the mothers of Turf Lodge rather than Gerry Adams whose analysis led me to write pessimistically at the end of this visit that we would not be able to beat the IRA permanently.

In October 1978 John Stanley, the young MP for West Malling in Kent, and I spent a fortnight in southern Africa as the guest of the South Africa Foundation. They put together a good programme, not biased in favour of the apartheid Government. In Johannesburg executives of Anglo-American and other businesses tried to persuade us that they constituted an irresistible force for change. We drove round the huge black township Soweto and talked to Nthato Motlana, one of the black

ANC leaders not in exile. My recollection of that first visit to Soweto was of a forlorn black bank manager in new but empty premises. The Lutheran Bishop Manas Buthelezi gave us a vivid picture of life in the township: '10 or 11 in each house, trains you catch by throwing someone else off, kids who play in the streets because in the house there is no room for anything but sleep'. Both he and Motlana were clear that black South Africans would always refuse to be expelled from South Africa to the mythical homelands which were their destination under the theory of apartheid.

I visited my godmother Irene Camerer, frail but dignified with magnificent white hair. She stood definitely at the other end of the South African spectrum to those we had so far met. Of Scottish birth, Irene became close friends at school with my mother, before marrying a Munich businessman. She had lived unscathed in Germany through the war and its immediate aftermath, but with her husband and growing family emigrated to South Africa soon after. Her son Alexander had stayed with us in Cheyne Row. He and his lively wife Sheila were keenly interested in politics – and in a political settlement. Their blond children were learning Zulu. Sheila later entered parliament and became a minister in F.W. de Klerk's Government on the progressive wing of the National Party. In all my visits to South Africa the Camerers acted as a hospitable unofficial foil to the briefings which poured in from all groups and parties.

In Pretoria we coincided with the British Foreign Secretary David Owen. He and the Americans led by Cyrus Vance were pressing the South Africans on early and free elections in Namibia, which South Africa still administered under the old League of Nations mandate. When John Stanley and I called on the Prime Minister P.W. Botha we found his office in full crisis over Namibia. Private secretaries dashed in and out of our meeting, and Botha left us for a few minutes to say goodbye to Owen and Vance. Sallow, friendly, radiating a feeling of power, he himself was unfussed. He told us several times that there was no such thing as a black South African; after three days in the country we knew enough to recognise a rubbishy conclusion, not enough to know how he reached it. In Botha's anteroom we bumped into the administrator of Namibia, Judge Steyn, who immediately invited us to visit the front line in Ovamboland in northern Namibia, where the South African army was trying to repel SWAPO guerrillas infiltrating from Angola. Before Namibia we spent a day in the Zulu capital Ulundi, with their leader Chief Mangosuthu Buthelezi, with whom I had several tortuous dealings in later years. In a torrent of words he explained how he rode two horses, being both leader of Inkhata, the Zulu National Party, and Chief Minister of the homeland of Kwazulu created by the white apartheid Government. When I knew him later he was still riding two horses – Inkhata and an uneasy place in Mandela's black ANC-dominated Government. On our way to the airport in Pretoria we called on President Vorster. He was brought back late and sweating from his afternoon walk to meet us. 'He is like a big old jungle beast. Africa was slow slow. Eventually sense, esp. economic sense, would prevail over communism. Long stories.'

We were whisked in an army plane up to Ovamboland, where an odd situation prevailed. An election was being held at the same time as a war. The nationalist movement SWAPO was fighting the two campaigns simultaneously, rather as Sinn Féin and the IRA used both the ballot and the bullet box in Northern Ireland. A moderate, multiracial alliance called the DTA were their main opponents. That evening we discussed election tactics with the DTA canvassers in the South African army base, a fact which in itself suggested that they had a limited popular base.

> Up early. Breakfast with an odd lot. A pilot thrilled because good old Smithie [Ian Smith – Rhodesian Prime Minister] yesterday bashed Nkomo's base in Zambia – and a tedious old Afrikaner schoolmaster saying how Afrikaner and African love each other. Military briefing by Col. Lambrecht. Soviet weapons [captured from SWAPO] on display, also Jason, a teacher who defected to SWAPO and was recaptured. By helicopter up to advance base. Inspect a kraal; also dogs which detect land mines. Sand and bush and young soldiers. As usual armies impressive and sympathetic. Specially flown back to Windhoek by County Administrator General over salt pan.

The round of politicians in Windhoek that afternoon was less interesting. Next day we were in Cape Town, faced with the contrast between on the one hand the beauty and comfort of Table Mountain and the Mount Nelson Hotel, and on the other the pathetic squalor of the Crossroads township.

So many people have written about the beauty, miseries and talents of South Africa and South Africans that it seems trite to add more. I returned several times in the next twenty years. Of all the countries which I have visited on what might be called political tourism, South Africa has stirred and attracted me most.

After an argumentative day in Lusaka we found our way to Rhodesia, then in the last years of minority white rule, beset by sanctions, isolation and black revolt. Blinds were lowered and lights extinguished in our Boeing as we descended into Salisbury; guerrillas with hand-held SAM missiles were active around the city. Once again our talks with black and white Rhodesians covered a wide range. The Rhodesian minister who usually handled contacts with Englishmen was P.K. Van der Byl. Several of my colleagues on other occasions were overwhelmed by what they perceived as wit and charm. I differed: 'The most offensive and ignorant person in authority whom I have ever met. A false Englishman in the manner of Ribbentrop. Against elections, against everything except intrigue and condescension.'

General Walls, the army commander, briefed us on his campaign against the guerrillas led by Nkomo and Mugabe. He struck me as frank but not first class. He described a military deadlock, though he would not use the word. He hoped that elections would provide an outcome which military force could not manage. Next day in the old Cecil Hotel in Umtali the army and police commanders were gloomy. The farms were emptying fast, and they had only one 'fire force' in the area to deal with the 'gooks' or 'terrs'. From a hilltop we looked out over Mozambique, beautiful in the spring sunshine. We could not see the mines laid in a vain attempt to prevent the trafficking of men and arms across the border.

At another military post at Mount Darwin we met for the first time the bitterness towards Britain of the white farmers. They saw themselves as defending a way of life derived from us, which we had deserted – 'but they are releasing in 20 mins some of the tensions of 6 years of war, bullets in the bedroom, fearful intimidation'. There was no such bitterness from Ian Smith, the Prime Minister, when we saw him back in Salisbury, though he looked old and was distant in manner. He galloped through his points in half an hour: yes, there would be elections; yes, there could be UN and British observers; yes, he was still willing to negotiate. There was no reproach over British sanctions against his regime.

Our last call was on the supporters of Bishop Muzorewa, who the West then hoped would win the elections. They were pleasant, voluble and eager to campaign – but the bishop himself, instead of leading them on the spot, was conducting a leisurely visit to Europe.

The main change in my private life during this period was the purchase in 1978 of a ground-floor flat in Inverness Terrace, which runs north from the Bayswater Road just short of Queensway. Since the sale of 40 Roehampton Gate in 1972 I had relied in London on spare bedrooms in the houses of various friends. The boys were beginning to need a base in London, and for myself I had begun to want more space and privacy. The choice of Inverness Terrace was not universally approved. The area was thought by some to verge on the sleazy, and there was no particular charm in the flat itself. But it served its purpose. I enjoyed coming back to that quiet privacy late at night from the Commons or the airport. I even enjoyed waking to find a small platoon of Nick's friends sleeping on the floor in the big Victorian sitting room. Huddled under blankets or overcoats, they would give me a polite Etonian 'Good morning, sir' as I stumbled over them to make toast and coffee. In the early evening, if I was back in time, the same very young men might queue in front of me in dinner jackets politely requesting me to tie their black ties for them.

My sons and I had the usual bachelor problems of lost keys, flooded bathrooms and exploding oven, but such incidents on the whole endeared the place to us. We took summer holidays together – in Wales, Brittany and the Loire valley. During several summers around this time we spent a week or so at Le Mortier some ten miles north of Tours. The daughter of the house and her Scottish husband, Catherine and Allan Law, had been friends of ours in Rome, and were always hospitable. Catherine's mother lived in the big house, the Laws in a dower house across the lawn, but we all ate together. The centre of the day for Madame was the arrival of the conservative newspaper *Le Figaro* from Paris about noon. Silence fell while she digested the latest movements of the Bourse and whatever was that day's evidence of the relentless decline of civilisation. Nick remembers that when Mitterrand won the presidency in 1981 she simply folded the paper and remarked, '*C'est la fin.*' Only French was permitted at her table. These visits were an excellent education for the boys and myself.

I spent almost every weekend in my small cottage at Westwell. Many meals, particularly at Christmas and Easter, were spent with Tatiana and the boys at her house in Black Bourton seven miles away. There was never any question of our coming together again, but, partly because we both knew that, the tension had gone from our relationship. I enjoyed the privacy of Westwell, but there were disadvantages. The cottage was hard to heat, the winter of 1978/9 in particular was long and snowy, and for the first time the word 'lonely' began to appear in my diary.

PART V

JUNIOR MINISTER

14

THE FOREIGN OFFICE

On Friday 4 May 1979 Margaret Thatcher became Prime Minister; in the next two days she framed her Government. I have always disliked being slave to a telephone which might not ring, and on the second day abandoned it in favour of a lunch for bankers in a marquee ten miles away from Westwell. On return to the cottage I was telephoned by a colleague, whom even now I shall not name. Roughly of my seniority, he was already showing impatience verging on indignation at the silence of his telephone – which, as it turned out, never rang for him. Having counselled patience, I turned slightly shocked to weeding dandelions out of the lawn. About teatime the Prime Minister, in dulcet tones but briefly, asked me to serve as one of the ministers of state at the Foreign Office. I accepted with enthusiasm. 'So another chapter and another step. I only want to make one more, i.e. to serve in a Cabinet. Lord C[arrington] rings and seems genuinely pleased. Sup. with T[atiana]. Boys ring.'

The next four years at the Foreign Office, three under Lord Carrington, one under Francis Pym, were the most carefree of my ministerial life, thanks mainly to the style and character of these two Foreign Secretaries. Cabinet ministers in my experience fall into three main classes. One set are useless and kept going by their civil servants: they do not last long. Another set are centralisers. Loving detail, they gather it relentlessly into themselves. Such ministers can thrive only if they have trained their minds to absorb formidable quantities of facts and figures and transmute them into decisions. Two examples of this style in my time were Geoffrey Howe and Leon Brittan, which suggests to me that it comes most easily to lawyers. Serving later under Leon

Brittan at the Home Office, I marvelled at his mastery of a complicated agenda. The third set prefer to delegate responsibility to others. They try, never with total success, to push most detail away from their desks, and concentrate on the core of each problem. They use the time and energy thus saved for the personal handling of whatever seems most immediate or important. That was the style of Willie Whitelaw at the Home Office and Peter Carrington at the Foreign Office. It was later the style which in the same jobs I derived from them – partly through conscious choice and partly through necessity. My mind does not easily retain or digest masses of detail. I do not play bridge, and my children have always beaten me at chess.

A minister of state under Peter Carrington enjoyed the best of all worlds. He was given wide discretion over where he went, whom he saw and what he said. He knew that he would be backed up by the Secretary of State, and that if anything became too rough he could refer upwards for a decision, which would be quickly made and simply phrased. Peter Carrington held frequent meetings with his ministers and substantial business was mellowed with gossip. We came to know our colleagues well and understand one another's problems. He used to good effect three very personal weapons: wit, pretended ignorance and half-pretended pessimism. 'Science was invented since I was at school' was a remark at the beginning of a discussion in his office of a complicated nuclear problem, during which he showed full mastery of its technical aspects. I know of no enterprise undertaken by Peter Carrington which he did not launch by telling friends and colleagues that he was bound to fail. His main achievement at the beginning of his tenure was to steer a settlement of the interminable Rhodesia problem past the rocks of the Prime Minster, the Lusaka Commonwealth Summit and the Lancaster House Conference. At each point he would confide in us that the next stage was almost certain to prove a disaster.

His senior colleague, also in the Cabinet as Lord Privy Seal, was Ian Gilmour, with whom I worked easily and in ever closer contact. These two cabinet ministers often talked in private of their acute frustration in dealing with the Prime Minister. They regularly exploded with exasperation against her performance at some conference or cabinet meeting. Gossip writers who heard indirectly of such explosions suspected, then and later, rebellion and treachery. That is to misunderstand the political process. This use of the safety valve does not prevent ministers working loyally and effectively under leadership which they sometimes find maddening.

As a result of their experiences, added to my own, I began to form a clearer view of our leader. When dealing privately with an individual, particularly someone in difficulty, Margaret Thatcher could be exceptionally perceptive and helpful. When over fifteen years I took foreign visitors to see her I was always impressed by her natural attentiveness and good manners, markedly better than my own. But in official meetings of all kinds with her colleagues she was usually authoritative to the point of abruptness. When crossed in argument she would dart off into a thick smokescreen of irrelevancies or even resort to personal rudeness, including to subordinates or others who had no means of defending themselves. There was no deliberate desire to hurt, simply a determination by hook or by crook to get her own way.

Peter Carrington and Ian Gilmour reacted in different ways to this phenomenon. Ian Gilmour disagreed with her on almost every political issue. Unlike Peter Carrington, he held strong views on social and economic policy and thoroughly disliked as un-Conservative the free market dogmatism which he believed Margaret Thatcher was imposing on the party. Ian could be formidable in deploying personal charm or forceful with argument, but he decided that these were assets wasted on the Prime Minister. It was clear to me and everyone in whom he confided that he would not stay long in the Government; it was simply a question of whether he should jump or wait to be pushed. The push came in September 1981.

Peter Carrington had a different approach, relying on his seniority and natural mastery of international problems in which the Prime Minister knew she was inexperienced. When I pressed him to take a bigger role in domestic politics, he replied that he had no time. This was true, but not the full answer. By limiting himself to foreign affairs he maximised his influence. Four times during her premiership Margaret Thatcher was persuaded into crucially important decisions which ran counter to her original instincts: the Rhodesia Settlement (1980), the European Budget Settlement (1980), the Anglo-Irish Agreement (1985) and the Single European Act (1986). In her memoirs and private conversations she shows that to some extent she came to regret all these decisions once she no longer carried the responsibility of office. All four were clearly in the national interest. The first two were brought to a successful close by Peter Carrington. In this and other respects I learned much from him.

By chance I was a witness of the crucial day on the European Budget. With a handful of Foreign Office officials I had been summoned to Chequers on 30 May 1980 to discuss the Middle East. We wanted the Prime Minister to be more forthcoming towards the right of Palestinians to determine their own future. She was, as expected, reluctant. Margaret Thatcher was hostile to Menachem Begin, the Israeli Prime Minister, and to Yasser Arafat of the PLO on the same grounds: namely, that both were guilty of terrorism. But Arafat's offence was still current, and anyway her instincts were always favourable to Israel. But her attention that day was elsewhere. When worried, she was rarely discreet in relaying to one minister her distrust of others in the team. She had left Peter Carrington and Ian Gilmour to carry forward the battle to reduce Britain's contribution to the EEC Budget, and was agitated by what she had heard overnight of their work. At twelve-fifteen Peter arrived at Chequers, brick red with exhaustion, accompanied by Ian Gilmour and private secretaries. The Prime Minister broke off our desultory argument on the Middle East, and hustled her two cabinet colleagues into the Hawtrey Room to discuss the EEC Budget. I paced up and down the rose garden while officials drew up a minute for me to sign summarising the flexibility which we wanted on the Middle East.

The argument on Europe which raged beyond our hearing in the Hawtrey Room is vividly described by Ian Gilmour in his book *Dancing with Dogma*. The combatants eventually emerged at two-thirty, and we ate a strained lunch together. As ever the Prime Minister was a thoughtful hostess. To my surprise, she returned to discuss the Middle East with us for twenty minutes, and even more unexpectedly accepted my minute. Perhaps because she had just been so rough with Peter and Ian she felt a conciliatory twinge towards the Foreign Office. The policy she then approved was later carried forward by Peter Carrington into the European Venice Declaration, one of the landmarks in the Arab–Israel dispute. Margaret Thatcher, having let off steam, was later persuaded to accept the Carrington–Gilmour deal on the European Budget as a success for herself – which indeed it was. Without her previous vehement determination we would never have done so well.

Having acted as the party's spokesman on Europe in opposition, I had hoped to handle European matters in the Foreign Office, but they fell to Ian Gilmour, which left me, as I wrote, with 'the stodgy end of the pudding'. I need not have worried. One of my first tasks was to renegotiate the Lomé Agreement, which governed trade and aid between the EEC and the ex-colonial countries of Africa, the Caribbean and the Pacific (ACP). Negotiation dragged through a night in May, and another in June 1979, despite the brisk, housemasterly chairmanship of the Council of Ministers by the French Foreign Minister, François Poncet. The Charlemagne Building in Brussels, where ministers met in my time, became a prison, its inmates starved of fresh air and exercise. To avoid disgrace among my European partners, I exceeded the maximum aid figure in my brief, and had to telephone Nigel Lawson at the Treasury for permission to go higher. These were all useful lessons. In the small hours of one night the Zambian representative denounced colonialism for ten minutes, until, still in full flow, he collapsed forward into a deep sleep, head in hands. The EEC held all the cards, and eventually the bargaining petered out.

We had to sign the new treaty in Lomé, the capital of Togo, a sleazy ex-French dictatorship in West Africa. The European ministers hung about in a luxury hotel, while the ACP tried to wring some final concessions out of our negotiation. I wrote a chapter of a novel, and read Trollope's *Three Clerks*. Eventually the President–and self-styled Founder–Guide of Togo decided enough was enough. In the square on the way to the Maison du Peuple several thousand people were dancing and singing. The huge hall was packed with young party militants wearing T-shirts and pants emblazoned with maps of Europe and Africa. The signing ceremony took a long time. Each of the sixty-eight signatories was greeted by a long chant in his honour, the whole hall standing, wiggling, waving hankies. This happened to me three times as I had to sign for Kiribati and the Solomon Islands as well as Britain. It was very hot. A banquet followed with excellent wines, repulsive food and three further hours of dancing and chanting. In my minute to Peter Carrington I described the scene: 'As the noise and excitement grew the President–Founder–Guide, who was and resembles a wrestler, sat impassive behind his glass of mineral water, like the Emperor Seth in *Black Mischief* . . . It is rather a scandal that something as important as the ACP–EEC relationship should be centred on this disagreeable little dictatorship.'

By this time I had settled into the routine of ministerial life, junior division. I would occasionally slip away at lunchtime and swim in the RAC's amazing pool, which was a perk at the time for MPs, or perhaps just for ministers. Every day at the Foreign Office was filled with meetings and meals, organised with quiet firmness by my first private secretary, Charles Humfrey. I began seriously to eat for my country, but preferred a prosaic working lunch or dinner at Carlton Gardens or Ten Downing Street to the long-drawn splendours of the Mansion House or Guildhall. The wives of aldermen constantly told me how much our overseas guests enjoyed and envied the City's traditions of processions, gold plate and loving cups. My impression was that most of them were longing for their beds. I am glad that in recent years Lord Mayors have curbed the ceremonies. In Britain high pomp is best left to the Royal Family; this is one of the advantages of monarchy.

Mere ministers of state were expected to respect the demands of the government whips in the Commons and turn up to vote when requested. I had no regular Labour pair at this time, and our majority was small. My diary was thus constantly at risk. I enjoyed Foreign Office Questions every fourth Wednesday in the early afternoon, but had little enthusiasm for late nights or all-night sessions. Dipping on one such long evening into Disraeli's *Life of Lord George Bentinck*, I wrote on 7 February 1980, 'No one would write such purple passages about our dreary

House of Commons now.' The next week there were guillotined votes on an Education Bill from 4.30 p.m. until 2 a.m. I lay on a mattress in my tiny office in the basement of the Commons, emerging every hour or so at the clamour of the Division Bell to join again the press of stale bodies in the Division Lobby. The next day was crowded with meetings and media appearances.

Only once did I have to carry serious legislation. In 1980 under pressure from the Americans we agreed to introduce limited sanctions against Iran. The Trade Minister Cecil Parkinson and I managed the Bill together. There was a muddle over whether sanctions would apply to existing contracts. When I remarked to the Prime Minister on the bench one day that I felt bruised by press criticism on this, she went out of her way (metaphorically) to cuddle me, telling me that my main speech on the Bill had been a masterpiece.

At the end of December 1979 Russia invaded Afghanistan. On Sunday 30 December Peter Carrington entertained Margaret Thatcher to lunch at Bledlow, his house in the Chilterns. It was a social occasion not without incident, for the Filipino staff handed round with the fish the stuffing intended for the jugged hare. The Prime Minister was firmly excluded from the gentlemen's conclave over port, but held her own conclave later with Peter and myself in his study. She was at her most reasonable, and told us how much she liked to be argued with. There was no need for argument with her that day over the aggression against Afghanistan; but it took the Atlantic Alliance several weeks to organise a not particularly convincing response.

As part of that response I was, with others, given the task of frustrating the forthcoming Olympic Games in Moscow. This was the most foolish task with which I was ever entrusted as a minister. I knew little about the world of athletics, but enough to realise from the start that neither administrators nor athletes were likely to abandon for political reasons an occasion in which they had already invested so much work and ambition. After another meeting on 16 January I was dissatisfied with the way I put the argument: 'I am too cocky, voluble, and not persuasive.'

The International Olympic Committee refused to shift the Games from Moscow, so it became a question of persuading British contestants to boycott them and putting together an alternative. On 17 March twelve countries (a puny fraction of the total) met in Geneva to carry forward these ideas. I chaired the meeting alongside President Carter's representative, Lloyd Cutler. The Americans wanted a television spectacular as a rival to Moscow, but through lack of support the concept dribbled away. The press and the Commons mocked us. I saw David Bedford and other athletes in vain. I wrestled at greater length but no greater success with Seb Coe's father, who was also his trainer. Peter Carrington held two equally unfruitful sessions in June with the chieftains of the British Olympic Committee. It was impossible to shift them, to talk of peace, war and justice: the discussion soon turned to the holiday arrangements of Geoff Capes, the shot-putter. I wrote a final, eloquent article in the *Daily Express* on 27 June asking athletes to play their part in making the world a bit safer by 'staying away from the scramble for Moscow medals'. All in vain; with the gallant exception of the equestrians they almost all went. Seb Coe, Steve Ovett and Allan Wells won gold medals.

On 30 April 1980 Iraqi terrorists had seized the Iranian Embassy in Princes Gate. The following drama showed the British governmental machine at its best. An operations room was at once organised in the Cabinet Office in Whitehall; Willie Whitelaw as Home Secretary took charge. Peter Carrington was in Washington and for six days I represented the Foreign Office in almost continuous discussion in that windowless room. The Prime Minister appeared among us twice but made no attempt to take control. It was the first time I had seen Willie Whitelaw as a taker of decisions, as opposed to a moderator of discussion; I was impressed. At a private meeting in the Home Office with the Metropolitan Police Commissioner David McNee and myself he said he was determined not to let the gunmen go, even if they released the hostages unharmed.

In Princes Gate the terrorists' demands shifted through the weekend. We felt bound to follow up their request to see a group of Arab ambassadors. On the afternoon of Sunday 4 May I saw the Kuwaiti and Syrian Ambassadors and the Jordanian Chargé d'Affaires. I invited them to present themselves outside Princes Gate and invite the terrorists to give themselves up. They asked if they could offer a safe conduct. When I refused, they declined to help. Three hostages were released over the weekend, but the underlying deadlock continued. The SAS were busy installing themselves next door in the Ethiopian Embassy, which rapidly filled with gadgets. The terrorists, like any normal Knightsbridge residents, complained that the noise of drilling kept them awake at night. The dismayed Ethiopian Ambassador, with a train of children and servants, had to be expensively accommodated in a hotel.

On Monday, a bank holiday, I learned that the Jordanian Ambassador had returned to London. He was the Arab representative I knew best, and I tried unsuccessfully to get him into action that morning. Because it was important to keep the terrorists in play, we persuaded the BBC to broadcast news of my meeting with the Jordanians at noon. They told me afterwards that it was the dullest news item they had ever led with.

I went back to Inverness Terrace at lunchtime. While I was devouring a pizza an official rang from the operation centre to report that shots had been heard from inside the house at Princes Gate. I hurried back to the bunker in the Cabinet Office; Willie Whitelaw drove up from Dorneywood in twenty-one minutes. It was not clear what the shots meant; no bodies had been produced. The terrorists again demanded to see the Arab ambassadors. I tried the Jordanian once more, but he refused to budge. Willie Whitelaw was superb. Legally the Commissioner of Police, representing the civil power, was responsible for maintaining the peace. Commissioner McNee needed to be satisfied that all peaceful efforts by his negotiators had failed before he could call in the military, which meant the SAS. Willie summoned a few of us into a private room. We agreed with McNee that either a second shooting or the showing of a body would be enough to trigger an attack by the SAS, who were now ready. Meanwhile I was urged to persevere with the useless ambassadors. I talked to the Algerian Ambassador in French, simply so that the BBC could calm the terrorists by reporting that a diplomatic effort was continuing. In the late afternoon the siege suddenly ended. A body appeared. As had been agreed, the attack was ordered. We watched on television the immediate and complete success of the SAS. The Prime Minister and whisky appeared almost simultaneously, and there was much relief. Perhaps we had taken too much for granted the superb professionalism of the SAS. It was they, not the ministers and officials gathered in the Cabinet Office bunker, who did the trick.

My work mainly covered North Africa and the Middle East, which I visited many times over those four years. Personalities change more slowly in that area than in the democratic West. Many of those whom I met as Minister of State were still near the top of their pile when I became Foreign Secretary ten years later. One who did disappear in that interval was President Bourguiba of Tunisia, the founder of his independent country. In May 1981 I called on him in his palace outside Carthage.

An amazing and useless interview of 50 minutes. The old man, a fine head, champing jaws, harangues us about the war, cannot be coaxed beyond 1943. Finds and reads a long and remarkable letter which he wrote in prison in 1942 predicting allied victory. Twice he reduces himself to tears. Once he climbs on a chair to show on a map where Cap Bon [scene of the expulsion of Axis troops from North Africa in 1943] is. Four-fifths ridiculous, one-fifth moving.

We were trying to stimulate British interest in a rather successful small country which was anxious not to be regarded as a preserve of France. I got to know well the British Ambassador's house off the road between Tunis and Carthage. He alone of our ambassadors ran an orchard and small farm abundant with olives and oranges and donkeys. In the old days he had a railway station to himself. The house itself is celebrated for the blue tiles which line the walls of each main room, notably the big reception hall at the entrance, over which a young Queen Victoria presides in a preposterous equestrian portrait by D'Orsay.

I hope all is still as I have described it. Several such embassies are the despair of the Treasury and of occasional Foreign Office ministers with narrow vision who measure the entitlement of ambassadors in cubic metres. They would like to confine the less important representatives of Britain to small suburban villas. Luckily the legal and political complications of disposing of a historic embassy like Tunis often prove insuperable.

Peter Carrington asked me to take over from him the task of accompanying the Queen on her state visits to Algeria and Morocco in October 1980. After breakfast on 25 October we stepped out into the courtyard of the British Embassy in Algiers and watched the royal yacht *Britannia*, portly and Hanoverian, find her way into the great harbour, HMS *Apollo* escorting while the shore batteries saluted. For the next fifteen years, *Britannia* was a character in my life, of which more later. The only problem in Algeria was the absence of any instruments with which the Queen could tackle in public a roasted lamb with a shiny hard skin, scalding hot. She scrabbled with her fingers, and it hurt.

Morocco was a different matter. That state visit has gone down in legend as a disaster. The view of the British press was that King Hassan behaved with deliberate and grotesque discourtesy to the Queen throughout. The truth is more complex. The visit had, like all its kind, been meticulously planned in advance minute by minute by British and Moroccan officials. The King took no notice of these plans. In a mixture of vanity and social fright he set out to devise the visit himself from scratch. He was cross, for example, to find that for security reasons the Queen could not travel in his royal plane, a fact of which his advisers had presumably been too scared to tell him. He piled so many extra coloured lights into his palace garden in Rabat that the whole system fused. The Queen, wearing tiara and diamonds, sat in a huge red and grey Rolls-Royce for thirty-five minutes until the signal came to proceed. Through these days the greater the chaos the more relaxed was the Queen.

The next day was much worse. The royal impresario, beside himself with nerves, took the Queen through endless suburbs of Marrakech, standing and waving to the crowds. We headed for a plateau in the desert, and arrived at 2.30 p.m. for lunch. Hundreds of tents had been pitched in a great semicircle. There were a thousand horsemen preparing their display, and about as many officials – but no lunch. The King disappeared, and the Queen was left for an hour and a half alone in a pavilion in full view of the press. The only refreshment was offered by a waiter who knelt beside her, and, showing a hidden flask, whispered, 'Cognac, Majesté?' The King, meanwhile, was busy compounding confusion in the background reorganising everything to produce a bigger and better lunch, which finally appeared at 4 p.m. The cavalry charge which followed was a success, and everyone went to bed in the Hotel Mahmounia exhausted but in reasonable spirits.

I was woken early by a call from London reporting that the British press had given the King no mercy for the chaos of the day before. The King did not know this when we travelled with him in the royal train to Casablanca, sentries posted at regular intervals along the railway line through the desert. I learned then why there needs to be a minister accompanying the Queen on state visits: she deftly diverted to me the King's political remarks. Indeed, we made good progress on a British bid for a steel mill in Morocco, and the King offered to help extricate a British citizen, Mr Sparkes, from prison in Iraq. In the afternoon things turned sour. The King sent his sinister Minister of the Court, General Moulay, to request that the Queen's dinner for him on *Britannia* be postponed by one hour. Although Moulay did not explain this, for security reasons the King was always dodging about from one palace to another, and had decided to spend that night some distance from Casablanca. This meant that 8.15 p.m. would be too early for him. Having consulted the Queen, I told Moulay that she could not alter the time since so many people had already been invited, but would quite understand if the King arrived, say, half an hour late.

The King arrived fifty-five minutes late, in a foul temper, with a prince or two who had not been invited. He had obviously heard about the London press. At dinner he sat on the Queen's right, and I on his right. All three of us talked in French throughout. To the Queen, of whom he was clearly in awe, he spoke social nothings about royal persons known to both. To me he hissed in a low voice so that the Queen should not hear. First, the British steel mission must be postponed. Second, he was not satisfied with the British Ambassador, who should be replaced as soon as possible. When I asked for a reason he said he was not obliged to give one, then added that the ambassador had made a mess of preparing the list of the decorations which the Queen would bestow at the end of her visit. I said that the list had been agreed with his ministers, to which the King replied that the ambassador's whole attitude was wrong. Perhaps we could say that the climate of Morocco did not suit him. Warmed by his own anger, he said it was intolerable that we had refused to alter the timing of the dinner. We should not behave as if it were 1904 (when the French took over Morocco). We were not treating him as a gentleman. He added that the Queen was charming and her reception in Marrakech had been marvellous. He could organise crowds, but not the smiles on their faces. But he would not eat her bread and salt without saying what was on his mind.

The conversation faded away, but left me, as I thought, with a problem. The King, however unreasonably, had clearly as head of state asked that our ambassador should go and had refused to withdraw the request. The ambassador, Simon Dawbarn, who had for two years reported sympathetically from Rabat on the King and his deeds, was to be knighted by the Queen on *Britannia* the next morning. There was obviously some risk of a further public relations disaster if the King persisted. After dinner the Marines as usual Beat the Retreat on the Casablanca quayside. As we watched from the deck of *Britannia* I told Prince Philip what had happened. He laughed loudly, and suggested I do nothing at all. It was excellent advice. At the farewell ceremonies next morning the King grimaced affably, and without unsaying any of his tirade at the banquet, told me that he was in touch with Baghdad about our prisoner. When I arrived back in London the Prime Minister decided, rightly, that we should not try to correct the record, but let the storm blow itself out.

I met the King of Morocco several times in later years. He never referred to our dinner conversation. Highly intelligent and personally brave, he ran his country well by the standards of his time, but autocracy became loneliness became unreality. By insisting on total subservience from all around him, he cut himself off from any flow of reasonable advice.

The countries which border the eastern Mediterranean and its hinterland used to be called the Levant. I became familiar with their capitals and rulers, but tried to remember that this was superficial knowledge. Each of these men had learned how to speak at international conferences and receive foreign visitors in the lingua franca of modern diplomacy. But each of them in their own land had to govern a volcano, the nature of which I could only glimpse, and it was that task, not their chats with people like me, which mattered in their lives.

Distances were small, but each country had its distinct character. In October 1979 in Damascus I listened to the immense expositions of the Syrian President Assad on the future of the region. Grizzled, tired, with a smile which ran out of friendliness as it stayed fixed hour after hour,

Assad ranged relentlessly from platitude to platitude. The monologue, which could last up to an hour including interpretation, hardly varied in its quiet obstinacy year by year. Only an expert ambassador sitting beside me could detect some changed resonance or new phrase which might suggest a shift of policy.

On that first visit I was driven west through the austerity of the Syrian hills, where scruffy soldiers stood beside a dug-in tank, a heap of shattered cars or a dead donkey, down into the Bekaa valley of Lebanon with a different political culture. The provincial governor offered a lunch of many courses and wines, served by waiters in white gloves, and attended by a mass of notables, most of whom had composed a speech of welcome in French. This prepared me for Beirut. Friends who knew that city and its mountains in their heyday speak of it with affection. I always disliked it in the days of its degradation through civil war. A city can be forgiven for being battered into ruin by its own citizens and their outside enemies. That happened to Belfast, but I never felt that Belfast lost its character. In Beirut vulgar wealth and ruinous hatreds existed side by side. I disliked listening at embassy parties to Lebanese ladies, fresh from lavish exile on the Avenue Foch in Paris, deploring 'mon pauvre Liban' as they twisted the emeralds on their fingers. On my first visit in October 1979 Beirut retaliated against my dislike. I had eaten something amiss one evening, and woke feeling frail. While being driven in the ambassador's Rolls through east Beirut to call on the Foreign Minister, I was suddenly overcome. The heat was stifling and the police siren inexorable. I just had the strength to tell the Rolls to stop and stumbled out into the ruins of a shelled courtyard with a stall of drinks among the rubbish in one corner. Feeling like hell, I vomited against a wall, and then became conscious of a grubby face bent over me: 'Seven-Up, monsieur? Très bien pour le mal d'estomac.' Heaven knows how long his sticky bottle had been open, but it did the trick. My verdict on the visit perhaps reflected this humiliation: 'Shan't come back to Beirut in a hurry. A raddled wounded whore still whoring.'

By contrast I became fond of Jordan, as both a tourist and a politician. There is no need here to sing the praises of Petra, Jerash and the Wadi Rum, or the oddness of the Dead Sea. I was attracted by the strong British flavour which Jordan's rulers gave to their version of Arab life. The streets of Amman were as clean as those of Guildford; the sentries marched and saluted with the precision of Aldershot. Jordanian politicians admitted me to their jokes and gossip in a way which would have been inconceivable in any other Arab capital. Several times a year in Amman or London I would see the King's brother, Crown Prince Hassan, whom I came to like and admire. One year he and I broke away from the routine of diplomatic exchanges and watched the Grand

National together on television in the Lamb Hotel at Burford. The King, too, was amazingly accessible to a mere minister of state, in London, in his house near Ascot and in his palace in Amman. King Hussein was one of the three most polite men I have ever dealt with. (The others were Sir Alec Douglas Home and Nelson Mandela; all three came from a strong traditional inheritance and never had to worry about who they were.) King Hussein called everyone 'sir', including Margaret Thatcher, who was at first surprised, but came to accept it as understandable. Several times we met at times of great strain for himself – for example, when we were at odds over the Gulf War, or when he was being treated for cancer. He often spoke gloomily, but never raised his voice in anger. When listening to that quiet voice through the years I tried to keep in mind the pressures at work on him from past and present – the assassination of his grandfather in his presence in Jerusalem and later of his cousin King Faisal in Baghdad, the battle with Arafat up and down the hills of Amman in 1970, the humiliation of three wars with Israel, the lack of resources of his neat kingdom, above all the need to keep the loyalty of the regiments on which his dynasty depended. He made mistakes, but, against many expectations, kept Jordan together and earned the deep respect and affection of his people.

I never felt equally at ease in my dealings with Israelis or Palestinians, and never enjoyed my visits to Jerusalem, Tel Aviv or the West Bank. On both sides I was conscious, as later in Ireland, of highly intelligent people devoting their minds to destructive argument, keen to humiliate well-meaning visitors who wanted to help but who could easily be tripped up on some detail of law or history.

On my first visit to Israel in December 1979 I had an unremarkable talk with Prime Minister Begin and a more interesting session with General Dayan, then out of office. He looked ill, his famous black eye-patch flapped on his face, and he no longer filled his clothes. He thought Israel should withdraw unilaterally from the West Bank, keeping only frontier troops, and let the Palestinians get on with ruling themselves. If only . . .

Now I will collect my courage and write what I came to believe about Israeli policy – not then on my first, ignorant, visit in 1979, but gradually over the years. I do not know when the Western world began to turn from resentment of the Jews as usurers and murderers of Christ towards guilt at the sufferings inflicted by Christians on Jews. Although Shakespeare puts genuine eloquence in the mouth of Shylock, the emphasis is still on Christian resentment not Christian guilt. The authors of the Balfour Declaration in 1917, which is celebrated as the founding document of Israel, were anxious to mobilise Jewish support for the Allies in the Great War. But they were also conscious of a debt of guilt for past persecution which could in part be paid by allowing the creation of a Jewish national home in Palestine. The debt of guilt was enormously increased by the suffering of Jews in the Holocaust.

My wife and I have seen Auschwitz. No one can now reputably dispute the wickedness of the Holocaust or the enormity of the suffering. The Jews once again, and much more dreadfully, were the specific victims of persecution. But does that fact create a special moral status for Israel among the nations? Does it entitle Israel to reject or evade criticism of behaviour, including its own acts of persecution, which in other states would be condemned? Israeli politicians and publicists do not openly assert that unique suffering entitles Israel to unique exemption from criticism; but in some cases their arguments and actions seem to have that foundation. Official visitors to Israel are conducted to the Holocaust Museum in Jerusalem near the beginning of their visit. It is an excellent museum with an awful message for visitors to absorb. That message should be about the universality of suffering and the need for a decent international order, not about a special status for Israel.

Our television screens have often been filled with images of Israeli tanks crushing their way through the towns of the West Bank in retaliation for recent suicide attacks on Israel. Nothing can excuse the suicide bombers, and from my experience in Northern Ireland I recognise that mixture of anger and hopelessness which the relatives of innocent victims are bound to feel. But pictures of Israeli tanks confronting teenagers armed with stones are reminiscent of images of Soviet tanks crushing dissent in Berlin, Budapest and Prague in 1953, 1956 and 1968. Those images helped to destroy for ever the sympathy which many felt before then for the Soviet Union as a past ally and victim of Nazi aggression. Similar images of Israeli oppression distort the memory of past Jewish suffering.

Israel is entitled to security. In a narrow land which its neighbours three times tried to destroy, that entitlement requires special guarantees and probably a friendly armed presence as a guarantee on the ground. But there has been no attack on Israel by her neighbours since 1973, and none is in practice conceivable now, so strong in favour of Israel is the military balance of power.

Israel has been rescued from serious international criticism partly by incoherent leadership in the Arab world, and in particular the in-adequacy and corruption of the regime run by Chairman Arafat in the West Bank and Gaza; and partly by the reluctance of the United States for its own domestic reasons to use the decisive power to influence Israel which it undoubtedly possesses. As I write, President Bush is stirring himself to a fresh effort, which will require much patience and political courage.

Twice during these years I visited Baghdad and saw Saddam Hussein. My report to Peter Carrington on the first of these visits on 12 July 1980 gives the flavour.

At 115° in the shade the annual revolutionary celebrations in Baghdad are not on the whole to be recommended for pleasure, but they illustrate quite well the nature of a disagreeable but powerful regime. Ministers (a few) and revolutionaries (a crowd) are gathered from across the world, housed in a luxury hotel, fed, lectured and invited to dine with the President in the garden of the huge palace built for King Faisal. The revolutionary groups were a bizarre lot (Puerto Ricans, a good many Africans, etc.) and they come largely, I imagine, to say thank you for last year's cheque and negotiate next year's. J. Nkomo (Rhodesia Patriotic Front) was there, munching silently under the palm trees. Saddam Hussein looked well, but he has a killer's smile, and murder continues to be one of the main techniques of government . . . The regime is basically nasty, and I do not think we should run after them.

But it made sense to keep in touch. A year later I had a more formal conversation with Saddam Hussein. He told me that the Revolutionary Committee had recently decided that relations with Britain should be improved. I speculated on the reason for it and the increased oportunities for civilian trade. Iraq was by then at war with Iran, though I found on that visit that the most the Iraqis hoped for was to hang on to the territory they then held. Contrary to later legend, we did not ourselves hope or work for an Iraqi victory. To us, both Iraq and Iran were run by unpleasant and potentially dangerous regimes. Total victory by either would increase the danger. In London Peter Carrington and I argued for caution in supply of arms to both sides. The British Government allowed, indeed encouraged, trade with Iraq, within limits which were constantly argued about between the Department of Trade and the Foreign Office.

Saudi Arabia was of equal importance to us as the leader of the Gulf States. When they visited London and wore European clothes, the princes and ministers of these states were ordinary men, mostly uninspiring. But at home, robed in white, faces partly concealed, surrounded by soft-spoken courtiers and officials, operating in magnificent modern palaces, they conveyed an impression of authority if not always of wisdom. Visitors learned to behave as if they too took for granted the vast carpets, the fountains, soaring arches of white marble, stupendous chandeliers, the clicking of beads, the array of juices, the tiny cups of bitter coffee. I admit that I enjoyed these visits and the leisurely intellectual jousting with rulers and ministers which was their justification. These were by no means democrats. Their fathers or grandfathers, in some cases they themselves, had begun life as desert chieftains squabbling over camels or some small oasis of date palms. Now, thanks to oil, they were among the richest men in the world. Western pundits had forecast incessantly that they were bound to be swept aside by the pressures of modern life. Yet there they still were, always anachronisms, always apparently doomed, yet presiding over the peaceful subjects in 1970, 1980, 1990 and 2000. They outlived many of their critics, changing without appearing to change, exercising ancient skills of leadership which Westerners found baffling.

Of these, the most baffling, because the most private, were the Saudis. Every now and then something would happen to show how sensitive the Saudis were to their portrayal in the Western media. In April 1980 the British TV company ATV screened a programme called *Death of a Princess*. The film described in lurid detail the way of life of junior members of the Saudi Royal Family and the execution of a princess for adultery. The Saudis were appalled. The Foreign Office explained (as we had to explain endlessly in all parts of the world) that in Britain freedom included the right of British citizens to say, write and broadcast horrible things about our friends as well as our enemies. Such utterances were not government policy, but Government could not stop them. The Saudis were deeply unimpressed, and threatened the collapse of our relationship with them. Our ambassador, James Craig, was forced to leave. We could not apologise for a broadcast which had nothing to do with us; on the other hand, we could not sit back and see our position in Saudi Arabia destroyed. It was decided that I should go out as a sort of John the Baptist to make straight the path for a visit by Peter Carrington. If I were snubbed, it would be a bore for the British Government, but not a disaster.

I flew in a Saudi Tristar without alcohol on 26 July. Looking out of the plane at Jedda airport I saw a helmeted police guard standing to attention, and a stately figure in white robes standing on a carpet. This seemed a good omen, but I was still not at all sure what to expect. The next day I flew over the desert to Taif and was installed in the huge Inter Continental Hotel, where a message told me that Prince Saud, the Foreign Minister, would probably receive me in the afternoon. The hotel suite was as usual filled with bowls of dates, chocolate and nibbles of all kinds. The flight had been hot, and I needed to make myself presentable. As I stood under the shower, there came a frantic rapping on the glass door. The Foreign Minister would see me at once. I scrambled out of the shower to dress, but as I pulled up the zip of my trousers it broke. My suitcase with another suit was back in Jedda. There was no time for repair, so I conducted a rather important conversation in a posture which experts had told me was offensive in the Arab world: one thigh firmly clamped over the other. It seemed to me that the gaping alternative would be considerably more offensive.

Prince Saud, it turned out, did not want to talk about the offending film. I was not asked for something I could not give, namely an apology. He had persuaded the King to call off the dispute and begin to repair the damage. James Craig could return to his embassy; trade could gradually revert to normal. It became clear to me that Prince Saud wanted something himself from the fracas, namely a pattern of high-level consultation with Peter Carrington on all the problems of the Middle East. This was easy, a gift as welcome to the giver as to the recipient. That evening I had the first of many meals with Prince Saud in the Crown Prince's house at Taif. Tall, handsome and always dignified, Prince Saud looks what he is, the son of a king. As I write, he is still Foreign Minister, the wisest and now the most experienced in the Arab world. Heavy other duties have been heaped on him from time to time, and I have never understood how he managed to cope, given the oblique and time-consuming way in which the Saudis take decisions. But even after I resigned in 1995 he welcomed me as if he had unlimited time for gossip with an old colleague. I do not think I ever heard him say a foolish thing.

A tragic episode told me more about the British press than about Saudi Arabia. On the night of 20 May 1979 a British nurse, Helen Smith, was found dead in Jedda. After investigation the Saudi police concluded that she died by accident, having fallen from a balcony where a party was being held. Her father Ron Smith and others believed that she was murdered. A British jury returned an open verdict. Around Helen Smith's death there sprung up in Britain a lurid farrago of stories and accusations. Into the pot were stirred elements of sex, murder, the secret service and high diplomacy. I have in front of me an account of these accusations and the way we handled them written by my private secretary, Stephen Lamport. It is too long to reproduce here. I will just summarise what I learned from the event. We were not sufficiently robust in our rebuttals of nonsense, because I listened too attentively to the caution of our legal advisers. The British Vice-Consul, Mr Kirby, was called to the scene of Helen Smith's death and wrote a report of what he found when he arrived. On legal advice we at first refused to publish this report. By withholding it we fed the suspicions of skulduggery and a cover-up. The reason for not publishing the report, which was made available to our own police and to the coroner, was simple. Kirby recorded that alcohol had been drunk at the party which Helen Smith had attended. Since this was illegal in Saudi Arabia, by publishing the report we might have got other British guests at the party in Jedda into serious trouble.

There was a long legal wrangle before an inquest was held here on Helen Smith after her body had been returned to England. It was widely supposed that the Foreign Office was struggling behind the scenes to prevent an inquest. In fact my officials and I were strongly in favour of one, but I was advised by lawyers that it would be wrong for me to do anything which might be interpreted as an attempt to influence the coroner.

The main lesson I learned from this affair is the emptiness of the old proverb that there is no smoke without fire. The magazine *Private Eye* emitted volumes of poisonous smoke in its attempt to show that somewhere there had been real villainy. I had until then felt indulgent towards *Private Eye* (which my friend Andrew Osmond helped to found) and amused by its wit. But their handling of the death of Helen Smith changed my mind. The cruelty with which for sport they blackened the reputation of Vice-Consul Kirby stuck in my throat.

This episode had no effect on our relations with the Saudis, who regarded it as an irrelevant argument between immoral foreigners. The main sufferer was Helen Smith's father in his grief and anger. He refused my suggestion that he should refer the matter to the Ombudsman, who was competent to examine the circumstances and would have had access to all our papers. The matter dragged on miserably for many months. Smoke can do a lot of harm before it is finally established that there is no fire.

Of all the Gulf States, Oman was closest to Britain. Since my first visit there with Ted Heath in 1969 Sultan Qabus had come to the throne and set about the modernisation of his country. He needed our continuing help in dealing with rebels in the Dhofar hills. Our relationship with this proud and sensitive man had to be handled with great care.

Here, as in Tunis, I was captivated by the history and architecture of the British Embassy. A four-sided courtyard in the style of the Government of India in the nineteenth century, the embassy stood on the curve of the Bay of Muscat at the edge of the old city. The external staircase leading up to the living quarters was decorated with sketches and photographs of many past consuls-general. The dates below each of these were crowded together. Before air-conditioning and antibiotics the intense summer heat and associated illnesses killed off the servants of the British Empire at a rapid rate. On the ground floor hung the bell from a merchant ship torpedoed in the bay during the war by a daring Japanese submarine. Outside the courtyard stood a celebrated flagstaff; an escaping slave, by hugging it, gained his freedom.

I enjoyed the big, bare, whitewashed bedroom I was given whenever

I travelled to Muscat over the next decade, with a fan rotating slowly from the ceiling. Breakfast and the sun-down drink were taken on the first-floor terrace, looking out across the bay to the Portuguese forts which guarded its entrance. A magical place, but with a weakness: it was next door to the Sultan's principal palace. Although it was not his style to speak about this to me directly, his ministers for several years told me that His Majesty wanted to demolish our embassy to extend his already huge residence. I feigned forgetfulness and enlisted Margaret Thatcher on my side, having learned by now that whatever her misgivings about the Foreign Office, she always wanted to keep our traditional embassy buildings in their ancient splendour. The Sultan promised her to let us stay in possession until the year 2000, but alas the hints from his ministers soon recurred. The Sultan offered to finance for us a new modern office, and a big new ambassador's house on a rock above the Al-Bustani Hotel. There came a point when it was politic to yield to this generosity, and the Sultan fulfilled his promise meticulously. When the old embassy was being evacuated I drank a final mournful whisky on the terrace overlooking the bay.

One never knew in advance of visiting Oman where the Sultan would be. British ministers might be received in the capital Muscat, or in the south at Salalah, or somewhere in the desert between. On my first visit in February 1981 the royal helicopter whisked me nearly 200 miles south of Muscat to a simple encampment of green army tents and Range Rovers, far from any habitation. Here the Sultan would stay for a week, while his subjects came in over the sand dunes with greetings and requests. He received me in a small tent without any furnishing except several carpets, on which we sat for nearly an hour and a half. Cramp comes easily to my Anglo-Saxon frame and I shifted about uncomfortably. The Sultan sat at ease, serene and faintly smiling. He was obviously conscious of a debate in London and among his own advisers as to whether he really needed the Chieftain tanks on which his heart was set. Coconut juice was served, and we were invited to refresh our hands in the smoke of incense. The Sultan, always friendly and lucid, analysed the affairs of the Gulf. I had already learned that in that part of the world there is little interest in asking a ruler or president about the state of his own country, since the answer is always that everything is fine. If, however, you ask about the state of the country next door, you may get a flow of revealing gossip.

The next candidate for ordeal by carpet that day was the UN Secretary-General, Kurt Waldheim. I was asked to wait during his interview so that the same helicopter could take us both back to Muscat. When Waldheim emerged from the tent, we were taken in a Range Rover a discreet hundred yards from the encampment. He and

I discussed the Palestine problem as standing side by side we peed into the Empty Quarter. My visual memory is that on this occasion Waldheim wore a black frock coat. That cannot be true, but the thought reflected his personality. I knew nothing then of allegations about his pro-Nazi past in his native Austria, but always found him bleak and starchy.

In April 1981 I went with Margaret Thatcher on a tour of the Gulf. As always on such expeditions with her I lived in a tense but enjoyable atmosphere of argument and admiration. The Prime Minister looked superb in the costume specially devised for a female prime minister visiting Saudi Arabia, which transformed her into a modern version of the late Queen Alexandra. She handled all her conversations with courtesy and charm. I remember particularly our call on Prince Abdullah, now the Crown Prince, but already in 1981 in charge of the important National Guard. She swept up his marble staircase, magnificently Edwardian in dark blue from a hat and veil down to her ankles, while the sentries saluted in amazement. She had been thoroughly briefed about our ambition to win the contract for the new National Guard hospital. There was one remaining difficult point concerning, if I remember right, the status of British personnel who would help to run the hospital. Prince Abdullah had evidently already decided to give us the contract, and he made no mention of the difficulty. Characteristically Margaret Thatcher refused to avoid it. To my dismay she plunged into a forthright explanation of our view on the matter. Prince Abdullah must have been puzzled; the Prime Minister was jumping a fence which was no longer on the course. But he did not take up the point, and we won the contract.

Though this was Margaret Thatcher's first visit to the Gulf, that did not prevent her holding and expressing strong views. Her son Mark was not officially part of her entourage, but he popped up from time to time, and in support of his business interests handled himself in a way which I found embarrassing. The Prime Minister took seriously the flattery of Sheikh Zayed of Abu Dhabi, who solemnly told her that he had gained more insight on our policy from Mark Thatcher than from the British Ambassador, David Roberts. The latter had hosted the annual Queen's Birthday Party in his courtyard and there was a great turnout of sheikhs from all parts of the Emirates. David and his staff wore the traditional Gulf rig for British officials: namely, short sleeves and cummerbund. This was neat and cool, but Mark told his mother that it looked old fashioned and patronising. Alas, there was something in this view. The Prime Minister, whose own behaviour was impeccable, could not be persuaded that Mark's commercial ambitions were mainly of interest to the Gulf rulers because he was her son.

If Mark's presence was an irritant, Denis Thatcher was a god-send. He was the perfect consort, able to cope with any situation which was drifting out of control. One evening in Qatar the British Ambassador's wife, who was German, fell into argument at her own table with the Prime Minister on a point of fact about the operation of a British oil company. Neither lady was qualified to speak with expert knowledge, but both dug in stubbornly. Later it transpired that ambassadress was right and the Prime Minister wrong, but that was not a conclusion which could safely be drawn that evening. Denis resolved the growing awkwardness by taking his wife firmly to bed about midnight. In the morning tempers had cooled, and the truth prevailed.

The climax of the visit came in Oman. Sultan Qabus received us in his southern capital Salalah. The palace there, built by Taylor Woodrow on the site of the old souk and customs house, had been furnished by Aspreys. Leather-bound volumes of Trollope and Dickens decorated each bedroom. The Sultan was sunny and talkative. We were flown in helicopters up into the Dhofar hills above Salalah, still troubled by rebels armed from the adjoining communist state of South Yemen. We stood in rising mist on the edge of a deep ravine which marked the frontier. 'Is that still ours down there?' asked the Prime Minister, pointing with imperial gesture towards enemy territory far below her.

During the first three years of Margaret Thatcher's Government my personal life settled into a regular pattern. When I was not at the Foreign Office or abroad, my time was spent either in the dark, slightly dismal flat in Inverness Terrace or in the tiny cottage at Westwell. As best I could, I stood alongside my three sons as they successfully climbed the rungs of English private education. Nicholas won an exhibition to Exeter College, Oxford, decided to read classics, and in the intervals of a vivid social life could be found in Inverness Terrace, deep in Cicero while the radio blasted out pop music at full volume. Tom thrived at cricket. A photograph enshrines a moment which would stay in my memory anyway. Parents' memories are odd things, selecting occasions by tests of affection, pride or sadness which are hard to explain. On a June afternoon Tom, bat in hand, is coming back off Upper Club at Eton up the slight slope to the pavilion with his friend, William Russell, after a successful innings. A borderline case, Tom was told that he could have a place at Pembroke College, Oxford, if he decided within the next few hours to read either theology or Arabic, both subjects being unfamiliar. Tom plumped for Arabic and the course of his life was changed; as I write he is Her Majesty's Consul in Jerusalem. Five years younger than Tom, Alexander needed the most attention. After a temperamental time at his prep school he prospered at Eton under the care of Nigel Jaques.

Al and I went on summer holidays together, for example in 1981 to the coast of northern Spain. A wet week was redeemed by a brilliant walk among the Picos de Europa. Hurds become hungry rather fast and the holiday became notorious in our family for our dismay at finding the doors of the hotel restaurant in Spanish fashion still tight shut at nine in the evening.

The feasts of Eton were central to much of the time spent with the boys. These occasions had altered in the direction of safety and gentleness in the thirty years since I had first known them. There were no longer fireworks after the procession of boats on the evening of the Fourth of June. On St Andrew's Day the Wall Game was still fought between collegers and Oppidans, but stronger rules against savage behaviour had made unnecessary the heavy protective sack which I had worn. The sun now shone through the brilliant glass of Evie Hone and Piper in College Chapel on the candidates for confirmation as the Bishop of Lincoln laid his hand upon them.

In 1981, to my great pleasure, I was asked to become a fellow of Eton in place of Peter Carrington, who had completed the fifteen-year stint laid down in the statutes. I had heard that Foreign Office officials were at the outset baffled by the cryptic 'P and F' which appeared every two or three months in his diary, always for a Saturday morning. An obscure sport? A clandestine assignment? Certainly these dates had to be protected from foreign or prime ministerial interferences. I soon understood why. The meetings of provost and fellows were a pleasant therapy for an overcrowded life. We met in Election Chamber under the chairmanship of the provost. We were surrounded by a selection of the glamorous portraits with which well-to-do young Etonians, on leaving the school, thanked the headmaster in the late eighteenth and early nineteenth centuries. A simple wooden statuette of our pious founder, King Henry VI, stood on the table. Immediately above us the bell of Lupton's Tower sounded each quarter a loud reminder of passing time. The provost, Martin Charteris, needed no such advice. By a tradition which he had founded himself, it was laid down that after our meeting but before we walked in our gowns to lunch in College Hall we should adjourn to his drawing room for a stiff gin and tonic. There was therefore no time for tedious delay; we moved through the agenda with despatch.

Unlike some other school governors, the fellows of Eton are not simply ornamental. The school was thriving; decisions affecting millions of pounds passed through our hands. During my time, after much debate we set in hand the huge project for a rowing lake at Dorney, now a major asset for sport in the whole of southern England. Each year we took two big decisions: what we should pay the masters and what fee

ith Mama and Tatiana at the marriage of Rose Nicolson and Richard Luce,
pril 1961 – some six months after we were ourselves married. (*Portman Press*)

A later photograph of Andrew
Osmond, my fellow author, with
whom I started collaborating in
1966.

China: as a young diplomat with Alan Donald in the Western Hills, 195⟨

China, with Edward Heath in 1974 . . .

. . . and with Margaret Thatcher in 1977.
(John Dixon)

eter Carrington and his Foreign Office ministers at Dorneywood, March 1980. Standing
e Richard Luce, Peter Blaker, myself, David Trefgarne, Neil Marten and Nicholas Ridley;
eter Carrington and Ian Gilmour are sitting. *(Crown copyright)*

Iargaret Thatcher looking the part on her visit to Crown Prince Fahd of Saudi Arabia
1981.

Judy and I are engaged, March 1982. (*Daily Mail*)

As Northern Ireland Secretary with Margaret Thatcher and Irish Prime Minister Garrett FitzGerald (centre), and, left to right, Peter Barry, Dick Spring and Geoffrey Howe. An Anglo-Irish Summit conference at Chequers, November 1984. (*Corbis*)

n of the fair: as Home Secretary with Nigel Lawson at the National Exhibition Centre, ovember 1988. (*Birmingham Post*)

he office of the Foreign Secretary. (*Anthony Osmond-Evans*)

Eton: tree-planting by the Provost and Fellows, January 1990. Martin Charteris is wielding the spade.

The 2 + 4 talks on German reunification, Bonn, May 1990. From left to right: Markus Meckel (East Germany), Hans-Dietrich Genscher (West Germany), Eduard Shevardnadze (Soviet Union), James Baker (USA), Roland Dumas (France) and myself. (*Schambeck*)

On the steps of the
Foreign Office,
announcing my intention
to run for the leadership
of the Conservative
Party. (*Daily Mirror*)

rt of my team for the leadership election, November 1990 – not a bad bunch. (*Press
sociation*)

In conversation with Prime Minister John Major at the start of a G7 summit in London, June 1991. (*Press Association*)

Foreign Office ministers and our attempt at a jolly Christmas card, 1991. Standing behind me are, left to right, Lynda Chalker, Douglas Hogg, Mark Lennox Boyd and Tristan Garel Jones. (*Anthony Osmond-Evans*)

we should charge the parents. The two decisions were related but not automatically, for it was up to a point possible to subsidise the fees out of the wealth of the foundation, normally allocated to capital projects. The politics of this annual debate were complex. An alliance formed between the representatives of the masters who felt that Eton must pay enough to attract the best, and those fellows for whom, as they moved in the rarefied atmosphere of banking and high commerce, a few extra hundred on the fee seemed insignificant. Those of us who belonged to the professional classes became indignant, arguing that Eton must not price its fees out of the range affordable by, say, civil servants or country gentry. The lines of debate shifted each year. Among those who on the whole favoured modest fee increases would be the head of the Civil Service, Robert Armstrong, Tony Lloyd (by now a law lord) and myself. Tony could become so vehement that, in the spirit of our ancient rivalry, I told him that we and the parents did better when he was unable to attend. In the days of high inflation the percentages at issue were large, and the consequences for parents dire. As the Conservative Government tackled inflation, the proposed fee increases fell sharply, and passion drained out of our annual debate. In any case Martin Charteris kept feelings well in hand with the necessary dose of wit and anecdote. Sometimes he would insist on time for one of his own pet projects. For example, we would wander about School Yard arguing about the precise pattern of cobblestones best suited for its repair. The notion that the yard should simply be grassed over was at once rejected as unhistorical, but also as depriving the fellows of a rich topic for discussion.

Martin Charteris was succeeded as provost, while I was still a fellow, by Antony Acland, already a close friend. My fifteen years as a fellow of Eton, following my years there as a pupil and as a parent, added much to the interest of life.

During these years I wrote with Andrew Osmond our last joint novel. Longer than its three predecessors, *War without Frontiers* was originally to be called 'Eurokill'. Drawing on the *événements* of France in 1968, it describes an attempt by a group of anarchists to subvert capitalist Europe. Running through the book is a powerful analysis of the motives of terrorists, as particularly displayed in their leader, Rosa. This part, the best in the book, was entirely Andrew's work. Indeed, he did most of the writing, and this time in the publisher's contract was recognised as the major partner. This shift was inevitable because of my workload at the Foreign Office, but it made for a less easy partnership than on the first three novels. Andrew, writing and rewriting, became impatient with himself and with me. He rightly felt that my mind was mostly elsewhere. I like the character, which I devised, of the European Commissioner

Patrick Harvey, but it was a relief when *War without Frontiers* was finally put to bed, and our friendship was relieved of this stress.

In the summer of 1981, though distant from the fray, I heard rumblings of the argument in the Cabinet between the Prime Minister and the 'wets' over economic policy. Margaret Thatcher moved swiftly to reassert her authority. On 7 September Ian Gilmour, the quietest but toughest of the rebels, told me that on holiday in Italy he had composed his letter of resignation. The same day I bumped into Peter Carrington at the top of the Foreign Office staircase. He said that the Prime Minister intended to sack Ian. He had argued to her that I should be promoted to take Ian's place as the second Foreign Office minister in the Cabinet, but she had said she wanted to move me as Minister of State to another department. He had requested that if Ian went I should stay; I had written to him three weeks earlier that I did not want to be shunted sideways. On 10 September I urged Ian to resign on his own initiative, in a dignified way. I knew that whatever happened I would not be taking his place. He replied that it was too late for dignity, and four days later he was sacked. Humphrey Atkins, who took his place as Lord Privy Seal in the Foreign Office, was always courteous to me in the few months that we worked together. But by then I felt that I knew the ropes and he did not, so deference to his opinions did not come easily.

On 2 April 1982 I represented the Foreign Office for the opening at Cambridge of the annual Anglo-German Conference, called Königs-winter after the village on the Rhine opposite Bonn where it was held in alternate years. I looked forward to an idle, even idyllic, semi-academic weekend, until news arrived of the Argentine rape of the Falkland Islands. As scheduled, I entertained German Christian Democrat MPs to lunch in the old kitchen at Trinity. The waiter dropped on the floor a huge dish of crème brûlée, the pudding for which my college is famous, creating an awesome mess. The omen proved accurate. Taking over Peter Carrington's slot at the formal dinner that night, I had to explain to the amazed Germans where the Falkland Islands lay on the map and why they mattered.

Next day the hideousness of the Falklands debacle became clear. The islands were firmly in Argentine hands. The British Government, and in particular the Foreign Office, was humiliated. The chances of a successful outcome, through either diplomacy or war, seemed hopeless. I had never handled the question in the Foreign Office, and my personal interest derived from my parents' visits to and fondness for the Falklands a quarter of a century earlier.

On 3 April Peter Carrington told me that he had decided to resign, but the Prime Minister argued him out of it. The next day, a Sunday,

Richard Luce, the junior minister in direct charge of the Falklands, told me that he was himself determined to resign, but he urged me to telephone Peter Carrington to persuade him to stay. I tried this at some length, arguing that his influence overseas was unique, and he should not resign because of an impending *Times* article or *Panorama* programme. I even cried in aid Trollope's thin-skinned Prime Minister, the Duke of Omnium, who trembled at the mere hint of a bad press. But the next day's press clinched the matter, and Peter's friends fell silent as he resigned. Whether he would have done so if he had been able to fight his corner in the House of Commons I do not know. But, seated on a pinnacle in the Lords, he found his position hopeless.

His successor as Foreign Secretary, Francis Pym, was the best available choice. A man of sound judgement, a skilful, undramatic parliamentarian, cautious, experienced and firm, he deserved and received the loyalty of those around him, including myself. Like Peter Carrington, he was usually pessimistic in conversation, but *his* pessimism had deeper roots. Peter Carrington's gloom was not exactly invented, but he used it as a tactical weapon to prepare the way for his own energy and skill. Francis Pym had plenty of both qualities, but they were obscured and hindered by his dark view of every prospect. A particularly thick fog surrounded his dealings with the Prime Minister.

Once Francis asked my advice on something which was particularly troubling him. The Prime Minister had suggested he cross the street to Number Ten for an informal talk, without preparation or agenda. I thought it extraordinary that he found this extraordinary. I knew that such informal meetings had been at the heart of Peter Carrington's relationship with Margaret Thatcher. Later, and with greater justification, Francis fought hard against the creation of a foreign affairs unit at Number Ten. Tony Blair has now formed two such units. The earlier battle ended in a draw: Margaret Thatcher appointed one senior foreign affairs adviser, Sir Anthony Parsons, an ex-ambassador to the UN, whom we all liked and trusted.

During the hectic Falklands days I saw Margaret Thatcher several times, always as a spectator. I was never involved in any operational questions. On 6 April she talked to junior ministers about the crisis. Some of those present expressed cautious doubts about the use of force, and Margaret left the meeting muttering the words of Henry V: 'He that hath no stomach for this fight, let him depart.' In private that day she was friendly with me, virtually apologising for not making me Foreign Secretary. There was no need for this; quite clearly the new Foreign Secretary had to come from outside the Foreign Office. On 19 April she asked me to lunch with the Cabinet at Number Ten in Francis Pym's absence abroad. I described her line that day as 'distraught and diffuse'.

She criticised the Foreign Office for failing to see how fast Argentina was slipping into the Soviet orbit, given that fascism and communism were essentially alike. This was a new and unsustainable line of argument; most Ministers, led by Willie Whitelaw, urged her not to develop it in public.

I believed, and believe now, that Margaret Thatcher's instincts on the Falklands were entirely sound, and that this was her finest hour. Once she was credibly advised that the recapture of the islands was feasible she cut through many understandable misgivings and carried the policy through to success. Just before the crucial decision I drove with her to an Anglo-French dinner at Hopetoun House outside Edinburgh. She had a cold and her voice was husky. She said a decision on force was needed within three or four days, and thought we should take it. Although, to me, she praised Francis Pym, she said she had been upset earlier by the questioning stance of Willie Whitelaw. She missed Peter Carrington, who argued with her but had strong powers of analysis and decision. She was pleased that I had told a French journalist that we would if necessary keep the islands indefinitely. At the dinner the French Prime Minister, Pierre Mauroy, emphasised his support. Two days later President Mitterrand did the same. This was the first time I had seen Margaret Thatcher and President Mitterrand together: 'A mask face, which comes to life and flickers attractively at rare intervals.'

It was a relationship which fascinated me then and eight years later. Either on this or on a later occasion in the summer of 1982 we had been advised from the Elysée that Mitterrand on a visit to Number Ten would urge us to be conciliatory to the Argentines. The Prime Minister, upright and tense in her chair in the Cabinet Room, was ready to resist this passionately. But Mitterrand began quite differently: '*Alors, madame, vous avez montré encore une fois ce que nous français avons appris depuis des siècles – on ne peut pas plaisanter avec les anglais.*' The Prime Minister, complimented on her own and Britain's courage, relaxed, and all was easy. The President had planned it all. Normally I resist explanations of events based on a theory of conspiracy; but I would make an exception of any event connected with the arch-conspirator François Mitterrand.

Throughout the Falklands crisis I kept in touch with my mother in Wiltshire, knowing her strong affection for the islands and islanders. To my surprise, she was not in favour of the war – not because she had any feeling for the Argentines, but because she thought it was bound to destroy the simple pastoral style of life which had attracted her. She did not live long enough to see that the fear was unfounded. The islands have indeed changed, but for the better. She would have enjoyed visits and letters from the modern islanders and been glad of their progress.

My life at the Foreign Office during 1982 and 1983 was full of travel. On top of routine meetings in Strasbourg, Brussels and Geneva, I visited Muscat five times; consorted with the British regiment stationed on the outskirts of Beirut; called on President Nimeiri of the Sudan in his palace at Khartoum and his house at Ascot; conversed hesitantly with Mrs Gandhi in Delhi and escorted her to the musical *Cats* in London; trampled through the valleys of Nepal and the mountains of Sri Lanka to see how we spent our aid money; jolted over the rugged roads of Yemen; addressed Afghan refugees in a marquee outside Peshawar promising them food and tents when what they really wanted were guns to fight the Russians; paid the first ever ministerial visit to the Maldive Islands, bumping my knee painfully on a coral reef. I do not feel defensive about this ministerial tourism. In a world of nation states Britain retains interests and carries out scattered activities around the world. The success of these interests and activities still depends largely not on international conferences, but on policies and personalities on the ground. Personal encouragement on the spot of what we are attempting and personal knowledge of those with whom we deal can make all the difference. Ministers today spend too much time nattering to one another at conferences and too little on this bilateral diplomacy, which should be the main job of junior ministers in the Foreign Office.

After this portentous defence, I have to admit that these expeditions were huge fun. I was lucky in choosing as my private secretary for this period Stephen Lamport, later private secretary to the Prince of Wales. Stephen's quiet competence and companionable good humour added spice to many bizarre visits. We worked so well together in official life that we decided to try our hands at a joint novel. The plot was conceived at the Mount Lavinia Hotel in Sri Lanka and rapidly matured over many long plane journeys. The result, published in 1985, was *Palace of Enchantments*, and describes a way of life not wholly unlike what we were doing at the time. To placate the permanent under-secretary at the Foreign Office, we had to remove the Sudan from the plot and substitute an imaginary African country called Meridia.

I saw less of Margaret Thatcher during this time, except in various episodes of the protracted argument which we had with her on Middle East policy. The Arab League wanted to send a delegation round the leading capitals of the world to carry forward their peace initiative. From their point of view, it was essential that this delegation should include a Palestinian from the PLO, though not Arafat himself, and that it should be received by the British Prime Minister. Margaret Thatcher was strongly opposed, arguing that the PLO was simply a terrorist organisation. Her refusal became public, and began to damage our interests. On 4 January 1983, after she had disagreed on the point with

Francis Pym, I was given a chance to deploy the argument. The Prime Minister's mood matched the sunshine pouring into the parlour at Chequers and she heard me out, before again disagreeing. Her refutation of the Foreign Office case had become somewhat complex. Her difficulty was that she regarded both Prime Minister Begin of Israel and President Mugabe of Zimbabwe as terrorists and yet was ready to meet them, so she had to argue that she would not meet a terrorist unless he was head of government. This was an awkward stance, which recalls Sir John Harington's quip: 'Treason doth never prosper; what's the reason? For if it prosper none dare call it treason.' It must be reasonable to test whether there is a chance of detaching violent yet influential leaders from their violence and converting them into politicians. Successive British Governments have applied that test to both the PLO and Sinn Féin, and the test continues.

We wore down the Prime Minister over the PLO. On 18 March 1983 I escorted the Arab delegation on a red carpet lined with guardsmen in grey overcoats from the Foreign Office to Number Ten. All behaved admirably. King Hussein of Jordan, leading the delegation, spoke at length but without controversy; the Palestinian was polite and prudent; the Prime Minister listened and entertained them all to lunch with her usual charm. It was one of Margaret Thatcher's strengths that once she had taken a decision she carried it out in style, shelving for the moment any previous reluctance. She did not sulk herself, and disliked the habit in others.

Towards the end of this period, I became the Foreign Office component of the Government's successful campaign against CND and in favour of defensive nuclear weapons. For the first time I worked with Michael Heseltine, who presided over our meetings, usually wearing a yellow pullover, from a sofa in the Ministry of Defence. As part of the campaign, I debated up and down the country, at non-party meetings, and learned new techniques, for example at the Worcester Diocesan Synod on 12 March 1982.

> Am matched against Dr Greet, pacifist and eloquent. A uni-lateralist amendment is moved, and a series of rather strong youngish clergy orate somewhat gracelessly for it, a ludicrous brigadier against. The Bishop of W. inept in the chair, the Suffragan of Dudley and his Polish wife virulently wrong. After some tactical manoeuvres I speak again, better, and the amendment is lost 59–74 and we adjourn to buffet lunch and coffee.

Perhaps I can describe here a day of small personal humiliation, such as Boswell slips into his journal at regular intervals. Somehow I acquired a reputation later for smoothness and calm, but I was and remain by nature clumsy and inept. I had spent most of the night of 7 February 1983 in the Commons, and attended a short debate on child custody about 6 a.m. On the way to a meeting called by Michael Heseltine that morning on the nuclear campaign I absurdly banged my nose hard against the roof of my official car. The result was a hideous mess. I bled copiously in Michael Heseltine's bathroom and into tissues on his sofa. That afternoon there was a meeting in the Foreign Office on the coming deployment of British troops in the Lebanon, and I began to flake. My next engagement was to escort the Prime Minister of Nepal to tea with our Prime Minister. I apologised to her for my gruesome nose. Margaret Thatcher said she had noticed nothing, adding splendidly: 'we keep the lights here soft and low'. A cream cake was served as the two prime ministers talked in armchairs upstairs in the drawing room. I tackled the cake with my fingers and quickly got into another mess. 'There is a fork, Douglas,' said the Prime Minister gently, as her Nepalese counterpart expounded in detail his request for aid.

On 9 May 1983 I was in the Hague, arguing with the Dutch about the deployment of nuclear weapons. Stephen Lamport brought in a message saying that the British General Election was to be held on 9 June: 'Damn. There go my last weeks in this amazingly pleasant job, the round peg in the round hole.' I guessed that I was likely to be moved after four years in the job, but had no notion where. The Dutchmen and I then walked through the vast tulip gardens of Keukenhof. It was my last Foreign Office expedition for six years.

But by then had come a great change. For seven years Judy Smart had been my constituency secretary, patiently working with four colleagues in the big ground-floor room of an eighteenth-century house in Old Palace Yard across the road from the House of Lords. Judy knew about Parliament; she knew about the Witney area, for her family home was a farmhouse at Cokethorpe; she quickly came to know about me. I depended on her, not just for the steady flow of Oxfordshire letters, but increasingly for other things, often connected with the three boys. When necessary she would pick one up or deliver him to school, or organise my holiday with them. I came to rely too thoughtlessly on her mixture of kindness and good sense. I stood on the edge and was slow to dive. Gradually on my part one set of feelings grew into another, warmer and stronger. In summer 1981 I had asked Judy to marry me. She hesitated, and I cannot blame her. She was taking on a man nineteen years older, with three sons from his first marriage, who followed an uncertain, consuming and potentially destructive career. Her mother, who at one time shared Judy's misgivings, came round to my side. She told me that these hesitations were in character, but once Judy had made up her mind I could be certain that our marriage would be sure as a rock. My mother-in-law got it right. My life, which had been narrowing without my knowing it, began to broaden again in every respect. We were married in the Registry Office at Wantage on 7 May 1982, and blessed immediately after in the church near her parents' home at Chaddleworth. I owe it to Judy that I then became, and remain, a happy man.

15

THE HOME OFFICE

The General Election campaign of 1983 was a good one for me. I enjoyed getting to know, in early summer sunshine, the other towns and villages added to my constituency by the Boundary Commission. My association was more at ease with itself than in 1979. For the first time in an election I campaigned elsewhere: in Bolton, Grimsby, Fife and Dundee. But it soon became clear that my race was not so much with Labour or Liberal opponents as with my wife. It ended as a dead heat. On the morning of polling day, 9 June, Judy went into the John Radcliffe Hospital in Oxford just after I began my round of polling stations and Conservative committee rooms. At Chipping Norton I learned that she had been advised to stay in hospital. The baby, already late, seemed to be on its way. In the afternoon I broke off my tour, went to Oxford, and remained with Judy until our son was born at 2.30 a.m. by Caesarean. I was probably the only election candidate that evening not to attend his own count. I thought that I had made a proper and virtuous choice of family in preference to politics. Judy draws a rather different conclusion: she remembers through the haze of anaesthetic the sound of my Roberts radio announcing Conservative victories at her bedside. Politics had not been banished, just muffled for the occasion.

Waking late at Westwell next morning I sleepily turned on that same radio and heard the National Anthem before the news. It could hardly be the BBC triumphing at a new term of Conservative government. It turned out to be Prince Philip's birthday, and that clinched the domestic argument. Philip our son became.

After a Saturday and Sunday spent in uncertainty on my part, Margaret Thatcher telephoned at lunchtime on Monday. Stephen

Lamport had already passed me a rumour circulating among the government drivers that I was to move sideways to be Minister of State at the Home Office, and this proved correct. The Prime Minister praised my work at the Foreign Office, and said that wider experience would do me good later. I did not bless her at the time. The Foreign Office gave drinks that evening for Francis Pym, who had been offered merely the Prime Minister's support for the speakership of the Commons, a job which he did not want, which was not in her power to give and which went to Bernard Weatherill. I walked straight from that party to see my new chief, the Home Secretary Leon Brittan. We began at once to discuss the legislative programme of the Home Office.

When Margaret Thatcher said she was moving me sideways to broaden my experience, she was rationalising, as prime ministers do, a decision which had other and simpler roots. I was merely a small piece in the big jigsaw puzzle of ministerial appointments which she had to finish in a hurry. Prime ministers do not complicate their lives by devising subtle career patterns for junior ministers. They know that luck and necessity, not forethought, will decide these matters. Nevertheless, she was quite right. My political career so far had been remarkably unbalanced. As a professional diplomat and a Foreign Office minister I knew something of that world. From my time with Ted I had gained an overview of the political scene. I was friendly with most of the leading characters. Though never one of her intimates, I had seen more of the Prime Minister since 1979 than most junior ministers. I had experience of constituencies, Central Office and the political side of the media. From this, some commentators wrote as if I were already qualified for cabinet rank, and perhaps I thought so myself when the telephone failed to ring over that June weekend. But I had never tackled specific and detailed issues of domestic policy, never faced a hostile press campaign, never steered a substantial Bill through the House of Commons.

Those gaps in experience were painfully filled over the next twelve months. The Home Office in 1983 handled a more bizarre ragbag of unconnected matters than it does today. As the senior Minister of State I found myself at once coping with criminal justice, the police, the regulation of broadcasting, civil defence, gambling, racing and anything else which happened at the time to need a ministerial presence or signature. Each of these subjects had its own hierarchy within the Home Office, and its array of pressure groups outside. All these personages, though friendly, worked in blinkers. They believed that theirs was the only subject strictly worthy of my attention. The matters on which they briefed and badgered me were wholly unfamiliar. There were no days of handover from my predecessor and no training of any kind. The British system throws infant ministers into the pool and expects them to swim.

Several of the subjects had a strong legal component; I had read no law. At the age of fifty-three I found myself a clumsy apprentice who must nevertheless at all times maintain the appearance of mastery.

The Home Office was not a reactionary organisation. On many of the matters I have mentioned officials were in favour of change, provided, of course, that the Home Office initiated that change and kept a proper control of its results. The level of intelligence, measured by academic learning rather than worldly shrewdness, was higher than in the Foreign Office, but the Home Office at that time did not really believe in communication. It was acknowledged that ministers had to make speeches and broadcasts, but these occasions should be restricted to the minimum. The vocabulary in which the Home Office discussed its problems was not much help in dealing with the outside world – or in gently leading a new minister to find his own place in the fortress of Queen Anne's Gate.

In the early months my red boxes sometimes filled me with gloom verging on despair at night as I sat in Judy's house in Hammersmith, which we used as our London base. I wondered if I would ever get to grips with these intricate submissions, sometimes scruffy in appearance, usually turgid in tone. The summer of 1983 was boiling hot, our London house small, and baby Philip noisy. Paternity leave had not been invented. By bad luck, this was almost the only time in my ministerial career when I did not have at my side a private secretary whom I could invite to become a confidant and friend. I had to rely on a certain natural stubbornness to keep me going.

Leon Brittan could have been forgiven some exasperation at this point. He was lumbered with a Minister of State nine years older than himself who had acquired a reasonable reputation at the Foreign Office but who seemed unsuited for the job he had now been given. Leon possessed a first-class legal brain, had served in the Home Office before, and held every issue at his fingertips. The pile-up of work was formidable. Leon would have been justified in politely pushing me to the margins and getting on with all important matters himself. If that had happened, then the fear I wrote into my diary a week after joining the Home Office that I would never reach the Cabinet would have come true. Leon's style was centralising in the sense that he liked to know everything that was going on and took the main decisions himself. But he involved me fully in his meetings, listened patiently to my naïve views on criminal justice, delegated to me just the weight I could carry, and showed officials that I was to be treated with respect.

The main burden was the massive Police and Criminal Evidence Bill, derived from the report of the Royal Commission on Criminal Procedure chaired by Lord Phillips. This is not the place for an analysis of the substance of the Bill as it was not in any way my creation. I simply led the team which in the end got it through the committee stage of the Commons. It is enough to say that among other things the Bill transformed what happened on the street and in many police stations between the police and an alleged offender. When and on what conditions could a police officer stop and search someone in the street? How long could an offender be held without charge? What were his rights to legal advice? How could he complain about police behaviour? On these and many other similar points practice varied across England and Wales, and the Royal Comission urged that they be covered by statute and no longer left uncertain in common law.

One version of the resulting Bill had begun its course through Parliament but had fallen when the General Election of 1983 was called. The new and ambitious Home Secretary was not content with the previous draft of the Bill which he inherited. This was a task exactly suited to Leon Brittan's talent. In meeting after meeting he went through every point of substance. On one day in July 1983 I went to five separate policy meetings in his office in Queen Anne's Gate. Painfully I raised my knowledge of criminal justice to the point where I could understand Leon's exchanges with officials. Gradually the new vessel took shape in dry dock. The launch was performed efficiently by the Home Secretary at second reading in the Commons on 7 November. I wound up the six-hour debate without disaster, though put out by the Labour tactic of the evening, which was to chat insolently among themselves during my last ten minutes, creating a buzz loud enough to harass me but not loud enough to lead the Speaker to intervene.

For weeks I dreaded the next stage, when I would be out on my own, steering the Bill clause by clause through standing committee. Leon Brittan, under opposition pressure, had agreed nominally to serve on the committee, but until the end made only fleeting appearances. The committee stage began on 17 November and dragged on slowly until 29 March the next year. During this time I was a slave to the Bill. Whatever else I did, the Police and Criminal Evidence Bill lurked darkly at the back of my mind. With several embarrassing stumbles, I learned the art of defensive advocacy. At one time we seemed hopelessly stuck on Clause 1; a whole morning was spent in a commotion on the power of the police to stop and search in a public place. Was a garden a public place? The lawyers on the committee excitedly roamed to and fro, raising all kinds of improbable hypotheses, and we were forced into retreat.

Ken Livingstone and his far-left Greater London Council had earlier tried to raise a popular tumult under the slogan 'Kill the Bill' on the spurious grounds that it gave the police tyrannical new powers. On the other flank the police themselves, their federation being represented in the Commons by Eldon Griffiths, feared that they would be tied down in excessive bureaucracy designed to safeguard the suspect.

From time to time my spirit flagged. Outside the committee I was encouraged by my predecessor Patrick Mayhew and by the shrewd, calm advice of the permanent secretary, Brian Cubbon. Inside the committee I relied heavily on the other junior minister, David Mellor, the young Member for Putney, a character now lost to politics. David was tougher and quicker than myself at the infighting of committee work. During that winter, as later when I was Home Secretary, I came to respect his skills. From stories I heard in both periods, he did not entirely reciprocate my admiration. Despite this I tried not very successfully to persuade other young ministers that although his tongue was rough and his ambition obvious, David Mellor should be considered a rising star. He lacked tact but never courage, and I have experience of his personal kindness. He is a natural broadcaster, but politics is poorer without him.

My other rescuer was the Labour Shadow Home Secretary, Gerald Kaufman. Gerald had the sharpest tongue of any Labour politician. Though not a dislikeable man, he enjoyed being disliked. He was a politician through and through, but in the old style. Not for him the pink-cheeked hypocrisies of New Labour. He had learned his trade in the bowels of the old Labour Party and practised it in the service of Harold Wilson as Prime Minister. He was a cynic who loved intrigue, but deep down there was a sentimental core. He wrote the funniest book available on the art of being a minister. He and I jousted in several capacities over the coming years, until we became mellow elder statesmen together on the Wakeham Royal Commission on Lords reform. At close quarters, for example during the committee stage of a Bill, he could usually outwit me, but he lost the advantage in artillery duels on policy across the floor of the House. During these early encounters on the PACE Bill I learned two important facts about Gerald Kaufman. First, that he kept his word once given; and second, that he hated working late at night, an emotion connected with his abiding love of the cinema. The Government was making such slow progress on the Bill that we arranged for the committee to meet in the evenings. Gerald contrived a burst of great anger at the first of these late conclaves, and I had to scurry back from a meeting in Lambeth Town Hall to appease him. The direct result was an agreement on the date when the committee would complete its work, and this was exactly honoured. Never before had a Bill been examined in committee for as many as fifty-nine sessions, and the Labour team issued special badges to all of us in commemoration.

We at no time threatened to cut short debate with a guillotine, an act of self-restraint almost inconceivable now in these less parliamentary times. Ours was not a party Bill but a genuine effort to sort out dangerous vagueness in the criminal justice system. I made with Leon Brittan's consent many concessions in committee, and was criticised for this by the whips and others who thought that a minister's job was to ram a Bill through Parliament with minimum change. Now that in the Lords I see Bills coming to us from the Commons ill-digested, with whole clauses not discussed at all, I look back on those fifty-nine sessions of the PACE Bill, if not exactly with pleasure, with a certain satisfaction.

The police were nearer the truth than was Ken Livingstone in their criticism of the Bill. It added to their paperwork, particularly as the original codes of practice attached to the Act have multiplied over the years. But without an Act of this kind the police would have been at the mercy of increasingly critical courts. Later, as Home Secretary, I saw too many examples of earlier miscarriages of justice to have much faith in the old system before PACE, which made it easy for some police officers, yielding to temptation, to cut corners and secure convictions by unjust means.

Though it did me good, this was the only job in my political life which I did not enjoy. I looked around for possibilities of escape, and they came sooner than I could have expected.

PART VI

THE CABINET

16

NORTHERN IRELAND

For the Hurds, the second weekend of September 1984 was tedious. We were house-hunting, so far in vain. The cottage in Westwell was too small to accommodate both a minister of state struggling with red boxes and Philip, now fifteen months old and growing fast. I worked in a neighbour's quiet dining room and took Philip blackberrying. 'Feel a bit low – no house, no promotion, not enough money – but not desperate.'

Relief was at hand in the form of promotion. It was common knowledge that Jim Prior had had enough of Northern Ireland; the Prime Minister was looking for a new Secretary of State. Some newspapers mentioned my name as a possibility and because of this I had already consulted Judy in case the call should come. We knew, though only vaguely, that this particular form of promotion to the Cabinet would greatly complicate our lives. There would be much bucketing about in a small plane with a small child, there would be some danger, and under police protection we would lose our privacy. Neither of us thought that any of this should stand in the way of the adventure should it be offered to us.

On Monday 10 September the Prime Minister asked me to go round to Number Ten about noon. She looked tired, and was fussing around the furniture in the upstairs drawing room, shutting off the partition which can divide it. She said she wanted someone in Northern Ireland who was intelligent and tough. She knew that I was the former, and Peter Carrington had told her I was the latter; would I take it? When I accepted at once she perked up, I suppose because she had thought I might ask for time to consider. She talked for a minute or two about the financial burden of protecting the Province, and analysed the character of Enoch

Powell ('flawed in some ways, but worthwhile'), who had by then put his baleful talents at the service of the Ulster Unionists. Then she summoned a bottle of hock, and also Willie Whitelaw, John Wakeham and her two parliamentary private secretaries for a small festivity.

Foreseeing hectic days, my first journey as a cabinet minister was to Trumpers to get my hair cut. Because of a constituency meeting in Witney that evening I drove alone to Oxfordshire. It was the last time I was to drive a car myself for ten years, except on holiday in Italy. As I turned into the back lane which leads down a lime avenue past the cottages at Westwell, I could see a group of police officers gathered outside our gate. I was at once folded within the embrace of protection, friendly but stifling, particularly for someone with a taste for occasional solitude and silence. My journey next morning to the Northern Ireland Office in Admiralty House was in an armoured police Jaguar, cramped for lack of leg room and slow. It took me months to accept that it was just not possible to open the windows of my car and banish the human fug which accumulated inside.

That morning my predecessor Jim Prior briefed me at Admiralty House for about half an hour, and then I was whisked to Belfast in an HS 125 jet. It is a foolishness of the British constitution that there is no provision for a proper handover from one minister to his successor. Often this would not be possible because of party differences or some sudden commotion, but Jim's move had been signalled for weeks. There was no reason why he and I could not have worked in harness together for, say, a fortnight so that I had a feel for the job before I had to take decisions or make policy statements.

Recently, when asked with others to examine the arrangements at Lambeth Palace we found the same defect. Incoming and outgoing Archbishops of Canterbury have passed each other with a friendly Anglican wave or a cup of tea, but no substantial handover. The latest handover at Lambeth went better. I am less sanguine about reforming the British Government.

By the afternoon I was propelled on to the steps of Stormont Castle to hold a press conference. Standing between the heraldic beasts which flank the stone staircase, I felt like a doomed French aristocrat facing a bloodthirsty mob. In my experience the Ulster press corps competes with that of Hong Kong for persistent cruelty. Intelligent and well informed, both groups find it hard to suppose that any matters other than those of their relatively small community can be of interest to serious people. The Hong Kong corps narrowly wins the prize for difficulty because although the interrogators have memorised their questions in English, they often cannot understand the answers, with the result that their victim is bombarded with the same question several times.

I knew little more about the Province than any other conscientious follower of public events. Suddenly, dressed in a little authority which might or might not be brief, I had to assume the manner of a proconsul, and a proconsul exposed to constant public examination by journalists longing for him to stumble.

The next day, after eating my first and daunting 'Ulster fry breakfast' (which masses on one plate just about every food which can be fried), I was whisked to Aberdeen, and then in a bus with other reshuffled ministers to Balmoral. Most of us were bulky men; in turn we knelt on a rather small tartan footstool before the Queen to receive our seals of office, which were then at once removed for safekeeping.

Back in London that night I had to telephone Nigel Jaques, Alexander's housemaster at Eton. Special security arrangements were apparently needed there because of my promotion to Ireland. The outside drainpipes on his house were coated with a sticky substance to deter intruders. Al's schoolmates put up helpful notes in their own windows: 'To the IRA. This is not Hurd's room.'

The next days were spent, not before time, in intensive briefings in both London and Northern Ireland. The excitement slowly subsided into routine. Judy and I sorted out the mechanics of what for me was a four-razor existence – Westwell, Judy's house in Hammersmith, the official flat at Stormont, and Hillsborough. By the end of September: 'The great change is for the better. A job with real responsibility sweeps away most of the misgivings building up since June 1983 in my mind about my own capacity. Of course a run of bad luck or mistakes would bring back the old nervousness . . . After three weeks the excitement and pleasure still win, and Judy in her own way shares them.'

The job of Secretary of State was a mix of normal and strange, as befitted the nature of Northern Ireland. The Westminster commentators who dusted off and reissued the phrase about it being a political graveyard missed the point. It was hardly this for a newcomer to the Cabinet. More important, the job offered a challenge to my ability and resilience. I use the word 'challenge' in its proper sense implying excitement and a worthwhile aim, not, as often nowadays in business jargon, as a weary synonym for 'rather difficult'. With the help of my fellow ministers based at Stormont, I was running a province of one and a half million people under direct rule. The Prime Minister and my cabinet colleagues allocated me a sum of money each year and expected me to get on with it. Occasionally I had to argue the case for extra help for the big employers – say, Harland and Wolff or Short Brothers – but the less the colleagues heard from me the better.

An elected assembly existed at Stormont, which gave the local politicians a platform but no real power. It was sensible for the minister to keep in touch with its committees. I learned to distinguish between Ian Paisley the demagogue, who regularly denounced me as a traitor, and Ian Paisley the farmers' representative who would chat quietly and knowledgeably for an hour on my sofa about pig prices and the green pound. Usually when I find myself dealing with a personality with divided characteristics I try to push what is negative into the margins. I tried this approach with Ian Paisley but it had no chance. The negative element in his character lay at the centre and drove forward his extraordinary energy. He devoted himself to persuading Unionists that the United Kingdom to which they were loyal had a Government which was bent on betraying and destroying them. There could be kindness in his behaviour, but there was nothing positive in his beliefs. Sophisticated people smiled at him as a bit of a joke, and in his genial moments he carried himself accordingly. But he was never a man with whom a senior British government minister could do serious business.

I was lucky in my ministerial colleagues. Rhodes Boyson, who arrived with me as the senior Minister of State, had built a reputation at home as a stern right-winger. Something which the Prime Minister must have said to him gave him the notion, which he explained to me at our first meeting, that he was there to look after Unionist interests, in contrast presumably to my supposed sympathy for Dublin. This was not at all my idea, and I heard no more of it. Rhodes Boyson settled down to his portfolio looking after industry and economic development. Two of the other ministers were high-flyers, though one with a damaged wing. Nick Scott, who never concealed his attachment to the left wing of the Conservative Party, was a good communicator, always a dangerous talent in Ireland. His phrase-making attracted the suspicion of the Prime Minister. Nick felt that he deserved promotion to the Cabinet, whereas both Jim Prior and I had to exert ourselves to prevent him being sacked. We did this because he was an excellent minister with well-balanced judgement in handling the crucial relationships with the police and the army. The other high-flyer, Chris Patten, was already a friend, and I came to rely on him as a confidant in matters well outside his portfolio of housing and health. Because under direct rule there were no local authorities with substantial power, Chris enjoyed himself approving such matters as the excellent design in a deep red brick of Belfast's new subsidised housing estates, set among many trees.

In October 1984, as an example of the fruits of direct rule, I opened the magnificent bridge across the Foyle at Londonderry. There the other dimension of Northern Ireland, discord and fear, could not be concealed by official protocol. The security services were agitated because news of my visit had been reported in the press. For safety I was supposed to fly by helicopter, but the thick mist over the hills of Antrim prevented this. We drove into Londonderry past the statue of Queen Victoria, her hands amputated by a bomb. The young Mayor was shaking with nervousness. I was not allowed to drive across the bridge, but snipped a tape at one end, resolving to come back on a less tense occasion.

I never myself felt physical fear in Northern Ireland. Those who protected me did not conceal the fact that they were unlikely to be able to save my life in an ambush, but could probably kill or catch my assailants afterwards, which might or might not act as a deterrent. I am a fatalist about my own safety. Without contesting in principle the regime imposed by my protectors, I tried, particularly at home in Westwell, to wriggle out of some of their rules, for example the one forbidding a solitary walk in familiar woods and fields.

There was tension too next month in Armagh. At the prison a number of convicted murderers, good looking and voluble, took me to task for the practice of strip searching. The two cathedrals of Armagh gaze sadly at each other across a rift. The Church of Ireland cathedral was empty except for banners from the Somme and tablets in honour of dead Fusiliers. By the time we reached the Roman Catholic cathedral dusk was falling. As I admired the modern altar with its clasping arms of granite a man slipped through the shadows towards me, evading my protection officers. He dragged a lad behind him, and, lifting the boy's hair, showed a hideous scar on his scalp. He shouted at me through the gloom that this was the result of a bomb for which the largely Protestant Ulster Defence Regiment was responsible. For a moment there was confusion as the two were hustled away. Cardinal O'Fiaich appeared smiling, and escorted me to his house near by. There, it being four o'clock in the afternoon, he produced two kinds of Irish whiskey, himself drinking Old Paddy (the one from the south). In Ireland these choices are not accidental. His housekeeper reinforced the hospitality with tea and a huge apple pie, and the tension dissolved in food, drinks and talk.

My colleagues and I learned to consume huge quantities of all three commodities in the course of our duties. Northern Ireland is full of institutions and institutional meals. The helpings are more generous, the courses more numerous, the speeches and the vegetables longer-cooked than across the water in Britain. Often on these slow, genial occasions, where everyone knew everyone else in the tight merry-go-round of Ulster life, one could forget entirely what was happening outside in the street: the army patrol in darkness a mile or two away in the Falls Road, the conspiracies being hatched in the Maze Prison, the bomb laid in the culvert under the road, or the mortar loaded on to a lorry and parked within range of a police station.

I was at dinner in London on 28 February 1985 when news began to come in of such a mortar attack on the RUC station at Newry, on the border. I was in the town next morning, in steady rain, to see the shattered Portakabin canteen in which nine police officers had died, then the lorry still fitted with the tubes for the mortar shells. It was the worst security disaster in my time in Northern Ireland. In the immediate aftermath a hush descended in people's minds. Newry is a Nationalist town; its Social Democrat councillors knew that the whole town, not just the police, suffered when the Provisional IRA scored a hit. The Unionist leaders whom I saw at Stormont that night were also quiet. It took twenty-four hours for the usual political hubbub to resume. Paisley denounced me for being in England making a statement on Newry in the Commons on the day the police officers were being buried.

Then and after I felt close to the men of the Royal Ulster Constabulary. Two of their officers were physically close to me every hour of every day. Protection seemed somehow less onerous in the Province than in Britain, perhaps because it was obviously more necessary, perhaps because it was carried out with wit and a lighter touch. As with all police forces in my experience, the higher the rank the more defensive became the relationship. Sir John Hermon, the Chief Constable of the RUC, was experienced and effective. I never quarrelled with him, but though I saw him often and he talked at length I never felt that I knew his mind. He gave me the plain facts of each situation as he saw them. But there seemed to be layers of feeling and perception which he kept from me. Though a professional police officer, he had been given a job packed with political complications. Moderate himself, he knew that I was no zealot; but he preferred not to share his preoccupations fully with me. Sir John had no difficulty in enthusing me about the RUC as a whole. He invited me to take the salute at their annual passing-out parade at Enniskillen within a month of my arrival. On a fine autumn morning the young cadets marched and counter-marched on the square in front of the dignified headquarters dating from the Napoleonic Wars. There was no doubting which Ulster tradition they mostly represented – blond, short in stature, with sharp noses and clear blue eyes under the rakish tilt of their caps. Their ancestors had been tough Presbyterian Scots, who had crossed the sea to better themselves. But that was a long time ago. Taking tea afterwards with proud parents and sisters I had a sense not of prejudice but of families genuinely offering their best to their country, which in their lives had a double identity: both Irish and loyal British.

There was a similar flavour to royal visits. The Duchess of Kent came most often. Though her face was already strained with worry, she seemed at ease in Northern Ireland, able to do good by communicating natural sympathy to people in different kinds of distress. In January 1985 she launched a Blue Star refrigeration ship from alongside the two giant cranes of Harland and Wolff which are the welcoming landmark of Belfast. The frosty sunshine, the swept-tidy dock, the police band playing the National Anthem, the crowd of schoolchildren waving Union Jacks as they cheered when the champagne bottle cracked, the background of hills behind the city white from the previous night's blizzard – conspired to create for me a moving summary of what for many people Ulster was really about.

By then I knew that there was another side to the story. Blue Star had got their investment timing wrong, and Harland and Wolff would need yet more subsidy to complete the ship just launched. The men working at Harland and Wolff or Shorts who decorated their workbenches with Union Jacks and royal photographs were making a statement not so much of loyalty as of exclusion: Nationalists were not welcome.

So far, I have written as if we were simply administering a status quo. Indeed, that was a large part of my life. The Provisional IRA could be held in check, but neither the army, the RUC nor the intelligence services believed that they could be crushed out of existence without a marked increase of cooperation from the Irish Republic. And that was hard to imagine. The attempt to get the local politicians to share executive power had failed in 1974 when Paisley's protests paralysed the Province and the Labour Government let Ted Heath's Sunningdale Agreement collapse. Later political initiatives had produced the Assembly, but that was a body for talk not action. The Unionist majority was divided between those led by Paisley who wanted devolution without concessions to the Catholic minority, and those like Enoch Powell who wanted full integration with the rest of the UK. Despite the personal courage of their leader John Hume, the members of the leading Catholic party, the SDLP, looked anxiously over their shoulders at the men with the guns and bombs. There was no scope for political initiatives in the short term to replace direct rule.

But gradually, too slowly, the mood was changing. The reforms introduced by the British Government through direct rule lessened discrimination. British and European investment brought a better way of life within the reach of many. The Falls Road and the Shankill Road in Belfast, the Creggan and the Bogside in Londonderry were still desperate places, with the desperation deliberately dramatised by the extremists in both communities. But people such as Liam Bradley gave me some hope. Anyone would know at once from his first name that he was a Catholic. Like his father before him, he farmed a foothill of the Mourne Mountains in County Down. His father had lived in one side of the square stone farmyard alongside the animals, and his mother refused to leave her old home. But Liam had built a new bungalow further up the rocky slope in a style reminiscent of the Costa Brava. With government and European help he had cleared the bracken and installed forty-five Friesian cows. The Secretary of State, arriving in this spotless home just before ten in the morning, was treated to many cream cakes and photographs of Liam's four children at their first communion. Granny appeared, the neighbours gathered with many cameras, the cream cakes led on to brandy, and it was hard to get away. Liam and his wife had no difficulty in receiving a British minister or later in coming for a drink with us at Hillsborough, in a way inconceivable for his father. In moments of gloom I used to remember the Bradleys.

Throughout my time in Northern Ireland a semi-secret negotiation was being conducted with the Irish Government on the future of the Province. The fact of the negotiation was known, but not its content. It began before I was appointed, and continued after I left, until the Anglo-Irish Agreement was signed in November 1985. But the crucial stage was reached while I was Secretary of State. This continuous negotiation was in the hands of our cabinet secretary, Robert Armstrong, and his Irish counterpart. He acted under the close supervision of the Prime Minister, the Foreign Secretary and myself. Each of us from time to time had a go at talking to the Irish ourselves, and the three of us met often with Robert to concert our position.

Margaret Thatcher had no great enthusiasm for the subject. In general she wanted to preserve the Union but had no particular regard for Unionist politicians, with the exception of Enoch Powell. Her main concerns were the danger to British troops and the cost of the Province to the British taxpayer. She regarded the Irish in Dublin rather as she regarded the British Foreign Office: she could be charmed by individuals but looked on them collectively as too subtle and soft. Because, unlike her successors John Major and Tony Blair, she did not pay continuous attention to the subject, at the opening of each meeting on Northern Ireland she tended to begin from square one and to repeat ancient themes which had been discussed and dealt with long before. I do not know how many times she began a conversation with me by saying that the answer might be to redraw the border so as to be rid of areas which were substantially Nationalist, and retain a loyal and impregnable Unionist province. Repeatedly I had to tell her of the tribal map of Belfast hanging in my office at Stormont. The map looked as if an artist had flung pots of orange and green paint haphazardly at the canvas. There was no tidy dividing line. The intertwining of the communities was hopelessly complex. The same was broadly true of Londonderry, and four of the six counties of the Province. The term 'ethnic cleansing' was not yet in vogue, but ethnic cleansing on a brutal scale would have been needed if repartition were to have any effect. Moving on, the Prime Minister would then excoriate Irish ministers and the Irish police (the Garda) for their feebleness in dealing with the IRA. Her main aim in negotiation was to shame and galvanise Dublin into effective anti-terrorist action, making as few concessions on points of interest to them as was compatible with that objective.

The Foreign Secretary, Geoffrey Howe, was prepared to go a long way to meet the Irish. Contrary to the conspiracy theories held by Unionist politicians, he never argued or authorised his officials to argue that the ultimate objective should be a united Ireland. He was, however, prepared to contemplate a system of joint authority by which the Irish and British governments would together govern the Province, with a strong degree of devolution to local politicians working together. He valued the willingness of the Irish in certain circumstances to contemplate repealing Articles 2 and 3 of their constitution, which treated the six northern counties as part of Ireland. If the Irish Republic changed its constitution so that it no longer proclaimed the unity of Ireland as a given fact regardless of the wishes of the majority in the north, the Unionists might relax their inbred suspicions of the Republic's intentions. Working closer to the coalface, I doubted this. I argued that even if the Irish could deliver this constitutional change (which must be uncertain since a referendum in the Republic was needed), it was not a prize which could command a high price from us. The Unionist suspicion of the Republic would not be transformed by the alteration. For my part I wanted an agreement, though my reasons for this were rather different from the Prime Minister's. After listening to the RUC and the army I had little faith in any sudden transformation of the Garda, particularly in the border counties of the Republic, into an effective anti-IRA force. For me, the essential advantage of an agreement would be the admission for the first time by the Irish Government that *consent* was the key to the constitutional position of the north.

It seemed clear to me that Irish unity could come about legitimately only if the majority in the north consented; otherwise Dublin would have to accept their right to continue as part of the United Kingdom. This was a statement of both democratic principle and practical reality. Eighteen years later, it seems a platitude, but at that time the case for Irish unity seemed so strong to the Irish political parties, to the Americans and to the British Labour Party that all these players were reluctant to concede that the Unionist majority in the north had the right to block it.

In return for the Irish acknowledging the principle of consent, I was willing to offer them not joint authority but a right to be consulted and to give advice on certain key aspects of the governance of the Province, including security. We would be giving them in theory what they already had in practice. The Irish Foreign Minister, Peter Barry, often telephoned me in the morning to complain about some minor overnight incident near the border in Armagh or Fermanagh which had not yet been reported to me. I could have done what Paisley always told me to do: namely, tell Barry that this had nothing to do with him, and slam down the receiver. I did not see who would have benefited from such a response. So long as it was clear that the power of decision lay with the British Government, I could see the merit of a bargain which formalised an Irish right to be consulted and comment in return for the big prize of their acceptance of consent.

At the back of my mind, though not paraded in argument to anyone, was an instinctive hope that Northern Ireland would remain in the United Kingdom. I never accepted the assumption shared by more than one of my predecessors as Secretary of State, and common among officials in the Foreign Office, that the unification of Ireland was in the long run in Britain's interests. I shared the irritation felt by almost all British practitioners at the way the Unionists played their hand. But with a somewhat romantic sense of history I was glad to see the red, white and blue bunting at Harland and Wolff, the Union Flag over government buildings, the crown on the RUC cap badge, and on the staircase of Belfast City Hall the huge picture of the Battle of the Somme in July 1916, on the first two days of which 5,500 Ulstermen died.

I kept quiet about my personal preference because I knew that the principle of consent had to go deeper than the wish of a majority in the north to stay in the United Kingdom. The consent of the Nationalist minority was important too. The majority had to abandon the truculent assumptions which had distorted Unionist rule from Stormont between 1922 and 1969. They had to respect the rights of the Nationalist minority and find a way to share power with them within the Province. The Secretary of State could help or hinder this slow, necessary process; he would certainly hinder it if he went around proclaiming *his* preferences for the future.

A tragedy in the autumn of 1984 could have destroyed the Anglo-Irish negotiations. The Conservative Party Conference at Brighton would begin on 12 October with a debate on Northern Ireland to which I had to reply. The party leaders gathered the night before in the Grand Hotel, but Judy and I were not among them. Tatiana's father Benedict Eyre and his wife Dorothea had invited us to stay some twenty miles away at West Burton, where I had spent many happy weekends during my first marriage. Neither of them was well, the house had become too big for them, and sadly they had decided to sell. This was therefore a farewell visit. Summoning up memories of past festive details at his dining-room table, Benedict produced a 1973 claret, then port and whisky as we reviewed the world. I had to deal with a box of work about Robert Armstrong's negotiation, and hone my speech for the conference.

Just after five in the morning the police arrived at West Burton to tell us that a bomb had exploded in the Grand Hotel. They knew no details, nor whether the conference would go ahead. I sat at the kitchen table scribbling a new speech in case it was needed. About two hours later I was told that the conference would proceed, but I should not yet go to Brighton myself. When eventually my police protectors were authorised to move we were close to the hour when I was supposed to be on my feet in the Conference Centre replying to the first debate. Judy and I were driven at high speed through the roundabouts which ring Brighton, then past the shattered Grand Hotel. The Conference Centre was full of rumours of friends and acquaintances dead or injured. The Northern Ireland debate and my reply to it were inconsequential. All eyes were on the Prime Minister, who was fiercely applauded that afternoon not for what she said but for what she was.

Among all of us at Brighton depression set in later in the day, as the rumours of death and injury turned into facts. We had all said the necessary things, and this process had sustained morale for a few hours; but the realities hit hard. We were driven back to London but the police refused to let Judy and myself stay at our London base in Hammersmith. This small two-up, two-down terraced house, built in the 1870s for the workforce (much of it Irish) which manned the factories and built the railways of West London, had worried them for some time. Although the names of the nearby pubs, the Lord Nelson and the Havelock Arms, were reassuring, they thought that the area still had an Irish flavour, and it was not possible for them to guard permanently the front and back of our home. So they took us, tired, sad and rather cross, to Westwell. In the next weeks they persuaded the Home Office to buy from the Metropolitan Police a considerably larger, and more easily protected, home in South Eaton Place, which became our London home for the next five years.

The Brighton bomb, without altering any of the basic facts of power and politics in Northern Ireland, underlined the continuing cost and danger. Neither the Prime Minister nor any of us suggested that the Anglo-Irish talks should be broken off; but prospects were dim. On 25 October I went to Dublin for talks with Peter Barry, the Irish Foreign Minister.

He drones on about specific grievances, frontier roads, etc. Then dinner alone with him and Noonan, Minister of Justice. A real

debate and a gloomy one. They are not prepared to consider a
security package which would give them a say (consultative) in
Belfast. Their fundamental criticisms of the RUC are unacceptable.
They are prepared to make a heroic heave on Articles 2 and 3 of
their constitution, but this is not much good to us. Noonan
negative on security cooperation. The tone is perfectly civilised, the
content depressing.

That was eventually where the argument rested through another year of
discussions at different levels. The Foreign Office would have liked to
move a little further towards joint authority, but the Prime Minister,
supported by myself, felt that we had gone far enough. The
disagreement between the two governments broke out into the open at
the Anglo-Irish Summit at Chequers on 18 and 19 November. My tactic
at this stage was to say generously to the Irish that we did not ask them
to change their constitution, in return for which concession they would
accept a more modest role in Belfast. This is what eventually happened,
but we made no progress at Chequers.

The Prime Minister liked her Irish opposite number, the Taoiseach,
Garrett FitzGerald. He was a man of ideas and integrity, a courteous
academic with a strong historical understanding. These were all qualities
which Margaret Thatcher valued in individuals, even when she
disagreed with their conclusions. But Garrett FitzGerald was also long
winded, and the Prime Minister lost patience. On the Sunday Chequers
was shrouded in thick fog. Margaret Thatcher began once again to talk
about a redrawing of the border. As she and Garrett FitzGerald
exchanged misunderstandings downstairs, the other Irish and British
ministers conferred in the Long Gallery in front of a good fire. The
Prime Minister began to compare the Nationalists in the border counties
with the Sudeten Germans in 1938; the Taoiseach looked grey and sad.
The summit petered out with an empty communiqué.

As often happened with Margaret Thatcher the drama came not at
the meeting itself but at her press conference afterwards, which she held
at No. 12 Downing Street after the Irish had gone home. I sat
embarrassed at her side. Artlessly, and turning to me at each point for
corroboration, she listed three ideas which had at one time been put
forward to solve the problem, and then eliminated them in turn: united
Ireland – that's out; confederation of two states – that's out; joint
authority – that's out. It sounded as if these three ideas had just been put
forward by the Irish at Chequers and rejected. Nothing at foggy
Chequers had been as precise as that. Nothing the Prime Minister said
was new, but the hardness of her three 'outs' created a shock in Dublin
of the kind the Irish rather enjoy, and momentary delight among the

Unionists, who were then dismayed that the Anglo-Irish negotiations continued.

By the summer of 1985, though, these negotiations had reached no conclusion, and I began to worry about rising Unionist resentment. The Irish had insisted that the content of our meetings should be secret, and in particular that we should say nothing to the politicians in Northern Ireland. Margaret Thatcher too had insisted on this at the outset. John Hume and his SDLP colleagues were no doubt content with what they learned from their friends in Dublin, but apart from some broad generalisations we kept the Unionists in the dark. This built up a huge grievance. Indeed, the eventual Unionist indignation against the Anglo-Irish Agreement was founded less on its content than on the fact that it had been secretly negotiated. Certainly the chances of reaching agreement would have been reduced if we had told the Unionists, and therefore the world, about each discussion. The Irish would have been particularly vulnerable because of their willingness to discuss with us, albeit unprofitably, the amendment of their constitution. Nevertheless, I felt that the secrecy was beginning to stack odds against a good outcome.

On 25 July the Cabinet met to discuss the negotiations. The mood was cool and uneasy, and this began to affect the Prime Minister's handling. The discussion was saved by Norman Tebbit. Because his wife had been badly injured and he himself hurt in the Brighton bombing, there was special power in his voice and his support was crucial; any opposition from him might have scuppered the negotiations. He agreed that they should continue. My own feelings that day were, I wrote, 'as ambivalent as any'. In coming years I disagreed with Norman Tebbit on most subjects under the sun, but I never forgot his steadfastness that day. With the Prime Minister and Geoffrey Howe I devised a compromise based on the fact that Jim Molyneaux (leader of the largest Unionist party, the UUP) and Enoch Powell were both privy councillors.

That evening Jim Molyneaux and Enoch Powell called on me at my request in my room in the Commons. Both men wore dark suits in the sticky heat, and the mood was correspondingly formal, though quite amicable. I offered to give them information on the Anglo-Irish talks on a Privy Council basis, which meant that they could not have disclosed particulars to colleagues. Molyneaux was inclined to agree, but Powell advised his leader to decline, and there was no outcome. It was true, as Powell pointed out, that knowledge which could not be shared would tie their hands in opposing an agreement. It was also true that if they had known how innocuous, so far as they were concerned, were the terms on which we were prepared to conclude with the Irish, their worries insofar as they were genuine might have been assuaged. Enoch

Powell preferred the darkness in which his theories about a conspiracy between the Foreign Office and the Americans to undo Ulster could hatch and flourish.

I never came close to understanding Enoch Powell. He was the only adversary in the House of Commons who ever seriously worried me. Others were nimble and could disconcert me for a moment, but Powell, by his appearance, voice and choice of words, radiated an authority which I had no immediate resources to match. We were almost neighbours in South Eaton Place, and he was invariably courteous to my wife. But I never held a friendly conversation with him, and never understood the admiration verging on worship which he inspired in intelligent commentators. I saw at first hand the harm done in turn by his negative eloquence on immigration in 1968, on Ireland in 1984/5 and throughout on Europe. It was a tragedy that such patriotic fervour, deep learning and forceful talent should have been dedicated to detecting non-existent conspiracies and upholding different causes of the sour right.

The cabinet discussion on 25 July had been on the basis of a joint paper by Geoffrey Howe and myself, recommending that the negotiations had a chance of success and that Unionist opposition, though strong, would be containable. Though some of my officials in Stormont were more anxious, we did not believe that the extremists, led by Paisley, would be able to mobilise again the industrial action which had destroyed the Sunningdale Agreement in 1974. In a crude way this assessment, which proved correct, was a measure of progress already made over those eleven years. My successor, Tom King, was in charge when the negotiations finally succeeded that autumn.

Most of the individuals who kept Northern Ireland going were in a vague way Unionist by background and inclination, and we ministers got on well with them as we worked together on practical matters. But I could not be satisfied in my dealings with Unionist politicians. I received wiser advice from the church leaders of the main denominations. At one time I had hopes of Paisley's young deputy Peter Robinson, who had a sharper mind. I invited him to dine alone with me at Hillsborough in the hope that hospitality would unlock a closed spirit. He accepted, but would not touch wine or whisky and I got nowhere. Jim Molyneaux was correct and courteous, but locked into the past, and apparently incapable of any flight of imagination which would separate him from the negative influence of Enoch Powell.

The Unionists had a genuine grievance against the secrecy of the negotiations, but when the agreement was reached they failed to see that they had gained a huge success in the recognition of consent. They remained suspicious and curmudgeonly. It was not until David Trimble emerged in the next stage of the peace process that they had a leader with a sense of the future as well as the past.

I had this damaging Unionist experience in mind eight years later when I supported Chris Patten in deciding that discussions with the Chinese about any changes to his constitutional proposals for Hong Kong should not take place before the Hong Kong people knew what the proposals were.

Looking back over diaries and official papers, I can recall these political exchanges and my growing fascination with the subject. But, left to itself, my memory fastens most easily on the house which Judy, Philip and I came to regard as our home in Northern Ireland. Hillsborough Castle would not be a castle in England. It is the former country mansion of the Downshire family and stands in gently rolling country about half an hour south of Belfast, at the top of the High Street of a small English-looking market town. Behind the house, falling away to the lake, a big garden is notable for its trees. It contained the biggest rhododendron bush in Europe (or the world, depending on one's informant). This huge object seemed, if the phrase can be excused, to be resting on its laurels, as if satisfied with its size without seeing the need for any great annual display of blossom. The garden, true to its loyalist character, boasted a collection of trees planted by different royal visitors which must be unique. The more mature beeches seemed taller, wider-spreading and in summer greener than their English equivalents. Upstairs a small flat and kitchen had been carved out for the Secretary of State and his family. Downstairs the state rooms were in our day somewhat dark and formal, before our successors Tom and Jane King brightened them up.

If Judy was in England I used to work by myself in one of the downstairs rooms at Hillsborough, with the help of whisky and a cigar. A lamp shone on my box, but the rest of the room was in half darkness, through which I could see the outline of the Lavery portraits of Carson and Lord Londonderry on the walls. The staff, in particular the young butler David Anderson, seemed to relish looking after a family. Philip, still a baby, was in the immediate care of an English nanny, Diana Watts, who enjoyed the company of our protection officers. She was not in the least scared of the IRA, but was not so good with cows.

Judy quickly developed a role of her own. Nowhere was very far from anywhere else and often we would criss-cross the Province in a day, perhaps coinciding for a word in a lay-by, after Judy had opened a small business and I had visited a couple of police stations. Because of Hillsborough, we were able to encourage family and friends to visit. New Year's Day 1985 was sunny after frost. Tom and Al, my second and third sons, walked with me across the waist of the Mountains of Mourne from west to east in three hours less five minutes. Judy's parents bought a promising steeplechaser from a trainer at Downpatrick.

On 22 April 1985 my mother had a heart attack while driving her car through Burford. I visited her in the John Radcliffe Hospital at Oxford, where she seemed rested and self-confident. It was ten months since we had celebrated her eightieth birthday at Westwell. We were to spend that weekend with the Abercorns at Baron's Court in County Tyrone. On the Saturday evening I had a long telephone conversation with Ian Paisley. A few days before he had denounced me as an arrogant dictator; on the telephone he asked me considerately and at length about my mother. That night a second thunderbolt struck her in hospital and she died just before midnight. After the service of cremation at Swindon there was a family gathering at her house, the Old Oxyard in Oare. For the last time we drank vermouth as had been her custom out of strange, small, coloured glasses. We inspected her painting studio which also contained the old wooden fort and big toy tanks, worn out by two generations of battle between Hurd boys. We visited the boys' bedroom with its silver box still full of ancient biscuits. Later we placed her ashes in the churchyard at Winterbourne in Julian's grave.

Judy was often sick through that summer of 1985, carrying our second child. Watching the Caesarean operation through a glass screen at the John Radcliffe on 5 August, I was amazed at the small object which was held up for our inspection. It was a girl. Jessica had a brother Philip, and three half-brothers. On the Hurd side her father, grandfather and great-grandfather had only brothers. She had broken the trend, and we were delighted. Her name was chosen after delay and some tussle. I had wanted something to remind her of Northern Ireland, where she had been conceived, but there were frowns and pursed lips over each name suggested, first names being one of the most obvious dividing factors in the Province. Life moved on, and within a few weeks Northern Ireland was no longer part of our present lives.

I was worried about houses. As a family we were now bulging out of the medium-sized cottage at Westwell into which we had moved three years earlier. Judy and I knew exactly where we wanted to live and bring up Philip and Jessica. Just off the duck pond at Westwell, two hundred yards from our cottage, behind two stone pillars, stood a sturdy farmhouse called Freelands. It was by traditional social standing the fourth house in the village, humbler than the Manor, the Rectory and the Dower house. It had been occupied in the past by the most important of the tenant farmers who leased the land from Christ Church, Oxford. In the nineteenth century the farming family had been dissenters, filling a meeting room at the back of the house on Sunday evenings with a congregation as big as those gathered for evensong in the church a few yards up the slope. A stream ran in winter, past the house and a garden then dark with yews, through a big farmyard, and alongside the two barns which had by our time been converted into houses and sold off.

In 1985 Freelands was owned and lived in by the sculptress Cecily Whitworth. A witty, vague lady of much charm, Cecily lived alone with donkeys which had the privilege of ravaging her garden. Her health was frail and in theory there was much to be said for her moving to, say, Oxford, where she would be closer to friends and family. But Freelands was full of artefacts of all kinds, including Cecily's sculptures, whole and unfinished. The confusion of the house was so great and so long-standing that the chances of Cecily moving seemed remote. Anyway, there was nothing we could do about it. Our need was so pressing that we had to look elsewhere.

So while still in Northern Ireland we bought a Victorian house, red brick with a Gothic porch, at Longworth, a village outside the constituency but by only a couple of miles. Trudging round its empty rooms with my father-in-law Sidney Smart, who combined imagination with shrewd common sense in these matters, we thought it would do. By the autumn of 1985 the time had come to spend serious money making the Longworth house habitable. The sums did not add up, particularly against the background of my family of five children, which collectively was just halfway through the process of its education. I considered leaving politics at the next election so that I would have ten years trying to earn something for old age. At this stage I had jogged along and saved nothing.

Then, unexpectedly, Cecily Whitworth offered us Freelands. But the price seemed high, and of course I had just bought the other house at Longworth. On New Year's Day 1986, cross because undecided, Judy and I wandered round Freelands drinking red wine: 'Each room is on a different level, but it has some magic which Longworth lacks.' This magic overcame our doubts. There was no point in an official survey, which would just irritate our already raw nerves. We pulled up part of the dining-room floor, found water immediately underneath from the adjoining stream, and put the floor down again. There was water too in the cellar. By now I knew Judy well enough to be sure that one project of improvement would follow another relentlessly through the years at Freelands. The financial sums, like the pump in the cellar, still did not work, but in February 1986 we bought the house for £240,000 and have never for a moment regretted it.

We now owned two country houses and a financial crisis, so we were extraordinarily lucky to find a buyer for the house at Longworth. I had been cast into deep gloom by the news, not revealed before, that a covenant gave public access to part of the field and yard beside the house. But after an anxious few months a purchaser appeared who was not put off by the covenant, and we received exactly what we had paid for the house.

At the end of August 1985 I broke my ankle, jumping at a stupid angle from a garden chair as if I were a sprightly teenager. I was punished with plaster and crutches and for some three months hobbled about in pain. Margaret Thatcher remembered this when she telephoned me on 1 September: 'Are you sitting comfortably?' she asked, as if introducing *Children's Hour* on the radio. 'I want you to listen carefully to what I am going to say.' Then she offered me the Home Office. I was amazed; there had been no hint, no gossip. She continued with an unlikely tale that she was moving Leon Brittan to Trade and Industry because she wanted more attention paid to these subjects. She asked me to explain this to Leon, as if that were my responsibility rather than hers. For me it was a marked promotion, and I at once accepted. But on reflection that night both Judy and I were sad: 'Mixed feelings for us both as job is hardly begun, and there are many things and people we are fond of. Esp. for me Hillsborough and my Stormont office.' By the next day these feelings had intensified: 'It is a crazy system. I am good at <u>this</u> job now, and v. unsure of the next.' And the day after that I wrote, 'I definitely wish I had stayed in NI. Not that we were poised for success, but I was on top of the job and ready for danger.' On my way to the airport on impulse I paused to say a prayer for the Province, alone in St Anne's Cathedral, Belfast, where I had preached a Lenten sermon earlier in the year. The Dean, vigilant at his post, bustled down the aisle to wish me well.

For nearly a quarter of a century, whatever else I was doing, I could not forget that I was the Member of Parliament for Mid-Oxfordshire or (as it was later christened) Witney. That hard-won fact was the foundation of my political career, and also the occasion for a steady stream of work throughout those years, irrespective of whichever government post I held. Foreign colleagues were amazed in an interval of some international conference to watch me signing replies to individual constituents on their personal problems, and to learn that I had earlier dictated these replies myself. My German colleague, the Interior Minister Herr Schauble, was moved once to expostulate: *'Die Kanalisation von Frau Schmidt* [Mrs Smith's plumbing problems]' could not be the proper responsibility of a minister. I explained proudly that under the British system they were precisely that, adding that this gave me a series of snapshots of what was happening in England outside the narrow realms of politics. This was not entirely accurate, since those who wrote were hardly typical of the population. Nor were the individuals who came to my surgeries, which I held one Saturday morning each month in different towns and villages. I never quite dared to follow the advice of my predecessor Neil Marten, who used an hourglass filled with sand which measured exactly the fifteen minutes to which each constituent was entitled. When the top half of the glass was empty his constituent was courteously shown the door. Assuming about eighteen constituents in a morning, I reckoned that one of these would be tearful, one angry and one unhinged; sometimes all three conditions united in the same person. I came to know well the different rooms in different towns, usually ancient, in which I spent these hours. Some constituents came expecting me to welcome them because they voted Conservative or to refuse help because they did not. But at the heart of our system of first past the post elections held in single-member constituencies lies the concept that the Member of Parliament represents people of all shades of opinion. He is landed with them, and they are landed with him until they decide otherwise. I relished the conversations and the relationship which grew up through the years out of this fact. By the end there was no village and hardly a street in any town where I could not remember some incident or controversy, or some individual to whom I had listened. Even now, when someone speaks of the withy beds of Clanfield, the toll bridge at Eynsham, the policing of Shipton under Wychwood, or the gravel pits round Standlake, old memories stir. I shall never drive north on the A44 from Oxford without telling any fellow passenger that the roundabouts between Begbroke and Yarnton were the result of several years' pressure from a devoted Member of Parliament.

In 1983, as I mentioned earlier, the Boundary Commission had cast its pencil over the borders of my constituency, moving it west and a bit north. It became more homogeneous and slightly more Conservative. I lost Otmoor and the eastern outskirts of Oxford, but gained Woodstock, Chipping Norton and the valley of the Evenlode. I lost red brick and gained Cotswold stone, though there was still plenty of variety.

Even in apparently similar Cotswold stone villages I quickly learned the differences. Some of these were historical: Leafield boasts a big church with a dominant spire, but Sir George Gilbert Scott built it as late as 1860 and there is no manor. That stretch of countryside was wild; it belonged to the royal hunting forest of Wychwood. For centuries it was unenclosed and a refuge for outlaws, gypsies, poachers and other persons inclined to radical politics. Other differences were more modern. The small towns of Charlbury and Bampton look much the same – a fine church, financed from the medieval wool trade, one street of small shops, schools, pubs, fine moderate-sized stone houses, council estates at the back – but their political characters were quite different. Charlbury brimmed over with progressive argument. Meetings there were hot with opinions about global warming and Third World debt. The United Nations Association ran a local branch from a house in Church Row. Bampton, by contrast, was staunchly Conservative, well to the right of its Member of Parliament, but too polite to press any points of difference, except when the local rates rose intemperately.

Over the years countless meals, large and small fairs and feasts, grumbles and achievements, polling stations and committee rooms, a few tears but more laughter, occasional anger but also loyal support were the strands in weaving a relationship of respect and affection – mine for my constituents, and sometimes, I hoped, theirs for their Member of Parliament.

17

HOME SECRETARY

My latest change of office in 1985 involved another expedition to receive new seals from the Queen. All cabinet ministers involved in the reshuffle travelled north together on a sort of works outing on 5 September. A slow Andover plane stopped at Carlisle to pick up Willie Whitelaw. An even slower bus drove us from Dyce airport to Balmoral through showers and sunshine. My broken ankle made me more than usually awkward, but somehow I managed to get down on the dreaded tartan footstool in front of the Queen, swear my loyalty and rise again without disaster. At lunch I sat next to her: 'As soon as she opens her mouth the shrewdness and fun emerge.' Afterwards we inspected the greenhouses.

But on the whole my new life was sombre. The volume of paperwork suddenly doubled; on the first weekend as Home Secretary I ploughed my way through four red boxes. I was now belatedly grateful to Margaret Thatcher for having given me an apprenticeship as Minister of State at the Home Office two years earlier. If it had not been for that experience I would have found the complicated subjects and the dense, allusive Home Office prose style hard to take.

For the first time I found myself dealing with personal files on which only the Home Secretary could take the required decisions. Fortunately I no longer had the task (which had distressed many of my predecessors) of deciding on death or reprieve for condemned murderers. But I alone, with advice but without shared responsibility, had to decide on such matters as the length of life sentences, alleged miscarriages of justice, deportation orders, and appeals by police officers against disciplinary punishments. These last were quite frequent, sometimes two or three at the bottom of a box. At the end of a long day there was a temptation simply to tick off the recommendation of officials or the junior minister who had seen the file just before me. But the future livelihood and happiness of a police officer and his family might have depended on that tick. Wearily I would turn to the detailed story, the accusation, the denials or attenuating circumstances, and so imagined myself momentarily in the shoes of both prosecution and defence.

On 9 September 1985, just a week after I became Home Secretary serious rioting broke out in the Handsworth district of Birmingham. I went there next morning. The Chief Constable of the West Midlands, Geoffrey Dear, a tall man of cool, reserved manner, quickly gained my confidence. But the lunch which he hosted dragged on too long. Labour councillors buzzed about trying to be helpful. I was anxious to see Handsworth for myself, but partly as a result of this impatience I got there too early. The rioting was not over and flared up briefly when I arrived. I found myself arguing with a group of black youths in Lozelles Street when once more missiles began to fly. I was not hit, but the police hustled me away as fast as I could manage with my injured foot.

I talked to disgruntled Asians on a corner, then to frightened whites down a side-street. Both these communities were scared that black violence would turn away from the police on to them. I met the firemen who had been in action for many hours, and at a meeting with community leaders urged them to issue a statement calling for calm. The young local MP Jeff Rooker was shrewd and forthcoming. A local GP beckoned me into his surgery and urged me never to relax the law on cannabis. The violence died, and my day dribbled away in a string of TV and press interviews.

September stayed hot and sultry. The police in London warned me that this was weather for trouble. People gathered on the steps of their houses as if in Harlem, New York. On Saturday 28 September the police shot a black woman in Brixton, and there was a riot by evening. This time I let several days pass before I went there. Meanwhile, I tried to mobilise local MPs and community leaders to work with the police to prevent further trouble. On 1 October, 'Two exhausting hours with Lambeth Consultative Group – weary depressed erratic people, and tho' I try hard I cannot raise their self-confidence.' Worse soon followed in North London. On Sunday 6 October a police officer, Keith Blakelock, was killed while trying to contain violence on the Broadwater Farm council estate in Tottenham. I lay awake that night in South Eaton Place with a raw throat, listening to the police sirens in the streets as reinforcements moved up to Tottenham. Next afternoon I visited wounded police officers in Whittington Hospital – 'cheerful young men, bashed this way and that . . . Plunged in gloom about this country.' Two months later Judy and I went to Police Constable Blakelock's funeral in St James's Muswell Hill.

The three riots of autumn 1985 made a deep impression on me. There was no marked economic misery and no specific political cause in those areas, or other cities which were also troubled to a lesser extent. I felt no sympathy for the rioters, many of whom turned quickly to looting when for an hour or two they had a free hand. But condemnation was not enough. Deep hostility to the police, racial tension between blacks, Asians and whites, endemic crime, drugs and sleazy, run-down housing estates combined to produce a sullen, hopeless mood easily sparking into criminal violence. Public services in these areas operated with gaps and imperfections concealed in official figures. I have tried never to forget in my interesting and comfortable life that there is a dark, sometimes desperate, underside to British society. It is the job of the Home Secretary to make sure, in many contexts and on many occasions, that he and his colleagues act in knowledge of that fact.

Gradually a routine took shape at the Home Office. My office at the top of 50 Queen Anne's Gate resembled the lounge of an ocean liner of the 1950s. The deep armchairs, occasional tables and ambitious potted plants looked as if they were anchored to resist the next transatlantic gale. Though lacking charm, it was an excellent room for meetings and it is for meetings that I remember it.

I realised that the Home Office contained many able officials who shone more convincingly in oral discussion than when writing their recommendations in the stilted prose style of the department. The minutes which filled my boxes were detailed and thorough. Every eventuality was examined in turn; the trees multiplied, the wood disappeared. Yet these same officials, when called to a meeting in my office, quickly discarded trivia and explained what was important. There was no difficulty in inviting junior officials, for their seniors believed in letting the youngsters have their fling. My permanent secretary at the outset, Brian Cubbon, did not pretend to direct every ring of the circus, but was quick to focus on any important point which had been neglected in discussion, or the point exaggerated by an enthusiast. I was also lucky in persuading Edward Bickham to continue as my special adviser. He took charge of my political comings and goings, as he had in Northern Ireland. There was no question in those days of political advisers directing policy, but Edward was always at hand for the occasional word of quiet wisdom.

The House of Commons rarely had anything important to discuss on a Friday. This was thus the right day for official expeditions out of London. These usually ended at Westwell so that on Saturday I could hold a constituency surgery, or in some other way show West

Oxfordshire that I was still among them. The possible menu for these days of Home Office tourism was ample – police, prisons, probation, television, radio, cable, race relations, gambling, racing, civil defence. The Conservative Party too had to be found a place somewhere in the day.

I give one example from my diary (from 1989) to show how this worked out.

> To Birmingham by train. Cross at alteration of programme. Heavy rain all day. To Smethwick first, an amputated church, now mostly Asian toddlers on slides upstairs and a spick and span community restaurant downstairs. Encouraging. Then a marquee and tycoons and Jill Knight [Conservative MP for Edgbaston], open Birmingham Safe Deposit in Edgbaston. Commiserate with G. Dear [Chief Constable] on not going to NI [as Chief Constable of the Royal Ulster Constabulary]. Broadcast on Richmond result before it is known – better than a disaster. [This was the by-election in which William Hague entered Parliament.] To Villa [Aston Villa Football Club] and Doug Ellis [the Villa Chairman], a nice man bounding with ideas, a cricket centre, a classroom, no. i.d. cards. To the Art Gallery, ludicrous Pre-Raphaelites. To the Central Mosque, a crowd, tension, TV light and heat. Muslims explain the insult of *Satanic Verses* [the just-published novel by Salman Rushdie]. I expound. Some disappointment and tendency to shout, but well handled. To Lady Guernsey's luxurious bath at Packington Hall, and routine [Conservative] fundraising in magnificent Pompeian room. To Nuneaton, braised chicken upstairs, a lively informal friendly simple meeting in big clubroom where forever Christmas [a conservative club which never took down its decorations]. Quite a day – enjoyable. Westwell.

The Home Office was a giant bran tub in which were hidden many unrelated packages of work, some big, some small, waiting to be unwrapped and dealt with in turn. Some of these were projects wrapped up by others in the past, others were thrust into the tub by unexpected events. Many of them required unwrapping in Parliament. During my five years as Home Secretary I spent more active time in the Commons than in the rest of my twenty-three parliamentary years put together. From practice I became more confident as a performer. Although this was not always possible, I preferred to choose my own words rather than rely on a text written by officials. I knew that clever opponents like my Labour shadows Gerald Kaufman and Roy Hattersley could catch me out on points of detail, and I studied to move back as soon as possible to the underlying argument which could rally support. I learned to volunteer a statement rather than have it forced from me, and how to use courtesy as a weapon against interruption. I began to enjoy parliamentary life.

There is a difficulty in describing here the packages which I drew from the bran tub. Each of these would need a chapter of its own to do it justice. Circling round are veterans or historians who regard their particular subject as crucial, but I must move on soon to the two biggest packages in my tub: broadcasting and crime. So with a paragraph or two on the other subjects, I apologise to those who will regard such treatment as superficial.

What, for example, is to be said about the Shops Bill? There was an overwhelming case for liberalising the 1950 Shops Act, with its restrictions on Sunday shopping which were confused and widely ignored. The Government's Bill, based on the Auld Report, had been introduced in the Lords in November 1985, and I tried to enthuse Conservative peers on its behalf: 'Those who are awake are receptive, tho' my presentation is not first class.' There was no serious trouble in the Lords, but after that clouds gathered fast. In the country the trade unions and the churches mobilised opposition to the Bill on the grounds that it was a threat respectively to workers' rights and Christian civilisation. Unusually we spent the second weekend of December in London, and this began badly. At early service in St Michael's Chester Square the priest not only used insipid Rite A from the new prayer book, but prayed against the Shops Bill. The Rector of Witney, brave man, was staunch for the Bill, and one Witney lady who knew America well remarked that the differences between that country and Britain were that in the States on Sunday the shops were open *and* the churches full.

My speech at the second reading on 14 April 1986 began with a dull technical explanation of the Bill, but perked up in the middle. I remarked that the attempt to ban Sunday shopping by law was relatively modern. At the high moment of the Victorian Sunday, when Mrs Proudie and Mr Slope railed against Sabbath-day travelling, there was no effective law forbidding shopping on Sunday. Nor had civilisation entirely collapsed in Scotland because there was no such law. It was a mistake to wheel in the criminal law to regulate an area which was not for most people criminal. Such arguments are obvious platitudes today, but that afternoon we were faced with many Members of Parliament who had committed themselves against the Bill before hearing the debate. I wandered into a minefield on procedure. The Conservative MPs were whipped to support second reading – that is, the vote on the principle of the Bill – but had been promised a free vote when it came to amendment of detail. When questioned, I gave an additional undertaking that we would not guillotine the Bill (that is, introduce a timetable to limit discussion of clauses). Calculating on the spur of the moment at the despatch box, I felt that this was a safe assurance, since the number of rebels in our own ranks made it inconceivable that we would get the votes for a guillotine motion. If they were against the substance of the Bill, they certainly would not help me on procedure – nor would Labour and Liberal MPs, regardless of their views on substance. But I had no authority from colleagues to give that undertaking. They were dismayed, though Ken Clarke, winding up the debate, made a grand job of rescuing the procedural arguments. On substance we had been doomed from the start, and second reading was lost by fourteen votes.

I know of no other modern occasion on which a cabinet minister has been defeated when proposing the second reading of a government Bill. The odd thing was that no one particularly cared. The immediate headlines next day were embarrassing for me but swamped by news of President Reagan's air attack on Libya. I was relieved not to face a detailed and probably doomed examination of the Bill in committee. The prestige of the Government was hardly dented. The law continued to be an ass Sunday by Sunday until common sense eventually prevailed.

Unlike the Shops Bill, the Firearms Bill of 1988 became the law of the land, but with difficulty. We acted after Michael Ryan ran amok in the small Berkshire town of Hungerford on 19 August 1987, killing sixteen people with his Kalashnikov. I knew Hungerford well. It was in my father's old constituency, a quiet town of antique shops with the Kennet River at its foot, close by the old Bath Road that we had travelled often as children. Sixteen killed by a Kalashnikov in Hungerford – the news seemed unbelievable when it reached us on holiday in Italy. On 23 August Judy and I visited the Hungerford police station, the peaceful, dim little road where all those people had been shot down, and in Newbury the widow of one of them, Police Constable Brereton. A few days later we went to his funeral.

I have never been good at showing public grief, or finding immediate words to express it into a microphone. I believe that inside myself I feel as much sympathy as most for the bereaved and the suffering. Like everyone else, I try to enter into and share what they are living through, but outwardly I can look and sound constrained and stiff – a result, I think, of both generation and temperament. This is a handicap for a modern politician. My voice does not easily tremble with emotion and when my eyes fill with tears it tends to be on unexpected, even trivial, occasions.

The pressure for tough and immediate new firearm legislation grew fast. We were criticised by the Opposition for taking our time. I told the

House of Commons in December 1987 what we had in mind, and the Firearms Bill trundled painfully through Parliament in the first half of 1988. Compared to the law today, it seems a slight measure. I disliked being pushed into legislation by a single tragedy. On the other hand, the Hungerford killings forced me to look for the first time at the state of the law on guns.

All my life in England I had lived in a house which contained shotguns, though by now I had myself given up shooting. I had not the slightest prejudice against legal owners of any firearms. But the rules when examined seemed definitely lax. It seemed odd to me, for example, at a time of rising concern about crime, that the police had no idea how many shotguns were held in this country or by whom. Shotgun owners grumbled over the new requirements for a register and police inspection of safe-keeping. But the real burden of the proposed law fell on those whose firearms would in future be forbidden, including, for example, full-bore self-loading rifles and burst-fire weapons. Douglas Hogg (the Minister of State in charge of the Bill) and I soon discovered that our officials knew less about the technicalities than they supposed. The Labour Opposition urged us to go faster and further; but a group of Conservative backbenchers led by Hector Monro (MP for Dumfries and Galloway) mobilised an expert lobby against the details of the Bill. When I briefed Roy Hattersley, then my Labour shadow, on the eve of my announcement I knew that as a skilled politician with a developed sense of mischief he would praise me next day in order to get me into the greatest possible trouble with the Conservative backbenchers. I talked that day to Max Hastings, a keen shot and editor of the *Daily Telegraph*. He was fed up with the whole subject, but observed that since we were where we were I had better get on with it.

So we did, suffering several setbacks and long nights in the Commons. On 23 May, 'To HoC Firearm Bill 7–1.45 a.m. Fairly grisly. Douglas Hogg handles it all, and well. But combination of our 26 rebels and Labour and Willie Ross [Ulster Unionist drags] it out, bed 2.15.' Two days later, after speaking to the Conservative Women's Conference and giving lunch to the Omani Minister of Information, 'On to Firearms Bill, speak on guillotine, which falls 12.50 a.m. Our rebels go to bed, a Labour/small party rump of 30 keep us up and voting till 5.15. V. tedious but not mortal. Bed 5.45 a.m.' It never occurred to me that ten years later a Government would so emasculate the proceedings of the Commons that ministers could go to bed at their convenience even when in charge of an uncomfortable Bill. I accepted the occasional all-night session as part of the price of serving a rigorous parliamentary democracy.

I hoped, as I told the Commons, that the 1988 Firearms Act would last twenty years. I was wrong. In 1996, after the killing of sixteen schoolchildren and their teacher in Dunblane, Michael Howard, then Home Secretary, introduced a further Bill, banning 80 per cent of handguns and heavily regulating the remainder. The pressure from the Dunblane parents against firearms received overwhelming public support and achieved an unfair Act which destroyed a sporting activity far removed from the Dunblane killings. By then, a backbencher again, I expressed doubts in the Commons and privately to Michael Howard, but did not want to lead a revolt in the last days of the Parliament and of my years as an MP.

In April 1989 another disaster also became tangled with legislation. On Saturday 15 April 96 people were killed and 170 injured at the Hillsborough football ground in Sheffield. Liverpool fans crowding in to watch the FA Cup semi-final with Nottingham Forest were crushed behind the security fence designed to protect the ground from hooligans. On Sunday I flew to Sheffield with the Prime Minister in a cold helicopter. We were both miserable. Our ear pads prevented conversation but she had already agreed that Mr Justice Taylor should lead an inquiry. We were briefed first by the Chief Constable of South Yorkshire, Peter Wright, who was pale and inarticulate. 'To the dreary litter-strewn ground at Hillsborough, with the fearful little gate and bent barriers. Then to the two hospitals. In intensive care youngsters on ventilators fight against death or brain damage. Relations sit round, touching. More youngsters, bruised but revived and talkative, tell stories. Young special [constable] of 19 breaks down. Clearly there was one, perhaps two, police blunders.' Margaret Thatcher and I went round the hospital wards together. In one of them a young Liverpool fan lay unconscious, surrounded by his family. No press or television were present. My whole instinct was to stay away from the family group round the bed, and leave them to their private anxiety. Margaret thought differently. She went straight to the bed, took the mother's hand and placed it on the unconscious boy's arm. 'Leave it there, dear,' she said. 'That's what he needs.' The Merseyside family must have been amazed at this appearance from an alien world, a Tory leader whom they had probably been taught to detest. But she was right. The boy died a few days later. The family will remember, I am sure for good, the sudden and practical sympathy of a woman who happened to be the Prime Minister. I recall the incident whenever I hear banal accusations of heartlessness against Margaret Thatcher.

Ministers spent a lot of time that summer arguing among themselves how the Hillsborough tragedy and the Taylor Inquiry should affect the legislation on football safety which we had already introduced. More interesting now is the place of Hillsborough in the dreary growth of the blame culture in this country. When such a disaster occurs it is clearly right to find out as fast as possible what happened and to examine the causes, so that everything possible is done to prevent another disaster. This may mean removing incompetent people from their posts. Less valid is the search for scapegoats who are to be ruined in public because of mistakes which they or their subordinates made before or during the disaster. Lawyers and the media leap into this search, which brings them direct financial benefits. Natural grief is exploited. The families of victims are encouraged to press for what is called justice, with the undertone that justice may include financial compensation for themselves, as if money cured grief. Headlines become everything. Understanding and forgiveness are excluded, or treated as eccentric if some brave victim dares to show them. There is no such thing as a wholly safe football ground, or train, or major surgical operation, or a human being cool and confident in all conditions of stress. Too many vultures hover over our public life, profiting from the fact that in moments of pain we forget the realities of risk. If the Chief Constable of South Yorkshire that Sunday morning was pale and inarticulate, it may have been in part because he saw clearly the years of accusation and explanation which lay ahead for his force.

Sometimes a surge of reforming change continues beneath the surface regardless of which party is in power. One such surge was the increasing outflow of information from Whitehall. Margaret Thatcher was accused of presiding over a secretive Government, and it is true that she had no belief in disclosure as a virtue in itself. But steadily under her reign departments and public services opened their doors. I instituted at the Home Office whole-day meetings at which outside observers and commentators were invited to cross-examine senior officials, for example on the trends and meaning of crime statistics. Later I strongly supported William Waldegrave in the Cabinet when he proposed the early release of papers from the intelligence services.

The same tide carried into law three important liberalising measures. As it happened, I was in charge of all three Bills, two as Home Secretary and one as Foreign Secretary. We reformed the Official Secrets Act; we brought into the open and placed on a statutory basis all three intelligence services – namely, MI5 (internal), MI6 (external) and GCHQ (communications). At lunch on 8 January 1987 Sir Anthony Duff, director of MI5, persuaded me that the time had passed when the Security Service (MI5) could successfully operate on the basis that it did not exist. The pretence had worn threadbare, making it increasingly difficult to recruit and retain men and women of quality for the service. He thought that it would take two years to persuade the Prime Minister and Robert Armstrong (cabinet secretary) of the need. By April, Robert

Armstrong was on board, but he and Geoffrey Howe still thought we were a year away from convincing the Prime Minister. In July she agreed that we could draft a Bill, though without commitment on her part to accept it. In April 1988 she agreed to the Bill. Parliament was rather easier to persuade than the Prime Minister, and the Security Service emerged into daylight.

Margaret Thatcher rightly believed that the secret work of the Security Service was crucial in dealing with foreign espionage, terrorism and subversion. She hated the constant leaks about its work and accusations against its officers. It was not easy to persuade her that it would still be possible to run successful secret operations from an organisation whose existence had been revealed. I am sure that we would not have succeeded without the advocacy of Tony Duff. He was one of those good-looking grand-mannered officials who could exercise great influence over her once they had gained her trust, as he had done during the Rhodesia negotiations of 1980.

Six years later from the Foreign Office I introduced and carried a similar Bill bringing into the daylight the external agency, the Secret Intelligence Service (MI6), and the Government Communication Headquarters (GCHQ) at Cheltenham.

The reform of the Official Secrets Act caused much more trouble. Our underlying concept was simple. The existing Act, drafted in a hurry in 1911, contained the famous Section 2, a catch-all clause making it a criminal offence to disclose any official information without authority. This went absurdly wide, and we proposed to abolish it. This would remove from the scope of the criminal law the great mass of official information. It would no longer, for example, be a criminal offence to leak a budget secret. But certain defined areas would continue to be protected, provided that it could be proved that disclosure would harm the national interest. There was one exception to this test of harm. In the case of members and former members of the security and intelligence services we would retain an absolute obligation on them not to disclose any information about their work.

It would, I suppose, have been naïve to expect that this reform would have been welcomed by reformers. The Prime Minister and, I think, just one backbencher worried that we might be going too far and putting national security at risk. All our other critics argued that we were not going far enough.

In June 1988 I was helped when introducing the White Paper containing our proposals by a spate of newspaper articles beforehand suggesting that we were going to introduce draconian measures. We were said to be about to propose that ministers, not juries, would decide whether a particular disclosure seriously harmed the national interest by issuing a ministerial certificate to that effect. In 1979 the Labour Government had made this proposal, as had the earlier Franks Committee. But I had decided that it was better to be more liberal than our predecessors and leave the matter plainly to a jury. This was a topical point since a jury had recently acquitted a civil servant, Clive Ponting, in the teeth of a judge's summing up which had pointed the other way. Some commentators supposed that I had arranged inaccurate forecasts of the White Paper so that people would be pleasantly surprised when it appeared; but neither I nor the Home Office was as clever as that.

On second reading of our Bill in December 1988, having made some concessions since the White Paper, I argued that ours were conservative measures, since they aimed to protect the citizen from specific and grave dangers. 'However they are also radical reforms because they open windows that have remained closed and cobwebbed, because they define clearly what has been confused for a long time, and because they strike a balance that is designed for today.'

The press in their hearts prefer leaks and speculation to open disclosure. They would rather have closed windows which they can smash than open ones through which news can pass without drama. But they were bound as a matter of principle to argue that we had not gone far enough. Some, indeed, said that I was tightening the rules. So did the Opposition, as was inevitable. The 1911 Act had tried to protect so wide an area that its fortifications were in practice crumbling. My Bill would tear down the crumbling walls, but by closer definitions erect rather more effective walls to safeguard the small area still protected.

Much of the debate turned on the question of whether members of the security services should be able to plead that their unauthorised disclosure had been in the public interest. The most powerful advocates of greater reform were a group of libertarian Conservatives, including Jonathan Aitken, Rupert Allason and (most eloquently) Richard Shepherd. The last of these indeed tried to pre-empt our Bill with one of his own, which we had defeated only with difficulty. He was a likeable, persistent man who did not listen much to the argument of others, but who easily worked himself up into a storm of principled rage. Since genuine indignation was rare in the Commons, it attracted sympathy and admiration. In all my friendly clashes with Richard Shepherd over the years, on these matters and on Europe, I never found much Tory blood in his veins: he was a pure liberal, with a contempt for pragmatism and compromise. Such men and women are needed in Parliament, but not in huge numbers if the Queen's Government is to be carried on.

The Official Secrets Bill was pushed forward through the obstacles by

John Patten as Minister of State. It had to be guillotined, so that debate would end at a fixed time, so on 22 February 1989 I would write:

> Made a good 10 minute [speech] on Third Reading. Hattersley and MacLennan rude, but the troops filing through lobby are in good heart. We just managed to contain rebellion. Argument constantly flowed against us, and the regiment we raised, though constant, were intellectually feeble. But we got by ... I watched the HoC clocks ticking towards 10 with exhausted relief ... Jonathan Aitken, the ablest of all our critics, gives champagne (for me [it was Lent] orange juice) and smoked salmon in Lord North Street for his team and indeed most of mine. Box – Bed 12.30.

The tide of disclosure has continued to surge forward with much new legislation on freedom of information and data protection, and the intelligence services have learned, as I hoped, to float successfully on that tide. If I were making the arguments again now, I would make a bolder distinction between press, Parliament and public. Individual citizens are entitled to penetrate bureaucratic obstacles and obtain official information directly related to their family and themselves. Parliament is entitled to probe into secret places on their behalf. But the claim of the media (the written press in particular) to be the theoretical guardians of our liberty has worn thin as their integrity and accuracy have diminished.

Some of the packages in the Home Secretary's bran tub brought welcome light relief. The Channel Islands and the Isle of Man, while intensely loyal to the Crown, are not part of the United Kingdom; their occasional dealings with the United Kingdom Government were conducted through the Home Secretary, who was expected to visit them from time to time. He also accompanied the Queen when she visited, as she did the Channel Islands in May 1989. The whole panoply of a state visit was deployed – reception, a banquet on *Britannia*, the Marines Beating the Retreat, fireworks, and of course loyal and then royal speeches. On Guernsey I completely lost my voice and the Queen sent me to bed with aspirin and linctus. It had been a testing day. One small boy in St Peter Port told me to do up my shoelaces and another, thinking I was lost, said, 'This way, Sir Geoffrey.' Knots of half-clad, cheering subjects waved Union Jacks at every corner of the winding roads, with an enthusiasm shown in England only at times of jubilee. In the Channel Islands it is always jubilee.

Jersey, Guernsey and Sark are well known to British visitors. For me Alderney, the least pretty of the Channel Islands, was the most interesting. Its hospitality is famous; on the other islands they say that the haze which sometimes shrouds Alderney airfield consists mainly of gin fumes. The Germans bundled the inhabitants off the island in the war and turned it into a camp for forced foreign labour working to build the Atlantic Wall: 'Respect the confused little memorial for the slave dead of 1940–5. The survivors still creep each summer to the scenes of their misery.'

For the Home Secretary the main problem on Alderney was Her Majesty's Breakwater. This was constructed to harbour the Channel Fleet during one of those strange panics about a possible French invasion which occasionally beset Queen Victoria's Government during the early years of her reign. The Channel Fleet had gone but the magnificent breakwater remained, as imposing as Paddington Station or the St Pancras Hotel. But by 1986 the seas which constantly batter it were at last having an effect. As I paced the breakwater that year I contemplated a high estimate for its repair and wondered how we could persuade the islanders to carry the cost. The seas, though thorough, are slow. This is the sort of problem which appeared in the Home Secretary's red box once every four or five years, but I hear it has at last been happily resolved.

Several other pleasant duties were connected with the Queen. I stood alongside her on the dais inside Buckingham Palace during investitures and read out the names of those about to receive knighthoods. Pronunciation needed care, particularly the Chinese names from Hong Kong.

Each newly consecrated bishop of the Church of England had to kneel before the Queen in Buckingham Palace and repeat in her presence an oath which the Home Secretary read out to him sentence by sentence. It was a splendid Tudor composition designed to weed out anyone who had got thus far while still harbouring disloyal or papist tendencies. One mildly progressive bishop suggested to me that I might set in hand a modernisation of this oath. It was thought anachronistic that bishops should have to declare that no foreign prince or potentate hath any jurisdiction in this realm of England. Having briefly considered the matter, I was clear that I should not meddle. Sometimes the real problem on these occasions was not the wording of the oath but the frailty of the footstool compared with the bulk of the bishop. Having survived this ordeal, the bishop found himself in lively chat with the Queen, who knows and cares about the personalities and practices of her Church.

Another duty was to attend on the Queen with the Foreign Secretary at the arrival, at either Victoria Station or Windsor, of a visiting president or monarch. The Queen greets the visitor, and then introduces him or her to these two ministers, in this case two middle-aged men with slightly frizzy grey hair and glasses. Once, like the boy in Guernsey, she got us mixed up and introduced Geoffrey Howe and myself by our wrong offices. After that, although in reality she knew perfectly well which was which, I could detect a wary glint in her eye as she approached us down the ceremonial carpet, King or President at her elbow. A slip of that kind once made is easily repeated. Another hazard of this occasion concerned dress. Certainly morning dress was required, but with a grey waistcoat (Ascot and weddings) or a black one (more solemn)? On the first occasion I wore grey, Geoffrey black. Each of us being a humble person, we both decided that the other had got it right, so the next time I wore black, Geoffrey grey. This could have gone on indefinitely. I cannot remember for sure on which colour our private offices harmonised, but I think it was grey.

More important was the ceremony at the Cenotaph on Remembrance Sunday. The Home Secretary was responsible for this because until the 1960s his office had fronted Whitehall opposite the monument. I had first to inspect the contingents of police, fire and ambulance services drawn up in the Foreign Office courtyard before they marched in the parade. Then I escorted the Queen from the courtyard through the old Home Office to the door leading out on to Whitehall. Timing had to be exact, conversation limited.

I always found the Cenotaph service deeply moving. I never knew it to rain. Beethoven's slow march while the wreaths are laid, the slow fall of individual leaves from the plane trees in the autumn sunshine, the two minutes' silence, the measured sound of Big Ben, finally 'O God Our Help in Ages Past' have often made my eyes prickle. The sense that all over this country at exactly the same time people are gathering for the same purpose at their own war memorials gives the event a special power. At one time I thought it would be better for the parade of veterans to take place in front of the Queen rather than after she had left Whitehall. The proposal did not find favour, though changes have been made to give royal recognition to that particularly moving part of the ceremony.

I managed to keep up some of my old contacts abroad by accepting invitations to discuss international terrorism and security. In January 1988 I revisited Morocco. My host was Driss Basri, who as Minister of the Interior for ten years already knew most of the King's secrets and was the main single prop of his power. I had not seen the King since the brouhaha of the Queen's state visit eight years earlier, and did not know how much of our tense encounters he would remember. Basri took me to see the King in the old French hill station at Ifrane, set in oak woods with traces of snow on the alpine-style roofs. The royal chateau was like the set of a provincial pantomime, lots of tracery, pink Venetian glass and mounds of chocolate and crystallised fruits, into which the courtiers tuck. Then up flower-lined stairs to upper chamber with marble and running water and a brown informal figure in jacket and slacks and sweater up to neck. He has bad cough and is full of antibiotics and smoking hard through a holder. Very amiable and of course clever, a likeable deprecating smile. The importance of tradition, the Royal Family, Mrs T, Gorbachev, etc. Am given a Cross of Commander of Alaouite Order, orange, with star and button.

The King played the trick of displaying simplicity in the middle of courtly splendour, both contrived by himself. Basri, the toughest man in Morocco, crouched before his King and slobbered over the royal hand in gratitude for every word tossed in his direction.

Another entertaining call was on Silvio Berlusconi, the future Italian Prime Minister, in his modern library in Milan. He was noted then as now for his control of Italian television. He gave a sparkling account of his philosophy of democratic television without rules. Explaining that in Britain I was the minister concerned with broadcasting, I asked him politely about certain risqué programmes for which his channels were famous. He explained with much emphasis that nothing could conceivably go amiss. Three controls were in operation: a network of advisory committees, five daughters who were to him the most precious objects in the world, and a group of nuns who were in the habit of telephoning him in the middle of the night on any matter of importance. In Rome I delivered a speech in Italian, having some trouble with subjunctives, and called on the Prime Minister, Giulio Andreotti. It was his seventieth birthday and I gave him an original copy of *The Times* for that day in 1919. We talked about drugs and immigration.

These were subjects which increasingly drew European ministers of the interior together in what was then known as the Trevi Process, but later developed into one of the intergovernmental pillars of the Treaty of Maastricht. During one such meeting at Lancaster House in London in October 1987 I persuaded the Princess of Wales to join us for a meal. 'Goes quite well – a bit stilted at first. D. Mellor makes a good presentation (on drugs). The Princess is quick and very willing, but no depth of knowledge,' which was hardly surprising.

A few months earlier the Princess had told me at a private party that she was willing to come to this occasion, if I really wanted it. As was her gift, she smiled at me as if her consent was the result of my own personal involvement, nothing to do with official advice or the state of her diary. Encouraged, and egged on by Judy, I then asked her to dance. I did not know that Lester Lannin's big band had the habit of going on and on and on without pause, changing tunes without stopping. Once I realised this, what was I to do? All my upbringing told me that I could not suggest to royalty that I had had enough, certainly not to this particular princess in my arms. On the other hand, there seemed no end to it, and my dance steps are awkward and limited. After what seemed an age, the Princess suggested, with what in others would be called a giggle, that we might sit down. Although I would not count myself among the very many who claim to have been her close friend, we were easy together from that day on.

I was grateful for the historical structure which in my day put broadcasting policy within the Home Secretary's empire. Most of my life was spent considering police, prisons and the criminal justice system with the professionals concerned. These were dedicated men and women; the matters we dealt with were intellectually gripping as well as hugely important to the country's welfare. But they related to the gloomy underside of British society – victims, criminals, prisoners, law courts, drugs, slum housing estates, poverty. Off duty the police cracked jokes, refilled their glasses and sang lustily. Judges and magistrates and prison governors no doubt did the same, though I was less often invited to join them. But the subject matter of their professional lives was sombre and was handled in that spirit.

There was nothing sombre about broadcasting. Britain had blessed itself with a successful and popular system of both radio and television. The BBC and the independent system competed with reasonable good humour. The top practitioners were witty men (there were very few women) with successful backgrounds and more success to come. They dressed loosely and enjoyed good meals. Men like Michael Grade, Paul Fox, Dukey Hussey and Jeremy Isaacs, to name a few, were not naturally austere. In short, my duties led me into a comfortable, talented, often cigar-smoking sector of British society.

This was certainly not a static sector, for as a result of technology and changing popular tastes, broadcasting was constantly expanding. It was the job of the Government to provide a framework in which this expansion could take place without undue distress or uproar. I told the broadcasters a few weeks after taking office that I had already noticed there was no such thing as calm in the broadcasting world: 'You live, because you like to live, in something between a breeze and a storm.' There was plenty of controversy about changes in the structure. Large claims were made and great principles invoked by all those who merely wanted a larger slice of the growing cake. In my heart I could not persuade myself that the many and complex issues in this controversy were hugely important. I enjoyed the continuous debate, its exaggeration, the zest and occasional malice with which it was conducted. Any change proposed to the minutiae of broadcasting organisation was described by some as the dawn of a golden age, by others as the death of civilisation as they knew it. In my speeches I adopted a deliberately teasing tone which I would never have used on anything to do with crime or immigration. In this book I have on the whole abstained from quoting my own speeches. If I indulge myself a little in this chapter, it is because some of these efforts on broadcasting were fun to write and deliver, in contrast to the monotony of most policy discussions. Those with whom I dealt teased me back. I hope they did not resent, though they must have noticed, that I was not engaged heart and soul, night and day in the search for the perfect broadcasting system, which is no doubt laid up in heaven.

Some of my colleagues in the Government felt more deeply. On no subject were there less conclusive meetings, more ministerial man-oeuvring, more compromise conclusions, more decisions reached in July but reopened in September.

The anvil on which we hammered was Professor Alan Peacock's report on the financing of the BBC. His committee, composed of serious men and women with strong opinions working under a lively leader, had ventured well beyond their terms of reference and set off a general debate on all broadcasting matters. Peacock published his report in June 1986. The Prime Minister set up a special group of ministers under her chairmanship to reach the necessary conclusions on policy. The committee, christened Misc 128, began work that autumn. Autumn turned to winter, 1986 became 1987 became 1988 became 1989. With difficulty we limped forward, through parliamentary debates and a select committee report, through a mass of representations from pressure groups and interested parties. Looking again at the documents, I recall again the tense, almost theological arguments of Misc 128. This was for me the paradox of broadcasting as a political subject: lively people and a bouncy, successful British activity provoked a set of notably arid arguments when their problems reached Whitehall.

The most powerful intellect on Misc 128 belonged to the Chancellor of the Exchequer. Nigel Lawson had long studied broadcasting from a principled point of view. He favoured as much freedom and deregulation as technology would allow, and then a little more. He believed that many of the arguments for public service broadcasting were bogus, and that over time the market, being the safeguard of freedom, should be allowed to prevail. David Young, in charge of Trade and Industry, broadly shared this view, but came to it largely from a commercial and technological angle. He wanted the greatest possible opportunities for the new industries of cable and satellite. The attitude of the Prime

Minister in the chair was more complex. She disliked the BBC. This was partly because she thought that it disliked her and distorted its reporting accordingly. More fundamentally, she believed that the BBC licence fee was intellectually contemptible and morally wrong. Why, she asked me repeatedly, should people be unable to watch programmes on the independent channels ITV and Channel 4 without paying a licence fee for BBC programmes which they might not want to watch at all? She accepted in principle both the market arguments of Nigel Lawson and the pro-technology arguments of David Young.

Her difficulties came a little further down the road. For the Prime Minister, though a free marketeer, was no libertarian. She felt a strong sympathy for Mrs Mary Whitehouse, then just past the peak of her campaign against violence and sex on television. Margaret Thatcher favoured a strong new law against obscenity. In particular she wanted to retain, or even strengthen, the existing regulations on the content of broadcasting. Brian Griffiths, an influential member of her policy team at Number Ten, brought a Christian approach to the problem. Behind the scenes he strongly encouraged the Prime Minister in her efforts to free the broadcasting market place, cut the BBC down by several pegs, and yet still regulate content.

The Home Office as the lead department had the responsibility for drawing coherent and realistic proposals out of this plethora of meetings. It was slow work. Sometimes I had to reassure the outside world that we were not entirely stuck, for example in a speech to the Royal Television Society in September 1987: 'The commentators have been leaping merrily ahead like hares in this race, but, rest assured, the tortoise of government is on its way.' Inwardly I was not so sure. The problem was not with any one of my colleagues as an individual, but with what happened, or failed to happen, when we met together in the dreaded Misc 128. Eight months after I commended the progress of the tortoise I wrote after one dilatory meeting, 'Once again . . . We move one step forward and two back, and are farther than ever from a broadcasting policy. No White Paper this summer, probably no Bill this autumn. Affable but wholly inconclusive.' I developed the technique of talking through the agenda of important meetings separately in advance with Nigel Lawson, David Young and Margaret Thatcher. It seemed the only way to achieve movement. None of them was unreasonable when tackled in the right way on a particular point, in the absence of others.

I could not have managed without the patient help of Tim Renton, the Minister of State specifically responsible for broadcasting. In the background hovered the formidable presence of Willie Whitelaw, who had forgotten more about broadcasting then I ever learned. As Home Secretary he had worked closely with the BBC, and had created Channel

4. Until 1988 he was Deputy Prime Minister, and even after he retired from the Government I knew that *in extremis* I could invoke his help in dealing with any proposal which I thought ruinous. The Home Office officials who advised me were sometimes criticised for remoteness from the hurly burly of actual broadcasting. They were certainly far from radical in their instincts, but they brought powerful and shrewd minds to bear on each problem and I was glad that they were not themselves part of the world of cigar-smokers.

I would weary the reader if I listed the twists and turns of the debate. The Peacock Committee, to my great relief, had come down against forcing the BBC to accept advertising. Their free market instincts led them down a better track: they wanted to achieve the sovereignty of the consumer by moving steadily towards a system of pay per view. The new technologies, they argued, would multiply choice and television viewers would eventually pay through specific subscription only for what they wanted to watch. Eventually the licence fee would fade away, but a limited range of quality programmes could be financed by the taxpayer through a body like the Arts Council. Meanwhile, given the limited choice immediately available, BBC and ITV should continue, but ITV franchises should be opened up for competition instead of being arbitrarily allocated by the Independent Broadcasting Authority. Finally the report agreed that television programmes, like books, should be subject only to the law of the land as regards content, not to any specific regulation.

I was too cautious in my opening holding statement on the Peacock Report, and had to correct the balance to show that our minds were open. I teased the BBC by remarking that the licence fee was not immortal, but in fact, strongly supported by Willie Whitelaw and Tim Renton, I was clear that for the foreseeable future it should remain. The Prime Minister, deprived by Peacock of any hope of financing the BBC through advertisement, had no immediate free market solution to offer. Indeed, we agreed quite quickly that the BBC licence fee should be indexed, bringing to an end the almost continuous negotiations between the Home Office and the BBC about the right figure.

There was much in the Peacock Report on which we could build. While we wrestled painfully with the details in Misc 128, I tried to set the scene in public on 9 July 1987, using, I must now admit, an excessive range of historical comparisons: 'We are not a band of Cromwellian soldiers defacing the statues and smashing the stained glass in the shrines of British broadcasting. But neither do we fall on our knees and worship, nor believe that every side chapel is perfect, every priest and acolyte indispensable.' I supported the Prime Minister in her open criticism of the inefficiencies of the present system against those who regarded the search for improvement as barbarous. On 21 September 1987 she held a seminar at Number Ten. The different potentates gathered and spoke rather too obviously in their own interests. To her dislike of the BBC was by now added a conviction that the independent system was equally outdated and even more inefficient. I agreed and had said so publicly in a speech three days earlier: 'To improve efficiency . . . is not to mimic the Goths, Visigoths and Vandals as they closed in on Rome.' The allocation of franchises should certainly be more competitive and transparent, since 'the members of the IBA [Independent Broadcasting Authority], men and women of talent and total integrity, have been made to look from time to time, through no fault of their own, like the late Duke of Newcastle bestowing his boroughs'.

As I pointed out in the same speech, one of the problems for Misc 128 was that the technical scene never stood still: 'The sage deliberations of Whitehall and Westminster are constantly interrupted by ingenious entrepreneurs bustling through the door with some new idea, some new technological discovery, which, they say, transforms the whole scene and compels us to start afresh. There will never be a moment when everything stops moving so that we can click the shutter and get a clear picture of the scene.'

The following year a classic example of this held us up for several weeks. David Young, almost two years after we began work, produced a new plan for putting up in the sky the second BBC channel and the independent Channel 4. This would, he argued, encourage the emerging industry of satellite broadcasting and at the same time free valuable terrestrial spectrum for development of pay per view. My advisers were appalled. More political in this case than the politician who produced the scheme, they pointed out that existing licence payers would suddenly find themselves having to pay for services which were currently covered by the licence. No doubt it would be possible to tinker with the figures, but the plans seemed to combine maximum dislocation with minimum benefit. One official produced a classic Home Office put-down at the end of a long minute: 'If I may express a personal view I fear that if the White Paper were to advocate the scheme expressed in the attached draft then the Government would be widely seen, and not only in the broadcasting industry, as having taken leave of its senses.' Somehow this plan had to be kept away from Misc 128 or confusion would become total. David Young and I met with our close advisers in July in a pub at Silchester. The Treaty of Silchester was agreed, and honoured. David dropped his plan; I made concessions on the method of allocating ITV franchises.

So the tortoise lumbered on. In September 1988 I sent a draft White Paper to colleagues with the conclusions reached at the most recent Misc

128 meeting in July. The Prime Minister at once began to reopen issues which I had thought settled. She worried that the result of reform might be to strengthen the BBC by weakening its commercial competitors. She worried in particular that ITN, the independent news service which she favoured, might fade away if exposed to the free market, leaving the BBC with a monopoly of news. She sent Brian Griffiths round to the Home Office; he and I then wrestled for an hour to work out a formula to protect ITN. A final set of compromises was agreed in Misc 128 on 20 October and the White Paper issued a fortnight later. A Bill was afterwards drafted which became the Broadcasting Act of 1990. The BBC in its essentials was preserved, though rightly directed to commission independent producers to make a substantial share of its output.

There had been a long-running tussle about Channel 4, which Nigel Lawson wanted to privatise. While agreeing that Channel 4 should sell its own advertising, I resisted privatisation on the grounds that the particular remit of the channel to innovate would wither away if the main aim of its management was to maximise profit. The argument dragged on; in the end Channel 4 was not privatised and became a non-profit-making trust.

The messy part of our proposals was the arrangement for allocating ITV franchises. We proposed that applicants for a franchise should have to pass a quality hurdle, after which the franchise would go to the highest bidder. In June 1989 after further interdepartmental argument, I was glad to announce a substantial strengthening of the quality threshold, a concept for which I was grateful to George Russell, the ingenious and equable chairman of the Independent Broadcasting Authority. My statement was 'long, cunning, low key, comes on late and goes smoothly'. I was no longer Home Secretary when the Bill was examined in the Commons. David Mellor, by then Broadcasting Minister, made skilful concessions and the Act, though still imperfect, came out rather better than had seemed likely during its growth in the womb of Misc 128. But it has failed in one of its purposes: to maintain a lively, varied independent TV system with deep local roots. Broadcasting in the provinces now seems as bland and homogenised as the architecture of many town high streets.

The pace of broadcasting has quickened since Peacock reported in 1986. Satellite and cable are now part of daily life. The excitement now surrounds digital TV; once again policy-makers in the Government have to wrestle with ever-changing expert forecasts as well as the ups and downs of commercial fortune. So far as I am concerned, the BBC has in these years drawn too deeply on the reserves of admiration which I felt for it. The corporation still does splendid as well as silly things, but the proportion of rubbish has grown to an extent which seriously undermines the relaxed 'why not leave it alone' defence of the licence fee. Increasingly the BBC treats us as if we all suffer from the same induced foolishness as one of its studio audiences. It has not used its reprieve well. There is a stronger case now than there was in 1986 for cutting back the licence fee until it covers only the cost of true public service broadcasts which would not otherwise be made. How and by whom that frontier is fixed might occupy a future Misc 128 for several happy years. But the Peacock Report, with its emphasis on consumer sovereignty based on pay per view, was always intelligent, and has become more realistic with the passage of time. As a result of our decisions the BBC licence fee may have gained a reprieve, but it does not possess immortality.

18

CRIME

The life of a home secretary is dominated by crime. He cannot abolish crime; he cannot even accurately measure it, for all existing measures are flawed. But he is conscious of crime as a cloud which hangs over many lives, including those lived in relatively secure circumstances but blighted by fear. Victims of crime and the larger numbers resentful and fearful of crime look to the Home Secretary for relief, and blame him if it is not forthcoming. His advisers will produce statistics and dotted lines on graphs extrapolated into the future, showing, for example, that crime will increase as households possess more stealable objects, or as the age group with the greatest propensity to commit crime increases in number. These observations are of only academic interest to him, since he cannot use them in his defence. Whatever the level of crime, it is unacceptable; his foremost task is to relieve the damage and the unhappiness which crime inflicts on society.

The front line against crime is long. The Home Secretary controls only one or two sections of it, though he hopes to influence others. The line begins with prevention of crime, then extends to detection and the relief of victims, then to punishment, then to imprisonment and its consequences. The overwhelming interest of the public, spurred on by the media, is in the punishment sector. The public believe that the judicial system of punishment is more lenient than it is, and that crime can best be cured by making punishment more severe.

In 1985, when I became Home Secretary, the focus of this debate was still the simple question of capital punishment. Parliament had abolished the death penalty sixteen years earlier, yet in the mid-eighties I could hardly attend a meeting outside Westminster without someone arguing from the floor that it should be reinstated. Sometimes there were amplifications, as on 9 May 1986. 'Lunch with businessmen in Loughborough pub – they tend to favour castration of rapists and shooting prisoners off roofs.' But usually there was just a straightforward plea for the death penalty, a view shared by the majority in opinion polls.

On most political subjects I understand opposing points of view and can be swayed by them. I often look for a way of reconciling differences rather than pressing an absolute view of my own. As a young man I caricatured this tendency in the brilliant diplomat Sir Pierson Dixon, my chief in New York, but I recognise it to a lesser extent in myself. For me, capital punishment was always an exception to this rule. Long before I became Home Secretary I was used to tackling the question in my own constituency. I decided early that it was pointless to think up a compromise. I simply had to say that I objected to the death penalty and explain why. If Conservatives or the West Oxfordshire electorate wanted an MP who voted for the death penalty they could choose one to replace me. What they could not do was complain that I had equivocated or misled them. After I became Home Secretary I had to transfer this stance from Oxfordshire to the national scene.

I used the conventional arguments against capital punishment. Men and women could be hanged who were later found to be innocent. There was no proof in the figures that hanging was a deterrent. The modern media would certainly make celebrities out of doomed criminals and their families, producing the opposite effect to that desired. In Northern Ireland the death penalty would *increase* support for the IRA. I firmly believed these and other arguments. But my underlying conviction was and remains simpler. It is just wrong, it seems to me, for human beings to sit down in cold blood and decide in the name of justice that other human beings should be killed. It is not for us to make that final decision about the worthlessness of a fellow creature. I understand why my parents' generation grew up with a different view; I understand why people in other and different societies think otherwise. But if I find myself differing on this with someone of my own age or younger in my own country, then that is for me a barrier between us.

The question came up in the House of Commons while I was Home Secretary in 1987 and 1988. Like their predecessors in earlier Parliaments, these were excellent debates. There was always a free vote; no Government could enforce a whip, or wished to do so. The standard of speaking was high on both sides of the argument. Votes could turn on what was said. Emotion was genuine, not confected to score points. The first debate in each Parliament was tense, because the opinions of the new members could not be accurately known in advance.

On 7 June 1988 as usual I drafted my own speech on capital
punishment, but discussed it that morning in Queen Anne's Gate with
officials and other ministers. Although I disliked Housman's poetry for
a reason already given, I wanted to quote an evocative verse from *A*
Shropshire Lad:

> They hang us now in Shrewsbury jail:
> The whistles blow forlorn
> And trains all night groan on the rail
> To men that die at morn.

My civil servants were in favour but two seasoned parliamentarians,
Douglas Hogg and my parliamentary private secretary David
Heathcoat Amory, advised against. Rather crossly I cut it out. The
speech that afternoon went quite well, and the vote against capital
punishment even better.

Much harder were the debates each October at the Conservative
Party Conference. These debates, not specifically on the death penalty
but on crime and punishment in general, were notoriously difficult
for Conservative home secretaries, particularly those with a liberal
reputation. Rab Butler and Willie Whitelaw had both run into storms.
A party conference is designed to generate extra political energy beyond
that of every day, which can propel party members forward for another
year of devoted activity. When there is a Conservative Government
that emotion is supposed to encourage ministers and discredit the
Opposition. But Conservative delegates are not creatures of the machine.
They are willing to show their loyalty, indeed they usually overdo it
when it comes to the leader of the party. But at some point in those
strange artificial days the mounting pressures in Blackpool, Brighton or
Bournemouth find an outlet which is not part of the design. The
delegates erupt once, but usually only once, break the harmony of the
week, give pleasure to the media and for the moment to themselves.

In my early days these eruptions were on Rhodesia; in my latter days
Europe. In the eighties they were on law and order.

Each year I prepared a speech to reply to the coming debate at the
conference. The speech would be conceived in the calm of Queen Anne's
Gate. Civil servants would supply reassuring facts and figures showing
progress and achievement. My special adviser Edward Bickham, with
help from junior ministers, would turn this into a draft of roughly the
right length. In London it looked fine, just needing translation into my
own words and some touch from me of what passed for eloquence. But
in the hotel room of the conference headquarters in Blackpool, Brighton
or Bournemouth a few hours later the same text seemed worthless. I had

entered into a different atmosphere: tense, exciting, exaggerated. The measured prose of Whitehall had to be transformed. I could only guess what the nature of the coming debate would be. My speech had to allow space for impromptu replies to points made from the floor. The preparatory work of maybe three months had to be reshaped in a day or at best two. Judy, Edward and others did their best to keep me calm. Judy gave me a new tie at the conference each year.

In my short story published as 'Ten Minutes to Turn the Devil' I portray a minister wrestling to finalise his conference speech. I try there to convey the weight of uncertainty, mingled with the excitement of a coming contest.

'Good luck,' everyone says as you cross the hotel lobby to your car. You feel that they are bidding you farewell on your way to the guillotine. Once you are there on the dais in the Conference Hall things improve. As delegates begin to speak, you long for the moment when you are called to reply. At that moment skilful engineering ensures that the lectern with your speech on it automatically rises towards you. The chairman utters words of benevolent introduction. The Prime Minister at your side mutters the final 'good luck', and you are off. Within twenty minutes you will have soared or flopped, and it will be over for another year.

In 1986 at Bournemouth I flopped, or at least that was my impression. The candidate for the Isle of Wight thundered away about capital punishment, but in my speech I dealt with other issues. Everyone noticed the omission. The conference as a whole went well; Margaret Thatcher received a stupendous ovation. Afterwards I roamed round Corfe Castle thinking I was a dud among stars. Next year at Blackpool went better.

> Up 6.30 for all the pre-speech interviews . . . Tiff with TV-AM who produce unannounced a 90-year-old burgled lady from Liverpool . . . We deal with long refinements of speech. Practise on autocue. Am very nervous and scared, coming after three months of tension. No way to live a life. 3 glasses of white wine at one of the endless TV parties. Conference speech. The Monday Club [a right-wing group] in full voice for c.p. [capital punishment]. Start poorly but on c.p. they heckle and I respond. This goes well, middle section fades a bit. Good applause . . . Willie moved and avuncular. The general verdict very good.

Most of the audience that year rose to give me a good standing ovation, but the Prime Minister at my side remained seated. She found herself in an impossible position. Most of the emotion in the debate had been about capital punishment, on which she disagreed with me. But the moment she decided to remain seated she must have recognised how this would be perceived. I lingered for a while among a small group of friends and colleagues behind the stage; there were loud congratulations and some backslapping. Suddenly Margaret Thatcher appeared on the stage stairs above us. 'I do not think it could have been better done,' she said to everyone present but to no one in particular, and passed on down the stairs. It was one of the few occasions when I saw her embarrassed.

Next year at Brighton, 'usual broken night and rising solitary panic . . . A debate fuller of crude hangers than expected. Turn it round and despite my feeble preparation, with an otherwise skilful speech gain a reluctant standing ovation. Tom King sets the pace, MT the last to stir, does nothing to commend speech, as usual lacks political generosity.' Her physical posture that year was described as 'a crouching ovation', but my comment about generosity was unfair. A small but significant incident followed, which showed her dilemma. Margaret Thatcher, though herself strongly pro-hanging, criticised the conference chairman for calling in the debate too many people who agreed with her. She was reasonably content with a situation in which she could record her own views, whether at the conference or in the Commons, without any chance of their prevailing. She certainly did not want the pressure for a return of capital punishment to reach a point where she felt forced into action. Not once during my five years as Home Secretary did she even begin to suggest that her Government should change the law to restore hanging.

Indeed, to an extent which surprised me, the Prime Minister left me alone to cope with problems of law and order. On some issues, such as the poor quality of police leadership, she let me have her strong views. In general I realised that she favoured a tough line and strong penalties. But whereas on broadcasting she chaired the relevant committee of ministers and constantly intervened on all matters of policy, on this wider and more important sector she held back. She also supported me in some decisions, particularly on prisons, which she must have found unpalatable. From time to time we met at Number Ten with only a private secretary present; she listened carefully and showed understanding. With the single exception of the party conference speeches, I have nothing to complain of in her handling of our relationship.

The last of these conference speeches, at Blackpool in 1989, produced the usual emotions. 'Mope and fret more or less alone in our bedroom of the Imperial [Hotel] on 3rd floor from 10 to 2. Rehearsing and getting bored with speech. Prawn open sandwich. Debate on law and order 2.35. Am, as before, in a dumb and miserable fear. A soporific debate, only one mumble on hanging. Start slowly, get going in middle to an extent which carries me through literary peroration. As usual the relief to have it over is gigantic.' On this last occasion the Prime Minister used a remedy for her embarrassment (and mine) which had been available all the time: she stayed away.

Questions of punishment might dominate the headlines, but they were only part of the effort against crime. For the first time we supported help at the taxpayer's expense for the growing victim-support movement. Much new effort went into prevention. We encouraged neighbourhood watch schemes, which multiplied fast. I spoke often about these schemes and hoped they might develop into a general mobilisation of community effort. Near the end of my time as Home Secretary, in October 1989, there was a 'Visit representatives of 35 N.W. schemes in South Blackpool. Talk to each of them, as nice a school-roomful as you could imagine.'

Experience shows that I placed more weight on the concept than it would carry. Neighbourhood Watch was particularly attractive to me because it fitted well into ideas about citizenship which I was pushing at that time. Recent research showed clearly the link between crime and the physical nature of our cities. Earlier in 1989 in a speech in my own constituency I had pointed out that 'It is not in mean and dark Dickensian slums starved of resources that crime is at its most desperate. It is in and around tower blocks created at huge public expense. People were pushed into a vertical collective, deprived of their natural sense of community, surrounded by grubby grass, given a subsidised rent and told to be happy.' In the same speech I listed some of the public projects being carried forward in our cities by my colleagues, members of the Thatcher Government which is sometimes accused of having been interested only in the material prosperity of the individual.

The police are of course central to the effort against crime. We had just revolutionised their operating methods in the Police and Criminal Evidence Act. They needed a period of digestion, and on the whole in my time they got it. We were committed to increase police numbers. In her conference speech in October 1985 Margaret Thatcher included a rhetorical flourish about never economising on the police. The TV camera switched momentarily to record me saying something to the Chancellor of the Exchequer, Nigel Lawson, sitting beside me. A lip reader could have caught the words, 'That will cost you a bob or two.' So it did, but he paid up, both in terms of numbers and the relatively generous system of calculating police pay.

After the riots of 1985 and the growth of football hooliganism the police received fresh powers in the Public Order Act of 1986. I spent a great deal of time at police meetings at this time. The police are at all levels a wary profession, though their caution is disguised by lavish hospitality. Gastronomically speaking, diplomacy is an austere profession compared to policing. In terms of quantities of food and drink consumed by way of public duty, the police forces of England and Wales almost matched the public sector of Northern Ireland. Meals hosted by the police with many courses, sing-songs, a great array of professional jokes, crackers and funny hats at Christmas all became part of my life. So did the conferences at the three levels of police associations – chief constables, superintendents and the Police Federation. The conferences of the last could be particularly formidable, as in 1988:

> Early to Scarborough for Police Federation, broadcasting twice in the drizzle outside King's Cross. One of the big hurdles of the year and I am frightened and wonder for the Xth time why I do this job. Received up the double staircase at the Royal [Hotel]. Leslie Curtis [chairman] (his final conference), very affable, delivers a hard, almost offensive speech about Edmond Davies [whose generous report on police pay was the Ark of the Covenant for the Federation] without real bite. My speech, on which I worked hard, is a success in the circumstances, some applause, a murmur of dissent only when I announce the total of 800 extra police this year [of course, they wanted more]. A great relief. Interviews. Huge lunch, of course, beef Wellington. Escape to York, Viking Museum, Castle Museum, Clifford's Tower, all fun.

Gradually, I hope I established a good working relationship with the police at all levels. I enjoyed my pastoral visits. I liked the autonomous structure of police forces, each under its own chief constable. Keith Oxford in Merseyside, James Anderton in Greater Manchester, Kenneth Newman in London were characters in their own fiefdoms, leading forces with individual traditions. When these men entered a room they brought power with them. That did not make them easy to deal with, but I would not have had it otherwise.

Every chief constable worth his salt is in private uneasy about the quality of leadership available to the police in the future. The Prime Minister wanted to return to the Trenchard system of the Metropolitan Police before the war, with cadets earmarked from the start for senior ranks and trained at a police version of Sandhurst. I was clear that the police as a whole would be demoralised by what they would regard as a backward step. They treasured the thought that every chief constable had started as a bobby on the beat. I was sure they had to improve the quality of recruitment and selection and also the speed of promotion, so much time was spent on this. Unease grew with evidence that rules had been broken and corners cut by the police in collecting evidence in the Birmingham and Guildford terrorist cases. The police grumbled against the new rules of the Police and Criminal Evidence Act but could hardly deny the need for them. Meanwhile, there was much to see and applaud. In December 1987

> Geoffrey Dear [Chief Constable of the West Midlands] shows off his boys – a helicopter in which we fly to West Bromwich, a Jaguar with a video camera, and the A.S.U. [Active Service Unit] which takes the paperwork from a PC and gives it to pretty girls, saving the PC two hours a day to clear up more crimes, fill the prisons and eventually bring down the crime figures, all of which is happening in West Bromwich. Large lunch as usual, w. cut glass 2 gins, 2 wines, amiable Labour chairman etc. Talk to undercover agents who smashed Zulu Warriors gang, violence entirely for violence's sake.

For most of the public, 'filling the prisons' was an undiluted good. As the West Bromwich police pointed out that day, and as Michael Howard always pointed out later when he was Home Secretary, burglars could not burgle while they were in prison. In the jargon they were 'incapacitated'. But there were several other sides to that story. The idea that the clanging of the prison door behind an offender provides a happy ending to a story of crime is widespread, but wrong. The tangled problems of our prisons took up ever more of my time at the Home Office. Several times we seemed on the edge of catastrophe.

The Home Secretary does not control the size of the prison population. That depends on the decisions of magistrates and judges in the courts, acting within the framework of penalties laid down by Parliament. The Home Secretary is expected to provide whatever prison places are needed as a result of those decisions, to keep the prisoners securely locked up, and to provide education and training to improve the chances of their getting a job and going straight after release. The planning processes in Britain are slow, new prisons are unpopular wherever you place them, and in my time even when permission had been given for a new prison the interminable grind of government procedures slowed down the actual construction. This all meant that the prison-building programme begun by Willie Whitelaw after years of neglect and continued by Leon Brittan and myself lagged behind the increase in men and women sent to prison by the courts either on conviction or on remand awaiting trial. Prisons became overcrowded, and close to overflowing. I had to juggle with unwelcome expedients to prevent disaster.

This juggling would have been easier if the prisons themselves had been in good shape. But we were caught in a pincer, one claw being the growth in the prison population, the other the inadequacy of the prison service. This was dominated by the Prison Officers Association, which still cherished the narrow and destructive instincts which had discredited the trade union movement as a whole in the 1970s. The system was full of wasteful practices. In particular prison officers thrived on a tradition of excessive overtime which cost a fortune and was fundamentally inefficient. The POA leadership exploited the difficulties of the service in order to buttress their position and in some cases reduced prison governors to subservience. The management of the service was reluctant to confront the union, which was capable of industrial action, or rather inaction. That could put prisons at risk and bring about what management most feared: disorder, a breakdown of security, and escapes.

I quickly learned how this could happen. In April 1988 the Home Office was negotiating pay and conditions with the POA. The average earnings of a prison officer were £15,000 a year (of which 30 per cent was overtime), which in those days was quite some distance from poverty. Nevertheless, in some prisons the officers began to take industrial action. On 29 April staff took control of Gloucester prison and refused to obey the governor's orders. I directed that there should be no further negotiations until normal working had resumed. The prisoners took advantage of this situation, which they could follow closely on the radio. Copycat riots broke out next day in several prisons. The first reports which reached Lord Glenarthur, the Prisons Minister, and myself said that several people had been killed. As the evening wore on it became clear that this was not so, but Northeye Prison in Sussex was set on fire. There was already serious trouble at Lewes and Bristol and good reason to suppose that this might spread. I decided to make an immediate statement that night to the Commons. This was most unusual, but I thought it would put me in a stronger position next day if the situation became really desperate. The Speaker agreed, but kept the whole exchange to twenty minutes. My statement and answers to supplementary questions were short and factual. Gerald Kaufman tried to put the blame on me, but this was not the mood of the House. Simon Glenarthur and I moved gloomily to the operations centre which had been set up at the prison service headquarters in Cleland House. We spent two hours listening to reports from prisons across the country. It was the worst night of my time as Home Secretary. No one was dead, yet, but it still seemed possible that the whole system might collapse. The mood at Cleland House was different from that in the Commons. The leaders of the prison service were furious with the irresponsibility of the

POA, whereas MPs had tended to stress the difficulties under which their prison officer constituents laboured.

Next day, to my huge relief, the drama began to drain out of the situation. Those involved on the ground, both prisoners and prison officers, saw the abyss and drew back. The Prime Minister was understandably concerned, given the scale of the disorder and the fact that it came as a surprise. She wanted to invoke the general Whitehall machinery for public breakdown, but prison disorder was unique and in practice had to be dealt with accordingly. This included a deal with the POA which we called Fresh Start. We would recruit new officers and do away with the ludicrous system by which an average prison officer worked sixteen hours of overtime each week. We estimated that under the old system 15 per cent of the money spent on prisons was wasted. In May 1987 I reported to the Prime Minister that we had reached agreement with the unions. At this stage I was opposed to bringing in the private sector to manage prisons. Guarding Her Majesty's prisons still seemed to me a matter for Her Majesty's servants. I hoped that the complex rationalisation of pay and conditions embodied in Fresh Start would alter attitudes within the POA and bring them into the world of modern management. Not an unreasonable hope, given the transformation which was already occurring in the police service – but a vain one.

Meanwhile, the other claw of the prison pincer was closing in on us. In June 1986 I sent a minute to the Prime Minister on a theme which I was to repeat to many different audiences over the next three years. I asked her to impress on colleagues that while as Conservatives we knew that stiff prison sentences were needed for serious offenders, we also needed tough, practical, alternative forms of punishment outside prison for less serious offenders. Margaret Thatcher underlined the argument with her pen, and acknowledged the minute. She did not comply with my suggestion, for it was not in her character to make this liberal point in any speech of her own.

By the beginning of 1987 the prison population stood at 46,350, some 2,600 more than a year before. On 9 February I warned the Prime Minister that we faced a fairly tense scene over the next few weeks and months. By March the total was at 49,100, close to the total capacity of the system if you crammed as many prisoners as possible into a cell, and held many of them hundreds of miles from their homes and families. In a minute I warned, 'The danger of a breakdown of control in a grossly overcrowded prison or prisons is very real.' No relief would come from the prison-building programme until after the summer, and I cautioned that I might have to come to colleagues for difficult decisions at short notice.

Meanwhile, we dealt with the overflow by holding prisoners in police stations. This was an inevitable but thoroughly unprofessional practice. Both services suffer from it: the prison service is charged large sums by the police for the use of their cells, while valuable police officers are distracted from their proper job of dealing with crime. By July 1987 the total of prisoners in England and Wales was 51,029, of whom 648 were in police cells. There was no particular rhyme or reason for this summer surge; it bore no relation to the figures of recorded crime, which were rising less fast than they had been. On 2 July I held a long and crucial policy meeting at the Home Office. 'Devise outline plan, including some 50% remission. Could be politically lethal.'

On 13 July the *Guardian*, to my dismay, leaked a version of the package. Next day it was ready for the Home Committee of Ministers. To my surprise, the Prime Minister was not particularly concerned about my politically awkward proposal to increase remission of sentences for good behaviour from one-third to one-half of sentence. She was more concerned with the cost of prison building and the consequences of an agreement I had reached with the Defence Secretary George Younger to take over the army camp at Rollestone in Wiltshire, which could hold 360 prisoners. George Younger, having been helpful on this main decision, was niggardly over any involvement of army personnel. This was evident when the Cabinet discussed the plan on 16 July: 'George Younger has let the brass roll over him, and is unable to produce a single cook or bottlewasher for Rollestone. Fortunately, this issue on which we have spent so much time is secondary and when Cabinet side with GY it is not a disaster. PM handles it all perfectly well.' Around lunchtime I told the POA leadership what was involved. Then I briefed some of our backbenchers in my room at the Commons. They were dismayed and critical, something to which I was unaccustomed.

My new parliamentary private secretary was David Heathcoat Amory, a quiet, good-looking Old Etonian, nephew of a Chancellor of the Exchequer, Member of Parliament for the cathedral city of Wells. David belonged to the solid centre-right of the party. His views on the European Union are markedly more negative than mine, but I came to respect his shrewdness and thorough approach to every problem. When David uttered, which in those days was not often, sensible men stopped to listen. On this occasion he told me that this was the most difficult statement I would have to make in the Commons. He set about rallying support with his usual determination. As a result the statement went reasonably well and the press next day, though poor, was not disastrous. I had avoided what our backbenchers most feared: namely, executive release, freeing prisoners on the mere say-so of the Home Secretary. Instead, I had expanded an existing scheme, remission for good behaviour, to allow the estimated release of 3,500 prisoners convicted for less serious offences.

One or two people complimented me on my courage, but not much of that was required. Since the decision had become inevitable, it was better to present it in a straightforward way without spin.

The crisis of overcrowding eased, but any hope of peace and quiet in British prisons took no account of the baleful influence of the POA. By the autumn they were taking industrial action again, and there were 1,000 prisoners in police cells. I persuaded the Prime Minister and the Cabinet that we needed to take disciplinary measures against those involved. Willie Whitelaw was obviously anxious about the consequences. On 22 October I informed the National Executive Committee of the POA that we would suspend from duty men who were not working normally, but found them 'inconsequent and intransigent. I am running a big risk.' Several diary entries from the next five months give some indication of just how much of a risk: 'News from prisons still very edgy, Wandsworth obdurate . . . Wandsworth suspend industrial action, . . . but we are not through yet . . . Prisons filling ominously fast despite my sacrifice of July [extended remission] . . . Woken by children at 3 a.m. and lie fretting about prison population.'

In the spring of 1988 I visited Dettingen Barracks at Camberley, the second army camp which was transformed into a prison. This time George Younger had provided cooks, but there was still a problem. Prisoners spend a lot of time thinking about food. They develop sophisticated ideas and form passions, perhaps as a substitute for other thoughts and passions denied them. There was no question of their accepting the army recipes of overcooked meat and veg and chips with everything. This was a battle the army cooks were bound to lose.

I was now ready to involve private firms not just to build prisons faster than before, but to manage remand centres. The Commons Home Affairs Select Committee had brought back encouraging reports from the United States. It would be a further step to allow private firms to manage convicted prisoners, but I was by now ready to experiment. Despite Fresh Start, the POA continued to frustrate all efforts to cope with overcrowding and improve prisoners' regimes. If private firms, free of the burden of the POA, could deliver higher standards, that could be an advantage huge enough to overcome my earlier doubts.

Seven years later, when I was out of office, the broadcaster Jon Snow asked me if I would take his place as chair of the Prison Reform Trust, a leading charity in this field. After sleeping on the idea, I accepted. Of all the tasks in the Home Office bran tub, managing the prisons was the most exasperating and arguably the most important. Like almost all the tasks which a minister undertakes, I left it in mid-air, for successors to carry forward. More than ten years later at the Prison Reform Trust I was able to watch what was happening and occasionally to apply a spur. The POA, now faced with competition, was tamer. New prisons, state and private, were on the whole impressive. Prisoners no longer had to slop out their cells. Perhaps, but only perhaps, there was more public understanding. But, as I write, the prison population is at a new record level (72,800), and prisoners are again held in police cells. Magistrates and judges still lack confidence in non-custodial sentences. Politicians and public are still tempted to believe that prisons are palaces of luxury, or warehouses into which we can simply pack people whom we want to forget. We have a long way to go.

There is a fascination about prisons which is hard to define, but goes deep into human nature. Bad men and women are subjected to strict authority and out of that tension may come a useful sense of community. The visitor does not sense this in a prison of the 1960s, designed like a bad hotel, all small rooms and corridors with many right-angles. But that sense of community is evident in the great Victorian prisons, as in modern prisons which mimic on a smaller scale their star-shaped radial concept. In such prisons with long lines of vision from a centre nobody feels far removed from anybody else. This is helpful to both staff and prisoners. There is much amiss but also something special at Leeds, Manchester, Preston, Wormwood Scrubs. Of the Scrubs I wrote: 'four great grey parallel liners, strong and turreted, and the amazing chapel athwart them. Then a clutter of accretions and the mistakes of planning continue to this day, so that neither kitchen nor hospital is tolerable.' At Durham the ancient prison confronts the rock on which castle and cathedral stand. Not long ago, building a fresh structure inside the walls, workmen disturbed the graves of men hanged in the prison long ago. Alongside the skeletons were small, empty glass jars, now displayed in the chapel. Prison staff must, contrary to rules, have placed or allowed relatives to place small posies of flowers beside the bodies at the moment of burial.

Commentators who write about past penal policies look up newspaper cuttings and without much probing describe me as a liberal home secretary. I am not ashamed of the label, but I doubt if it is accurate, at least during the early years of my tenure. Rather, I looked on the penal system as just one part of the wall of protection of the citizen against crime. Wherever the wall was shown to be crumbling it was my job to repair it, without spending much time considering the philosophy of the repair work. Thus, after argument with lawyers led by the Lord Chief Justice, I persuaded Parliament that the Attorney General should have the right to appeal against sentences which seemed to him over lenient. I strengthened the laws on the carrying of knives, the ownership of guns, and vexatious behaviour in the street. As regards juries, with others I persuaded the Cabinet not to accept Lord Roskill's recommendation to abolish jury trial in serious fraud cases; on the other hand, I dismayed liberals by doing away with the right of the defence to challenge members of a jury without giving reasons. On the urging of the police, I opened up the question of the right of a defendant to silence but was not able to persuade enough people that in certain circumstances a jury should be able to draw conclusions from such silence. All these decisions still seem to me common sense, but no particular pattern of either liberal or punitive thinking runs through them.

I specifically repudiated the liberal tendency to excuse crime because of the circumstances of the criminal, as I outlined in my party conference speech of 1986: 'Even more strongly should we reject the idea that crime is the inevitable result of unemployment or bad housing or poverty. These are evils in themselves – but the notion that a riot or a rape or a murder is somehow justified as a cry of protest can only take root in a society which has lowered its own standards of thought and behaviour.' Two years later I talked about a minor riot in Lincoln: 'There is no question here of deprived, unemployed victims of discrimination or something called Thatcherism. In Lincoln that night . . . we have seen disturbances caused largely by youths who were white, employed, affluent and drunk.'

As time passed, I learned and thought more deeply on these matters. After the 1987 General Election I was confirmed as Home Secretary and by then was confident in the job. That autumn, and again in 1988 and 1989, I called meetings of my advisers, both ministers and officials, to Leeds Castle in Kent. All of us found it easier to think when away from the immediate problems which burdened our desks. We looked across the whole range of the Home Office effort. We worried about the causes as well as the detection and punishment of crime. Parents, teachers, the media – which were the more effective in influencing whether a teenager grew up straight or crooked? If, as I increasingly thought, the family and the surrounding community of friends and neighbours were the key to an individual's development, then imprisonment (which took offenders away from these influences and absolved them from all family responsibilities) was justified only when society clearly needed protection from a particular offender. Of course, this thought matched our day-by-day worry about prison overcrowding, but was not driven by it. As well as concentrating with other departments on the initiatives under the Safer Cities programme, we began to focus more intensely on punishment outside prison, in the community. This was not easy. One promising possibility based on tagging was unreliable because the tags did not work properly. (They came into their own after 1997 when the Home Secretary, Jack Straw, used them to reduce his own problem of prison overcrowding.) Punishment in the community would be administered by the probation service. But neither the magistrates and judges who passed sentences nor the probation officers themselves regarded that service as an instrument of punishment. The probation officers had to be coaxed out of seeing themselves as concerned simply with welfare. This process of policy-making and persuasion has been thoroughly and sympathetically described by Lord Windlesham in the second volume of his work *Responses to Crime.*

I was greatly helped and stimulated on this front by John Patten, who joined me as Minister of State in 1987. His academic background qualified him for the intellectual fisticuffs that were inevitable when dealing with lawyers and other professionals. He was a bold pugilist of another kind in the House of Commons. His wit and ingenuity kept me going through many a long meeting.

The work of ministers and officials continued after I left the Home Office in 1989, and bore fruit in a White Paper and then in the Criminal Justice Act of 1991. The wheel of debate turns. It does not often bring to the top entirely new ideas, but in each decade different weight is given to familiar considerations as policy is formed. Now we are back in the search for effective punishment outside prison and rehabilitation within. More widely, we look again at the effort against crime as a whole, beginning with the family, the school and the community, moving on through the different parts of the penal system and now rightly concentrating on fitting the released prisoner back into the community as a law-abiding citizen. If I were holding an away day at Leeds Castle now I would ask those present to concentrate on the notion that for society the most important moment in an offender's life is not when he enters prison but the day he leaves it.

There were some men and women in prison for whom the question was not how they were treated but whether they were guilty at all. Over the Christmas holiday in 1986 and at the same season in 1988, I spent many hours at Westwell poring over the details of three criminal cases. I was not a judge, but I had been put in the position of one. The cases of the Birmingham Six, the Guildford Four and the Maguire Seven arose from terrorist murders committed by the IRA in England in the 1970s. In all three cases juries had found the defendants guilty and judges had accordingly sent them to prison. As the years passed, increasing doubts were expressed about the merit of these convictions. These doubts spread beyond the ranks of the Irish Nationalists and their natural sympathisers on the left. Well-established journalists such as Robert Kee, two former home secretaries, Roy Jenkins and Merlyn Rees, two distinguished law lords and Cardinal Basil Hume took up the cases between 1986 and 1989. Their pressure was directed not on the juries or judges who had convicted and sentenced the defendants, but on the Home Secretary. I had to consider with as much care and thought as I could where my responsibilities lay. Hence my decision to take the files home quietly over the two Christmases, shut away from the pressures and distractions of other work.

Men and women had been murdered by terrorists. Other men and women had been locked up as the murderers. Not many years earlier, convicted murderers would have joined the victims in death, having been hanged by the neck in accordance with the law. Now in the 1980s they were alive in prison. The exercise was no longer ghoulish and academic. The future in this life of human individuals rested on it, as well as the reputation of justice.

In theory the Queen could exercise the prerogative of mercy and release some or all of the prisoners on the advice, which she would accept, of her Home Secretary. In practice it seemed to me inconceivable that a politician under political pressure should ask the Queen without any further legal process to reverse the findings of judge and jury. There was another way. The Criminal Appeal Act of 1968 gave me the power to refer back cases to the criminal division of the Court of Appeal if I thought fit. In effect, I would be ordering a retrial.

I could not properly consult my colleagues in the Government, say the Lord Chancellor, the Attorney General and the Prime Minister; nor, obviously, any of the judges. There could be no collective responsibility; the decision was solitary and mine. I could, however, take advice from within the Home Office, where a division, C3, existed to handle cases of alleged miscarriage of justice. These officials were shrewd, meticulous and fair-minded. They had a high feeling for their responsibility as my advisers. They regarded their job as lying close to the core of the Home Office tradition of dignified thoroughness.

In 1987 I took my first decisions on these cases. In preparing to announce these decisions to Parliament I received a detailed draft statement from officials. I set it aside and wrote my own text in lay language. I wanted to set out plainly for everyone how I saw my job in such matters. After referring to pressures on the subject I told the Commons on 20 January:

In responding to these pressures, a Home Secretary must never allow himself to forget that he is an elected politician and that under our system the process of justice must be kept separate from the political process. It is open to others to say, 'If I were trying that case as a judge I would have given a different summing up,' or, 'If I had been on that jury, I would have reached a different verdict.' But it is not open to the Home Secretary simply to substitute his own view of the case for that of the courts. It would be an abuse of his powers if he were to act as though he or those who might advise him constituted a higher court of law. A different situation arises, of course, if new evidence or some new consideration of substance is produced which was not available at the trial or before the Court of Appeal. In any civilised system of justice there must be a means by which a case can be reopened so that new matters can be assessed alongside the old evidence by due process of law.

I believed, and believe now, that under the system which then existed this was the only reputable way in which I could use the powers I possessed. On that basis I referred the Birmingham case in January 1987 to the Court of Appeal on the grounds that there was new evidence casting doubt on the scientific test used during the trial. I refused to refer the other cases, the Guildford Four and the Maguire family, on the grounds that there was at that stage no new evidence to justify this.

The Court of Appeal began to review the Birmingham case. Pressure mounted on me to change my mind on the two other cases. In July 1987 Cardinal Hume led a powerful delegation to see me to press their argument, and they were supported by *The Times* in a leader. One of the consequences of the policy I had set out in January was that it was never possible to slam the book shut and announce, definitely and for ever, that those convicted would stay convicted. These were not ancient cases. It was always possible that new evidence would come forward to justify a reference to the Court of Appeal. Indeed, through 1987 and 1988 new pieces of information were produced which had to be assessed. I asked the Deputy Chief Constable of Avon and Somerset police to look at these, independently of the Surrey police who had handled the original Guildford case.

In January 1988 the Court of Appeal delivered their verdict after reviewing the Birmingham case. Emphatically they reaffirmed the original verdict of guilty. The Lord Chief Justice, Geoffrey Lane, announced this in terms which suggested that I had been weak and foolish to refer the case back to them.

In September 1988 Cardinal Hume asked to see me again about the Guildford and Maguire cases. As Roy Jenkins had warned me, he felt passionately, and would not give up. I decided that it would be courteous to go and see him in his own study, at Westminster. There were just the two of us in the room. This made it easier for me to say something which had been on my mind for some time. He and I were both particularly concerned about the well-being in prison of Carole Richardson, a young woman who was one of the Guildford defendants. I said that I did not find the new evidence on the case compelling and felt certain that the Court of Appeal would reaffirm the guilty verdict if I referred it to them, just as they had done with the Birmingham Six. It would be more difficult to get Carole Richardson early release on compassionate grounds if a review was pending or if the Court of Appeal had again proclaimed her guilty of murder.

I was not trying to outflank the cardinal. I understood his belief reaffirmed that day that all the defendants were innocent. I was not going to change that, but I wanted him to understand my own thinking. This made some impression. Cardinal Hume said that he would no longer press for a reference to the Court of Appeal. He did not specify that day what he wanted instead, but a fortnight later he suggested that I might use the royal prerogative of mercy or set up a tribunal under the 1921 Tribunals Act. It did not seem to me that a tribunal would get anywhere, the Act having been devised for quite different purposes. As for the prerogative of mercy, it would put me in exactly the position which I had repudiated before the Commons in January 1987. I, a politician under public pressure, would be usurping the position of the original jury without any legal process to justify this, even though such a legal process was available.

Some, including Roy Jenkins, had argued that the charged mood in the country in the 1970s after the terrorist attacks had distorted the attitude of the original juries. But that was precisely the kind of political argument of which I was suspicious. Who was I to say that because of a change in political atmosphere we were wise in 1989 whereas juries in the 1970s were foolish? Public attitudes shift constantly. I could not prove that these judges and juries had been careless of the evidence before them, and I could hardly base a decision on the argument that society had become more tolerant of terrorism since the month after the atrocities of Birmingham and Guildford.

My dealings with the cardinal were courteous throughout. He never raised his voice, used dramatic language or questioned my good faith. But I could have no doubt of the dignified strength of his belief that the Guildford verdict was wrong.

The ground continued to move under my feet. The solicitors Birnbergs provided new evidence which the cardinal had seen but I had not by the time of our meeting on 8 September. On 29 December, having worked through the papers again, I decided, despite the rebuff which they had given me over Birmingham, that I must refer the Guildford case to the Court of Appeal. In a minute to Margaret Thatcher in the new year I explained why: 'I do not believe any point separately would justify referral – together they do.'

In February 1989 an entirely fresh and damning piece of evidence came to light. It was discovered that there were two versions of the record of the original interviews made by the Surrey police, at which the defendants had confessed. The version used at the trial was later and fuller than the original, the assumption being that it had been doctored to help obtain convictions. A new police inquiry through the summer of 1989 was conclusive. The Attorney General on 12 October asked the Court of Appeal to quash the original verdicts. The Guildford and Maguire defendants were released, but clearly that was not enough. There would have to be a judicial inquiry into what had gone wrong. I pushed hard for this to be set up at once. I tried to get hold of the cardinal but he was in Lourdes. My officials wanted to delay setting up the inquiry because it might prejudice any prosecution of the Surrey police for perjury. The Lord Chief Justice held the same view, more strongly. But Patrick Mayhew (as Attorney General) and I had supped full of delays by this time.

The matter of an inquiry was not one for me alone, but for the Government as a whole. Geoffrey Howe was in the chair of the necessary ministerial meeting on 19 October, and had his own doubts. But Patrick and I rammed the argument home and the inquiry was agreed. Luckily the Prime Minister was in Kuala Lumpur at a Commonwealth summit, or we might have had a bigger problem. I made a statement that afternoon in the Commons, which was quiet and receptive. Afterwards I gave thirteen television interviews on the trot: 'Reasonably satisfied at having put some limit to the disaster.' That was certainly the most that could be claimed.

Sir John May led the inquiry, which was later swallowed up in the Runciman Commission on judicial procedures. Leaving my desk at the Foreign Office in 1991, I gave evidence to the May inquiry. I argued strongly that the Home Secretary should no longer handle these matters. An independent body was needed to decide on references to the Court of Appeal. The wheels continued to turn slowly. The Birmingham verdicts eventually collapsed in 1991. In 1995 the body which I had recommended – namely, the Criminal Cases Review Commission – was authorised by Parliament. No future home secretary in such cases will find himself asked to act as a judge.

I have one further comment. It is sometimes said that the Home Office and I were moved by a desire to protect at all costs the reputation of the police and the judiciary. This thought was buttressed by a foolish remark of Lord Denning to the effect that the whole system of justice would be shaken if the verdicts were reversed. I had no respect whatever for the *obiter dicta* of Lord Denning in old age. I never held the view which he describes. I came from outside the legal profession and found that an advantage. By the time of these events I had no exaggerated respect for either police or judges. I had handled the passage of the Police and Criminal Evidence Act in 1984 which provided procedural safeguards against the kinds of abuse which had been perpetrated by police officers in the Birmingham and Guildford cases before the Act was passed. But whatever the police and judicial procedures, justice will always depend to a large extent on the integrity of the individual police officer. There can be no cover-up for breaches of that integrity; any such cover-up, far from maintaining the system, is bound to undermine it.

The decisions facing the Home Secretary rarely fall tidily within the ordinary confines of party warfare. There are usually no handy signposts marked 'Conservative Way' or 'Left-wing Way' which can excuse a minister from doing his own map-reading. On the question of ancient war crimes there was certainly no signpost. Evidence began to emerge of serious crimes committed in the Soviet Union and Eastern Europe during the Second World War by men who had then served or fought alongside the Germans, and were now living in the United Kingdom. Of course, by 1988 such men were in their sixties, seventies or even eighties. Their crimes, if they had been committed in the United Kingdom, could still have been subject to prosecution even forty-five years later, since we have no Statute of Limitations. Though time under United Kingdom law may obscure the evidence, it does not pardon the criminal. But the alleged crimes had not been committed here but in Latvia or Belarus or thereabouts. The question was whether we should change our law to bring these crimes within the reach of British justice.

My first instinct was cautious, even negative. I disliked the peremptory nature of the pressures being brought to bear. But I knew I had to keep my mind open. In February 1988 I asked Sir Thomas Hetherington, the former Director of Public Prosecutions, and Mr William Chalmers his Scottish equivalent to investigate the allegations. The report of these cautious, highly experienced men reached me in June 1989 and came as a shock. They showed evidence of horrific killings on a very large scale. I was well aware of the difficulties, but I was not prepared to evade them by extraditing those concerned to face the Soviet version of justice.

Many favoured doing nothing, as had been my earlier instinct. But my mind changed. On 13 July I confided to my diary, 'All those who have read the Hetherington report (including the Prime Minister) v. reluctantly believed we must act on it. All those who haven't (i.e. Judy and the 1922 Executive) don't. It will be a major tussle unlike any other.'

I understood the difficulty of getting evidence of a calibre to convince a jury beyond reasonable doubt that some apple-cheeked old gentleman living peacefully in a bungalow outside Edinburgh was the man who had forty-five years before ordered the machine-gunning of Jews standing by the trench which they had just dug as their grave. In a minute to the Lord President, John Wakeham, I voiced this concern: 'Whether any prosecutions, let alone convictions, would follow if we persuaded Parliament to change the law is a different matter. I nevertheless believe that it will be very difficult for us to justify total inaction.'

Cabinet took the question on 20 July ('All reluctant, all resigned to some action. They water down my formula a bit, but it is bearable'). The watering down consisted of insisting that there should be a Commons debate before the Government produced a Bill.

Usually my decisions have been pragmatic and have sometimes included sitting on the fence for some time. On this occasion the Prime Minister shared my view. But it was not she who pushed me off the fence. As usual in Home Office matters she left me to make my own proposals. The shock of the prima facie evidence of atrocities persuaded me and then my colleagues that we must bring such crimes within the law. In 1990 the Lords threw out the resulting War Crimes Bill, which was no longer my responsibility. Geoffrey Howe, then Leader of the House of Commons, wanted to drop the Bill. He thought that we had already shown our sense of outrage simply by introducing it, and need not use the Parliament Act to overrule the Lords. Rather feebly I agreed with him, but the Prime Minister and David Waddington, by then Home Secretary, felt we must persevere, and the Bill eventually became law. There have been two prosecutions under the War Crimes Act of 1991: one was abandoned because of the ill health of the defendant; the other resulted in a conviction and a sentence of life imprisonment. Looking back, I believe that I was right to push ahead in 1989 and wrong to wobble in 1990.

19

THE CONSERVATIVE PARTY

My political life now ranged well beyond the Home Office and the constituency. On the first Sunday of January 1986 we went to lunch with the Howes at Chevening. The Westland tempest was brewing. The issue was outwardly simple: should Westland, our British manufacturer of helicopters, collaborate with an American or with an Italian firm in the next round of production? That debate contained military, legal, industrial, but above all political strands which it became impossible to disentangle. Margaret Thatcher batted for the American solution; the Defence Secretary, Michael Heseltine, for the European. The Prime Minister's dual role as both umpire and passionate protagonist turned a secondary procurement decision into a political crisis. The Foreign Secretary talked to me after the meal in an alcove behind the piano at Chevening; he absentmindedly upset a glass of port. Geoffrey Howe thought it would be very damaging if Michael Heseltine resigned because of his preference for a European solution. We agreed that the issue should if possible be used to restore collective discussion in the Cabinet.

Willie Whitelaw briefed me on the telephone next morning. Everyone, he said, was now hysterical, but at least the Prime Minister had agreed that there should be proper cabinet discussion. On 7 January I wrote a letter to Margaret Thatcher, which I did not send because I was given an opportunity to talk to her directly on the 8th. I used the unsent letter as a brief. 'It would be dangerous and damaging if Michael Heseltine were to leave the Government. Your authority has to be clearly upheld, and this must obviously include what you have written and said on the subject. These considerations cannot now be easy to reconcile.' I suggested a collectively agreed statement on defence procurement, including different strands which at the moment seemed in conflict, but which were in fact all essential, including encouragement of competition and value for money, of private British industry, and of European cooperation. 'I hesitate because I know well your dislike of fuzzy documents – but you have sometimes recognised that they are necessary.' The Prime Minister took this well, and most unusually went on to consult me about cabinet changes involving the retirement of Sir Keith Joseph from Education. Next morning the Cabinet met 'to shelve the Westland argument peacefully . . . and ends with Heseltine stalking out and resigning. Neither he nor she intended this. [That is still my view.] But she mishandled him yet again, and he in rising anger refused to listen to all offers of compromise about how and what statements should be cleared by Cabinet Office – a shame.' As often happens, the final breakdown came on procedure: Michael Heseltine mistrusted the inner machinery of government as biased against him.

I have since come to know Michael Heseltine well, and now count him as a friend. But at this time I found him hard to read. He made no effort to enlist me as an ally even though I knew that we had several points in common. We both held a generous view of the role of the Conservative Party in social matters; neither of us denied the importance of government action in carrying this through. We both believed strongly in Britain's role in the European Union, though Michael carried his enthusiasm for integration faster and further than I did. But our temperaments are different. Michael was a cavalry leader, relying on the excitement of a charge to carry him to success. Under that impetus he was ready to travel a long way with radicalism. For example, I was surprised and dismayed by his vehement desire to transform the structures of the Civil Service which had always been part of my working life. Michael relished and I disliked the scent of danger. I remember later walking with him to a meeting of ministers called by John Major to take a suddenly needed decision of Bosnia. 'Isn't this fun?' Michael said as we hurried down the corridor in the House of Commons to the Prime Minister's room. I stared at him in disbelief, being deeply worried and gloomy. Michael's enjoyment had nothing to do with the issue; he was simply elated by the feeling of crisis which depressed me.

The Westland drama of 1986 wandered on into its final act. The party and Number Ten gave me for a few days a leading role in handling radio and television. As often happens, the storm began to focus on a side-issue: namely, Leon Brittan's decision to publicise part of a confidential letter in which the Solicitor General Patrick Mayhew analysed some inaccuracies in a letter written by Michael Heseltine. But as usual the rest of life continued and the drama had to be fitted into its routines. I spent the night of Friday 24 January in Lancashire and spoke about drugs policy to Conservatives in Bolton.

The next day:

The headlines roar as everyone decides whether the PM is now a target. Up at The Last Drop, a stylish and successful place in New England style, good breakfast with Edward [Bickham, special adviser] whose company is a pleasure. Beautiful drive over the moors to HM Prison Preston. A brisk strict governor, no proper sanitation or workshops. Trot round quite happily, savouring nasty dinner, admiring Victorian radials in their new colours. Businessmen visit at Bury, nice Alistair Burt [MP]. Moss Side, blacks in shopping centre to discuss development. They are quiet and a bit dull. A Vietnamese leather factory in Salford. Dumped at Manchester (Reform) Club to rest, but flee from its discomforts to Piccadilly Hotel, where dictate – bath – rest – ring Judy. Speak to NW Annual dinner of FCS [Conservative students] at the Club under Liberal stalagmites, fireplaces, photographs. About 80 young, obsessed with persecutions by Left in Manchester University and Poly. Speak on cities. Back briefly to Piccadilly, write to Tom. The sleeper, not really necessary, but the height of solitude.

So I bumped south through the night in my cell, arriving at Euston early on Sunday morning. This would not be a day of rest. I had been selected to appear for the Government on what was then the most influential political programme on television. The interviewer on *Weekend World* was the former Labour MP Brian Walden, well known for stubborn persistence in search of a story.

The Westland situation had deteriorated further. The Prime Minister had made a clumsy statement in the Commons on Thursday which had led on Saturday to Leon Brittan's resignation as Secretary of State for Trade and Industry. I was driven to Ten Downing Street to confer with the Prime Minister's officials on the line I should take on television. They assured me that there were answers to all the outstanding questions, but the more they explained these answers the more complicated they seemed. Margaret Thatcher appeared for five minutes. As happened when she was tired, she did not draw breath. She wanted me to attack Michael Heseltine; I listened, but resolved to do no such thing. (She was keen on the same misguided tactic when Michael Heseltine next challenged her in 1990 as will be shown later.) More usefully, Edward Bickham then punched me with the questions Brian Walden was likely to put. The interview went well. Brian Walden was very professional, I held my ground, and the general reaction was excellent. Willie Whitelaw telephoned congratulations on the way I had steadied the uneasy ship.

A helicopter flew me west through the wintry sunshine of the Thames Valley to a family lunch of roast beef with Judy's parents at Chaddleworth. I learned later that the staff at Number Ten were not entirely happy with my broadcast. They appreciated my defence of the Prime Minister but noted for the future my emphasis on the importance of proper cabinet government.

The next was the last of the extraordinary Westland days. Senior ministers (in my diary I call them 'the greybeards') gathered round the big table in the government whips' office at No. 12 Downing Street. A scene followed which would have been inconceivable both earlier and later. We went through and largely rewrote, in her absence, the draft speech which the Prime Minister was to give in the Commons that afternoon. Over two hours we made substantial changes, while she waited in humble mood upstairs. Leon Brittan meanwhile peppered us from outside with demands to know what was going on – naturally, as he was preparing his own resignation speech. The Prime Minister accepted our changes and the debate began. 'Kinnock poor, MT gets through quite well. It is a clumsy story, but is out now, and its very clumsiness convinces.'

I continued in several broadcasts my steadying task but the drama was over. My Sunday lunchtime effort on *Weekend World* had helped to convey the necessary atmosphere of calm and reason. On the evening of the debate, John Patten 'surfaces to say that he and Chris Patten and William Waldegrave think that at the right time I should throw my hat in the ring [for the party leadership, which at the time, of course, was not vacant]. Flattered, as this is a very strong group, but of course fantasy – life will now subside.' It did . . . for a time.

Five months later the Prime Minister invited me to join her newly formed strategy group. For the first time in twelve years I became involved in the central direction of the Government and the Conservative Party. The circumstances however were quite different. Before 1974, as Ted Heath's political secretary, I was way down the pecking order, but in practice close to the inner thinking of the leadership. In 1986 I was far removed from the Prime Minister's inner thoughts but senior enough to be included in her formal or semi-formal discussions about the future. Our first meeting on 30 June at Number Ten gave me the flavour. 'All over the shop – MT skittish and omniloquent, never lets Geoffrey Howe finish a thought. We scamper from themes to policies to PR points to hatred of the BBC and back again. I am the only one to favour anything on service and neighbourliness.'

This particular group never became particularly important, but its composition showed how complete had been the revolution in the party in favour of the right. Although they were very different in their approaches, I regarded Margaret Thatcher, Nigel Lawson and Norman Tebbit as instinctive hardliners on most subjects. John Wakeham, the Chief Whip, was silent except when it came to procedures or personalities. Willie Whitelaw was close to retirement, though still powerful when he chose to exert himself. Geoffrey Howe's deteriorating relationship with the Prime Minister already limited what he could achieve. I could not by myself redress the balance, but I set myself to talk in public about the themes which I had already raised with colleagues without response. Many ministers – for example, Michael Heseltine before he resigned, Ken Clarke and Ken Baker, as well as myself – were carrying out policies based on service and neighbourliness. It would be damaging if the official rhetoric of the party reflected solely the individualist philosophy of the Prime Minister. Individualism and the associated emphasis on wealth creation were a necessary component of modern Conservatism, but not complete as a portrait of the party nor sufficient as a theme for the electorate. So my long-suffering constituents and such audiences as the Bow Group and the Coningsby Club heard a good deal from me in these years about social cohesion.

I looked for an occasion to reach a wider audience and found it on the bicentennial of the birth of Robert Peel in February 1988. Peel had fascinated me since his biographer Professor Kitson Clark talked about him at Cambridge in his rooms alongside the Great Gate of Trinity. I consulted the latest biographer Norman Gash, and arranged to speak at Tamworth, where Peel had launched the first manifesto of the modern Conservative Party in 1834. Peel's old house had disappeared except for a tower, being replaced by a rather disagreeable entertainment centre: 'Winking lights, quantities of nasty food, pink sugar round the sorbet. But all v. friendly.'

My main theme at Tamworth was 'the active citizen', working in all the voluntary associations which were a strength of British society. The fruits of economic success could turn sour unless we brought back greater social cohesion, as Peel and the Victorians had done in their time. Our policies in the cities were not an extra or a luxury, they treated a disease of the heart. It was not enough to maximise personal wealth, though our approach was in contrast to the socialist attraction of lying back and waiting to be taxed by the state. Warming to this theme in the *New Statesman* a month later, I wrote, 'perhaps even in these columns one can suggest that the WRVS (Women's Royal Voluntary Service) has worn rather better than the Webbs'.

The Tamworth speech and active citizenship went well in the press;

the Prime Minister even muttered a friendly comment on the bench in the Commons the following week. She had no objection to me talking on these High Tory lines; indeed, she was in favour of anything that got the party positive headlines. It was just that she could not bring herself to think like that herself, and, being an honest woman, she would not speak what she did not think.

Five days after Tamworth I spoke and answered questions at an informal meeting of the General Synod of the Church of England, chaired by the Archbishop of Canterbury, Robert Runcie. This had never happened before, and was good fun. I saw no reason why the Church of England and the Tory Party should be at loggerheads. The old partnership of parson and squire was over, but the Church of England was and remains the biggest single example of the voluntary associations which I had praised at Tamworth. Some of my colleagues criticised the Church's manifesto, 'Faith in the City', as some sort of Marxist tract, but this was nonsense. The Church placed and continues to place rather too much confidence in bureaucratic solutions to social problems, but the thrust of its analysis was the same as mine – and by creating its own Urban Fund it was following its mouth with its money.

When Geoffrey Howe and I had discussed Westland behind the piano at Chevening we had agreed to press for a return to proper cabinet government. But nothing happened, except that Margaret Thatcher recovered her poise. Government decisions and cabinet discussion continued much as before, the two being too often distinct. The Prime Minister became increasingly overbearing towards Geoffrey Howe, who had been her close political companion in the early years of her Government. Willie Whitelaw retired; he had warned me at the time of Westland that Margaret Thatcher would never learn to chair a meeting as others did. There was only one way in which Margaret Thatcher could perform as Prime Minister; it was either that way or someone else.

The myths go too far. It is not true that the Prime Minister intervened to govern the affairs of every major department. On the contrary, it was perfectly possible for Nigel Lawson, myself and others to run our departments as we thought best, remembering that there were certain hobby horses which the Prime Minister liked to ride, and that she did not like to be surprised by bad news (such as a prison riot). Provided that precautions were taken on these points, ministers would find Margaret Thatcher quick to understand and support decisions which they took. Indeed, she preferred decisive ministers to those who waffled around trying to guess her mind. Nor were there doctrinal inquisitions or hunts for heresy. It was possible for a minister to choose different hymns from the Tory hymnal and sing them out loud. She had her own favourite tunes and a favourite choir to chant them for her, but she knew there were others. Nor was the Cabinet a collection of hired nodders, as in P.G. Wodehouse's stories of Hollywood. Some ministers were indeed courtiers; others only talked to their own briefs. But there were generalists like Norman Tebbit, Nigel Lawson and latterly myself who could find their individual voices on matters outside their department.

After the defeat of the 'wets' in 1981 and the consequent reshuffle there was no concerted effort by any group of ministers to challenge the Prime Minister's version of events and policies. Offhand, I can think of only one significant exception: namely, the success of Geoffrey Howe and Nigel Lawson working together to force the Prime Minister to compromise on British entry into the European Exchange Rate Mechanism before the Madrid summit in summer 1989. It was characteristic of the system that though both these ministers were friends of mine as well as colleagues, they did not seek my help, or indeed force any serious discussion in the Cabinet. Within months each of them separately fell into serious trouble with the Prime Minister which led to his resignation. Again, neither kept me more than sketchily in the picture, until after the event when each turned to give me his account of what had happened. I do not particularly blame them. The Prime Minister operated on a radial not a collegiate basis. She was open to frank debate with individual ministers and did not expect always to get her way, but cabinet meetings were essentially for routine discussions and the occasional ratifying of decisions reached elsewhere.

One consequence of this system was the long life of the community charge or poll tax proposal. My diary is full of hissings and rumblings on the subject. In 1987 during the General Election campaign I walked round Birstall Market near Leeds in support of Elizabeth Peacock. 'They are all upset by the community charge, which I always thought was the Exocet. Write to Tebbit [Party Chairman] on this.' I sat on the ministerial committee which examined the detail. It was the detail that mattered. I remember well ferocious meetings I had endured in West Oxfordshire against the old rating system. People wanted a change and the principle of the community charge was not offensive. It was just that every time we considered hard figures they were unacceptable to this important group or that. I was no expert and no enthusiast on the subject of local government finance. I supported those who tinkered with the figures and the timescale, trying to make the proposition less disastrous – and as a result more expensive to the Treasury. Nigel Lawson has said that he lobbied me to oppose the whole idea. I remember grumbling with him, but so long as Margaret Thatcher was in power, running the system as she did, a policy with which she was identified could be amended but not reversed. The lady, famously, was not for turning.

*

In July 1989, as in many a July, there was talk of a reshuffle. One of my bilateral meetings with Margaret Thatcher was fixed for 17th. 'She is cheerful and friendly, her mind not on HO affairs, and I make some progress on police and broadcasting matters. She makes no mention of reshuffle, except obliquely at very end to say how good that HO is quiet. Tell her to touch wood.' It is worth noting her choice of words: 'quiet' was not what she wanted from most departments. But she had been Prime Minister for ten years. She knew that a home secretary (like a Northern Ireland secretary) who brought her no bad news was as good as she was likely to get.

A week later the first seismic rumbles through Whitehall began to herald the reshuffle. On 24 July Number Ten rang my office to say that the only change at the Home Office was that we were losing Douglas Hogg on promotion ('So I stay, somewhat wearily, but surviving'). I felt a twinge of jealousy at the news later in the day that John Major was succeeding Geoffrey Howe as Foreign Secretary. I had made no secret that this was a job I would like.

Next morning I was at the Palace helping the Queen to invest nineteen new knights bachelor. It proved an eventful morning. One knight fell off the footstool and another was wearing a turban so big that the Queen could not slip the riband of knighthood over his head. When I got back to the Home Office I found the rumour surging round Whitehall that Geoffrey Howe had been offered my job the day before. The press wanted me to be amazed and resentful. I was genuinely unflustered. I knew that the Prime Minister thought I was doing a reasonable job because she had just told me so. She obviously had a big problem on her hands in dealing with Geoffrey Howe's reluctance to leave the Foreign Office, so it was not amazing that she had tried to tempt him with the Home Office. I had done the job for four years and would no doubt have been offered something else worthwhile. Anyway, he had turned down the idea.

I spent much of the next day trying to persuade Geoffrey Howe that he could make something important out of the deputy premiership which he had been given, and John Major that the Foreign Office was not such an awful place as he at first supposed. Andrew Turnbull, the Prime Minister's main private secretary, telephoned to take me through what had happened in Margaret's desperate conversation with Geoffrey. If he had accepted the Home Office, I would have been offered the job of Lord President of the Council and Leader of the Commons – which I certainly would have accepted. On the following day I went over to No. 11 Downing Street to see what Nigel Lawson made of all this. He said that there should be an inner cabinet, but the Prime Minister would never agree, so the bunker mentality would continue. We agreed that he,

Geoffrey and I should meet in the autumn to discuss, perhaps with the cabinet secretary, Robin Butler, how collective government could be revived.

The autumn came. Nigel Lawson and Geoffrey Howe went. The return of collective cabinet government had to wait another year.

20

Summer Holidays

During these years we established a pattern of summer holidays as a family without really thinking about it. The pattern was irregular and sometimes interrupted by crises. During the late eighties and early nineties we usually spent as a family one week in August with Dennis and Bridgett Walters at their home, La Cappellina near Lucca in Tuscany. (Dennis, as a backbencher with a special interest in foreign affairs, had encouraged my career ever since my days in the Conservative Research Department.) Then we would adjourn for another week or fortnight sharing a cottage in Devon with our friends the Negrettis.

The contrast between these holidays was formidable. Pisa airport was in those days an unsophisticated institution. The sniffer dog employed by the Italian authorities to track drugs prowled openly among the suitcases on the single carousel. One year, in front of a crowd of British tourists, this dog whimpered enthusiastically round an elderly but innocent suitcase of mine until it was hurriedly pulled off by the police officer sent to greet the British Home Secretary. I remain surprised that no one earned a pound or two by photographing the incident for some British tabloid. Free of the airport, I tried to remember the way through the outskirts of Pisa and drove the hired car either north on the *autostrada* or directly over the hills which separate Pisa from Lucca. Either way, within an hour we passed through the straggling village of San Leonardo and watched anxiously for the sign 'Materiali Edili'. We had to turn sharp left in front of the builder's yard up the narrow avenue to La Cappellina. This was the farmhouse bought long ago by the journalist and Independent MP Vernon Bartlett, visited twice by me during my time in Rome, and now transformed by Dennis and Bridgett. We usually arrived, inconveniently for our hosts, just at the start of the siesta hour. The routine of the household remained constant throughout the years. At first Judy and I came alone; later, when Philip and Jessica were with us, we were allocated an apartment with its own little kitchen, above the chapel in honour of the Virgin which Dennis had rescued and had reconsecrated.

I have known many swimming pools, but the one at La Cappellina, where Judy and I began each day, remains firmly on the shortlist of favourites. It was protected by a grove of bamboo on one side and a slope of olives beyond, with surrounds of thin red bricks in Roman style, and a view over the house to the wooded hills across the valley. In a dry year forest fires often crackled and glowed along these slopes. We watched small planes bombard the flames with inadequate canvas bags of water, and hoped they would not exercise their right to replenish from our pool.

The Tuscan morning might be spent sampling the varied pleasures of Lucca, an ideal city for shopper and tourist. Judy and Jessica would patrol the via Filunga, noting particularly where the 'Fin Stagione' signs suggested ripe bargains. I might lead Philip, mildly complaining, across the Roman amphitheatre to the medieval Torre Guinigi. Or we might all bicycle through the trees on the top of all four sides of the pink city walls. Around noon the rendezvous at the end of our exertions would be the café at the corner of the Piazza San Michele which specialised in ice creams. As we wrote postcards St Michael, on the tip of the exaggerated façade of his church, would continue to ward off plague from the city.

The nature of my protection had to be negotiated at the start of each holiday. My British police teams left me at Heathrow, but they had to warn the Italians of my arrival. The captain in charge of the *carabinieri* would present himself, cane under arm, on the lawn of La Cappellina, salute our hostess, sip coffee. I would ask for the maximum privacy. He would offer the maximum protection. We then negotiated a treaty. Most years we would be left at peace at La Cappellina, but would notify the police of expeditions beyond. Once I broke the treaty and was ashamed. We made a shopping expedition to Lucca, having failed to notify the police. At the end of the shopping I stood on the descending escalator of the Standa store clutching parcels. I was horrified to see the captain of *carabinieri*, still dapper, approaching me on the ascending escalator. The matter was resolved in a civilised manner: we each averted our gaze as we sailed past the other. Quite apart from my breach of the treaty, each of us knew that Standa was a cut-price store which the other might think fell beneath our dignity.

The lunches at La Cappellina are remembered by my family for the special excellence of eating Italian dishes with local wine in flasks, under a pergola through which filters the Tuscan sun. The Hurds were traditionally greeted by risotto tricolore, in the Italian national colours, zucchini and home-made tomato sauce surrounding the rice; my special greed for osso bucco would be acknowledged later. The siesta was deep.

Later, while others played subtle tennis, I often climbed the slope of olive trees and scrambled through the hedge down to a narrow lane which led past the cemetery up to the village of San Ginese di Compito. Behind the large, modern church a narrow terrace looked out over the valley of the Arno. On this terrace olives had been planted to commemorate the boys from the village who had fallen in the Great War. Each had his tree and his tablet: Isonzo 1916, Caporetto 1917, Piave 1918. The olives of San Ginese are gnarled now, and their roots have split or displaced the tablets. The village also lost men during Italy's tortuous involvement in the Second World War; these are commemorated here by a shiny rhetorical monument, much less poignant than the shabby individual stones of the Great War and the olives looking across towards the mountains of Carrara. I found this terrace poignant and went there each year. In a short story about Bosnia I later transported the terrace to a village near Sarajevo.

On one evening of our week at La Cappellina we would take Dennis and Bridgett to dinner, probably at the El Cecco restaurant in Pescia, noted for the variety of its mushrooms which came opportunely into season towards the end of August. One night we would all dine with the Gilmours. Ian Gilmour and Dennis Walters were old friends, their friendship cemented by dedication to the Palestinian cause. Ian and Caroline spent part of each summer at their house, La Pianella, to the west of Lucca, where they entertained a flow of congenial house guests. Crafty and competitive tennis would be followed by hours of badinage over dinner in the garden. This expedition involved a fearful hazard: namely, the ascent and descent of the steep, rocky, tortuous road which led up to the house from the main road. Shaken by this awesome experience, we would emerge to find Roy and Jennifer Jenkins or Sara Morrison or the economist Bill Keegan sipping wine on the Gilmour terrace in Olympian calm. House guests, once exalted to the summit, rarely ventured down the mountain until their final voyage to the airport and home. Dinner guests had to enjoy themselves as best they could, trying to forget the terrifying, almost vertical descent in the dark which would be necessary before they reached their beds.

Back at La Cappellina one or more of the Walters children would usually be staying alongside us. At the Ferragosto holiday the magnified noise of village celebration would force its way down through the olive grove, and the younger members of the party would go up the lane to dance among the coloured lights. Dennis and Bridgett, unlike the Gilmours, entertained Italian friends. The veteran columnist of *Corriere della Sera* Dino Frescobaldi would come to discuss European politics gravely with me under the pine tree at the edge of the garden. A favourite guest was Harold Acton, aged and softened since I had first met him at La Pietra twenty years earlier. He often arrived late from Florence, sometimes blaming this on the communist affiliation of his chauffeur. He retained a clear memory, exquisite courtesy and a tendency to emphasise his consonants. But it was difficult now to persuade him into the vein of delicate malice about past friends and enemies which had once marked his conversation. Now over eighty, he drank much wine during the evening, then accepted with dignity a guiding arm to steer him down the path to the waiting car.

The household at La Cappellina has been dispersed; the routine is no more. There are personal sadnesses in this, alongside happy memories of what were for me ideal interludes of rest and revival during the most crowded years of my life.

Nepeans, a cottage on the coast of South Devon, could hardly have been more different. No one in the days when we knew it could have called it a comfortable place for a holiday. No swimming pool, no tennis court, indeed no outside facilities at all except a child's swing reached down a path beset by nettles. No pergola, just a log shed, the wall of which provided some shelter for barbecues against wind and rain. No olive groves, but a beech wood pressing in on the cottage from three sides. No indoor elegance, but a meter which (in the first years) had to be fed with fifty-pence pieces to achieve hot water in the tub hiding under the eaves of the single cramped bathroom.

Yet it was a magical place for which my children have often pined. On its fourth side the cottage looked through blackberry bushes out on the wide estuary of the River Erme about half a mile before it joined the sea. At low tide it was possible to ford the river without difficulty. But the flood came in ferociously, applauded by a great audience of seabirds, gulls, egrets, oyster catchers – and a heron. Before breakfast, usually alone, I would amble in a dressing gown down the muddy path past a Victorian tea house on the river's edge to a small, sheltered beach. There would be no one in sight, except perhaps a man walking a black Labrador on the far shore of the estuary, too far to be bothered by nakedness. The swim was most fun though a shade dangerous at the ebb, when I had to aim upstream at such an angle that when struck by the force of current and tide combined I would be carried on to a spit of sand and pebble and not swept out to sea.

Nepeans is on the Flete Estate owned by the Mildmay White family. Its centrepiece is the beach at Mothecombe round the corner from the Erme Estuary, set in a semicircle between rocks jutting out from cliffs crowned with turf and copses of beech and hazelnut. On the top, at the edge of the hamlet of Mothecombe, two elderly ladies kept a shrine of pilgrimage: namely, a tearoom without modern trimmings in the old schoolhouse. After crab races on the sand, beach cricket, and defence of castles against the tide, the ice cream and soft drinks at the blue-and-white schoolhouse were reached up a steep sandy path through blackberries and two fields of sheep. We were allowed to use another path up through the sheltered gardens of the big house and to harvest the windfalls from their orchard for purposes of blackberry-and-apple pie. At the August bank holiday the Mothecombe Estate played cricket against the village of Holbeton on the ground at Flete itself, which looks towards the distant tower of Ugborough church.

In simplicity rather than comfort we shared Nepeans with the Negrettis. Lucinda had been at school with Judy. Her husband Simon is a formidable tennis player and the organiser of successful sporting occasions of many kinds for the children. I lack both skills. Guy and Gipsy Negretti are much of an age with Philip and Jessica Hurd. Negrettis and Hurds rubbed together well year after year in the cramped cottage. My particular duty was to tell smugglers' stories 'from the head' when the children were in bed. It was easy to drum up the necessary shivers of pleasurable fear when wind and rain were beating at the bedroom windows of Nepeans as my smugglers and revenue men fought it out in the estuary down the path. Devon at this time was beginning to devise wet-weather entertainment for its visitors, but on a really torrential day there was nothing to beat Dartmoor, and the trudge against the wind up to the desolate reservoir. While at Nepeans we and the Negrettis constantly complained about the weather; once we had left we quickly, under pressure from our children, began to plan the next visit.

Out of affection, the Mothecombe beach and the ladies' tearoom appear in my novel *Image in the Water* as the scenes of a youthful indiscretion which wrecks the Home Secretary's career.

PART VII

FOREIGN AFFAIRS

21

Germany and the End of the Cold War

The cabinet meeting on Thursday 26 October 1989 passed serenely. I had half expected that the Prime Minister would complain because while she was at the Commonwealth summit in Kuala Lumpur I had as Home Secretary persuaded ministers, despite opposition from the Lord Chief Justice, to set up an inquiry into the handling of the Guildford case. Silent on that subject, on others she was cheerful, even chirpy. On my left Nigel Lawson seemed quiet but not morose; as usual we exchanged light-hearted slips of paper commenting on the proceedings. He had told me some weeks before that he was having difficulty with the Prime Minister's wish to appoint Professor Walters as her economic adviser, but had given no hint since then of a crisis. I was amazed when the Prime Minister rang late that afternoon to offer me the Foreign Office, following Nigel's sudden resignation and her decision to move John Major from the Foreign Office to replace him at the Treasury. Still in a state of shock, she made no attempt to explain her thinking, as she had when sending me to Northern Ireland and the Home Office. Indeed, her inner feelings showed when she added: 'You won't let those Europeans get away with too much, will you, Douglas?'

I missed Nigel Lawson in the Cabinet. As Chancellor of the Exchequer he radiated authority. It helped that he had put on weight since I first knew him. It helped also that, though he had the quickest mind in the Cabinet, he habitually spoke with slow gravity. Each word seemed fully weighed and evidently the result of deep reflection. Occasionally he would summon me to his sitting room in No. 11 Downing Street. He would then explain *ex cathedra*, evidently turning difficult concepts into childlike language for my benefit, why it was important that the Cabinet next day should agree to spend less money or concur with whatever was his current analysis of the economic scene. This gravitas was quite compatible with an irreverent wit and an admirably balanced view of the humble though fascinating place of politics in human affairs.

I had now accepted the job as Foreign Secretary which I had long desired, but which by then I thought had passed out of reach. 'Ludicrously rapid farewells at HO, withdrawal symptoms, things are going well there, and a good team.' After a protracted Asian dinner at the Portman Hotel I went home to South Eaton Place, drank whisky and put on Beethoven's seventh symphony.

Being now more self-confident on such matters, I decided not to cancel a speaking engagement next day at Exeter, to which was linked a visit to my third son Alexander, then living in one of those remote, untidy farmhouses beloved of students of that university. On Saturday Geoffrey and Elspeth Howe came for tea and soggy cake at Westwell. Geoffrey, increasingly disconsolate as Deputy Prime Minister, told me much about recent matters of which I had no idea. In particular he narrated the battle which he and Nigel Lawson had fought with the Prime Minister before the Madrid summit in the summer to prevent her throwing over the idea of Britain joining the Exchange Rate Mechanism at the right time.

I was no longer an isolated chieftain running a department which, though important, did not in 1989 lie within the heart of the Government. From now on I was at the centre. Twice in the next weeks Tristan Garel-Jones, whom I did not yet know well, impressed on me that if there was ever a serious contest for the leadership of the party a group of MPs would expect me to stand. That sounded, and at the time was, unreal. I needed to concentrate on the Foreign Office.

The move at once lightened my burden of paperwork but the briefings given me by Geoffrey Howe, John Major and William Waldegrave (by now Foreign Office Minister of State) dispelled any notion that the life of Foreign Secretary would be one of luxurious ease. During each week of the next five and three-quarter years I handled a bundle of diverse matters, and talked with handfuls of people from all over the world. There was no single week when I focused on a solitary matter. If I write about these years in chronological sequence it will be impossible for the reader to follow any single subject coherently. Each chapter will become, like my life, an untidy tangle of different threads. That will not do. So I have to write separately about different subjects. If the book is not to stretch into intolerable length, I must miss out many matters altogether. That will vex some specialists but I hope not the general reader. More worrying is the fact that this subject-by-subject structure will disguise the reality of everyday life: namely, the tangle of meetings, paper submissions, telephone calls, journeys, surprises, hours of boredom, anxiety or relief all mixed together in the Foreign Office. I find this tangle hard to describe nowadays to pleasant academic students who write about once a month to ask for comment on particular events or policies. I almost always try to help, but they are surprised, even scandalised, if it emerges that in my memory or my diary there is only some tiny vestige of the particular matter to which they are devoting a year or more of study. It is not only research students who get this wrong. The fatal defect of the Scott Report on arms for Iraq was the failure of that experienced judge to understand the inevitable atmosphere and pace of modern government. The pell-mell of modern diplomacy has to be lived through to be understood.

In October 1989 I was returning to an office and a service which were thoroughly congenial to me. This was not merely a matter of individual friends. I was nearly sixty, the retiring age for British diplomats. Antony Acland was British Ambassador in Washington and Alan Donald in Peking, but otherwise most of my contemporaries in the service had left or were on their way. But I knew and relished the feel of the service and the way it set about its business.

Although there were individuals whom I thought inadequate and habits which I disliked, I reject the crude, generalised condemnation of the Foreign Office which is scattered through the memoirs of ministers such as Margaret Thatcher and John Nott. I do not believe that as Foreign Secretary I was run by the professionals; nor, I hope, was I arrogant in imposing my ignorance on their knowledge. Some ministers stand aloof from those who work for them, either because they are suspicious of their motives or because they regard stiffness as a badge of authority. But a foreign secretary spends hour after hour close to a handful of officials in planes, hotels and conference rooms across the world. He shares success, disaster and tedium with them. He learns to know their handwriting, their taste in fiction, their appetites, the problems of their children, and whether they snore. Aloofness in these circumstances naturally gives place to friendship and to me at least it seemed foolish to resist this process. I benefit greatly to this day from the results. I still regularly see and correspond with about a dozen individuals who worked closely with me during these years. In old age it is a great refreshment to count on a batch of friends, perhaps not in their first youth, but twenty-five or thirty years younger than myself.

Most of these were professional members of the Foreign Service. But the Foreign Secretary also needs help across the wider range of domestic and European politics. Michael Maclay and Maurice Fraser acted as my special advisers when Edward Bickham left to better himself. They directed my party political life. On foreign policy they hovered discreetly in the background, not raucous and self-promoting like some special advisers more recently, but ready with a nudge or well-phrased comment if they thought the professionals were leading me astray from my own (or their) convictions.

I spent between a quarter and a third of my time abroad. Some of this was repetitive, and certain routines established themselves. The Foreign Affairs Council of the European Union met on Mondays once or twice a month, either in the graceless Charlemagne Building in Brussels or on the Kirchberg outside Luxembourg. Daylight and fresh air, decent food and leisurely conversation became rare commodities on council days. It was as if one had to dive into a grubby swimming pool of a temperature difficult to predict in advance, from which it was impossible to escape for twenty-four or thirty-six hours. For Brussels I established a routine which at least softened the discomfort. I used to fly there late on Sunday afternoon from Brize Norton, a ten-minute drive from home. Our permanent representative at the EU, John Kerr, in 1992 took over the fashionable and heavily gilded house on the rue Ducale facing the royal park, which had been occupied for many years by the British Ambassador to the Kingdom of Belgium. A separate chapter would be needed to describe the manoeuvre by which that protesting ambassador was deprived of his centrally placed palace and shunted to a perfectly agreeable Art Nouveau house on the rue Henri Pirenne a couple of miles away. Its author was the Minister of State, Tristan Garel-Jones, who chooses to regard it as the climax of his Foreign Office career. I connived at the decision, and certainly benefited from it. John Kerr used to assemble for Sunday supper half a dozen or more of his staff, young and old from different Whitehall departments. Sunday supper in the rue Ducale was not a question of scrambled eggs. Over a proper meal with good wine we ran through the agenda for the council next day, and quickly spread ourselves into a review of the state of Europe and the world. Cheered by these exchanges, and fortified next morning by exceptional croissants and a brisk walk among the statues in the royal park, I was in reasonable state for the dreary plunge into council business.

Once a year I spent a week at the UN General Assembly in New York. This involved making a speech on behalf of Britain to the General Assembly itself. It is just possible, standing there at the world's rostrum, to persuade oneself that once a year the world is listening to Britain's words, delivered *urbi et orbi*. In reality, each member state, being allotted eight or fewer seats, normally fills just one with a junior diplomat to report home in case anything dramatic occurs. The seats of the speaker's own delegation are full, as may be those of any country which expects to be so insulted that it will have to muster an impromptu walkout. Otherwise, the speaker's words fall on a disappointing wilderness of wood and shiny leather.

Outside the chamber, New York becomes a bustling diplomatic fair, during those early weeks of each autumn UN General Assembly. Confidential meals and meetings in hotels and delegation offices fill each day as the members of different regional groupings confer with one another, usually in generalisations not very different from those uttered in the Chamber. More useful are bilateral meetings which can be slipped in without attracting the media attention that would otherwise complicate them. I could quietly meet Ali Akbar Velayati, the Iranian Foreign Minister, to test whether there was any longer a threat from his country to the life of the novelist and British subject Salman Rushdie. I could each year spend several hours formally discussing Hong Kong matters through interpreters with the Chinese Foreign Minister, Qian Qichen. On one of these occasions I scored an unexpected linguistic success. Over forty years my knowledge of Mandarin had faded almost to nothing, but one day a flash of memory told me that a senior Chinese official had just whispered to his minister that the agenda item we were discussing could be postponed to the next day. 'No,' I interrupted in English, 'I am sure we should settle it now.' The Chinese were shaken, though only temporarily, into believing that I had been able to understand *all* their private mutterings. If only diplomacy were always so simple.

Since I had attended Selwyn Lloyd in the Waldorf Astoria in 1956 both traffic and prices had multiplied in New York, so that it was no longer sensible for the Foreign Secretary to lord it alongside the Americans in their favourite hotel. I always stayed in the UN Plaza Hotel opposite the UN itself, and swam twenty lengths each morning in its big pool at the top of the building looking towards the Secretariat and the East River. This habit of swimming before breakfast when I was abroad grew on me. I did not conscript a companion; if she was there Judy nobly accepted this as a wifely duty and there was usually a complaisant private secretary good for a ten-minute gossip as we swam side by side in the pool. Some of these swims stick in the memory: with John Sawers in a tropical downpour in Singapore; with Richard Gozney freezing in Pretoria, each of us urged on by pride and hoping that the other would cry off; with Christopher Prentice in a sauna in Finnish Lapland; with John Sawers again when we were caught by the cameras in white hotel dressing gowns leaving the beach during my last summit at Cannes. These were three private secretaries different in background and temperament, each for a year or two closely bound hour by hour into my life, condemned to share its moments of anxiety and enjoyment.

I usually flew across the Atlantic by British Airways, sometimes, if time was short, out by Concorde in the morning (a two-lunch day) and back overnight by Boeing. For other destinations the method varied. Elderly RAF VC10s were available, very safe as we were often told, but internally beginning to disintegrate in small ways. Doors jammed, ceilings dripped, fittings came away in your hand. Their real disadvantage, however, was price. The mysterious Thatcherite concept of the internal market had reached the Royal Air Force. They proposed to charge the Foreign Office huge fees, apparently taking into account not just the cost of the flight itself, but every penny spent on training the pilot and the sergeant who served the sandwiches.

My private office rose to the Thatcherite challenge and scoured the world for cheaper planes. Richard Gozney, my main private secretary from 1991 to 1993, became a buccaneer of the travel business. Sometimes the vehicles which he chose were bizarre. On one occasion we flew the Atlantic in an Arab plane, rich in gold taps and computerised information on the exact direction of Mecca. We discovered that after dropping us the crew would fly at once to Jedda, in breach of every conceivable regulation on safe working hours. The RAF began to enter into the same entrepreneurial spirit. When about to fly to Tokyo, I noticed that we were loading huge quantities of Coca-Cola on to the VC10, beyond the limited likely demand from my associates and myself. It was explained that the refuelling fee at Novosibirsk, in those days part of a disintegrating Soviet Union, was US$25,000 in cash and a quantity of Coke. At Novosibirsk, lifting the cabin window shutter, I saw a fleet of jeeps approaching down the tarmac through snow and darkness. Officials in fur hats stamped their frozen feet and negotiated with our crew at the back of the plane. The jeeps departed; nothing happened; we seemed entirely in the land of Dr Zhivago, at the mercy of whatever nebulous authority temporarily controlled these empty wastes. Eventually the power of Coca-Cola and dollars prevailed and we moved on.

I have always enjoyed the act of travel, regardless of purpose or destination, and particularly when a spice of waywardness flavours the proceedings.

At home, too, routines slowly established themselves. In January 1990, after some alterations and redecoration, we moved into the Foreign Secretary's residence in Carlton Gardens. For all of us this was a happy home. The two lower floors kept their formal flavour; the rooms were big enough for different kinds of official entertaining, without the somewhat oppressive grandeur of Lancaster House. The two upstairs floors became a family flat, just a comfortable size for Judy, me and our two young children. It was possible, as we proved on Philip's sixth birthday, to use the blue drawing room as a cricket pitch – though with a ball of soft foam and huge penalties for hitting a picture. My private office showed its usual versatility by providing Christopher Prentice as both bowler and umpire.

My first months back at the Foreign Office overflowed with good news. The Soviet Empire was disintegrating, the countries of Eastern Europe gaining real independence, the Cold War ending. The symbol of this change was the breach and then destruction of the Berlin Wall. On 16 November 1989 I was the first Western minister to visit the newly opened crossings of the Wall. In the Potsdamer Platz I was jostled by the friendly crowd into stepping over the line with East Germany. I shook hands with an East German border guard because it seemed the natural thing to do; luckily there was no Foreign Office lawyer at my side to warn me of the grave diplomatic implications of this irregularity though legal minutes buzzed to and fro afterwards. The Brandenburg Gate was still closed, and I walked parallel to the Wall as far as the Reichstag through happy schoolchildren to whom British soldiers were serving coffee. All I had to do was congratulate and be glad in the good-tempered confusion of that day. But something more rigorous was required in dealing with the consequences, in particular the rapid German thrust towards unifying their country.

Britain, with her allies, had supported the reunification of Germany in many declarations over many years. The transformation of the Soviet military zone into a separate German state (the German Democratic Republic) created a destabilising division in the heart of Europe, which was made much worse by the nature of that state. The East Germans were kept as prisoners within a communist system which depended on Russian military power. No technical skills, athletic successes or mass parades could disguise that fact. As the prison walls crumbled in 1989 it was natural that Germans should begin to concentrate on reunifying Germany as a free democracy. Her allies were expected to encourage in practice a process which they had long supported in theory.

That, however, was not the view of the British Prime Minister. William Waldegrave had warned me in advance what to expect. I listened many times during those early weeks to outbursts of her anxiety and irritation. With characteristic honesty she explains the reasoning in her memoirs. She did not seriously believe that Chancellor Kohl was a new Hitler, or that a united Germany would coerce Europe into a fourth Reich under the jackboot. But she argued that unification would unbalance Europe by adding fifteen million disciplined Saxons and Prussians to what was already Europe's leading economic power. The crux of the argument was the nature of modern Germany. The Prime Minister did not understand the total change which the disaster of defeat had brought about after 1945. She knew some Germans well, but they seemed to be mainly bankers and academics. She had not experienced the German political process at close hand, for example in the Anglo-German discussions each year at Königswinter. Nothing had entered her own life to erase vivid memories of the German past. She did not believe that Germany would subordinate itself to a process of European integration. Given new strength, Germany would be tempted to assert once again, though no doubt by different means, a dominance over others.

This line of thought seemed to me deeply mistaken. It was likely to lead us into an effort to prevent or postpone German unification which was bound to fail, to our own great disadvantage. I was new to the job, but understood the Prime Minister well enough to know that she would not resent argument. Equally, it was clear that she would not easily or quickly change her mind. She was supported by several of her close advisers, notably Nick Ridley, Secretary of State for the Environment, for whom Germany's overwhelming economic strength was the key. Nick, intelligent, self-confident, unhappy without a cigarette, was by then established as one of her inner circle. She enjoyed his irreverent, jargon-free approach to any problem. There was no understanding at the time that unification, far from adding hugely and at once to Germany's economic strength, would impose on that country a social and economic burden which even today has not lifted.

In the first weeks all I could hope was to dampen the Prime Minister's hostility. In this I was helped by the German Foreign Minister, Hans-Dietrich Genscher. This subtle and experienced politician was the first of my foreign colleagues to take trouble over the new British Foreign Secretary. On my first official visit to Bonn he took me after two hours of talks to watch Wales play Germany at football in the huge Cologne stadium. I noticed that German ministers sat on a simple bench and were treated with less deference than British ministers would be at home. I led him across Downing Street to see Margaret Thatcher on 29 November, immediately after Kohl had launched the ten-point programme for unification which deeply troubled her. The Prime Minister was tired and talkative, but not aggressive. Genscher coped well with the arguments to which he had answers – for example, the need to respect NATO – and avoided the rest. Margaret encouraged him to come and see her again, which he did in February 1990. Genscher told his officials afterwards that he had been surprised to find how often I ventured into the discussions with points of my own. I never felt any urge to conspire with him against my Prime Minister's views, but he knew the score, and kept in close personal touch through the awkward months ahead.

Meanwhile, the situation worsened. My officials were warning that we seemed to be more pro-Russian than the Russians. They pointed out that Gorbachev was showing no sign of intervening to prop up the communist regime in East Germany and that we were in danger of seeming to prefer Europe as it was, divided and half-communist, to the Europe 'whole and free' of which the US President George Bush was already speaking. I became somewhat irritated with my officials and our ambassadors in Europe for not realising my difficulty with the Prime Minister – and that if we were not careful our position could deteriorate still further.

Already I was hearing at Number Ten about the parallel with the years 1904–14, when the British, French and Russians had joined in an entente to check German ambitions. This mischievous mining of history was carried further by President Mitterrand at the European summit in Strasbourg in December 1989. Although Margaret Thatcher distrusted Mitterrand, she enjoyed his company and admired his sense of history. At Strasbourg, as was his habit, he juggled with ideas when talking to her, summoning up the same thought that, as in the past, Germany could only be restrained by Britain and France acting together. But this was just intellectual play. I always enjoyed Mitterrand's company, until his illness closed in on him; his was the most subtle intellect of any politician I encountered. But his constant juggling with ideas, phrases and historical comparisons was a pastime, not a prelude to action. Before she met Mitterrand again in Paris a month later I warned Margaret Thatcher in a long minute that in public he was speaking in favour of unification, and there was no evidence of any serious French effort to check its impetus. Our aim, I believed, should be to influence the terms of unification not to stop it. My French colleague Roland Dumas argued throughout that the remedy for any worries about a united Germany was to tie that country firmly into European integration. This was the policy which Mitterrand was quietly pursuing by persuading Kohl to accept a single European currency. It was a view which held no attraction for Margaret Thatcher.

On 23 January I visited East Germany and was impressed by the modest yet determined Christian groups of dissenters in Berlin and upstairs in the Nicholaikirche Leipzig: 'They have the future of Europe unwittingly in their hands.' Reporting at Chequers the following weekend, I found the Prime Minister still aggrieved by what she thought of as German selfishness for promoting unification regardless of the effect on Gorbachev's domestic position. But that day she talked of a transition phase rather than total opposition. After lunch President Bush telephoned. 'A vision of MT upright in chair in her dull study, looking out over grey rainy rose gardens, two hyacinths, bracelet occasionally striking against desk as she scribbles, receiving, questioning and not welcoming the news of substantial US [troop] cuts in Europe. Feel sorry for her, a "rout" she says.' The Americans were not only backing early German unification, but themselves weakening what she saw as the essential stabilising US presence in Europe.

On 6 February I had the first of several meetings that year with Kohl in the Chancellor's office in Bonn. Communication between him and Margaret Thatcher being virtually non-existent, each was willing to compensate by extending courtesies to the other's Foreign Minister. For seventy minutes alone with him except for an interpreter and his collection of marine specimens, I listened to Kohl's indignation against an article by Margaret in the *Wall Street Journal,* followed by twinkles of good humour and an immense ramble through his early life and underlying beliefs. He said he could never be accused of nationalism. He wanted Britain to be inside the circle of European decision-making and would never make an anti-British statement. I warned him against rushing too fast into unification and he promised to be flexible about dates. He asked me to act as his political contact. He would try to avoid surprises such as his sudden ten points, adding however that he would win any competition with Margaret Thatcher over the practice of consulting allies. When I next saw him a month later he was beaming and spoke of good spirits in the air. In May he took me further into his confidence about his political debates at home. The West Germans he said had become greedy. They were wrong to complain about the cost of supporting the East Germans. It would simply mean postponing the third covered swimming pool in places like his own home town.

These meetings set the tone for my dealings with Kohl over the next five years. He was never a man for graceful courtesies and would take little notice of me at big conferences. But in his own office, as he repeated the stories of his own father and childhood, emphasised again and again his admiration for Churchill, quoted and requoted Thomas Mann's phrase about aiming for a European Germany not a German Europe, he became for me a large, familiar and sympathetic figure. I never blamed him for driving ahead with unification as fast as he could. That was legitimate leadership; in his position Margaret Thatcher would have done the same. It was for Gorbachev to make his own calculations about Gorbachev's future. Kohl could not be sure how long Gorbachev would be able and willing to concede what Germany needed. He saw the opportunity, and knew it might be fleeting. The window was narrow, he scrambled through it, breaking a little glass on the way, but less than might have been expected.

The Prime Minister delivered her last tirade against German unification in a cabinet meeting on 8 February. My talk with her that evening was friendly, but she brushed aside my arguments and continued to talk about the need to work with the Russians against Kohl. On the threshold of a big international meeting in Ottawa I felt that she had dealt me a negotiating hand without any worthwhile cards.

Happily, the next week proved a turning point. In theory we met at Ottawa to discuss an open-skies treaty; in practice this became a diplomatic fair, like a UN General Assembly in New York. Out of a series of conversations came an American proposal that problems with German unification should be settled in a group composed of West and East Germany and the four occupying powers: the USA, the Soviet Union, Britain and France. The idea of the 2 + 4, though criticised by the smaller European countries who were left out, was a godsend to me. It came close to Margaret Thatcher's own ideas on procedure. In place of ad hoc and confused conversations, we held in different capitals during the next seven months a series of well-prepared meetings at which Britain sat by right, with an orderly procedure conducted by foreign ministers. There was no longer a danger of deals, particularly any affecting NATO or the rights of the Poles, being done behind our back.

Margaret Thatcher had one more shot in her locker. Characteristically (though this runs counter to the general caricature), she preferred not to have to rely on her own instinctive opinions but buttressed these with outside expert support whenever possible. In March 1990 she invited a group of highly respected academics to Chequers for a seminar on Germany. This gathering has passed into popular history for the wrong reasons. The Prime Minister as usual began with a robust statement of her own anxieties, but found little support. 'They none of them shared her extravagant suspicions of Germany, but this just makes her flail about more. All good humoured but they are half amused, half depressed by her prejudices.' A full record was kept by her private secretary, Charles Powell. Weeks later this record leaked to the press. Charles wielded a vivid pen, and it was his account of the Prime Minister's views which caught the imagination. Less noticed was his final and correct conclusion that the weight of the evidence and the argument at the seminar favoured those who were optimistic about life with a united Germany.

Somewhat reassured on procedure, perhaps slightly damped down by the Chequers seminar, Margaret Thatcher was next powerfully influenced by the way the substance of the discussion was going. Far from turning soft on NATO – for example, by flirting with ideas of a demilitarised eastern Germany – Kohl held absolutely firm. A united Germany must be a full member of NATO. We knew how difficult this would be for Gorbachev to accept, given the convictions of his military. We were not surprised that for a time at the 2 + 4 talks his Foreign

Minister Eduard Shevardnadze put forward rival ideas to please Soviet opinion and attract the softer elements in German politics. Margaret Thatcher worried less that Kohl would weaken, more that he might lose power to the German Social Democrats who came into her category of 'wobbly'. For Margaret Thatcher there were always plenty of wobbly people in the world, inhabiting an unsatisfactory limbo between virtue and vice.

A week after the Chequers seminar (but before the leak of Charles Powell's record) Kohl came to London. The Prime Minister exerted herself to make the visit a success. At the press conference after our relatively anodyne discussions the two leaders united against the media, each rejoicing visibly at the points the other scored. I carried away the conviction that at heart they respected each other. It was just that they were no good in a room together.

The 2 + 4 talks on unification proceeded smoothly through the summer. The only hiccup at home was caused not by the Prime Minister but by Nick Ridley, who in July gave an interview to the *Spectator*, which as published was crudely anti-German and quite contrary to the policy of the Cabinet to which he belonged. Charles Powell moved quickly and persuaded Nick, who was on an official visit to Hungary, to withdraw what he was alleged to have said. 'Am content with this, and got PM to read it out in Cabinet. Later media and advisers a bit wistful as if I should have pressed for his resignation. But he is not an enemy, nor I an executioner. Backbenchers surge around and there is a wide view that he should go. But I bet PM will stick with him.' Next day the storm continued to blow around Nick Ridley. On a beautiful, cloudless evening Peter Carrington was delivering the annual lecture of the Ditchley Foundation in a yellow marquee outside that amazing house in Oxfordshire. I put a few innocuous words into my vote of thanks to reassure the Germans about our policy. A couple of journalists galloped away to manufacture a story. Nick resigned the next day, and I was told later that the Prime Minister felt I had helped to push him over the edge. This was not so. I had accepted his withdrawal of his silly piece in the *Spectator* and never pressed that he should go. I thought the mini-crisis was over, and was trying to mop up. Judy and I were on good terms with Nick and his wife, who lived not far from us in the Cotswolds, at the Old Rectory in Naunton. Judy had worked for Nick at one time, and our television room is hung with landscapes which he painted. The Cabinet was short of members like him with lively wit and a range of interests outside politics. He had earlier supported European unity. Disappointed by the lumbering bureaucracy of the EEC, he switched to total hostility. This was a matter for him, so long as he did not try to run foreign policy.

The last year in which the Soviet Union held the key not just to the German question but to the whole course of international affairs was 1990. That key was still in the hands of Gorbachev, whom I went to see for the first time that April. I was ushered into a hot, high-ceilinged room in the Kremlin with curtains excluding the sun and any prying eyes. Gorbachev bounced in from another meeting, his eyes bright with pleasure at his own cleverness and success. He was in good spirits and teased Leonid Zamyatin, the Soviet Ambassador in London, with that not very funny brand of brutal Kremlin humour which in Stalin's time had proved lethal to recipients. He added little to what I already knew about his German policy, but spoke of the pressures exerted on him by the Soviet military. The great of this world are sometimes stirred to particular emotion by some relatively minor personality. Gorbachev that day had been irritated to distraction by the bearded Lithuanian leader Vytautas Landsbergis, who had lectured him at length on first principles. After criticising Landsbergis and instructing me briefly on Soviet economic policy, Gorbachev said that he had not spoken so freely to a Westerner for a long time. Since he hardly knew me, I doubt the truth of this. Gorbachev, unlike Yeltsin after him, had abandoned the heavy communist method of discourse. He enjoyed trying out ideas and darting from one subject to another, and I suspect he found Western interlocutors, including our successful ambassador, Rodric Braithwaite, more apt for this purpose than his own colleagues.

Judy and I dined that night with the Soviet Foreign Minister Eduard Shevardnadze and his wife. The four of us were alone with an interpreter in their small flat crowded with the mementoes of a party career. Shevardnadze's white hair and mastery of any brief gave him a dignity which never deserted him. That evening he spoke in a soft-voiced, friendly way, but neither then nor in many later talks did I feel he was letting me into his real mind. Occasionally at 2 + 4 meetings, or more often at the press conferences which followed them, he would flush with indignation at some remark, allowing the pressures under which he lived to break through his usual self-containment. Talking to him years later when he was President of Georgia, both in his presidential palace in Tbilisi and at a meeting in Berlin to celebrate the tenth anniversary of unification, I tried to probe below the surface. He and Gorbachev had come to the conclusion that Soviet foreign policy was a disaster, that the communist regimes in Central and Eastern Europe must be abandoned to their fate, and the West approached for a new friendship based on trust. This change in foreign policy was more sweeping than anything Gorbachev himself contemplated inside the Soviet Union. Its speed and completeness surprised us all. Huge risks were taken with the Soviet military establishment, and indeed with a public opinion schooled to believe that NATO was an instrument of aggression. I wanted to understand what combination of intellectual analysis or moral compulsion drove them on. I cannot say that I found a full answer. The disastrous Soviet intervention in Afghanistan after 1979 and the dishonest efforts to justify that adventure were part of the explanation which Shevardnadze gave me. More generally, both he and Gorbachev felt such a revulsion against the ruling system despite their own successes within it that they decided to seek a different kind of success through leading a fundamental change.

On the night of that supper in Moscow Shevardnadze's wife showed a different truth about Soviet life. She looked what she was: the majestic daughter of a Soviet general. In 1937 her father had been taken away and shot under Stalin's orders. His daughters wept, knowing that he was innocent. Yet in 1953 when Stalin died they wept again. In the intervening years Stalin had led Russia to safety through great suffering in the Patriotic War.

The same lesson struck me from a different angle a few days later on my first visit to Leningrad. A foreign minister often finds himself laying wreaths. Usually my concern would be to avoid a clumsy mistake and remember the drill which our military attaché had muttered into my ear a few minutes earlier. It was not always easy to summon up the suitable emotion. The war cemetery north of Leningrad was a different matter. Two young Russian soldiers marched my wreath in front of me. I fixed my eyes on the pockmarked backs of their necks as we moved down the immensely long path which leads from the museum at the entrance of the cemetery to the Statue of the Mourning Mother up several steps at the far end. There is no question of individual graves. On either side of the path, lined by bushes bare that spring day of any roses, large funeral mounds contain massed corpses. These had been picked up and shovelled together by the trucks which toured the city streets each morning of the wartime siege. There are no names, no crosses. A distinguishing badge on each mound indicates only whether it holds civilians or soldiers. Behind the mounds a dead march sounds from leafless trees. More than a million Russians lie there. There is no sense of heroic victory, just a massive proof of suffering and the steadfast endurance for which Russia is famous. After glimpsing what the city had endured as Leningrad it surprised me that they were returning to the old name St Petersburg.

I was back in Moscow six months later for the last session of the 2 + 4 talks. The question of Poland's western border had at one time seemed troublesome. The Poles wanted the border guaranteed by treaty so that the Germans would never have a pretext for trying to regain the lands which they lost in 1945. Kohl was at first reluctant for domestic political reasons but yielded. By September 1990 we were preoccupied by the Gulf crisis, but 12 September had been fixed as the date for signing the agreement on German unification. A final argument blew up the night before on the right of non-German NATO troops to exercise in the former East Germany after unification. Our negotiator on this matter, John Weston, with my approval pushed the argument for this late into the evening. The Americans, who sympathised with us, left Weston to make the running. German officials agitated themselves into a worry that this disagreement would prevent the signature of the agreement next day. They alarmed Genscher who in turn woke up the American Secretary of State, Jim Baker. This late night flurry was unnecessary. I had no intention of allowing a relatively minor argument to get out of hand. The Russians would lose a lot of face if there was no signature next day and it made negotiating sense to press them up to the last minute. At a dour autumnal breakfast at the French Embassy next morning the four Western foreign ministers agreed a compromise formula which the Russians accepted with minutes to spare. We all signed on time. Gorbachev gave us a lavish lunch, and talked at length about every aspect of his policies. 'So self-confident that he persuades [us] within the four walls; outside all is slipping.' Next day I called on the man into whose hands the power was slipping. 'Back to call on Yeltsin – a dictator in waiting. Unsighted on detail but vigorous and entirely confident. Enjoy the joust and learn that he will win over Gorbachev.' The second half of the prophecy was right, the first half wrong. He outmanoeuvred Gorbachev, but did not become a dictator. I was misled by Yeltsin's authoritarian manner. His words were often rough, as were his tactics; but there was a good sense behind both which held him back from exercising dictatorial power.

22

DESERT SHIELD

The first day of August 1990 was meant to be my last at work before a summer holiday which was scheduled for the next three weeks. There was something seductive about the final week of summer work. The catalpa trees in the House of Commons courtyard were in full flower, a sign that Parliament was on its way to the long recess. The daily diary was no longer packed. These were days for tidying up, occasions for seeing people or tackling subjects which might have been neglected in the normal turmoil. In that week I held policy meetings on Antarctica, Cambodia and European Community institutions. I saw my Labour shadow Gerald Kaufman, and the heads of the two intelligence agencies for which I was responsible, MI6 and GCHQ. I visited the dentist and took my children to the Canadian circus Cirque du Soleil. The family then disappeared and I was left alone in Carlton Gardens without a kitchen, which was being decorated, or a corkscrew, which hampered my end-of-term gossip with Chris Patten. Having signed off with a final telephone call to the Chancellor of the Exchequer, John Major, I went down to Westwell. I woke next morning, looked out on our ancient oak tree and was glad it was holiday. I turned on the radio. Iraq had invaded Kuwait.

The Prime Minister was in Aspen, Colorado, with President Bush. Back in London Geoffrey Howe and I did what seemed necessary. Kuwaiti assets were frozen before the Iraqis could seize them, and a plan for sanctions against Iraq approved. On the 3rd I telephoned Margaret Thatcher in Colorado. She praised my brisk handling of the immediate situation, and commented that she was stuck pointlessly on a mountain. In fact, as emerged, she was doing an excellent job. She never claimed that she made George Bush's Iraq policy for him in those days, but she accelerated the moment when he decided and declared that Iraq's aggression must not stand.

That was our guideline for the next six months. One way or another Kuwait must be freed. Forty years earlier we had fought a war in Korea to reverse an act of aggression. The same principle, even more blatantly, was at stake here. Of course we were also influenced by our friendship with the Kuwaitis, and by the economic importance of the Gulf to the West. But this was not a war for oil. If we and the Americans had been solely interested in cheap oil we would have settled quickly with Saddam Hussein. We would certainly not have embarked on a war which left the Kuwaiti fields blazing and disabled. This was a campaign of principle, made politically more palatable because it was undertaken for a friend. The best way forward was peaceful, through diplomatic pressure backed by economic sanctions. In case that failed we needed to prepare force, beginning with air strikes, moving if necessary to attack by troops on the ground. Looking back on all the meetings held in the Cabinet Room under both Margaret Thatcher and John Major, I recall several difficult decisions on particular aspects of policy. But there was none of the intellectual and ethical questioning which later beset our policy on Bosnia. In that later conflict we were operating under a new and as yet unformed doctrine of humanitarian intervention in the internal affairs of a foreign country. Questions of analysis and doubts on policy cropped up at each stage. In the Gulf we were operating under the familiar necessity of resisting and reversing the aggression of one nation against another. We took greater risk in the Gulf War than in Bosnia, but I do not recall any of our main decisions as particularly controversial among ourselves, or indeed in my own mind. Each decision seemed to flow inexorably from the last until we achieved the final liberation of Kuwait.

The first weeks of August were spent in an uncomfortable limbo between work and holiday. As planned, I took the family for one week to Tuscany and another week to Devon. Both weeks were thoroughly disrupted by fax and telephone. There was much concern for British citizens trapped in Iraq and Kuwait. A meeting at NATO headquarters in the middle of this period gave me an opportunity to discuss over sandwiches with Jim Baker, the American Secretary of State, how we could best put together a coalition of the willing against Iraq, which would need to include most Arab states. For months I had been alongside Jim Baker in the 2 + 4 talks on Germany, still not concluded. I already respected the authority with which he spoke, and his knack of cutting without rudeness through diplomatic complications to the necessary conclusion, usually couched in a salty Texan phrase. From this time forward we worked together in close confidence as friends. Over these sandwiches in Brussels I tried to worry him about the position of Jordan, which was shifting against us: 'The King has to pick his way between his people and his friends, no fun.'

The Prime Minister, like the Hurds, was trying to combine holiday with work, and finding it difficult. She was staying with friends at Constantine Bay in Cornwall and invited us all over from Mothecombe on 13 August. The house was full of police and secretaries. Margaret Thatcher piled the children's plates with jellies and hovered over me as I telephoned the Foreign Office from the garage. She was in defensive mode that day, emphasising to me as a lawyer to a layman that our aim must be to resist the aggression against Kuwait, *not* to overthrow Saddam Hussein and install a new government in Baghdad. She later changed that view, indeed forgot that she had ever held it. After comings and goings in London and Paris I snatched a final weekend in Devon at our cottage haven. The last day, 26 August, was typical.

A well-composed day. Chess outside after breakfast. A slim chance for peace and diplomacy, pray for this at Holbeton family service Rite B with Lord of the Dance type hymns [examples of modern liturgy which I dislike], big much restored church. To Mothecombe as sun comes out, swim. Amazing colours as last year, much excitement over a baby mackerel caught in the shallows, refuses freedom, barbecued. Flete cricket match. Write review of Len Deighton. Walk fast back from Flete to Nepeans [cottage] one hour – Dumas rings. Pasta, Gewürztraminer, treacle tart after smugglers' tale for the children.

My next job was to rally as best I could the Arab components of the coalition. This meant a tour of the Gulf. On 1 September, 'Call on Sheikh Zayed [ruler of Abu Dhabi]. 1¾ hours. His Old Testament cadences rise and fall. Strong against Hussein, and Arafat is finished. [Neither the first nor the last time that particular prediction was made.] A wreck of a fine face, but he is full of vigour and history. Most enjoyable.'

It was a help that none of the main characters in the Gulf had changed since I knew them as Minister of State ten years earlier. The Sultan of Oman was serene and analytical in Salalah, and gave me a gallon of specially prepared lemon perfume. The President of Yemen I had not met before; he was favourable to Iraq, and we had the sharpest argument that I have ever had with an Arab. The ruler of Kuwait sat in forlorn exile in the lonely comfort of the Sheraton Hotel up the hill at Taif in Saudi Arabia, where my trouser zip had broken ten years earlier.

As usual I waited for hours in Jedda for a summons to King Fahd of Saudi Arabia. Again as usual it came late at night, just as I had begun to despair. He talked for eighty minutes uninterrupted except for interpretation. The Saudis, like all the Gulf rulers, felt frightened and betrayed by Saddam Hussein, and wanted to see an end to him, but with the least possible fuss.

King Hussein in Amman next day was seeking vainly for a middle way. He had told Saddam Hussein that he was against Iraq's annexation of Kuwait, but felt she should have access to the Gulf.

This robust diplomatic activity of mine played well at home. Tom King (now Defence Secretary) and I were given an ovation when we talked to a crowded meeting of Conservative backbenchers on 6 September. The press was kind. I felt that personally I was at something of a peak, which would not last. There was plenty else going on. In September we finally settled German unification. I visited Tokyo and carried out my usual rounds at the UN General Assembly.

After speaking at the party conference in Bournemouth I flew to Cairo, and paid a disastrous visit to Israel and the West Bank. As Robin Cook found later, hardliners in both those camps are skilled at laying little traps for visiting foreigners. An Israeli member of the Knesset leaked an exaggerated account of something I said at a closed meeting about a Palestinian state. Palestinians took offence and boycotted my planned meeting with them next morning. It might have been the other way round. For years such futile and negative sparring by clever people had served as a substitute for leadership. October also included an equally disastrous European summit in Rome recorded elsewhere. John Major finally persuaded the Prime Minister to join the European Exchange Rate Mechanism.

But most of the time my mind was on the Gulf. One way or another Saddam Hussein would have to give up Kuwait. I was anxious that peaceful pressure should be given a full chance, partly because it might after all induce him to withdraw but also because the coalition of the willing would be most effective in war if all governments and public opinion could see that war had been truly the last resort. By contrast the Prime Minister, in a change of mood since August, was inclined to a military campaign as soon as we were ready. She was particularly scornful of discussions at the United Nations, and this led to my last disagreement with her. Margaret Thatcher, together with many Americans, argued that Article 51 of the UN Charter, which authorises self-defence, gave us full and sufficient cover for responding to the Kuwaiti request for help in recovering her independence. This was true in law, but politically inadequate. Remembering Suez, I felt that it would be wrong to commit British troops to a war denounced by the official opposition. The Shadow Foreign Secretary Gerald Kaufman, who was throughout cooperative, made it clear that Labour support depended on a specific Security Council resolution authorising the use of force. This was the view of France and other European Governments.

Crucially, it was also the basis on which President Bush relied for support in Congress. Jim Baker was therefore an ally in the argument; in fact, he led it. He and I went over the ground together at the Foreign Office on 9 November before I took him across to see the Prime Minister. Jim Baker was a powerful advocate and a trusted friend; Margaret Thatcher did not resent the fact that he and I had conspired together. After a little more than an hour the argument was over, and we were authorised to secure a UN resolution. As Margaret Thatcher argued through those weeks, there was the danger of a Soviet veto, and an even greater danger of the authorised resolution being amended and messed about by half-hearted professional diplomats in New York. But our own professional diplomats did a good job, and the first Gulf War unlike the second was launched on the clearest and soundest foundations, both legal and political. But between the Gulf diplomacy and the Gulf War we lived through a drama of our own in British politics.

23

The Departure of Margaret Thatcher and a Leadership Contest

The last year of Margaret Thatcher's premiership was ominous for Britain in Europe. I was not opposed to her policy of robust insistence on British interests, even at the expense of European progress. Instinctively I disliked the tactics of the swinging handbag on which she prided herself. But I had to admit that through these tactics she had gained a notable and lasting reduction in our budget contribution to the EEC. Moreover, she had shown leadership of a highly pragmatic kind when in 1985/6 she promoted the European Single Market and accepted in return a degree of majority voting which went well beyond the practice in Ted Heath's time. She knew the European leaders better than I did, and on the whole treated them in private with courtesy and occasional flashes of charm, even when she disagreed with them. Although, for example, she opposed just about everything that the President of the Commission Jacques Delors stood for, she respected his intelligence and commitment to Europe, just as he respected her force and courage. Meetings between the two were fascinating; both became expert in probing without attacking the other's position, and finding subjects which they could discuss intelligently without the need for fisticuffs.

But Delors had no say in the most important question for Britain in Europe in 1990: namely, whether Britain should join the Exchange Rate Mechanism. Geoffrey Howe, as Foreign Secretary, Nigel Lawson and now John Major as Chancellor of the Exchequer had worn down the Prime Minister. She was retreating step by step from her opposition to the ERM. Most businessmen, the trade unions, the Labour Party and much of the press were in favour of joining. By the time I became Foreign Secretary only the date and the rate remained to be settled.

The running in this argument was made by the Chancellor of the Exchequer. As usual the Treasury kept the matter tightly in its own hands. The tradition of Treasury exclusiveness, so baleful in the crisis when we left the ERM in 1992, was also evident when we joined in 1990. I felt no resentment at this, and no desire to become more closely involved. The foreign policy advantages of joining were clear. Within the ERM we would have a more effective say, not just in the handling of currencies, but across the whole range of European economic decisions. But these advantages, though definite, never seemed to me decisive. Whether, when and at what rate we should join were matters to be settled to the best advantage of the British economy. Unlike Geoffrey Howe, who became Foreign Secretary after a successful period as Chancellor, I had no experience which entitled me to speak with confidence on financial matters. At every point when called on to do so I supported the new Chancellor, John Major, with whom I was keeping in close touch, and for whose judgement I by now had strong respect. He and I had begun to meet for occasional lunches at the Mijanou restaurant in Ebury Street when I was Home Secretary. In July 1990 with our wives we went with the Prime Minister to a massive G7 summit in Houston, Texas. Margaret Thatcher was in her element, revelling in the heat, the knots of cheering spectators in the streets and the opportunity to make speeches about freedom. In the intervals of superbly organised meals, including a barbecue and rodeo with much country music, the foreign and finance ministers were set to work out compromises on aid for Russia and on the General Agreement on Tariffs and Trade negotiations. The Majors and Hurds found time for a couple of irreverent lunches together in our hotel. His and my views and political instincts were similar. I was learning to appreciate the mixture of public caution and entertaining private indiscretion which marked John Major's approach to politics: 'I like and trust him more and more.'

On 4 October John Major came to breakfast at Carlton Gardens, talked about public expenditure, and also the Exchange Rate Mechanism, but he said nothing specific about a date for entry. I left for one of several tussles at that time with the Prime Minister about discussion of Iraq at the UN. 'PM increasingly Boadicean, is now definitely of the war party . . . The argument is strong but not heated.'

In the afternoon a message came asking me to cross the street and see the Chancellor. John Major told me we would join the ERM next day. I was slightly surprised, not at the news, but by the fact that he had not mentioned it over the boiled egg that morning. 'He is by nature more secretive than I. But pleased.' In his memoirs John Major records his own tussle with the Prime Minister that day, which resulted in the date of entry being unexpectedly brought forward after he had breakfasted with me.

In the background the EEC was preparing to move on through stages from the ERM to a single currency. John Major had launched in June 1990 his scheme for a hard ecu which would function in parallel with national currencies, and might (or might not) eventually be successful enough to supplant these currencies for most purposes. The thought that this crucial choice might be made by consumers through the market rather than by politicians always seemed to me attractive. Such a scheme had earlier been in Nigel Lawson's mind. I do not know whether it would have worked if we had introduced it earlier and pushed it harder. What is certain is that by June 1990 it was too late. Our partners regarded it as a device of the ingenious British to evade an uncomfortable decision. As a Spanish minister remarked: 'Good proposal, wrong country.'

The Italians held the EEC presidency in the second half of 1990, their Prime Minister being the veteran Giulio Andreotti. It was no secret that Andreotti, under the silly system by which each six-month presidency aims at a triumph for the holder, was anxious to fix a date for the intermediate Stage 2 of Economic and Monetary Union and to press on towards Stage 3, the single currency. Andreotti called a special EEC summit for October 1990 to discuss the matter in Rome. Italy in those days was the most enthusiastically integrationist of the large EEC members. The question was whether the others, in particular France and Germany, would want to press ahead at that speed. It was important to impress on them the difficulties this would cause for us.

The Germans were the key. The Genschers came to stay with us at Chevening on 29 July, and we took them to see Verdi's *Falstaff* at Glyndebourne. We strolled round the water lilies on the lake, accompanied by Genscher's biographer, and picnicked in the walled gardens. The 2 + 4 negotiations on German unification were moving smoothly, and there was no need to discuss them in detail. But on EMU I warned Genscher not to back us into a corner, and he seemed to take the message. My return visit was to his home town in Halle not far from Leipzig in East Germany. Genscher enjoyed walking me through the streets and showing his obvious popularity with citizens who greeted him: '*Alles gut, Herr Bundes Aussenminister?*' '*Alles gut, Frau . . .*' Handel was born in Halle, and there was plenty of his Anglo-German music that evening in the Town Hall to match our *Falstaff*. But the important business had been done that morning. As already described, personal contact between Helmut Kohl and Margaret Thatcher had ebbed to vanishing point, and I found myself acting as a go-between. In Bonn on

26 October I warned the Federal Chancellor against pressing in Rome for a date for the start of Stage 2. He reiterated he would be flexible. He would never make an anti-British statement. He wanted Britain to be within the inner circle of European decision-taking, and was confident we would be. He became more gloomy when I argued that the summit should establish a European position on the GATT round of world-trade talks which would have meant winkling the French out of their protectionist corner. But I came away reasonably reassured.

The next day the Prime Minister and I arrived in Rome in pouring rain. While the Prime Minister lunched with Mitterrand I found the grave of Gussie our terrier (*d.* 1964) among the acanthus by the aqueduct in the garden of the Villa Wolkonsky. The summit, shorter than most, began that evening in the Palazzo Madama. 'Horrid, as they all are, and this one pointless.'

Early on Sunday morning, 28 October, Margaret Thatcher and I looked through the draft conclusions for the summit which the Italians had just circulated. It was clear that Andreotti and the other Christian Democrats had persuaded Kohl at their pre-summit party meeting to press harder and faster on EMU than Kohl had indicated to me. Margaret Thatcher left me to handle the relatively mild conclusions on political matters and erupted against the EMU section.

The exchanges round the table were bad-tempered, her press conference that afternoon worse. On 30 October she made a balanced statement on the summit to the House of Commons but lost that balance when answering questions from MPs afterwards. My diary shows that I sympathised with her main position. I have never conjured up any personal enthusiasm for a single currency, and in 1990 accepted entirely the case for delay and avoiding fixed dates. Whereas on German unification the Prime Minister was plain wrong, on this I thought she was broadly right – but that her tactics, in particular her occasional rough and overstated arguments, would produce the wrong results. 'Typical Foreign Office,' she would say when confronted with any argument that her tactics would alienate individuals and governments with whom we needed to work. The paradox in autumn 1990 was that the harsh immediate reaction to her tactics did not come from the continent but from our own backbenchers. Many cheered her loudly on that raucous afternoon in the Commons on 30 October. They agreed with the substance of what she stood for, but on reflection a few days later were no longer ready to back her judgement.

In his diaries, Alan Clark disarmed criticism by acknowledging his drawbacks as an inconsistent and unreliable colleague. The one political constant which he claimed for himself was loyalty to Margaret Thatcher. On 29 October 1990, the day after the Rome summit, Alan Clark came to see me in my room at the Commons to say that Margaret Thatcher must go and I should take her place. This meeting is not recorded in his published diary.

Of course, doubts about her European tactics formed just one tributary of the stream which swept away Margaret Thatcher. A bigger torrent was the protest against the poll tax. On 14 March 1990, after a dreary day replying to indignant letters from the constituency, I wrote, 'we should have stopped it a year ago'. And the next day, after a meeting of ministers, 'speak out on community charge, too late of course, but the rules must be changed hereafter. We are in the deepest pit yet, the bitter letters pour in.' There never seemed a right moment to reverse policy. We had a particular difficulty in West Oxfordshire, where eighteen Conservative councillors resigned from the party on the issue and sat as Independents. Instead of abandoning the principle, some of the best minds on both left and right of the Cabinet set themselves to find ways of relieving the pain which it would inflict on different types of people. We spent hours working out these reliefs, which became increasingly expensive but showed no signs of calming public hostility. We must all share a responsibility for the erosion of cabinet Government which produced this disaster.

On a personal level Margaret Thatcher and I got on well, though I was never an intimate. She had given me three cabinet positions, and supported me pretty well in all of these. Being in her company was itself an adventure – stimulating, unpredictable and usually fun. One had to think fast and speak straight. I knew her well enough to reject the continual accusations of heartlessness. She had accomplished amazing things for this country, and deserved to leave the political scene with dignity. On the other hand, I felt that her very success was spoiling her judgement. She was less inclined to listen to anything except applause. In her the brake which in all of us imposes a pause between what we think and what we say was wearing dangerously thin. Particularly when she was tired, she talked too much and without reflection.

In short, I believed she should either change her methods or go. I still hung on to the possibility of change in her, the need for which I had indicated during the Westland crisis four years earlier. But if that failed, she should go of her own accord, not be pushed.

The party conference in Bournemouth that October was a pretty nauseous affair. In early days I had relished the annual dose of undiluted politics which the conference administers. As Home Secretary, I had worried deeply about my own obligatory speech, a hurdle which I might or might not clear successfully. I came to dislike heartily the final session where the leader of the party gave a long, contrived speech and received a long, artificial ovation. This applause was particularly tumultuous and particularly false in October 1990. Although John Major later improved the form of this event, I have never attended a party conference since I left office in 1995. There has been no need and no temptation.

On 1 November 1990 Geoffrey Howe telephoned to warn me that he had decided to resign, about an hour before he did so. I tried to dissuade him but in vain. The job of Deputy Prime Minister should have given its holder the opportunity to insist on precisely the change in method of Government which we needed. His relationship with the Prime Minister by this time ruled that out. Geoffrey was by then Margaret Thatcher's longest-serving ally in the Cabinet. He had stood by her with courage when Chancellor of the Exchequer and scored some of the most important successes of her Government. The scorn with which she later treated him not only offended him; it was proof of her failing political judgement.

On 13 November Geoffrey Howe made his lethal resignation speech. Afterwards I saw the Prime Minister alone. She was baffled and wounded. Unusually she did not begin with any statement of her own position, but waited for me to speak. I said she was hard to work with, but most of us wanted to try, even though she found it difficult to argue without causing offence. This was taken in good part.

Michael Heseltine at once declared his intention of standing against Margaret Thatcher for the leadership of the party. At the urging of Ken Baker, the Party Chairman, I made some early television appearances that morning in support of the Prime Minister. John Major came to breakfast, grey with a heavy cold and much pain in his tooth. It was clear from what he said that he might well decide to stand for the leadership if Margaret Thatcher withdrew. This came as no particular surprise. My close political friends – Tim Yeo, John Patten, Chris Patten, William Waldegrave and Max Hastings – were urging me to do the same. I still thought that Margaret Thatcher would soldier on and survive. On 16 November at Batley in Yorkshire I made a speech which in effect said to Margaret Thatcher, 'Stay and change,' particularly by uniting the party on Europe. When harried by reporters I repeated that I would not stand against Margaret Thatcher, which they took as implying that I would stand in a second ballot if she had withdrawn. In fact I had not made up my mind; it was still a hypothetical question.

The contacts and manoeuvres of the next few weeks have often been described. Such accounts made arid reading afterwards except to those who took part, and sometimes even to them. I can honestly say that in the first of these weeks Margaret Thatcher's political future was of greater interest to me than my own. Of course, I would have liked to be Prime Minister. That still seemed a remote possibility, though I was warmed by the encouragement of that handful of younger friends whom

I liked for themselves and knew to be wise as well as honourable. They were now backed in their advice by some senior backbenchers. But Margaret Thatcher's future was the theatre of the moment.

On the weekend of 17 November I worked on my boxes at Chevening, in the first-floor study with the Berlin tapestry, looking out through a drizzle over the lake. We walked up to the ridge with its keyhole of trees, dodging journalists. My third son Alexander arrived from Exeter University, very cheerful; he, Philip and I played snooker before supper ('This job really much more agreeable than that of PM').

Should the Prime Minister go to Paris the next week for the Conference on Security and Cooperation in Europe summit or leave that to me and spend her time at home drumming up support against Michael Heseltine? I had no doubt that she ought to go to Paris. I had little confidence in her tearoom techniques, particularly as her idea of campaigning at this time was to pour scorn on Michael Heseltine in a way which did her more harm than good. Instead of appearing rattled, she should stick to her plan to represent her country. She took this advice and for one last time we set out together on the Sunday evening.

Monday and Tuesday in Paris were diplomatic days, beginning for me with kippers from the Isle of Man at the British Embassy and television interviews. The Prime Minister signed a treaty, and attended the portentous CSCE summit of thirty-four governments. I talked separately with my French, German, Turkish, Italian and Canadian colleagues. In short it was another diplomatic fair, useful not for the speeches being made at the conference itself but for the opportunity to talk privately in nearby hotels and offices.

On these two days the prevailing subject was Margaret Thatcher's future, on which I was cross-examined from all angles. 'There is much personal sympathy for MT here, even among those, Kohl, Mitterrand, whom she most exasperates. Impossible not to share this. There will be pressure on J. Major to stand if she falters, as on me. I hope she doesn't [falter] as at last I think she may be manageable. Cognac and cigars and jokes. Ring J. Fireworks across the Seine. *The Longest Journey* [E.M. Forster].'

It was not possible to tell from Margaret Thatcher's own bearing that anything was amiss, except when on Tuesday we lunched with the Dutch Prime Minister and Foreign Minister, Ruud Lubbers and Hans Van den Broek, both of whom she liked. Anxiety made her talk to them particularly fast.

In the early evening the news of the first ballot reached Paris: 204 Members of Parliament had voted for Margaret Thatcher, 152 for Michael Heseltine and 16 had abstained ('Dammit, she is pushed into second ballot by a handful, the worst result'). There are plenty of telephone lines into the British Embassy in Paris and they buzzed. After talking to those closest to her, not including myself, Margaret Thatcher darted out into the embassy courtyard and announced that she would fight on into a second ballot. Two close intimates of hers – Peter Morrison, her parliamentary private secretary, and Bernard Ingham, her press secretary – suggested that I might go out a few minutes later and speak in support. I had been the first to sign the paper nominating her for the first ballot, and there would be no logic in refusing to nominate her for the second. So I said as much in the courtyard: 'The Prime Minister continues to have my full support.'

That was not the end of the day. The French had organised a huge dinner out at Versailles, preceded by a performance of the ballet. The Prime Minister had much on her mind and much telephoning to complete. We sent a message to President Mitterrand that for reasons he would understand the Prime Minister would be somewhat late for his hospitality, and would be grateful if he would not wait for her; she would join the proceedings as soon as she could. When eventually we arrived at Versailles, in pouring rain, Mitterrand had, out of courtesy, ignored the message and waited. Exhausted but serene, Margaret Thatcher was escorted past President Bush, the King of Spain and an array of other dignitaries to the front row of the theatre in the palace. The ballet was followed by a protracted banquet in the Galerie des Glaces, transformed that night into the most splendid dining room in Europe. The Prime Minister carried herself magnificently. All eyes were upon her as course followed relentless course. They looked on her as some wounded eagle – who had herself wounded many in the past, but whom none wished to see brought down, unable to soar again. Dazed myself, I wondered throughout how she must be feeling. I never felt greater admiration for her than on that night.

The practical problem on such massive occasions is always getting away. It was past midnight and still raining. There was a long queue for the cars. Protocol required that kings and presidents should leave before mere prime ministers. President Bush, sacrificing his position, told the protocol officer to call the car of the British Prime Minister. He went up sharply in my esteem. That night I wrote: 'I think she will persevere, keeping me and J[ohn] M[ajor] out, and either win or lose by a whisker.' Although I had not finally decided to stand if she withdrew, the idea was growing fast in my mind.

The French were particularly attentive to Margaret Thatcher next morning. Their Prime Minister, Michel Rocard, presented her with elaborate wooden maps especially crafted for the conference. By afternoon we were back in London. Margaret Thatcher began her famous final series of individual interviews with cabinet colleagues. My turn came towards the end of these, at 5.15 p.m. Nothing had happened in the last twenty-four hours to cancel my pledge of support given in the embassy courtyard. I simply advised her not to attack Michael Heseltine in a way which was bound to damage herself as well as the party.

I went to bed that night knowing next to nothing of the impact made in these interviews by other cabinet members such as Ken Clarke and John Gummer, who had told her she would lose. The noisy enthusiasm of the sycophants a month before at the party conference and of the parliamentary party was strong in my memory. I still thought she would stay, fight and narrowly win. Influenced by what had happened in Paris, including the amazement of all foreigners at our strange proceedings, I also believed (and still believe) that a prime minister of this country should lose office through a vote in the Commons, or in a General Election, but not by a putsch from within the governing party.

Next morning, Thursday 22 November, Peter Morrison rang me early to say that Margaret Thatcher was withdrawing. Judy then urged me to announce my candidature at once. She remembers my reply: 'But today is Margaret Thatcher's day; my campaign starts in earnest tomorrow.' I had made up my mind, but did not realise how fast things would move.

Margaret Thatcher announced the news to the Cabinet. The room filled with emotions so complicated that no one expressed any of them successfully. I do not believe that anyone round that cabinet table actively disliked Margaret Thatcher. Her strained manner showed a personal sadness which touched all of us. We knew that this really was a historic occasion, and some of us tried to reflect this in terms of thanks and farewell. Margaret herself cut short this unsuccessful scramble for suitable words, worried, I think, that it might lead to the shedding of tears, and not just her own. But there was also a suppressed sense of excitement. The moment the meeting was over a new chapter would open. Either Michael Heseltine or one of us would become Prime Minister. There would be other changes. Not one of us, except Margaret herself, could be sure what we would be doing in a fortnight's time. All we could know for certain was that the style of government with which we had been familiar for eleven years would be fundamentally different. There was some discussion that day among the whips about tossing a coin or reaching some private agreement between John Major and myself on one of us as a single candidate. This quickly fell through. We were both entitled to stand as alternatives to Michael Heseltine, and since we were close colleagues with similar views there should be no unseemly bitchiness between us. It was sensible for both names to go forward. I launched my effort on the Clive Steps outside the Foreign Office at noon.

This final phase of the Conservative leadership contest lasted only five days, from Thursday to Tuesday, though in retrospect it seems much longer. It must rank as one of the most friendly struggles of recent times. No great issues divided us. John Major and I communed together by telephone on most days. Although I did not then know Michael Heseltine as well as I do now, there was no hostility between us.

In my memory the campaign was at first conducted in many interviews with top journalists and television in the garden at Westwell or round the village duck pond. Although at that time only MPs had the vote in a leadership contest, they would obviously be swayed by press and public impressions of the candidates. On Monday 26 November my campaign moved to my room at the Commons, where I saw about thirty Members of Parliament individually. One of them, later a stalwart critic of mine on Europe, asked me for a job if I won. The others focused on the poll tax and Europe.

From the first day, 22 November, my tactical problem had been clear: 'John Major's bandwagon begins to roll.' The great bulk of those MPs who had supported Margaret Thatcher to the end were swinging to John Major. The speed and extent of this movement surprised me. Looking back I see three main reasons. First, Margaret Thatcher encouraged them to vote for John Major, believing wrongly that his views on policy and the nature of politics were virtually in-distinguishable from hers. I still do not understand how she came to think this, but out of a mixture of guilt and affection among MPs her advice had some effect. A dozen years later I found myself sitting next to Margaret Thatcher at dinner. After I had listened to her familiar complaints about John Major's premiership I ventured to ask her why she had urged everyone so strongly to vote for him. Lowering her voice so that the rest of the table could not hear, she replied, without any malice but in sheer forgetfulness: 'I will tell you in confidence; he was the best of a *very* poor bunch.' Second, my views on crime and punishment and Europe offended some, though not all, of our right-wingers, whereas John's were largely unknown. Third, he seemed to them a pleasant and talented candidate, more likely than me to win for the Conservatives a fourth term of office at the next election, which had to be held within two years.

It was on this last point of electability that I made the main mistake of my short campaign. The press were anxious to create some excitement in a contest which for them had gone flat with the disappearance of Margaret Thatcher. They fastened on the thought that I was an out-of-date sort of candidate – a patrician, upper class, a toff. Some of John Major's helpers may have fanned this flame. It threatened to burn my campaign badly. I reacted with flustered denial. I drew on the facts of my early life and background. Everyone close to me knew that I was far from patrician, that my suits were made in Swindon rather than Savile Row. In vain I showed them my rolling acres, all ten of them. In vain I mentioned my scholarship. In vain I explained that in my boyhood my father had been a tenant farmer with no capital, that my brothers and I earned pocket money planting potatoes and harvesting flax. These statements, though true, made things worse. It looked as if I were pleading a humble, poverty-stricken background. How could that be reconciled with the fact that I was an Old Etonian, and the son of a peer; in short, a toff? A few commentators, in particular Simon Jenkins in *The Times*, got it right. I came not from a patrician background but from the traditional professional middle class. My tastes and instincts were those of Barsetshire, not the Dukeries. I had been lucky in my family, my upbringing and my education, but that did not make me a toff. Towards the end I got the argument right myself by asking in public what the hell this was all about; I was standing for the leadership of the Tory Party, not some demented Marxist outfit. It would have been better to take that line, and only that line, from the outset.

Given the flow of the right wing of the party to John Major, my only hope was to attract some of those who on the first ballot had voted for Michael Heseltine. They included old friends of mine like Ian Gilmour and Dennis Walters. Most of these had long shared with Michael Heseltine strong disapproval of Margaret Thatcher. By contrast I had served in her Government and supported her up to the moment when the trapdoor opened beneath her. Michael Heseltine had spent four years in the wilderness, or at least roaming the country from one melon and chicken supper to another. It was natural that they should stick to him. Moreover, they were far from certain that my heart was really in the struggle. In this they were not alone. I was not sure how to deal with the suspicion of half-heartedness. It was true that I had not lain awake at night for years in advance plotting and pining for this hour. It was also true that later when the hour had passed without success I lost no sleep in cursing my failure. But during the competition itself I was entirely committed to my own cause. I enjoyed those odd, slightly comical days (though Judy says they felt like hell) and hoped they would lead to triumph. I repeated to myself the argument with which his private secretary urged Lord Melbourne to become Prime Minister against His Lordship's view that it was likely to be a bore. 'Why damn it, such a position never was occupied by any Greek or Roman and if it only lasts two months, it is well worth while to have been Prime Minister of England.' 'By God, that's true,' said Melbourne. Although not quite so self-evident as in 1834, the remark was still true enough. None of the three candidates ranted and raved during the contest, but I was thought to be particularly cool, even detached. I think that on a good day I was as strong a communicator as the others. For some years afterwards my individual poll ratings, for what they are worth, were regularly the highest of any minister. But I was never apt at putting together strong emotions and throwing them at the public. I had no intention of leasing from some public relations firm a hot new personal style for the purpose of becoming Prime Minister. Anyway, I don't think it would have worked.

If the number of my supporters stubbornly refused to grow, I was happy with the strong team around me. It was good to win the approval of senior colleagues like Tom King, Patrick Mayhew and Peter Brooke. Also with me day by day was a group of younger politicians, working enthusiastically and I hope enjoying themselves in the process. I could not have hoped for a more lively or ingenious crew than the two Pattens, Tristan Garel-Jones, William Waldegrave, Tim Yeo and Edward Bickham. I borrowed some of their energy; the mistakes were mine. They would have been the nucleus of a good Government. I still enjoy their company and am proud that they once wanted that Government to be led by me.

The end came without surprise, disappointing but without disgrace. The final count was: John Major, 185; Michael Heseltine, 131; Douglas Hurd, 56. Technically there could have been a further ballot, but the political message was clear. Both Michael Heseltine and I at once rallied behind John Major. I dashed across the Foreign Office to the Clive Steps where I had begun my campaign and announced that it was over.

Next day the new Prime Minister discussed his Cabinet with me. I then tried to make a witty speech collecting the *Spectator* award as Parliamentarian of the Year, made a Commons statement on the Gulf and saw *The Barber of Seville* at Covent Garden. Within hours I was on the Concorde to New York. The world had not stood still for our leadership campaign. Jim Baker and I had agreed on the telephone the text of the draft Security Council resolution authorising the use of force if necessary against Iraq. On Thursday 29 November we carried the resolution in the Council by 12 votes to 2 with 1 abstention (China). There was no Soviet veto; it was a triumph for the leadership of Jim Baker.

Would I have made a good prime minister? Who can tell? I would have enjoyed it more than John Major did. I would have chosen rather different ministers, promoting the team just mentioned, but at once trying to reach a personal working relationship with the ablest right-wingers, notably Michael Howard, Peter Lilley and Michael Portillo. Whether this would have worked, I cannot be sure. I would have set myself the same main aims as did John Major, in particular to put Britain back at the heart of European discussions and to recreate a nation 'at ease with itself', on the lines I had sketched as Home Secretary. What followed

gaggle of European foreign ministers and, standing in front of me, President of the
European Commission Jacques Delors.

MODS AND ROCKERS

to battle with John Major. Riddell's take on the Conservative Party Conference, Brighton,
October 1992, and the Maastricht Bill.

Talking to America: with George Bush and James Baker. (*White House*)

ith Bosnian President Izetbegovic in Sarajevo, July 1992. Behind us, Keith Low and
ancis Cornish looking anxious.

aiting for the Sultan of Brunei: Home Secretary, Foreign Secretary and Prime Minister at
ictoria Station, October 1992. Fingers crossed. (*Newspaper Publishing*)

Constituency days: the new parliamentary candidate for Mid-Oxfordshire at a Conservative rally at Shotover, 1973. The Prime Minister smiles, but is the platform with him? (*Oxford Mail*)

May I rely on your support? Campaigning for the 1992 General Election in Great Tew.

Still at his post . . . Richard Gozney, my private secretary, about midnight in Holyrood Palace at the European Summit, December 1992.

My Foreign Office team in June 1993 on the ramparts of Luxembourg: Christopher Prentice, Robert Culshaw, John Kerr, Francis Cornish, myself and John Sawers. (Half hidden at the back is Detective Rick Clark.)

Our last diplomatic banquet, in the Durbar Court, June 1995, with Tim Earle and Brian Burrows of Government Hospitality just before the off. And Garland's cartoon for the menu cover.

...evening, Kent, the official residence of Foreign Secretaries. (*Anthony Osmond-Evans*)

Philip and Jessica at Chevening, 1990.

Nick, Alexander and Tom at the christening of my first grandson, Max, May 1991.

Our home at Westwell.

Judy on her way back from leukaemia in the garden at Westwell, spring 1999. *(Mail on Sunday)*

would have depended mainly on events but partly on the style of the premiership. Having watched at close quarters three prime ministers – Ted Heath, Margaret Thatcher and John Major – I know that I would have tried to do the job quite differently from all three. I admired them, but none of their styles would have suited me.

The first chapter of my novel *Image in the Water* describes the memorial service in Westminster Abbey of Simon Russell, Prime Minister. Reflecting as part of Fauré's requiem is sung, a cabinet minister in the congregation remembers Russell answering a question about the premiership at a press conference:

> Being Prime Minister is not a matter of climbing mountains and planting silly little flags marked Russell on the summit. It is more like navigating a river in a clumsy boat full of passengers, a winding river with sandbanks, white water, rocks, even cataracts at some points, and tidal towards the end. Your aim is to convey your passengers safely to their destination. They are eating, drinking, playing computer games, only occasionally sparing you a glance or a thought. They blame you for the weather as well as for the rubbery soufflé at lunch. Your only reward is the satisfaction of eventually steering their ship safely into harbour. Then you can apply to the company for another voyage, which is what we are doing in this General Election.

This I believe.

Another minister in the congregation remembers something that Russell had said:

> Simon Russell, whom he had much respected, had once passed on to him what he had described as the most closely guarded secret of the premiership, that it was not really hard work. The Prime Minister did not face each day the compulsory grind of departmental business. The fixed duties of the office by no means filled the week. Except at times of national crisis there were many hours for the Prime Minister to dispose of as he or she wished. Of course, prime ministers themselves always disputed this. They were likely to be persons of great energy. Not since Baldwin resigned in 1937 had Britain had a really lazy prime minister. The others had filled the time by constant and often unnecessary intervention in the affairs of departments, then complained of overwork. Prime-ministerial time, Russell had argued, should be better employed in leisurely strategic thought, touring the country to gain first-hand impressions, and consulting wise opinion from outside politics.

This last statement is a bit exaggerated, but has a kernel of truth. This country would be better governed if prime ministers did their best to hold themselves back. They do not need to catch every headline or christen every meeting they hold as a summit. At first they might lose out in terms of personal prominence and effectiveness. In time the country might feel more at ease, knowing that something which could be valuable in an emergency – namely, the full force of the Prime Minister's authority – was better kept in reserve, instead of being paraded before them for their daily applause.

24

DESERT STORM, A NEW PRIME MINISTER AND EUROPE

The change of Prime Minister made no difference to our policy as we moved towards war. John Major was as resolute as Margaret Thatcher about the need to free Kuwait. On 27 December I joined him to discuss the Gulf during his first weekend as Prime Minister at Chequers. By then I felt that the Americans wanted a war, whereas I still hoped that Saddam Hussein might be induced to withdraw without one. 'But this is academic since we agree that if SH pulls out he cannot be attacked, and if he stays he must be.'

A month earlier we had secured the planned Security Council resolution authorising the use of force if necessary. Jim Baker followed up with a meeting in Geneva with Saddam Hussein's representative, the portly, unscrupulous Tariq Aziz. Baker did not hope for any success with this, but it was important to show that every reasonable effort had been made to get Saddam Hussein out of Kuwait by peaceful means. Baker kept in close touch with me during January. I managed to clear the path for him by heading off a separate European initiative, and then something similar from France. Hans Van den Broek, the Dutch Foreign Minister and a strong Atlanticist, was a powerful ally in this. He and I agreed that American policy was in essence reasonable, and that only Saddam Hussein would benefit if every post brought a new initiative and every plane to Baghdad a new well-meaning emissary.

At home the new Prime Minister and I knew we must do our utmost to keep the Opposition on board. It was inevitable, perhaps in a democracy even right, that there should be individuals in all parts of the Commons who questioned and criticised the line we were taking. But if

British servicemen were to risk their lives in action they needed to know that the great mass of parliamentary and public opinion supported what they were being asked to do. This involved several private meetings with the Shadow Foreign Secretary, for example about the timing and handling of Commons debates. Gerald Kaufman, usually waspish and aggressive in debates on other matters, kept a strong sense of proportion on anything to do with the Gulf, respected my confidences to him as a privy councillor, and did his best to help.

My earlier visits up and down the Arab world over the previous ten years proved their worth in these first few weeks of 1991. None of us managed to persuade King Hussein of Jordan to change his refusal to join the coalition of the willing which we had built against Iraq. I had another go with him in Amman in January. First I tackled his brother Crown Prince Hassan, along with the new Foreign Minister, Taher al-Masri,

> in camel coat like them all, pleasant Palestinian. Hassan a bit sharp and scores debating points of low value along with real problems of oil and refugees if there is war. Throughout that day waiting on news of UN Secretary-General in Baghdad. Talk then walk to lunch with HM. As ever amazingly courteous but unmoved – willing to talk about the rosy future, hardly about the crisis. He and his brother have reversed roles, the King the dreamer, the C.P. [Crown Prince] the realist.

But we kept the Jordanians from committing themselves the wrong way even if we could not enlist them as an ally.

The Saudis needed constant encouragement and reassurance. I was in Riyadh on 10 February. King Fahd spoke to me for eighty minutes without stopping. I recorded a genuine feeling from this meeting that we were in the same trench, though the Saudis worried about the consequences of a war launched from their soil by mainly American troops against another Arab nation.

A sub-theme of my foreign visits at this time could have become embarrassing. Long gone was the British tradition of financing our allies in time of war. In 1991 we expected well-to-do friends to finance us, and it became part of the job of the Foreign Secretary to make this clear. It seemed best not to beat about the bush. I begged my way round the world and the results were surprisingly good. On 30 January in Bonn Chancellor Kohl was in generous mood. 'I have never known him so energetic, beaming, ebullient. Very friendly to J.M. [John Major] and me. Anxious to work together on Turkey, party unity in Europe. Gives me DM800 million and asks if it is enough. I find him and his opinions comfortable.' At the meeting with King Fahd already mentioned he too promised obliquely to help. He was not the sort of man to mention figures in an audience chamber filled with princes, but the figures came right. During the same visit, on 9 February I besieged the Sheraton Hotel in Taif where the exiled Kuwaiti court dragged out a melancholy existence surrounded by jagged hills and goats. 'The Ruler as usual slight and hunted. He gives me £600 million just like that.'

Air attacks on Iraq had begun on 17 January. The Gulf Committee of Ministers gathered regularly at Number Ten. During its meeting on 7 February I suddenly noticed that there was no glass in the two sets of windows in the Cabinet Room fronting the garden. It was a mild day and I had felt no cold, but thought it odd that John Major should have held our meeting there when reglazing was obviously in progress. There was time for this thought to form in my mind before we heard the crump of the IRA mortar shell which had landed in the garden a few yards away. Somehow a lorry had managed to park in Whitehall outside the Banqueting House, from which the IRA had fired – the same tactic as had destroyed the Newry police station during my time in Northern Ireland. There was a small flurry of ministers for a minute or two. I can remember no words of either heroism or panic. No one struck an attitude. We just wanted to get back to normality as soon as possible. We adjourned to the nearby Cabinet Office Room, from which the management of the Iranian Embassy siege had been conducted, and our meeting resumed in good order.

The ground attack on Iraq began on Sunday morning, 24 February. We were at Chevening, the aconites bright round the edge of the lawn. We went to church, and during an inadequate service I thought about the war. 'Soothed by the sense, from the war memorial and hymns, and names of servicemen from the parish, that this is a sound tradition . . . no role for me in these next warrior days.'

The warrior days were few. On 27 February after a one-day visit to Portugal, I flew to Washington, and walked in cold sunshine on Roosevelt Island with my old friend Antony Acland, now British Ambassador. In the early afternoon I was at the White House, which was hosting an informal gathering of the ruling group of the administration – the President, Vice-President Don Quayle, Jim Baker, Brent Scowcroft, the President's security adviser, Secretary of Defense Dick Cheney and Colin Powell, the Chief of Defense Staff. Photographers were mobilised to appear in waves; each heard and snapped the President thanking me for the unstinting help he was receiving from Britain. The afternoon then took what was for me an unexpected course. The great men discussed the war informally in a way unlikely to happen in Britain in the presence of an outsider, even an outsider representing a close friend. The President was told that the military news was excellent: the defeated Iraqis were pulling out of Kuwait, pounded by Allied bombers as they headed for Iraq through the Mitla Pass. President Bush heard that the American pilots were not enjoying what they called a turkey shoot, massacring men on the ground who put up no resistance. The President said more than once that he was anxious to avoid butchery. The war was won; the question was whether we should end it that day or tomorrow. I said that we British were ready for another day or two of operations. Colin Powell reported that the Allied Commander-in-Chief, General Schwarzkopf, judged that our objectives had been achieved, and was willing to stop on either day. No one expressed a contrary opinion. The discussion ended inconclusively. Later that same day Jim Baker told me that after I had left the Americans decided on an immediate ceasefire, and the President had telephoned John Major and President Mitterrand to this effect. I slept poorly in the plane home that night, changed into a clean shirt at Heathrow, and drove straight to Number Ten. I found that the Ministry of Defence and the Prime Minister's security adviser, Percy Cradock, were put out by the speed of the ceasefire, having expected another day of war during which our bombers could have knocked out more Iraqi tanks and crippled the Republican Guard, the mainstay of Saddam Hussein's regime.

But that was the extent of disagreement. No one either in the White House on the 27th or in Number Ten and Whitehall before or afterwards contemplated driving on to Baghdad and deposing Saddam Hussein. In the West we hoped and expected that the ruin of his policy in Kuwait would lead to his downfall. And not only in the West; one Arab leader emphasised to me that he hoped Saddam Hussein would end up either dead or banished. But no one in a position of serious authority argued at that time that we should change the purpose of the war once we had won it, and use our strength for an objective different from the one for which it had been gathered.

There is a crucial point here. Some years later I heard President Bush argue it before an interviewer in Texas. 'With whose husband, brother, boyfriend', he asked, 'was I supposed to push on to Baghdad?' Our troops would probably have had to stay there for years to sustain whatever Iraqi Government we had put together. The President had in effect made a contract with the US Congress and the American people to risk American lives so that a straightforward act of international aggression should not stand. He would have broken that contract at the last minute if he had added a new aim, a new obligation and a new risk. The same was true within Britain, in Europe and in the Middle East. The coalition of the willing had been put together easily and fast because of its simple purpose – to reverse the aggression against Kuwait. If we had changed the purpose the coalition would have dissolved. We could not have secured a new Security Council resolution to that effect. Without such a resolution the British Government would have lost the support of the Labour Party and broken the national unity which was crucial for the morale of our troops. No one doubted Saddam Hussein was a wicked man who had done terrible things to his own people and to others. It would be better if he went. We had no illusions about him and no secret desire to sustain him. But we were not going to war to rid the world of an evil ruler. We were acting very specifically to reverse an act of aggression. Only professors of hindsight, a numerous band in this case, can argue the opposite case. For us at the time enlarging the purpose of the war was not an option.

I liked and honoured President George Bush Sr in all my dealings with him. He was straightforward throughout the Gulf crisis. He gave the world the measured, firm and reasonable American leadership which we need on such occasions and to which we can readily respond.

By this time my colleagues and I in the Government were getting used to our own style of leadership. The arrival of John Major at Number Ten in November 1990 brought a change of style rather than of policies. The poll tax began its inevitable slide towards the rubbish bin, but otherwise we continued, because we believed in, the Conservative policies of the last ten years. However, we used a different tone of voice.

The difference of style in the Cabinet was so striking that Chris Patten described it as liberation. We had become used, as I have described, to a cabinet system in which decisions revolved round the will of the Prime Minister. That will could be shaped, even drastically altered, in discussion with colleagues, usually outside the Cabinet Room. Most of us had learned how to use the shaping tools at our disposal. Our success in government had depended in large part on our success with the Prime Minister.

The new Prime Minister deliberately withdrew from this dominant position. No longer did any serious discussion in the Cabinet begin with a statement of the Prime Minister's views. John Major usually reserved himself for the summing up, before which he took trouble to ensure that all significant voices round the table had been heard. Margaret Thatcher had begun with the assumption that no reasonable person could disagree with her. More precisely, that was the assumption with which she found it useful to start a discussion, even when she knew it would prove inaccurate. The assumption provided her with the high ground in a discussion. John Major preferred to manoeuvre on the plains. Of course, the new Prime Minister held personal views on most subjects, even if not so absolutely as his predecessor. But he preferred not to overawe opposition with the assumption that it could not exist. Instead he lured it out into the open, exposed it to criticism, and thus weakened it so that with luck it could be finally disposed of in his summing up. For this he needed allies and a plan. For example, he might ask me as part of his choreography in advance of a cabinet meeting to make a particular point or put a specific question on domestic policy. I usually agreed, unless my ignorance of the point at issue would make it ludicrous to intervene.

For me there was a greater change. I found myself for the first time intimate with the inner thoughts of a prime minister. True, I had been close to the heart of Ted Heath's thinking on many matters, but it was not in his nature to pour out his personal anxieties to anyone. Although I developed an effective working relationship with Margaret Thatcher, I was not, and did not seek to be, one of her intimates. Before the autumn of 1990 I had come to know John Major reasonably well, and at intervals we had talked frankly together. Once he had defeated me for the premiership I received day by day a flow of confidences from him on all subjects, personal and political. These usually reflected anxiety, and sometimes despair on whatever he thought lay ahead of him. I was not alone in this. I quickly learned that several others were trusted in the same way.

It is not difficult to decide how to handle John Major's confidences in this book. They were given to me precisely as confidences. They relate to people still alive and active, notably himself. It would be wrong to set them out week by week as they poured in on me. Even if that were not so, they would mislead the historian, just as they misled at the time those who caught a glimpse, but only a glimpse, of the way he ran the premiership. John Major was in the habit of talking, even to people he did not know well, in terms of pessimism, of self-doubt, of complaint against the malignity of his enemies, of his colleagues or of the fates in general. Some took this as proof of his inadequacy. Rather, as I learned, it was a technique, a mechanism of management by means of overflow. I do not mean that what he confessed to me was bogus or invented. His anxieties were real, but only part of the whole. He relished the job at the same time as he complained about it. More than that, behind the parade of complaints I learned to recognise an essential integrity and confidence in his own ability to handle matters. In some foreign matters where he and I worked hour by hour, side by side together, I often found him more patient and more competent than I would have been in his chair. Once or twice, for instance over intervention to help the Kurds in 1991, I found something extra – a generous imaginativeness based on firm principle – which carried him beyond my own judgement into decisions which turned out to be correct.

Quite often I disagreed with John Major. To a surprising extent, we differed on personalities. There were a few friends of mine with whom he found himself at war. There were others distrusted by me who captivated him. His reaction to the media was different to mine. He was easily upset by small personal stories, particularly if they affected his family as well as himself. He used to telephone me at seven in the morning about some tawdry piece in a tabloid, which I had not read and would probably never have read if he had not rung.

By 1990 I had come to the conclusion that a number of worthwhile journalists were genuinely interested in the truth of a subject; to them it was sensible to speak often and openly. There were many more, right across the spectrum, who were either determined in hostility or else ruthless in search of a story true or false. No one in this second group would be interested in reporting that the Prime Minister or Foreign Secretary was getting it right, so there was no point in bothering with them. I therefore feigned a calm which I did not always feel in the face of a hostile press. I still think this is the best available tactic. On balance over my political career I had a fair run, phases of unfair criticism being matched by times of exaggerated praise. By contrast, John Major felt that the whole media owed him a fair hearing. When denied this, he practised techniques of complaint, of indiscretion and of flattery which were on the whole unsuccessful. Although I had disliked several of the absolute aspects of Margaret Thatcher's reign, I felt that John Major could have used the authority of his office more often than he did to reach the British people over the heads of the media.

These were differences which he and I thrashed out in dozens, perhaps hundreds, of conversations held all over the world between November 1990 and July 1995. I enjoyed the feeling that he trusted me, even though this had its inconveniences. Like all prime ministers, he had only a hazy idea of where his colleagues were likely to be, or in which time zone they currently resided. One Sunday morning I was sitting relaxed in a wooden chalet by a remote lake in Quebec Province admiring the autumn brilliance of the maples. The news came that the Prime Minister wished urgently to speak to me. There was no telephone in the chalet. My Canadian host and my private secretary, Richard Gozney, assumed a crisis, and bustled to solve the technical problems. Eventually, after much effort and ingenuity on their part, I was led up through the woods to an isolated rock in a clearing overlooking the lake. Contact was triumphantly established by radio telephone, amid some buzzing and clicking, with the ever-efficient Downing Street exchange. It turned out that the Prime Minister wished to chat inconsequently about the London morning papers.

I enjoyed John Major's company and supported what he was trying to do. I tried throughout his premiership to help and sustain him. Out of our different backgrounds he and I believed in the same concept of calm, generous-minded Conservatism which could be accepted by a nation at ease with itself. Such tactical disagreements as I had with him were by comparison insignificant.

This was certainly true of European policy. European ministers throughout 1991 were preparing the new draft treaty which it had been agreed should be submitted to the summit of presidents and prime ministers at Maastricht in December. These negotiations have often been described in detail which I need not repeat. Here again our partners found a change in British style, rather than substance. In particular John Major and Helmut Kohl liked each other so there was no longer a gap in relations with Germany at the highest level. But our main aim remained the same in 1991 as it had been in 1990: we were not willing to commit Britain to join a single European currency. In practice there was no way in which we could prevent others going ahead if they so desired. We wanted to see progress in establishing a common European voice in foreign affairs, but not at the price of allowing that voice to be shaped by majority voting as opposed to unanimity.

At the heart of the negotiations lay the fundamental question how the EU* should grow. The Monnet doctrine still held sway among the high priests of Europe. Jean Monnet's long and successful experience as a practical administrator had led him to believe that gradually, sector by sector, the nations of Europe should transfer power to supranational European institutions – coal and steel first, then nuclear energy, then the common market, then the single market, next the single currency. We would, he thought, move to the harmonisation of taxation and no doubt welfare, pensions and the rest, until we had created what he was not afraid to call a United States of Europe. Jean Monnet saw Britain as an important member of this enterprise. Only in this way could Europeans prevent the disasters and seize the opportunities which his analysis clearly revealed.

More than half the European ministers with whom I negotiated in 1991 still held to this doctrine, and others who did not really believe it used the rhetoric associated with it. The French, for example, who disliked the European Commission and had no intention of giving up either their national nuclear deterrent or their permanent membership of the UN Security Council, were adept at clothing their aims in the familiar phrases of European integration. No such option was open to

---

*From this time on it is correct and convenient to refer to the European Union in place of the European Economic Community.

me, and anyway I believed that the Monnet doctrine had just about run its course. The supranational institutions of the EU had in some areas justified the confidence which governments, including Margaret Thatcher's, had placed in them. For example, it made practical sense for the European Commission to negotiate on behalf of us all in international trade negotiations, thus achieving through our unity a rough parity of power with the US or Japan. But in other areas the Commission was overreaching itself with excessive interference and regulations. Speaking in Brussels in November 1991, I coined a phrase which others have often repeated, criticising the Commission for 'inserting itself into the nooks and crannies of everyday life'. Our aim was to prevent European leaders from being presented at Maastricht with a draft treaty which simply transferred a fresh bloc of policy-making to the supranational institutions as if this were still the only way in which the EU could progress.

During these meetings I came to know and like the President of the European Commission, Jacques Delors. I disagreed with him widely but respected the painstaking clarity of his thinking. It was a pleasure at the end of a ragged discussion of some abstruse financial subject among European ministers to listen to Jacques Delors, sometimes impatient, usually with a flash of wit, as he shepherded Europe towards an agreement. My note of a private dinner he gave me in Brussels in September 1991 gives the flavour of our meetings.

> He speaks in English, which is a brake, but it is enjoyable – in fact I enjoy the company of an honest highly intelligent man. His analysis of USSR even more sceptical than ours. On IGCs [the inter-governmental conferences preparing the new draft treaty] we differ strongly on majority voting in foreign policy, which I know to be wrong – and to some extent about our let out of EMU, and our handling of Dutch text. He says he has not seen Mitterrand since July, and deplores his ambiguities.

The EMU reference is to the negotiation being conducted for us by Norman Lamont, John Major's choice as Chancellor of the Exchequer. We were aiming at the opt-out eventually achieved by which the single European currency went ahead, but was not binding on Britain unless we so decided. The reference to the Dutch text was more immediately relevant to me. The Dutch, who held the EU presidency during these critical six months, were impatient with long meetings and slow progress. They feared that the British were entangling everyone else in compromise and that the purity of the process of European integration was being lost. The day after my dinner with Delors, abandoning the unfinished text on the table, the Dutch put forward a new proposal on political union which in a straightforward way would transfer substantial power to the supranational centre. 'We all fall on the new Dutch text. I can wait till the Danes, Luxembourgers, Italians have done their work. Even Delors and Genscher desert poor Hans, who reacts stubbornly, but in the end good humouredly to defeat 10–2.'

I liked Hans Van den Broek, the Dutch Foreign Minister. We disagreed on this matter and later on Yugoslavia, but he had given me powerful help over Iraq earlier in the year. The evolving European political system, like the Westminster system, enables political disagreements to coexist with private goodwill because they all happen within a shared framework. Hans Van den Broek's English education enabled him to play cricket with my children on the lawn at Chevening.

After his setback in Brussels, Van den Broek entertained his European colleagues in a castle near Utrecht. By this time as a diversionary tactic, we had concocted an Anglo-Italian paper on defence with the help of their Foreign Minister, Gianni di Michelis – a large, long-haired Socialist, the acknowledged expert and author on the subject of Italian discos. Gianni de Michelis was known for his intelligent but long-winded interventions in our discussions, which usually began with the phrase 'Molto brevemente . . .'. We discussed the Anglo-Italian paper in the castle, after our French colleague Roland Dumas had allowed his old-fashioned bath to overflow, soaking down into the Dutch bedroom below. (If this book is ever to end, I must not wander too far down the infinite paths of diplomatic gossip.)

Meanwhile, at home the Prime Minister and I were trying to build some British self-confidence on European matters. Margaret Thatcher, who had never lacked such self-confidence herself, was already giving out the information that her successor (whom she had helped to select) was bound to lack it. At the party conference in Blackpool in October 1991 I tried to counter this: 'We are grown-ups in the Community now, no longer frightened by shadows on the wall. We are well able to take care of ourselves and promote Britain's interests.' I underestimated the power of the shadows on the wall.

But the party conference went well, as did the preparation at Westminster and in the country for Maastricht. By now I had the ingenious and entertaining help at the Foreign Office of Tristan Garel-Jones as Minister of State for Europe. He and I began to sketch the concept of Europe as a temple, not a tree. Under the old Monnet doctrine Europe would grow slowly like a tree, with a single central trunk and many branches. We saw the new EU rather as three pillars: one supranational, but the other two (foreign affairs, and home affairs and justice) intergovernmental. These would be based essentially on agreement between nation states, with no monopoly of initiative for the European Commission, and no jurisdiction for the European Court. Far from fading away, the nation states would remain the essential sources of authority in most sectors of European cooperation. In addition, the treaty would lay down, in what was called the 'subsidiarity clause', put together by the Germans and ourselves, that we should only act collectively as Europeans where action at a national level would not meet the need. This was heresy to the high priests of the old doctrine, but this heresy was for the first time included in the Treaty of Maastricht and has shaped the course of Europe ever since.

The Prime Minister became increasingly anxious about the prospects. He was determined not to open himself to any later accusation of deception. The Cabinet was taken carefully through the negotiating position. So, to an unprecedented extent, was the House of Commons, in a two-day debate beginning on 20 November. I called on Margaret Thatcher in her office on the first morning of the debate: 'faintly chaotic, but a good atmosphere. She is in the midst of [preparing] her speech and we talk entirely about the EU. She will vote for the Govt tomorrow, but mobilise huge forces against us after Maastricht if we sin.' The Prime Minister opened the debate on that first day ('Very clear, detailed, unexciting, but never loses the House and succeeds. Kinnock [Leader of the Opposition] flounders and we pour salvoes into a stricken vessel'). I led on the second day. By this time Margaret Thatcher had argued in public the need for a referendum on the outcome of the conference. Privately John Major was already flirting with the idea of a referendum on the single currency. He failed to carry colleagues on this at the cabinet meeting of 21 November, so nothing could be said in the debate. I was not at that stage persuaded by his argument for a referendum and felt that my own speech and the debate as a whole went pretty well without this dangerous ornament.

A week before Maastricht, John Major and I spent three hours in the Hague with the Dutch Prime Minister, Ruud Lubbers, who would chair the summit. The preparatory work was almost complete. Thanks to the earlier defeat of the Dutch centralising draft, the texts on the political part of the treaty were not too bad, though there were rhetorical phrases which would cause trouble later. On the economic side, it looked as if Norman Lamont had just about succeeded in negotiating with his colleagues the principle of a British opt-out from the single currency, though its precise terms were unknown. Late in the day a new difficulty had arisen. Our European partners were determined to include a social chapter in the treaty which would provide a legal basis for Union legislation on a wide range of labour and welfare measures. Michael

Howard, as Secretary of State for Employment, was the responsible cabinet minister in London. There was no question of him acquiescing in the text as it stood. I sympathised with him. Either the chapter had to be drastically amended or we had somehow to negotiate a second British opt-out. At our meeting in the Hague, 'Lubbers friendly and Jesuitical [that had been his education] probing our final position. Moves on the Social Chapter. Increasingly our isolation appears, but that can't be helped.'

And so finally to Maastricht itself. A mountain of documents had been prepared in all Union languages. We foreign ministers and our colleagues the finance ministers thought that we had worked hard in the preceding months. But the main burden had fallen on officials, and in our case particularly on John Kerr, British Ambassador to the EU. He appeared to enjoy every minute of this pilgrimage, and with the help of his wife Elizabeth proved amazingly robust under the strain. For the next four years John Kerr was never far from the centre of my life. I sometimes felt that he was himself the centre of British government. Schooled in the Treasury and the Foreign Office, he knew the ways of both British and European bureaucrats. Hardly an important move was made or appointment proposed without John Kerr either being its author or knowing its provenance and likely outcome. John Major christened him Machiavelli. In both the literal and metaphorical sense he quickly filled any room he entered with smoke. He did not like problems to be simple, but none was so intricate that his ingenuity could not find a solution. His hinterland of kindness and wit ranging far beyond his job made him a prized companion at all hours of day and night. He had no personal vanity, boasting only that his small stature made it possible for him to advise the Prime Minister from a crouching position concealed by the conference table, during the crucial moments of some summit discussion at which only heads of government were supposed to be present.

Sunday 8 December 1991 was a day of sunny frost at Westwell. I read the Gospel at Holy Communion, took a long walk with Jessica on her pony, signed Christmas cards, and read Owen Chadwick on the Church in the nineteenth century. After lunch I was driven to Heathrow and flew to Maastricht with John Major and Norman Lamont. None of us had the slightest idea whether the summit would succeed. John Major said he was modestly pessimistic; but that was his style.

We stayed in a brand-new hotel, sparse but adequate. On the first day of the conference the presidents and prime ministers staked out positions. Lubbers was excellent in the chair, and with John Major's help prevented any part of the discussion of the draft treaty from getting out of hand. It was a day of sighting shots; the hand-to-hand engagements were for the morrow. That night I thought everything was still in the balance, and might fail.

The hotel breakfast next day was grisly, almost as rough as the Prime Minister's mood as the British delegation ate together. He talked of the conference breaking down. But once the meeting began and he was in harness again John Major pulled steadily for agreement all day, sustained by Norman Lamont and myself. I cleared up the difficult points on foreign affairs and defence, and Norman reached agreement on the British opt-out from the single currency. The danger was of breakdown on the Social Chapter. I was present at a long conversation between the Prime Minister and Lubbers. Later, without colleagues, he toiled over the ground with Lubbers and Kohl. We could not accept the Social Chapter as drafted. Our partners could not accept our much diluted alternative text. Neither we nor they wanted a second British opt-out. Never was ingenuity more necessary among weary men. Lubbers met the moment with a device by which our partners would agree the Social Chapter among themselves without Britain being involved at all. Throughout the Dutch Prime Minister was shrewd, infinitely patient and courteous.

That was the turning point, but not the end. Back at the main conference table it fell to me to conduct a series of final bitter arguments about relatively minor points in the text which we wanted changed. The British, being better briefed on detail than most other delegations, were notorious for this kind of nit-picking. That evening Kohl and Mitterrand, anxious for their beds, were particularly irritated with me. But perseverance paid off, and we ended about 1 a.m. with a defensible text. The Prime Minister held a press conference and we were in bed by two-thirty. My dreams were dominated by the apparition of Lubbers talking fast and low in Dutch.

In diplomacy it is almost always a mistake to describe a negotiating success as a triumph. The words 'game, set and match' used by John Major's spokesman after Maastricht did much more harm than good. Negotiation, unlike tennis, is about compromise. Absolute phrases can antagonise your negotiating partners abroad without convincing your critics at home. The preparatory work by Norman Lamont and myself, guided by John Kerr, had gone reasonably well. But in Europe one can never tell what will happen when such work moves to the great ones at the top table. They tend to know less of the merits of each question and worry more about its politics. Some of these great ones, I shudder to recall, have small compunction in scorning the work of their own ministers. At Maastricht one relatively new issue, the Social Chapter, had not been prepared in any detail. But as it turned out the Prime Minister used his good humour, his modest manner and his grasp of detail to achieve a remarkable result for us all at Maastricht.

There was no great European activity in the first six months of 1992. We were preoccupied with preparing and winning our fourth consecutive General Election victory. In February I was one of those in the Cabinet who cast doubt on the magic of a cut in income tax as an election winner. I did not agree that tax was as decisive an issue as most commentators believed. I campaigned hard for the party, sailed with our candidate round Aberdeen harbour, canvassed for a pessimistic Chris Patten in Bath, was snubbed in the market square of Nottingham by a socialist seller of daffodils, and advised the Prime Minister, this time unnecessarily, to be more authoritative in manner. I was helped throughout by Edward Bickham, shrewd and efficient as ever. It seemed to rain most of the time, and the polls were adverse. In West Oxfordshire I kept up the tradition of town and village meetings, and found plenty of friendliness under the umbrellas. I constantly had in mind the precedent of June 1970 when we had won against all perceived odds. Nevertheless, we seemed likely to lose. I prepared to hand over the Foreign Office and No. 1 Carlton Gardens to Gerald Kaufman.

As I mentioned earlier, the Sultan of Oman had given me a very large jar of lemon perfume concocted by himself. Since it was strong, I used only a tiny dab as aftershave each day. I had worked out a superstition that I would shave in the bathroom at Carlton Gardens until the Sultan's lemon essence ran out; then I would have to leave. There was still an inch or two at the bottom of the Sultan's jar in April 1992. That was just about the only good omen. By the 7th, 'This vexing campaign nears its end. Like my army career I find it both disagreeable and irresistible, longing for it to be over, yet regretting its passing.'

After the usual pastoral round of villages on polling day, 9 April, I went to the count in the Witney Sports Centre. From the radio I learned that we had lost Cheltenham and Bath, but surprisingly held the seat of Basildon in Essex which had become a sort of token because of the attention paid by social analysts to what they called 'Essex man': the typical new Tory voter who had ensured our success through the 1980s. 'Handfuls rather than regiments of casualties. The experts, marvellously confounded, begin to shift their estimates towards a working majority, which we amazingly achieved. My own result 2.15 a.m. – majority up from 18,000 – 22,500. Then we drove to London and Central Office. Greet Chris Patten who has been brave and stylish in defeat [his in Bath]/victory [his and ours in Britain]. Then PM arrives fr. Huntingdon, tired, but of course buoyed up, and performs well.'

A few days later I took my family as our tradition required to the Old

Berkshire point-to-point on Lockinge Down, it being Easter Monday. 'For once a perfect spring day. White baps and cheese and ale at back of Range Rover on grass. Walk the course after first race. P[hilip] and I win 70p on favourite later. Sun gleaming on massed cars of triumphant Tory England. Saluted still on the wave of Election victory.'

One of our first tasks was to carry the domestic legislation which was necessary to ratify the Treaty of Maastricht. The argument within the Conservative Party was not extinct but it had died down, and Europe had played no big part in the election campaign. The opponents of the treaty had lost their two most powerful advocates: Margaret Thatcher and Norman Tebbit were no longer in the Commons. I was fully occupied that spring with Turkey, Hong Kong, Macedonia, Prague and a visit to the Gulf and Egypt. On 21 May the second reading of the Maastricht Bill carried in the Commons after a good-tempered debate. The way through to ratification seemed tedious but sure.

Ten days later all was confusion. Under their constitution the Danish Government had to hold a referendum on the treaty. The Danish politicians were confident. Their Foreign Minister, Uffe Ellemann-Jensen, was a keen advocate of European integration and had been somewhat impatient with my cautious arguments during the negotiations. The main Danish political parties, the employers and trade unions had campaigned, albeit lackadaisically, for a yes vote. On the evening of voting day, 2 June, we began to realise that they had got it wrong. John Major held an impromptu and inconclusive meeting. The Maastricht Bill was due to start its next stage in the Commons the following day. 'Do we scrub, postpone, persevere with the Bill? The PM begins cautious, ends brave . . . but it's a mess. Chablis and quiche at home. Bed 1.'

I was due to broadcast on the *Today* programme on BBC Radio 4 early the following morning. Just before the appointed time the Prime Minister rang and warned me not to mention that we intended to proceed with the Maastricht Bill that afternoon. It was a wise decision. At meetings later that day the whips and Tony Newton, the Leader of the House, were clear that the two dozen Conservative rebels who had voted against the second reading would now be powerfully reinforced. Opposition to Maastricht, which had seemed hopeless, was now full of promise. The treaty could not come into force without the Danes, and the Danes had voted no. The British Government would now be pressed to abandon the Bill, and the treaty. The Prime Minister made a statement that afternoon rejecting this analysis. We would stick to Maastricht and proceed with the Bill, but not now. It was enough said for that afternoon, but we were in confusion. 'PM . . . deals fruitlessly with questions . . . Sit exhausted with him for an hour in his HOC

[Commons] room, Minerva docet in stained glass [I always disliked that room which I seemed to visit only at moments of crisis]. He wolfs a bacon sandwich and we wander round and round.'

From then on there was a Danish problem and a British problem. The Danish problem proved easier to solve. Elleman-Jensen telephoned that evening to say that what the Danish Government needed was time and resolute partners. If we hung on till autumn there might be another chance. The next day a NATO meeting had been arranged in Oslo. We spent most of the time in the margins talking about the EU and Denmark. Our other partners were indignant against the Danes and strongly against any renegotiation of the treaty to suit them. I found myself alone in pointing out that we needed the Danes and must help their Government persuade the people. So began an effort which was led by British diplomacy until it brought success at the Edinburgh summit in December. With the Danish Government we identified what seemed to be the main reasons why their electorate had voted no: for example, a dislike of the single currency and a worry about the vague defence aspiration in the treaty. To alter the text of the treaty would be to throw the whole process of ratification back across Europe into the cauldron. Could we find other ways of reassuring the Danish people on their sore points? They had the last word, but there was nothing illegitimate or undemocratic in trying to meet their misgivings. Through the months lawyers laboured, ministers conferred, diplomats dug in to the detail. Eventually a document emerged which worked. As an example of a complex technical achievement of modern diplomacy among democracies, I would put near the top of the list the bringing round of the Danes between June 1992 and their second and favourable referendum the following spring.

The British problem proved tougher and took longer to resolve. 'We are holed below the water line,' I confided to my diary on 5 June 1992. There was no serious question of our abandoning the Bill, but we drifted in confusion for several weeks about timing and procedure. I had a rough encounter with Conservative backbenchers on 24 June. The vociferous critics rushed out of this private meeting to brief the press, while our friends stayed silent and embarrassed. But gradually the Prime Minister asserted his authority and we decided to reintroduce the Bill in the autumn, after the Irish and French had held their own referendums. On 1 July we took over the presidency of the EU from the Dutch. It was not to be a calm six months.

I managed to snatch one of our traditional weeks of holiday at La Cappellina in Tuscany and another equally traditional week at Mothecombe in Devon. But that July and August also included our London conference on Yugoslavia, visits to the disintegrated fragments of that country, the shaping of Chris Patten's plan for Hong Kong, a summit in Munich, a swing round South East Asia, and visits to South Africa and Kenya.

By September sterling was in trouble, but the early days of that crisis passed me by. It was the custom of each presidency to hold an informal meeting of foreign ministers for long-term thinking, and I chose Brocket Hall in Hertfordshire for ours. As usual, long-term thinking was submerged in a torrent of talk on immediate problems, notably Yugoslavia and the imminent French referendum on Maastricht. On Saturday afternoon we played croquet according to rules derived, I hope accurately, from their childhood by Mesdames Dumas and Delors, and listened to a performance of *The Merry Widow*. Only Jacques Delors seemed concerned about the currency markets. Back in London I realised that the pound was on the edge, but as usual there was no collective discussion. Once again currency matters were regarded as sacred mysteries entrusted only to the Prime Minister and the Chancellor of the Exchequer. At that time we were discussing whether we should intervene militarily in Bosnia, and if so how. The width and openness of these debates about life and death in Bosnia, in which several ministers and Parliament were repeatedly involved, were in sharp contrast to the secrecy on currency matters. I knew nothing of the brief which Norman Lamont took to the crucial meeting of finance ministers in Bath, or of his plans for handling the Germans, who appeared to hold the key to success or disaster.

Wednesday 16 September, described in my diary as 'a day of gloom' and in the history books as Black Wednesday, began with a meeting to discuss what we would do if the French voted no in their referendum on Sunday. Because Number Ten was being refurbished, the Prime Minister was working in Admiralty House. I crunched across the gravel just as I had done in the same direction during the Cuba crisis thirty years earlier. We met in the dining room, with flocked wallpaper and pictures of naval battles, all victories, where as Home Secretary I had not long before entertained chief constables of police. The meeting and the day were immediately absorbed by the currency crisis. The laymen present – namely, Ken Clarke, Michael Heseltine, Richard Ryder (Chief Whip) and myself – found ourselves taking part in the high-pitched climax of a play, at the earlier acts of which we had not been spectators, let alone actors. We were told late in the morning that every minute of discussion cost the reserves £18 million, that every remedy had been tried and that we should immediately suspend British membership of the ERM. We were none of us in any position to gainsay this advice. I argued, and others agreed, that if this was to happen our partners should be told and the rules of the ERM followed. It could not be sensible to act in a way which would destroy trust in all our other decisions. Failure was one thing, panic another. While this was being done Richard Gozney and I walked round the lake in St James's Park.

Later I was back at Admiralty House, this time with the Home Secretary Ken Clarke munching sandwiches in the drawing room, gossiping of this and that in the sunshine. There was absolutely nothing for us to do. As Ken later remarked, we were additional doctors brought in at the last moment simply to witness the death of the patient. Eventually Norman Lamont reported the failure of his last effort to save the pound by raising interest rates, and we agreed to suspension. 'PM and Lamont both calm, esp. PM, and I admire their coherence in disaster.'

Disaster it certainly was. Foreign Office officials urged me to argue at the cabinet meeting next day that we should re-enter the ERM as soon as possible. To my surprise, Norman Lamont was also in favour of a formula to that effect. It seemed to me quite unrealistic, but the Chancellor's formula was agreed. In reality we had for the moment neither an economic nor a European policy. On the 20th the French voted yes by a hair's breadth in their referendum, but for us that solved nothing. The whips were gloomy, as only whips can be, about the prospect of getting the Maastricht Bill on the road again.

Our difficulties were underlined when I chaired a meeting of EU foreign ministers at the UN in New York on the 21st. Relieved at the French vote, my European colleagues were enthusiastic for pressing on with Maastricht and suspicious when Tristan Garel-Jones and I muttered our doubts and intimated the mortality of our own Government. They thought we were piling on the gloom to disguise our own lack of will. This was one of several occasions when it was a distinct disadvantage to hold the presidency. In the chair I had to allow the passage of a declaration which went a good deal further than was politically wise for us at home.

The next day I tried to explain our dire political plight to the new German Foreign Minister, Klaus Kinkel, then flew to Gatwick overnight, sleeping well in a DC10. I had just finished a bath at 1 Carlton Gardens when Stephen Wall arrived from Admiralty House. Stephen, having been my private secretary, was now the Prime Minister's. Calm at all times, trusted and liked by both of us, he was an ideal intermediary. He told me something that the Prime Minister obviously wanted me to know: namely, that he had spent part of the previous day drafting a letter of resignation. That indeed was the main theme of a series of meetings that day at Number Ten, ending with a steak which I ate alone with John Major that evening. The Prime Minister said that he felt shabby to be still in office after the collapse of two main Government policies. He enjoyed a world outside politics; maybe the time had come to rediscover that world. The position seemed to me different and clear, as I tried to explain. John Major had been right not to ask for or allow the resignation of Norman Lamont a week earlier after Black Wednesday. He and the Chancellor had operated the ERM policy together, and if one must, both would have to go. But we now had to resurrect the Maastricht Bill if we were to carry any weight anywhere at home or abroad. John Major was essential for this. If the Bill failed that would be a different situation: then *I* would feel bound to resign, and I implied that he would need to do the same. This was not, I think, the view of some of his close advisers, who thought he could soldier on without the Bill. I inferred that he himself agreed with me, but the point was fortunately never put to the test.

That autumn the hurdles came close together. On 24 September the Commons debate on the crisis was wound up by Norman Lamont. I never believed that he was the right choice for Chancellor of the Exchequer, but that evening and in the next few days I was full of admiration: 'excellent, a speech of real verve and courage'; 'shows obstinate courage under v. heavy fire'.

The Prime Minister was coming fast to realise that his position depended on pressing ahead with the Maastricht Bill. Much would depend on the tone of the party conference in Brighton. The crucial debate on Europe was to be held there on 6 October. The day before I was driven to Brighton, rather silently and sleepily with Judy beside me. I tried to build up my speech into a real warning of the danger the party was facing. All my old anxieties about the party conference speech returned as I paced up and down declaiming to an empty hotel bedroom. The next day the organisers did me a good turn by calling to the platform Norman Tebbit, who delivered a sneering attack on our policies and on the Prime Minister. Tebbit was well received and effective. As I listened to his negative arguments, the spirit of contradiction rose strongly inside me, and I longed to be at him. I sat impatient as speaker followed speaker until at last my time came. The Prime Minister, sitting beside me, scribbled a note, which I kept:

Douglas
Good luck!
Give 'em hell – and don't worry about causing offence.
John
How can they expect us to break our word?

This advice proved sound. Anyway, my blood was already up. After a few minutes the hall began to turn in our favour. In plays and films the director often has to show a crowd changing its mind under the influence of oratory, as for example when it listens to Mark Antony on the death of Julius Caesar. Usually the film director makes individuals in the audience applaud one speaker and a few minutes later the same characters applaud his opponent with expressive gesticulations. That is not what happens in real life. On a question like Maastricht the audience is divided, with a large section undecided and ready to be swayed. Norman Tebbit did not persuade the pro-Europeans, but he cowed them into silence so that he appeared well on top. I did not persuade the sceptics, but I roused our supporters, and so brought the solid undecided centre on to my side. I warned of a split in the party, like that over the Corn Laws in 1846, if we continued as we were going. That afternoon in Brighton and on one or two other rare occasions, I felt the exhilaration which comes from carrying with you hundreds of your fellow humans who had started somewhere else. It was the best conference speech I made, and I could not have done it without the provocation of Norman Tebbit. It was a great relief to wake up next morning for the first time in weeks without an incubus. The day included a conciliatory chat with Norman Tebbit.

The next hurdle was a European summit in Birmingham. This needed particular preparation at a time when in our weakened state any fresh controversy might be fatal. The French were sparring with the European Commission on the crucial world-trade negotiations in GATT. Leon Brittan was the commissioner in charge, a strong liberal in trade matters, and led the necessary bargaining with the Americans on behalf of us all. The French suspected him of preparing to betray their agriculture. On 10 October I spent three and a half hours with the President of the Commission, Jacques Delors, in Brussels and found him as a Frenchman much torn on the subject.

> Lunch in rue Ducale. He is exhausted, so speaks French, a good idea. [On such bilateral occasions vanity often prevents the most sensible course: namely, talking in one's own language and listening in the other.] He over dramatises – Danish position a disaster (not true). French Government will fall and riots in the countryside if there is GATT agreement etc., etc. Take him thro' Birmingham plan. Warn him his own as well as French standing at stake if GATT fails . . . He takes this all very well. Indeed he is a pleasure to do business with.

The Birmingham summit a week later on the 16th was overshadowed by a big row over the Government's plan to close coal mines, and strange ructions on public spending between Norman Lamont and colleagues in London. 'The only good thing about day is Birmingham itself – like a lady without beauty who has organised herself into elegance.' The sparkling new buildings in which we met made a strong impression; Helmut Kohl told me it was the best-organised summit he had known. One tiny incident sticks in my mind. Emilio Colombo, now Italian Foreign Minister, had been as a young man a faithful acolyte of the high priests of the Monnet doctrine. He knew every phrase and concept of the true faith of European integration. But now he was old and sleepy. At Birmingham he woke up while we were discussing a declaration with the phrase, intrinsic to the new Maastricht doctrine of subsidiarity, that the EU should intervene only when it was clearly necessary to act at the European level. Colombo seized the microphone and protested that the limitation was a betrayal of the European ideal. The more we acted as Europe, the better. No one took the slightest notice. President Mitterrand continued the discussion as if nothing had been said. We lived in the post-Maastricht world. Supranational rhetoric now belonged to nostalgic outsiders: at the heart of the EU the great ones knew better. I wished that some of our sceptics had been there to see how the weather had changed.

Clumsily we hoisted the Maastricht Bill out of the ditch and back on to the road. It was not clear whether the engine would start. We decided that we needed a Commons vote, in the jargon a 'paving motion', before we proceeded with detailed examination of the Bill in committee. It was far from clear that we would win this vote, which was set for 4 November. Richard Ryder and his fellow whips thought a week in advance that we had only a 30 per cent chance of success. The morning of the debate was taken up (I almost add 'of course' because this is the way of the world) with the visit of the Sultan of Brunei, a friend of Britain of great financial importance, but notoriously silent. The Prime Minister had to converse with him in the morning, then 'PM haggard, strides up and down the bishop's waiting room [at Number Ten] agonising on Maastricht. He knows and I know that the Whips say we are going down. I think he had decided to resign [if we lost] though he does not say so.' Judy and I trundled off to Lancaster House to give lunch to the Sultan and his wife. One look at her led me to remark in my diary, 'To say that she is "interested in jewellery", as the brief does, is the understatement of the year.' My mind was not on the royal jewellery or the Sultan's monosyllables but on the wind-up speech which I had to make that evening. The Prime Minister opened the debate well, and it proceeded against the dramatic background of an uncertain vote. For once I enjoyed my wind-up speech and the good reception it achieved. There were two votes, which we won by margins of six and three.

Champagne and jubilation followed, but were spoiled for me by the news that Michael Heseltine had, with John Major's agreement, made a deal in the lobby with a backbencher, Michael Carttiss, which may (I still think *may*) have clinched the vote, rather than my own golden eloquence. Michael had undertaken that we would not hold the third reading (the final stage) of the Bill until after the Danes had voted again. He had muttered something to me on the bench that we should think about such a concession, but I had brushed him aside as I concentrated on putting together my wind-up, a job which can only be done alone in a hurry at the last minute. He then talked to the Prime Minister and, I think, got his general assent.

This was the sort of last-minute change of policy which is justified only if it succeeds. This one worked on the night, made me cross for a couple of days and caused a general rumpus. In the end the two processes, Danish and British, came together in time, quite naturally the following May, though that is not something Michael Heseltine could conceivably have known as he conspired successfully in the lobby that November evening.

The final summit of our presidency was held in the royal palace of Holyrood in Edinburgh. The contrast with Birmingham and its modern buildings was total. Everything in Holyrood was dark and old except the interpreters' booths. We conferred under the dark gaze of the job lot of royal portraits put together by one of the Stuart kings who felt an urgent need for ancestors. My own office contained a crimson four-poster bed. The weather was wet and cold, the cold particularly formidable in Edinburgh Castle where we entertained our partners to lunch. The powerful effect of Edinburgh on our visitors was reinforced by the Queen's banquet on *Britannia*, anchored a few miles away at Leith. Two days earlier the Prime Minister had announced in the Commons that the Prince and Princess of Wales were to separate. Yet there the Princess was, bestowing that special mixture of beauty and charm which melted men's bones. Presidents, prime ministers and foreign ministers as they dined could make no sense of what was happening in our Royal Family, but were content to bask for an hour or two in an extraordinary radiance.

Talking late with the Prime Minister that night back at the Caledonian Hotel we were far from sure that the summit would succeed. This was John Major at his best. Complaining and foreseeing failure all the time, he relished the job of ringmaster in a four- or five-ring circus. He enjoyed mastering the briefs and persuading colleagues round each difficult corner. As usual, though there had been much preparatory work, nothing would be finally settled until everything was settled. The Danish question lingered. We had promised what we called a 'decision' covering what we believed were the Danish difficulties. The word 'decision' (less than a treaty amendment, more than an ordinary Council conclusion) had kept the lawyers happily on the hop for several weeks. Would colleagues accept it, would it be enough for the Danes? There was a brouhaha over Macedonia. The Greek Prime Minister Mitsotakis rehearsed eloquently but unconvincingly to me in private, and to the conference at large, his country's grievances against her new, weak, highly vulnerable neighbour. The main commotion was about money. On the one hand, we were determined to bring the EU budget under control by fixing a firm ceiling on expenditure as a proportion of the gross national product. On the other, we had to agree, under the heading of 'cohesion', on help already promised to the poorest members of the EU: namely, Spain, Portugal, Ireland and Greece. The Spanish Prime Minister Felipe González was the most demanding, Helmut Kohl and the Germans, as the chief paymaster, the most resistant. When late on the last night Kohl, in what he mistakenly supposed to be a whisper, uttered the word 'Felipe' and bundled the Spaniard out of the room into some private fastness, we knew that the end was near. But before that John Major had listened and talked and listened again in private meetings, edging each participant towards agreement. I did the same on the lesser issues. At the last minute, when weary ministers gathered to finalise the conclusion, there was a noisy outbreak at the end of the table. The Dutch and the Luxembourgers, usually the closest of companions, started fighting on an obscure point about the site of a European institution. John Major managed a final act of pacification. We got to bed at 3.35 a.m. I have a photograph of my private secretary Richard Gozney at his desk during these last hours, pen in hand, surrounded by paper, fast asleep. The British presidency, begun shakily in June, disrupted by Black Wednesday, had ended in reasonable success.

These processes of bargaining and cajoling which reached a peak in Edinburgh sometimes earned the European institutions a bad name among those who have not thought the matter through. The alternative would be either a super-state or a Europe in which everyone shouted and disagreed from fixed positions.

I will spare the reader the long further travails of the Maastricht Bill. The Government faced a political alliance of Conservative sceptics and the Labour Party, which when fully mobilised had the votes to defeat us. But each part of that alliance had reason to be embarrassed at their own behaviour, which usually prevented them putting out their full strength. Most, though not all, of our Conservative sceptics hesitated before joining with our opponents so far as to wreck the Government, which they had just been re-elected to support. The Labour Party was in theory in favour of the Maastricht Treaty, but, unlike the brave pro-European Labour MPs in 1972, could not resist the opportunistic temptation to give the Government hell on specific issues, even though this put ratification at risk.

Our difficulty was that our case was essentially defensive. It was hard to argue any triumphant advantage to Britain from the Treaty of Maastricht. Our arguments about intergovernmental pillars, about subsidiarity, about a common foreign and security policy were perfectly sound, but rang no bells with public opinion. We spent much of our time showing that, given John Major's two opt-outs, the treaty would do Britain no harm. We could not be forced into a single currency or into legislation under the Social Chapter. But these negative arguments did not amount to a battle-cry.

Our sceptics were not so much concerned with specific promises of the treaty as with their fear of a super-state and their resentment of the pretentious, interfering ways of the European Commission. Theirs was not so much an offensive against Maastricht as an attempt to regain ground which had in their view been conceded to Europe by Ted Heath at the time of accession, and (though both they and she were un-comfortable about this) by Margaret Thatcher in the Single European Act.

The Prime Minister, as his Brighton note to me showed, took a straightforward line. He and the rest of us, with the consent of a properly consulted Parliament, had committed ourselves to a treaty. The electorate had just given us a vote of confidence. It would be deeply damaging, indeed unthinkable, to go back on our word. I agreed with this. Moreover, I saw the EU as a huge historical achievement compared to anything Europe has ever seen. By historical standards it was still young – imperfect and often irritating because we had not yet learned the art of working effectively together. Rhetoric had run ahead of achievement, but that was an argument for moderating rhetoric, not for abandoning achievement. If we had scrapped the Bill and so refused to ratify the treaty, we would have remained a member of the EU. But we would have plunged it and ourselves into a period of bad-tempered confusion. Probably our partners would, after a time, have recovered from our act of sabotage and put together a treaty of their own with a single currency, and other provisions going further than Maastricht. We would then by our foolishness have helped to bring about the nightmare which had always alarmed our predecessors: a continental union influencing British lives at almost every turn over which we had no control. Irrespective of whether we then drifted out of formal membership of the EU, we would have reduced ourselves to a weak, though no doubt pretentious, nation wedged between the United States and Europe. Each would pay us courteous attention for old times' sake, but their important dealings would be among themselves. By doggedly sticking to Maastricht and steering it through to ratification, we averted this danger.

In July 1993 we at last entered port, but not before we had hit one more sandbank and floated ourselves off with difficulty. The Conservative Eurosceptics and the Labour Party came together with maximum force on the question of the Social Chapter and the opt-out we had gained for Britain from obnoxious legislation. They had failed to separate the Government from the treaty of Maastricht, but both groups were now in a state of reckless emotion. After all the months of wrangling they saw victory just in sight and were not over-scrupulous in planning their last push. The Conservative rebels were so keen to ditch the treaty that they did not mind voting in favour of a left-wing Social Chapter and destroying the Government. The Labour Party were so keen to destroy the Government that they did not mind ditching the treaty which they were supposed to favour. John Kerr in Brussels and Foreign Office officials produced various wheezes whereby we would legally dodge the issue. We could, for example, use the royal prerogative to ratify the treaty and deal with any social legislation separately. These notions found no favour with the Prime Minister, who by now was fatalistic. On the morning of the next crucial vote, 22 July, the Chief Whip reported to the Cabinet gloomily on the prospects, as was his wont. The Prime Minister cut short discussion. We met again in the Commons just before the vote. Ken Clarke proposed, and Michael Howard supported him, that if we lost we should move straight next day to a vote of confidence framed in a way which would enable us to go ahead with the Bill as drafted. Michael Howard's loyalty to the Government prevailed over his dislike of the treaty, and this scuppered the objection of the other Eurosceptic ministers.

A few hours later we duly lost the vote by eight, and the vote of confidence was set for next day. We were not clear that night how our rebels would react. In the heat of argument they had given the impression that the destruction of the Bill was more important to them than anything else. Now there was a short pause. They had to consider coolly whether they wished to destroy not only the Bill but also the Government. Ministers spent the morning seeing individual MPs. I gave coffee to Bill Cash, the most voluble of our critics. He rambled, was not sure, but clutched at the smallest possible olive branch: namely, my promise of a longer meeting at which he could expound his views at even greater length. This was quite a heavy price, but on balance worth paying. Then I saw Trevor Skeet, another backbencher, who rallied to us. At twelve-thirty Michael Spicer called on the Chief Whip and myself to say that the rebels would support the Government in the vote of confidence, requiring only a courteous acknowledgement in my speech which I would have given them anyway. By now I was becoming quite adept at the tightrope art of the wind-up, and managed to unite the party by teasing the Liberal leader, Paddy Ashdown. We won by thirty-nine votes. The Prime Minister's gamble had paid off.

On 2 August we ratified the Treaty of Maastricht. The heavens did not fall. Ten years later the Queen is on her throne, the Prime Minister remains at Number Ten, the Chancellor of the Exchequer increases taxes from No. 11, we can invade Iraq, we can keep the pound as long as we like, and for better or for worse the future of Europe remains essentially in the hands of the elected governments of European nations.

I was often struck by the lack of self-confidence which otherwise robust individuals in Britain felt when faced with individual European issues or the general question of our future in Europe. They seemed to read in history that we would always be worsted by continental Europeans except when we were fighting and killing them. Nelson and Wellington were to them the key figures, not Castlereagh, Palmerston and Salisbury. Our continental partners thought otherwise. This contrast came to bear on me personally when I flew out as Foreign Secretary for a Council negotiation. In the English Sunday papers at Westwell I would be represented as foolish, unintelligent and slow, about to be outwitted and gobbled up by those devious, subtle continentals. By the time I touched down at Brussels I had become the highly briefed, sophisticated, not too scrupulous Englishman coming to argue his way to a better deal than Britain deserved.

As I reread this account of European policy it sounds too defensive. It is true that I was not thrusting forward enthusiastically into a visionary future for Europe. Indeed, I spent a good deal of time damping down European rhetoric and discouraging the ambitions of keen integrationists. But that was because such unrealities threatened something already achieved: namely, British membership of the European Union, or, more precisely, prevented that membership putting down roots of respect and commitment in British soil. To our vigorous membership of the most hopeful organisation Europe has ever seen I felt and feel a robust commitment which comes from both brain and heart.

This commitment surfaces at different times in different ways. When I sit in the sun in the Piazza San Michele in Lucca, espresso in front of me on the iron-fretted table, *Corriere della Sera* on my knee, I feel at home. When some years ago I flew from Teesside to Rotterdam, a route unfrequented by diplomats and ministers, and listened around me on the crowded plane to the buzz of all the pursuits and pleasures carrying young people to the continent, I understood what the European single market was about. What to my parents and once to me had been unusual expeditions needing much thought and preparation were to my fellow passengers as normal and everyday as travelling to London. That was the real meaning of the phrase in the treaty about 'ever closer union of peoples'. The same thought penetrated even into the Council Building in Brussels, despite its long hours, airless rooms and revolting coffee. I cannot remember exactly what text we were arguing about in the Council of Ministers one evening, except that it concerned an agreement with Turkey. The discussions had seemed endless and were at times cross as ministers stuck to their briefs and the presidency failed to break the deadlock. Around midnight, just as we began to despair, a way through was found. As we agreed what our negotiator could offer the Turks, there was a spontaneous round of applause from all corners of the table. We were clapping our own success on this small occasion but also the idea which had brought us into the room. Instead of fearing the Turks, defending Vienna against them, intriguing and fighting against one another over the disposal of their empire, we had come together as one Europe to negotiate with them in friendship. To denounce or deny this kind of progress is absurd.

That was a small example of a thought always at the back of my mind through the irritation and inefficiencies of EU life. I profoundly disagreed with those who thought that Britain, which had shared the past of Europe, should cast herself out of its future.

The debate on Europe sputtered on, fanned into flame by particular controversies. I will not describe here our veto cast against the Belgian Prime Minister, Jean-Luc Dehaene, as a candidate to succeed Jacques Delors as President of the Commission; nor the fracas about the European Finance Bill and our attempt to discipline our rebels. I pick out one commotion which again damaged the Government, produced the sharpest disagreement which I ever had with John Major, and caused me much anxiety and vexation – all over a matter which turned out to have no practical importance.

Britain, since Margaret Thatcher's time, had supported the enlargement of the EU; in 1993 the candidates in the waiting room were Sweden, Finland, Norway and Austria (though Norway later backed out). Enlargement required certain changes to the treaty. One of these concerned the arrangements for voting when a vote was needed. The principle of weighted voting, with bigger countries, including Britain, possessing more votes, was not in question. The number of votes allocated to the new members was easily agreed. The problem arose over the number of votes which a minority would have to muster in order to block a decision. It was in theory reasonable that if the total number of votes increased with enlargement, the number required for a blocking minority should also increase to keep the proportions the same. Some said the new blocking minority should be twenty-seven; others, including Britain, preferred to stick at twenty-three.

At first the QMV (qualified majority voting) question seemed a minor part of the enlargement discussions which included more practical problems such as fish and finance. Most of the larger states were with us in preferring a blocking minority of twenty-three, and John Kerr in Brussels thought that we would end up with a reasonable compromise at or close to our own position.

As the meetings multiplied two movements gathered speed. The German, French and Italians proved no longer ready to defend twenty-three, whereas my colleagues were almost unanimous in regarding twenty-seven as a humiliating disaster. In countless meetings in Whitehall, every department except the Foreign Office harped on the need for Britain to have the strongest possible chance of blocking objectionable legislation. It is true that William Waldegrave, a mild sceptic but Minister of Agriculture, pointed out that on agricultural matters we needed majority voting and a weak blocking minority if we were to have any hope of reform. The same was true of many single market issues. The number of occasions on which Britain was in serious danger of being outvoted had proved and was always likely to prove very small. Nevertheless, my colleagues dug our ditch. Some of the most strenuous digging was accomplished by Michael Heseltine and Ken Clarke, usually my strong allies on European matters.

I began to feel hemmed in with no room for manoeuvre. My diary entry for 8 March 1994 gives the flavour:

> As nasty a birthday as I recall. Imprisoned in the Charlemagne [Brussels building where the Foreign Affairs Council met]. No progress on QMV – we argue at lunch. No useful compromise to hand. PM and colleagues miscalculated in supposing the Germans would compromise rather than spoil enlargement. They don't move from 27, tho' we dangle compromise before them. I shd. not have allowed this to happen. [My only ally was Spain but this alliance could involve penalties.] In parallel on fish the Spaniards fight a magnificent rearguard action (Solana [Foreign Minister] and Westendorp [deputy]) using arguments for access to Norway which are wholly ridiculous. Feel ashamed not to be helping the Norwegians. 4 meals running in the Charlemagne, much nasty Greek wine [Greece had the presidency]. Speak from the prison to Judy and John [Sawers, now my senior private secretary] but little comfort. Pangalos [my Greek opposite number] a clumsy chairman

and Kinkel [German ditto], though friendly to me and rightminded, try to bully the Spaniards, which is an error. Escape finally, tail between legs, no conclusion. Bed 12.

Up to then the only blessing was that the press had not grasped this issue. But as March proceeded, this changed and the newspapers began to sniff danger. The Prime Minister and I appealed separately to the Germans, without success. I had recently helped Klaus Kinkel at a German political meeting of importance to him and he had then in thanks told me to let him know if in return I ever wanted him to put a stone into my garden. The German phrase was new to me, and puzzling, but I wrote saying now was the moment for the stone. I argued with my colleagues – including the Prime Minister – for some flexibility but they refused. The difficulty about standing absolutely firm had nothing to do with embarrassment to myself or anyone else. Agreement on this point had to be unanimous. If there was no agreement, we would be blocking the entry of the Scandinavians and Austria into the EU. Their entry was one of our main objectives. We would abandon it – and for what?

On 14 March John Major called yet another meeting in advance of the next Council discussions in Brussels. 'Confirm my negative riding orders for tomorrow. I say I could not defend destruction of enlargement. Commonwealth drinks at Marlborough House. Bow Group usual reception at Christies. Feel PM is destroying my job under me. Take Judy to film *Shadowlands*. C.S. Lewis, slow, beautiful sentimental.' Next day in Brussels was fruitless. 'I feel like a bank with a run on it, using up assets fast.' A long talk with John Major that day was mainly on his own anxieties on wider matters. But in the Cabinet on the 17th with his help I at last secured some flexibility around the figure of twenty-five. This would probably have clinched the matter if I had been given it a month earlier; but the subject was now out of control. Yet another meeting in Brussels on 22 March; after a hopeful start, I got nowhere, though the Spaniards under Solana's leadership stayed firm. Next day, 'The cloud I so much dread won't lift. Talk to PM and succeed in depressing him. PM says (four eyes) [i.e. no one else there] we musn't divide over this, first time in 3½ years.' But he himself was digging the ditch deeper by combative remarks in the House of Commons which were loudly cheered by our Eurosceptics. One of my private secretaries recalls: 'I think the time you were most angry and depressed in my years with you was when you emerged from one of the interminable Council lunches in March 1994 on QMV to be told what the Prime Minister had just said in Prime Minister's Questions. You shook your head in disbelief and went quite grey ... Just when you thought it cannot get worse, it did.'

As already noted, the informal meetings of foreign ministers away from Brussels were intended for wise strategic discussion, but often hijacked to settle stubborn issues of the moment. The presidency decided to refer QMV to the informal meeting which they were organising in the hill town of Ioannina in northern Greece. I travelled there by way of Plymouth, where the Conservative Central Council was meeting. My speech was not in tune with their mood, but in *my* mood I felt this was tough on them rather than on me. Angry and fed up, I argued in the strongest terms yet that there was no glory in isolation for its own sake. 'That is yesterday's game, these are yesterday's toys. Let us put them back in the toy cupboard. Britain against Europe, *Britannia Contra Mundum*, cannot in our saner moments be our rallying cry.' We must fight hard for a good agreement, not for a glorious defeat.

Ioannina may be an agreeable, even exciting, town when visited in leisure and with enthusiasm. It held no charm for me and I do not want to see it again. The hotel was nasty. On the second day ministers were taken to an island in the lake. In a monastery we were shown paintings of saints being tortured in various ways and eventually beheaded. Throughout these experiences the saints presented notably mild expressions on their faces. I tried to follow their example.

Because it was an informal meeting, the normal range of officials was excluded. My companions at Ioannina were Judy and John Sawers, the first always stalwart, the second proving himself a true comrade in arms. We were about as far removed as was possible in Europe from the ordinary comings and goings of communication within a government. We were required to settle a question which had frustrated us in many earlier meetings, without any new element which could break the deadlock. It was not a question of huge importance to others, apart from the Scandinavians and Austrians who were becoming impatient and anxious. Ministers, the party and the press had made it of critical, perhaps lethal, importance at home. 'We have put second things first and will suffer grievously.'

I managed to persuade Pangalos in the chair to discuss QMV in a small group. This excluded the French, who became cross. The Belgians and Dutch were equally vexed. It was not clear after the first day whether any progress was possible. The Spaniards were by now ready to settle, but Solana held back out of solidarity with me. Kinkel did his best to put a stone in my garden, but it was a small one. The hotel was too constricted and uncomfortable for private discussions indoors. Judy recalls looking out of her window at groups of anxious ministers forming and re-forming among the paths and bushes outside, reminding her of the last act of *The Marriage of Figaro*. On the second day, Sunday 27 March, I had breakfast alone with Jacques Delors in an alcove of the hotel restaurant. I warned him that if things went on as they were we might soon find for the first time one of the main political parties in Europe (my own) taking a firmly anti-EU line. He took this seriously, said he trusted me, and promised to try to help on the side by softening the social legislation being proposed by Brussels, which was another serious cause of contention. But this was of no immediate help. That morning we worked out a formula to resolve the QMV dispute. The blocking minority would be twenty-seven, but there would be a delay for further consideration with a view to reaching agreement in any case where the minority registered between twenty-three and twenty-six votes. The Spaniards, who had been staunch throughout, accepted this formula. I said I could only undertake to refer it to my colleagues. I had no illusion that they would find it palatable.

That Sunday evening I drank beer with John Major back at Number Ten. He was weary and sour. His instinct was that we must ask for more; I thought we had got all we were going to get. He perked up as we began to think about how the problem could be handled tactically, a field in which he always enjoyed exercising his talents. But the press next morning was lousy. The Prime Minister telephoned early to say that he thought it impossible to proceed. I was back with him at 8.45 a.m.; he suggested that we ask Ken Clarke, by now Chancellor of the Exchequer, to join us from next door. This was a shrewd move, since he knew that Ken had resisted all my appeals and firmly argued that we must hold to twenty-three. I set out my reasoning to the two of them. Ken had come to the meeting expecting to be urged by both John and me to accept my compromise. Instead he found us at odds. He at once said that if the Foreign Secretary's assessment was that the Ioannina compromise was the best we could get, I must be supported. This was a decisive moment.

That afternoon I answered a question in the Commons and set out the position. This went surprisingly well and two colleagues wrote notes of congratulation. The Prime Minister rang before midnight in conciliatory vein. I went to bed with just a hope that the cloud might lift.

Cabinet next day was far from easy. The Prime Minister before the meeting showed privately that he still hoped that I would change my mind. When I presented the compromise he expressed no personal opinion at all. Discussion was sombre and he scribbled a note: 'Douglas, As bad as I feared! Do you wish to respond/answer the questions?' I did so, and eventually the majority backed me, with the usual Eurosceptic ministers arguing fairly but without passion against the compromise.

The Prime Minister could have swayed the Cabinet by offering to pursue the matter in Europe at his own top level, but did not do so. He understood that this would not work, and would put him in serious danger. Instead he volunteered after the cabinet decision to make the necessary statement himself in the Commons accepting the compromise. This was a miserable business for him, particularly because of his own robust statement a week earlier. The episode altered his own attitude on European matters, or rather hardened a change which I had seen taking shape in him for some time. He and I quickly returned to mutual trust and our close, joky way of working together, but from then on I knew that on Europe his enthusiasm was likely to be several degrees cooler than my own, which was rarely itself red hot.

As far as I can discover we have never had to use the facility which we achieved in the Ioannina compromise. The difference between twenty-three and twenty-seven votes turned out to be nugatory. The Spaniards used it, I have been told, to delay a decision on animal welfare which we were anxious to see carried. The whole issue was, as I had expected, unreal. We should not have allowed the molehill to become a mountain which in turn produced an avalanche.

I have come across a chart of possible events which I scribbled at Chevening on 20 March, and then kept with me during the Ioannina meeting.

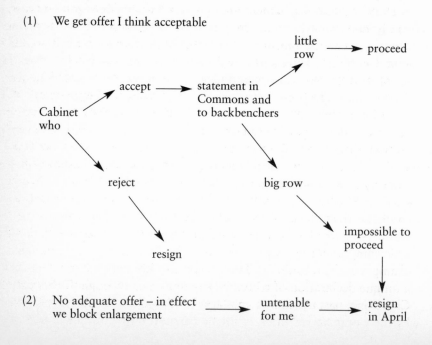

(1)   We get offer I think acceptable

little row ———→ proceed

accept ———→ statement in Commons and to backbenchers

Cabinet who

reject

big row

resign

impossible to proceed

(2)   No adequate offer – in effect   untenable ———→ resign
we block enlargement ———→ for me   in April

John Sawers saw this scrap of paper and sent it back to me with a yellow slip: 'Terrible document. Returned for ever.' I never spoke on these lines to the Prime Minister but his memoirs show that he guessed. Three of the four possible scenarios would have led to my resignation.

Chevening deserves at this point a fuller mention because of the growing part it played in my life.

In the symphony of British political history during the eighteenth, nineteenth and twentieth centuries the name Stanhope sounds repeatedly like the note of a distinguished minor instrument. James Stanhope commanded, with mixed fortunes, against the French in Spain while Marlborough was defeating them spectacularly at Blenheim and Ramillies. He became Prime Minister to George I at the time of the South Sea Bubble. The family intermarried with the Pitts; Lady Hester Stanhope was niece and hostess to Pitt the Younger before wandering off into the East. The third earl was an amateur scientist who sympathised with the French Revolution; the Kentish gentry christened him Citizen Stanhope and refused to call. The fifth earl served in Peel's Government, wrote a long history of the Peninsular War, and pressed successfully for the setting up in 1854 of the National Portrait Gallery. The seventh earl rose to become First Lord of the Admiralty in the 1930s. His wife died early and he had no children. In his old age, contemplating the end of his dynasty, Lord Stanhope devised a scheme which would prolong the family's public service beyond his own death. He created and promoted in 1959 an Act of Parliament under which a trust would administer the family home at Chevening and place it at the disposal of the Prime Minister, a cabinet minister or a member of the Royal Family descended from George VI. Failing any of these, Chevening as a residence would be offered to the Canadian High Commissioner or the American Ambassador. The present Prince of Wales looked at Chevening but had other ideas. By convention successive foreign secretaries have, without expense to the taxpayer, used Chevening for whatever mix of rest, work and pleasure suits their character and circumstances.

This bald account does not convey the reality. I never went to Chevening without being amazed all over again at my good fortune. General Stanhope's victories over the French in Spain had been less emphatic than those of the Duke of Marlborough in Germany and Flanders, and the generosity of the nation was less sensational. Chevening is not as magnificent as Blenheim. It provides a first-class example of the tradition of English country-house building rather than a unique declaration of triumph. You approach through the hamlet of Chevening, past the church and farm buildings, into a courtyard flanked by the Georgian red brick of the house on three sides. The fourth side

442 DOUGLAS HURD: MEMOIRS

looks through iron gates on to a lime avenue to the ridge of the North Downs a mile away. On the opposite south side of the house an uncluttered lawn leads to a lake; to the right lies a patterned rose garden and a maze. The total is dignified, welcoming and very English. Although it was much bigger than any house I could ever have thought of living in, we never felt awed by Chevening. I always preferred its understated simplicities, its abundance of light and space, to the dark complications of the house used by prime ministers at Chequers. The latter is fascinating to visit, but suffers from an overflow of history.

We never turned Chevening into a family home. The rules of the trust wisely discourage this by laying down that the pictures and furniture of the Stanhope home are not to be changed. That may be one reason why it did not suit Prince Charles. Anyway, we had a home already; we had just completed work on Freelands, which was proving a success. Our time at Chevening would be limited and possibly short. It would clearly be a mistake to put down roots. Thanks to the understanding of the trust, and the hard-working friendship of our housekeeping couple Paul and Hilda, we had no responsibilities at Chevening. We spent roughly one weekend there each month and three Christmases.

From the professional point of view the usefulness of Chevening was its informality. I used it for entertaining foreign colleagues whom I wished to get to know away from their briefs and officials. Whisky late at night beside a generous log fire in the drawing room was the beginning of several working friendships. There are different levels at which a foreign secretary may deal with his overseas colleagues. It is perfectly possible to jog along at meeting after meeting in a routine relationship of politeness, even cordiality. But sometimes a moment arises, usually at short notice, where you need a deeper understanding. Will X stand shoulder to shoulder with you in a difficulty? How much weight will his routine expressions of friendship and regard carry when it comes to the point? For example, I badly needed and received Spanish support in the tense EU argument just described in the spring of 1994. Months before I had used Chevening to get alongside the new Spanish Foreign Minister, Javier Solana. He had his own reasons for sharing our argument, and I am not claiming that the Chevening whisky influenced what he did later. But the recollection of that informal evening spent in his company influenced my judgement of whether he would remain alongside, as he did, when the going got tough.

My German colleague Hans Dietrich Genscher turned Chevening to his own advantage. He arrived in a helicopter, frightening the geese by the edge of the lake. He brought not only a private secretary and a photographer but his biographer, a form of one-upmanship which I was unable to match.

I used Chevening to drag my senior advisers away from their routines as Foreign Office under-secretaries or ambassadors and invite them to think irregular thoughts. Other government departments used it when we were not there. There was already a tradition that the Chancellor of the Exchequer devised his budget in the library at Chevening, surrounded by his Treasury knights, who combined after dinner to sing madrigals. Those were the days when Treasury knights still had some say in the budget, as well as a taste for madrigals.

But my stronger memories of Chevening are personal: of working on red boxes upstairs in the tapestry room overlooking the lake; of rowing children on that lake, pushing through the green weed which every summer baffled the trustees, and scrambling ashore on one of the islands; of competitions after lunch in the maze whose leggy undergrowth provided gaps through which unscrupulous small children could cheat; of morning service in the church, though the hymns were pitched too high for the Hurd family; of the dining room with its unbroken line of Stanhope portraits, the most beautiful by Ramsay; of spring walks through lambs into the valley to the north. That walk, past the stile erected by Geoffrey and Elspeth Howe, culminated in sharp ascent on a staircase of railway sleepers to the keyhole cut in the beech trees on the ridge.

Or, perhaps most vivid of all, the return journey of the same walk at Christmastime. In wind and rain we looked for holly with berries from the hedgerow near where old maps showed the summer house of the Stanhopes. Just past that point Chevening came into sight. The big redbrick house fading into the dusk below us was saved from darkness by the warm light in the windows which promised tea, the big wooden jigsaw puzzle of the World which we kept for Christmas (three pieces missing), then snooker with Philip, and only the first glance at the boxes which would have arrived from the Foreign Office by this time but could wait for tomorrow.

25

CROATIA AND BOSNIA

For four years, from the summer of 1991 to the summer of 1995, Yugoslavia and its successor states could never be far from our minds. For me it had a particular character among several heavy problems which had to be handled at the same time.

This was not because of its huge importance for British interests. Britain had no substantial commercial or strategic stake in Croatia, Bosnia or the other states which had made up Yugoslavia. From time to time half-hearted attempts were made to justify our peacemaking efforts by talking of the danger of a general war. Certainly there were other piles of combustible material lying around: Kosovo which flared up after my time, and also Montenegro and Macedonia which so far have been subdued. But the chances of a big war blowing up out of Yugoslavia were never great.

The particular flavour of the Croatian and then the Bosnian crises compared with other problems which crossed my desk was of bitterness, mingled with doubt. Yugoslavia broke up in a way disastrous for its people. The boundaries of most of the states within it included large ethnic minorities. History had made the mixture. There was no way of peaceably redrawing the boundaries so that each state was ethnically tidy. There were thus three possibilities: the different communities had to learn to live together in harmony within the present boundaries; or the boundaries could be changed by military conquest; or people could be moved by force through 'ethnic cleansing'. Everyone outside Yugoslavia preached the virtues of the first solution once we had recognised that Yugoslavia as a single entity was doomed. But inside the two largest communities, the Serbs and Croats, hankered after a mix of the second and third solutions – military conflict accompanied by ethnic cleansing – with the Serbs in the lead in forcefulness and savagery.

The bad news from Yugoslavia was not continuous during those four years. There were periods of calm and a few of hope. But all the time a fuse was quietly burning its way towards the next set of atrocities. I came to dread the subject; my heart sank when it led the news bulletins. This dislike did not lead me to turn away. I learned later that I was criticised by my officials for spending so much of my time nagging away at it. International conferences, minutes to the Prime Minister, telephone calls to foreign colleagues, planning papers, meetings in my own office – all these fill the files to overflowing.

There was another big difference between Croatia/Bosnia and other problems. Most of the latter were morally and intellectually clear cut. They might well be complicated and operationally difficult, but the line which I thought we should follow was straightforward. That was true of German unification, the Treaty of Maastricht, the Gulf War, Hong Kong, the Falklands and a mass of lesser matters. My own mind, being neither subtle nor original, likes to cut to the centre of a problem and identify a way forward with which I am morally and intellectually content. I found this extraordinarily difficult with Croatia/Bosnia. We seemed to be working our way through a tangled thicket without paths or signposts.

The great majority of those with whom I dealt shared this feeling of fog and frustration. That was true of most Britons, continental Europeans and Americans. There were some individuals who from the beginning believed that there was no tangle, just a clear, well-posted path. On 27 June 1991, the day that Slovenia and Croatia declared their independence, I was at a European summit in Luxembourg. I noted sardonically in my diary, 'MT telephones me and issues instructions.' It was seven months since Margaret Thatcher had ceased to have that right. It was less than two years since she had landed us in considerable danger by her equally forthright but mistaken view of German unification. Throughout the four years of war in Croatia and Bosnia Margaret Thatcher impressed on me in letters, telephone calls and meetings her strong conviction that the question was a simple one of aggression by one country, Serbia, against the others; we should deal with Milosevic the aggressor as she had dealt with the Argentines and as all of us had dealt with Saddam Hussein. She was not alone, though almost all those who shared her view shared something else with her: they held at the time no responsibility for taking decisions and bearing their consequences. This did not in itself make them wrong. A minority in Britain were deeply stirred in a way which forced respect. One had to go back to the Spanish Civil War to find such a passionate, deep-seated distress about events in a foreign country, together with anger at the apparent passivity of the

British Government. In particular I remember my meeting at the Foreign Office with Miloska Nott, the Slovenian wife of my former cabinet colleague John Nott. Lady Nott was impressive because she spoke softly and because she was backing up her views with the practical organisation of help for Croats expelled by the Serbs from their homes.

But the indignation of individuals never coalesced into a sustained national movement. In a way I was always waiting for this. Individual passions ran so high that I half expected them to ignite opinion as a whole, but this never happened. My colleagues in government and all parties in the Commons were, with individual exceptions, sceptical of the need for even the limited intervention which we undertook. They found the complicated situation in former Yugoslavia hard to understand and the characters in the drama unsympathetic. A decision to commit British troops to fight a war in Bosnia would have been deeply unpopular at all times. Lesser decisions – for widespread bombing or for supply of arms to one of the parties – would have been easier to carry through, but there was never any decisive pressure on us to act against our own judgement as ministers.

Since the end of the Bosnian war, the individual voices of criticism have swelled into a chorus. Hindsight is a powerful tool. Milosevic initiated the war in Bosnia, he also helped to end it at the Dayton Conference in 1995. Because of Kosovo, he then threw away the opportunity (which his rival President Tudjman of Croatia seized) of moving his country towards the European mainstream. He was brutal from the beginning, as the ruins of Vukovar show. In hindsight it looks to some as if there was never a chance, that he showed villainy and intransigence throughout and that all diplomatic dealings with such a man were doomed. That is not my view. We had no illusions about Milosevic who dealt throughout in calculations of power and pressure. It was our aim to press him in the right direction. It took too long, and in the end he calculated wrong.

Since Dayton the doctrine of forceful intervention for humanitarian reasons in the affairs of other countries has led to military action in Kosovo, Timor and Sierra Leone. As I wrote in 1997, 'we are all interventionists now'. The latest interventions in Afghanistan and Iraq were essentially for self-defence, but a strong humanitarian justification had its place in the argument. But what is now settled doctrine was for almost all of us ten years ago arguable and obscure. We acted throughout in good conscience, though that is not itself a justification for particular decisions. We made mistakes. The war eventually ended in a peace treaty which satisfied no one, but has justified itself by lasting for eight years. That peace took four years to achieve. During this time British and European efforts saved many lives, but many others were lost. The tangled thicket was not our invention, it was real; but our effort to hack through it needs to be described with humility, particularly at those points where a different choice might (but only might) have led to a quicker peace.

I never believed that those who fought the wars in Croatia and Bosnia were historically bound to hate and kill one another. Neither there nor in Ireland did I think such hatred and killing inevitable. I had never visited Yugoslavia before the crisis, and claimed no expert knowledge, but the young Yugoslav men and women whom I had known, some of them quite well, had been precisely that – Yugoslavs. After the first meeting or two I realised that they were also Slovenes, Croats or whatever, but they acted and talked, and for all I could tell thought, as Yugoslavs. Nor did that seem remarkable. After all, I thought of myself as British rather than English. Yugoslavia had been on the map since 1919, first under kings, then after the bloody commotion of the Second World War under Tito. I had read of these wartime commotions and did not suppose that Yugoslavia was a haven of harmony, but Tito had built it into a substantial country. Yugoslavia was well respected in the world because of his successful defiance of Stalin, and the skilful diplomacy which somehow made him one of the leaders of the Third World. The unravelling of the country after his death was not an inevitable disaster, but the result of shortsighted greed for power.

I sometimes find it easier to think things through by writing a story about them. Early in the Bosnian war I put together a short story called 'The Summer House'. Its hero is a medium-rank Yugoslav civil servant working in the provincial forestry department in Sarajevo. A Serb, he builds and shares a summer house with his neighbour and fellow civil servant, a Croat. The savage history of their village is obscurely recorded in its cemetery, but 'in 1991 reality was the Forestry Department, the journals on plant disease, the intrigues for promotions and postings, Mr Tomic's accounts, his boy's football matches'. Talk of new war starts, and is dismissed. But then real war sweeps down on the hero, swallows up his son and his neighbour, and leaves him at the end with nothing except some experience of bureaucratic life and of tree diseases. I tried to trace the decline from his humdrum European life to savage tribal warfare, in a brief and pale reflection, I suppose, of Golding's *Lord of the Flies*. It is my best story.

Four years later I spent a few days in Vukovar making a series called *Search for Peace* for BBC Television. Vukovar, built gracefully on the Danube in solid Habsburg style, lies within Croatia but was assaulted and largely ruined by the Serbs in 1991. While I was there I began a story of a Croat soldier who escapes from that siege with his wife and gets a job as a waiter in a hotel on the Adriatic. When the war ends he is sent back to his home only to find it partly occupied by a Serb family which had in turn been ethnically cleansed by Croats from their home in the Krajna. The story, called 'Home to Vukovar', turns on how they react to their discovery.

I worked hard on these two stories. They are an attempt to trace the direct impact on human beings of the events which for me were a matter of paper, telephone calls, endless meetings and much wrestling in my own mind.

In September 1991 the first decisions were needed early. Yugoslavia disintegrated. I was faced at a meeting in Brussels with a proposal that the Western European Union should send a peacekeeping force to Croatia. The WEU was a European defence institution set up at Anthony Eden's initiative in the mid-fifties after the collapse of the project for a European Defence Community. It had served a political purpose then, but by 1991 was in search of a role. It seemed clear to me that this was gesture politics, on a par with the empty proclamation by our Luxembourger President at this time that the crisis in Yugoslavia was the hour of Europe. No one proposed for a moment that European troops should fight their way into Croatia or impose a settlement. All would depend on a ceasefire and the consent of both Croats and Serbs. At this stage, for different reasons, neither we nor the Germans were willing to commit ground troops. The French, I thought, had their own agenda, as I noted on 30 September: 'The French really want a big European army in Yugoslavia and an Anglo-French protectorate. Dumas [still the French Foreign Minister] tells me it is all a continuation of World War 2.' President Mitterrand around this time took me even further back in history: '*Mais vous comprenez, Monsieur le Ministre, c'est quatorze encore une fois.*' He implied that once again, as in 1914, it was for Britain and France to hold back the Germans. As already recorded on German unification, Mitterrand enjoyed playing with historical analogies, but had no intention of turning them into policy.

Throughout these years the French were characteristically agile. They worked with us pretty well as the only other serious military power in Western Europe, admitting us to their outer but not their inner thoughts. They had no sympathy for Milosevic but much for the Serbs, because of the First rather than the Second World War. They distrusted the German influence over Croatia, wanted to keep the Americans at arm's length, were willing to take risks, and above all wanted France and French policy to shine.

I had warned the Prime Minister on 17 September that we could not exclude absolutely and for ever the deployment of British troops in Yugoslavia. By now Peter Carrington, who had been asked to represent the EU, and separately the US Envoy Cyrus Vance were beginning the long, tortuous attempt to negotiate settlements between Serbia and the other states of the former Yugoslavia. Two of these, Slovenia and Croatia, had fought off Serb attempts to coerce them into submission. In the autumn of 1991 the question arose whether the West, and the nations of the EU in particular, should formally recognise these two as independent states. There was no problem about Slovenia, where fighting had stopped and where in any case the population was almost entirely ethnic Slovene. Croatia was very different. Peter Carrington, and indeed just about everyone involved except the strange constellation of the Germans and Margaret Thatcher, distrusted the intentions of President Tudjman of Croatia towards the large Serb minority in his country. Peter Carrington and a legal arbitration commission headed by a Frenchman, Robert Badinter, were trying to negotiate guarantees for ethnic minorities which would be a condition for international recognition of the new states. They had not yet completed their work with Croatia, and were anxious that EU states should not recognise the new nation until they had achieved those guarantees. The Secretary-General of the UN, Javier Pérez de Cuéllar, shared this view. But the Germans were in a hurry. Their public opinion, horrified by the Serb attack on Vukovar and growing atrocity stories, pressed hard for recognition as the only form of protection we could offer the Croats. It was about this time that Hans Dietrich Genscher advised me that as a general principle Germany, in view of its awful past, could not afford to find itself on the wrong side of any moral issue. He had Croatia in mind.

That was, of course, to oversimplify. An underlying German sympathy for Croatia went back to the days of the Austro-Hungarian Empire, and less reputably to the help which ruthless Croat nationalists had given to the Axis in the Second World War. More important, the peculiarity of the German attitude to Balkan troubles was beginning to emerge. There was a similarity here with the United States. For different reasons, the two countries where public opinion was most vehement against the Serbs were those countries which felt able to do least on the ground to check them. The Americans throughout rejected the idea of sending US troops to the former Yugoslavia. The Germans were equally opposed, partly for legal objections based on one interpretation of their constitution, but mainly for reasons of history. Chancellor Kohl once told me that, whatever the legal position, it would be disastrous to deploy German troops in any country which had been occupied by the Germans in the Second World War. This included everywhere in Yugoslavia. Hans Dietrich Genscher probably had little difficulty in synthesising all these considerations within his subtle and experienced mind. His successor, Klaus Kinkel, found the frustration almost intolerable. I often realised that his instincts were for a tougher line against the Serbs, but he had to bite back his words in the knowledge that he could not deliver.

As 1991 drew to a close German pressure for recognition of Croatia and Slovenia increased. I felt in private and on 26 November said in public that recognition was a matter not of principle but of timing. Croatia had in effect secured her own independence. It would be foolish and against our normal practice to deny that fact indefinitely by withholding recognition. On the other hand, Peter Carrington and other wise heads continued to urge delay so that they could continue to use recognition as a bargaining weapon with Tudjman.

It had been agreed that the Foreign Affairs Council should discuss the subject in Brussels on 16 December. The morning was spent debating aid to Russia and signing agreements with the Poles and the Czechs to pave the way for their eventual membership of the EU. Peter Carrington began the Yugoslav debate with a clear statement of the case for delay in recognition. I supported him at length. As the discussion continued in the Council Room there seemed to be a majority against immediate recognition. But this was not a matter for majority decisions. Nor was it something which the EU would do collectively. Recognition was (and is) a matter for individual states.

The account in my diary chimes with the reporting telegram sent from Brussels: 'Dumas inexplicably silent. Genscher stubborn. Then we dine [which meant that our official advisers were no longer present] and it gets worse. Gianni de Michelis [Italian Foreign Minister] storms and shouts, but actually provides the driving force for compromise.' The emerging compromise was that we should as individual states recognise not at once but a month later, on 15 January. The next question was whether recognition should then be automatic or could be further delayed if Robert Badinter and his commission tabled a negative report on his discussions with President Tudjman about Croat guarantees to their Serb minority.

> Insist on break. Ring PM to say Germany calling in her Maastricht debts. He at once and rightly says settle. Before that confer with Dumas who is tired and evasive as ever. We agree to argue for a chink of discretion if the Arbitration Commission produces a negative. Genscher accepts this, then retracts [he told us that he had telephoned Kohl who rejected the compromise]. Finally a tiny chink of opt out remains. Hans Van den Broek [Dutch Foreign Minister, in the chair] unhappy. Dumas, far too late, shows signs of fight. We settle 1 a.m. Press. To airport, to find it fog-bound. Bed [still in Brussels] 3 a.m.

So there it was, fairly typical of many long days of negotiation in Brussels, though most were on lesser subjects. We held to the agreement and recognised Slovenia and Croatia in mid-January. The Germans had recognised at once.

Peter Carrington and others said and continue to believe that this was a wrong decision which undermined their pressure on Tudjman, and also led to the premature recognition later of Bosnia, thus precipitating the Bosnian war. In general, British policy in these years has been attacked for being too mild towards Serbia. It is thus a trifle odd that the individual decision most often picked out for criticism went against them. I doubt the automatic connection with Bosnia, where there were different considerations, and am not at all clear that we would have helped the peacemakers by denying for a few more weeks something which was already an established fact: namely, the independence of Croatia.

The final negotiations of the Treaty of Maastricht had taken place a fortnight earlier. The Germans made no attempt at Maastricht to force the pace on Croatia and Slovenia. They did not raise the matter at all. It had already been agreed that the Foreign Affairs Council should discuss the matter after Maastricht but before Christmas. No deal, formal or informal, was struck at Maastricht on recognition. But at the crucial meeting on 16 December in Brussels Genscher reminded me, as I told the Prime Minister, of the undoubted fact that he and Kohl had been helpful in facilitating John Major's negotiating success at Maastricht. Now, so ran his argument, it was the Germans who were in political difficulty and it was our turn to help them by agreeing to the recognition of Croatia and Slovenia. This argument carried weight with the Prime Minister and myself. It did not seem sensible to carry the argument on recognition to the point of an angry disruption of the EU. I was (and remain) fairly confident that the Germans would have recognised in mid-December whatever anyone else did. Peter Carrington was disconsolate in the following weeks that we had let Tudjman off the hook, perhaps exaggerating the strength of that hook. He was by now concluding that, in Milosevic and Tudjman, he and Vance were dealing with two twisters whose undertakings were worthless.

Gradually the crisis shifted to Bosnia and the British involvement increased. In April 1992 my colleagues reluctantly agreed to send a modest field hospital of 300 men. Through that summer a miserable pattern began to establish itself. By this time the Bosnian Serbs, having refused to take part in a referendum on Bosnian independence, began to besiege Sarajevo. They shelled the city, but never launched a ground assault. They agreed to ceasefire after ceasefire, each of which broke down in a welter of mutual recrimination. Stories of Serb atrocities began to shock the world. Peter Carrington carried on his efforts manfully, but in private indicated that he had had enough. The

Americans became restive but not to the point of action. The pressure grew to find an answer through some form of European intervention.

This was also the summer of the Danish referendum on EU membership, and of the sterling crisis which ended on Black Wednesday.

For the next three years, British policy on Bosnia was essentially in the hands of three ministers – John Major, Malcolm Rifkind, Minister of Defence, and myself. We liked and respected one another. Although from time to time we differed on the right response to particular situations, we shared a general approach. We were emphatically not pro-Serb, or pro-anyone. We believed and said that, although there were no innocents among the leaders of the former Yugoslavia, the Serbs bore the main responsibility for originating the war in Bosnia and for continuing it. For that reason we supported economic sanctions against Serbia alone. Nevertheless, this was also a civil war, given that 90 per cent of those taking part were Bosnian Serbs, Bosnian Croats and Bosnian Muslims. We believed that our aim should be to detach Milosevic from the Bosnian Serbs, not to force all Serbs into a defiant laager. We supported the UN arms embargo imposed unanimously in September 1991 on all parties. We were keen to build up the humanitarian effort in Sarajevo and elsewhere, and slowly accepted that this would need military protection if it was to be effective. We faced colleagues in the Cabinet who, while not openly challenging our judgement, were reluctant to see greater British involvement. This reluctance was even more evident in the general feeling of the House of Commons. We disliked the idea of military intervention on the ground to throw back the Bosnian Serbs and impose a solution by force. Since the Americans and Germans had excluded themselves from any such action, it would in essence be Anglo-French, and we were not ready for that, being far from clear how it would end. We believed that peace could be achieved only by negotiation backed by pressure. We did not exclude air strikes, but, after listening to much professional advice, doubted if they would be effective without follow-up on the ground.

I shared, but was not satisfied with, this analysis. I am sure that was also true of my two close colleagues. I certainly cast around for additional or alternative tools. I discussed with Peter Carrington the possibility of recarving the frontiers of the former Yugoslav states, but we found this impracticable. We repeatedly considered how best to ease the pressure on Sarajevo. We tried to keep allies and partners together – hence, for example, a visit to Paris on 15 July 1992, 'to beard Dumas at Quai over divisive way in which they were undermining Carrington. D. is very affable but unrepentant, willing that C. should take the lead provided he leads us towards the French direction, i.e. a big conference in Paris.'

That July Britain took over the European presidency for the usual six months. Yugoslavia was high on our list of preoccupations, and I needed to visit the area and meet the leaders. On the 16th I spent two hours with President Tudjman in a modern villa built by Tito in the hills above Zagreb. Tudjman, like Tito, was fond of protocol. Immense hussars in splendid uniforms clanked impressively about the villa. A shrewd man, Tudjman almost persuaded me that he was not as villainous as he had been portrayed. He relaxed after a stiff start, and (falsely as it turned out) said he had no designs on the integrity of Bosnia. Afterwards I was driven south to the zone patrolled by our white-coated EU monitors. The Croatian war was over, and villages shattered by shells were beginning to return to normal, with the help of the UN Protection Force and these monitors.

Next day a Hercules flew me steeply down into Sarajevo airport, over green, cloud-shrouded hills and red-roofed villages. It was not a happy day. The air force was commanded by the Canadian General MacKenzie, then in his last days in Sarajevo. I found him tired and biased against Bosnians, that is, the legal Bosnian Government dominated by Muslims. Once I had inspected the huge hangar full of UN stores to be distributed to refugees, a French armoured car drove me into the city and the Presidential Palace. I was told to put on a flak jacket, and regretted it. Wearing it I felt silly rather than safe. I was warned by the UN that a mortar would explode near by some time during my talk with President Alija Izetbegovic, and it did.* The atmosphere of distrust and double talk was pervasive.

This was the first of my several meetings with President Izetbegovic. Usually I am quick, sometimes too quick, to assess a character, but I never knew what to make of him. He seemed to combine the dignified, the pathetic and the devious in proportions hard to quantify. We had quite a good talk that morning. I disliked the walkabout which followed, partly because of the flak jacket, mainly because of the huge army of cameramen into which I was steered. Izetbegovic at my elbow was anxious for shots of me against shattered walls and broken windows. Richard Gozney, my main private secretary, who was meticulous in overseeing such occasions, was not with me. 'By vexatious misunderstanding (no Richard), don't stop outside hospital with him [Izetbegovic] and this causes offence. Press conference, not too bad, but I am too brusque' as sometimes happened when I felt harassed.

The following day in Belgrade I called first on Prime Minister Milan Panić, until recently a businessman in the USA:

---

*David Owen records the same phenomenon on his first visit to Sarajevo seven weeks later.

a phenomenon, a clown with Jimmy Carter principles, parachuted into the Balkans by Milosevic, but now running amok with a mixture of idealism and commercialism. We have a lively set-to trying to channel his enthusiasm for peace and human rights into the actual situation in Bosnia and Kosovo. Then to the Patriarch, small, white bearded, saintly back to first principles. Then Milosevic for an hour, very hard in self-justification, a stream of untruths about past and present, no Serbian troops in Bosnia, ample human rights in Kosovo, but prudent and half consenting about future. Debate here both more defensive and more open than in Zagreb.

It was my first meeting with Milosevic. He was less grand and easier to talk to than Tudjman, his English being perfect. The combination here noted of untruthful defiance on the past and caution on the future marked most of our discussions. Milosevic was quicker-minded than Tudjman, but in the end his judgement proved worse. Both being unscrupulous and unreliable men, Tudjman salvaged and Milosevic wrecked his country.

I rounded off the tour that same day in Macedonia, where as President of the European Council of Ministers I had to defend the indefensible delay, caused by Greek intransigence, in recognising and helping that new country. 'I have no case and stick to it modestly. All redeemed by delectable moussaka and trout and white wine half way up Vodno mountain with ['Kiro] Gligorov [the President] on lawn under trees. They treat me undeservedly well.'

My host in Albania, the final stop on the tour, was President Sali Berisha, whom I had met improbably at a Conservative conference in Blackpool. He drove us up into the hills to the Skandarbeg Castle and Museum. The President was keen to show off his popularity, but I judged that he was more waving than waved at. After a huge lunch we walked in our town shoes through a village, chosen by us at random. The peasants were startled but not particularly enthusiastic as they tended their baking-hot fields and muddy irrigation channels. Here, indeed everywhere, were the famous concrete bunkers erected like monstrous white mushrooms on the orders of the former crazed dictator Enver Hoxha to defeat the combined assault by troops of NATO and the Soviet Union which he daily expected.

Next day, in another world in Brussels, my shoes cleaned, I chaired my first Council of Foreign Ministers. We were told that yet another ceasefire in Bosnia had collapsed. There seemed no respite:

Jessica's 7th birthday, but a deeply gloomy day. The clamour and emotional pressure for intervention growing fast here and especially in the US. Our prudent stance looks feeble and inhumane. Yet I cannot think that air strikes would settle anything much, and a ground operation to deal with snipers etc. would be interminable. Worry now that UNPROFOR [the UN Protection Force] will withdraw from Sarajevo. A lot of telephoning produces reasonable instructions to Washington and New York on extending humanitarian role.

On 18 August we agreed to send a British battalion group to Bosnia to help escort the humanitarian convoys. We also decided that the time had come for a substantial diplomatic effort to resolve the situation, or at least shift it into a different gear. The London Conference on Yugoslavia brought together the Americans and Europeans, the UN and the main parties in the fighting. It went better than I had expected.

David Owen took over from Peter Carrington as the main EU negotiator. It was not a job in which anyone could be expected to persevere for long. I had difficulty at first with Roland Dumas over this, but the other governments welcomed David. 'Wholly different to PC. Will be a pain to us doubtless, but in a good cause.' I did not know David Owen well, and was familiar with dire tales of his abrupt behaviour to subordinates as Foreign Secretary under Jim Callaghan in the late seventies, and later of his wayward dealings with the Liberals and his fellow Social Democrats when they tried to build a viable third British political party. I discounted most of this. I had always enjoyed his energy and open manner of debating. Dumas was objecting because recently David Owen had publicly supported air strikes against the Serbs. The Prime Minister, a strong advocate of his appointment, believed that he would grapple open-mindedly with the realities once he got to know them; and so it proved.

John Major was at his best presiding over a big conference. As a technical feat, his chairmanship of the Yugoslav Conference in August 1992 was only matched by his chairing of the EU summit in Edinburgh four months later – both held at a time of acute political strain for him. He worried about the disorder of it all, the petty arguments about seating and interpretation, but he knew how to stifle the worst and stimulate anything even half good in the main actors.

Entirely consumed at Y. Conference, which stumbles towards success, thanks to the hard work of our team dealing with characters, issues and documents of amazing complexity, and to the high skill of PM in the chair. He is the best Chairman I have known. Izetbegovic is persuaded into talks, Karadzic [Bosnian Serb leader] into a unilateral decision to stop heavy weapons, Dumas into accepting David Owen, Boutros Ghali [new Secretary-General

of the UN] into and out of sulks, Germans and Dutch ditto. Final
hesitations about tabling a paper on Serbia triumphantly resolved.
I play a secondary part, fending off the lesser characters,
interposing here and there. Finish about 8.30 p.m. with a clutch of
documents and a little hope.

Next day, 29 August, I went back to an interrupted holiday in Devon
clutching that hope.

On 25 September the Commons debated Serbia. I reported that the
London Conference had ruled out alteration of boundaries in the former
Yugoslavia except by agreement, and established the principle of minority
rights. I was clear that the Serbs bore the largest responsibility for starting
and continuing the war, which was why the mandatory sanctions applied
only to Serbia. I analysed the possibility of air strikes. They would be
morally justified, and I did not rule them out in the future. But when
addressing the House I raised doubts about their effectiveness:

> Given the terrain, given the weapons being used for most of the
> killing, given the way in which civilian and military, Croats, Muslims
> and Serbs, live side by side, and the likelihood that military action
> of this kind would immediately bring to an end the humanitarian
> activities of the Red Cross and High Commission for Refugees, we
> and our other allies and partners have come down against that
> option each time that it has been considered. It would be easy, I fear,
> to increase the casualties without stopping the conflict.

A fortnight before this speech I had listened to a sombre military
briefing about the danger of British forces being sucked remorselessly
into an open-ended and ill-defined commitment in which they faced
significant risks. We were warned, for instance, that the Bosnian Serbs
held several hundred portable surface-to-air missiles which could be
used against Allied aircraft.

Three months later the scene had barely altered. I wrote an article for
the *Daily Telegraph* between Christmas and the New Year, partly to clear
my own mind. After describing the life-saving work of our troops and
aid workers I talked about David Owen (for the EU), and Cyrus Vance
(for the UN) who were about to produce their plan and map for the
three ethnic components of Bosnia to accommodate Bosnian Muslims,
Bosnian Croats and Bosnian Serbs within one country.

> Peacemakers are invariably mocked until they succeed. 'It is only
> talk' they are told, which of course is true. But it is also true that
> talk – a negotiated settlement – is indispensable to peace. War

cannot be the eventual arbiter between Serb, Croat, Muslim or Albanian any more than it can between Israel and the Arabs. They can fight for months or years but there will be no outright accepted winner. A peace process is as essential in the one set of disputes as in the other ... I have always distrusted the idea of military intervention by the West to force a settlement in Yugoslavia. I still do, but the Serbs should note a change. They have brought even those who hold that view to the point where we can imagine armed action against them to prevent a general Balkan war.

I made many speeches and broadcasts and wrote many articles about Bosnia in these years. This particular piece with its heartfelt endorsement of diplomacy, coupled with a warning about the use of force against the Serbs, accurately summarises the balance in my mind.

The comparison with Israel and the Arabs has often returned to me. The most frequent criticism of our policy in Bosnia is that we were timid, allowing years of suffering and oppression to pass without effective remedy. The critics imply that the lesson has been learned. But as I write, the cycle of suffering and oppression between Israel and Palestine continues unchecked. Hardly a day passes without the killing of innocent individuals. A future generation of critics blessed with hindsight will certainly compare the two situations. We laboured then for peace, they labour now; the tools remain blunt, the work slow.

At the turn of the year we began to focus on the arrival of the Clinton administration after the defeat of President George Bush. The Republicans in their last months, with Larry Eagleburger as Secretary of State, had shown themselves more active. Clinton had promised, without precision, to be more active still. At my suggestion the Prime Minister called a seminar on Yugoslavia at Number Ten on 22 January 1993. For once he was not at his best in the chair. Distracted by other problems, he stuck too closely to the agenda and did not allow discussion to range widely. But it was useful to have in the same room David Owen, our chiefs of staff and our ambassadors at the UN and in Washington. We noted that public opinion here was less exercised than in other countries. The reports of our troops and aid workers who saw what was happening on the ground helped to balance the oversimplified belief, widespread in Germany and the United States, that the Serbs were uniquely guilty. David Owen reckoned that the chances of his new plan succeeding were 50–50. Much would depend on the new US administration endorsing his map, which meant telling Izetbegovic that he would not get any more from them. We discussed additional sanctions against Serbia, and the pros and cons of limited air strikes against the Bosnian Serbs. David Owen still favoured these, but the general view was that air strikes were unlikely to change policy, and were valid only if the target itself was important for checking the Serbs. We all strongly opposed lifting the arms embargo as a counsel of despair. By now Britain had 2,600 troops on the ground in Bosnia, more than any other country. We had delivered 13,000 tons of goods and greatly reduced the number of potential Bosnian deaths from hunger that winter.

We tried to influence the new administration as they slowly appointed their top officials and shaped their policy. In February the Prime Minister in Washington pressed the Vance–Owen plan on President Clinton. In April Owen and Vance scored a breakthrough: they persuaded all the leaders, including Milosevic, to accept their detailed plan for Bosnia. At a meeting in Athens on 1 May even Radovan Karadzic, the stubborn and disagreeable Bosnian Serb leader, was pushed to agree, subject to the agreement of the Bosnian Serb Assembly at a meeting to be held a week later. David Owen felt, with justifiable pride, that the bloody Bosnian war just might be over at last.

The Americans were thinking on different lines. It was arranged that the new Secretary of State, Warren Christopher, should tour Europe to expound and consult over a new American policy, beginning in Britain. The Prime Minister, Malcolm Rifkind and I received him at Chevening on Sunday afternoon, 2 May. We met upstairs in the room with the Berlin tapestries which I used as my study, and continued work over dinner of asparagus and underdone beef.

Throughout our time together in office, Warren Christopher and I worked well in harness. Later he came and stayed with us at Westwell, and I took him to watch cricket at Blenheim, which he found incomprehensible, and tennis at Wimbledon, where he was thoroughly at home. He had quite a different temperament from Jim Baker. No jokes, no Texan aphorisms, no racy stories from the past, no forthright assertion of authority – but a quiet, persistent voice, courteous manners from a past generation, and a good lawyer's ability to master the detail of a subject without losing its essential core.

But Warren Christopher puzzled us that day at Chevening. American policy-making is not carried out in the dark. The British Ambassador in Washington, Robin Renwick, operated well upstream, with contacts which alerted him to the way thoughts were moving long before they reached the President. John Major's Foreign Office adviser, Rod Lyne, had already established a good link with his counterpart in Washington, Tony Lake. We knew that the new administration was focusing on the case for lifting the arms embargo and supplying weapons to the Bosnian Muslims. The Prime Minister had already sent Clinton a message questioning the wisdom of this and saying that we would rather, though reluctantly, examine the separate argument for air strikes. Yet when

Warren Christopher presented his case he showed no sign of acknowledging this correspondence, but began the argument as if from the beginning. Economic sanctions, he said, were too slow in operating on the Serbs. The arms embargo worked against the Bosnian Government. The President believed that the embargo should be lifted and the Bosnian Muslims supplied with what they needed. The United States would actively help in procuring arms for them in Eastern Europe. The President acknowledged that the immediate effect of the 'lift' might be a Serb offensive, to gain maximum advantage before the new arms reached their enemies. This might be deterred by NATO air strikes.

The Prime Minister, supplemented by Malcolm Rifkind and myself, explained why we opposed lifting the arms embargo. Since this is one of the two key arguments in the whole debate about Bosnia I will pause briefly to set it out. Rereading the papers, I can feel rising again in my mind the strong mix of arguments and emotions which made me and many others so emphatic against 'lift'.

The mandatory arms embargo on the whole of the former Yugoslavia was passed unanimously by the Security Council in September 1991 when the fighting was still confined to Croatia. Everyone accepted that once the Bosnian war got under way the embargo created an imbalance in favour of the Bosnian Serbs, given the artillery and other arms which they inherited from the Yugoslav National Army. At first sight, and some saw no further, it seemed only fair to correct that imbalance.

The first difficulty was legal, but led back into reality. The embargo, mandatory under international law, could be lifted only by another Security Council resolution. Russia, because of its veto, would have to assent. The only change to which the Russians could conceivably agree would be one which lifted the embargo from everyone. Arms would then freely flow to all the warring parties. Whatever advantage the Bosnian Muslims might gain would be less important than the fact that Bosnia would be awash with arms. Answering a question from me, Warren Christopher made it clear that the Americans believed that the Croats as well as the Bosnian Muslims should receive arms. Indeed, geography made it impossible to imagine a serious supply of arms to the Bosnian Government in Sarajevo which did not pass through Croatia, and the Croats would want their whack. But at this stage the Bosnian Croats were almost, though not quite, as ruthless as the Bosnian Serbs in their determination to dominate a large slice of Bosnia as their own.

'Lift' would mean in practice the withdrawal of the increasing humanitarian effort and of the growing number of mainly European soldiers protecting that effort under the UN flag. There were some, including David Owen in some moods, who believed that the humanitarian effort prolonged the war; though David with the rest of us believed that 'lift' would be the surest way of doing that. What was certain was that Bosnians of all backgrounds, who would otherwise have died of malnutrition and exposure, were kept alive over three winters by the work of the UN. This work would have come to an end if we had opted to intensify the war by 'lift' instead of trying to end it. Eventually, as we shall see, even the Bosnian Government, the hottest exponent of 'lift', agreed that it should be postponed for that reason.

There was, however, a more fundamental argument against 'lift' which was hard to put across but which moved me strongly. We were trying not just to keep people alive by providing food and shelter, but to end the war which was ruining their lives. While Warren Christopher was putting the case for 'lift' at Chevening it seemed as if the Owen–Vance plan was going to work. It was frustrated a few days later when the Bosnian Serb Assembly rejected it. Peter Carrington's earlier efforts had also been frustrated; so were later plans and enterprises for peace, whether mounted by David Owen, Cyrus Vance and others in Geneva, or by imaginative soldiers like Michael Rose and Rupert Smith on the ground. But they and we had to keep on trying. The war would not end through military victory but through a negotiated peace. Pressure, as well as diplomacy, was needed to achieve that peace. But 'lift' was not pressure for peace but a vote for war. As I had written in the *Telegraph*, 'we could of course withdraw our troops, end the humanitarian effort and let the cocks, fully spurred, fight it out in the cockpit. Before 1914 that was the way of treating the Balkans; it did not work very well.' We had to do better.

Later I used an even sharper phrase to the same effect. Sometimes phrases occur to me which I know I ought to suppress not because they are untrue but because they are *too* apt; they strike deep and are dangerous. I was in a plane, flying I cannot remember where, when it came to me that what the proponents of 'lift' were after was not a negotiated peace but 'a level killing field'. The echo of Cambodia gave the phrase its strength; each side would after 'lift' have the wherewithal for years to produce heaps of skulls in the manner of Pol Pot. I asked David Martin, then my parliamentary private secretary, whether I should use the phrase. He said I should use it if I felt it, and I did. But it was too sharp; it shocked rather than educated. Some critics with deliberate obtuseness wrote that I must have been arguing for an *un*level killing field. That is nonsense. I was arguing for an end to killing, for continuing to feed the hungry and for finishing the war by negotiation.

Nowadays, as the arguments become blurred and oversimplified, the case for 'lift' has become more widely accepted. Indeed, as the months passed, the peace effort flagged and the war continued. I came myself to believe gloomily that 'lift' might be inevitable. But it is worth recording that at the time the arms embargo was overwhelmingly accepted as right. The Labour Party accepted it; so did the most effective of our parliamentary critics, the Liberal Democrat leader, Paddy Ashdown. So did the Europeans, with occasional German reluctance; so did the majority in the Security Council. No one could accuse David Owen of timidity or overcaution. In a long memorandum to the European foreign ministers in April 1993 he argued the case against 'lift', concluding, 'It might salve people's consciences for a few weeks, but it could be a fatal step towards a wider Balkan war.' I would have stressed 'longer' rather than 'wider', but the point is the same. This whole argument stretches well beyond Bosnia to the underlying question of the responsibility of politicians, particularly politicians who call themselves Christian, for the lives of those over whom they have a fleeting influence. This thought lay close to the heart of what I believed I was about as Foreign Secretary.

Warren Christopher left Chevening that night courteous but disappointed. Unfortunately, the British press got hold of the idea that we thought he had presented his case inadequately. This was not true; he had argued well for a mistaken policy. Warren Christopher had hardly picked up our admittedly reluctant willingness to go along with air strikes as a check to Serb, or conceivably Croat, attacks in Bosnia. We saw this as an alternative not a supplement to 'lift'. The concept had been discussed by ministers on 27 April and in a full cabinet meeting on 29 April. Ken Clarke, Norman Lamont, Peter Lilley and others were puzzled and unwilling, but there was enough support for the recommendation of the three ministers most closely involved. It was the first of many such discussions over the next two years.

Perhaps it is reasonable to insert here once again the thought that life was not all Bosnia. For example, 5 May was

Cold and bright. A tense day. Pick up specs from Mr Pope in Wimpole Street. Walk to BBC. Give evidence for 2 hours to Select Committee on Bosnia. Waffle more than usual, partly from fatigue, partly to give little away. Shrewd Labour questioning. Give lunch to Mandela at 1 CG [Carlton Gardens]. He has shrunk a bit, but is as ever courteous and more forthcoming than usual. Talk almost entirely about the complex relationship with Buthelezi [the Zulu leader]. Last day of report stage [in Commons] on Maastricht. I have to conduct the retreat and acquiesce in Amendment 2 on Social Chapter. Do this with some elegance but no fun. After our surrender the debate peters out and escape to LHR [Heathrow] at 9 instead of 10. Long flight to Budapest to join the Queen in ghastly modern dark guesthouse – J[udy] and John [Sawers]; at first jolly, then sleepy.

At this time there was a change in Paris which eased my life considerably. Alain Juppé replaced Roland Dumas as Foreign Minister. It was impossible to dislike Roland Dumas: he was charming, intelligent, with an experience and interests which ranged far outside politics. He was warmly hospitable to the Hurd family when we visited him at his home to the east of Bordeaux, though possibly apprehensive that our two boisterous children might do terrible things to his slender Giacometti. But I never felt that I was in his confidence.

When I first breakfasted with Alain Juppé at the Quai d'Orsay on 2 April 1993 I wrote, 'nimble and friendly, not a great man'. Later the praise would have been more emphatic. I enjoyed the subtlety and sharpness of his mind, even though he never overflowed or revealed much in the way of personal feeling. We had some tough arguments on European matters, but he proved a reliable and intelligent colleague on Bosnia at a difficult time. I am not entirely sure that my admiration for him was fully reciprocated, but I hope he enjoyed in his own buttoned-up way our close work together.

David Owen believed that we could have imposed his plan on the Bosnian Serbs after they rejected it. I fully supported the plan but did not see how in practice it could be imposed by force. David Owen was sure that Milosevic had made a genuine effort to bring round the Bosnian Serbs, and his book *Balkan Odyssey* provides evidence of this. But the relationship between Milosevic and the different Bosnian Serb chieftains was murky. It was necessary to pile the pressure on Milosevic by direct discussion and through sanctions. He must be forced to bring the Bosnian Serbs once again to the table, this time to accept the Vance–Owen plan or a variation, and see it through. This eventually happened, but in changed circumstances and after my time.

Meanwhile, to David Owen's indignation, the Americans were ignoring his plan. Once again they puzzled me. I was invited at short notice to Washington and found myself at a meeting on 21 May with Warren Christopher and our Russian colleague, Andrei Kozyrev. The Americans had decided that we needed to involve the Russians more closely. They produced a rambling draft document which they had agreed with Kozyrev. Its striking characteristic was that it neglected the Vance–Owen plan, and emphasised the need to check further Bosnian Serb advances, rather than induce them to withdraw to the Vance–Owen map. I too was keen to involve Kozyrev, and relieved that the pressure on 'lift' was relaxed. But before going any further I needed to talk to Juppé. I saw him in New York that night and we both flew back to Washington the next day with a clutch of Anglo-French amendments to keep alive Vance–Owen and the prospect of Serb withdrawal. These were mostly accepted, but by then the damage had been done. The *New*

York Times had published the original Russo-American draft. From New York I had talked on the telephone with a morose David Owen, who already knew the facts. In his book he deals generously with what he regards as our connivance at the torpedoing of his plan by the Americans. He puts his finger on one essential point: he and Cyrus Vance had a mission to Bosnia; Alain Juppé and I had to consider the whole partnership between our countries and the United States. These were different perspectives. We had to judge how far we could carry out reasonable disagreements with the Americans on Bosnia without endangering the wider partnership.

Another difficulty soon became apparent. David Owen has an American wife, and knows America well, but he had a knack of rubbing Americans up the wrong way. He enjoyed crossing the Atlantic, charging up the beach with guns blazing and telling them what was what and where they were going wrong. It is usually absurd to generalise about such a varied country as the USA, but there is one characteristic about its leaders which David ignored: they admire and sometimes practise blunt speech, but it is almost always within a framework of accepted thought which they regard as correct. They are ill at ease with forceful, intelligent Europeans who come whirling at them from outside that framework, dealing in paradoxes and complications. Peter Carrington was the kind of European diplomat whom they expected and admired, though he came from a very different background to their own. They sometimes found it difficult to know what to make of David Owen.

Within days we were engaged in negotiating a Security Council resolution declaring so-called safe areas. Of all the episodes in the Bosnian tragedy, this is the one I find least easy to defend in retrospect. The French took the initiative, clutching at the concept of safe areas as a short-term expedient to save the Muslim enclaves in the Drina valley in eastern Bosnia from a new Serb onslaught. I discussed this with Juppé in Paris on 1 June: 'We are in a rhetorical nonsense on safe areas in Bosnia, but he rationalised it well, and we remain bound together.' From a visit to Romania and Bulgaria I sent instructions to David Hannay, British Ambassador at the UN, trying to water down the phrasing of the motion so that it carried less of an unrealistic commitment. On 4 June, 'Eventually fly home, trying to devise a new Bosnia policy. Safe havens resolution passed, unlikely to work. Dine on board, all tired. Westwell at its best, summer evening light, stream down to a trickle.' Presumably because I was tired, I used the word 'haven', which we had excluded from the text of the resolution because it was felt it created too absolute an impression. On Monday 7 June I reminded an office meeting in London of our earlier view: that the safe areas policy needed three factors for success – a Security Council resolution, which we had achieved, a degree of local consent, which was absent, and substantially more troops with a proper UN–NATO agreement on command and control. The question arose whether we should contribute more men ourselves. I felt strongly and David Owen agreed that we had done more than our share already. We were urging the Pakistanis, Indians, Iranians and some Latin Americans to build the UN force to the level which their commander said was required to carry out the new concept. This was originally estimated as meaning 32,000 additional troops, but even the later concept of a 'light minimum' of 5,000 proved unworkable.

The French were criticising the Americans for not putting men on the ground. David Owen was criticising the Americans for opposing his plan. Warren Christopher rang me early one morning to criticise David Owen for his criticisms. I took the call naked in a bedroom in Luxembourg, a defenceless posture which somehow made explaining David more difficult.

In the absence of extra troops the safe areas resolution, though it worked in the short term, was a bluff, which, as Malcolm Rifkind pointed out, could easily be called. The Bosnian Muslim Government knew this well, but the rest of the world did not. Once it was clear that the UN could not raise the extra troops we should have admitted as much and changed the resolution. The motion was ambiguously worded and it has been argued that there was no commitment in it to protect or militarily defend the areas if the deterrent effect of the UN presence did not work. Nevertheless, I should have backed my own scepticism at the time and held back the French from letting rhetoric outrun reality. As it was, we fell back on the concept of NATO air strikes to deter and if necessary punish the Bosnian Serbs for future attacks. In practice this was not enough.

The miserable pattern continued. David Owen and Cyrus Vance laboured away at fresh negotiations in Geneva and the local capitals. A new Contact Group including the Russians began to elaborate its own plans for a settlement. Nothing matured. On the ground fighting flared up and died down repeatedly. Absolute victory was beyond the reach of any party, but so was absolute peace. There were no heroes, but the Bosnian Serbs fell below all others in bad faith and cruelty. Michael Rose in his book *Fighting for Peace* tells in detail how he spent the year 1994 commanding the UN force. A stylish optimist who ten years earlier had shown me round West Belfast, he tried in a brave and colourful way to put into practice the principle of a UN peacekeeping force committed to peace without making enemies, but in the end it was not enough.

I pick out some personal recollections.

In January 1994 I visited the British troops in Bosnia. New snow was weighing down the pines on the hillsides flanking the road which our engineers had built to carry relief supplies from the base at Tomislavgrad up to Vitez. The road was almost Roman in its importance. Our Land-Rover drew into a muddy siding to let a great convoy of empty British and Danish trucks return south for more supplies. At Vitez the Coldstream Guards were in charge. Serb artillery was not far away in the hills, but the main task of our troops was to keep Croats and Muslims from attacking one another. Experience of Northern Ireland made this a natural task, and the soldiers had organised a memorable Christmas for local children. I slept in a bare room with a naked light bulb but no hot water, and this seemed apt. A cock crowed repeatedly. Next day General Rupert Smith jolted with my private secretary John Sawers and myself in a Warrior armoured car to the main UN headquarters at Kiseljac. We stopped at one point where a Malaysian truck had fallen into the river, and again when our Warrior broke down. It was cold in the Warrior and impossible to see out of it. Rupert Smith read a Mary Stewart novel; John and I concocted a short story about a Warrior journey. All in all, I found what I expected – no sudden ray of hope, but the British army doing well a professional job which they thought worthwhile – 'but no British interest can justify them staying for ever'.

Saturday 5 February 1994 was an outstandingly beautiful day at Chevening; snowdrops and aconites were massed under the trees in front of the lake. In the afternoon I heard of the shell which had landed in the market square at Sarajevo, killing sixty-eight people. As usual there was dispute as to who had fired it, but the assumption had to be that it was the Bosnian Serbs. From a clinical point of view, nothing had changed. The shell which had destroyed these innocent lives did not alter the military, political, legal or even moral situation with which we were wrestling. We already knew that all sides were capable of such an act of careless cruelty, and particularly the Bosnian Serbs. But we do not live in a clinical world, and on balance we should be glad of the fact. I was enough of a politician to know at once that the situation had fundamentally changed. I spent that weekend at Chevening on the telephone. As often happens, the first questions were procedural and, as is also common, the chosen procedure affects the substance. At my request David Hannay in New York sounded out his French and American colleagues with a view to immediate NATO action. They concurred that NATO rather than the UN Security Council should tackle the matter, and I flew to Brussels on Sunday night, cancelling a planned visit to South Africa.

The French and Americans proposed a NATO ultimatum to the Serbs to pull their guns back from Sarajevo. The Prime Minister and I were clear that we should go along with this, and John Major called a meeting of the Defence and Overseas Policy Committee of senior ministers for 5 p.m. on Tuesday evening, 8 February. He made the case for the ultimatum, but it soon appeared that most colleagues were against us,

Michael Portillo and Michael Heseltine in particular. Malcolm Rifkind was just back from Bosnia, very conscious of the difficulties on the ground and of the view of Michael Rose, who was busy negotiating a local agreement on Sarajevo airport. He was not ready that afternoon to go along with the Franco-American idea of an ultimatum to the Bosnian Serbs. The Prime Minister tried to sum up the discussions in favour of the plan, but this failed and he went off to a meeting in Leicester.

We were left in a thoroughly uncomfortable position. The NATO Council was due to meet next morning. Our representative, Sir John Weston, needed instructions; we had none to give. During these next hours, as often over this period, I was helped and sustained by the professional skills and good sense of two Foreign Office officials: Pauline Neville-Jones and my private secretary John Sawers. I talked to Malcolm Rifkind, and to the Prime Minister on the telephone; our triumvirate was reunited. I tried to get hold of Warren Christopher, who rang back after midnight. I thought it best to explain frankly how we stood, or rather didn't stand, and he was understanding. Eventually I got to bed. Earlier that day I had had to deal with the visiting President of Armenia ('unremarkable') and give evidence to the Foreign Affairs Select Committee of the Commons on Hong Kong ('uneventful').

Under a tactic agreed with John Major, I called on Michael Heseltine in his ministerial office in Victoria Street early next morning. Michael liked to operate by listening and speaking. There were no papers in his office, but elegant furniture and distinguished modern pictures. One of the benefits of proper cabinet Government is that you work closely enough with colleagues to know whether to trust them on difficult matters where your own first reaction is against them, but where the responsibility is theirs. Michael Heseltine heard me out and immediately accepted what I said. (I had to draw on the same reserve of personal confidence with Ken Clarke in the Ioannina crisis a month later. But that day on Bosnia it was the Prime Minister who tackled Ken and won him round.) That made a majority. With minutes rather than hours in hand, Sir John Weston received his instructions to support the French and the Americans. The historian relying on official papers will not hear of this commotion. The official record of the Defence and Overseas Policy Committee meeting concludes with the decision arrived at on Wednesday morning rather than the indecision of the meeting itself on Tuesday afternoon.

That was not the end of the episode. We still had to get the full Cabinet to ratify the decision we had made and to carry the Commons. On the Wednesday afternoon I began to hear a groundswell of criticism from the Commons against our stand. Thursday had to be another day of persuasion. Ted Heath was one of the strongest critics of British or

NATO intervention in Bosnia, which he thought would just make things worse. I took coffee with him in Wilton Street on Thursday morning. He agreed to see Robin Renwick, British Ambassador in Washington, to get a professional view of the American position, and remained blessedly silent for the rest of the day. I saw Paddy Ashdown and David Steel from the Liberal Democrats, then Jack Cunningham, the Labour Shadow Foreign Secretary. Labour spokesmen caused me no difficulty at all during this period, but on the whole I preferred talking with Paddy Ashdown, who consistently pressed for a more forward policy on the ground, while supporting the arms embargo. He was critical but knowledgeable and I always learned something from seeing him.

The Cabinet later that morning caused no problem, all the doubting ministers having had their say on Tuesday. I worked on my Commons statement and ate sandwiches at the Foreign Office with George Jones from the *Daily Telegraph*. At 3.30 p.m. I stumbled somewhat with some sentences in my statement and the left-wing Labour MP Dennis Skinner (a strong opponent of intervention) thought that my heart was not in what I said. But it went well enough, and our backbenchers, about whom I was most worried, were acquiescent. Then to the Commons tearoom for further persuasion, then a party meeting of backbenchers upstairs, where Malcolm Rifkind and I stonewalled against the doubts. 'We are at the mercy of events now (and there is no truth in Sarajevo) and I especially.'

That wave, like many others, rose then subsided without ever breaking on the shore. Michael Rose's airport agreement held for a time and next week the Prime Minister and I flew to Moscow to hear Boris Yeltsin's complaints about being kept in the dark on our Bosnia policy.

Several months earlier I had minuted to the Prime Minister: 'more than any country, at some cost to our reputation, we have been the realists in this. We should continue to insist on realistic objectives and timetables.' That remained true throughout. But part of realism was maintaining the Atlantic Alliance, and that meant keeping our disagreements with the Americans within bounds. Our triumvirate of ministers was very conscious of this throughout, particularly the Prime Minister. Of course, we were sometimes irritated by the Americans, who were strong on policy but weak on risk-sharing, just as they were irritated by what they saw as our excessive caution. Some critics, drawing on hostile American sources, have exaggerated the strains which resulted. Strains there were, but the leaders on both sides of the Atlantic deliberately kept them under control.

A minor episode not up to now reported illustrates the point. In the summer of 1994 Manfred Worner, Secretary-General of NATO, died after a long, sad illness. There was urgent need of a successor, not least because of NATO's growing role in Bosnia. In the first ten days of September the French, Germans and Americans took separate initiatives to let me know that they would welcome me as the next Secretary-General. I talked to the Prime Minister, who was alarmed. He knew by then that I would be resigning before long, but he was not yet ready to replace me. It would look, he thought, as if I were leaving a sinking ship. As always he spoke highly of the help I gave him, but would not have been John Major if he had not also mentioned that we might lose the Witney by-election which would follow my move to NATO.

I politely declined the approaches, though they certainly meant that I would have got the job if I wanted it. I was flattered and tempted, but after fifteen consecutive years as a minister I did not really want to start a new career abroad on top of a new bureaucracy. I mention the episode here because the Americans would certainly not have supported a candidate for NATO who they thought was endangering the Alliance over Bosnia, particularly at a time when Bosnia was NATO's main preoccupation.

The main achievement of 1994 was the agreement that spring by the Bosnian Muslims and Bosnian Croats to stop fighting one another. This was a notable success for American diplomacy. It further isolated the Bosnian Serbs and marked a turning point for Croatia itself. Tudjman made the strategic choice which eventually Milosevic rejected: to guide his country away from traditional nationalist ambitions towards the European mainstream.

The principle of a NATO presence and possible air strikes against the Bosnian Serbs had been accepted. The practice proved difficult to work because of the so-called dual key. This was not simply a bureaucratic encumbrance. It was arranged that the UN must agree every time before NATO struck, given that a strike would affect the safety of UN forces, including British, on the ground. But the two cogs did not mesh easily. The fact that most of the major players were members of both NATO and the UN was less important than the fact that the two organisations were run by different kinds of people with a different ethos. The NATO command, sitting in headquarters far from the zones of conflict, was usually keen to get on with the job. The Secretary-General of the UN, by then Boutros Ghali, believed that the whole enterprise in Bosnia was distorting the UN away from equally pressing tasks in the Third World. His representatives on the ground were keen to prevent the UN force from appearing one-sided, since that would in their view make them useless and offend one of the main principles of UN peacekeeping. From the Gorazde crisis onward, governments wrestled to turn the key in the lock, but often the right moment had passed before agreement was reached.

In July 1994 Alain Juppé and I flew to the area. This was designed unusually as a joint Anglo-French mission. We travelled together, spoke to each interlocutor in harmony. He briefed the British press, I the French. After seeing Tudjman in Zagreb, we dined there with the UN representatives. They 'reproduce pure milk of peacekeeping doctrine – air strikes, new exclusion zones, lift of arms embargo, [in their view] all v. damaging. But this calm message never reaches Washington.' After a reasonable talk in Sarajevo with President Izetbegovic, we ventured by helicopter to the Bosnian Serb capital at Palé, pleasantly set in a green gorge, consisting largely of chalets in the Swiss style. I found their leader Karadzic villainous and rhetorical, and we had a rough talk. He was proud of his appearance, in particular the bouffant hairstyle, and also of his intellectual prowess, which seemed negligible. We decided to beard him in his lair, but our aim was not to bring him round but to persuade Milosevic to desert him. We attempted this next day. There was no pomp or grandeur about Milosevic; he received us in a dull office with a huge sofa. By agreement with Alain Juppé, I took the lead in wrestling with his arguments and using the inadequate carrots and sticks at our disposal. 'He will, I think, do his best by his villainous lights, but probably won't be enough.'

We were at it again in December. This time Alain Juppé took the lead, stressing the urgent danger to Serb interests if General Mladic, the Bosnian Serb commander, continued to make life impossible for UNPROFOR. 'Milosevic, alert as ever, a good debater, says he'll do his best. All this with many present. Upstairs in his office he expounds his plans for outnumbering and outwitting Karadzic.' He was talking of votes in the Bosnian Serb parliament in Palé.

It was hard to know what to make of Milosevic's detailed account of his dealings with these Bosnian Serb politicians. I do not suppose that the details were truthful, but the slow process by which he was brought to betray his allies was in hand. The Bosnian Serbs depended on Serb support but were not his creatures, and had defied him in rejecting the Vance–Owen plan in 1993. They had allies of their own in Belgrade, more extreme than Milosevic. But sanctions were at last beginning to bite hard on Serbia and he could hope for their relaxation if he acted against Karadzic. Milosevic was quick in debate but sometimes slow in deciding. These considerations were maturing in his mind, but he had to be jolted more robustly before he took his decision.

I found these two joint exercises with Alain Juppé instructive in their own right. On one of them he sat on one side of the aisle in the front of the plane and I on the other. My officials from the back plied me during the flight with several volumes of careful briefing. Each subject was flagged and annotated. Juppé had nothing with him, except the texts of the relevant Security Council resolutions, which he seemed to memorise.

I asked my officials later why they cluttered me with all this verbosity; was it not better to leave me to clear my own mind as the French had left their minister, maybe with just an essential text or two? I learned that Juppé rebuked his officials just as strongly; why was he humiliated with silence while the British minister was fully briefed for any conceivable contingency?

Both the British military and we at the Foreign Office began to know French ways more intimately because of the pressures which we shared. The French were by now the chief troop contributors, with the British second. At all levels, civilian and military, they operated on a looser remit than we did. The President (whether Mitterrand or Chirac, from 1995) would take a sudden initiative and achieve headlines for France and himself. It was for others to work out the consequences. French ministers operated on the principle, which they share with newspaper editors, that no one will remember in a month's time what they said today. Consistency was therefore unimportant; in a month's time it might be right to launch quite a different plan. Like the Americans, they were bold in proposing military initiatives, even though they, unlike the Americans, would have to face the results on the ground. But they were then ready to listen to laborious explanations by our professionals of the consequences, and agree that they had not thought through their proposal. It would not quite be true to say of them, as of our King Charles II, that they never said a foolish thing and never did a wise one, because their commitment and staying power through the Bosnian crisis were notable. But there was a flavour of eloquent showmanship about their activities which sometimes exasperated and once or twice impressed us, their main partners.

As 1994 wore on the strains on existing policy intensified. The nuts and bolts which had (just) kept the different plates of the policy together were breaking or wearing out. It might not be safe or sensible to keep British troops in Bosnia much longer, and the threat of withdrawal skilfully used might at last bring about peace. The Americans too were in a state of flux, beginning to think more in terms of a negotiated peace, and no doubt the Bosnian Government realised this.

On 23 September I met Michael Rose at RAF Brize Norton on my way home from a conference in Germany. By good luck it was possible to invite Kofi Annan, now of course UN Secretary-General, but then the head of UN peacekeeping in New York. At Brize Norton Rose, supported by Annan, set out again his passionate belief in the impartial UN peacekeeping operation and disbelief in undermining that operation with more robust bombing. He told me something I did not know: that the Bosnian Government was wavering in its demand that the arms embargo be lifted at once. He writes that I was in a good mood that afternoon because I was looking forward to a rare weekend of leisure in Oxfordshire. Not quite so: it was the weekend of Yeltsin's visit to Britain. His Foreign Minister Kozyrev stayed with me at Westwell; he and Yeltsin castigated us next day about our failure to give Milosevic adequate incentives to compromise.

Michael Rose had persuaded himself of the merits of a policy which, despite his personal charm and skill, was falling to bits around us. But one thing he told me stuck in my mind and I needed to test it with the Bosnians themselves. If they, the main proponents and supposed beneficiaries of 'lift', were going cool, that would simplify the situation for us, and for the American administration, which was under constant pressure from Senator Bob Dole, Margaret Thatcher and other partisans of 'lift'. There was an immediate opportunity in the margins of the UN General Assembly which as ever was mainly useful as a diplomatic fair. After consulting Alain Juppé I saw the Bosnians on 27 September. There was no doubt that if they were wavering it was because they at last accepted that 'lift' would involve the immediate withdrawal of UN troops. There would be no place for peacekeepers if our policy was to back one side in the war. The Bosnians had consistently criticised UNPROFOR and hinted that it was worse than useless. They were now up against the real prospect that it might disappear. It was time for them to choose.

The Bosnians told me that they were willing to postpone any call for lifting the arms embargo for six months. They wanted no Security Council discussion because they knew that the majority of the Council was against 'lift'. They wanted an assurance that we would keep our troops in Bosnia meanwhile. I said that we would, so long as their mandate was achievable and the risk did not become unacceptable. If the latest peace proposals foundered, then 'lift' might become unavoidable. I had become gloomily resigned to the likelihood of 'lift' not as part of a peace effort but as a result of that effort's failure.

The three principal Bosnian leaders were present at that meeting. Although I never exactly warmed to President Izetbegovic, I was coming to respect his dogged patriotism. I had no time for Muhamed Sacirbey, the Bosnian Ambassador to the UN who became Foreign Minister. His good looks and eloquence were powerful on TV and with Bosnia's warmest partisans, such as Margaret Thatcher. He was conciliatory in private, bitter in public. I knew nothing then of the corruption charges which he later faced, but he was never a man with whom I wanted to do business. The Prime Minister, Haris Silajdzic, on the other hand, I admired. He was rough with me in private as well as in public, but clearly genuine, more so I think than any other Balkan politician I dealt with except the Macedonian President Gligorov.

An uneasy peace prevailed in Bosnia into the spring of 1995, secured by a ceasefire agreement which was set to last until the end of April. We were all deeply concerned by the dangerous stagnation on the diplomatic front. I was clear that our policy had run out of hope. On 13 April I sent a minute to the Prime Minister, sketching two possible policies if large-scale fighting broke out again. We could sit it out in Bosnia, hoping that something would turn up. UNPROFOR and the British part in it would then become institutionalised. This would suit the Americans, the Germans – and the Bosnian Government, for whom UNPROFOR now acted as a partial shield, protecting them to some extent from any massive Serb riposte to their attempts to regain ground. But this prospect could not appeal to the French and ourselves. Our military had been extraordinarily skilful and lucky so far in avoiding casualties. This could change at any moment. A few mortar shells on any of our positions would do it. UNPROFOR was caught again, as in 1994, between the dangers of pretending to a muscular role for which it was not equipped and being humiliated by Bosnian Serb provocations. So far we had been right to judge that the good which UNPROFOR did outweighed the risks. But I did not believe that we should stay trapped indefinitely in such an exposed situation.

We could, I went on, reduce our exposure by concentrating our forces and reducing their number. This might be the safest course, but arguably would simply reduce British influence without really diminishing the danger. A more radical option would be for the French and ourselves to tell all concerned that we were willing to stay through the summer but withdraw before the winter of 1995; and that at the same time the arms embargo would then be lifted. We would argue that the international effort in its present form had run its course, and matters should be brought to a head. The summer should be used to galvanise all concerned, to negotiate a settlement while there was still time. 'If this tactic were successful, we should move into an implementation phase. This would almost certainly still involve a UK presence on the ground but with a different and more constructive function. If it failed, we should need to be ready to carry out our threat of withdrawal.'

David Owen, who had already signalled that he wanted to give up his mandate, had been urging for some time that we should bring matters to a head. Alain Juppé was thinking on similar lines. That I, being by nature more patient or perhaps just more sluggish, than either of them should come round to this view was a sign of desperation, to which was perhaps added a touch of exhaustion. The Bosnian tragedy had sputtered on and on and on, we had worked strenuously, and it seemed endlessly, to bring it to an end, but it was settling down into a hopeless fact of life. The Balkan politicians thrived, and in some cases made money out of their intransigence. Meanwhile, the Bosnian people suffered – and British soldiers were each day at serious risk.

The Prime Minister, Malcolm Rifkind and I discussed my paper on 26 April. They both argued against my plan. The Prime Minister in particular felt that we had to soldier on ('PM's arguments on Bosnia a decent appeal to our international duty. PM at his best and somewhat shames me'). I worried that out of a decent desire to stick with our duty we were once again just waiting for something to turn up. But this time something did.

Meanwhile, fighting had broken out again when the ceasefire agreement expired, and we were back with the old problems of the dual key which failed to turn in the lock. Parliamentary restiveness reappeared. On 3 May I was pressed in the Commons to withdraw our troops and this was backed later privately by Iain Duncan Smith (now Leader of the Opposition) and Bernard Jenkin (now Shadow Defence Secretary).

On 7 May potentates gathered in London in large numbers to celebrate the fiftieth anniversary of Victory in Europe. At Buckingham Palace I drank three glasses of champagne before lunch: 'An error. At table with Kohl, usual flow of generous spirit and acute egocentricity. Tudjman who promises me no more military adventures' – again. The Croats were then busy ethnically cleansing the Serbs who had the misfortune to live in Croatia.

The Bosnian Government asked for air strikes against specific Bosnian Serb positions. The request was referred to the UN Secretary-General and refused. I disagreed with this refusal and wrote to Boutros Ghali accordingly, which unsettled him without settling anything else. During a political visit to Glasgow on 11 May I wrote in my diary, 'Bosnia as usual unsettled. MOD/UNSG [Ministry of Defence/UN Secretary-General] block air power. PM blocks withdrawal, so we don't have much of a policy except Pauline [Neville-Jones] toiling away in contact group.' Four days later I was in Paris and congratulated Alain Juppé on becoming Prime Minister. 'As usual friendly and sharp. He is determined to get France out of Bosnia, unless things improve, wants to work with us.'

The situation round Sarajevo grew rapidly blacker. The Bosnian Serbs reacted to NATO air strikes against their ammunition dumps by taking UN observers hostage, and then thirty British soldiers in Gorazde. The whole concept of UNPROFOR, for long fragile in the absence of agreement, was breaking down.

As often happens, the crisis came to a head on a Sunday – 28 May.

Sun and cloud at Westwell . . . work, except a few minutes' bowling to Philip. A load of papers, ring Pauline, Malcolm and John

[Sawers]. Gradually options become clearer in Bosnia, but prospects remain v. down. Grasp every minute of Westwell, honeysuckle and lilac fully out, leave at 4, John at FCO, then officials, then OPD at Number 10. Mood turns robust, our instincts coincide, and we decide to reinforce, though to PM's mild annoyance I argue this is likely prelude to withdrawal. Round and round, Heseltine the most critical. We are on the edge of catastrophe . . . But PM on same line as 26/4 [26 April – recorded above]. Leave before meeting ends. Sandwiches in [Hawker Siddeley] 146 to Brussels. Cigar and whisky here and go over ground. Should fresh troops be UN or NATO or national etc., etc.? Bed 1.30.

The British and parallel French decisions to reinforce were the first of the turning points that summer. At the NATO meeting next morning colleagues were impressed by the news that we were at once sending artillery and engineers to Bosnia and preparing to deploy a mobile air brigade to provide UNPROFOR with a much-needed reserve. Warren Christopher asked the crucial question: would UNPROFOR now act against Bosnian Serbs if they proved obstructive? Malcolm Rifkind and I reviewed the situation at Chevening on 5 June with Carl Bildt, the former Swedish Prime Minister, who was about to be appointed at our suggestion to succeed David Owen as the EU representative in Bosnia. Malcolm and I wrote a joint minute to the Prime Minister, arguing that we must not raise too high expectations about the effect of our reinforcements, that our troops would still need some degree of local consent if they were to do their job, and that we should still keep in mind a threat to withdraw. My own pessimism was still hard at work, but on 13 June I was able to announce the release of all our hostages.

As it turned out, 1995 was not to be a repetition of 1992, 1993 and 1994. Attitudes and the situation on the ground were changing. The British and French decision in May to provide UNPROFOR with artillery and a mobile reserve was one of the crucial changes. But already the military tide had turned, particularly in favour of the Croats, who were taking their revenge for Vukovar by expelling the Serbs from western Croatia. The Bosnian Muslims were attacking Bosnian Serb positions.

The Americans too were on the move. President Clinton was alarmed at the news that the safe withdrawal of UNPROFOR from Bosnia would require the temporary intervention of a large number of troops, most of whom would have to be American. Richard Holbrooke became his principal operator. Bold in speech, enjoying the risks he took, uncluttered by the weary experience which depressed the rest of us, Holbrooke was occasionally exasperating, but never at a loss. He professed great sympathy for the frustration of Alain Juppé and myself with past American policies, though he probably regarded us as semi-extinct volcanoes so far as Bosnia was concerned. He was impatient of texts, legalisms and the need to consult allies, but also of the shibboleths which had prevented the Americans from making effective contact with Milosevic and Karadzic. If these two villains were necessary to the making of peace, then obviously he and his chief lieutenant Bob Frasure must, he concluded, deal with them.

The end of the story fell outside my term at the Foreign Office. The Bosnian Serbs under General Mladic played into the hands of their enemies by brutal attacks on Sarajevo (with a second murderous shell on the market) and the massacre at Srebrenica. The Americans reached the scene with formidable energy. The difficulties of the dual key were brushed aside by regrouping the reinforced UNPROFOR. NATO air strikes were renewed with greater effect. The siege of Sarajevo was lifted, and eventually all the parties were dragged to sign a peace agreement at Dayton, Ohio, in November 1995. It was a peace which pleased no one, but it ended the war, and no one has yet destroyed it.

I saw Milosevic once more, in July 1996. After I left the Foreign Office in July 1995 I was appointed to the Board of the National Westminster Bank and became deputy chairman of its subsidiary NatWest Markets. Some time after this appointment I learned that one of the projects being negotiated by NatWest Markets concerned the privatisation of Serb Telecom and a possible agreement to advise the Serbian Government on the management of their debt. During these negotiations I flew to Belgrade to see Milosevic, keeping the Foreign Office fully informed. The conversation was partly political, partly to discuss the relationship with NatWest. This meeting happened after the Dayton Agreement, but before the Kosovo crisis, that is, in an interval when sanctions were relaxed. In 1996 it seemed possible that Milosevic might follow Tudjman's example and move his country towards a liberalised economy and a freer political system. Without political and economic liberalisation no lasting relationship with NatWest was possible. There was no such liberalisation and the relationship withered, leaving the privatisation of Serb Telecom as its only outcome. This was a legal and legitimate deal, but the visit was a mistake, not interesting enough to justify the embarrassment it later caused.

I have tried plainly to set out what happened over Bosnia as far as I was concerned, in particular what I felt, and why I acted as I did. I have not on the whole entered into polemic, leaving others to judge. I have written about the most argued points, for example the recognition of Croatia and Slovenia, the role of UNPROFOR, the safe areas resolution and the arms embargo. I have admitted mistakes and misgivings where I feel them. There remains one question unsettled in my own mind. In the summer of 1995 the Anglo-French reinforcement of UNPROFOR and the American insistence on more energetic air strikes were effective in ending the war. Would they have been equally effective in 1993 or 1994? Or did they for their success need other factors which were not present earlier, for example war-weariness everywhere, the turn of the military tide on the ground against the Bosnian Serbs and the final willingness of Milosevic under the burden of sanctions to drag his allies into a peace settlement? No one can be certain of the answer to that question.

Two years later Western leaders acted more quickly and decisively in Kosovo than we had in Bosnia. This was the other wholly humanitarian operation by British forces in recent years, leaving aside the smaller examples of Sierra Leone and East Timor. Mistakes were made in Kosovo and innocent people killed there and in Serbia itself. But the Albanian majority were rescued from Serb oppression, and the territory given a semi-colonial status under UN governance. Those responsible learned what they believed to be the lessons of Bosnia, and their relative success has tilted opinion towards supposing that by similar methods we could have rescued Bosnia earlier. The circumstances, the advice and the general arguments at the time were different and I have tried to set these out fairly, without being wholly certain of the answer to my own question.

There can be no final thoughts on this matter, but I add one more. As time passes and I grow older I become more suspicious of the straightforward, violent solution to international problems. By this I mean the suggestion, often urged in comfort by commentators, that miseries and dangers are best remedied by actions whose immediate result would be the killing and maiming of individuals, many of whom will be innocent. It is argued on such occasions that the more distant effect of the use of force will be the sparing of lives and the curing of miseries and injustice. That may be so; it is foolish to be absolute in such a calculation. But a strict burden of proof, for example the Christian test of a just war, is required of those who send others to kill and be killed.

Appeasement was a term of praise between the two world wars of the twentieth century; it is a term of abuse today. But the peacemakers have their ration of praise, in phrases which have come down through twenty centuries and will be remembered when the arguments of today are forgotten.

26

HONG KONG

During this time Hong Kong was living its last years as a British colony. The Joint Declaration negotiated with the Chinese by Margaret Thatcher and Geoffrey Howe in 1984 provided that Hong Kong should pass to Chinese sovereignty at the end of June 1997. It would then hold self-governing status under the famous principle of two systems (communist mainland, capitalist Hong Kong) in one country (China). No one ever supposed that this transition would be easy, but few questioned that it was necessary.

I had become fascinated by and devoted to Hong Kong during the years when I lived in Peking in the mid-fifties and this feeling persisted during my visits in the seventies. Hong Kong and New York were two places which it was a thrill to approach. The excitement was partly visual – the pleasure of seeing skyscrapers massed on a rock and a harbour alive with the bustle of trade. This was combined in Hong Kong with the spice of danger, as the plane threaded its way down through cloud, mountains and buildings on to the old airport runway at Kai Tak. When approaching both cities I also felt what could clumsily be described as a cultural challenge. Down below me, about to join my life again for a few days, was a thriving, varied community of some of the most energetic and talented people on earth. There would be hazards as well as pleasures on each visit, but in neither city could my stay conceivably be dull.

The success and appeal of Hong Kong depended on the fused characteristics of both British and Chinese. It was sad to think that the British part in Hong Kong life was dwindling and in the official sense would soon come to an end. My dealings with the Chinese on the necessary preliminaries to the transfer of power were long drawn and exasperating. But neither nostalgia nor exasperation shook my acceptance of the Joint Declaration of 1984. It was the best agreement that could have been reached given the realities of power. We just had to get on with carrying it out as best we could in the interests of Hong Kong.

By June 1991 I had decided that the next and last governor of Hong Kong should be a British politician. This was no criticism of the governor then in office, Sir David Wilson. A dedicated and experienced Scot, David Wilson and his wife Natasha were popular in Hong Kong. They represented one of the last flowerings of that tradition of wise British students of China, who enormously respected the Chinese people without deceiving themselves about the difficulties of dealing with its Government. But the last years of the colony would be different, perhaps dramatically different, from those that went before. Because in 1997 the actual transfer went smoothly though sadly, it is easy to forget that this might not have been so. Either the Chinese authorities or some groups in Hong Kong might have overplayed their hand. This danger increased sharply after the killings in Tiananmen Square in Peking in 1989 which shocked and alarmed the people of Hong Kong. It seemed sensible to have in Hong Kong a governor who was accustomed to dealing with party politicians, whether in London or Hong Kong, and who was demonstrably close to the most senior British ministers.

I told David Wilson of this decision, but the choice of a name was left until after the British General Election of April 1992. On the eve of that campaign I wrote to the Prime Minister and included the names of various candidates in the letter. My preference was for Francis Maude, on the assumption that he might lose his very marginal seat in Warwickshire.

Francis was my choice mainly because of his record as Minister of State in the Foreign Office when we handled together the crisis of the Vietnamese boat people in 1989. This was the most painful episode in my first months as Foreign Secretary. The Hong Kong authorities had traditionally accepted as political refugees Vietnamese who had found refuge in that well-ordered place from the war and subsequent poverty of Vietnam. But by 1988 the numbers had become so great that the Government of Hong Kong changed its policy. Camps were set up and return to Vietnam encouraged. The boat people had become deeply unpopular in Hong Kong as a burden. The Chinese Government, while doing little to prevent the Vietnamese boats from creeping round their coastal ports to Hong Kong, argued that this was a problem created by British feebleness which must be cleared up before the British left. Conferences and diplomacy produced no adequate answer. My immediate predecessor as Foreign Secretary, John Major, began to move in favour of forced repatriation of those Vietnamese who had not been persecuted at home but simply came to Hong Kong to better their lot. The Americans, whose hostile policy towards Vietnam was one reason for the country's poverty and the outflow of boat people, began to object on humanitarian grounds to what we intended. Despite this, I decided in December 1989 that we must begin to fly even unwilling Vietnamese home from Hong Kong. There were by then 57,000 boat people in Hong Kong. This seemed the only way of deterring larger numbers from risking the voyage. We also needed to put paid to the stories current in Vietnam that once in Hong Kong the boat people would be generously treated and perhaps offered a golden life across the Pacific in California.

This was one of the few occasions when I was conscious of murmurings of anxious dissent among my own officials. Two of those closest to me, my senior private secretary, Stephen Wall, and Antony Acland, by then British Ambassador in Washington, were much disturbed. The British press was overwhelmingly hostile. The operation was tricky and uncertain. All depended on what happened when the first plane was loaded with boat people and took off. Francis Maude, as Minister of State, was in charge of the details. Throughout he remained calm and convinced that we were right; his steadiness was a great help to me.

On 12 December in the small hours of the morning fifty-one boat people, escorted by riot police, boarded the aircraft bound for Hanoi without any serious disturbance. I made a statement in the Commons that afternoon. As usual many other things were crowded into the same twelve hours. That morning we had a big argument among ministers at Number Ten about passports for Hong Kong, of which more soon. I lunched alone with the Prince of Wales at Kensington Palace and discussed just about everything. I sat beside the Prime Minister as she made her statement on the EU summit at Strasbourg the week before. Finally I got to my feet on Hong Kong. The Opposition attacked me fiercely and the press was hostile next day ('Turmoil runs high over boat people. Feel justified in what we did, but feel weary at what is said and written').

For a day or two I was treated by liberal people as a descendant of the Gestapo and imitator of the Holocaust. But gradually the policy justified itself. The Vietnamese who returned were not persecuted. The Americans muttered but fell silent and finally lifted their economic embargo on Vietnam. If we had wavered in December 1989 the problem would have worsened, to no one's benefit. Because we persevered, there was no crisis in 1997; the boat people had gone home or to other countries with space to receive them, including Britain.

On that occasion the criticism came from the left in Britain, but almost at once the next Hong Kong drama got me into trouble with the right. The Chinese professional classes in Hong Kong, including the civil servants, were alarmed at the prospect of communist rule. They did not shout or demonstrate, but quietly began to make their arrangements to emigrate, for example to Vancouver or Australia. A real danger took shape, that the colony would before 1997 lose a high proportion of the people who made it work and would be essential to the place after the transfer of power. Paradoxically, the best way of persuading these people to stay was to offer them the right of abode in Britain. They would then have an each-way bet. If things went well, and two systems in one country worked as advertised, then they could stay at their jobs in Hong Kong and keep their right-of-abode documents in their private safes. But if life became intolerable, they would be able to find another home in Britain. The question for the British Government was the total number to whom this right could be given. I hoped for 100,000 individuals with their families. My successor as Home Secretary, David Waddington, was sympathetic on the principle but not on the numbers. We settled eventually at 50,000 and I announced the figure to the Commons on 20 December 1989. There was a substantial row.

I had as Home Secretary gained some experience of the sour right in my party. It is necessary to distinguish between the generous and the sour right. The generous right believes in the whole tradition of the British past, in particular of the British Empire. The sour right concentrates on what is negative and exclusive. I believe the sour right has done more harm to the Conservative cause in the last fifteen years than any other group, individual or factor. On this issue the generous right could be persuaded that the imperial tradition required generosity as I tried in the Commons on 20 December: 'This is just about the last main chapter in the story of this country's empire. I am rather keen . . . that the last chapter should not end in a shabby way.' The sour right would have none of that. They were simply concerned with the danger of large-scale immigration. We were discussing professors, teachers, engineers, civil servants, most of them with ample means to house and feed themselves wherever they went. The sour right conjured up a nightmare of thousands of penniless Chinese descending on Britain, swallowing up jobs, homes and welfare benefits. It was a campaign of which Colonel Blimp and the old imperialists would have been ashamed. Once again Francis Maude (himself of the generous right) and I had to wear down our critics one by one. This was hard work. Margaret Thatcher, though wobbly at first on numbers, backed her ministers wholeheartedly when the crunch came. After all the noise the necessary Bill passed the Commons relatively easily. The Government of Hong

Kong had a difficult job allocating the right of abode among the different groups, but managed it. The new policy, as intended, helped many valuable people to stay in Hong Kong and smoothed the transfer of sovereignty in 1997.

Francis Maude was moved to the Treasury in 1990. He did lose his seat in the General Election of April 1992, and my diary shows that he was still in my mind as a possible Governor. But another casualty on that day shone as a brighter star. Two days after polling day the Prime Minister, after consulting me on his cabinet reshuffle, suggested on the telephone that Chris Patten, having lost his seat in Bath, might be offered Hong Kong. Others were suggesting that we contrive a by-election, probably in the safe seat of Chelsea, so that Chris could quickly return to the Commons. That weekend was full of conversations on the subject. The hazards of a by-election were just too great; the age for such devices was past. More important from my angle, the advantages of Chris Patten in Hong Kong grew in my mind each time I thought of them. I totally trusted his judgement and integrity. He was in the same relationship with the Prime Minister as with me. I knew by now that the rocks ahead, both in Hong Kong and with the Chinese in Peking, would prove formidable. Chris Patten is powerfully persuasive and a leader of men, two gifts which do not always run together.

On Monday 13 April at Number Ten I talked this over with the Prime Minister and the Chief Whip, Richard Ryder. By this time John Major was in different mode. The exhilaration of his own remarkable election victory had subsided, and he was back in his natural state of mixed foreboding and fascination with his job. He wanted Chris Patten back in the Commons so that he might eventually be in a position to succeed me at the Foreign Office, and more immediately so that he himself could continue to rely on Chris's day-by-day political advice. Richard Ryder and I repeated the argument against a contrived by-election. By this time Chris and Lavender Patten were well aware that the governorship was on offer. The two of them ate a supper of smoked-salmon pasta with Judy and myself in the kitchen at Carlton Gardens that evening (it is one of Judy's best dishes). I pressed him quite hard, and he promised to reflect during a few days' holiday in France. On a visit to Turkey ten days later I heard that Chris had accepted the governorship of Hong Kong, 'to PM's sadness and my gladness'.

On Sunday 26 July I went again to Hong Kong. My third son Alexander was working there for Hong Kong Telecommunications. We arrived in a bizarre Saudi charter plane (one of those hired by Richard Gozney on sound Thatcherite principles to undercut the RAF) from Manila, a city which always depressed me.

An immediate uplift of spirit. Drive with Chris to Government House. Repose. Then on the *Lady Maureen* [the Governor's yacht] to silver mine on Lantau [the biggest island in the Hong Kong group]. Al . . . is v. cheerful, and attentive. Good lunch on board. Walk from silver mine to Discovery Bay, very hot. Waterfalls, a cave, a shelter for cows, then we lose track and plunge into maquis, ravines thick with thorns and obstructions. Eventually a grateful waterfall where we bathe feet. Down to Discovery Bay (90°) where A. provides Coke and tea and fruitcake in his pad on the first floor. He seems v. happy. Back by police launch, amazing shifts of light and mist and shadows on harbour. Looking back to ships against backing of sunset and Lantau is a Turner painting. Swim at GH with R[ichard Gozney] and Stephen [Smith, assistant private secretary]. Round table for political discussion. Goes well. The Pattens v. happy. A gold day.

I learned afterwards that my private secretaries noticed that I had lagged behind in the heat on the track down to Discovery Bay. They worried at this symptom of tiredness. Every now and then during these years I did feel exhausted, but never for more than a day or two. My private office never ceased to ply me with mountains of work, which was what I was paid for, and relished.

Next day, after swimming again with Richard, I drove and walked about Hong Kong with the Governor – a container terminal, a monastery full of rather nasty treasures, a housing estate, an old folks' home, a shopping centre, a meeting of the local District Board. This was a 'walkabout' in the professional political sense. We were part of an election campaign with no election. Chris Patten had received huge publicity on his appointment, and because of his open approach was already, a few months later, a popular celebrity. Crowds quickly gathered, chattered and applauded. Mothers held up their babies for the Governor to touch. Cameras, private and media, clicked and flashed without cease. I was witnessing the beginning of a phenomenon which helped to explain the exasperation with which the Chinese authorities viewed the last Governor of Hong Kong. It was not just that they disliked his proposals; they detested his popularity. Colonial governors in their view should be stiff and unapproachable, in uniform and plumes. A popular governor, at his best when working a big Chinese crowd, was incomprehensible and not to be accepted.

Years later, after the transfer of power, I was recognised in a Hong Kong shopping mall. A shopkeeper, tense with excitement, pulled out from a private drawer two photographs of Chris Patten and offered them to me free of charge, on condition that I promised to encourage him to come back to Government House. Chris does not greatly resemble Bonnie Prince Charlie, but that lady shopkeeper was certainly a Jacobite.

I do not want to go into all the Hong Kong issues which crossed my desk, for example the tedious but crucial financing of the new airport. I must find space for the constitutional argument which particularly embittered our dealings with the Chinese. In 1990, well before Chris was appointed, we had reached agreement with the Chinese on the arrangements for elections to the Hong Kong Legislative Council the following year. For the first time in 1991 there were eighteen directly elected members out of a council of sixty; it was envisaged that at the next elections in 1995 there would be twenty. These figures were included in the Chinese Basic Law which was, in effect, the Chinese constitution unilaterally devised in advance for Hong Kong. Politicians in Hong Kong had pressed me for a higher element of direct democracy. To my advisers and myself it seemed a big step forward to have persuaded the Chinese to accept that there should be any directly elected members at all.

It was up to the new Governor to put forward proposals from Hong Kong for the next set of Legislative Council elections due in 1995. It was hoped that the councillors elected then would serve a full four years, thus providing continuity through the transfer of sovereignty in 1997. In the jargon of our diplomacy, this concept was called the 'through train'. I did not discuss possible proposals with Chris Patten before he went out. I recognised that he would need time to work himself in and consult with the main interested groups in Hong Kong.

On 15 September 1992 Chris Patten was back in London to present his plan to a restricted group of ministers. It was not an ideal moment for calm reflection on the future constitution of Hong Kong. We were in the depths of the sterling crisis which ended next day in our falling out of the ERM. King Hussein of Jordan and the Prime Minister of Ukraine were both in town and requiring attention. Nevertheless, we had a good discussion, precursor of many others on the same lines over the next three years.

Chris Patten's proposals were ingenious, but far from revolutionary. They built on the progress already begun in moving Hong Kong towards democracy. He did not challenge what had already been agreed with the Chinese: namely, that the number of directly elected councillors should increase only slightly, from eighteen in 1991 to twenty in 1995, a third of the total. But he changed the basis of the so-called functional constituencies under which groups representing the different professions of Hong Kong chose councillors to represent them. There were to be thirty of these legislators from functional constituencies, half the total.

Chris Patten and his advisers in Hong Kong proposed that the number of electors in these functional constituencies should be substantially increased. The last ten seats were to be filled through nomination by an Election Committee, and Chris proposed that this committee should be composed of members of district boards who were already themselves directly elected. Chris Patten has described his as 'a programme that represented most people's second-best option'. It was a marked yet still cautious move towards full democracy. It disappointed Hong Kong democrats. Because the Chinese Government chose to be enraged by it, the plan is sometimes thought of as a provocative leap into the dark, but a look at its contents shows otherwise.

Back in London at the meeting of ministers on 15 September Michael Heseltine as President of the Board of Trade objected to the proposals on understandable mercantile grounds. Michael always had a romantic view of the possibilities of trade with China. Had he dealt with these matters in the nineteenth century he would have echoed the hope then expressed by optimistic merchants, that 'a new world was opened to their trade so vast that all the mills in Lancashire could not make stocking stuff sufficient for one of its provinces' (Lord Elgin's speech to the merchants of Shanghai, March 1858). There had been endless disappointments since 1858, but now at last the dream was becoming reality. A stable Chinese Government, interested above all in building prosperity, was welcoming foreign trade and investment. The race was on for huge commercial advantage in the new China. Was Britain at exactly the wrong moment to hobble herself in that race because of obscure constitutional arrangements in Hong Kong which could be of only fleeting interest to the people of the colony soon to pass under Chinese rule? That was Michael's argument, which Chris and I, with the Prime Minister's help, contested successfully that day. But we heard it often again thereafter. It was strongly supported from outside by Ted Heath, whereas Chris could count on the wholehearted support of Margaret Thatcher, from whom he was separated on almost every other political issue.

Chris Patten was to launch his proposals in Hong Kong on 7 October. Until then they would be secret. On 25 September in a talk lasting more than two hours at the UN in New York, I unveiled the plan to the Chinese Foreign Minister, Qian Qichen. Always a cautious and disciplined interlocutor, he made no comment of substance. That was not surprising, given the complexity of the plan. But interestingly, in view of what happened later, he made no comment either on procedure. He did not complain that afternoon that we had no right to go ahead with announcing constitutional plans without Chinese approval.

Just before Chris Patten launched his plan, the Chinese in Peking asked him to hold back. When, despite this, he went ahead, the sky turned black. Thunderbolts and hailstones rattled around him. No abuse was too severe, no argument too extreme for his critics in Peking. The Governor's popularity in Hong Kong grew; the Legislative Council approved his plans; the British Government gave him total support; but the controversy with Peking continued in different aspects for three years. We managed to ring-fence the dispute and carry on reasonably with our dealings with the Chinese on other matters. Despite some mutterings, there was no conclusive evidence that our trade with China suffered. But against this background progress in the necessary practical discussions with the Chinese on the handover of Hong Kong was painfully slow.

What irked the Chinese was not so much the content of the election plans as the way they were handled. The proposals launched on 7 October 1992 were precisely that – proposals to be discussed with the Chinese and if necessary amended. At all times we in London and Chris Patten in Hong Kong accepted that we were committed to consult the Chinese in this way and were willing to consider their views. The Chinese wanted something more: namely, secret discussions in advance of publication, and a veto on the result. They claimed that this was the procedure to which I had already agreed in the correspondence which embodied the agreement covering the earlier election in 1991.

I was genuinely startled when the Chinese made this claim. My recollection of the earlier agreement was that we had consented to consult with the Chinese on the next stage, which is what we were doing in the autumn of 1992 – but not that we had agreed to secrecy, let alone a veto. I would not have consented to any such undertaking without serious thought and discussion with colleagues. When we examined Chris Patten's proposals in the Foreign Office in September 1992 before he put them to ministers, none of my advisers drew my attention to any correspondence with the Chinese Government in 1990. Nor had they briefed Chris Patten on the point or shown him the correspondence before he left for Hong Kong in the spring. I was relieved that the House of Commons Foreign Affairs Select Committee in March 1994 concluded that there had indeed been no undertaking of the kind the Chinese claimed.

But for some wise and experienced old China hands the question was essentially political rather than legal. I remembered Percy Cradock as a sparkling performer at the Cambridge Union. There he paraded his left-wing views with outstanding panache and wit. I met him again now as an adviser to the Prime Minister, sober and buttoned up though still capable of a caustic phrase. He had served as British Ambassador in

Peking and had been invaluable to me in reaching the agreement with the Chinese on the 1991 elections. With increasing intensity he argued that we should again seek agreement with the Chinese in secret. To varying extents this was the view of several others whom I liked and trusted, in particular my friend of more than thirty years' standing Alan Donald, now in turn British Ambassador in Peking. To them was later added the voice of Geoffrey Howe, main author of the 1984 Joint Declaration under which we were operating. It was the only major disagreement I have had with Geoffrey Howe on a matter of policy – or indeed on anything else.

I disagreed with this view and did not allow it to prevail. This was not simply because of loyalty to Chris Patten. He had never asked and I had never promised support for everything he proposed. In the summer of 1995 the two of us argued quite hard on the timing of agreement on the Court of Final Appeal, a point connected with a triumphant trade visit to China at that time by Michael Heseltine. But on the main issue I thought he was right.

The doubting officials knew a great deal about China and believed that a sophisticated relationship of trust with Peking was more important for Britain than fleeting arrangements in Hong Kong. But I felt that they did not know Hong Kong as it was emerging. I had been exposed on several visits to the reality of modern Hong Kong and the rapid growth of its civil society. Although they often criticised me, I respected such Hong Kong democrats as Martin Lee who had already proved their credentials by standing for the handful of directly elected seats. Being proud of Hong Kong, I did not regard its future freedom as a secondary matter. It seemed to me inconceivable that Geoffrey Howe, had he been in my place in 1992, would have tried to negotiate the future constitution of Hong Kong in secret behind the backs of its people. Certainly we should be ready to compromise, since Chinese consent and the 'through train' would be a valuable gain. Certainly it was true that the Chinese would have the power after 1997 to upset whatever we had done. But under the Joint Declaration the responsibility for these matters was still ours until the flag came down. I agreed with Chris Patten on his fundamental thesis – that it was our job to carry forward what we had (perhaps belatedly) begun in stimulating democracy in Hong Kong, and that this involved being as open as possible both with Hong Kong and with its future master in Peking.

Although by 1997 I was two years out of office, Judy and I were invited to the transfer of power ceremonies. We flew with a batch of British notables in a chartered Boeing. I described the next three days as 'a cascade of mixed emotions with champagne'. The most poignant was the first evening, when we said goodbye to British rule at Government House. The garden was too small for a massive ceremonial farewell. Indeed, both Government House and its garden, which when I first saw them in 1954 dominated the harbour, had for years been diminished by the press of skyscrapers around them. The Hong Kong police, as ever dapper and emphatic, marched and counter-marched. A lone piper was picked out by a spotlight on the roof. There was 'Land of Hope and Glory', then the National Anthem, then tears. The next night we dined for the last time on *Britannia* with the Prince of Wales. *Britannia*, her escort HMS *Chatham* and the Royal Marines Beating the Retreat on the quayside after dinner – indeed, all the symbols of imperial power, including Government House itself – seemed puny against the backdrop of a great modern capitalist city, now slipping sideways to become part of the most populous country in the world.

On the actual day of transfer it rained, then drizzled, then rained again. We sat behind the Pattens and heard Chris give his final, excellent farewell. After the banquet I stood next to Guido Di Tella, the Foreign Minister of Argentina. 'I know what you're thinking,' I said, as through a rain-streaked window we watched the fireworks over the harbour. 'But you will never see this in Port Stanley.'

Through those days, like the Pattens, I was not in a jocular mood, but powerfully moved by conflicting thoughts. I was vexed that some of my British colleagues went to the swearing-in of the new Legislative Council, a pale shadow of the more robust democracy which we had begun to introduce. I disliked the goose-stepping of the People's Liberation Army, and the easy way in which the Hong Kong audience on the first day of Chinese rule fell in with President Jiang Zemin's communist technique of signalling when he wanted applause at different points during his speech.

It had thundered all night, and rain clouds were still heavy over the harbour. But on the whole it had gone well: the ceremonies of 1997, the slow process of transfer to China, the negotiations of 1984 which launched that process, indeed the whole period of British rule. In 1842 we had almost by mistake taken some barren rocks and fishing villages, and then helped millions of Chinese to transform Hong Kong into one of the great cities of the world.

27

THE WIDER WORLD

The British Foreign Secretary lives humbly in a vast world theatre of many stages, on each of which a long play is being performed. He finds himself called to one stage after another, clutching a part which is sometimes significant for that drama, sometimes just a word or two as part of a chorus. Some of the stage props become very familiar. The Charlemagne Building and my summer and winter quarters in Brussels, the suite and swimming pool in the UN Plaza Hotel, the Laura Ashley decoration upstairs in the British Embassy in Washington and the big Lutyens dining room full of congressmen and senior journalists, the gilded salon and small coffee cups of the Quai d'Orsay were all part of my life. My roles in other dramas came round less often, and I can pick out just one or two.

The limits to the doctrine of humanitarian intervention are shown starkly in that I could not honestly list Rwanda among the major preoccupations at the Foreign Office. Yet in Rwanda in 1994 the Hutus were massacring and expelling the Tutsi minority on a scale which dwarfed the suffering in Bosnia. Rwanda was a small African country, formerly under Belgian rule, with which we had been little concerned. News came through imperfectly and late. We were heavily preoccupied with Bosnia. We sent army engineers to support the transport of the small UN force in Rwanda. I remember the Belgian Foreign Minister Willy Claes telephoning in agitation early one morning to tell me that ten or more Belgian soldiers of the UN force had been killed in one explosion and the Belgian Government had decided to pull out. The French, for their own reasons, launched a limited military intervention, 'Operation Turquoise'. It never occurred to us, the Americans or anyone else to send combatant troops to Rwanda to stop the killing. I record this as a bleak fact.

Later, much regret was expressed for the West's inaction. President Clinton, in expressing his own remorse, indicated that the lesson had been learned and that in future the West would not stand idly by. I believe this is proven nonsense. For several years now the Congo has been convulsed by civil war. It has been pillaged by its own politicians and by the armies of its neighbours. The UN, backed by the West, has tried to find a solution – by sustained diplomacy, as we tried in Bosnia. No Western power has contemplated military intervention to impose a solution by force. The doctrine of humanitarian intervention will never be universal; it will always depend on time, place and circumstance. That is why universal rhetoric, however generously meant, is unconvincing. We deceive ourselves with our own speeches.

We succeeded at this time in putting some modern strength into our dealings with India. Because of history, we could not avoid becoming entangled in India's old and angry dispute with Pakistan over Kashmir. The Pakistanis were always anxious to tempt us in as mediators. They were adept at inveigling a British minister with flattery mixed with accusation. At one moment in their discourse we were flattered as the only people who deep down understood the Kashmir problem; at the next moment we were accused of creating it. In either case we were told that it was our duty to intervene. Prime Minister Nawaz Sharif, mild voiced and deceptive, tried this out on me in October 1992. In January 1995 his successor Benazir Bhutto was more subtle.

On arrival in Pakistan from India I had been besieged by journalists at the airport, and let slip some comment that the ancient Security Council resolutions on Kashmir in favour of self-determination were just that – ancient – and not likely to prove of much practical use. The Pakistani press next morning was savage and predicted that the Prime Minister would administer a strong rebuke when I called. Instead she was cool, beautiful and sophisticated, putting on her Oxford-inspired performance as an honorary member of the British establishment. She was mild on Kashmir, and even admitted that some violence there might have been stimulated from Pakistan, but not, of course, from any government agency. She used to the full a technique which I remembered from an earlier encounter in the Ritz in London, when I had called on her one hot day as a sweating and dishevelled Home Secretary. Her veil was only loosely secured so that it slowly slipped back from her face. Each slow unveiling of her flawless complexion and exceptional nose and forehead lasted about two minutes. When this was complete, she allowed just a second or two for admiration, and then pulled the veil forward, with a gesture as if mildly rebuking it. So the performance started again. I was glad to be a spectator of this enjoyable exercise, but it rather took me away from my brief. I was not entirely surprised to read in the Pakistani press next morning that the Prime Minister had given me a savage ticking off for my indiscretion at the airport, a matter which she had not in fact mentioned at all.

In May 1991 I went to India with the Prince of Wales for the funeral of Rajiv Gandhi. I had met Rajiv Gandhi in London before he was Prime Minister and we had got on well. Our acquaintance had not blossomed once he was promoted above my level. We arrived at the funeral pyre outside Delhi at 3.20 p.m., but nothing happened for an hour and a half. It was blazing hot and there was no cover. Ted Heath had equipped himself with a black umbrella, which though incongruous gave him protection denied to Prince Charles and the Prince of Orange. They sat immobile in white uniforms in the front row, trying to avoid conversation with Yasser Arafat across a gangway. Chanting began and continued uninterrupted until the arrival of the coffin and the slow lighting of the pyre. A helicopter sprayed petals on the coffin. There was dignity in the farewell rituals of the Gandhi family, and in the Last Post.

Six months later I was back in Delhi for several days of talks with Indian ministers. I became fond of the great yellow and red sandstone buildings designed by Herbert Baker to line the Raj Path up to Lutyens' Viceregal Palace. Tough chieftains of the Congress Party held sway as ministers, dispensing expensive licences and planning permissions in the offices from which the British had once governed India. Sparrows flitted down the high corridors between the offices and the courtyard. These corridors contained screens against the sun but also electric fires, bad pictures, a host of bearers, messengers, petitioners, tea-makers – and others, in the tradition of centuries, just waiting for something to happen.

Prime Minister Narasimha Rao once received me alone in his sunny garden in Racecourse Road. He sat with me there alone quietly for an hour as the light faded. Tea and biscuits shimmered across the lawn. Above us a wounded kite was set on by its fellows; butterflies were active among the flowers. Rao, serene in a grey suit, talked softly about the integrity of India. It was a familiar tale – if concessions were made to Muslims in Kashmir, India might begin to disintegrate into its different religions. I said that from outside what seemed lacking was an effective elected voice from Kashmir itself. He said that would come, in six months or so; but first they must hold successful elections in Punjab. Nearly two years later I saw Rao again. He had aged, wore a blanket around his shoulders, and was exhausted from the election hustings. If anything, his views on Kashmir had regressed.

*

A smaller drama in which we played a larger part concerned Argentina and the Falkland Islands. The war was over, the Falklands were more British than ever. I knew enough about them from my reading and from my parents to understand that this would not change. On sovereignty there could be no compromise. There was no point in playing with ideas on the subject as the Foreign Office had done before the war. But Argentina would not give up her claim, which was deeply embedded in her political structure. It was an important and (then) relatively prosperous country with traditional links of friendship with Britain. Could we rebuild our relationship sector by sector by pushing the question of sovereignty over the Falklands into the background? We could and we did. I was lucky in my Argentine opposite number, Guido Di Tella. Cultivated, devoted to his pictures, widely read, Oxford-connected, he knew Britain well. We shared a friendship with Thomas and Anthea Gibson, who lived in the Manor across the duckpond from us at Westwell, but also owned an estate to the south of Buenos Aires alongside a host of good-looking cousins, who had settled in Argentina at the beginning of the century.

My first visit to Argentina in January 1993 began in long talks with Di Tella in Buenos Aires. He took me to see President Carlos Menem, who did not pretend very hard to be other than what he was – a cheerful and successful buccaneer. He and most Argentines had no appetite either for renouncing their claim to the Falklands or for trying again to seize the islands by force. So within limits Guido Di Tella was given a free rein. It had long been the Argentine argument that union with Argentina was in accord with the true *interests* of the islanders. I argued with Di Tella that everyone must have regard to their *wishes* as well. If he came close to accepting this, it was because he fancied his own chances of bringing round the islanders by friendly persuasion. Unlike the Spaniards, who treated the people of Gibraltar with harsh contempt, Di Tella set himself to find the key to the Falkland Islanders' hearts. If it were a matter of money, that could not be exorbitant since there were less than 2,000 of them. If it were a matter of trust and friendship, he would show the way, if necessary islander by islander. The baffled islanders became accustomed to his friendly messages, both general and to individuals on birthdays or other anniversaries. He prided himself on even the smallest evidence of success. Once he attended the Conservative Party Conference and found a stall manned by a Falkland Islander. He interpreted as a diplomatic triumph what must have been the immediate reaction of a nice lady faced with the sudden advance of a courteous foreigner. 'She shook my hand,' he told me in triumph. 'She actually shook my hand.'

After the meetings in Buenos Aires we were flown south to the

Gibson *estancia*, set in the pampas among Aberdeen Angus cattle and flocks of ostriches. Shallow pools were frequented by ibis and flamingos. It was the last of my trips with Richard Gozney whose passion was ornithology. He left behind in the mansion of the *estancia* a list of one hundred different species which he identified in that weekend. I have never known a place so dominated, even for the ignorant, by the calls, colour and movement of birds.

My protection officers, reconnoitring the place in advance, had assured all concerned that I certainly would not ride a horse during my stay. They had even procured a pony and trap for my use. They had to be proved wrong. Luckily I learned quickly that when riding in Argentina it was right to do most of the things which we had been taught to avoid on the farm at Rainscombe long ago. Argentine horses did not trot. I should keep one hand on the reins with the other on the saddle; the more I looked like a sack of potatoes, the better. A sore backside was a small price to pay for pride regained.

The Falkland Islanders were understandably deeply suspicious of the Argentines and reluctant to have any dealings with them. I was sure it would be a mistake for us in London to try to nudge them forward. We should do nothing to revive their old distrust of the Foreign Office. Di Tella's postcards and telephone calls on wedding anniversaries would certainly not bring them round. If the facts of geography and economics softened island attitudes, well and good. If not, the cost of the garrison was a price we British just had to go on paying to defend people whose only crime was that they wanted to stay British.

One fact of economics was the domestic life of the ilex squid. This fish, much loved by Far Eastern gourmets, is born, travels, spawns, travels again and dies, all with a reckless disregard of international sea boundaries. It seemed to show no understanding of the complications it created as it swam in and out of contested British and Argentine waters. The prosperity of the Falklands began to depend increasingly on revenue from the licences paid by fishing trawlers from Korea, Taiwan and their neighbours. But the fish were an asset shared with Argentina. The case for cooperation with the Argentines, in research, in the terms of each licence, in patrolling against poachers, became strong. We began to negotiate seasonal agreements in these matters, the islanders joining in the discussions.

Against this background Judy and I visited the Falklands in April 1994 after three days in Brazil. The army briefed us at their base at Mount Pleasant, then a helicopter flew us over bright coloured roofs into Port Stanley. My spirits, which had been low, revived smartly. There was not the slightest problem of cultural identity. Witney, it is true, had no Government House, and contained more than five times as many

Britons as the whole of the Falkland Islands, but the dinner that night with the councillors and the public meeting next day in Stanley were entirely familiar. A full hall, a few potential hecklers at the back wearing doubtful expressions, a polite introduction and muted applause, attentive, upturned faces, a slow start to questions but then a good flow, hearty, rather relieved applause at the end – we might have been at an election meeting in Oxfordshire.

There was no doubt about my message: that we were wholly committed to the islands. The question mark hanging in the air concerned oil. If the incessant drillings offshore produced economically viable quantities of oil what – if any – arrangements would have to be made with Argentina? Would the whole feel and character of the islands change? I pushed the question back at them. Most of them, I knew, felt that it would be foolish to leave the oil in the ground; but the timing and condition of extraction, and the degree of necessary cooperation with Argentina would have to be worked out with the islanders themselves. The drillings turned out to be indecisive, and the questions remain in the air for another day.

Judy and I were flown with John Sawers to Sea Lion Island, the most southerly of the Falklands and the richest in wildlife. A tiny hotel and an adjoining farmhouse gave the human race suzerainty over grey and golden sea lions, gross, slightly menacing elephant seals, and gentoo penguins – amazingly agile in the water, but on land clumsy slum dwellers in squalid colonies. As we found later in the Galapagos, none of these birds and animals had any real fear of humans. Walking on Sea Lion Island is not easy because of the mountainous tussocks of grass, under which on occasion the peat has smouldered for several years. Unhealed scars of the 1982 war still show themselves on every island. We flew over the wreck of a Skyhawk plane destroyed by a Sidewinder missile, and found on Sea Lion Island a memorial to HMS *Sheffield* opposite the point where more than a hundred miles out to sea her tow-rope had fatally parted. Next day we climbed the hill above Darwin and imagined the moment when Colonel Jones had lost his life and won his VC.

Lunch in the Community Centre at Goose Green was exactly like a similar occasion in Oxfordshire – straightforward, generous food and beer set out on trestle tables. I presented a silver cup and received a thick sweater in return. It was hard to grasp that this friendly room had been the prison into which the Argentines had pushed all the civilians in Goose Green and held them for many days uncertain of their fate. The folk there, and others in Stanley, spoke often and warmly of my father and mother and their visits in the fifties and sixties. I left Goose Green with a prickle at the back of my eyes.

In the VC10 on the way home to England I began, as was my habit, to sketch a short story based on the last few days.

The year which began with that journey to the Falklands produced winds as sharp as any that blew round the islands. During 1994, alongside the problems of the EU, Bosnia and Hong Kong, I had to face the damaging consequences of a decision I had taken hastily three years earlier. In 1991 I had been confronted with a formal minute from Tim Lankester, permanent secretary of the Overseas Development Administration under my jurisdiction, in which he informed me that the ODA could no longer support the financing from our aid budget of the Pergau Dam in Malaysia. The figures had changed since the project had been authorised and in his view it was no longer economically viable. This was a matter of which I knew nothing. I made quick enquiries and found that Margaret Thatcher as Prime Minister had in 1988 formally committed us to the project in a letter to Mahathir bin Mohamad, the Prime Minister of Malaysia. Mahathir was a prickly, awkward person, and Malaysia an important country. But, quite apart from the danger of offending him, the point of principle seemed clear. The British Prime Minister had made a promise which, as can happen, turned out afterwards to be frustratingly expensive. Tim Lankester had done a proper job in pointing this out. My job as Foreign Secretary was to calculate the overall national interest. To break the last Prime Minister's word would be a damaging breach of faith, which we would live to regret. But we had a new Prime Minister, and it was prudent to consult him. The paper was passed to Number Ten. John Major by return of post accepted my view, and I issued the necessary formal instruction to the permanent secretary, Tim Lankester, to proceed with the project. Silence fell, but not for long. It emerged that the promise of finance for Pergau had been linked, in conversation and correspondence, with a negotiation conducted with Mahathir in 1988 by Margaret Thatcher and the then Defence Secretary, the late George Younger, which included a Malaysian undertaking to buy British defence equipment. Geoffrey Howe, then Foreign Secretary, had quickly pointed out that a linkage between an aid project and arms sales was contrary to stated British government policy. After correspondence in Whitehall the Malaysians were told that the two issues must be treated as separate, and both went ahead on that basis.

Coincidentally, Mahathir picked a row in 1994, not with the British Government, but with the *Sunday Times* for its comments on his policies, and began a boycott of British goods. As charities connected with aid began to campaign against the Pergau Dam, I found myself in a thoroughly disagreeable position. I was defending a wasteful project on grounds of good faith and friendship with a man who was busy kicking us in the teeth. Lynda Chalker, the Aid Minister, though loyal throughout, was deeply unhappy, not least because her own high reputation in that office was also at stake.

Worse was to come. While in Brazil on 7 April 1994 I was deeply dismayed to hear from John Vereker, who was Tim Lankester's successor as permanent secretary at the ODA, that not just the wisdom but the legality of financing the project was in question. This was entirely new. It was one thing to have a political row with the Labour Party and the aid agencies, in which I had strong arguments on my side and the party with me. It was quite another to be hauled before the courts on a point of law. There are some politicians who thrive on personal involvement in legal disputes; I always hated the thought of such tussles. Tim Lankester in 1991 had not raised any legal point; he, I and the Prime Minister had dealt with the matter simply as one of policy. The Government now resisted an action on legality brought by the World Development Movement, and lost. The court's ruling was not that it was illegal to finance the Pergau Dam, but that it could not be done out of the aid budget.

In such matters it is better to act quickly, decisively and without bluster. The Treasury allowed us other funds to finance Pergau, and a number of smaller projects which I found might conceivably be open to similar objection. They would not compensate the ODA for the money already spent in Pergau, and I had a rough but not disastrous ride in the Commons on 13 December. The press next day was slightly better than I had expected.

Looking back, I can see that it was a mistake to act so quickly in 1991. If I had called an office meeting and summoned papers, no doubt the temporary link with arms sales in 1988 would have been revealed. Conceivably Foreign Office lawyers might then have raised the legal doubt which surfaced in 1994. I would have had to think more carefully about the cost of keeping Margaret Thatcher's word.

The Pergau episode vexed me greatly at the time. It spoiled what was otherwise a creditable record which Lynda Chalker with my support had built up on aid. The British aid projects which I saw in South Africa, Bangladesh, Kenya and elsewhere were different in quality from Pergau, and convinced me that the generalised criticisms of aid as a waste of money were unfounded.

It had become clear to Lynda and myself that a major shift of policy was needed. The effectiveness of our aid programme had in the past been argued largely in terms of the totals provided. It had been thought impracticable or in bad taste to say too much about the governance of the countries which received our aid. In 1990 we introduced a concept of good governance and respect for freedom as a condition for future aid. As Clare Short found out in carrying this policy forward, it is essential if our aid is to work well, but hard to carry through. Lynda Chalker's knowledge of and devotion to Africa carried her successfully through several sticky occasions.

Throughout these years the drama of Russia was playing to packed houses. My role, a minor one, was to second the Prime Minister in developing the role for Britain which Margaret Thatcher had established as Gorbachev rose to power. On each of several visits I came to know reasonably the two main players with whom I had to deal.

Andrei Kozyrev, Yeltsin's Foreign Minister, seemed at first immature; neither his officials nor I knew what to make of him. He was young, joky and unsure; it seemed as if he had grown up uncertainly in a gap between the old Soviet Union and the new Russia. This was wrong. He began to speak frankly to me, in Moscow, in New York, at Chevening, once overnight at Westwell, in the margins of other meetings. I realised that he was, as I wrote in 1993, 'brave, humorous and principled'. He lived in the old military and diplomatic jungle inherited from the Soviet Union, knew that the other beasts intrigued against him, and never believed that he would last long. But he hung on, thanks to Yeltsin's continued favour, which was a credit to both men. He advised me to speak bluntly to Yeltsin without diplomatic frills, and clearly did so himself. Alone with me over brandy and cigars in Stockholm in February 1995 he urged us to take a tougher line and persuade Yeltsin to sack his Defence Minister. He worked at every stage to avoid collisions with the West.

Andrei Kozyrev represented the Arctic port of Murmansk in the Russian Parliament and invited me there in May 1994. It was, I wrote, 'the nastiest bit of God's earth I have ever visited'. It happened that two of our embassy interpreters in Moscow were pregnant; neither would come to help me in Murmansk because of their fear of nuclear contamination. It was dramatic to stand on the hill overlooking the harbour into which our battered Arctic convoys had once limped. But every human habitation in Murmansk seemed new, uncared for, already decaying and hideous. Kozyrev and I conferred with our staff in a modern hotel: 'He is soft voiced, sometimes rambling, neither vain nor stupid.' Outside the hotel window the Arctic sun always seemed about to set, but for hour after hour never did so – or not at least until after much vodka and many toasts with the Governor of the Province, the Mayor of the City and the Admiral of the Northern Fleet.

Next day the admiral received me at his naval base. The contrast between military and civilian conditions seemed stark. I was briefed, embarrassingly, to exclaim 'Good morning, Sailors!' in Russian as I came aboard to the contingent drawn up on the deck of the flagship;

they replied with a welcoming roar. There was plenty of space on each deck, elegant marquetry in the wardroom, an abundance of chessboards, vodka and snacks round every corner. The admiral had just received his first official visit from a British submarine. He asked me whether we really expected British sailors to live in such cramped conditions. I am not sure whether the doomed Russian submarine *Kursk* was with the Northern Fleet that day. But there was already a question whether the fleet, however impressive at anchor, was still capable of putting to sea, let alone serious naval action. Chessboards, marquetry and vodka are not the main requirements of a navy.

John Major rightly took the lead in dealing with Boris Yeltsin, for example in quickly supporting him during the coup in August 1991. But I was usually there in support, and from time to time Yeltsin was ready, as Gorbachev had been, to see me without my chief. I once called on him in the Kremlin when he expounded in forceful terms his policies on the economy and the creation of a commonwealth to replace the Soviet Union. He admitted that Gorbachev had deceived us about Soviet troop numbers and biological weapons. He was interrupted during this meeting by an official who presented him with a portentous sheet of vellum for his signature. Yeltsin apologised for the interruption. The paper was, he said, an urgently needed decree (*ukase*) governing the status of intellectuals in the new system. Only in Russia, I think, would showmanship have taken this particular form.

Yeltsin did not proceed by reasoned argument. He would begin a discussion with an emphatic statement of the Russian position, banging the table with his fist until the glasses (there were usually glasses) shook alarmingly. But more than any politician I have ever known he was sensitive to the atmosphere of a meeting and in particular to the way in which he himself was treated. John Major was adept at noticing and making use of these shifts of mood. At the end of a good meeting Yeltsin would bang the table again and restate the Russian position – except that it would have moved. Position A and later the different position B were expounded with equal force by the man who at the time was in sole charge of foreign policy. What he lacked in intellectual subtlety he remedied in native political shrewdness. He could understand and respond to the problems of others. For example, at a meeting at Number Ten in January 1992 he refrained from pressing us to reduce our nuclear force of Tridents in line with the reductions he was negotiating with the Americans. That day, 30 January 1992, was a record for me and perhaps for any foreign secretary in that I lunched with the ruler of one superpower (Yeltsin in London) and dined with the ruler of the other (Bush in New York).

As the Western position in Bosnia hardened against the Serbs, we might have run into serious trouble with the Russians. I do not believe that Yeltsin cared a jot for Milosevic or the Serbs, and Serb political influence with the Russians as fellow Slavs was sometimes exaggerated. But he did not like being excluded and kept in the dark, because that was public humiliation. John Major's visit to Moscow in February 1994 began rather testily, partly because Yeltsin had a cold, mainly because we had just stiffened the NATO line on Bosnia without warning him in advance. After my meeting in Murmansk with Andrei Kozyrev some weeks later, I tried out on Yeltsin in the Kremlin the formula 'no vetoes, no surprises'. This meant that we must be free to do what we wanted, but would keep him informed. Yeltsin snorted, being at the time slightly cross with me for saying in public that Russian troops should pull out of Estonia. But, having reflected, he came back to the formula, approved it, and refilled my glass.

The climax of this stage of our relationship came with the long-planned visit by the Queen in October 1994. The backdrop of Moscow made sure that the visit would be spectacular. The prize on the first day was won by the gold-clad Patriarch and the basses and baritones in the Uspensky Cathedral in the Kremlin. But the cautious Russian authorities did not at first get the hang of the possibilities. They still regarded unregimented crowds as a security problem, not an opportunity. Instead of letting a crowd gather, they closed Red Square in Moscow so that the Queen and Yeltsin wandered through it without much sense of purpose. Once we were in St Petersburg the mood changed. A regiment dressed in eighteenth-century uniform paraded outside the Catherine Palace. There were excellent fireworks against the blue and white northern sky. Crowds gathered and waved as the Queen drove through the city to *Britannia* anchored on the Neva. My voice foundered that night, but the courtiers cured me by insisting on kippers and honey for breakfast on board. The visit in cold sunshine to the Tsars buried in white marble across the river in the Cathedral of St Peter and St Paul gave me a clue to the growing success of the visit. While the Queen was in their country the Russians were searching around for a clue to their own history. Part of their history once again made a deep impression on me as I watched the Queen and Yeltsin walk the long path between the mass graves (one million two million, no one knew) in the cemetery. The trees as before played Beethoven's 'Dead March', and veterans of both countries gathered around the memorial.

That night Yeltsin dined on *Britannia*, sitting on the right of the Queen, with myself on his right. He had obviously been carefully briefed – no vodka, only two toasts, no hugging of the Queen. I sensed a certain unease at the beginning of the meal. Yeltsin sniffed and tasted the white wine which came with the first course. Incapable of concealing his feelings, he shoved the glass aside in scorn. When the claret came ten minutes later he sniffed and tasted again – and liked it. Within seconds his glass was empty. There loomed before me one of the great diplomatic decisions which shape the fate of nations. In the ordinary run of events he would have to wait at least five, perhaps ten, minutes for a refill. It was in my power to change this – but once the routine was broken it could hardly be reinstated. Yeltsin would absorb unlimited wine from then on. There were dangers in this and I pondered – but claret was not vodka, and there were only two hours more of Yeltsin's presence on the royal yacht. No great harm was likely in that time. It seemed better to have him brimful and happy than abstemious and depressed. I summoned the footman and the glass was refilled. It paid off. Yeltsin became more friendly to me and full of praise as we talked about Ukraine and the future of NATO. He told the Queen several times that he was uncertain whether to stand again for the presidency. She took a certain amount of this, then remarked quietly that after listening to him she had come to the conclusion that he would stand. He thought this perceptiveness deeply impressive and roared with laughter. When the time came for him to propose her health he waved away the gavel, and banged us into silence with his giant fist. The evening was a great success.

After the Marines had Beat the Retreat John Sawers and I slipped off to a hotel because we needed to leave early next morning for Estonia. Judy remained as farewells were made and *Britannia* sailed, slow and brightly lit, down the Neva to the sea, past roads and bridges crowded with waving and cheering Russians. Judy thought this a fine example of a royal floatabout.

The Queen's visits abroad are normally covered by court reporters as extensions of her activities at home, with the usual emphasis on appearance, dress, weather and small eccentricities of behaviour or speech on the part of her hosts, herself (very rare) or (in particular) Prince Philip. It is true that the visits themselves day by day have little political content but they are the climax of a process, or more accurately a summary of a whole relationship. When foreign secretaries and ambassadors talk, as they often do, of relations between two countries they really mean their own comings and goings, the political disputes and convergences of governments. Prime ministers range a little wider, especially if like Churchill or Thatcher they come to represent in their persons a particular idea or experience. But in big countries thousands of Britons are scattered through the land in all kinds of activity, commercial, benevolent or just personal. Only when the Queen comes are these people and their lives brought together as representing Britain in Germany, France or wherever. Only the Queen summarises the past and the present of the whole relationship between Britain and that country. Her presence in a city or a village carries with it a unique charge of interest and emotion.

I saw this happen repeatedly across the world, sometimes to the astonishment of my sophisticated advisers. On the visit to France in 1992 the Queen and her party were driven by car through flat, empty countryside. We were late and moving fast to regain time. A group of old women in black stood at a lonely crossroads miles from anywhere. I cannot imagine how they knew when and where to gather that summer afternoon. They could have seen only a blur of a royal profile. In the following car I caught the flare-up of delight on their faces and lip-read the simple message passed one to another: 'C'est la Reine!'

Not that it was all smiles and delight. Quite often there was history to be remembered, even exorcised. In October 1992 as part of her visit to Germany the Queen at Dresden attended a service of reconciliation in the Kreuzkirche. It was forty-seven years since the RAF had devastated that church and that city. The controversy had fallen away, risen again, did not disappear. After much argument in Britain the Queen Mother had just unveiled outside St Clement Dane in the Strand in London a statue of Lord Harris, head of Bomber Command, chief architect of the policy of mass bombing. The Queen had never been to Dresden, which before 1990 had been part of communist East Germany beyond the possible range of a state visit. It seemed to me inconceivable that she should pay her first visit to a united Germany without going there.

But that morning I had doubts. The service in the church was just right. The preacher, Simon Barrington Ward (long before my successful rival for the Rosebery Prize at Eton), was Bishop of Coventry, a city devastated by the Luftwaffe. He had for years led the way in reconciliation with German Christians. But the crowd in the square as the Queen left the church was large and ominously silent. A few faces and a shout or two were hostile, but it is the silence which stays in my memory. The Queen was driven to Leipzig and a noisy, enthusiastic welcome. The silence was from Dresden, not from Germany. But she had come and said her prayers in the Kreuzkirche. The silence would not be repeated today. Afterwards I wrote to the Prime Minister:

> The Queen has fared well here. The half-morning at Dresden was always going to be vulnerable to a few dozen people, and so it proved. But if Dresden had been ignored everyone would have known why and felt the gap. The equation was right – yes to the Queen Mother at the Harris service, yes to the Queen at a reconciliation service at Dresden. The reception in Leipzig was amazing.

In May 1995, in another bombed German city, another piece of history was recalled. I went with the Prince of Wales to Hamburg to remember the surrender of Germany fifty years earlier. In the amazing Rathaus the Bürgermeister and the Prince discussed the springs of human cruelty over port and orange juice respectively. Next day the Prince spoke to 20,000 Germans gathered in the square. He had memorised the entire speech in German. I had difficulty in persuading him to say a few sentences in English for our own TV crews. Hamburg is a highly sophisticated city; but that crowd will remember the Prince and the anniversary of VE Day.

I had the opportunity to talk with the Prince on Foreign Office matters quite often in London or at Highgrove. He wrote and telephoned me, in a way which seemed wholly reasonable and welcome, when something weighed on his mind in my sphere of action.

The Prime Minister and Robert Fellowes, the Queen's private secretary, kept me informed in general terms of the rift between the Prince and the Princess of Wales. Indeed, the Queen herself could be surprisingly candid on the subject in private. But I was not required, and had no inclination, to cut off my or the Foreign Office's links with the Princess. She was almost painfully anxious to continue overseas visits with our blessing. This subject, like everything to do with the Princess, raced out of control in the press. As far as I was concerned, there was never any question of her having a formal appointment as a roving ambassador. The good causes with which she was associated wanted her help overseas and she was keen to provide it. In theory a difficulty might arise after her separation from the Prince when foreign governments failed to recognise the distinction between Princess Diana as an official representative of Britain and Princess Diana as head of a particular charity. For example, when she visited Cairo for a charity, President Mubarak asked her to call and of course she responded. When quite separately I arrived there a few days later I was charmed to find on my dressing table in the embassy a long letter in the Princess's hand telling me what she had been up to. There was never any real difficulty. The Princess came to the Foreign Office and I called at Kensington Palace. She was not in the least interested in politics. She never discussed any aspect of her private life with me, except once Prince William's education. She looked to me for support in just one matter important to her: namely, her overseas work. I was glad, or more accurately enchanted, to give it.

The last state visit on which Judy and I went with the Queen was the climax of a difficult and important reshaping of policy. Under Margaret Thatcher Britain had opposed general sanctions against the apartheid regime in South Africa. Partly because of the Prime Minister's habit of debating head on with her opponents, the Conservative Government had gained the reputation of sympathising with apartheid and working for its survival. Those close to events knew better. Certainly the white South African Prime Minister knew better, for Margaret Thatcher had often lectured P.W. Botha privately on the need for change, and in particular for the release of the African National Congress leader Nelson Mandela from his prison on Robin Island. Mandela and his two main lieutenants, Cyril Ramaphosa and Thabo Mbeki, knew this too, though they disagreed with us passionately on sanctions. After F.W. de Klerk succeeded Botha as Prime Minister apartheid began to sink, but not at all in the way which I and many others had feared.

Having watched the French forced out of Algeria, the Portuguese out of Angola and Mozambique, and Ian Smith defeated in Rhodesia, I never thought that apartheid in South Africa would survive. But I feared months, perhaps years, of destructive revolution ending in a bloody change. Instead quite a different process got under way – a slow grind of political machinery of meetings, documents, breakdowns, public abuse, then return to the negotiating table.

During these years I watched in public and listened several times in private to two men in charge of dismantling a doomed yet apparently still powerful system; one was in the Soviet Union, the other in South Africa. Gorbachev and de Klerk were quite different personalities. Gorbachev, with Shevardnadze's help, had convinced himself that the Soviet system was morally and intellectually wrong. Unlike Yeltsin, he hoped to preserve both the Soviet Union and the leading role of the Communist Party, but only by totally transforming them. He changed because he had decided it was right to change. De Klerk underwent no such conversion. I never heard him say that apartheid was wrong. He convinced himself that it was bound to fail, a different proposition; he reached this conclusion while the regime was still in full physical control of South Africa, and this was the crucial point. By acting quickly he bought the whites precious time to adapt to the coming transfer of power.

When I first visited South Africa in March 1990 the Government was edging towards 'talks about talks' with Mandela and the ANC. After seeing de Klerk I wrote to Margaret Thatcher that he 'was unruffled and in command of his own policies. He told me that he was in a hurry but did not intend to commit suicide. The violence in the townships continues and Mandela continues to talk about armed struggle. Because of these facts de Klerk would probably lose an election tomorrow [i.e., an election with the existing white electorate]. But, like Gorbachev, he has to press on and will certainly do so.' In July 1991 I was there again and found de Klerk 'v. impressive – quick, rational, convincing.

A delicious lunch, esp. the rock crab. Then Mandela at ANC in Jo'burg. He is in strong physical and mental form ... is passionate about township violence as an obstacle to talks. This is de Klerk's weak point, the failure convincingly to check violence, thus he encourages false suspicions of conspiracy.'

Because of history and a shortage of friends, de Klerk and his colleagues were glad to pour out their minds to us. More difficult was our task of building a relationship with Mandela, but slowly we managed it. I did my best to help over township violence, which mainly took the form of clashes between the supporters of the ANC and Zulus. On my visit in 1991 I landed from a police helicopter on a playing field under the hills above Durban, and scrambled over rocks to visit people living in ruined shacks which either the ANC or Inkatha had burned out months before.

There was violence both in Natal and in the townships round Johannesburg where Zulu workers were gathered into grim hostels. The key to Zulu attitudes lay with Buthelezi, their chief and the leader of Inkatha, their political movement. Over the years he proved adept in playing white against black fears to the benefit of his own position. The Prince of Wales had found spiritual gifts in Buthelezi which sadly eluded me. I learned to treat him as if he were an Arab ruler: that is, after some initial compliment I let him speak uninterrupted for half an hour or more. Once he had delivered what was on his mind it was possible to insert some thoughts of one's own.

The British could act as an audience and sometimes as an interpreter between these forces working against all odds to create a new nation. The British Ambassador, first Robin Renwick then Tony Reeve, was able to gather into his house a wider range of South Africans, including white and black militants on the same evening, than anyone else in South Africa. All sides wanted us to help them put together the new nation in practice on the ground long before they had reached agreement on its constitution. Robin Renwick formed a team of young British Foreign Service officers to run our programme of 250 projects and 1,000 scholarships. More than once I visited our projects in the Alexandra township outside Johannesburg, for instance in July 1991: 'Admirable health centre in bright colours. Present bats and pads to demon black cricketers, readmitted today to international game. Crèche run by Chris Patten's sister-in-law. The place is not policed, a strange mixture – overweening brick hostels [where the Zulu workers lived], modern flats, original houses swamped by squatters' shacks, new black middle class on slope beyond.' When I asked in the local hospital what particular equipment I should send them from our aid programme, the answer was a burns unit. The lack of police and abundance of cheap alcohol produced fights, paraffin stoves were knocked over and the results were disastrous. When the burns unit arrived a patient in the hospital sent me a long poem of thanks.

Gradually de Klerk and Mandela brought the rainbow together, and power was transferred to the majority. At the British Embassy on 9 May 1994 de Klerk made his last speech as State President. There was a huge accumulation of emotion that evening and next day. Dull would he be of soul who could not understand the immensity of what was happening. Hatred and fears which had dominated the scene for a generation were overcome – not abolished, but put to one side. A ruling class which had seemed at one time impregnable, at another doomed to violent destruction, turned out to be neither. A set of rulers representing the black majority did not wade through slaughter to a throne, but received authority in a dignified ceremony from their former oppressors. Mandela made his followers sing the Afrikaner anthem 'Die Stem', as well as their own, 'God Save Africa'. Across the valley of Pretoria swept the fighters and helicopters of the South African air force, received with an immense cheer as the crowd suddenly realised that these were now *their* planes.

Inevitably there was much waiting before and after the ceremony. John Sawers devoted himself to finding beer for the British delegation. Somewhere there is a photograph of Prince Philip in a panama hat, the Archbishop of Canterbury in purple cassock and myself gratefully swigging Castle beer from cans in the grateful shade. It was as happy a state occasion as I can remember.

The Queen's visit the following March was something else again. No one could tell in advance how it would go. True, we had built a satisfactory relationship with Mandela and his Government of National Unity. But that was a matter between politicians. A state visit would involve the Queen with the mass of South Africans. Not everyone in the cities and townships had received cricket equipment or a burns unit from Britain. Would they remember the old bitterness about sanctions, or the even more distant days of the British Empire? The Queen herself was as ever serene, but we all knew there was an element of gamble in this visit, with high stakes for her and for Britain.

The tone was set in Cape Town at the service in St George's Cathedral. 'Praise my Soul the King of Heaven' has never been more fully outpoured. Archbishop Tutu, resplendent in cape and robes, broke down the formality with a jolly service. The next day the Queen drove to Port Elizabeth. 'Amazing day. Some 70 km of roads [through the townships] all save perhaps 2 lined with excited and applauding crowds, mostly young, many schools, black, coloured, white in succession, flags, dancing and shouting. Unique.' As before in South Africa, I was amazed by the way children in spotless white shirts and dresses spilled out of grim shacks and dirty streets. In tearing spirits they raced before us along the dusty roads.

Britannia was by now anchored in Durban harbour for the Queen to give dinner to Mandela and his ministers. Chief Buthelezi was in excellent form that night, doubling up with laughter at his own jokes. On the last evening there was a farewell at the City Hall. 'Queen and Mandela on balcony. Below, a big crowd and impi dancing furiously and a bull donated. Eventually away, the impi flanking the cars, banging and stamping splendidly in the drizzle. Final 3 national anthems at airport and Queen away in her 767. The best state visit ever.'

The Queen had remembered but most of us had forgotten a distant event which weighed heavily in her success. As Princess Elizabeth she had broadcast on the wireless from Cape Town on her twenty-first birthday, while with her parents on their visit as King and Queen of South Africa. In that high, serious voice of her girlhood she had solemnly pledged herself to the service of the Commonwealth. Time and again this broadcast was recalled by high and low during those days in 1995. The Queen was not just visiting South Africa; she was coming *back*, after an absence of nearly fifty years during which most of South Africa had been largely exiled from the world, from its sports, its trade, most of its social contacts. Now the Queen was back, the fruitful rain fell, Nelson Mandela was in the President's house, and all might yet be well.

I must cut short these accounts of royal visits, and of the royal yacht *Britannia*, about both of which I am sentimental. I will forbear from describing in detail the weekend of leisure during a state visit to the United States spent cruising round the coast south of Florida with a royal picnic one day and a storm the next. I put the storm into a short story, removing the Queen and transforming *Britannia* into a luxurious drug smuggler. I published this in a newspaper, wrongly supposing that the courtiers also present in the storm did not read the *News of the World*.

More soberly I would argue that the decision to scrap, or rather not to replace, *Britannia* was prize foolishness. It happened in a way which did no credit to our political system. For years ministers had pondered the future of the royal yacht. The Royal Family, though devoted to *Britannia*, were in no mood to ask for her to be refurbished or replaced. Narrow-minded admirals were not keen to carry the modest cost on their sector of the defence budget. Ministers discussed and delayed. Finally on the edge of the 1997 General Election John Major and his colleagues announced that they intended to spend £60 million on a new royal yacht. The election was in everyone's mind. The Labour Party had not been consulted. They leapt at the chance to oppose what they described as an extravagance. Tony Blair developed a refrain during his election meetings: 'One thing we will not do is follow the Tories in promising £60 million for a royal yacht.' Once elected he allowed more than ten times that amount to be wasted on the futility of the Millennium Dome.

I kick myself that in my time I did not arrange for Labour shadow ministers to travel on *Britannia* and experience the character and usefulness of the ship. Of course, there was pleasure and relaxation on board for the Queen, her family and those with her. That seemed on the whole a good thing. There was practical commercial benefit as well. I spent a day on *Britannia* in the yellow waters of Bombay harbour, no member of the Royal Family present, watching Indian businessmen troop aboard to sign contracts for British industry. In Kuwait harbour I watched the Prince of Wales chair an economic seminar, which everyone of note in the city attended. It is inconceivable that either of these events would have succeeded half as well if held in a hotel or an embassy. Such events could be more amply provided for in a new ship.

The case is not essentially commercial. *Britannia* represented a connection between Britain and the sea which seemed natural, moving and powerful to anyone who experienced it, whether during a state visit or at other times. On 5 June 1994 the Queen sailed for France to celebrate the fiftieth anniversary of the Normandy landings on D-Day. On a sunny morning *Britannia* was escorted out of Portsmouth harbour by a mass of little boats, their crews enthusiastic and cheering. Then she passed great ships in review – our aircraft carrier *Illustrious*, the American *George Washington*, the *QE2*, the *Canberra*. In mid-Channel she sailed between two lines of warships representing the wartime Allies. As we approached, each ship cast a wreath into the sea. I stood beside President Lech Walesa, tears streaming down his cheeks, as the Polish destroyer dropped its wreath of red and white into the waves. On deck I said to John Major with some force that this proved the case for a royal yacht. This was maybe not quite logical, but it was right. The politicians fumbled then, but it need never be too late.

28

CLOSE OF A CAREER

During 1993 I began in a desultory way to consider my future. I had been Home Secretary; I had failed to become Prime Minister; I was wholly unqualified to be Chancellor of the Exchequer. I enjoyed the way of life of Foreign Secretary, and still felt the wind in my sails; but for how long? I was keen to leave the Foreign Office at a time of my own choosing, preferably by surprise and earlier than most people expected.

But what, if anything, after that? I did not want to slide downhill. There was only one other government position which could conceivably be attractive, and John Major offered it to me. On 18 January 1993 he asked if I would consider at some future date becoming Lord President of the Council to fill the role occupied by Willie Whitelaw under Margaret Thatcher: that of general confidant and mentor of the Prime Minister and supervisor of the progress of government. I was flattered and thought hard. I agreed with what John Major was trying to do, and worked easily with him. I had learned his little ways, as he had mine. For example, if he was about to disagree with me about something I would first know this if he remarked that I was looking a little peaky. I was already receiving from him (although I was not alone in this) copious draughts of speculation, lament and self-criticism as he contemplated past, present and future. But at the age of sixty-three I did not want to begin another big government post. I wanted to write novels and perhaps find a City job which would for a few years bump up my income. To coin a phrase, I wanted to see more of my wife and family, particularly Philip and Jessica, then ten and eight years old.

On 4 February I declined John Major's offer and told him that I would like to retire from the Foreign Office some time in 1994, whenever suited his convenience.

I tried to take an intelligent interest in the domestic political scene. I sent John Major a minute in May 1993, which was a digest of many conversations with him during the year. I suggested that summer 1993 was the right time to define the extent to which he wanted to alter the thrust of Thatcherism: 'Left to itself the Government and Party machinery will continue down the old road, away from public opinion.' On merit I favoured privatising the railways, but not the Post Office. On public services, 'I am impressed by the harm which can be done in the public services by the overcrowding of scrutiny, market testing, agencies etc. These are all valuable techniques. Piled on top of each other on the same people at too rapid a rate they cause alarm and inefficiency. There are some horror stories which probably never reach you.' I argued that we should make a bid to win back the professions, notably the teachers and the doctors. We needed to revive local government and attract better people to stand as councillors: 'Ted Heath used to call in regularly the Conservative leaders from the great cities. They were people of stature. It might be worth your doing so again, in the hope of building them up into something more substantial.' I listed ways in which we could build up civic pride, including in London: 'Deregulation now makes parts of London look like Mexico City.' All this I would write again today ten years later, with a flood of fresh examples.

After touching on crime and prisons, I homed in on machinery and presentation:

I worry about this. There is a case for a hands-off Prime Minister like Callaghan, concerned with the outlines, not the detail. I doubt if we shall ever see such a Prime Minister again, but I do not believe the Prime Minister should handle as much detail as you do. If, like yourself, the Prime Minister is determined to master detail, then the present machinery is plainly inadequate. One answer might be to revive the CPRS [Central Policy Review Staff; better known as the Think-Tank, this reviewed government policy from 1971 to 1983] in its original form, i.e. a unit under a person of substance functioning in Whitehall, with full access to papers, giving Cabinet (or, in a later version, simply the Prime Minister) a radical critique and unorthodox proposals to be considered alongside those from the government machine, in tune with the thrust of policy ideas which you have laid down. Alternatively, or in addition, you might consider having a Minister of State in your office (an idea which I put forward in the 1970s). Probably brought into government as a peer, he would perform in Whitehall and with the party the same sort of task which your PPS performs in the Commons – eyes, ears and voice. This would be revolutionary and he would need to be without personal ambition. Margaret Thatcher made a weak attempt at this with David Wolfson as Chief of Staff. Churchill had Lindemann, but only on one aspect. The concept is worth looking at again. I am sure it could be defended. Alternatively, or in addition, you might consider an inner group of the Cabinet, formal or informal; not dealing with topical issues, but with the overall sense of direction, meeting, for example, once a quarter at Chequers for half a day under your chairmanship.

You are better than any recent Prime Minister at question and answer. This advantage must be fully maintained and exploited. But it does not provide the emphatic and authoritative aspect of leadership. It seems to me that without sacrificing anything or taking a false position, you could identify, say once a month, a Prime Ministerial occasion where _you_ set out what _you_ intend. You could ring the changes between:

(i)   a Commons speech;
(ii) a substantive and well-worked speech;
(iii) a press conference at the QE2 [Conference Centre], beginning with a statement.

I am in favour of breaking the pernicious stranglehold of the lobby on policy presentation. They are _not_ a good filter for your views.

I did not spend 1994 or the first months of 1995 brooding over retirement. As already described, the war in Bosnia reached its final spasm. It was always absurd to suppose that the European Union would be quiet, particularly in any sector of its life which mingled with domestic policies.

There was one particular task which the Prime Minister asked me to carry out for him in private. He had become increasingly attracted to the idea of promising a referendum on a single European currency. He believed that by specifically giving the electorate a vote before Britain could enter he could drain the poison out of the dissensions within the party. The Tory warriors could put away their weapons, or at least most of them, saying, 'We needn't slaughter ourselves any more, it will be for the people to decide.' I was at first reluctant. I had thoroughly relished the referendum of 1975, but as a unique event. We had stood firm in resisting a referendum on the Treaty of Maastricht as a whole on the solid argument that we lived in a parliamentary democracy. Parliament existed to take the nation's decisions, great or small. We had after sweat and tears managed to ratify the treaty on that basis.

But the Prime Minister persisted, as was his wont, and wore me down. The abolition of the pound would, it could be argued, be unique. It would directly affect the way of life of every individual in Britain. And the political advantage for an embattled Government would be great. We would outflank the Labour Opposition and half silence our own Eurosceptics. In November 1994 I gave way, mainly because I wanted to sustain John Major, and John Major badly wanted to promise a referendum. He set me to put pressure on cabinet colleagues. A Sunday night supper at Number Ten showed the extent of the problem. The two strongest pro-European ministers, Ken Clarke and Michael Heseltine, were definitely against a referendum, and so remained despite my efforts. Nor did I have more luck with the Eurosceptics. On 14 December I tried with Michael Portillo after a vote in the Commons. He was cool, intelligent and courteous, but we got absolutely nowhere. Eventually I had to report failure to the Prime Minister. It was not until 1996, after I had left the Government, that he prevailed over his colleagues and gave the promise of a referendum on behalf of the Conservative Party. Tony Blair felt obliged to follow suit. That referendum promise has set the framework for debate on British membership of the single currency ever since.

In January 1995 I fell into a pit. There was no special reason. *The Times* and the *Daily Mail* had been sniping at me for some time as part of their Eurosceptic stance. On 26 January the Overseas Policy and Defence Committee of the Cabinet discussed a general paper I had circulated on policy in the EU. 'My paper and that by officials criticised quite briskly, especially by Howard and Portillo, and the friends are either silent or not v. effective. The PM loquacious and on the whole helpful, but in central position. In the end the work will be roughly within the framework I proposed.' I went off to give lunch to the new Dutch Foreign Minister. 'An odd chap, and like all of us vain. A long way from us on substance of Europe. But friendly in intention.' These stray comments show where the pieces were on the board. The Dutch were strong for further integration. I wanted the EU to stay roughly where it was and make a success of what it already had in hand. The sceptics wanted to pull back powers to nation states. None of this was new. The piece which had moved, though only a square or two, was the king. John Major did his best to cheer me up as I floundered in the pit, but his personal stance had become more sceptical. His most popular moment on Europe since Maastricht had been when he had vetoed the candidature of the Belgian Prime Minister, Jean-Luc Dehaene to succeed Jacques Delors as President of the Commission; his worst had been when the Cabinet agreed to the Ioannina compromise on majority voting. His own intellectual analysis of Britain's interests remained the same, but he would no longer show any personal enthusiasm for the EU.

The next day *The Times* led with a flaming story that I had been massively rebuffed by the Cabinet on the 26th. Someone had leaked a misleading account of the debate among ministers. The Prime Minister at once denounced the story as a travesty, ordered other ministers not to broadcast on Europe and did his best to back me up. Ted Heath and Geoffrey Howe unwittingly helped by criticising me for lack of enthusiasm on European integration. Gradually the sceptic press shifted its fire on to Ken Clarke, and I climbed, somewhat muddied, out of the pit. But the episode affected my timing, since I was keen if possible to leave the Government at a moment when neither I nor it was in worse than routine trouble.

I had another long but equally fruitless talk with Michael Portillo in mid-February, this time trying to find out where he thought the Conservative Party could realistically pitch its tent on Europe. 'V. hard. Has no tactic to remedy present disastrous strife. Says Ken's speech last Tuesday [I cannot trace this] has destroyed trust. Unwilling to help me find common ground. Says he has shot his bolt. But has no tactic, and I wear him down just a little. Polite but uncompromising. Box. Bed 1.' I must admit to some personal chagrin about this. Usually I find I can break through the reserve of another politician, friend or opponent; I can find enough trust at least to establish where we both stand. I could take no possible offence, but Michael Portillo's walls remained impregnable.

There was one other cause which I wanted to carry further before I resigned. Now that the Cold War was over it seemed time to look at our overseas policy as a whole. This was particularly important for the allocation of resources. At present the Ministry of Defence argued each year for its own budget. The Foreign Office argued separately for its much smaller budget, which had four components: namely, overseas aid, overseas broadcasting, the British Council and the Diplomatic Service. The armed services no longer needed to see the threat from the Soviet Union as the fact which overwhelmingly dominated their thinking. They could look at Britain's external position as a whole and consider how best to reinforce it. But that was also what the Foreign Office and its different auxiliaries existed to do. Instead of looking at defence needs separately, we should look at the overseas effort as a whole, and allocate our resources as a whole.

My colleagues soon perceived some special pleading in this. The Foreign Office budget was always under pressure and I had a reputation for fighting hard to protect it. Indeed, Ken Clarke once observed (I hope in jest) to the Prime Minister that he had mistakenly supposed that in negotiating with me on the Foreign Office budget he was dealing with a gentleman. I was having to open posts in the new countries of the former Soviet Union and Yugoslavia. I doubted whether it made sense to close and squeeze existing diplomatic posts to allow for this. Those responsible for the aid, broadcasting and British Council budgets argued a similar case. I believed that a comprehensive review of our overseas effort would relax the pressure on these civilian budgets even if it meant doing without one of the planned 'Euro fighters'. But my concern was more than budgetary. I believed, and believe, that this argument goes much wider. The most obvious example of the need for what is now called 'joined-up government' is in Britain's overseas effort.

I argued the case at a strategy meeting at Chequers in September 1994, and thought I made some headway. I walked Minister of Defence Malcolm Rifkind round Westwell village, and by the time we reached the churchyard felt I was getting somewhere. One difficulty was the reluctance which both he and John Major felt at holding any big review which included defence. They thought that this would raise unrealistic hopes or fears and throw up more divisions and difficulties than the Government could handle.

I tried again at another strategy meeting at Chequers on 13 January 1995. I was resisting one of the newfangled techniques invented by the Treasury for a fundamental review of Foreign Office spending. I undertook to accept the fundamental review of the Foreign Office on the understanding that it would lead to an enhancement of our effort to promote British exports, the English language and what is now called defence diplomacy. The Prime Minister was still against any overarching review including defence, but the minutes of the meeting contained a phrase about enhancing the civilian overseas effort. On his own recollection of the meeting, Kenneth Clarke challenged the minutes; the Prime Minister upheld them. But this bureaucratic triumph led nowhere in particular, and I had no time to reap the harvest, which (just possibly) that discussion might have sown.

But I could convey the general message to a wider public, and on this everyone helped me. We were fed up with the way in which EU matters dominated the news. Of course, this was partly our fault because of the newsworthy divisions within the Government on Europe. But Britain was a world power, albeit no longer a great one. We had worldwide assets, of which the English language, the skills of our armed and diplomatic forces, the position of London as a financial centre and our role in the Commonwealth were four of the most important. I felt that we should spend more time in public debating the nature of these assets and how we could increase them.

On 29 March, soon after the Queen's triumphant visit to South

Africa, we organised a full day's conference in the Queen Elizabeth Centre in London on 'Britain in the World'. This was meant to be something exceptional, and in the short term it worked. The Prime Minister, Henry Kissinger, the Prince of Wales, the Shadow Foreign Secretary Robin Cook and I all produced something a bit out of the ordinary, and the media responded accordingly. We were criticised by some in the press the next day for not focusing on Europe, but that was the whole point. 'There is a world elsewhere,' as Coriolanus said. For a few days I thought that we might have lifted our sights.

My immediate future became increasingly entwined with the Prime Minister's. On 26 May we both flew to Bonn for an Anglo-German summit. The news from Bosnia was appalling: NATO had struck at the Bosnian Serbs the day before, and they were retaliating with brutal shelling and taking of hostages. There was urgent need for the Russians to persuade Milosevic to press the Bosnian Serbs to hold off.

Chancellor Kohl fed us huge quantities of asparagus and white sauce. In our presence he roared genially to Yeltsin, who was in Minsk; given the latter's equal roar, there seemed little need for a telephone. John Major and I later had time to relax on the terrace of the British Embassy overlooking the Rhine. I had been briefed that he wanted to talk about the euro – whether we could promise a referendum, whether we could promise not to join the single currency even in the next Parliament. In fact we talked of none of this. John Major by now accepted that I was resolved to leave the Government in the summer. He talked positively about our working relationship, saying that only with me and Ken Clarke could he discuss politics in a relaxed way. I was anxious that he might think it ingenious to appoint a Eurosceptic to succeed me, and strongly recommended that instead the next Foreign Secretary should be Malcolm Rifkind.

The decision to reinforce Bosnia having been taken at the end of May, the pressures on me personally began to relax. Indeed, I thoroughly enjoyed the June summit of the Group of Seven at Halifax in Nova Scotia. 'An amazing place this, sunny with sharp northern light, fine workaday harbour, people an endless street party in shorts, waving cheerful and excited greeting at every car and bus. "O Happy Canada" says Kinkel [German Foreign Minister] contrasting with dour protest-ridden Germany.' In the evening the Cirque du Soleil performed by the waterside, there were jolly fireworks and the crowds continued large and high spirited.

The main theme of the Halifax conference was Russia, but our Prime Minister had to think mainly of the turmoil enveloping him at home. He had been badly roughed up at a meeting of mainly Eurosceptic

Conservative backbenchers in the Commons just before leaving for Canada. On the plane home he unveiled the thought that he might resign as leader of the Conservative Party and force a leadership election which would flush out his opponents. I supported the idea. He discussed it with me again on 20 June after I had briefly visited Madrid for one of the empty series of meetings on Gibraltar. He was keen that I should not at once announce my intention to resign, and I held off for three more days.

On the 20th Judy and I gave a dinner at Carlton Gardens for Henry Kissinger, who had just been knighted by the Queen. I had known and liked Henry and Nancy Kissinger for several years and we had stayed with them in Connecticut. Everyone in the West who was interested in foreign affairs owed him a debt, and he had given me particular help at the 'Britain in the World' conference that March. Soundings revealed to our delight that the Princess of Wales would accept an invitation to our dinner. This changed the nature of the occasion, given the number of people who wished to come and bask in the combined sunshine radiated by the Princess and the unrivalled philosopher of foreign policy. The Foreign Office had a list of possible guests; the British Ambassador in Washington had his little list; Judy and I had a list of our own. One or two individuals not on any list telephoned to enquire about invitations which they feared might have been lost in the post. But Judy and I held firm, refusing to transfer the dinner away from our house to the bigger, more official tables available at Lancaster House or Admiralty House. So it remained a very personal occasion. I remember it as good fun; Judy remembers a last-minute panic when the flowers ordered for the dinner table failed to arrive.

John Major announced on 22 June that he would challenge his opponents by resigning the leadership. By this time I was under a good deal of pressure to stay in the Government from people in the know. Every now and then, for example after the good day ending in the Kissinger dinner, I half regretted my decision, but only half, and it stayed firm.

At breakfast on the 23rd there seemed no reason to delay further:

Spend morning in FO peacefully telephoning my sons, heads of agencies, Chevening etc. Talk to a huge array of cameras by the Ambassadors' entrance at noon. Solana [Spanish Foreign Minister] and Warren Christopher ring. Leave after a sandwich and glass of wine. To Ludgrove [cricket match against Philip's school Summerfields] snooze under trees. P. fields in a floppy white hat. PM rings for no particular purpose – he too feels liberated. John [Sawers] rings to read PM's letter [charming]. Tea on Ludgrove lawn. Then, reluctantly, to Droitwich to form a [Conservative] Patron's Club.

Obituaries are usually kind; it is at a later stage that people make their own reputations and money by pulling a corpse to bits. There would be much to be said for a system by which we hover around for a few weeks after the announcement of death, time enough to hear some of the kind words in person and read the others carefully cut out, pinned together and placed tidily in one's in-tray. This is more or less what I achieved in June and July 1995. My resignation announced on 23 June would take effect when the Prime Minister declared his July reshuffle, which he did on the 5th. For me, though not for John Major, it was a sunny twelve days. I went with him to the European summit at Cannes, and swam from the jetty of the Hotel Carlton while he wrestled with the news that John Redwood had taken up the challenge to contest the leadership of the party against him. At my last Foreign Office questions in the Commons I turned away a small barrage of enjoyable compliments, of which the neatest came from Tim Rathbone. He began, 'As the only member of this House who has bought a second-hand car from the Foreign Secretary, may I . . .'. There were small farewell parties with champagne ('Ebb tide, no regrets, some sadness').

Meanwhile, the Prime Minister was once again fighting for his political life in the contest he had provoked. The two most powerful press millionaires, Rupert Murdoch and Conrad Black, were out to destroy him. On a party tour in Teesside and the West Riding on 30 June I found strong support for John Major among the party faithful; but they had no vote. I kept in close touch with Lord Cranborne, whom the Prime Minister had shrewdly invited to run his campaign. It is often sensible to be helped by someone entirely different from oneself. On 3 July, after talking to Robert Cranborne in the House of Lords, I supposed cautiously that John Major would gain the support of 200–240 of the 329 Conservative MPs. Robert said that no one knew his real intentions. I suggested that, provided he got a majority at all, however slight, senior ministers should encourage him to stay on. Robert agreed, and suggested that I should make sure I was at Number Ten when the news of the count arrived. I demurred, doubting if John Major would want to be surrounded at a difficult moment by a gang of gate-crashers.

Next morning Robert rang to say in a characteristic metaphor that the horse was shying at the fence. Alarmed, I did find my way to Number Ten (through the Cabinet Office rather than the front door), so as to be upstairs in the Prime Minister's private flat at five in the afternoon when the poll came through. The result was 218 votes for John Major. The more courtier-like of those present at once applauded vigorously and uttered loud congratulations. The Prime Minister stood silent by the mantelpiece. In recent days he had told me that he was seriously tempted to retire to private life. He must have had this thought again as he weighed in his mind a result which was above the worst but well below the best which had been predicted. 'I think it's enough, Prime Minister,' I said, rather after the rest. After a few more seconds he agreed.

I never seriously doubted that he would persevere, whatever the temptations to be rid of the torments visited on him by his party. That was his nature: he complained but did not quit.

Next day, to my relief, Malcolm Rifkind was appointed Foreign Secretary, after the last-minute hiccup which beset most reshuffles. I left the Foreign Office, and the individuals there of whom I was fond. The following evening, for the first time in sixteen years except holidays, I received no red boxes. On the 12th the Queen received me to take leave, and we chatted about the problems of the world. The next day I drove Philip, aged thirteen, down to Wiltshire. We went to see my brother Stephen, convalescing after a serious accident when he was trampled by one of his own cows. Then I took Philip for the first time up the Giant's Grave, and we looked across at Rainscombe Farm, which had been my home when, a great time ago, I had been his age. The wheel had turned almost full circle.

Envoi

Readers who have been carried this far by an interest in politics may want to stop on the day when I slipped away from the Foreign Office to watch cricket at Ludgrove. But this is a personal rather than a purely political story. My personal life was not obliterated along with my ministerial career in July 1995.

In the last eight years I have continued to bustle about the country and the world, to fill days with meetings and working meals, to make speeches, write books and scribble in my WH Smith diary every night. None of this is particularly important, but I have not subsided into a deckchair. I counted one recent year and found that I had slept that year in forty different beds. That is about average. Various ambitions are repeatedly postponed: I am still *about* to become a keen gardener, to cruise in the Aegean and to tackle Proust. In short I am still busy. This suits me.

My life at once lost focus. I was engaged not in one career but at any given time in a dozen unrelated activities. I still had an office and an efficient and benevolent secretary who updated each Thursday a list of five or six pages of future engagements. The people with whom I dealt on one thing had no knowledge of the others in my life. My fellow workers on the Prison Reform Trust knew nothing of those at the private bank Coutts, who knew nothing of Westminster Abbey or the work of the Archbishop of Canterbury, who knew nothing of the publishers Little, Brown, who knew nothing of the Mediation Charity CEDR, who knew nothing of the House of Lords or the Cambridge Foundation, and so on. Putting together a week out of these shifting components became a new art. I was never good at saying no to a well-written invitation, particularly if it involved travel, or meeting old friends, or talking to a young audience at a school or university.

The most important event of the years after leaving the Foreign Office has had nothing to do with any of the above. In 1998 Judy was finishing her four-year degree course in history at Birkbeck College in London. Rather remarkably, she had started this while still the Foreign Secretary's wife. She enjoyed this new world and in particular her fellow students, and worked hard at preparing for her final dissertation and examinations. This was a moment when everything seemed to be going well for the Hurd family – less pressure, more leisure, no worries. The sky was clear, dangerously clear.

During her last term at Birkbeck Judy began to struggle with aches and pains and what seemed acute exhaustion. At first this seemed easily explained by all the work that had to be fitted in at the eleventh hour before her exams. The first doctor she saw recommended a gin and tonic and some early nights. The symptoms remained, worsened, and she went for a second time to the surgery. A second doctor had a look. At once her life changed pace dramatically. She was hustled as if every hour counted into the John Radcliffe Hospital in Oxford. The consultant gravely told us both that she had acute myeloid leukaemia, and that her chances of survival were about 30 per cent. I was not sure whether Judy in her dozy state was alert enough to take in the enormity of what had been said in such a matter-of-fact tone of voice. It took me several days to absorb it, and to explain it to her friends and family, to Philip and Jessica (aged fourteen and twelve), and to myself.

Four heavy doses of chemotherapy, followed by an autologous transplant – the John Radcliffe in Oxford, spells in bed at Westwell, the Royal Marsden in Surrey – the quiet, rather pessimistic consultant followed by the bouncy, optimistic consultant, both men tireless and dependable in the National Health Service. The wards, the nurses, the trays, the shabby corridors, the recorded ups and downs of the white blood cells, the big hospital lifts which felt as if they were designed for goods not human beings, the soft noise of the saline solutions dripping towards Judy's veins in plastic tubes, the deaths down the corridor. Later the woolly hats which Judy wore at home on all occasions until her hair grew again, the endless washing of hands and worries about infection because treatment had destroyed her resistance. All these things and much else we experienced. We discovered that they are part of everyday life for many more people than we had supposed when Judy started down the road.

In the spring of 1999 I took Judy to the elegant and welcoming Hotel Tresanton in St Mawes. The Cornish wind was cold on the daffodils and I was not sure how Judy would cope with her first expedition of convalescence. We walked haltingly along the coastal path to St Just, and for the first time the balance in my own mind shifted to confidence in her recovery. Now, as I write, that recovery is as complete as is given to any of us. I dislike press headlines that so many thousand lives are 'saved' by a treatment or 'lost' to a disease. Deaths can be postponed, but immortality is not in the gift even of a tabloid newspaper. Through God's mercy, her own calm and courage and the skill of those who looked after her, Judy gained precious years; and all of us close to her are grateful and wiser.

In sickness or in health, Judy needs a project. Year by year our house at Westwell was improved, though never enough at any time to change its character. A boot room was added in the Gothick style. The kitchen and dining room were knocked together. A tennis court was created on the slope beyond the winter stream. Judy enlarged the garden lawn by slicing a haha through the nearest field, and bought the neighbouring slope which is crowned by a line of ancient walnuts. Compared to hers, my efforts were minuscule. I introduced cowslips to one slope and primroses to our copse. Nothing we have done transforms Westwell into anything more than a comfortable farmhouse, but gradually we have moulded it to our own family needs and wishes.

From my point of view, the most important change came when the police evacuated their post in the stable block. We could then transform that end of the building into a library. Stairs lead up to my study which is established where once the police held sway, with a window looking over the back garden to the house and another across the lawn up the bed of the stream past the oak tree. In the library books are ranged roughly by subject matter on principles known only to myself. Many of these are travellers who have circled the world with me. A few tattered veterans, including Pope, Sterne and Bishop Hurd's sermons were renewed at the height of my prosperity by a bookbinder in the Iffley Road, Oxford. In the study my filing system is even more abstruse; indeed, said by some to be anarchic. Reforming it is always one of my tasks for the future, perhaps coming before even the assault on Proust.

These changes were possible because for the first time in my working life I lived for a few years without money worries. When I resigned as Foreign Secretary in July 1995 I had no idea of my financial future – except that for two more years I was still a Member of Parliament, and was eligible for a ministerial pension. I started a new political novel, *The Shape of Ice*, and looked around. Within two months I accepted an offer from Bob Alexander, chairman of NatWest Bank, to become deputy chairman, NatWest Markets, with a non-executive seat on the main bank board. The world into which I then moved was strange. NatWest, having recovered from earlier mishaps, was at the time in imperial mode.

Its overseas ambitions grew under the enthusiastic direction of Martin Owen, my immediate superior as chairman of NatWest Markets. It seemed to them sensible to enlist a former Foreign Secretary who could keep open doors, particularly into the public sectors across the world in the heyday of privatisation. Established in Bishopsgate, I wisely recruited as my private secretary Julia Broad, who became for seven years the quiet but highly efficient organiser of my time. Julia had previously led a sheltered life within NatWest. Henceforward she was exposed to the charms and pressures of ambassadors, ex-prime ministers, archbishops and prison reformers, foreigners calling incomprehensibly from distant places and, of course, members of my family in and out of season.

At first my life with NatWest Markets ran smoothly. I visited many old haunts in a new guise – Moscow, Tunis, Rome, Tokyo, Jakarta and others – to sign an agreement or host a meeting. The meetings of the World Bank and International Monetary Fund each September, alternately in Washington and elsewhere, reminded me strongly of the UN General Assembly in New York. The proceedings at the core of the event were neither attended nor discussed by the mass of bankers who crowded into Washington or Prague or Hong Kong. We whirled about in a confusion of meetings, receptions and ostentatiously competitive meals. All the resources of twentieth-century technology were deployed to help us. Consequently, a high proportion of our time was spent in traffic jams or waiting for lifts; but at least while waiting we could jabber into mobile phones.

But NatWest Markets went wrong. A malpractice was discovered, but not acted on decisively. The board, which had trusted Martin Owen's enthusiasm in acquisition after acquisition, first turned cool, then took fright. There was a revolution, and Martin Owen left. NatWest itself entered a period of decline followed by eventual takeover. I stayed on the main board until I approached the leaving age of seventy, but my occupation, indeed my justification, was largely gone. I became happier, though less highly rewarded, when my job with NatWest was transformed into two smaller and separate positions with Coutts private bank and with Hawkpoint, the lively financial partnership off Bishopsgate who gave me an office and enabled me to keep Julia.

A job in the City but no car meant the Tube. My police protectors, like my private secretaries in the Foreign Office, believed that I would be incapable of successful travel after having depended for so long on their assistance. My private secretaries would have felt justified on the day when I tried to travel to Holland on Judy's passport, but the police officers still protecting me at that stage reassured their Dutch colleagues, and I recovered from this early setback. My protectors believed that on the Tube I would be constantly besieged by strangers wanting either an autograph or a punch-up. In practice, though quite a few fellow travellers in the early years recognised me, only a small number approached, almost all of them in a friendly way. My favourite was the Sikh at Shepherd's Bush Station who sold me a ticket with the remark, 'Time you were back at the helm, sir.' For a reason which I do not understand, most of those who struck up a conversation were from the ethnic minorities, blacks shouting, 'Hi, Doug!' from a building site, or careful approaches from Asians complete with CV or visiting card. After a time this usually became a matter of half recognition – people know they have seen me somewhere on television, and confer briefly among themselves as to who the hell I am. There are one or two places, particularly Hong Kong and Kuwait, where I was once on television so intrusively that what my children call 'the recognition factor' stays higher than at home. Waitrose in Witney still scores highest of all. None of this has ever caused me the slightest difficulty.

I did not contest the General Election of 1997. On my last evening in the House of Commons I said to myself, 'You have sat here for twenty-three years, your father before you, your grandfather before him. You must summon up some emotion as you leave.' I found a deep armchair in the Commons Library and gathered my thoughts. Opposite in another chair snoozed a Labour Member of about my age. He had, I think, been a junior minister in the Callaghan Government before 1979. The House was on an adjournment debate, the Library was empty, there would be no more votes. Probably no one had told him he could go home. I had a vision of him snoozing in that chair for the last eighteen years, waiting for something to happen. For all except the first and the last two or three years I had worked and bustled about as a minister. This had not happened through any great talent of my own, compared to his. The turn of the wheel had meant that at the age when I could be a minister, my party happened to be in power. For that I felt deeply grateful.

I remained in spirit more of a politician than a banker, and a politician mainly interested in foreign affairs. I enjoy belonging to the courteous, elderly political club called the House of Lords, and worked in John Wakeham's royal commission on ideas for its future. My own views on the subject are eloquent but extensive and would hardly fit in here. What I missed about daily, intensive politics was not the grind of taking decisions and defending them, but the automatic flow of fascinating information. In one of his books Max Hastings aptly called this 'the intoxication of access'.

If I wanted information after my resignation I could still get it. My Labour successors as Foreign Secretary, Robin Cook and Jack Straw, have been generous with their time. I have sat on their sofa in my old room at the Foreign Office, sipped their tea, listened respectfully to their views and noticed how the pictures have changed. Both have allowed me to pick the brains of their officials and our ambassadors overseas without hindrance. I learned that anyone in Britain with a serious interest in what happened yesterday in the outside world has to read the *Financial Times* or the *Herald Tribune*. But I missed the daily flood tide across my desk of information and analysis from all over the world.

As a minister I had been rather pompously scornful of the many international gatherings of the distinguished elderly. They wag their beards in comfortable hotels and discuss mournfully the state of the world for which they are no longer responsible. Now that I am on the other side of the fence I enjoy these occasions, particularly when the organisers attract some minister, international servant or governor of a central bank who is still in action and can bring into the conference room fresh air from the real world.

Sometimes I myself have been invited to make speeches. There is something particularly wayward about the way this works. I never reached anything like the fee level taken for granted by the top layer of international lecturers such as Henry Kissinger, Margaret Thatcher or John Major. Most of the speeches I have made have received no reward except expenses, a decent audience and dinner. But every now and then someone offers several thousand pounds for an hour of preparation and half an hour of delivery. This is several times what would be earned from a newspaper article. The *Financial Times* has offered me an occasional slot in their Personal View column, which I like for the company I keep there and the audience I can reach.

The Shape of Ice and *Image in the Water* are linked novels published during these years. They appealed to connoisseurs of British politics, an admittedly narrow band, but were well received. Because I was still writing, my publishers reprinted in paperback the backlist of my books, including those written with Andrew Osmond and Stephen Lamport, which had long been one of my objectives.

More unusual for me was the making of a three-part television documentary with the BBC under the title *The Search for Peace*. We tried to trace how peacemaking had evolved from the balance of power preached by Metternich and Bismarck in the nineteenth century, through the Great War to Woodrow Wilson and the League of Nations, on to Potsdam and the 1945 settlement, ending with the concept of humanitarian intervention and Bosnia. It is true, as is often said, that television rations ideas strictly. My producer, Matthew Barrett, an intellectual Wykehamist overflowing with ideas, was very clear that even a BBC 2 audience could not absorb more than three or four thoughts in one programme. But the process of making a documentary, the constant repetitions, the rephrasings, the professional discussions in planes and over cheap restaurant meals helped me to concentrate my mind. We went to places beyond my reach as Foreign Secretary. As an interviewer, sitting in his presidential palace in Georgia, I was able to pin down Shevardnadze on how he and Gorbachev abandoned the communist regime in East Germany. In Houston I asked George Bush about the ending of the Gulf War. I visited my uncle's grave on the Somme, and the spot from which the Archduke had been shot in Sarajevo. At a Ruthene Mass in a church fouled by the Serbs outside Vukovar I heard the UN general in charge remind the congregation from the altar steps that vengeance belongs to the Lord.

One advantage of retirement is that one no longer needs a view on everything. A minister, or indeed a Member of Parliament, by convention has to pretend, if not omniscience, at least a sporting knowledge of any topical subject. 'I don't know' is for them a dangerous phrase; 'I don't care' an impossible one. In retirement one can blank off huge sections of human life or philosophical enquiry and confess as much to a sixth-form audience.

A calmer view of life as a whole seems to be quite compatible with fiercer rage on minor matters. I have come to hate litter. Only fear of ridicule prevents me wandering all about London picking up empty crisp packets and soft-drink cans from gutters and pavements. As it is, I do this only occasionally and in our neat little street in Hammersmith. But on my regular walk to the Central Line Tube station I compose denunciations to the Hammersmith and Fulham Council on the squalid shambles that is Shepherd's Bush. Writing fierce letters on small things is one of the clearest symptoms of old age.

More insidious is the disintegration of thought. By this I do not mean that one becomes stupid or inarticulate. Rather, one's thoughts no longer have to hang together in a coherent whole. I have found myself following certain likes and dislikes without having to consider whether they are compatible one with another. On some subjects, for example anything to do with prisons, I find myself more liberal than before. In general, however, I seem to have returned to the instinctive conservatism of my youth, except that this is no longer automatically connected with the Conservative Party.

I could never vote anything but Conservative, and pay my dues to the local party both in West Oxfordshire and in Hammersmith and Fulham. Luckily I like the Conservative champions in both seats. The defeat of 1997 seemed to be inevitable because we had been in power for eighteen years and were disordered and exhausted. Much more remarkable has been the failure to recover from that defeat. This cannot now be convincingly explained by referring back to any enormities of John

Major's Government. The grip of the sour right on the party since 1997, and more especially on much of the pro-Conservative press, has, I believe, prevented the natural turn of the wheel in our favour. I have said this quietly from time to time but have no longer any zest for party political manoeuvres and combinations. Rather, I have marched fervently for the countryside, rejoiced at the success of the Golden Jubilee, preached at Harvest Festival in Westwell church and presented the award to Shipton under Wychwood as the best-kept village in Oxfordshire. This is a mellow conservatism which not even the Conservative Party can take from me.

Nick and Tom, my two eldest sons, have during this time worked overseas, and given us occasions to bask among Brazilian islands over Christmas, examine Petra and swim in the Dead Sea. Judy and I have ventured to the glaciers of Patagonia, and another year to Peru and the Galapagos. But I am beginning to feel some narrowing of horizons. It is as good to see my grandchildren playing tennis or football at Westwell as to visit them in foreign parts. *Re*visiting familiar places, even if undramatic, now has the edge. Taking the ferry to Skye, or watching the incomparable view of islands disappear in cloud then re-emerge in sunshine from Jacky Shaw Stewart's windows at Traigh now beats, though narrowly, the Galapagos. Part of this book was written in South Devon, on the estate where as recorded we rented for many years a holiday cottage. I had planned a hermit week, imagining a diet of soup and sardines from tins while I wrote and wrote. But Judy decided to come, then Philip, then friends of both. For old times' sake, Philip brought his crab lines and shrimping net as well as his new golf clubs.

Summer's lease was almost up, but not quite. Morning mist over the meadows and estuary quickly dispersed. We swam on Mothecombe beach in October as if it were August. We still stuffed our pockets with windfall apples and on the way up from the beach the ladies still served tea and flapjacks in the old schoolhouse. One has to allow for mists and then frosts and the gradual shortening of days, but there is a lot to be said for autumn.

INDEX